The New Chinese Astrology

Suzan[illegible] White is a recognized authority on Chinese and western astrol[illegible]es. She is the author of *Chinese Astrology Plain and Simple, Su[illegible] White's Guide to Love* and *The New Astrology*, a revolution-a[illegible] which combines western and Chinese astrological systems to [illegible] 144 'new' character types. All of Suzanne White's books ha[illegible]ome bestsellers worldwide. An American, Ms White lives and wor[illegible] both Paris and Buenos Aires. For consultations, e-mail her: Su[illegible]suzannewhite.com

Also by Suzanne White

Chinese Astrology Plain and Simple

The New Astrology

Suzanne White's Guide to Love

The New Chinese Astrology

Suzanne White

PAN BOOKS

First published 1993 by Macmillan

First published in paperback 1994 by Pan Books

This updated edition published in paperback 2008 by Pan Books
an imprint of Pan Macmillan, a division of Macmillan Publishers Limited
Pan Macmillan, 20 New Wharf Road, London N1 9RR
Basingstoke and Oxford
Associated companies throughout the world
www.panmacmillan.com

ISBN 978-0-330-45206-9

3 5 7 9 8 6 4 2

A CIP catalogue record for this book is available from the British Library.

Typeset by SetSystems Ltd, Saffron Walden, Essex
Printed and bound in Great Britain by
CPI Mackays, Chatham ME5 8TD

I dedicate this book to the promotion of compassion, understanding, education and brotherhood among all peoples everywhere.

Contents

Author's Note

The generic 'he'

Rather than make the difficult choice between the sexes each time I needed a pronoun to refer to the behavior of an animal sign, I have opted to use the 'generic' masculine pronoun throughout this book. Please don't be flummoxed when you read 'The Monkey's never certain if *he* wants his dinner at six or at eleven,' or 'The Dog has an abrasive tongue and *he* doesn't hesitate to use it on *his* adversaries.' I can explain.

In the beginning, I struggled with the following kinds of constructions: 'If the Tiger wants his/her life to be productive, he/she must learn to be disciplined. The Tiger lives lustily and always seems to want his/her cake and eat it, too. A Tiger never wants to alter his/her lifestyle to conform to a routine.'

Exhausting reading? Yes. And clumsy writing, too. Those interminable *he/she* and *his/her* references kept jumbling my syntax, cramping my style and, frankly, were driving this Tiger a little batty. So, except where I am specifically describing women, the generic masculine pronoun is used throughout. Obviously, the text does *not* refer exclusively to male animal sign behavior nor is a sexist slur intended . . .

Introduction

Let me explain . . .

I have always liked to begin my books with a little story about myself, about how I came to write this one and about who I am, indeed, to be assuming to write such a work. It may sound egomaniacal. It is. But here goes, anyway.

Those of you who already know me are aware that I first heard of Chinese astrology when I was a twenty-five-year-old skinny, self-pitying American fashion model living in Paris. There, through a hippie boyfriend, I met a grand old wizard of Chinese character divination who advised me to get out of modelling and into writing.

He did not tell me to get out of Paris, so I stayed there for a while and married. But ultimately I followed the old gentleman's advice and became a writer. First, I penned vapid, humorous articles about women's problems in women's magazines. Then, aged thirty-three, I batted out my standard purge first novel all about *me*. It failed. But that did not discourage me. The old Chinese man had been right. I was far happier as a writer than as a fashion model. So I sat down and wrote a book about, of all things, Chinese astrology! Amazingly, *Suzanne White's Original Chinese Astrology* did not fail. *Au contraire*! It was (and still is) a huge success – translations into all languages, enough money to eat for a few years and well . . . it worked.

After that I had two beautiful kids and started yet another big fat novel (this time about some fascinating people besides myself). Then, suddenly, before I could finish it, I got very busy being a recovering cancer patient. When I was well and strong again, I wrote another book about astrology. This time I served as matchmaker: I married the two types of astrology we all know best, Western and Chinese, into a system I call New Astrology. By now (1985) I had gained a reputation as an astrologer. I had even started reading charts, interpreting people's planetary configurations, adding in their Chinese astrological data. I was getting astonishing results. In the process I was finding out more and more about my favorite subject, Chinese astrology, and how it affects every part of a person's life. Not only was I still riveted by the accuracy of Chinese character reading but I was discovering how one's Chinese sign affects health patterns. I grew familiar with the five elements and how they govern the different years in which we are born. I learned about how Tigers get on with Dragons, and Goats with Snakes. I learned how to use Chinese astrology to help people understand themselves and their families, friends and acquaintances.

After fifteen years of study and experience, of toiling over obscure oriental notions, of juggling thousands of variables and applying them to real people, I had acquired so much new Chinese astrological wisdom that I decided to write a companion book to my first. My original book is really a primer. It gives a sound basis for understanding the skeleton of the Chinese astrological system. It is a readable, interesting and, in its own way, complete book. If you haven't already, I urge you to read it. But I wrote that book back in 1976. Today, I am a different woman. Not only have I gained new knowledge but I have met colonies of colorful new people whose behavior perfectly illustrates the influence of their Chinese animal signs. How could I resist wanting to share the best of a trove of stories about some of my new friends: Kathryn, the genius Monkey; Val, the arch conservative liberal Rooster; and Bill the Dog who barks overbearing customers right out of his tiny rural bookshop. Most of all, I want to tell you as much as I can about how this mystical system of Chinese astrology works and how it can help you to see your way through life's complexities.

It has been said that I am possessed of an uncanny intuition. Although I am a mathematical dunce, a loss as a logician, and can figure out absolutely nothing through cause and effect, I have always felt that if I follow my hunches, listen to my innermost voices, heed the little muse that lives directly over my right shoulder and urges me to 'Hurry up! Go ahead! Do it,' then I practically never make giant mistakes.

Why, then, do I insist on continuing to write books about Chinese astrology when I could be writing books about hunches or muses or innermost voices?

I have a friend in New York called Celeste. She is a professional astrologer and an impressive spook, *not* some abracadabra spirit worshipper weirdo. Celeste is her real name and her Italian Catholic parents certainly did not predict that she would choose at age thirty-five to become an astrologer. Celeste is a Sagittarius and a Tiger. Sagittarian Tigers do not fool around.

Last January Celeste came to visit me one afternoon in my winter quarters in Sag Harbor. She had heard of me through a mutual acquaintance who runs a metaphysical bookshop in our small Long Island town and had been told I was an astrologer, nothing more.

We had lunch and then repaired to my upstairs office to tinker with a complicated astrology program I had just put on my computer. Later, when we'd had enough of that, we went downstairs to sit in the living room, drink herb tea and chat.

Celeste, whom I had only just met, sat opposite me on the couch, sipping her steaming brew. 'I'm curious,' she said. 'Why did you decide to become an astrologer?'

I answered, 'I didn't. Astrology chose me.' My reply seemed glib but was the truth. I had consulted an astrologer in Paris, I explained, when I was young. 'After that it seemed there was no going back.'

'You mean you had no choice?' asked the concerned humanitarian Sagittarian.

'Well,' I began. 'I grew up in the sixties. Then I married a southern Californian with astrological leanings. Also, I am quite responsive to the wisdom of my intuition. Yet . . . I really can't explain it. Astrology is just part of life for me.'

'Do you ever feel as though you're being pushed into it?' asked Celeste with an inquisitive air.

Here was a new wrinkle. I nodded. 'Yes.' I clasped my hands and leaned towards her, interested. 'Yes, I do. All the time. I feel almost obliged to write about it. It's as though I may as well not even try to escape it. Chinese astrology is like a strong wind at my back.'

'Chinese astrology?' said Celeste, amazed. 'You mean you're a Chinese astrologist?'

'Yes. Well, I write books about Chinese astrology. Not often about Western signs. I'm not really an astrologer the way you are. I'm just a writer who dabbles in astrology.'

Celeste gave a short laugh and sat back against the cushions. 'Oh, boy,' she said. 'Oh, boy.' She sat forward, looked straight at me and said, 'Did you know that there is a little old Chinese man standing behind your chair?'

I wheeled around, glanced up and saw nothing. Turning back to face her I smiled. 'You were only kidding!' I was relieved.

'No,' she said. 'I am not kidding. I've been sitting here for half an hour wondering what that old Chinese guy was doing hanging around you like that. He's been there all day.'

I twisted my body again, trying to spy my Chinese companion. Once again I saw only nothing. 'Celeste, this gives me the creeps,' I said firmly.

Celeste reassured me. 'Oh, don't worry,' she said. 'Your Chinese man isn't evil. He is very, very happy. You are doing his work for him. That's what he's trying to tell you. "Hurry up! Go ahead! Do it!" he's saying.'

I didn't know Celeste very well then but have since learned that her visions are usually pure insight and can definitely be trusted. Thanks to her, I am confident that *The New Chinese Astrology* will be a huge success.

What is astrology?

Astrology is neither witchcraft nor magic. No serious astrologer claims to be able to predict exactly what will happen to whom when. And no astrologer worth his salt believes that preparing and interpreting astrological charts is absolutely scientific either. Yet we all know and accept that our individual astrological charts can be basic to learning about what makes us tick. But our personal horoscope gives nowhere near the whole story. The complete person, our real inner self, our soul, spirit, nature, *id*, ego, or whatever we call it, is not so easily accessible. Before getting to the bottom of our psyches, to understand our full range of emotions and character traits, we must find out much more.

Whether through astrology, psychology, phrenology, analysis, hypnotherapy, healing, numerology, tarot, I Ching or any number of other perfectly valid tools for developing self-knowledge, we almost never get the full picture. Try as we might, we usually only scratch the surface of who we really are, reveal only a single aspect or catch a mere hint of our total character. The quest for self-perception is long, arduous and often dead ended.

But we must be patient. We must not give up. Like detectives, we are well advised to keep a mental magnifying glass handy to examine our motives. In this way, diligently snooping behind our own scenes, we can discover new aspects of who we really are, find out how we can improve our personalities, foil our pet neuroses and alter destructive life patterns that we keep repeating to our own detriment. Painstakingly, during a whole lifetime, we should try honestly to assess our real character and make adjustments where we can to find peace of mind and to live in harmony with others and with nature.

Everything counts

Astrology can help. But it is not the whole answer.

Looking objectively at our individual natures we can readily see that from the day we are born, our selves and our lives are governed by hundreds of different influences. Each of us is a hotch-potch, a crazy quilt of varied component parts: astrology, heredity, geographical situation, environment, nationality, social class, economic stratum, religion, physical appearance, stamina, health, race, sex, and free will, to name but a few. Astrology helps to give us a basis. But we must try to take *all* the aspects of our complex selves into consideration.

Let's say you are the daughter of a Polish Jewish man and an Irish Catholic woman. You were born in Latvia but raised in Chicago. Your father started his career as a vegetable salesman pushing a cart in the street and ended up owning four supermarkets. You were raised in the Catholic faith and went to convent schools. You were never sick when you were small but you have inherited your father's allergies and now suffer from terrible hay fever. Your birth date is 12 June 1946 which makes you a Gemini/Dog. Your race is Caucasian and your sex is female.

Perhaps you feel that from the moment you discovered that you were born a Gemini/Dog, certain of your character traits became crystal clear. Maybe you can finally see why you have always been accused of being a worry wart and talking too much. But think about it. Being raised Catholic in a convent school can make you a worse worry wart than you already were. And having a Jewish father and a Catholic mother could inspire some insecurities or uncertainties as well. And being born in Latvia and unable to return there until the end of the Russian occupation means something, too. What am I getting at?

Just this. Please don't expect astrology to give you all the answers.

Count on me and my astrologer cronies to shed light on your crowded, complicated life. Don't be afraid to go looking in my work for clues to your strengths or character flaws. My job is to try to clear up your doubts about yourself, to show you how your Chinese astrological sign affects you.

But my job is certainly not to land on your window sill like some ungainly middle-aged Tinkerbell, wave my magic wand and zap your ailing refrigerator back into service. I cannot abracadabra your deeply ingrained, repeated and, in some cases, hereditary defects. I cannot put a stop to your insistence on hugging and nurturing a cherished neurosis. If you want to hate cabbage and carrots because you despised the noisy creaking of your father's vegetable cart, I cannot do anything about it.

Sometimes, people ask embarrassing questions of astrologers. 'Will I die young?' or 'Has my husband been cheating on me?' or 'Does my wife ever fantasize about the next-door neighbor?' or 'When is my baby due?' One reader wrote me a letter. 'Dear Suzanne White,' it began. 'Give me back my husband!' A caller from the central rural part of France rang up to say that he knew I had been reading his mail and that in the night I was burning his throat.

And while we're on the subject, here's one for you: a faithful reader from Zaïre sent me an expensive overland two-months late international money order for $20 requesting that I remove the evil spell from wife number three who had already borne seven of his children (whose magnificent classical-sounding names he had carefully listed), and who, it appeared, never felt like making love with him any more. I wrote back and said I was sorry but I couldn't help him. I mean, I am not a witch. None the less, I fervently believe in the value and truth of Chinese astrology.

Most astrologies are densely complicated. To know how to *do* astrology, one almost has to have studied it. Yet, there are parts of astrology that we can get close to fast. And these are the parts we will be using here. I won't be able to clear up all your doubts, but I will try to give you more than one clue to your real character. Once you have some clues, it's easier to solve your own mysteries.

As for me, I am convinced that when it comes to reading character, Chinese astrology works. I am not a missionary so I won't try to persuade you now. Rather, I suggest you read about your Chinese sign. If you don't find yourself in the descriptions, chances are you haven't been levelling with yourself about who you really are deep down. So if you don't identify with your animal sign at all, ask someone close to you to read your chapter. I'll wager they'll see more than one similarity between you and the Monkey, Rat or Snake you really are. And I will further bet that they will be able to help you to see yourself in a clearer light.

What is Chinese Astrology?

Is Chinese astrology anything like western astrology?

Like our own western astrology, Chinese astrology uses twelve different signs or symbols to define twelve basic categories of human being. Similarly to western astrology, the Chinese system uses a person's birthdate as the basis for his sign so in some ways the two systems are alike. Now, let's have a look at how they differ.

Astrology = astral + study = study of the stars
Zodiac = zoo + circle = circle of animals

We tend to use the terms astrology and zodiac almost interchangeably. Yet the Chinese zodiac is literally a circle of animals and is not very astral at all. Chinese astrology looks to philosophy, the calendar, the cosmos and the rhythms of nature for its ideas and predictions about events and character.

Western astrology, on the other hand, looks heavenward to the stars. Western astrologers chart the positions and movements of heavenly configurations to draw conclusions about both nature and the future.

Our own astrological signs are monthly. Each of our signs has a different heaven-inspired mythological name and corresponds to a period equivalent to a single moon cycle. If you were born in the moon cycle period labelled Aquarius, then in western astrological terms you are an Aquarian.

Chinese zodiacal signs are yearly. Each Chinese sign has a different animal name and corresponds to a period equivalent to an entire Chinese calendar year. If you were born in a year-long period which the Chinese label the Dragon Year, then in Chinese astrological terms you are a Dragon. Simple? Yes. Chinese astrology is so simple that you need only know the year of your birth to find out which of the twelve signs is yours.

In Chinese astrology there are no intricate charts to draw up or elusive rising signs to calculate. But there is one tricky aspect to consider. The Chinese New Year falls on a different date every year. This holiday can occur as early as mid-January or not until late February. So, if you were born in either January or February, that is, if you are either Capricorn or Aquarius in western astrology, please consult the chart on pp. xxix–xxxii to see whether your particular birthdate falls into the previous or the new Chinese year. Once you have determined your Chinese astrological sign, you need only read the chapter that corresponds to you and you're on the way to a better understanding of yourself through Chinese astrology.

The Chinese animal symbols are: Rat, Ox, Tiger, Cat, Dragon, Snake, Horse, Goat, Monkey, Rooster, Dog and Pig. These animals always appear in the same order.

At first, when I learned about Chinese astrology, I found the choice of these animals odd. Yet, when I thought about the agrarian society that existed in early China, it began to make perfect sense. The philosophers needed to make concrete their findings about how each of twelve individual years balances the power between Yin and Yang. They used familiar animals that were most characteristic of the style or tone of that year. Take the Ox year, for example. It's the second year of the twelve-year cycle. The Ox year is a traditionally slow-moving, hard-working yet docile year, suggesting a predominance of Yin over Yang. To depict it in the zodiac, the Chinese chose the slow and stubborn yet familiar beast of labor, the Water Buffalo or Ox, a Yin creature.

For the bombastic and festive fifth year of the cycle, they naturally chose the noisy mythical Dragon. The frisky seventh year is called Horse. Some of the animals are not so familiar to us now as they were back then in rural China. For example, we find rats despicable. Yet, in a barnyard setting, a rat is a very respected beast. Yes, he is invasive, but he is also powerful, protects his own and knows how to hoard food. In times of famine, the Rat is king. He takes first place in the zodiac cycle.

Since the beginning of recorded Chinese time, 2637 BC, the animal sequence has recurred faithfully every twelve years. It always begins with the Rat and ends with the Pig. And – to make things even more convenient for us twentieth-century Westerners – 1900 was a Rat year. That means that the next Rat year was 1912 and 1924, 1936, 1948, 1960, 1972, 1984 were all Rat years. Anybody born in any of these years is a Rat.

Surely by now you are wondering how a grown woman like myself dares go about proclaiming that all the people born in a single year are alike. I have heard this doubt expressed more than once. I sometimes wonder myself. I often ponder how and why it is that as early as 2637 BC, the Chinese began dividing time into periods of sixty years and then subdividing them by twelve (see p. xxvi), giving the individual years animal names and characteristics. It seems weird, doesn't it? Quaint and folkloric. I frequently ask myself how all the people born in one or another of these zoologically endowed years can have similar characters?

There is a legend that Buddha called all the animals in the kingdom together for a conference and only twelve arrived. He supposedly then rewarded each of his guests by naming a year after them. As the Rat had arrived first, he got the first year and so on down the line all the way through twelve beasts to the Pig who had come in last. Now that I have been actively involved in Chinese astrology for over fifteen years, I realize that the Buddha legend is only a legend. In an effort to sniff out the real beginnings, I have asked many scholars for a historical explanation of the origins of Chinese astrology and several Chinese sages have provided me with as many possibilities.

The one I believe and hence share with you comes from my esteemed friend and guru, a brilliant Vietnamese astrologer named Ngoc Rao. He taught me that Chinese astrology, in one form or another, was widely used all over the Orient from the fortieth century BC. It became especially popular between 2953 and 2838 BC under the Emperor Fu Hsi and again under Shen Nung who was born in the twenty-eighth century BC. The zodiacal system and its philosophies as we know them today were codified by Ta Nao, an able minister of Emperor Huang Ti, born about 2704 BC. It was made official in 2637 BC and was formally inaugurated, as were other historical events, at the sixtieth anniversary of the same popular Emperor Huang Ti's accession to the throne. For forty-six centuries thereafter, this system was used as the national standard and touched on all state affairs in China.

Rao knows a great deal about Chinese history and is an author and practicing astrologer. So, in so far as I can grasp them with my clumsy Western mind, I trust his facts. Also, I am satisfied with what

I have observed through using Chinese astrology over the years among my own clients and friends. No matter what started it or who was responsible for the first sign being Rat, the sixth Snake and the tenth Rooster, I am completely convinced. This Chinese astrology thing is a real, sane and functional tool for self-development. Besides, I don't know who invented thought or wisdom, metaphysics, rationale or poetry, but not knowing precisely where these things began doesn't stop me from using one or all of these abstractions to personal advantage almost every day of my life.

After all this time, I am still amazed by the uncanny accuracy of Chinese astrology. Maybe I am even hooked on it, because each time I add a name to my address book, I jot the person's Chinese sign next to his name. Each time I encounter a person in my business life or start an acquaintanceship with someone I try to guess his Chinese sign. Often I succeed. But if not, I unashamedly ask them what year they were born. Sometimes they tell me and sometimes they don't. But if they hang around for any length of time, sooner or later I make it my business to find out so I can add their name to my personal Chinese sign chart and start comparing their characters to the thousands of others already enrolled. If you are at all sceptical, I strongly suggest you make twelve lists of names of people you know and keep them up to date. Make some comparisons and observations of your own. Once you do this for six to eight months, you won't need any more convincing.

Over and over I have seen Chinese astrology work for myself, for my family and friends. In business, in love and in daily life, the evidence is clear. Everyone born under the same animal symbol has been allotted about the same destiny capital and will have about the same character traits. They'll have like strengths and weaknesses, comparable preferences and aversions, parallel health patterns and even medical predispositions. Their emotional make-up and reactions will be predictably similar, too. We are born with a certain wherewithal. What we do with our birth fortune is up to us.

People born in Pig years are all somewhat naïve and hate to say no; Rats are aggressive and talkative; Dogs loyal and anxious; Snakes altruistic and attractive; Dragons healthy and noisy; Horses independent and pragmatic; Goats dependent and creative and have no sense of time; Oxen slow and eloquent; Tigers rash and magnetic; Cats flee conflict and love tradition; Monkeys are entertaining and give lots of presents; Roosters are resourceful and bossy and adore clothes.

One thing is for sure. I did not invent Chinese astrology. But it is so damned clever and accurate and user-friendly that I sometimes wish I had.

Chinese philosophy in three easy lessons

Chinese astrology is a field of study which grew out of a philosophy. Chinese philosophy is often difficult for Westerners to comprehend. Because I want to share at least my own smidgeon of Chinese philosophy with you, I have tried to chop through the dense thicket of oriental thought and tidy up some of the branches. Here's what I have understood so far.

Chinese astrology has its origins in three very different yet interdependent philosophical concepts essential to Chinese thought: Yin and Yang; the five elements; and the Chinese calendar.

Yin and Yang

Yin and Yang are the two main opposite but equal oriental forces. The power of Yin is sometimes interpreted as passive, female, docile, receptive and society-oriented. Conversely, the Yang energy is said to be aggressive, male and socially indifferent. To the Chinese, everything in life is either Yin or Yang and the trick to achieving harmony is knowing how to balance Yin and Yang so they operate in synergy rather than clashing.

According to Chinese thought, any circumstance in the universe – a rainstorm, a night of love, a child taking its first steps, a wobbly bedstead, a frantic phone call, a dish of steaming pasta, a traffic accident, a dancing bride and groom or a washing-line in the sunlight – is the direct result of an energy balance or imbalance between Yin and Yang. Complicated?

Patience. Please hear me out.

According to Chinese philosophy, the world is a huge interdependent clump wherein absolutely everything is relative to everything else. Even tiny imbalances in nature can and will create commotion in the events of human life. In a given circumstance, when one of the two main life forces is disturbed, it displaces the proportion of Yin and Yang. The situation then becomes lopsided. This disproportion plays hell with harmony and our troubles begin.

So Yin and Yang are both basic to life and constitute the basis of life. They are the most important essential energies or forces in the Chinese thought universe. Naturally, each of the Chinese animal signs is either Yin or Yang.

The five elements – Wood, Fire, Earth, Metal, Water

To allow for movement to occur and bring about change, Chinese philosophy calls upon the five elements as agents of change and reaction. Change, the Chinese say, derives from the influence of the five main elements – Wood, Fire, Earth, Metal and Water – on the basic Yin or Yang balances. Like in the old rock, paper, scissors game we played as kids, each of these five Chinese elements has the ability to control and/or destroy one other of the elements and is always capable of producing the element that directly follows it. In the regenerative cycle of the elements, Water engenders Wood.

Wood is characterized by the color green. Wood heralds the beginning of life, springtime and buds, sensuality and fecundity. Wood's influence affects the liver, the gallbladder and, by extension, the digestion. Wood needs moisture to thrive. Its two opposite yet equal emotional forces are rage and altruism. The Wood person will be expansive, outgoing and socially conscious.

Wood in its turn, can create and nourish *Fire*. Fire's signatory color is red. Fire is hot weather, satisfaction of nature, aridity and dust. The tongue and the small intestine are the centers of attention in the Fire person's body. Fire makes heat which either warms or burns. The Fire person must constantly seek to balance a tendency to explode and possibly destroy, against a desire to create coziness and warmth. Passionate by nature, this impatient, ebullient person must strive to keep his flame under control.

Earth is created from the ashes of the Fire. Now we are in the soothingly satisfying late summerish cycle. Earth's favorite color is yellow, which represents the equanimity between beginnings and endings. The weather of Earth is mild or temperate. In the human body, Earth influences spleen, pancreas and mouth. Earth's two opposite but equal forces which need to be kept in constant balance are nurturing and smothering. On the one hand Earth gives care and allows for growth. On the other, Earth buries weaker souls under her too ample skirts and snuffs out their breath. Earth people are gifted for fairness and have the ability to commit themselves to protracted projects and complete herculean tasks with ease. They must struggle against a penchant for worry.

The Earth grows *Metal* in her veins. Metal says white and autumn. Metal is cool, crisp weather. Metal's effect on the body centers in the lungs and respiratory system. It only secondarily rules the large intestine and the nose. Metal people like to communicate. They need to keep a bizarre capacity for creating discord and a gift for sowing harmony in constant balance. Metal is the onset of winter. Its influence can sometimes add sadness or gloom to an astrological chart. Two of Metal's emotional forces are melancholy and romance. I see Metal as Wagnerian. Metal people must guard against a tendency to wallow in nostalgia.

Lastly, Metal begets *Water* – ground water trickling its way through layers of the Earth's ore. Water's color is blue. Its season is full-blown winter. Water is always moving, fluid, mutational. In our bodies, water's influence affects our plumbing systems, the kidneys and the bladder. The ear, too, comes under the spell of Water. Hence people born in Water-ruled years are frequently musical. They pick up on everything. Be it good or bad, they never miss a vibe. Water-ruled creatures are always very sensitive and sometimes even mentally fragile. The down side of Water's influence, then, is a stressful nervousness. To balance that fidgety, squeamish, overly sensitive side, Water endows its subjects with the noblest quality of all, kindness and sympathy. Sometimes too permeable, the Water-ruled must take precautions against drowning in the chagrin of those they see as less fortunate than themselves.

So, the five elements cause the commotion and are responsible for creating both balance and imbalance – for moving things around and making life interesting. These purveyors of change can be controlled or not, depending on how one manages them.

Each animal year of the Chinese zodiac has been assigned one of the five elements. That element turns up twice in the cycle before going away for another ten years. The five elements are always presented in the above order. Once we know this, we can understand how the elements directly affect us and pertain to our individual characters.

The Chinese calendar

The Chinese calendar year contains either twelve or thirteen moons. Unlike our fixed Gregorian calendar year which always ends *plunk* on 31 December and begins promptly at midnight on 1 January, the Chinese year is a flexible entity which never begins or ends on the same date twice in a row. The Chinese year may terminate any time between late January and mid-February on our calendar (see charts on pp. xxix–xxxii for specific dates). Just as on our calendar, the last day of the old Chinese year falls the day before the first day of the new Chinese year. For example, a Dog year ended on 7 February 1959, the Pig year directly following it started on 8 February of that same 1959. So, if you were born in January or up thru 7 February of 1959 on the Gregorian calendar, your birthday falls into the previous Chinese Dog year and even though we call 1959 a Pig year, you are still a Dog.

The Chinese divide up time differently, too. Our Gregorian or Christian calendar is made up of centuries that cover one hundred years and are subdivided by ten into ten-year periods called decades: 10 × 10 = 100. The Chinese have 'centuries', too, but they are only sixty Chinese years long. The sixty-year Chinese 'centuries' are subdivided into five twelve-year periods that I like to call 'dozencades': 5 × 12 = 60.

The Chinese are not in the twentieth century of their calendar. They are way ahead of us, not only because they started earlier and didn't base everything in their calendar on the birth of Christ, but also because they have shorter, sixty-year centuries. The Chinese entered their seventy-eighth 'century', dating from way back in 2367 BC at the sixtieth anniversary celebration of the Emperor Huang Ti, on 2 February 1984. The next Chinese 'century' will start in 2044.

The elements work by governing each animal sign once through the sixty-year 'century'. You will not come across a Water Dog or a Fire Horse more than once in sixty years. This fact alone accounts for sixty different basic character or destiny types. Further, when a learned Chinese astrologer drafts a chart for an individual person according to the oriental astrological system, he takes into consideration the month and the season, the time of day and the type of weather on the day of birth as well as certain astral configurations at the moment of birth. In all, good Chinese astrologers deal with a base of no less than 512,640 different possible personality charts. This means that only two people in a million stand a chance of being born with identical destinies.

In this book, we shall first approach an in-depth, yet jolly, understanding of the twelve basic animal signs – their character traits, their good and bad habits, their tastes and dislikes. We'll discuss their physical type, their health and their love behavior. Then, we will take a look at the sixty possible variations on these twelve human themes created by the governing elements' influences. Following that, we'll take a glimpse into the future and see how our particular sign will fare throughout the entire twelve-year Chinese cycle. Finally, we shall see how each of us gets along with the various members of the other signs.

I hope this jaunt through the byways of Chinese astrology as it applies to modern life will prove both amusing and useful. If not, drop me a line at the address below and I'll try to answer your queries or at least find you a real expert who can.

Suzanne White
Suzanne@Suzannewhite.com

The Chinese Calendar

Year	*Sign*	*Element*	*Year Begins*	*Year Ends*
1900	Rat	Metal	31 Jan 1900	18 Feb 1901
1901	Ox	Metal	19 Feb 1901	7 Feb 1902
1902	Tiger	Water	8 Feb 1902	28 Jan 1903
1903	Cat	Water	29 Jan 1903	15 Feb 1904
1904	Dragon	Wood	16 Feb 1904	3 Feb 1905
1905	Snake	Wood	4 Feb 1905	24 Jan 1906
1906	Horse	Fire	25 Jan 1906	12 Feb 1907
1907	Goat	Fire	13 Feb 1907	2 Feb 1908
1908	Monkey	Earth	3 Feb 1908	21 Jan 1909
1909	Rooster	Earth	22 Jan 1909	9 Feb 1910
1910	Dog	Metal	10 Feb 1910	29 Jan 1911
1911	Pig	Metal	30 Jan 1911	17 Feb 1912
1912	Rat	Water	18 Feb 1912	5 Feb 1913
1913	Ox	Water	6 Feb 1913	25 Jan 1914
1914	Tiger	Wood	26 Jan 1914	13 Feb 1915
1915	Cat	Wood	14 Feb 1915	2 Feb 1916
1916	Dragon	Fire	3 Feb 1916	22 Jan 1917
1917	Snake	Fire	23 Jan 1917	10 Feb 1918
1918	Horse	Earth	11 Feb 1918	31 Jan 1919
1919	Goat	Earth	1 Feb 1919	19 Feb 1920
1920	Monkey	Metal	20 Feb 1920	7 Feb 1921
1921	Rooster	Metal	8 Feb 1921	27 Jan 1922
1922	Dog	Water	28 Jan 1922	15 Feb 1923
1923	Pig	Water	16 Feb 1923	4 Feb 1924
1924	Rat	Wood	5 Feb 1924	23 Jan 1925
1925	Ox	Wood	24 Jan 1925	12 Feb 1926
1926	Tiger	Fire	13 Feb 1926	1 Feb 1927
1927	Cat	Fire	2 Feb 1927	22 Jan 1928
1928	Dragon	Earth	23 Jan 1928	9 Feb 1929
1929	Snake	Earth	10 Feb 1929	29 Jan 1930

Year	*Sign*	*Element*	*Year Begins*	*Year Ends*
1930	Horse	Metal	30 Jan 1930	16 Feb 1931
1931	Goat	Metal	17 Feb 1931	5 Feb 1932
1932	Monkey	Water	6 Feb 1932	25 Jan 1933
1933	Rooster	Water	26 Jan 1933	13 Feb 1934
1934	Dog	Wood	14 Feb 1934	3 Feb 1935
1935	Pig	Wood	4 Feb 1935	23 Jan 1936
1936	Rat	Fire	24 Jan 1936	10 Feb 1937
1937	Ox	Fire	11 Feb 1937	30 Jan 1938
1938	Tiger	Earth	31 Jan 1938	18 Feb 1939
1939	Cat	Earth	19 Feb 1939	7 Feb 1940
1940	Dragon	Metal	8 Feb 1940	26 Jan 1941
1941	Snake	Metal	27 Jan 1941	14 Feb 1942
1942	Horse	Water	15 Feb 1942	4 Feb 1943
1943	Goat	Water	5 Feb 1943	24 Jan 1944
1944	Monkey	Wood	25 Jan 1944	12 Feb 1945
1945	Rooster	Wood	13 Feb 1945	1 Feb 1946
1946	Dog	Fire	2 Feb 1946	21 Jan 1947
1947	Pig	Fire	22 Jan 1947	9 Feb 1948
1948	Rat	Earth	10 Feb 1948	28 Jan 1949
1949	Ox	Earth	29 Jan 1949	16 Feb 1950
1950	Tiger	Metal	17 Feb 1950	5 Feb 1951
1951	Cat	Metal	6 Feb 1951	26 Jan 1952
1952	Dragon	Water	27 Jan 1952	13 Feb 1953
1953	Snake	Water	14 Feb 1953	2 Feb 1954
1954	Horse	Wood	3 Feb 1954	23 Jan 1955
1955	Goat	Wood	24 Jan 1955	11 Feb 1956
1956	Monkey	Fire	12 Feb 1956	30 Jan 1957
1957	Rooster	Fire	31 Jan 1957	17 Feb 1958
1958	Dog	Earth	18 Feb 1958	7 Feb 1959
1959	Pig	Earth	8 Feb 1959	27 Jan 1960
1960	Rat	Metal	28 Jan 1960	14 Feb 1961
1961	Ox	Metal	15 Feb 1961	4 Feb 1962
1962	Tiger	Water	5 Feb 1962	24 Jan 1963
1963	Cat	Water	25 Jan 1963	12 Feb 1964
1964	Dragon	Wood	13 Feb 1964	1 Feb 1965
1965	Snake	Wood	2 Feb 1965	20 Jan 1966
1966	Horse	Fire	21 Jan 1966	8 Feb 1967
1967	Goat	Fire	9 Feb 1967	29 Jan 1968
1968	Monkey	Earth	30 Jan 1968	16 Feb 1969
1969	Rooster	Earth	17 Feb 1969	5 Feb 1970

Year	*Sign*	*Element*	*Year Begins*	*Year Ends*
1970	Dog	Metal	6 Feb 1970	26 Jan 1971
1971	Pig	Metal	27 Jan 1971	14 Feb 1972
1972	Rat	Water	15 Feb 1972	2 Feb 1973
1973	Ox	Water	3 Feb 1973	22 Jan 1974
1974	Tiger	Wood	23 Jan 1974	10 Feb 1975
1975	Cat	Wood	11 Feb 1975	30 Jan 1976
1976	Dragon	Fire	31 Jan 1976	17 Feb 1977
1977	Snake	Fire	18 Feb 1977	6 Feb 1978
1978	Horse	Earth	7 Feb 1978	27 Jan 1979
1979	Goat	Earth	28 Jan 1979	15 Feb 1980
1980	Monkey	Metal	16 Feb 1980	4 Feb 1981
1981	Rooster	Metal	5 Feb 1981	24 Jan 1982
1982	Dog	Water	25 Jan 1982	12 Feb 1983
1983	Pig	Water	13 Feb 1983	1 Feb 1984
1984	Rat	Wood	2 Feb 1984	19 Feb 1985
1985	Ox	Wood	20 Feb 1985	8 Feb 1986
1986	Tiger	Fire	9 Feb 1986	28 Jan 1987
1987	Cat	Fire	29 Jan 1987	16 Feb 1988
1988	Dragon	Earth	17 Feb 1988	5 Feb 1989
1989	Snake	Earth	6 Feb 1989	26 Jan 1990
1990	Horse	Metal	27 Jan 1990	14 Feb 1991
1991	Goat	Metal	15 Feb 1991	3 Feb 1992
1992	Monkey	Water	4 Feb 1992	22 Jan 1993
1993	Rooster	Water	23 Jan 1993	9 Feb 1994
1994	Dog	Wood	10 Feb 1994	30 Jan 1995
1995	Pig	Wood	31 Jan 1995	18 Feb 1996
1996	Rat	Fire	19 Feb 1996	6 Feb 1997
1997	Ox	Fire	7 Feb 1997	27 Jan 1998
1998	Tiger	Earth	28 Jan 1998	15 Feb 1999
1999	Cat	Earth	16 Feb 1999	4 Feb 2000
2000	Dragon	Metal	5 Feb 2000	23 Jan 2001
2001	Snake	Metal	24 Jan 2001	11 Feb 2002
2002	Horse	Water	12 Feb 2002	31 Jan 2003
2003	Goat	Water	1 Feb 2003	21 Jan 2004
2004	Monkey	Wood	22 Jan 2004	8 Feb 2005
2005	Rooster	Wood	9 Feb 2005	28 Jan 2006
2006	Dog	Fire	29 Jan 2006	17 Feb 2007
2007	Pig	Fire	18 Feb 2007	6 Feb 2008
2008	Rat	Earth	7 Feb 2008	25 Jan 2009
2009	Ox	Earth	26 Jan 2009	13 Feb 2010

Year	*Sign*	*Element*	*Year Begins*	*Year Ends*
2010	Tiger	Metal	14 Feb 2010	2 Feb 2011
2011	Cat	Metal	3 Feb 2011	22 Jan 2012
2012	Dragon	Water	23 Jan 2012	9 Feb 2013
2013	Snake	Water	10 Feb 2013	30 Jan 2014
2014	Horse	Wood	31 Jan 2014	18 Feb 2015
2015	Goat	Wood	19 Feb 2015	7 Feb 2016
2016	Monkey	Fire	8 Feb 2016	27 Jan 2017
2017	Rooster	Fire	28 Jan 2017	15 Feb 2018
2018	Dog	Earth	16 Feb 2018	4 Feb 2019
2019	Pig	Earth	5 Feb 2019	24 Jan 2020

The Relentless Rat

Illustrious Rat,

You lucky Rat, you. In China, Rats are very highly prized (and not just for supper). You are power hungry and know how to 'go for it'. Once you get those tiny Rat claws firmly around an honored position, you hold on for dear life. Leadership becomes you. People respect you. You seem so cool. You are fun-loving and sociable. But your private self is often fidgety and nervous. You need to talk problems through. Getting anxiety off your chest is as good as putting it out of your mind.

Some accuse you of being *too* communicative. Let's just say you talk a lot. You are not a willing idler. You're quick-witted. You speed through work to have plenty of time left to meddle in what others are up to. When dealing in delicate matters, you instinctively know how to keep your whiskers clean. Yet, you aren't a straight arrow. You would always rather zigzag your way to fame and fortune than trot the straight and narrow.

You tend to be picky. You are paradoxical. An odd mix of profligate and thrifty, saving everything from worn-out rubber bands to frayed shirt collars, just in case, then spending like a bandit on some extortionately costly bauble that you deem essential to your well-being.

You charm others into doing what you want. Winning friends and seducing lovers is child's play for you sexy Rat folk. Still, I don't see you as promiscuous: you are the marrying kind, you require a family. Run out and win yourself a flamboyant Dragon, a conscientious Ox or a trickier-than-thou Monkey mate. Steer clear of Cats and Horses. Youth is a jolly time for you, energetic Rat, but midlife can bring your downfall due to errors of judgement in love or business matters. If you deign to seek counsel from friends, your golden years should prove comfortable and cloudless. My advice? Stop fretting. You'll never starve. Crafty go-getters like you rarely do.

Your secret admirer,

Suzanne White

In the twentieth and twenty-first century all Rats were born between the following dates:

31	January	1900	and	18	February	1901
18	February	1912	and	5	February	1913
5	February	1924	and	23	January	1925
24	January	1936	and	10	February	1937
10	February	1948	and	28	January	1949
28	January	1960	and	14	February	1961
15	February	1972	and	2	February	1973
2	February	1984	and	19	February	1985
19	February	1996	and	6	February	1997
7	February	2008	and	25	January	2009

The Rat ID card

Lasting symbols have special powers. Enhance your self-image by surrounding yourself with tangible signs of your own identity and make these symbols known to your friends and loved ones. Use them daily and they will bring you luck, security and a feeling of personal worth.

Your best
color is warm ochre
flower is daisy
fragrance is sandalwood
tree is oak
flavor is piquant
birthstone is emerald
lucky number is 11

Your favorite
food is sweetbreads
animal is wild goose
drink is bordeaux (claret)
spice is coriander
metal is bronze
herb is rosemary
musical instrument is violin

The Rat is Yin

The Rat motto is 'I rule'

Sunny side up, Rats are charming, protective, compassionate, communicative, dynamic, familial, thrifty, skilful, sober, upright, attractive, idealistic, prosperous, experimental, calm, sensual, loving, talented, adaptable, open-minded, brilliant entrepreneurs.

But in their darker moments Rats may wax verbose, grow possessive, picky, defensive, excessive, addictive, fickle, stingy, bumptious, bossy, exploitive, anxious, argumentative, opinionated, overbearing and downright self-obsessed.

Rat tales

Legend has it that Buddha called together twelve symbolic animals for a power powwow. The Rat showed up first. As recompense for his alacrity, Buddha awarded him the honor of being the first sign of the Chinese zodiac. To know a Rat is to understand just how seriously each one takes Buddha's gift of first position. *Born leader* is a gross understatement. Rats are leadership *freaks*.

Rats are the people for whom the expression, 'Never a dull moment' was invented. They love fiercely, work intensely, play with the zeal of a driven golf ball, compete with everyone in sight (including themselves) and never stop talking. Rats have opinions on all subjects. What's more, they never cease to offer them. They insist on discussing every aspect and nuance of any idea, scrutinizing all the details and dissecting each shade of meaning.

Rats do too much, go in too many directions at once and are constantly at risk of scattering their efforts too widely, weakening the thrust of their central strength. Most Rats get more accomplished in twenty-four hours than the rest of us do in as many days. An engine inside their ratty little heads hums along in perpetual motion, jet-propelling them to achieve.

The name of the Rat game is 'herculean performance'. No half-way measures nor small potatoes for Rats. They are never satisfied with the mediocre. Piddling projects bore them. Routine stifles them. Only novelty and excitement stir the cauldron, causing their little Rat hearts to throb *kaboom, kaboom*. Daredevil plans, romantic callings entice and inspire them. Out of nowhere, *pouf*! Off flies your favorite Rat, following his heart instead of his hitherto reasonable head. Next thing you know he's running a war or diving for pearls. The Rat doesn't flinch at transplanting his entire family in Thailand for a year to learn the language and discover Thai cuisine, music and art. He feels adventure ought to be the norm – the more harrowing, the happier the Rat.

Although he can be thoughtful at times, it is rare to catch a Rat sitting quietly. These people are constantly, exaggeratedly, and with reckless abandon, on the run. Rats jump on the treadmill when they leap out of bed in the morning and never stop till they drop back into bed. 'Go' is their byword, action their hobby, drama the very soul of their existence. Rats need movement the way dogs need company. Anything less than whirlwind running, chasing and accomplishing depresses the Rat. If he stops whirring like an overwrought helicopter, he sinks and sulks, complains and drives everyone to distraction.

Rats are not easy but they are worth it – ask anyone who has a Rat for a lover, parent, child or friend. Rats revere and cherish those close to them, pay incessant compliments, remind their loved ones when to take their medicine, drive them to the mountains in the middle of the night for a ski jaunt, give up Sunday afternoon to hang kitchen cupboards single-handedly, advise on finances, decorating, or heartbreak.

Rats not only esteem and protect those they love . . . they take the necessary time to do so as well. They are past masters at giving undivided attention or creating individually designed moments just to please and encourage the person they adore.

Holding the job of close friend or companion to the Rat is also absorbing, time-consuming, exhausting work. Rats pick up on every trace of a new expression, and every sigh or smirk that you don't monitor yourself will be monitored for you by your Rat companion. When a Rat is talking to you, you dare not let your attention stray: 'Are you listening to me?' he asks. 'Am I boring you?' he worries.

Rat chat can be tedious. They need to talk but they are not attracted to the discreetly solitary game of monologue-in-the-mirror. They need an audience, feedback, so seek out someone they like and try to find a clever way to corner them for a good old natter. If you are so lucky as to be chosen as a Rat interlocutor, you are sure to be flattered – at first. In the beginning, you may even get a word or two in edgeways. Watch him operate, though. You tell your story and, charmingly, he comes right back with something – but only vaguely related. If he's angling to use up a lot of your time, he may even give you a second chance to try to redirect the conversation. But Ratso's hidden agenda calls for him to take over the direction of the *tête-à-tête* and ultimately monopolize it.

Stories you have heard before are a very important part of every Rat's repertoire. 'Did I ever tell you about the day Bernadette and I went to the supermarket and a Turkish chap in a long robe tried to steal our cart?'or 'I wonder if I told you about that man I dated in the sixties who liked to be beaten with spaghetti?' Because you know that your Rat desperately needs to re-recount his favorite episode, you sit back and listen raptly.

While you're at it, notice the intricacy of those lengthy preambles. Rats have a tendency to start all their personal stories in their mother's birth canal, tracing each developing molecule through infancy and childhood until finally, an hour later, they arrive at yesterday's gripping experience with the balding bank teller whose eyes are two different colors. If you have half a life to blow sitting around shooting the breeze, you should team up with a garrulous Rat. You will never be bored.

But you might be irked and infuriated by his occasionally pushy style. Rats have trouble accepting second place. Not only are they jealous of attention given to others, but they must be seen to shine and be thought of as the brains and soul behind everything. Back-seat driving is a Rat speciality. In company, Rats often try to usurp the dynamic of the group and because they are both seductive and aggressive, they accomplish this by the most divinely clever and slinky means.

Quick of wit and fleet of foot, Rats know better than almost anyone how to take their time, sneak up on their prey, focus on their target and pounce at the perfect split second. When first they join the group, Rats pretend to co-operate with the crowd, play all the socially necessary games, fitting neatly in like putty in a window frame. Then, when you least expect it, they rocket to a position of force, effortlessly zap the others into submission and perform a peaceful (but no-nonsense) takeover.

Richard Reventlow, my Rat friend in New York, gives arcane surprise parties for his unsuspecting wife, Sheila. Next year everyone is invited to Bali for her authentic Pacific birthday party experience.

But in group play, unless Richard-the-Rat gets to be the mother, he takes his dolly dishes and goes home in a huff.

I shall never forget the time I went to the cinema with the Reventlows. It was years ago but the feeling that went with the moment has permanently lodged in my left elbow. When we entered the lobby, Richard patiently waited to buy our tickets then motioned Sheila and me ahead of him and took back his three stubs from the man at the door. As we crossed the threshold of the darkened cinema looking for a seat, I was in the lead. I don't like to bother other people when they're already engrossed by being picky over seats, so I hastily opted for three on the aisle of the middle block. I started to sit down, silently beckoning my friends to join me as discreetly as possible.

Suddenly I was lifted from my half-sit by a gripping hand beneath my elbow. Then, I was ordered – yes, *ordered* – to, 'Come with me!' by the previously gentlemanly Richard Reventlow.

I resisted. 'No, Richard. This is just fine. Please sit down.' I tried to disengage my elbow from his iron grasp.

But nothing doing. Reventlow had something else in mind, seats that he, the self-appointed leader of this party, would choose. 'Follow me,' he said in a loud hiss.

This decision-making position, I could tell, was crucial to the bones of his Rat self. He felt that it was his job, his duty, his privilege and his responsibility to remove me from the role of pilot and assume his birthright – leadership.

I didn't want to make a scene so I followed him and sat down where he wanted me to. I might add that Sheila (who expects such behavior by now) trotted sheep-like behind us. I was furious. I had been transformed into a helpless child by this normally sweet man. Richard the Rat had turned into Hitler. I sat through the whole film in a white rage and vowed never to go to the movies with my friend Richard again. Of course this has had no impact on his takeover charms. When it comes to being captain even of a rowing boat, he (like all Rats) perseveres until the job is his. His ends very often justify his means: when he plays scoutmaster one always has a good time.

Being choosy about who runs the show has enormous advantages. Richard-the-Rat's need for ascendancy, his determination to be consulted above all others and to make the final decisions recently saved his wife's life.

One afternoon Sheila had a headache. It got worse and she had to lie down. The kids called Richard home from the office. He summoned an ambulance and raced his wife to the nearest hospital where they immediately did a scan. The attending doctor came out saying, 'Your wife is having a massive cerebral hemorrhage. Either I operate or I don't. It's up to you.'

Poor Richard, who always has every detail under control, who governs his life and his family's lives with loving care, was frightened. Thirty years of loving marriage and now this . . . Sheila was not even fifty. The doctor added, 'Before you decide, Mr Reventlow, I would advise you to think about the quality of her life. I'm afraid she will be a vegetable.'

Richard rose to the challenge. He looked the doctor squarely in the eye and said, in his best superman controlled voice, 'I want a second opinion.'

The doctor summoned a top brain surgeon who rapidly consulted the scans and magnetic resonance tests. 'I must go in there,' the big specialist told Richard. 'Now!'

The operation was a complete success. Thanks to Richard's insistence on making all the important decisions, Sheila is now writing her third book, as perky and fun-loving as ever. Richard's decision saved her speech, her wits and most of her motor control. The Rat is the subtle takeover chief of the whole world. The need to lead, decide, gain dominion and influence over others reaches to the very essence of Rat behavior. It can translate into bullying but the Rat's head honcho complex has its useful side.

The Rat craves social acceptance and peer approval. He spends much of his life seeking a place in society where he can feel both comfortable and loved for who he really is. Attention and affection, regular release of emotion and close companionship are essential to his equilibrium. However, as Rats are not easily open and intimate with strangers and tend to keep their counsel rather than tell the truth in delicate situations, they are frequently cut off from real friendship and camaraderie. And they are the first to wonder why. Rats may have a large circle of acquaintances but as they fear proximity, tend to be suspicious of easy intimacy and refuse to suffer fools; they may have only one or two good friends whom they trust and with whom they share innermost secrets.

Nothing makes the Rat feel worse than loneliness. The fear of isolation plagues him. If a Rat senses he is being ignored or suspects rejection by a loved one, he can soon become invested with a panic which drives him to indulge in excess. The Rat is not naturally promiscuous so sex is not usually where he seeks solace. But a rudderless Rat may readily take to drugs, overspending, gambling or drink and sometimes never return to a normal life.

The Chinese claim that Rats have an easy childhood and young adult life but that they make poor choices about love and money in midlife. The years between thirty-five and fifty-five can be tormented, uncertain and financially unrewarding for the Rat. However, the Chinese also say that Rats who gain wisdom through adversity can benefit from a comfortable and harmonious old age.

Rats are notoriously tight-fisted. They know how to earn money and are gifted in keeping it. As they are supremely opportunistic, they only invest time and emotion in exclusive relationships where there is something to gain. Once they earn money, they take it seriously. Rats are the original gold-pieces-in-a-sock-under-the-bed shekel-pinchers.

Contrary to their scrimping habits, Rats may surprise you with inordinate generosity. If a Rat takes a shine to someone, he is likely to lavish everything from exciting presents to flowery compliments and deafening applause on him in an effort to show his appreciation. Rats open their houses and arms to their loved ones for ever. 'Come, live with me. Yes. Stay as long as you like . . .'

Hospitality is no stranger to the Rat's panoply of good qualities. You are truly welcome in his home but don't be surprised if you are almost immediately pressed into service. 'Hey, Jack, you got a minute?' says the Rat, next afternoon.

Three hours later, when you're still trimming hedges or mowing lawns, remember that I warned you: never take up residence at the *Auberge du Rat Généreux* unless you are prepared to participate in *all* the projects Ratso thinks up. And watch out if you don't trim that hedge straight. Rats can be cranky as hell. There is a meticulous side to the Rat's character which wants every chore done correctly, flawlessly and without ado. He is impatient with sloppy work, intolerant of those who cannot do what he wants, and finds himself amazingly comfortable with those he considers fellow geniuses.

In public, Rats always appear cool and controlled. At first meeting, one is invariably impressed by their self-possession, how cheerful yet businesslike and serious their demeanor, how dashing, how serene and together they seem. Rat women take pains always to be well groomed and spiffily dressed. Rat men wear conservative yet extremely individualistic clothes, choosing rich natural colors and tying scarves or ties with the *savoir-faire* of a top-notch *couturier*.

But, for fun, sit next to a sedate Rat at a dinner party. Notice how the tablecloth keeps flapping about next to your neighbor's leg? You can be sure that the more sober and collected he seems, the more frenetically the Rat is jerking his leg. Rats are famous for hidden nervous tics. See how they operate in business meetings. Everyone is sitting composedly around a conference table. Watch the Rat. He always looks the most impressively serene. His placid expression belies no inner anxiety or displeasure. Yet, if you look closer, you'll see that he is fidgeting, snapping a rubber band or bending and reshaping a paper-clip. The Rat's secret jitters reveal his tension. Perhaps they help to minimize the stress or frustration inside.

Parties, social gatherings, political organizations and clubs always attract a preponderance of Rats. As he is compelled to obtain the acceptance of his entourage, membership and ascendancy in well-established, well-intentioned groups fire his imagination. Humanitarian efforts and charities bore him, but the Rat will involve himself – if only to be better accepted by his community. And because he reckons, he might be able to run for president of the whole shebang. Even the gentlest, most unassuming Rat is hungry for control and influence over others. Rats will do anything – cater to the needs of whoever it is who makes the group tick, flatter the ladies' auxiliary, regale them with funny stories, and send gifts for the holidays – to be noticed, earn respect and a chance at the highest office.

Besides being popular and amusing, the Rat is kind. He is also honest, intelligent, methodical, meticulous, versatile and flexible. His ability to sugar-coat bitter pills, talk people in and out of tight spots and offer sound advice is unparalleled. He is also an adviser whose irresistibly seductive sweet talk inclines people to share their secrets with him.

As for himself, the Rat prefers to remain impenetrably secretive about what's going on inside his head and heart. After all, he needs to gain ground, profit from the network of his friends and acquaintances, earn and keep material wealth and reach for power, which precludes the luxury of confiding in others. If he opens his own Pandora's box, too much of his soul will be revealed and the Rat will not only feel naked, but will inevitably become vulnerable to the onslaughts of enemies and competitors.

In China, Rats have a reputation for stinginess yet I have not noticed much avarice among them. There exists, however, a complicated set of financial priorities belonging exclusively to the Rat. First, when the bill arrives at the table, there is always an uncomfortable moment when the Rat pipes up saying, 'Well, well, here's the bill,' and everybody shudders. Even though he is frequently wealthier than all his guests and indeed often pays for the whole gang, the Rat is never easy-going about money.

Rats are drastically penny wise and pound foolish. They rush around the house tutting and scolding, turning down thermostats and switching off lights, or else they hoard sugar and flour in case the price goes up. Then they are complaining because their larder isn't overflowing with cases of champagne and race out to buy fresh strawberries in December. Rats spend lavishly on food, entertainment and drink. Their houses are always filled with excellent quality furniture and they always dress nattily. Yet, when it is time to put their hand in their pocket to help out a friend or contribute to a charity, their claws wither and fall helplessly to their sides.

But, yet, the Rat *is* among the most generous people alive. No Rat has lent me money but scores have lent me their houses, handed over their car keys and willingly shared their own network of acquaintances with me. Rat friends have long-term babysat *gratis* for me when I was ill. Rat doctors have gone out of their way to improve my life. My Rat lawyer has unselfishly saved me too many times for his own good. Rats have loved me intensely, without reserve. Rats are inveterate givers of fine gifts, throwers of extravagant parties, providers of ample *bonne cuisine*, labor and hospitality. Yet, no matter how you cut it, that little extra pin money that is expendable capital to you and me will for ever remain money in the bank to the incorrigibly frugal Rat.

Squandering money is not the Rat's strongest suit – indeed, Rats make poor gamblers because they are terrible losers. They shouldn't play at so much as the lottery because if they don't win they hate themselves for frittering away precious capital. Don't ask your Rat friends for a loan but don't hesitate to fall into their arms when you have a broken heart. They'll take you in, defend your point of view, hug you to pieces and feed you blind with advice. A Rat friend may never offer you his shirt, but he can always be counted on to cover your back.

When I was first in France I met a Rat woman named Irma Pride. Irma was about forty-five and I was twenty-three. We worked together in the same American Air Force base and school outside Paris. Irma was head of the GI recreation center on the base when I was a high school guidance counsellor. Irma was widowed; she lived with her three kids in an old mill house about ten miles from the base. I, and many others used to delight in having dinner with Irma and her family because, in true Rat fashion, Irma gave fabulous dinner parties. Like a true Southern lady from Kentucky, she also had a woman who cooked and served meals. Gracious and convivial are two words that come quickly to mind when I recall those long evenings around the fireplace, gossiping with Irma.

In those days, I shared a flat in Paris with a French girlfriend. It was an hour and a half's drive to work and I often spent my free time in the city. Still a kid, I had scorned such details as the base speed limit of ten miles an hour.

One rainy afternoon I sped on to the base from the French

countryside where the top speed limit was as many miles per hour as your car could move or no speed limit at all. I charged through the gate doing 30, waving a sunny hello to the nice military policeman manning the entrance. I was late (as usual) so I jumped out of my car and began gathering books to beeline for the office door. Just then, a big Mercury convertible drew up next to my car and parked. A tall guy in civilian clothes unfolded himself from the driver's seat and came towards me. 'D'you know the speed limit on this base, lady?' His eyes narrowed as he added, 'What's your name?'

I was pretty flippant in those days. He might have been asking me for my phone number. 'And what's yours, big boy?' I queried and started walking away.

A slow drawl came washing up behind me like a dense cloud of noxious gas. 'Ahm Buss Cones,' it said. 'Head o' the Air Police.'

It all came back to me then. This was the self-same guy I had rejected the previous week in the officers' club. He had asked me a lot of dim-witted questions about why I didn't live on the base and what I saw in French people who were obviously not on 'our' side. At that moment, I didn't give two hoots who he was. I was late and he was detaining me. I kept walking, head high into the wind, towards my building. He followed. 'Ah could pull yer license for this,' he threatened. 'This here's insubordination.'

I cannot tell you how exasperated I felt but maybe I had been driving a bit fast. 'I'm sorry if I drove too fast,' I snapped. 'It won't happen again.'

'Give me your license,' he said.

I refused. Flatly. Then I said coldly, with no respect whatsoever, 'Look, Mister Buzz Cones, why don't you just Buzz on over to your officer's quarters and put on your badge and your uniform before you start stealing my personal papers?'

Buzz phoned me about an hour later and told me to come over to his police shack and 'surrender' my license. 'If you want my license,' I shot back, 'send one of your goons over here to fetch it. I'm busy.'

After that the situation degenerated rapidly and Buzz sent an officer pronto to pick up my license. There I was. A long way from home and forbidden to drive my car. Where in the devil would I sleep?

After work, I sped over to the recreation center to spill my story to Irma the Rat. 'Then he said this and I said that and . . . I hate him!' I boohooed.

Irma shifted straight into Rat action mode. She dialled Buzz Cones's office at the cop shack and in her Kentuckiest patrician accent asked to speak to Captain Cones. 'Hullo theyuh, Mistuh Cones,' she said graciously. 'This is Mizz Pride, director of the recreation centuh.'

'Maham?' I could practically hear old Buzzy boy clicking his heels through the receiver.

'Buzz?' Irma went on in that condescending Southern lady voice, 'I have a little lady here in mah office. And, Buzz honey, she's sittin' here cryin' her eyes out over her license. She's General John White's baby daughter and she just keeps wantin' to call him up way over there in Korea where he's head o' the troops and . . . well, Buzz, she's mighty overwrought and she just wants to talk to her daddy in the worst way . . .'

My licence arrived within five minutes, carried by the officer who had wrestled it away from me an hour earlier. Ah, the cleverness of Rats.

Rats are not always devious. They are sincere, warm-hearted and gentle souls. That they so desperately seek dominion over others results from their strong fear of both loneliness and failure. Power over others ensures that others are present, swimming around in the Rat's personal pond, unable to escape his need for attention or depart from his sphere of influence. Although it is commonly thought that the chief is always the loneliest Indian, the Rat clearly does not see things like that. To him a solid leadership position – father, mother, boss, teacher, president – not only symbolizes success but promises lifelong companionship. Although the people-hungry Rat prefers to be loved and cherished by his constituency, whether or not his serfs and subjects adore or detest him is of little importance. What matters most is that he arrives at the summit and remains on top. Whatever the cost in loss of esteem or lack of respect, at least the Rat is surrounded.

What remains the single most glaring Rat weakness is a thorny complex about who he really is. Not visibly insecure or unsure of himself, the Rat is none the less a technicolor identity crisis. He presents a public picture of solidity and good fellowship, broadcasts confidence rays in public and seems fine in any situation. He is adaptable, flexible and usually not stubborn. But he is soooo nervous. Soooo afraid of losing, of not pleasing, of never having enough and of not being up to snuff that he lives in a perpetually precarious position of self-doubt which drums at his soul chanting: 'Who am I? Why am I here? Where am I going? What's wrong with me? How can I better succeed? How will I make people like me?'

Not only does he want to be perfect, but the Rat suffers for his lack of perfection. He regrets the indifference of every person he does not charm or attract. He vows that he will improve his approach, be nicer, kinder and find a way to inveigle everyone to like, appreciate, approve of and understand him. Perhaps this is why he is so relentlessly beguiling. He dreams of being loved solely for what he is and is prepared to perform valorous deeds or commit underhand finagles – anything – to ensure that he gets that much-needed loving acceptance. Yet, the Rat was born dissatisfied with himself. He would always rather be perfect than just plain 'fine, thank you'. He fears never being able to inspire a reciprocal relationship intense and unconditional enough to satisfy his need for unflinching, unswerving romantic devotion.

To alleviate this, he should give himself more latitude. He should drop his ego and his guard, learn to accept his mistakes, indulge himself in a few harmless peccadilloes and realize that he, too, has the right to be an ordinary human being. With a modicum of objectivity, a few years of introspective psychotherapy and possibly meditation, even the most ill-at-ease Rats can emerge as better balanced – not perfect, mind you, but better.

Rats are always seething with ideas and fomenting plans unbeknown to us mere mortals. Layer upon layer of shades of meaning, a shale-like spirit, friable and rich in density, camouflages rage or joy or other explosive feeling. Out of nowhere the Rat commits some act of spontaneity so outrageous and unexpected that we naturally begin to think of them as unpredictable. And so they are! Explosively so.

Dame Rat

Vivacity and dynamism characterize the female Rat's appearance. She is never classically beautiful, even-featured or smashingly attractive the way Snake or Pig women can be. But as anyone who knows can tell you, people find her animal magnetism and charm irresistible.

Because Rat women are exquisitely sophisticated and capable of finely honed quick-witted repartee, some claim they are less than feminine. They certainly are not pushovers for clever con men. Rats are women with mettle who know how they want to run their lives. They manage every detail of their existence from a tender age.

Nobody tells a Rat woman what to do or how to do it. She is a monster of personal integrity and aplomb. Doing things her way, she feels, is her prerogative and if she changes her mind tomorrow, she doesn't want to hear any flak from you about it. The Rat is her own woman. Influencing her is not a job for the lily-livered.

The Rat woman's facial features are rarely harmonious. She tends to be handsome rather than pretty and is more appealing for her personality. Her forehead is high and so are her cheekbones, which are also usually sharply contoured and jutting. The Rat woman's nose is of average size and either pointed or turned up, mouse-like. She has a smallish mouth. Her eyes are fairly large, close-set and distinctively shaped. She nearly always has a pointed chin which gives her face the shape of an inverted triangle. In youth, her body is agile and lithe. Her *derrière* is round, firm and fetchingly shaped. If she watches her weight carefully, Dame Rat can remain wasp-waisted and elegant until well past the age of sixty. However, she is a committed gourmet cook and adores entertaining guests to lunch and dinner where fine wines flow freely. This lady's will is not strong where resisting pleasure is concerned and, unfortunately, she often thickens by forty, even growing chubby in old age.

Rat woman's skin is fair but tans easily. Her breasts are small, firm and high. Her shoulders are well shaped and suited to wearing the most luscious of *décolletés*. Her limbs are long and muscular. She walks with her head held high and gestures gracefully. She is always bouncy and her gait has a youthful air.

In her early years, this woman is almost always a tomboy, preferring jeans, T-shirts and boots, and later wearing classically tailored suits and simple dresses rather than frilly skirts with feathers and furbelows. She either keeps her thick hair short and bobbed, or long and straight as she doesn't like hyper-feminine or exorbitant upswept coiffures. In her way, Dame Rat is content to be treated as 'one of the boys' and eschews the extra *politesses* she deems best bestowed on those whom she frankly considers sissies or prudes.

Because they can depend on her sincerity, men willingly treat Dame Rat as a chum, someone they can talk to openly and with whom they can be candid. She is never coy and rarely flirtatious, preferring to deal one to one with boyfriends, almost businesslike in her approach. In return, she is admired and revered by men and is seldom without an escort to accompany her through life.

Rat women are born social butterflies. They are not flighty but rather gregarious. Like their male counterparts, Rat females talk a lot, expressing opinions and holding forth on subjects of general interest to everyone within earshot. They are companionable creatures whose personable, easy-going nature appeals to and enlivens group meetings. Wherever she shows up, she is a welcome addition. She is anything but a loner and always invites amusing and controversial people to share her feasts.

The Rat woman is a thrifty spendthrift. When she shops she buys cartloads of bargain luxury items: pounds of caviare, cases of the best champagne and vintage wines. Yet she will drive a mile out of her way to pick up a case of cheap washing powder that she heard was as good as her usual brand which costs a penny more. She may spend a thousand dollars on a designer dress she is going to wear once but if she leaves her battered old polyester sweater at a friend's house during a visit to Hong Kong, she may telephone at peak time to ask the friend to slide it into a large manila envelope and send it to her by express mail.

My Rat friend Lucy Hayward always lives in the plushest surroundings, boasts the most elegant of wardrobes, gads about the world and travels first class everywhere. She has means but she still scrimps and hunts for new ways to save money on necessities. She makes all her four kids' night clothes, winter bathrobes and underwear by hand. She concocts her chubby husband's voluminous undershorts out of old designer sheets and makes her own silken slips and satin camisoles. She has stitched her damask table linens, her embroidered sheets and her curtains.

'I buy the fabrics wholesale,' Lucy confided to me one day not long ago, 'a whole bolt at a time. It's cheaper that way. If you buy six bolts at a go, they don't even charge for delivery,' she said, with a Rat-like smile of self-satisfaction.

Family comes first for Rat women. They hardly ever remain single. Social acceptance and belonging to a community lends security to the Rat lady's life. She is born with an exacerbated sense of vulnerability. No matter her birth position in the family, she perceives herself as an outsider, the one her parents didn't really want. When she grows up, much of her energy is spent in securing a home and then in building a family. Solid, unassailable protection from want is her first priority. The rest, she figures, will fall into place on its own.

About fifteen years ago, my British Rat friend, Ann Kennerty O'Donovan Grevin-Bill Barclay, chucked the last of her four husbands out of her London flat – not an easy decision for a Rat woman whose standards for marriage are impossibly high. She believes in conjugal bliss. To disparage him sufficiently and gain some comforting complicity from me, she said, 'He moved in little by little, with paper bags. So, to get rid of him, I stuffed his things into several new paper bags and left them out on the landing.'

The picture of poor Nigel or Ted or Percival or William coming home to a landing full of his personal effects stuffed into chic shopping bags was comical but rather sad. Poor Ann, whose intentions were so intensely honorable, had suffered too many romantic setbacks. 'Why?' I asked her. 'He seemed such a nice person.'

'I'll explain some day,' she said. 'I must go now. I'm about to feed the children,' and rang off.

Weeks later, in the middle of a dark windy night in Paris, my phone rang. 'Did I wake you?' Ann wondered. 'I'm sorry, Suzanne, but I wanted you to be the first to know.'

Know what? I thought. I had been through some fairly thorny times with Ann. On holiday in Ibiza she had got herself roughed up by a gorgeous American movie star. In the South of France with her old beau Charles from Scotland we'd had a fracas because he had tried to forge checks on her bank account.

'The bills are being paid again,' she said perkily. 'Isn't that super?'

I shook myself awake. Can any bills be so all-fired important as to ring me about them at 3.47 a.m.? Or is there some arcane British expression I don't know yet which when translated means, I've got a new lover or the maid is pregnant.

'Ann . . .' I said, as clearly as I could. 'What are you talking about?'

'Percival's come home,' she said, with a correct giggle.

I never cease to marvel at the direct manner in which the Rat woman deals with her finances – and her men. The key to her happiness and harmony in a household can be banked, spent, invested or used to pay her bills. A Rat's most devout wish is to live as lavishly and elegantly as possible. I don't know a Rat woman who would turn down a live-in maid, a house in the country with a swimming pool and a lifetime gift certificate for the *couturier* of her choice. Rat ladies love loot – to spend and to save.

Even when she is married, the Rat woman may continue to dally with danger in love. Falling briefly in love with rotters, taking in errant sado-masochists or deciding to reform hopeless drunks are just a few of her specialties. If she can blend her intense householding self with the gritty side that craves excitement and passion, the Rat woman may let down her perpetual guard and relax a bit.

Letting go is not easy, however. The Rat woman has few close friends and even fewer confidantes. Psychologically, she is pulled in different directions about the role of intimate friends in her life. As we already know, the Rat doesn't take kindly to prying. Her secret life belongs to *her*. She is wary of letting any significant intimate details show. As she stands tall, is well groomed and ultra meticulous about the manner in which she comports herself in public, Dame Rat may give a false impression of haughtiness or standoffishness to outsiders. Little could anyone guess that inside her heart she is sweating in a mire of self-doubt. Who would know that the sophisticated Lady Rat might be in great pain about her youngest child's unsightly acne or her husband's latest infidelities? I have never seen a Rat woman cry. Most of her complaining is done in private with friends or family she trusts.

There is, however, a form of Rat woman hysteria that I like to call 'terminal dithering'. It applies to every Rat woman I have ever known and involves marathon monologous communicating on any subject which might currently be bothering her. Perhaps because she is mostly circumspect and reticent, unable to share her innermost thoughts with just anyone, if you are chosen to serve as the lucky confidante of an unleashed prolix Rat woman, you are bound to get three or four earsful at a sitting. You may even have difficulty absorbing the volley of scrambled information she emits and grow enraged that she has nailed you to your own couch or telephone solely to air her opinions or tales of woe. Does she ever once ask, 'How are you? Am I boring you?' No. Once Dame Rat starts to enumerate Henry's faults or to dissect the zigzag patterns of Tom's snoring, you can be sure you're in for a real Rat run of stand-up problem-solving.

Rat women are publicly reserved, but they are not contemplative. Rats are Yin. The orientation is outwards, towards society, away from the soul. In much of their life experience, Rat women think of themselves as passive victims of circumstance. It is not easy for them to see how their own input affects a situation. They are loath to accept blame for their sometimes defensive reactions and quick to give out friendship-infraction tickets to both real or imagined adversaries.

The Rat woman's personal standards are high – too high for most people to measure up to and definitely too lofty for her ever to satisfy her own demands completely. To maintain rigid traditions and outdated social patterns in today's anarchic society makes life tense for Lady Rat. She is fundamentally honest and wishes that everybody had good manners, a well-developed sense of justice and fairness, a social conscience and a will of iron to carry out improvements in all areas of human endeavor. When she discovers that the majority of people litter roads with reckless abandon, that urban graffiti scrawlers are now called 'artists' and that her neighbor has started inconsiderately buzzing his new chain-saw during her Sunday tea parties, the Rat lady is outraged and disappointed. When she discovers that she is too busy to contribute time to a charity shop or too selfish to give up her evening TV show to visit an ailing aunt, she sinks into self-disappointment and begins to berate herself.

Lack of confidence is the Rat's big enemy. Sometimes, all the Rat woman needs to plunge her into free-floating anxiety and self-despair is one little setback. Her goal is security: social and material insurance are uppermost in her mind. Her soul cannot function properly unless she has stability. Of all the signs of the Chinese zodiac, Madame Rat might most benefit from psychotherapy. Occasionally, when she feels the hurdle is too great to handle on her own, she will welcome the therapist's ability to calm her down, help her accept her flaws and be less demanding of those she loves.

Once she has achieved a healthy equilibrium, the Rat woman can apply her many talents to a career. She is gifted for many pursuits, especially those involving detail and careful observation. Rat women are particularly talented for literature and many have become celebrated writers, George Sand, Katherine Mansfield, Charlotte Brontë, Mary McCarthy and Willa Cather to mention a few. They were all endowed not only with passion, sensitivity, a vast and vivid vocabulary, a clever turn of phrase but also that unique discipline so necessary to writing – long daily application of *derrière* to chair. A Rat woman who can find her way to a place in her head where she transforms her anxieties, ideals, observations and commentaries into readable text can launch herself as a writer. She has a remarkable capacity for dreaming aloud, culling the most profound meanings out of life events and for reinventing herself as a child, a man or another character who bears her no resemblance.

The Rat woman loves both animals and little kids and is usually loved by them. She might be a pediatrician, pediatric nurse, or kindergarten teacher. She might choose a career as a horse or dog trainer, a pet shop owner, a vet or breeder of cats or dogs.

Her charming personality makes her an ace salesperson: she instinctively knows how to impart her own enthusiasm for a product or concept to a customer or client. Her gift of the gab comes in handy here, too, as she can pick up on and talk about anything with anyone she encounters in the workplace. Her easy grace and natural manner sets them at ease, helps them to trust her and ultimately to buy from her. All fields involving socializing and chit-chat are perfect for the Rat woman, public relations, press attaché or publicity agent.

The Rat woman can also be counted among top businesswomen. She is persuasive and has the tenacity of purpose necessary to negotiate contracts and carry off big deals. With her inimitable Rat charm, she is an able seducer of clients and often lands some of the biggest contracts. Bosses like the Rat woman: unlike her male counterpart, she is able to accept a subordinate position. She feels happiest when her own skills are exploited to their fullest capacity. Titles are not as important to her as praise, consideration and recognition for a job well done.

Male competitors don't make her uneasy either. In business, she is confident and well equipped to hold her own. She is so versatile that she might choose from a wide scope of jobs such as journalist, literary or show business agent. She also makes an engaging, witty professor, guaranteed to be passionate about her subject. She could adopt a career as a public speaker, in radio or TV, on a lecture circuit, as an interpreter. In film-making, with her keen eye for detail, she could be an excellent editor or script girl. Dame Rat's methodical and diligent approach will enhance her chances for success as a secretary, accountant, librarian, researcher, laboratory assistant and legal, medical or dental assistant. Group or team efforts attract her too. Advancing the cause of a major joint venture through her eager participation is the Rat woman's stock-in-trade. She appreciates all the recognition her superiors can conjure for her hard work and earnest contributions and is inspired to work even harder each time she gains approval.

Despite the competent Rat woman's capacity for success, at heart she prefers the role of stay-at-home to that of bank president or hot shot property magnate. In her own house she feels safe from the vicissitudes of the outside world, secure in her habits and immune from danger. There, she has less emotional turmoil to deal with, fewer anxiety attacks and nervous collapses.

To the female Rat love is the stuff of life. Her health depends on a smooth-running love life. No matter how independent she may appear or the grandeur of her job or her prestigious diplomas, the Rat woman cannot live without a man in her life, her bed and her heart.

She is not a willing victim of macho men who mistreat women. She understands liberation and salutes the progress such movements have made for the betterment of women's lot. However, Rat women are not misanthropic. They love men and feel a serious kinship with them.

For the evolved Rat woman who has worked on gaining emotional stability, the ideal lifestyle may be to live in the shadow of some great mind or talent. She makes an excellent wife for a kindly, honest man who needs a brilliant mate. She knows how to care for him and wants to love him more overtly and passionately than he loves her. His job? To provide a receptive love object for her to revere and protect.

She always wants to be married. Love for her is meaningless if it doesn't lead to marriage or a long-term live-in relationship. Her standards for sex are exacting: she is interested in consistently high-quality intense lovemaking. Because she is so demanding and choosy, the Rat lady has trouble finding her ideal. His potential and background has to be well-nigh perfect before she can allow herself the luxury of investing her time and feelings in a relationship.

Her obsession with marriage as the only real objective for any self-respecting couple can hinder spontaneity in any love affair. If she meets someone who might be a *possible* long-term lover or future husband, she almost immediately lets it be known that her goal is marriage, settling down, having a family. Under the strain of such ponderous foreknowledge, many a potential fiancé will turn tail and leave Dame Rat in the lurch.

Rat women can become so desperate to be secure and settled down that they have been known to plot to steal a best friend's boyfriend or seduce a lover from a family member. Knowing that she can be guilty of man-swiping, the Rat woman has a tendency not to entrust her own husband or lover to any woman friend or acquaintance – even for the space of a conversation. At parties, she may even grow paranoid, clinging possessively to hubby's arm to discourage his defection to possible rivals.

Despite (or perhaps because of) all the plotting to land herself a husband, like her male counterpart Dame Rat sometimes remains single. She will claim that her spinsterhood is chosen, that she didn't marry because Mr Right never came along, but she probably set her sights too high, was repeatedly disappointed by the swains she met and finally decided it was better to be alone than settle for less than perfection. Instead the Rat woman acquires pets to spoil, adopts a niece or nephew or even an orphan on whom to lavish attention, love and money as a substitute for marriage.

If she marries (and she usually does), the Rat female hangs on to her home and family like a shipwreck victim to the last lifeboat. Even if she is unhappily married, she valiantly conceals her disappointment. She may rationalize that she must subjugate her own happiness to that of her children and claim that she stays with Harry the wife-beater for their sake. No matter their degree of compatibility, she is rarely unfaithful. The Chinese say that a Rat woman will only make extra-conjugal whoopee with a man of her own sign. She cannot resist the flirtatious Rat's advances and tumbles to his endearingly familiar methods.

Even though she wants more than anything to be attached to somebody she can call 'family' in a harmonious household, the female Rat is far from easy to live with. She's capricious, changing her mind at whim, her enthusiasms go in fits and starts and she never seems quite to know what she wants. If she admires her husband she will defer to his needs, subjugating her own. However, if she feels superior to him, she may misuse his patience, eroding his good nature because of her refusal to resist indulging herself. She may swamp her mate, trying to force him to measure up in areas he doesn't care about, and finally losing his love because of her incessant childish demands.

Dame Rat makes a superlative mother. She befriends her kids at an early age, showers them with affection and strengthens them with moral support. To her, her kids are the best, and even if nobody else does, she believes in them. Happily, too, she won't smother their personalities. She wants her kids to be healthy, educated and capable of taking on the world when they grow up. Although she may be protective she encourages them to stand on their own feet at an early age. She knows that motherhood is her strongest suit and doesn't lack confidence as she might elsewhere.

On the physical side of lovemaking, the Rat female is noted for her naturalness and ability to give herself to the man she loves. She is a sensual creature who adores sex for its own delicious sake and is eager to provide as much pleasure for her mate as he is capable of accepting. She loves to feel protected and will be most excited when she feels secure. She adores sexual variety but will rarely initiate new patterns. Her imagination is limited and she is cautious about showing aggressive behavior which she fears might seem unsuitable in a dutiful wife. Like her male counterpart, the female Rat's appetite is uneven: strong negative emotions, anxiety or a sudden dip in self-confidence may cut it sharply. The wise partner will exercise patience and not be afraid to cajole his lover.

The female rat is attracted to suffering. Because of a secret masochistic streak, she may marry a man much stronger than herself. Even though she may protest, she often prefers to live under a man's thumb, wriggle in his clutches and feel secure in his macho protectorate.

The Rat woman may act independent, carry off a marvelous career in some singularly masculine field, but underneath the cool façade of self-sufficiency, she lives for the love she will receive from and give to her husband, children and extended family. Without another to cherish and be cherished by, she is but a spectre, a woman who feels she has failed and who would rather be dead than thrust into enforced love limbo. The female Rat is a love addict: affection, tenderness, devotion and fondness are the only drugs she needs and she will do anything for her daily fix.

Brother Rat

The Rat man is definitely not the sleazy gutter-rodent type we might mistake him for. His outward appearance is one of his best assets. He is a distinguished, handsome, magnetic and charming gentleman. In China, the male Rat is also noted for his warmth and mostly sunny disposition. At first glance, he may seem too solemn – not taciturn, as he tends to be free with words – but a shade too ponderous and earnest. Don't be fooled. Beneath the Rat man's standoffishness lies a treasure trove of delicious surprises and a bottomless pit of spontaneity and wit.

Rat males are well designed. Even when their faces are not small or their features pointy, there is something rodent about the shape of the head. The cheekbones are relatively high, perched over elongated, hollow cheeks. His ears are large and his chin is usually pointed. His countenance is lively and his eyes twinkle merrily. His well-defined mouth is always on the verge of flashing a smile. Lots of Rat men like to sport facial hair and may wear thick moustaches and billowing beards.

Overall, one might say that the Rat male bearing is slightly effeminate. He feels compelled to be well groomed, sometimes dresses in a frankly dandified way and is more aware than he lets on of just how terrific he looks. In youth, his body is slender, agile, lithe and supple. He moves gracefully (and is made for dancing). He holds his head high, keeps his back straight and steps surely along, with a jaunty air of self-satisfaction and benevolence. Rat men inspire confidence. One would never be afraid to ask this fellow for directions or request that he help carry some bags up the steps. He emanates benignity and good manners.

Unfortunately, if he gives in to his gourmandise, later on in life he may become portly and red-faced. Any excess may destroy his good looks and even diminish his life expectancy. Yet he can remain young-looking well into old age if he monitors his intake of tasty treats, drink and tobacco. Older Rat men are just as pleasure-seeking as younger ones and often continue to exercise their virility late in life.

The Rat man is clever with his hands. Building, gardening, crafts and artisanal activities appeal to and challenge him. He's a willing potterer, content to spend hours in his workshop, listening to edifying music while conjuring a revolutionary new idea for a self-destructing plastic bag strong enough to carry rocks home from the market without splitting.

The Rat male's mind is fertile and full of hidden resources. He's able to solve the trickiest problems in a trice and act wisely in an emergency. However, if he loses confidence in himself or his abilities, the Rat male will sizzle himself into a major gut-level anxiety fit. Remember, he never appears nervous, concealing tension, so suddenly, with thunderbolt speed, he grows testy, mean or morose and is likely to commit rash acts or make ill-advised decisions. When confidence slips, he loses his capacity for good judgement and may well blunder into wrong-headed behavior.

As he is typically tight-fisted and meticulous, especially about money, he will almost always succeed at careers that involve ruse and/or calculation. He might make an excellent accountant, banker or tax inspector. His talent for detail will also serve him if he chooses to be a librarian, researcher, archivist or pharmacist. He is efficient and thorough in all that he undertakes but he often endeavors to ply a splashy myriad of unrelated and complex trades at once. He is forever attempting to accomplish the impossible, to please everyone who needs him and come out a hero in their eyes as well as his own.

As the Rat male hankers so for security, he sometimes lacks a sense of adventure in his work. He should be wary of professions that require him to prospect for clients or hard-sell reticent buyers. Even though he is an excellent salesperson, the male Rat needs to be liked. He will be unwilling to take the criticism that accompanies pushy or coercive tactics.

As these fellows make a point of being constantly on the move, jobs that allow for travel and mobility are preferable to desk positions. Rats make superior journalists, diplomats, travel agents, union organizers and salesmen. Because of their charm and willingness to take the initiative and pursue objectives through communication, male Rats also thrive where they use words. Advertising and speech-writing are two jobs tailor-made for the Rat's surefire success. When defending a viewpoint, pleading a cause or arguing for their own side, Rat men are persuasive and competent. They should never be afraid to try law, public relations, radio or TV anchor jobs.

Take my Rat lawyer, Maître Dayras. Since we met in 1965, our association has been arduous – but fruitful. Like many Rats, Dayras is a dignified character. He is a short, thinnish man but his bearing is immense. His voice is distinctively sharp and Rat-like. As soon as you walk into his office, you hear it tommy-gunning questions to associates or orders to secretaries. Everyone fears Dayras's scolding manner. And everyone respects him.

While Maître Dayras is speaking to a client, he continues signing papers, answering phone calls and reading briefs. He is able to concentrate on five or six areas at a time, has a memory like a bank safe and a will of tungsten.

I have sat behind him in many a court room, marvelling at his conviction, raptly listening to him beseech the court to understand just how wronged I have been. 'This poor woman was ill. A single mother of two small children. A well known writer of best sellers,' he rants. 'And this person, her *publisher*, sells a total of fifteen thousand books without reporting the sales to her, to avoid giving her so much as a *centime* of the profits.' For emphasis, he steps towards the three-judge line-up. His voice is hushed and confidential. 'When Madame White requests statements and demands payment from this so-called reputable publisher, he refuses. He says she is nothing but a money-hungry American!' Then he retreats discreetly, letting this last remark settle on all ears. He consults his papers once more and raises his head to say casually, 'This publisher was keeping Madame White's royalties. In his bank account. Earning interest on his writer's money . . .' he raises a stern finger, 'and he did this over a period of years! *Monsieur le Président*, this publisher laughed at Madame White's requests for accurate accountings and offered her a small monthly stipend. She needed the money. But, of course, she refused. He said that if she wanted justice she would have to take him to court.'

Dayras steps back, closes his file folder and finishes with, 'And so . . . here we are today, *Monsieur le Président*, in court.' From behind him, I cannot help but notice how superlatively he maintains the cool dignity for which Rats are famous: nose in the air, head cocked with penetrating interest. When I look down at his huge briefcase, I note with affection that, despite appearances, King Rat's inner motor is still speeding down the fast lanes of his mind. He only *looks* relaxed. Concealed beneath his lawyer's robes, Dayras's nervous right leg is bobbing up and down, fuelled by enough Rat nervous energy to light the Eiffel Tower for a week.

Dayras rarely loses a case. Until I knew about the Rat's iron-willed tenacity and strength of purpose, I couldn't explain his consistent victories. The Rat is relentless. When he gets hold of his prey he doesn't let go until the victim either cries uncle or dies. Rat determination is fearsomely effective and he is also optimistic: even if he loses a battle, the verbose Rat is never totally discouraged. He may step back a pace, but he refuses to give in. He holds his ground, reshapes his strategies. Then *thwack*! he offs their heads like a jet-propelled samurai in a hurry to get back to a hot tea ceremony.

Shrewdness is hardly foreign to the wily Rat man's character either. Give a male Rat a contract to land or a factory to run and you can be sure he will come up with the goods. Do not, however, be aghast at his deviousness. Rat males like to zigzag their way to paradise and have little time for conservative methods of operation.

It may behoove these agile-minded males to be self-employed. If they are disciplined about organizing, use their time wisely and have the strength and presence they can aptly carry off a single-handed enterprise. Male Rats hate to take orders: in most instances, if only to maintain their autonomy, these chaps will do precisely the opposite of what they are told.

Because they need to hold sway over others and wish to make a difference, leadership posts appeal to Rats. They make good politicians. They know how to wow an audience and are not above revelling in day-long baby-kissing sprees. Rat men glory in receiving full scale attention at home so what could be wrong with getting it from strangers?

Rat men are sensitive. They cleave to culture and enjoy intellectual pursuits. Art, knowledge-gathering and the absorption and creation of literature can provide them with opportunities for plying a lucrative as well as gratifying trade. Not only do they feel things deeply, but Rat men are exceptionally observant of detail and highly gifted for rhetoric. Historically, their show of literary talent is astounding: Shakespeare, Tolstoy, Nathaniel Hawthorne, James Baldwin, Truman Capote, T. S. Eliot, Ionesco and Lawrence Durrell were all born in Rat years.

The Rat male takes care of his own. He will be a good and willing provider for his family. He is also adept at managing investments and not infrequently makes a killing in the stock or property market. Of all the careers open to the Rat man, business probably suits him best. He is not only enterprising and astute about choosing his markets wisely, but has an infallible flair for recognizing a bargain. Better still, he knows instinctively how to buy at a low price and resell at a profit.

If a Rat man makes it through his middle life without making a huge error of judgement about either money or love, he will never want for the means to a satisfactory living. He is clever, strong-minded, always willing to put his shoulder to the wheel and unafraid of mingling with the masses.

Because they tend to be arrogantly inflexible, opinionated and slightly misanthropic when young, all male Rats should make a serious lifelong effort to implement their success by gaining self-knowledge. If, by the age of fifty, the male Rat has begun to understand altruism, assimilated a solid sense of his own worth and knows how to apply temperance and moderation he can expect to live a long, fulfilling and interesting life.

Rats love to be in love. This character is the most romantic and sentimental of the Chinese zodiac. When he loves, the frugal Rat becomes a monster of generosity. The object of his ardor will be crushed under presents, expressions of tenderness, glittering compliments, and often doubled over from laughing. She should be prepared to receive everything her Rat has to give – and more.

Probably the most salient feature of the Rat's approach to seduction hinges on his strength of purpose. When inspired to secure the favors of a woman he wants, the Rat throws his personal vector into first gear and commences the slow, unremitting journey towards winning her heart.

I recently had the great luck to be squired by a Rat gentleman friend, whose diligent approach was a discovery for me. It consisted, among more banal activities such as going to the movies and out to lunch, of a bounty of blandishments, Valentines, exotic rare wild flowers, ardent declarations and hot promises. He took me by surprise with his kooky phone messages, made me dizzy with his praise, left me giggly after long sneaky chats from the office. His attempts to gain my attention were positively enchanting. This tireless charmer was open-hearted, frank and even benevolent. I was not the least immune to the Byzantine tissue of pretty white lies he wove. The Rat 'getting to know you' process turned out not only to be thrilling, it was sexy and security-inducing too.

Yet despite their flirtatious methods and baroque seduction routines, male Rats are not deceitful Don Juans. The Rat male is in love with love. He needs full-scale attention and high-quality sex, craves loving care the way a baby needs its mother's milk. But he returns all the above in spades!

Remember, the male Rat never completely believes that he deserves to be loved. In an attempt to gain ardor and affection from the woman he loves, he will go any distance to keep her happy. All she has to do is love him and love him some more. Then he will provide all the fun, sensuality, security, joy and fidelity for a lifetime.

When they are young, Rats are often attracted to weaker, dependent females who see them as father figures,providers, supermen. The young male Rat is excited at the prospect of protecting his mate. He fills with benign machismo whenever called upon to play hero. Later in life, the Rat is more likely to be drawn to stronger, more vibrant, steadier women who can second him in his social and professional life. He is not a jealous lover and may even be quite proud when he notices that his pretty wife or mistress is attractive to other men. As long as he feels he is the one she considers superior, the Rat male breathes easy. He is moderately faithful as a mate, not for want of opportunity but because he wants quality love and passion, not an ephemeral one-night stand.

Although the male Rat can be selfish, where physical love is concerned he is a born pleasure giver. To satisfy his romantic dreams, sexual responsibilities ought to be held equally by both parties and reciprocal pleasure-giving experienced as often as possible. The Rat is sentimental and the idea of sexual communion joining two beings, fusing their bodies and souls, enthralls him and he aims for this union to occur each time he makes love.

His technique, too, is ever changing. Rats hate routine. They are forever peering into the darkest corners of their partner's mind to discover new ways of exciting their interest and their erogenous zones. Lingering foreplay and gentle words of love are the tools of the sexy Rat man's trade. He almost always takes the lead, initiating sex in unexpected ways – a chance middle-of-the-night caress, a surprise *tête-à-tête* in the early morning.

Because of his highly strung, nervous disposition and the perpetual hum of his inner turbine, his sexual appetite may be subject to fluctuations, perhaps even periods of impotence. A wise partner will learn how to cool the Rat's sizzling nerve endings with TLC, massage and soothing words of undying love.

When he enters a marriage or long-term relationship, the male Rat's intentions are always the best. He may be forced to act unethically in business or trickily in politics, but he has unflinching principles about family, which inspire him to strive to make his marriage work. He will be devoted to the well-being of his wife and the education of his children. If ever he is unfaithful he knows enough to keep his counsel. And no matter how passionate a Rat feels about an extra-marital lover, he will always choose to return to his wife rather than divorce. Family break-ups go against the grain of all that he believes in and stands for.

Rat men have a profound need to keep secrets. They don't like to tell their wives, girlfriends or even good pals the gory details of their private selves. They are willing advisers and gaily embark on sorting out other people's intimacies but their own remain an enigma. If you have a Rat man in your life, you may need to use some wily strategies to find out what is going on inside that little Rat noggin. Never confront him openly on a potentially incendiary subject: a cornered Rat is an angry, dangerous Rat. The surest way to this vital man's brain center is through love. Shows of affection, scores of tiny kisses on his tousled hair and plenty of listening between the lines will net you more secret information about him than any 'talking to' you might decide to give him.

Certain Rat men are crippled by the risk of loneliness and rejection. If he gets married or invests himself totally in somone he loves – the

Rat man is taking the risk of losing her. At the very thought of the heartbreak and loss, his inner motor shifts into overdrive, his digestion flashes *acid* in orange neon and his anxiety center registers a giant *tilt*. An especially tense and insecure Rat may find himself living the life of a frustrated bachelor.

The five Chinese elements and how they influence the Rat

The Wood Rat

1564 William Shakespeare
1804 Benjamin Disraeli, Nathaniel Hawthorne, Johann Strauss the elder
1924 Marlon Brando, Lauren Bacall, Sarah Vaughan, George Bush, James Baldwin, Truman Capote, Ed Koch, Charles Aznavour, Freddie Bartholomew, Eva Marie Saint, Doris Day, Stanley Donen, Sidney Lumet, Lee Marvin, Zizi Jeanmaire, Audie Murphy, Sidney Poitier, Hank Williams, Johnny Stark, Eva Gabor, Henry Mancini, Bea Arthur, Carroll O'Connor, Gwen Verdon

Wood settles a healthy coating of balm on the zigzag nervousness of the Rat character. Unlike other Rats, this one knows how to relax and take things as they come. His temperament is cooler than that of other Rats but, as though to camouflage his native stand-offishness, the gregarious Wood Rat exhibits more amiable charm and extroversion.

Most Rats worry about their image and care immensely about how others feel towards them but the Wood Rat seems to possess a more solid sense of his position in society. This added security allows him to demonstrate a carefree, open attitude and gives his personality an edge of merriment and devil-may-care that cohorts and members of the opposite sex find enchanting. He is jocular and even a bit lightheaded when serious issues are in the offing.

Wood gives this Rat a special talent in discerning both the beauty and the worth of art objects. Add this to his powerful business acumen and the Wood Rat may make a killing in antiques or become a respected art dealer. Or he may become an author of important literary works, a painter of no little renown or a world-class musician. He is inspired by his environment and sensitive to every nuance of aesthetic input which comes his way.

Ever conscious of his need to belong to a social group, the Wood Rat wears his iron-clad principles on his sleeve. He is forever making pronouncements about what he will and will not tolerate in his life and the lives of those he loves. He worries incessantly about his offspring and their progeny. He would probably commit a crime to protect them and shield them from earning a bad reputation.

Wood Rats have giant egos. They need approval, applause and encouragement almost more than they need food. Part of his open-door policy and seeming willingness to be flexible and understanding comes from his desire to be accepted by those to whom he extends his hospitality and with whom he agrees to cohabit. Leave him on his own to fend for himself without lending moral support to his projects or sharing his ideals and you will reap nothing but complaints and hard-luck stories. Wood Rats hate to be alone and feel justified in blaming everyone who doesn't give them what they need.

This person is usually successful at what he undertakes. He knows his limitations and intelligently aims only as high as he knows he can go. He is, however, socially frustrated. Although people outwardly like the Wood Rat, are willing to chat and hang out with him, go to his elegant home for dinner and pay him compliments, he feels slighted. He has few real friends. Although ostensibly he gives them every opportunity, people don't confide in him easily. Do they fear his sharp critical tongue? Or is it his lack of compassion? Either way, he feels left out. Perhaps he should curb his unfortunate habit of looking for bargains when he chooses his friends. Wood Rats take heed: love those you befriend for their hearts and not for what you think you can get out of their networks and you will be rewarded with the unconditional friendship and loyalty that you so covet.

The Fire Rat

1756 Wolfgang Amadeus Mozart
1816 Charlotte Brontë
1876 Pablo Casals, Sherwood Anderson, Willa Cather, Mata Hari

1936 Ursula Andress, Glenda Jackson, Dennis Hopper, Keir Dullea, Yves St Laurent, Dick Cavett, Kitty Dukakis, Vanessa Redgrave, Hal Ashby, Albert Finney, Jill Ireland, El Cordobes, Richard Bach, Alan Alda, Burt Reynolds, Kris Kristofferson, Suzanne Pleshette.

High-strung talkers, these rapid-fire Rats are fashioned of raw energy, laced with a giant injection of nerves and overlaid with a serious case of the jitters. No slouches need apply. Fire Rats will gnaw their way through game-players, false friends, snobs and charlatans. They want truth, beauty and justice – or else!

The Fire Rat is the apotheosis of all Rats. In appearance, he is a concentration of his busy-bee Rat brothers and sisters. He is like them in every way: outwardly calm, inwardly nerve-racked, protective, generous, greedy, charming, eloquent, persuasive and tough – except that the Fire Rat is more completely immersed in being himself than he is in being the person who pleases and cares for others. This characteristic, which some consider arch selfishness, sets him apart from the Rat who settles down, raises family and stays fettered to a boring lifestyle for the good of the family. Fire Rats want to build something wonderful they can irretrievably call *theirs*. They make passionate lovers and are swashbuckling pursuers of the romantic life. They gorge on passion and never stop nibbling on the bones of love.

Fire Rats are also brilliant intellectuals. Not only do they win all the glittering academic prizes, they are endowed with lightning quick perception. They can throw action into a passing thought before competitors have even noticed the thought was there. Obviously, this jet-propelled brain effortlessly outwits and out-maneuvers his adversaries.

As all success comes early and relatively easily to him, the Fire Rat grows quickly impatient with rejection, heartbreak and obstacles. When confronted with an imposing hurdle or major disappointment, he may find it hard to concentrate and will bolt to where the grass looks a shade greener and there are more folk to love him. He fears loneliness worse than death. He is impulsive and always searching for a new experience to distract and excite him. Whether as a palliative to frustration or in answer to a whim, the Fire Rat dives in head first, gobbles his way through the new situation, relationship or job, eventually discovering that he has been spreading himself too thin: the Fire Rat may have acquired three ex-wives and families, four lovers, several careers and a dozen hobbies. Now, he is caught in his own rat trap.

He can only learn from experience. Yet experience can be his enemy. Nobody who gets involved with the Fire Rat remains indifferent to his charm and bits of him are strewn everywhere. In scattering his forces, he can end up losing his grip on what he wants before he knows what he was longing for. As accepting failure or rejection is out of the question for Fire Rats, nervous breakdowns, severe depressions and mind-numbing drug abuse problems stalk this self-willed but fragile, well-meaning person's footsteps.

Physically, this Rat survives on his nerve: he is made of grit, stoicism and bravery. He pushes himself harder in every new enterprise, slogging to prove he can do more and get further. He hops out of bed at 6 a.m. to attack the day and falls dead into bed at 3 a.m. exhausted, but willing and ready to get up again three hours later and clobber the next day with the same axe. Unless he is forced to slow down, learns how to take life more philosophically and is applauded and encouraged along the way, the workaholic Fire Rat will chop till he drops.

Usually the Fire Rat wants to make and keep lots of money. If he finds, because of dispersing his energies, that he cannot do so, he will tear voraciously at himself, blaming his own weakness and regretting much about his previously faulty approach to life. Somehow, from the moment he locates the flaw in his former approach, he can begin to see his way clear to making a comfortable, sane living. As though by some miracle, he stops chewing holes in his stomach wall, changes his methods, espouses an entirely new direction and, although he is a deeply sentimental and honorable soul, dances merrily on the graves of his earlier tormentors. It may take this Rat a while to realize his potential, but when (and if) he finally decides to do so – watch out!

The Earth Rat

1768 François René Chateaubriand
1888 Irving Berlin, J. Arthur Rank, Barry Fitzgerald, Maurice Chevalier, T. S. Eliot, Joseph Kennedy
1948 James Taylor, Peggy Fleming, Prince Charles, Olivia Newton-John, Mikhail Barishnykov, Donna Summer, Gerard Depardieu

This is the grounded, no-nonsense Rat who gets to the top cleverly and fast. He seems to have known his goal from the day he was born, worked diligently to get the post he has always coveted and, by the age of forty, be there, sitting pretty and whistling a happy tune.

Something about the Earth Rat tells you straight away that he can deal sensibly with anything life places before him. He is strong-minded and demanding, always expressing his own priorities first, yet being unafraid to make concessions and negotiate where he cannot win. He is steadier than other Rats, more desirous of keeping the peace. His willpower is enormous: he can chomp through resistant detractors or inhuman workloads and come out fresh and ready for more.

Unlike most other Rats, the Earth Rat maintains his calm in the face of emotional turmoil. His philosophical view helps him to see through panic so as not to get scorched in the heat of the moment as other Rats so often do. Earth Rats are plodders. They get up at a reasonable hour, follow a disciplined routine and approach work and play with a measured, sensible intelligence. The rapaciousness of most Rats is absent; they are solidly trustworthy and remarkably soft-spoken. They may have unshakeable opinions and are persuasive talkers but Earth Rats don't feel obliged to force their ideals on others.

Earth Rats are congenial people. They love to eat and need to be surrounded. Throwing parties or small social gatherings is a major talent: they know instinctively how to match up compatible guests at a dining table. Despite their conviviality, you will not often find Earth Rats attending smart catered affairs in expensive restaurants: they feel more at home during cozy family receptions where their superior position as host is never in question and they can express themselves freely without fear of criticism.

Take an Earth Rat out of his hospitable home environment and you will discover that in daily life or business he is rather smug and self-satisfied. As he has always struggled hard to get where he is, he has a marked tendency to judge others as less industrious or eager to succeed, dubbing them layabouts and ne'er-do-wells without just cause.

Earth Rats often try our patience with their relentless pontificating and self-righteous speeches. But they are not always as sinless as they seem. When called upon to be protective of his family or caring about the one he loves, the Earth Rat is unbeatable. He can be faithful and tries to keep his own and his family's reputation pure. Yet he is a committed romantic and craves passion as much as the next Rat. His remedy for setback commonly takes the form of a little extra-marital fling or a secret affair. Is he fickle? Not really – just hedonistic and desperate to feel himself dead center in the thrall of love.

Earth Rats may carry prejudices to extremes. They may be catty, too, and will whine about the inadequacies of people they feel are less competent or successful than themselves. They hate not being loved and snivel when they feel left out or lonely. But of all the Rats, the Earth Rat is the most wholesome.

Some say that because of his judgemental tone and haughty air of superiority, the Earth Rat is cruel and unfeeling. Nothing could be further from the truth. This Earthy Rat is all heart. He may *seem* forbidding, but watch how he performs when it comes to kissing babies and openly displaying affection to his loved ones. Earth Rats love to build a homely nest and invariably keep packs of domestic animals. Their comfortable houses are always stocked with plants and pianos. Their kids are warmly socialized and look well fed and happy.

The Metal Rat

1840 Thomas Hardy, Tchaikovsky, Alain Duhamel
1900 Adlai Stevenson, Spencer Tracy, Clark Gable, Luis Buñuel, Mervyn Leroy, Helen Hayes, Julien Green, Kurt Weill, Aaron Copland
1960 Kenneth Branagh, Yannick Noah, The Duke of York, Daryl Hannah, Valerie Bertinelli, Sean Penn

The Metal Rat seeks to gain fortune and fame through influential contacts and applying his talents to shrewd networking. He is not as intellectual as other Rats but his street-wise instincts are more fully developed. He is the great persuader, who will stop at nothing to produce the outcome he seeks. When embarking on an eloquent chat-up session, the wily Metal Rat tirelessly seduces, cajoles and caresses his object until his goal is in sight and he can feel certain he's made his point.

This Rat is more profound than quick-witted. He takes achievement and 'getting there' too seriously. He never leaps before he looks at his landing pad a hundred times. He thinks things through, picking over each detail as he goes along. He's a ponderer and a trouble-shooter too.

Though he may absorb information slowly, the Metal Rat picks up hostility and grudges, registers pain and rage on his inner radar screen like quicksilver. Any profession where hunches and extra-sensory perception are useful will be a perfect vehicle for this sensitive soul's special talents. He might choose psychiatry, education, astrology, the police force, detective work, research or social work.

Such vivid perspicacity as he has may, however, backfire. He sees so clearly the flaws in someone else that he quickly becomes judgemental. These extra lucid evaluations can take some of the pleasure from his life, tear away illusion and youthful idealism. Some Metal Rats become pessimistic, possessive and materialistic, even paranoid about the way others treat them. Being so alert to others' mistakes makes him edgy and he is given to fits of brooding and pure pessimism. After a while, he becomes known for his crankiness and loses the capacity to laugh at himself. If he doesn't take steps in early adulthood to develop his objectivity and hone his social skills, by middle age, this Rat may develop into a jaded cynic to whom social acceptance is difficult to find.

Meticulous by nature, the Metal Rat detests anything slapdash or half-hearted. He thinks himself businesslike and tries to behave soberly when dealing with his fellows. He is economical and flaunts it at those he sees as wasteful or spendthrift. He dislikes lukewarm sentiment and deplores half-way measures, which he judges as lazy and slipshod. The Metal Rat cannot bear people who lack enthusiasm – especially if they lack it for him and his pet projects.

Curiously, though, this sometimes curmudgeonly person is overtly hedonistic. He loves food and eats a lot. He takes love and marriage seriously, seeking pleasure in sex with gusto, dexterity and skill. He usually has little enthusiasm for carousing but will occasionally get a little high at his own parties where he feels safe from the probing eye of the outsiders he considers so dangerous to his sterling reputation.

The Water Rat

1732 Franz Joseph Haydn, George Washington
1792 Gioacchino Antonio Rossini
1912 Mary McCarthy, Loretta Young, Roy Rogers, Curt Jurgens,

Garson Kanin, Gene Kelly, Paul Meurisse, John Cage, Eugene Ionesco, Michael Wilding, Laurence Durrell, Eve Arden

The aggressive Rat personality is pleasantly diluted with the influence of the Yin element, Water. To this Rat, ambition and the race for success are secondary. His first interest is to live a charmed life and move gracefully through its vicissitudes without emerging scarred and crippled.

The Water Rat is even more feminine than many of his fellow Rats. He favors elegant clothes and fineries such as gold earrings, diamond clips or rings – not often associated with hardier Rats. The Water Rat is gifted for giving advice, for which people seek him out.

Water Rats, especially women, love sweets. While they are unwilling to damage other important aspects of their health, they tend to binge on sugar and a tendency to obesity in middle age is common among them. The remedy would be to cut down on sweets, eat greens and replace meat with fish and grain dishes. Sugar not only fattens the Water Rat but it adversely affects the healthy function of his pancreas and his fragile nervous system.

The Water Rat has sound intuition and intellect: he grasps inner meanings and also knows how to solve human problems almost before they arise. He is a great one for pulling rank, one-upping his adversaries quietly yet effectively and beating enemies at their own game. Though never dangerous or cruel, he can destabilize the bravest of men by demonstrating his uncanny ability to see through opacity. His dreams are clear visions and often premonitory. Heeding their messages may save his intimates much pain.

This type of Rat is happy to live the comfortable bourgeois life. He is not rapaciously ambitious, yet he wants to live in comfort, even luxury, and seems less driven to work as hard as others. Prizes, jobs, important positions and even fame and fortune come his way without much effort.

Water Rats are not born altruistic. Evolving in the rarefied atmosphere of his plush home and immediate surroundings, this Rat sometimes forgets that there are poorer, less fortunate souls than he. Instead of improving his sophisticated central heating system, he ought, perhaps, to look at the lives of those who are in need of a blanket, a cup of coffee or even a pat on the head to keep going.

This Rat is always acquiring new knowledge, dashing off to take courses in hitherto unexamined subjects, and tucking into cultural events designed to impart arcane information to his already impressive personal storehouse. His mind is particularly fertile and able to synthesize abstract concepts into art. Many Water Rats write well, produce fine paintings and music and make a handsome living doing so. They often prosper because of their charm and attraction more than any application of elbow grease. Water Rats are not lazy – just a little smug that success comes their way because of their natural superiority.

This Water Rat can be a real trial to his entourage. Odd for a Rat, but he tends to laziness, is occasionally slovenly and sometimes shuns responsibilities, claiming they are better left to lowlier folk. Sudden outbursts of self-pity and -aggrandizement both annoy and confound those he lives with. Because of a basic contempt for the system, he is easily corruptible and somewhat venal in his outlook.

He is, however, patriotic, and loyal to family and friends, towards whom he is sincere and loving. He is able to face adversity with equanimity and courage. His sense of justice is well developed and he is willing to fight for what is right – so long as he doesn't have to stray far from his leather chair and panelled office.

Rat health

Rats enjoy a sound constitution, should and do live a long time. They are energetic, keeping their hands and minds active, and are not afraid of hard work. They invest themselves in the well-being and survival of their family, which guarantees that their interest in their surroundings will remain intense and their curiosity alive well into old age. People who love their families and are surrounded by them tend to live longer than those without anyone to love.

Perhaps because of his good health, the Rat develops a cocky attitude towards his body's needs which, in turn, begets an anarchic food intake schedule. Eating erratically with no respect for the quality of food he ingests wreaks havoc on his gastro-intestinal tract and on his jittery nature. Coffee, before, during and after meals or at any juncture of day or night, whisky and wine taken indiscriminately often in excess, sweets in the middle of the night or before breakfast, depending on the Rat's whim – all take their toll on his needy body's delicately balanced equilibrium. Yet with eating, as with all sensual pleasures, the rat is greedy.

All Rats have a testy digestive system. As they are anxious and tense, acid indigestion plagues them throughout the day and has been known to keep more than one Rat awake all night. Belching and heartburn are but two of the symptoms with which Rats live and they consume large bottles of viscous antacids liquid or endless cartons of those chalky mints to zap excess stomach acid. Wouldn't you think that Rats would prefer to curb their appetites for trash rather than soaking up all that dope? They don't. They stubbornly persist in ruining their health by devouring anything and everything whenever they like, and palliating the result with bromides.

If, however, he is to enjoy a long life and remain in good health, the Rat must learn self-discipline. He ought to take regular meals at set times, never eat late at night or between meals. He should attempt to reduce the quantities of meat, starches and sweets he consumes and he should never eat 'junk' or packaged foods. Alcohol should only be used in moderation: smooth dry red wines with meals, champagne on special occasions but certainly no beer, aperitifs or cocktails, which play havoc with his fragile stomach lining.

He can have fruit – especially citrus fruit – and he should prefer honey to sugar, wheat germ oil and wholegrain cereals to white rice or refined wheat products. Infusions of orange blossom will help this jumpy character to sleep. He ought to take vitamins – especially E and C. Rats love to abuse tobacco so they should add on a B-complex tablet and be sure to get lots of beta carotene.

If he learns to eat carefully, the Rat may be able to avoid stomach ulcers but as he usually refuses to listen to reason about his eating habits and incessantly suffers from turning his highly strung temperament inwards, he will probably have an ulcer or stress-related illness at least once in his life.

Rats succumb to many mental disorders. As they are workaholics, nervous breakdown and depression often threaten their equilibrium. If the Rat does not slow down and get himself in balance, he may be headed for a major breakdown or end up living in a mildly (or even severely) manic-depressive state. When all is well he is up with a capital U – cheerful, optimistic, talkative and impulsive – but in the face of a setback or difficulty, the Rat's morale plummets and he suffers from giddiness, constipation, muscular pain and arthritis and/or emotional gloom and doom which can bode clinical depression or even awaken suicidal tendencies.

The Rat is guilty of mistreating his fragile nervous system's good nature by over-indulgence – in physical work or study, playing a sport, falling in love, eating rich food, quaffing alcoholic drinks, recreational drugs, smoking tobacco, slurping ice creams or gobbling chocolates. It seems as though Rats cannot be satisfied by moderation. Too much hard work means that all Rats suffer from insomnia some time, made worse when they lose their grip on reality, worry about unpaid bills, or even about not getting enough sleep. After a few sleepless months of protracted exhaustion and anxiety, some Rats find themselves popped into ambulances and hauled away to the nearest nursing home or loony bin.

Combine his lifetime of consuming a rich diet with the Rat's congenital vascular fragility and you reap some impressive cerebro-vascular accidents – or strokes. Again, Rats must be vigilant, see their physicians regularly, heed advice about smoking and altering their frenzied work and eating habits. If they don't monitor their blood pressure and practice a skilled sport such as tennis, fencing, swimming or walking, the Rat puts his heart and arteries in jeopardy.

Traditionally, Rats contract more than their share of lung cancers, possibly due to their tendency to chainsmoke. Even though they have ample evidence of a weak, vulnerable respiratory tract, bouts of bronchitis, periodic coughing fits and morning phlegm plague the Rat. His lungs get easily congested and colds may prostrate him for weeks.

If, as is likely, he refuses to give up smoking, he should at least try to boost his respiratory system's capacity by horseriding, cycling, golf, swimming and other oxygenating sports. Secondly, both for his fragile chest and respiratory tract as well as to assist in calming his frazzled nerves, he should avoid living in cities or areas of high pollution in favor of the countryside, if possible, close to a forest where the oxygen is frequently renewed by abundant plant life.

Allergies are another delicate Rat affliction. Rat women especially experience reactions to every pollen, dust, mold spore and smoke allergen known to medicine. Her lungs are susceptible to alveolitis but her nose and bronchial tubes fill up and make her miserable when she has allergic reactions. Rats can be treated with drugs but would be better off taking a water cure at a spa in France or Italy. From the age of fifty the Rat's susceptibility to allergy diminishes so that often by the time he or she retires the body will be allergy free.

Most dangerous for the Rat's well-being and health is his utter scorn for symptoms. Either he is a coward about seeking painful treatment or else he truly believes that aching muscles, difficulty in breathing, pains in the feet and legs or bronchial distress, hyperactivity or gloom, if ignored may disappear. The Rat recklessly abuses his health and one day pays dearly for the arrogant assumption that he will live for ever in perfect fettle. Careless-living Rats often suffer from severely handicapping chronic illness after the age of fifty-five. If I dare venture an educated guess, life as an aggressive, restless Rat, incapacitated or confined to a wheelchair is probably a fate worse than the alternative.

Rat futures

What the Rat should expect from the next twelve Chinese animal years

2008, the Earth Rat year – Your year at last! Here begins a whole new cycle of Chinese animal signs and, as usual, you are leading the pack. Life will seem easier. Bumps and lumps will even out for you and people you thought you could never get along with are all of a happy sudden on your side. Watch out for a tendency to let down your guard and go slack where indeed you should be quicker on the draw. Romance will increase in intensity and want to become engagement. Commitment beckons. Then marriage is nigh. Don't hold off. If you feel you have found "The One", then tie the knot. It's all part of the plan because your main objective this year is to carefully plot out the next dozen years of your life. Where do you want to be in twelve years? With whom will you be living? How much do you want to be earning and will you prefer the city or the country? Make major long-term decisions in 2008. And don't look back. Life is too short to regret missed opportunities that are out of fashion anyway. Stay alert. Leap into new projects with your usual enthusiasm, but hold the reckless abandon.

2009, the Earth Ox year – Talk about hard labor! If you planned properly last year then you already knew that this would be a year to put all others to shame in the work department. You are not a layabout. Not by a long shot. But . . . as things looked so rosy last year, you might just have got out of the habit of pushing that rock up the hillside. In this new Ox year, you will need all the grit and determination you were born with to impress the Ox with your industriousness. You can be a huge asset to the plodding Ox. But you will have to prove yourself this year because Oxen do not tolerate idlers. If I were you, Mr or Ms Rat, I would not plan huge celebrations or throw wild shindigs in an Ox year. Pay particular attention to details in contracts and verify all incoming bills, invoices and even bank statements for slip-ups and errors in calculation. You are not on a losing streak. But you could fall victim to someone else's shoddy bookkeeping.

2010, the Metal Tiger year – The general climate of instability engendered by this Tigerish time is not your favorite. You are a security-seeker, a protector of your home and family and you like to be in control. You may even dream one day to exert power over your own destiny. The Tiger? He (or she) could not care less for security or safety. In fact, despite his natural leadership qualities, the Tiger does not actively seek power over others. So the tenuous atmosphere created in this changeable year promises to destabilize you and keep you very much more on your toes than most. If only you knew what to expect, it wouldn't affect you so thunderously. But in Tiger years nobody quite knows what's around the next corner. So my advice to you Rats is to roll with the punches. Don't make waves. Keep a low profile, all the time managing to steer things your way. If you play your cards close to the chest, your Tiger year can turn out to be a giant success. If, however, you flaunt the power-hungry side of your character, you may not fare so well.

2011, the Metal Cat year – You Rats will be needing all of your wily skills this year because the Cat and you are traditionally at odds. You are not wont to conceal feelings and just about never spare us the details of your moods. The Cat is a past master at skullduggery and clandestine behavior. He or she never wants to attract much attention or face up to conflict. The tone of Cat years is anything but straightforward. Instead it's quiet and effective and cooler than cool. You are forever moving and skittering about in an attempt to control and run things your way. Your very jitteriness rubs the Cat's fur the wrong way. This will be an excellent year for investment. Make it your business to do business; but keep your beady little eyes peeled for chicanery and theft. If you are not permanently attached, you could very well fall madly in love this year. If you do, then whisk your new heart throb off to a desert isle where the two of you can daydream about next year, which promises to bring far more felicitous vibes your way.

2012, the Water Dragon year – Breathe easy, my little Rat friend. The Dragon and you are old cohorts from way back. You respect the flamboyant Dragon's need for attention and never threaten to steal his fire. Your intelligent handling of Dragons is in fact legendary. You know how to let them shine while carrying on your own empire-building in the background. The Dragon year's tone is celebratory. The scaly beasts love to play host to casts of thousands at numerous festivals and gatherings of all variety. Any excuse for a huge commemoration. It's the Dragon's way – the more ceremonious the event, the more he or she enjoys watching people have fun. You don't mind playing charming guest among the Dragon's innumerable friends, all the while planning networking strategies of your own. Play hard this year and make hay while the Dragon's brilliant sun is shining on your life. Enjoy this hectic but lucky year. It is guaranteed to be one of your memorable best.

2013, the Water Snake year – This threatens to be a belt-tightening spell for you Rats. Commerce slows in Snake years. You won't go broke. But your income may diminish sufficiently to cause you a few sleepless nights. Put some cash away in a safe place. There is political unrest and global turbulence now, so get ready to hunker down and perhaps even shoulder new and different responsibilities. Your love life may cool somewhat during the months of June and July. The chill is but temporary, so don't lose heart. Someone in your direct entourage will want to concoct a damaging rumor and your private life may just be its subject. Certain people deem gossip harmless. But the tall tale in question carries more weight than a mere fib. It has the power to create scandal. Keep your whiskers peeled during the first months of the year so as to fend off any trickery you sense is in the offing. Also, be prepared to compromise where you might otherwise have refused to budge. Flexibility pays off in Snake years.

2014, the Wood Horse year – Rat and Horse typically quarrel – over everything from how money is spent to how to raise geraniums. Despite the Horse's odd attraction for you, as soon as you two strike up a relationship, the fight is on! Arguments can be productive. But in the case of Horse and Rat, perpetual spats take up much of your precious time and get neither of you anywhere positive. So rather than live this year in permanent tumult, try staying out of the limelight. Do not try to gain more power. (Leave political office off your list for now. Forget asking for a raise or bidding on that promotion.) If you are too visible and/or grabby in a Horse year, you might face both financial and emotional bankruptcy. The Horse hates to be dictated to. And you like to be boss. As you can see, this year bodes disruptive chaos – unless of course you wisely choose to stay out of the spotlight. As you will not be parading or appearing in public all that much, why not plan to have the cosmetic surgery you have been postponing in this Horse year? Next year promises to bring you back into the public eye. So you might as well do everything you can now to improve your appearance, spruce up your wardrobe and scissor that old-fashioned hairdo into some kind of contemporary shape.

2015, the Wood Goat year – In the Goat year, you will be sailing in smoother waters. You have had a couple of lean seasons of late which may well have cramped your style and dulled your creativity. But this year promises to relieve all of the stress connected with economic slowdown for Rats. Money will cease to be the most crucial issue. By June, you will feel more like getting out and showing off your sparkling social skills, attending parties and public events where your native charm is much appreciated. Of course, as soon as you stick out your furry little neck, someone gorgeous and lovable may hang him- or herself around it and be loath to let go. This new romantic interest could threaten an already stable marriage or long-term relationship. Beware of putting the steady home life that you so desperately need in jeopardy. Be polite. But firm. Shrug off the intense desire for a quick, passionate summer romance. The Goat year smiles on your fortunes and offers you renewed peace of mind. Don't blow it. Towards the end of the year, seek the financial advice of someone with more experience than you in the area you have in mind to invest in. Be it real estate or diamond mines, if you are new at it, heed the counsel of an older, wiser – and richer – cohort.

2016, the Fire Monkey year – Here comes fun! You and the Monkey always hit it off. Monkeys are partial to surprises and excitement. They take kindly to movement and enjoy action for its own sake. Monkeys are social animals. But . . . unlike you Rats, Monkeys don't really care about power. They are willing back-seat drivers who prefer to lurk in the wings solving problems and serving as the 'brains' behind an operation. So in Monkey years, you are free to take charge again. Go after that seat on the board. Run for office. Try to become the president of the world. Ask for dominion and you shall most likely receive your wish. One quick cautionary note: be prepared to flatter a family member who is most decidedly not on your team. The person in question may only be a distant cousin or a nephew by marriage, but they are of a jealous nature and will do whatever they can to bend your spokes. As they are sensitive to adulation and praise, go ahead and slather it on.

2017, the Fire Rooster year – Don't count on getting rich this year. The Rooster has a reputation for economizing in hard times. Do the best you can with what you have. That's the Rooster's message for Rats. Don't overspend. Catch yourself before you indulge in what appear on the surface to be 'bargains'. A bargain is only as useful as how much it subtracts from your budget. And budget you will in the Rooster year – or else! The good news is that this early in the year, you will be very close to falling in love. I cannot guarantee that this one will be the one with whom you will spend the rest of your natural life. It may indeed be merely a 'teaching affair' wherein you learn how to accept that certain independent aspects of a loved one's character will never mesh with your need to protect and to 'own' that person's full attention. Don't let my advice hinder your progress here. The love you bring to this union will be well spent as the lessons you learn will be crucial and useful for a long time to come.

2018, the Earth Dog year – Money worries fly out the window for Rats this year. You can breathe more easily now and even splurge on one or two lavish parties or luxury holidays. Do, however, use your time wisely for a new endeavor. It may not be a business venture or have to do with increasing your own income. Rather, I see you getting involved in a charitable pursuit of some sort which may set you back a few thousand of your local currency's biggest bills. Take it slow. Don't jump at the first opportunity to help starving populations or assist the undereducated girl children in a particular region you fancy visiting. Make certain that the charity in which you invest your good heart and fortune will use your money wisely and that the people who need it most will benefit. Research well before you give. Sparks may fly in your love life in 2018. You tend to be inflexible on matters which are key to your mate's emotional survival. Take all that he or she tells you more seriously than before. Be willing to discuss alternatives to the lifestyle you have previously been able to impose. Perhaps it's your lover's turn to call the shots for a while.

2019, the Earth Pig year – This is a lucky year for Rats. The Pig approves of you and encourages all of your moneymaking and wealth-amassing schemes. You will, however, have to be more cautious about health issues. You probably have a chronic condition of some sort – a nagging backache or palpitations or on-again-off-again nausea – that you have been successfully ignoring for quite a while now. This will be the year to clear up those symptoms. Get thee to a medical professional or accredited health practitioner before summer sets in. You will more than likely be required to follow some sort of new regime. Diet and exercise? Change of climate during allergy season? A new medication? Whatever it is, you must take it very seriously in order not to allow the condition in question to worsen and cause more serious problems later on. Your romantic picture will have improved – provided you were able to implement a more flexible viewpoint with regard to your significant other's needs.

The Diligent Ox

Hail, Diligent Ox,

A veritable Gibraltar. An indomitable fortress. This sign might have been called Bulldozer instead of Ox. You are an essentially temperate person who cares greatly for rigor, labor, strength of character and . . . results!

You can stick at a task longer and go at it harder than anybody. You spare no elbow grease. You hate to be beaten, so you simply never give up. Some may call you slow; others complain that you are clumsy. In fact, you move at your own sweet pace and refuse to be pushed or prodded by a lot of hot-headed fly-by-nights. You believe in simplicity and achievement. Levity in business exasperates you.

You are capable of profound, enduring love, yet romance leaves you cold. You prefer action to beds of roses and phials of exotic perfumes. You take life very seriously but life doesn't always return the favor. You don't normally talk much but you have a remarkable talent for story-telling.

If it's really results you're after, use that special flair. Chat up the conservative Rooster you've been longing to invite to dinner. Share some pink bubbly with a garrulous Rat or send dozens of white roses to a luxury-loving Snake. They are all well equipped to handle your peculiar brand of seduction. The first two eras of your life will be characterized by hard work. During the second adult phase a misunderstanding between you and a neighbor or colleague may cause a deep, long-lasting rift.

Don't lose heart. Your old age will be both long and healthy with peace of mind taking over after fifty as priority number one.

Advice? Yes. Lighten up. And stop judging others by your own high standards. You'll only be disappointed. Nobody (except you, my dear Ox) is perfect.

Enduringly yours

Suzanne White

In the twentieth and twenty-first century all Oxen were born between the following dates:

19	February	1901	and	7	February	1902
6	February	1913	and	25	January	1914
24	January	1925	and	12	February	1926
11	February	1937	and	30	January	1938
29	January	1949	and	16	February	1950
15	February	1961	and	4	February	1962
3	February	1973	and	22	January	1974
20	February	1985	and	8	February	1986
7	February	1997	and	27	January	1998
26	January	2009	and	13	February	2010

The Ox ID card

Lasting symbols have special powers. Enhance your self-image by surrounding yourself with tangible signs of your own identity and make these symbols known to your friends and loved ones. Use them daily and they will bring you luck, security and a feeling of personal worth.

Your best	***Your favorite***
color is dark blue	food is beef stew
flower is chrysanthemum	animal is bear
fragrance is Shalimar	drink is strong tea
tree is pear	spice is coriander
flavor is sweet	metal is copper
birthstone is lapis lazuli	herb is sage
lucky number is 1	musical instrument is tuba

The Ox is yin ***The Ox motto is 'I persevere'***

On the self-contained exterior, Oxen are patient, contemplative, skilful, dextrous, eloquent, confident, familiar, authoritative, industrious, sure of foot and eloquent.

But . . . pierce the Ox's thick hide and you will find prejudice, chauvinism, blind faith, pride, tyranny, pettiness, criticism, eccentricity, bigotry, conservatism, grumpiness – and, on occasion, violence.

The Ox and I

The Chinese animal after which this sign is named is the Water Buffalo. I renamed it for occidental readers when I wrote my first book. Now, I am a little sorry as I think Water Buffalo is a more fitting image, less domestic than Ox. But what's done is done, and Ox is the name we all now know.

It is always best to stay on the good side of Oxen. As old-fashioned hardliners, these tough people are without peer. They tend to classify almost everything into two basic categories, bad and good. If he is in an unusually jolly humor and willing to give nuance a chance, he might agree to see shades of meaning such as 'light' and 'dark'. But you won't catch Oxen going much beyond fundamentals. Oxen are steady, patient, long-suffering world-beaters who inspire confidence and admiration. They are phenomenally strong.

Some neurotically meticulous people examine every detail of their lives under a microscope. Oxen are neurotically meticulous people who observe all of life through the wrong end of a telescope, always opting to take the long view, to foresee every upcoming situation at a safe remove, calculating ahead the likely risks and results.

Oxen painstakingly pick over every detail. They watch every move you make. Not only are they careful observers but Oxen study, pore over, dissect, take out the stitches and sew the whole thing back up a hundred times, if necessary, before calling any job done. Oxen are proficient, competent, thorough and annoyingly accurate.

Perimeters and parameters are the Ox's best friends. Take away the confines and you scare him half to death. Just for fun, tell an Ox that in the new deal you're about to strike with him that you consider a contract unnecessary because you cannot tell him when, where or how much and that he must trust in your good faith and leave the rest up to old Lady Destiny. The imperturbable Ox will not comment. He'll walk away without a word. He'd sooner die than be a party to any such *unreliable* deals. Before embarking on any association or partnership, the Ox wants it all down on paper. It's tough to get him to go to a picnic without having the event scheduled weeks ahead, registered with the Patent Office and stamped by the Bureau of Vital Statistics.

However, although he will resist entering into any shared experience, be it marriage or a rumba class, once an Ox has decided to trust another individual, once he believes in their goodwill and good faith, he will never ask for another signed document. Then he will give of himself, his time, money, and blessings and will not doubt the lucky person who has passed the Ox test.

Getting through the Ox's tough demeanor to the diligently guarded but gooey center is a long exercise in perseverance and demonstrative rectitude. But if you succeed you've got yourself a valuable friend for life. It is unlikely that Captain Ox will take too many lifetime passengers on board because overbooking would diminish the quality of his services: as friends, Oxen feel obliged to perform faultlessly. They are caretakers, protectors, counsellors, money and hand lenders. Too many full-time friends would sink such a well-appointed ship.

Oxen are like litmus paper. Show an Ox a potential lover or associate, ask his opinion of a potential travelling companion or try out an idea for a project on him. You won't be sorry: Oxen are strong, silent and observant. While the new person (or idea) is chatting away, trying to impress, Oxxy will sit back, cool as Moscow, watching, absorbing every detail and clicking off a mental checklist of pros and cons as long as a Russian novel. If he thinks it stinks, he will tell you outright.

If you do win him over, the victory may not be entirely a blessing. Once admitted to the Ox family circle, one is obliged to live up to the honor. The Ox holds up his high standards as a model and severely judges those who do not aspire to maintain these same ideals.

One does not do mischief to an Ox with impunity. An Ox betrayed speaks even less than usual, paws the earth once or twice, and charges directly at the jugular.

He is ponderous but impulsive when angry, especially if he's been made a fool of. He is capable of fearsome rages. Oxen are too stodgy and proud to lose their self-control so don't usually turn the furniture upside down, but instead the slow-moving Ox will conjure up some long-lasting violence or mental torture. Revenge is a meal best eaten cold, but the angry Ox is a hungry buckaroo who prefers to begin his revenge with a hot hors-d'oeuvre and to continue eating heartily through all seven courses. Then he sends his enemies the bill.

I have an Ox friend named Marguerite. She's French and she's been a friend for nearly thirty years. When she and I first met I was in my early twenties and she in her early fifties. She had hired me as her English tutor and we became fast friends.

Marguerite is a smallish woman. She's neither frail nor chunky, but she is dense and built close to the ground. She has masses of straight white hair which she wears in a boyish bob that neatly frames her sure-featured *auvergnate* or country-French face. Her dark eyes are piercing but gentle. She's gruff, but as tender-hearted and warm-natured as the crème caramels she prepares so well.

When Marguerite and I are both in Paris, she calls me to talk on the phone every Sunday at 10 a.m. I couldn't remember to ring anyone at 10 sharp every week.

Marguerite and I knew each other well for fifteen years before she addressed me as 'tu'. One day she simply said, *'Tu viens déjeuner?'* – Come to lunch – friendly instead of *'Vous venez déjeuner?'* – Please come to lunch, Madame – courteous yet stand-offish. I was deeply touched by Marguerite's obviously well-calculated decision to use *tu*. Like anything that is hard to come by, when you break down an Ox's reserve, you feel like it's your birthday. Tears came to my eyes. Now, our friendship is inviolable, lifelong. If I'm sad or anxious, Marguerite invites me to visit her in her country *château*. When I score a victory, Marguerite's applause can be heard all over Paris. Marguerite is a true Ox, a brick. She wouldn't crack under torture.

When she was sixteen, Marguerite's widowed mother married her off to the youngest son of a rich man, a loutish rich kid and the family ne'er-do-well. Marguerite determined that she wouldn't let this enforced, but prosperous, marriage ruin her life.

Unfortunately a year later, after she had borne a child, Marguerite came down with tuberculosis. When she was sent to the mountains to a sanatorium, the husband's family told the hospital's head doctor they would pay him handsomely to give Marguerite drugs so that she would become addicted, perhaps die, and never return to the big house in Paris.

Marguerite was sick and depressed at the thought that she would either die or go back to her horrid in-laws. Gradually, they all stopped visiting her. She stopped eating and eventually succumbed to the fatigue caused by the worsening of the lesion on her lung. Soon, she was sleeping her life away, having decided they would all be better off if she were dead.

Marguerite told her doctor that she wondered why nobody ever came or wrote any more. She feared for her baby girl, believed the in-laws were trying to steal her child.

The doctor tried everything to get Marguerite to decide to get better. One day he told Marguerite about the bribes he had been offered. 'They may hope that you won't get well. Maybe they want your child.'

'You think they wanted you to let me die so they could take Paulette away from me?' whispered Marguerite.

'Something like that . . .' said the doctor. He left her alone then, advising her to reconsider.

Marguerite says, 'At first I was so shocked that I grew more and more ill. I felt so unwanted and unloved. I continued to starve and sank lower and lower. Then, one morning, I woke thinking about my two-year-old daughter. Although she was the image of her father, she had a sweet nature. I still ached with love for that child and I realized that if I let myself go any further I would never see or hold her again.

'The nurse had tried everything to get me to come back to life, including hand-squeezing raw meat to extract the blood and making me drink it.

'I hated that raw blood but the nurse insisted, assuring me that blood would build me up. All night I thought about my daughter and on that day in 1937 I said to my nurse, "Please, Mademoiselle, can you get me some beef blood?" You can imagine her shock at my request, but I knew it would make me strong.'

The pale young Ox woman rose to the occasion. Inside her mind, the Ox – the wronged, the betrayed Marguerite – felt tough, not physically strong, but Ox-strong, iron-willed. 'The nurse gave me fresh beef blood to drink three times a day, to build up red blood cells. Then, I ordered some bottles of red wine. I ate everything they gave me even though it often upset my stomach. I began phoning Paris and insisting on talking to my little girl. In a few weeks, I was walking around the hospital and in six months I walked out cured.'

And when Marguerite got home did she race up the huge front staircase, scoop up her child and run away for ever? No. The Ox takes the long view. Marguerite moved back into the big house in Paris and stayed there until, by subtly imposing her will and determination, she made the family accept her. She was finally able to prove to her spoiled husband that his brother and stepmother were trying to do him out of his share of the father's fortune. She pressured her father-in-law into building her a house where she wanted to live, hired the nannies *she* wanted, found the lovers and friends *she* needed and thrived amid the Philistines.

And what happened to them? The monstrous in-laws all died of heart attacks and strokes, leaving Paulette to inherit the handsome fortune of her father's side.

Now when I ask her advice about anything, Marguerite gives me the sound warning she gave herself years ago: 'Always remember to create your memories carefully because when you are old, your memories will be your best friends.'

Memories, traditions and customs are the Ox's security blankets. No one can accuse an Ox of being a vaporous dreamer who wastes his life concocting rattlebrained schemes and blazing trails to nowhere. The Ox is a thorough-going down-to-the-ground, go-ahead soul. He is not keen on such imprecise terms as 'seem', 'almost', 'perhaps', and 'we'll see'. The reality-loving Ox usually sticks to 'exactly', 'accurately', 'authentic', 'never'.

Oxen need order. At home, they equip shelves, cupboards and closets with hooks and special racks for every item. I save used Nescafé jars for an Ox friend who stores hundreds of items – screws, bolts, nuts, nails, bits of wire, sugar, salt, rice, buttons, paper-clips, *everything* – in them. Each jar is soaked to get rid of its label, then filled and re-labelled, sprayed with a waterproof coating to keep its marking from fading or peeling, then stored in its cupboard, with its sister and brother bolts or condiments, which is also labelled and locked.

This methodical habit of filing and sorting is not the Ox's only pet pastime: it is the Ox who switches off lights and shuts windows, secures doors, sighing when you forget. The way that others choose to live does not always suit the serious, economical Ox householder.

Oxen are veritable sponges for responsibility and duty. Ox children are good little boys and girls – sitting ducks for guilt-trip parents who admonish them not to forget to turn off the lights and never to let in drafts. Little Oxen listen, obey and remain perfect little home economists. Poor Oxen, they take everything sooo seriously.

Unlike the nervous Monkey, the belligerent Tiger or the skittish Horse, the Ox is not easily undone. A yellow and green fire-spitting elephant could suddenly surge into his headlights but the Ox would remain unswervingly steady at the wheel. Oxen hang on with their fingernails to every challenge they accept, tugging firmly and regularly at the stubbornest knots of each complex situation until they work them loose. Oxen are not ready, set, go-problem solvers like the Monkey nor do they dodge confrontation like the Cat. When the giant rock is rolling down the hill straight at him, the good Ox respectfully waits for the light to turn green. His goal? To be completely finished with one and perfectly prepared to go on to the next gigantic undertaking.

Oxen hate metaphysics. Poetry bores them. Quixotic fancy, whining self-pity and vapid self-examination drives them bonkers. Here's a sample conversation with a material-bound Ox:

You: Hi, Bill, have you seen Charlie lately?
Ox: Yes. He was at the PTA meeting last Tuesday.
You: How did he seem?
Ox: He was wearing a blue shirt, grey trousers and a blazer.
You: Oh, I see. Well, how was he looking?
Ox: He had on a club tie – silk – rep stripes: blue and red with small crests all over.
You: That's nice. But how did he actually look?
Ox: He was wearing air-cushioned Nikes, royal blue and white.
You: Had he been drinking?
Ox: Yes. Earl Grey tea with milk and two sugars.
You: I meant, drinking, like alcoholic-type-drinking. How did Charlie *look*?
Ox: Huh?
You: Did Charlie look *happy*?
Ox: I don't remember.

Oxen have remarkable memories and are capable of in-depth reporting on absolutely everything they observe – except for the metaphysical. They don't look for signs of emotional distress. They are not cold-hearted or immune to sadness but just don't know how to recognize sentiment.

Oxen are not repelled by the intangible. Rather, they have difficulty understanding what the rest of us find so gripping about it. Fantasy throws the Ox. He wonders what we see in flaky subjects like astrology and psychology and why we are sometimes lost in a daydream or transported by a new romance. You can wag enough romantic folderol to space out a whole herd of bison right under the Ox's snout and he will reward you with a truckload of indifference. Oxen prefer a drivel-free existence. Some more sensitive Oxen may try to learn to appreciate the metaphysical, relax a bit and sink into the hovering-nowhere pleasure that others know how to extract from a roam through a pleasant vacuum. But the materialistic Ox mind often remains immune to the abstract.

Because they are not keen on petty chit-chat and abhor small talk, Oxen love mottoes, proverbs and aphorisms. They need to be certain of what they are saying and are terrified to appear ridiculous, so often pepper their speech with clichés or maxims like 'All professions are a conspiracy against the laity,' or 'Time is money,' and 'Such is the nature of the human animal.'

Silly puns and tired jokes help the timid Ox feel more secure in company. Just as you can always count on your Ox friend to lend a hand in times of dire need, you can also be sure he will pop the ancient story about the foreigner who introduces one man to another saying, 'Here is Jack Larsen. He has a finger in many tarts.'

Nigel Jackson, the Ox who tells this story, is a close friend who I have heard tell it at least four hundred times in the last twenty years. As far as he is concerned, if it made someone smile in 1947, it's good enough to be repeated into the twenty-first century. Oxen refuse to make changes for the sheer pleasure of refusing to change.

Yet Oxen are rarely boring. If you can keep them talking news and current affairs, they have an innate ability – not often used unless called upon officially – to recount experience and teach us things. They are even eloquent, but don't often show it in private. Oxen are not gifted at rapping over a bottle of wine. When they deign to speak, it's with good reason. To avoid speaking but say what's on his mind, the shy Ox may become a writer, where he can express himself without being face to face with his interlocutor. Politics and trial law sometimes attract the Ox: a public professional life affords him a forum without the discomfort of *têtes-à-têtes* and allows him to keep intermediaries and a safe distance between him and the people he's talking to.

Stubborn refusal to budge is part of what gives the Ox such extraordinary strength. But it is also his Achilles' heel. The faithful Ox woman Anne-Marie, my kids' nanny in the sixties and early seventies, was a Breton woman who had come to Paris as a maid when she was very young. She resisted the temptations and dangers of life in the big city and finally married. She became concierge in my apartment building and to earn extra cash, she looked after people's kids.

All through their babyhood and early infancy, the rapport between my kids and Mémé, as they dubbed her, was harmonious. Anne-Marie called them her little golden treasures, spoiled and loved them. But when the girls were getting older, friction grew between them and Nanny. Daisy came home from school one day and announced that she had learned about how Christopher Columbus discovered America with three ships he got from the Queen of Spain. Anne-Marie was peeling potatoes for the family's soup and said, 'Christopher Columbus discovered America in a dirigible balloon. I saw it on TV.' Then she gave one of those typical Ox, condescending indulgent laughs that imply 'You poor, adorable fool.'

Daisy brought this strange news to me. 'Mom,' she said, 'did Christopher Columbus sail to America or did he fly?'

'They didn't have flying machines in 1492,' I said.

'I thought it seemed funny,' she said. 'But how can I tell Mémé that? She thinks Christopher Columbus discovered America in a dirigible balloon. If I tell her the truth she'll get real mad.'

Poor little Daisy. It was hard to accept that her beloved omniscient nanny was wrong about such a major issue. Losses of innocence are always jarring. All I could suggest was 'Honey, rather than upset Mémé, just let her think what she wants, OK? Just nod and pretend you agree.'

The Ox gets along best with himself and is capable of living a solitary life. When he's alone, the Ox finds a thousand little jobs to keep him productively occupied. Most Oxen are good fix-it people and prefer tinkering on their own to the demands of social interaction.

Oxen adore eating and often have problems keeping their weight down. But, with their iron self-discipline, they control the excess poundage through rigid dieting. As they don't mind routine, they are happy to be served the same dishes every day at the same hours. The Ox could enjoy soup on Monday, ribs on Tuesday, spaghetti on Wednesday, through to Friday's fish and Sunday's roast and start again with Monday's soup. His food, the Ox insists, must be of good quality and well prepared but variety is unnecessary.

People sometimes find the Ox a bit dull. With his plain tastes and deliberate ways, he can seem a drudge. He's judgemental and easily annoyed. He's either too close-mouthed or too long-windedly repetitive. Oxen are not flexible; nor are they happy-go-lucky hail-fellows well met. Jollity doesn't come easily to the humdrum-loving Ox and he's often accused of being a stodgy killjoy.

None the less, these dependable straight-shooters deserve admiration. Oxen carry through all their undertakings without complaining or snivelling. They always keep their word and rarely break the law. Oxen don't shirk responsibility, try to hold their families together, and pay their debts.

So if, once in a while, your favorite Ox creeps away inside himself and doesn't speak to you for days, don't call him a grouch. Give him a break. Try to help him to express himself. Entice him with food and wine, wrestle him to the floor, kiss him and tickle his ribs. Then, once you have him in your power, teach that rigid old Ox to dance or swim, ride a bike or even do aerobics. If you can cajole him past stubborn resistance and help him to enjoy himself, he'll be for ever indebted to you.

As for you . . . you've got yourself the best friend you've ever had – for life!

Ms Ox

Oxen are stalwart and tenacious. The female of this species is also devoted to basics. She has grounded her belief in the importance of family in tried and true methods and, although the Ox is a sign marked by solitude, most Ox women get married. Often, the Ox woman starts her professional life thinking that she will leave marriage and children to less driven and ambitious women. But this early choice is foiled by the impending Big Ben of a biological clock ticking away the fertile seconds, which is when even the most reluctant-to-commit Ox surrenders to her innermost need to foster and head up a family.

She is a nature devotee and, when she finally acquires her home in the country (she's not mad about city life), will grow her own herbs, vegetables, roses and fruit trees with a rigorous respect for Mother Nature's laws. The Ox woman also adheres effortlessly to the strict routines imposed by caring for others. She's the sort of organized householder who pops a pie into the oven before taxi-ing her immaculately dressed, perfectly behaved kids to and from school. Then she trudges home to take the pie out, replace it with a roast, and leave again to meet her husband's train. Later, when the whole crew gets home, the reliable Ox woman serves hubby's drinks, the kids' dinner, oversees homework and listens to his trial of the day and never gives a yawn of boredom.

The Ox woman cleaves to duty. However, her family obligations do not prevent her from having an important career. Take Margaret

Thatcher. As Britain's Prime Minister she worked tirelessly with a few close associates to maintain the conservative image she had of her country. She did not often say yes. Rather, in typically Ox fashion, Maggie Thatcher said NO – the resounding refusal of the She Bull stubbornly standing her ground. She could not have been more committed as a political leader while proving herself a successful wife and mother.

Despite great resources of energy, most Ox women (unless, like Jane Fonda, it's their profession) resist exercise. They are not lazy, weak or embarrassed about doing gymnastics, aerobics or running but they don't like to move quickly and hate to sweat. But they frequently sign up for classical dance classes and may enjoy taking the family on long hikes. Challenge sports, such as mountain climbing and long-distance cross-country skiing, may also appeal and, interestingly, tennis. The win or lose aspect of all her involvements is important to the Ox woman so if she's bitten by the winner bug the Ox woman goes all the way. She doesn't mind fighting in a hand-to-hand combat of skill and endurance but she doesn't see the point in vapid gymnastics for health.

Last year my Ox sister-in-law Carol turned from a butterball of post-partum chubbs into a lithe slender sports queen in a matter of two months. Always beautiful, Carol had had a miscarriage and felt depressed for a few months. She clung more than ever to home and guarded the one baby she already had with the zeal of a German Shepherd. Her pretty brown eyes grew rounder and cow-like and her waistline began to follow suit. Then one day – ta dah! – Carol discovered tennis. While staying at home, she'd seen some matches on TV and became excited by the prospect of winning at something that looked so difficult. Perhaps she also wanted to get back in shape but she's such a stoical Ox that she never complained about being unhappy or getting fat.

Carol went in for tennis the way hunters go after bear. Ox-sure of purpose and of foot and eye, she bounced and hit thousands of practice balls, perfected her backhand and, in a matter of weeks, started beating the lacy knickers off her opponents.

'I need a new racquet,' she told my brother one evening at dinner, 'a Prince. I'm entering the tournament and if I win I'll have to go on the road.'

'How much does a Prince cost?' asked her husband.

'About two hundred dollars,' she said calmly, dishing up dessert. 'And from now on I will be needing a full-time afternoon babysitter for Ryan and I'll be taking the car so you'll have to take the ferry to work.'

My brother knew his wife of fifteen years well enough not to argue. Like everything else she did, Carol took her sport to heart. Either she would do it right or she would not do it at all. He was ready to support her. Six weeks later she knocked out the previous year's champion.

Without challenge, the perilous temptation for the Ox woman is to allow her family's needs to overcome her sense of self. Unfortunately, after a few years as housewives, many Ox women grow dowdy and too fat or too thin and decide to pass off physical beauty as frivolous. If she finds her husband is losing interest in her sexually or beginning to stray, the Ox woman will usually turn a blind eye and dutifully apply even more energy to making their home and raising the children.

Of course she is jealous but she will not let it show. She takes it in her stride. She makes no effort to alter her habits or flounce up her appearance. She's sure of her position as wife and she will wait it out, hardly changing her attitude, smiling sweetly as though nothing untoward were happening beyond the perimeters of her skirts.

The Ox woman nearly always triumphs in the end. What she wants from marriage is not romance and passion, but a husband, family and a life after passion, which outlasts accidents and silly men's clandestine affairs. She doesn't fuss about Jim's Visa card bills for his candle-lit dinners with the odd blonde. Candle-lit dinners bore her, anyway, so why should she begrudge poor overworked Jim an occasional sally into faithlessness?

It is said that the Ox woman looks at sex as a sort of healthy indoor sport. She would feel ridiculous slinking around in clinging lamé dresses and teeteringly high heels, playing the seductress. Look at Jane Fonda. For a time, Roger Vadim, her French first husband, tried to turn her from a student activist into a sex symbol. She made *Barbarella* and other sex-bomb films, then left Vadim and became a tough-talking, hard-driving political figure. Suddenly she married her political partner, Tom Hayden, an apparent nobody, but whom Fonda loved fiercely. They had kids and she became an aerobics specialist and wrote books about how to keep yourself and your family healthy. Jane Fonda is a toughie and, like all Ox women, her charm is in her strength.

Think about it – Barbara Bush, Margaret Thatcher, Mary Tyler

Moore and Meryl Streep – rugged stalwarts one and all, women whose collective family crest might read (in Latin, of course) 'Rigor/ Endurance/Performance'. And think about the women you know who were born in 1901, 1913, 1925, 1937, 1949 or 1961. If one of them is not a tower of pure, unflagging might, please write to me about her and I shall examine her case in depth.

As virtue and righteousness are so important to her, the Ox woman is not guileful and rarely, if ever, malicious or gossipy. She will not stoop to chicanery or cheating to win favor or earn money. She will bear up in times of poverty but is not good at being without funds or comforts for a long stretch. The Ox woman requires at least a modicum of affluence to be happy. She's happiest when there is enough money for everybody to have the right shoes, go to the right schools and the right piano lessons. When there is not enough, she will not shrink from scrubbing a few floors to get more.

The Ox woman makes a wonderful parent. The only hitch is that if her kids don't live up to the strict standards to which she aspires and which she exercises, there will be trouble. She's intolerant and judgemental. The Ox mother will give hell to a kid who leaves school in the midst of his studies to 'find himself'. She's worked and made sacrifices for him and cannot understand why he won't do the same for her. Although she is usually not rancorous and would not take out her anger on him in petty ways, she's tough and may stop his allowance, pack his things and ask him not to darken her door again until he has come to his senses.

The Ox woman's physical appearance is often modest and unassuming. She is at least of middling height and may be quite tall, with shortish legs and longer arms. She is sturdy-looking with fleshy lips, a thick neck and large shoulders. Her bosom is often ample and her thighs are never skinny. She carries herself well and strides along, graceful, attractive and sure-footed. Her eyes are her best feature, lovely, deep and liquid, expressing the tender sensitivity that she rarely puts into words.

This character is neither morose nor over-preoccupied with her own anxieties. Her pleasant company is soothing and reassuring. Although she is slow and deliberate like her male counterpart, the female Ox is not taciturn and holds forth openly on subjects that directly concern her. She won't do much conjecturing, though, or try to solve the problems of the world. Even in conversation she sticks to basics. She has an excellent sense of humor and is able to laugh at her own foibles, which makes her fun to be around. Her ability to satirize is as well developed as that of the Ox male and she can be very funny and cutting when she needs to be.

The young Ox woman is easily swayed by the smell of money and success, yet because of her seriousness, she can be naïve about the rotting underbelly of the *real* world. As she is never deceitful, she cannot understand why anyone would cheat or lie to her. As she grows older, she becomes more sophisticated but in youth the Ox woman often has the wool pulled over her eyes by those less honest than herself.

The Ox woman clings to her family background as well as to the family she has created in adult life. She's forever taking the kids to her aunt's or looking after her cousin's kids during the school vacation. She calls her mother every week, takes her dad to the doctor and cheerfully visits her husband's ageing granny. All family festivities are held at the Ox woman's home. How does she find time to shop and prepare with such aplomb, goodwill and never seem flustered? She's an Ox. The thing she does best is maintain traditions and keep the home fires burning.

Her faults? The Ox woman is stubborn and not easily swayed. When determined about something, she won't give a centimeter; she must make her own decisions in her own time. She can be testy and will not be criticized. If she is feeling sensitive about herself or shaky about her position, she can become downright paranoid. Petty details will suddenly annoy her. She will rankle at the slightest comment on her dress or her hair. The Ox woman so desperately wants to be at the head of the herd and feels so responsible for everything and everyone around her that if she loses face or confidence, she is afraid the world will crumble around them all.

Another little female Ox secret – she doesn't care for cosmetics or perfumes and refuses to wear ruffles and furbelows. This is not a form of reverse snobbery or a scorn for beautiful things – the Ox woman adores real leather, fine china and elegant furnishings – but because she disdains fashion: she feels that *la mode* is too easy-come, easy-go. It has no staying power and therefore is not to be considered in her lifestyle. If she wants to attract a man, the Ox woman relies almost entirely on her natural, sturdy good looks, strength and her sexy, velvety voice. Her goal, remember, is not a raucous roll in the hay – it's marriage and the works or forget it, Buster.

Mr Ox

While I was writing this, Saddam Hussein was playing Russian Roulette and Desert Hopscotch with the hearts and minds of thousands of hostages and their families, taunting the world's leaders with his tough-guy schemes and undauntedly, stupidly, bullishly refusing to budge. I discovered that Saddam Hussein, born 28 April 1937, is an Ox. I was not surprised. In New Astrology, he is, as was Adolf Hitler, a Taurus/Ox. Stubborn is too mild an adjective here: obstinate; inflexible; bullheaded. Egomaniacally sure of his superiority, blind and deaf to reason, this guy is a public menace.

I immediately wanted to phone George Bush. I wished I had a hot line to Mitterrand's office. I felt I had inside information. Hadn't Bush compared Saddam to Hitler? I guess he didn't know how right he was. To attempt to resist Saddam with threats and harsh language, to try to daunt him with strong words and long-winded edicts and military measures was folly. With a guy like Saddam Hussein, you tread lightly, dip and dance, blind him with science. You talk sweetly, spar with him and watch for the occasional dropping of the guard. You treat him with a psychological velvet glove. You talk him through it and, after a time, you talk him out of it. But you do not defy him. When the Taurus/Ox sees his own brand of force heading straight at him, he becomes all the more determined to win – and even more dangerous.

I think it is safe to say that most Ox men are a curious combination of Saddam Hussein and Santa Claus. Of course, not all Ox men are potential Saddam Husseins, nor Taurus/Oxen bad guys. (Some nicer Ox-born Taureans are Gary Cooper, Jack Nicholson and Billy Joel.) The Ox's brute force, if used positively, can be gigantically benign. But the Ox man is a born hard-head. He's strong to a fault, obtuse and unbudgeable.

Now all good and bad pronouncements are relative. Let me qualify this over-simplistic assessment by adding that some of my best friends are Oxen. Nevertheless, I'm not going to tell too many deprecating stories about them or they might murder me in my sleep.

Look at some of the famous Oxen on the lists in the elements section: there are no small fry among them. Walt Disney, brilliant bigot; Adolf Hitler, murderous dictator; Idi Amin Dada, celebrated tyrant and infanticide specialist; Saddam Hussein, famous Bull shoveller dictator. There are, indeed, dictators in all the sign groups and perhaps this list is only coincidence, but – Napoleon was an Ox, so was Julius Caesar and, mind you, so was Johann Sebastian Bach. Ox is a rich sign for a man, full of potential greatness. But that power must be used positively or demon tyranny may set in, cement replace brains and the fight is on.

Also, check out how many actors, stand-up comics and TV personalities there are on the Ox-male list. Plenty. Presidents and statesmen . . . not too many: Oxen don't like to take political risks. Either they dictate or they don't play the game. Writers? Yes. Singers, too, and apt creators of social commentary, but few artists or poets: Oxen are not keen on anything fancy.

Even at rest they think about work. Firstly, they always endeavor to succeed with almost mindless resolve and have no time for frivolity unless it helps them achieve their objective. An Ox man will attend a party if he thinks he'll meet someone he needs to know for professional reasons. You might even get a recalcitrant Ox to go to a gym or take him on a shopping spree, providing you give him a sound reason as to how his participation in what he considers a waste of time will advance him.

Secondly, when they are pulling a wagonload of bricks and laboring to gain ground, they are also working at improving their property. Ox men adore acquiring land, buying houses, purchasing buildings and, in short, gaining ground. They have an almost holy regard for the earth and are especially pious if it belongs to them. Ox men will carry photographs of their *châteaux*, yacht and fleet of Mercedes in their wallets so that they can distribute them to folk they meet. Sounds awful – but don't misinterpret the Ox's ponderous handing out of show-and-tell photos, because he is not merely trying to impress. He is not an able one-to-one communicator. Timid and retiring, he does not improvise well and is incapable of thinking on his feet. The photo postcard hand-outs are only props to serve as tangible proof of his situation. The Ox man is not a hustler or much of a salesman. If he wants you to know that he is rich, loves sailing, golf, writing or singing, he will show you a picture of his house or a copy of his book or record. To the Ox man, the old saw 'Actions speak louder than words' saves him from confrontation.

Don't ever ask an Ox man the classic 'Do you love me?' question and expect a decent answer. You will only elicit blushing and brooding, or sulking and grouchiness. Cornering an Ox male is worse than cornering any Rat and it only makes him even more tongue-tied. Don't try to turn this Ox guy into a Latin lover – even if he is one, he'll act more like a Hun. If he does love you – and he is perfectly capable of great, undying, long-suffering love – the Ox man will demonstrate his love in the only ways he knows how: you may find all the wood you need for your fireplace for a year piled up outside your door, or a leather bankbook in your name with several thousand dollars deposited therein under your pillow, or a shiny new Range Rover in your garage. Usually he will not hand the present to you – he is too diffident or afraid of surprise to dare such a gesture. He is annoyingly timid, but enormously generous, with those he loves. But don't count on the Ox for cheap frills: he will never, like the spendthrift Monkey male, buy you a $1,000 nightie.

The Ox male is forever repairing, gardening, hammering, tinkering or pottering. He loves to take things apart and put them back together and gets a charge out of making broken things work again. The end result may not be aesthetically pleasing but whatever was broken is guaranteed to run smoothly again: even the most intellectual Ox man is gifted in manual work.

Ox men do not take risks. They like to be sure of what the prize is before leaping with all four hoofs into any project. They are cautious, prudent and get no pleasure from the uncertainty of being routed off the beaten path. Impermanence makes them uncomfortable. They would be happy in a world where the ephemeral didn't exist. The Ox man is neither a guesser nor a hazarder of opinion. He'd rather be late than wrong and deplores philosophical conjecturing and vain speculation. The Ox is a man of almanacs and atlases, road maps and compasses, dictionaries, thesauruses and encyclopedias. His home and/or office will be heavy with reference books and he will refer to them all the time while planning his next move.

Like his female counterpart, the Ox male never gives up his attachment to his origins. If he was born in Yugoslavia in the mountains and has subsequently moved to Iowa, he will always hanker after the mountains and may even insist on going back there to die. He's more interested in the past than in the future. He won't keep many pets and if he lives alone (which he often does) his furnishings will be sparse and no-nonsense. If he marries he usually puts comfort before attraction as he considers his sexual habits have little or nothing to do with those of his wife.

In love, the Ox male is constant yet physically unfaithful. He loves profoundly and supports and sticks firmly by his family commitments. He will always be there when his partner needs him. But the Ox man does not consider sexual love to be in the same league as married love and devotion. To him, love and sex are separate. He is sensual and loves the good life. He is addicted to comfort, fine food and wine and is fairly easy to please so long as these needs are seen to.

The sex act is so far removed from what he thinks of as love that the Ox male is capable of having sex with almost anyone, but he can only love very few people. The Ox male's emotions are intricately connected to his unyielding heart. His public image has little or nothing to do with his inner feelings and his secret self is unavailable for viewing by even his most intimate friends or lovers unless they're very lucky.

I had this experience with my pal Nigel Jackson, my boyfriend in the summer of 1974. For some unknown reason, he had been difficult with me for a few months. I tried to pry the reason out of him with wine, home-cooked meals, practical presents and night-time heart-to-heart chats. But Nigel remained mute. In time he brightened up, my curiosity lost its cutting edge and I gradually stopped asking him why he'd been so grouchy.

In March 1990 I met him for a drink. At some point, Nigel brought up the name of a person we had visited in July 1974 in Mallorca and I said, 'I can hardly recall what we did in Mallorca because you were so cranky that I was beside myself with anxiety, thinking I'd done something to cause it.'

The normally opaque Nigel had drunk a glass or two of our great American California wine and must have felt he could throw caution to the winds. He laughed, embarrassedly. 'That summer,' said Nigel, 'I was jolly annoyed.'

'But *why*?' I said.

'Val came for Easter to the South of France that year,' said Nigel. 'Remember? And he complained at least twice a day about the drive from Germany,' he added sternly.

'Yes. He drove all night after working a full shift at the hospital. He was bleary-eyed for days,' I put in. 'Was *that* why you were cranky?'

Nigel sipped his wine then looked over at me, red in the face at what he was about to admit. 'Yes,' he confessed.

'In July?' I gasped. 'It happened at Easter.'

'Yes,' Nigel said again. 'The more I thought about it the more it bothered me.'

Nigel had been annoyed at Val, an overworked doctor who was patently exhausted. It had taken me *fifteen years* to find out something so banal which I felt I deserved to know while it was happening. 'You really take the cake, Nigel Jackson,' I said, getting up steam to huff out of the restaurant. But then I looked at him. He was pale and perspiring, pulling nervously at his beard. He had opened up and *told* me what had been bothering him in 1974. I couldn't desert him now. I wouldn't do that to a dog – so why do it to an Ox?

'Nigel, sweetie,' I said as nicely as I could in my state of mind, 'I don't s'pose I'll live long enough for you to get around to telling me why you walked out of that restaurant in Juan les Pins in 1983, will I?'

'Oh, I should think not, my dear,' said Nigel, already comfortably covered again by his imperturbable behind-the-beard grin.

Ox men don't mean to be obtuse. But Lordy, they are masters of opacity, and sticks in the mud to boot. Yet the Ox is loyal, capable of great personal sacrifice for those he loves, and is deeply wounded when true love goes wrong. He can be vengeful and even dangerous when wronged.

The Ox man is not the type to freak out if his wife cheats on him sexually, but if she falls in love with someone else, leaves him and/or deserts the kids, the Ox can become dangerously depressed. Remember, he cannot show tenderness without feeling embarrassed. He keeps emotion in, turns it around a hundred ways in his head, but never seeks outside aid or even consults with friends. Eventually something gives, and it is very often his nerves. As the Ox man disdains nervous or psychosomatic illnesses, if he starts to crack up, he begins not to like himself. Then, he can be horribly cranky and, if pushed or constrained by people or surroundings, may become downright nasty.

Ox men are stocky and massive like their female counterparts but they are not as tall. Their muscles are powerful and, even if they are thin, they can carry heavy weights. The Ox is graceful and has an easy walking style but, as he is stiff of mind, if he's cross or embarrassed, he can be clumsy, stumbling or tripping, especially in public.

There is never much expression on the Ox man's face. If he can get away with it, he may even wear a beard to hide his expression.

Conventional as he is, the Ox man doesn't give a fig what others think of him. If he doesn't feel like wearing a tuxedo to a formal party, he will be comfortable showing up in corduroy trousers and a bush jacket. Generally, he is a conservative dresser and may wear the same brand of the same style of shoe all his life, buying new ones only when the old cannot be repaired. Although his eyes may twinkle, hinting at some hidden joviality, the truly jolly side of the Ox man is perceptible only when he is in an exceptionally good humor, feeling confident and well fed or even slightly tipsy. Mainly, he maintains a serious demeanor.

His hands are small and his feet turn slightly outward. His complexion is often swarthy and his hair abundant. He has, *naturellement*, a thickish neck and heavy shoulders. His mouth is handsome, rounded and full lipped. He's more interested in touching things than in talking about them and if he has an artistic bent it will often be as a musician or a painter. The Ox male also makes a fine actor or public personality. Not really an innovator, he prefers to have his dialogues or routine written for him as his strength is in expert delivery. The Ox is a born raconteur, despite his natural shyness, and if he has time to get his script down pat and can launch into it cold in front of an audience, this talented man is spellbinding.

The five Chinese elements and how they influence the Ox

The Wood Ox

1685 Johann Sebastian Bach, George Friderick Handel
1805 Hans Christian Andersen
1865 Rudyard Kipling, W. B. Yeats
1925 Malcolm X, William Styron, Gore Vidal, Richard Burton (actor), Lenny Bruce, Art Buchwald, Russell Baker, Johnny Carson, Sammy Davis Jr, Jack Lemmon, Robert Altman, Peter Sellers, Jonathan Winters, William Buckley, Mel Tormé, Merv Griffin, Mike Douglas, Idi Amin Dada, Howard Baker, Paul Newman, Hal Holbrook, Maureen Stapleton, Cliff Robertson,

Margaret Thatcher, Dick van Dyke, Dina Merrill, Elaine Stritch, Rock Hudson, Hildegarde Neff, Dorothy Malone, Tony Curtis, Mikis Theodorakis, Mai Zetterling, Barbara Bush, Julie Harris, Angela Lansbury, Patricia Neal, Shana Alexander, Edmond Gorey, John Erlichmann, Robert Kennedy, Rod Steiger

The Wood Ox is the heaviest-duty of the heavy-duty Oxen. The day that the Wood Ox is not working, studying, composing, or struggling to lift some monster weight, you may consider him dead.

But even in death, the Wood Ox is not the type to slip gently away, leaving us sweet memories of his romantic, lyrical spirit. When this person takes a dive all the water whooshes out of the swimming pool, leaving a humungous, *booming* memory of his weighty, creative and effective presence.

The Wood Ox is not everybody's favorite nice guy. *Au contraire!* He is what my mother used to call 'A real piece of work', a relentless fighter against all forces that he does not already control. In an effort to dominate, direct, gain superiority, and emerge as the controlling element in every undertaking, this dauntless, wily, brilliant, persevering person lets no obstacle discourage him. His motto is 'Progress *Gratia* Progress' – advancement for its own sake – and if you must walk over a few dead bodies along the way, well, says the Wood Ox, *c'est la vie.*

I knew a Wood Ox whose father made bricks in the French countryside in the traditional way, but no money. Aged eighteen, when my friend left school, she began working for her father in the office. She was sure her father was doing everything wrong, so she told him so. They fought. Oxxy packed her kitbag and left home. Four years later, her father fell ill. The brick business was in its usual teetering-on-the-edge state. Oxxy was called home to help out.

While her father lay ill, Oxxy went to the factory. She called on a bank or two, borrowed capital, bought cement-block makers, installed them, set the old brick salesmen to selling the blocks to builders and began accruing a fortune in profits. When a few former customers came in asking for old-style bricks, Oxxy told them that her father's company did not make them any more and that all the smart builders had switched to cement blocks.

When her father, who was not yet sixty-five, got better, he came back to work. But Oxxy had moved into his office, relegating him to a freshly painted anteroom. 'Papa,' Oxxy informed him, 'you can relax. Be my assistant.'

She had *retired* her father from his own business! And she is proud of it. She boasts of it. It is one in Oxxy's repertoire of *See How Wonderful I Am* stories.

Oxxy's father died – I suspect of a broken heart, but Oxxy doesn't see it like that. 'My father had no backbone. He used to take time off to dig in his garden. Sometimes, he would even go fishing. I had to save his business. Just to prove how weak he really was, after I semi-retired him, he sank into a black depression and he died before the next Christmas.'

I find this tale shocking. But for the Wood-born Ox, whose stomach is as strong as his mettle, there is no way but his way. There are no clever solutions other than his solutions. Nobody else works as hard as he does, so nobody deserves as much. He takes everything, puts his name on it and then lends it back to its rightful owners.

Wood Oxen are tough customers. But, though specialists in the art of domination they can be extremely generous. The Wood Ox loves nature, children and family and reveres those who know how to ply nature in return for her best bounty. Be they farmers or doctors, artists or householders, Wood Oxen will always help out those they feel are doing a 'good job', exerting all their strength and being successful.

One interesting side benefit to friendship with Wood Oxen is that often they are incredibly witty, seeing life satirically and communicating their ironic viewpoint. Although they may not deliver much romantic chit-chat in bed and are hopeless duds at candle-lit dinners, Wood Oxen possess sublime eloquence. When they use this gift to expand their presence and increase their own bounty, nobody is more effectively communicative. Wood Oxen always know how to choose the perfect phrase to describe the pain, the humor, or the sensation they experienced. If you're lucky enough to get one of these taciturn types to tell you a story, you're in for a treat.

Wood Oxen are frequently unaware that lots of people hate them. They disdain the feelings of those they do not like. You'll never hear one of these steel-souled people tell you how sorry they felt to have to divorce their spouse or quit on their boss or move far away from their ageing mother. Wood Oxen simply feel they should unremittingly go ahead. If they don't make many heartfelt friends but, rather, bevies of enemies, it doesn't matter. If friendship has to cost them one inch of headway, they will abandon the friend.

Although teamwork is hardly his speciality, the Wood Ox likes to be married and raise a family. However, at best, being the wife or husband, child or even sibling of this character is difficult. A Wood Ox can only be handled by someone who behaves weaker than he does. Don't counter what he says by a retort or a gibe. Never disagree with him. Don't answer when he orders you to bring him coffee, make love, walk the dog. Only your limp inertia can raise so much as a goose bump in this archly self-important person's polyurethane ego. He's got so much himself that he doesn't know what to make of lack of will. Trust me, act as though you agree with everything. Play obedient-pooch games, complete with whimpering if you must – but go on doing exactly as you please. If, in this disgustingly subservient way, you play your hand close to your chest, the Wood Ox is guaranteed to become your slavering servant.

The Fire Ox

1877 Hermann Hesse
1937 Bill Cosby, Dustin Hoffman, Warren Beatty, Billy Dee Williams, Anthony Hopkins, Robert Redford, Erich Segal, Jane Fonda, Jack Nicholson, Trini Lopez, Tom Courtenay, Ursula Andress, Merle Haggard, Sally Kellerman, Sandy Dennis, Tom Stoppard, David Hockney, Gary Hart, Mary Tyler Moore, Saddam Hussein.

The most pleasant way to open a description of the complex Fire Ox is to warn you that Fire affects the Ox in precisely the same way it affects dynamite, jet planes and helium-filled dirigible balloons. Where there is already a surfeit of latent power, the Fire element adds punch and leads to excess and even disaster.

Unlike other Oxen, the Fire Ox is impatient: like them, he wants to move ahead and get places but he has difficulty with the long view. Oxen don't often risk making fools of themselves. Most are born planners: they like to look through the wide end of the telescope and watch how things may happen from a good remove before lurching into the fray. The Fire Ox's telescope is on backwards.

Like most Oxen, this one knows he is intrinsically superior. Don't give it a second thought. The Fire Ox is better and more deserving of success, money and whatever else he sees, wants and takes. To the adorable Oxen cocktail of self-assurance, this creature adds an endearing new characteristic: moral self-righteousness.

Fire Oxen fear nothing – even ridicule – and will forge ahead brandishing slogans as though married to their moral exhortations, proselytizing speeches and 'enlightened' schemes until death do them part. It can be a terrible bore. It can even be self-destructive. But Fire Oxen will carry on, firebrands waving, wearing their moral indignation on their sleeves and often making fools of themselves. The flipside of this passionate-quest handicap is that the Fire Ox is often a genius, mightily successful and frequently accurate in choosing his targets. Warren Beatty, Robert Redford, Jack Nicholson, Bill Cosby, Dustin Hoffman and Mary Tyler Moore have all been exorbitantly outspoken, gone to the limit of their talents in many unusual areas of showbusiness and have all come up smelling like a dozen roses.

The Ox's strength, when coupled with Fire's pizazz and passion, makes for a fabulously effective human being. Also, work is no object: this person has extraordinary powers of endurance. Because he is lucky enough to think he is always right, he can be inconsiderate and clumsy. He is idealistic and not completely dishonest. He's a true fighter for his cause and will stand up for what he believes against all odds.

He's bolder than he is clever, more willful than he is tuned in to what's really going on. For this Ox, the battle is the best part of the war. He'd like a little glory, too, but he is not really after making the big coup or winning the lifetime victory so that he can settle down and raise a family. The war, for the Fire Ox, will never be over. Till death do him in.

Sadly this obdurate soul is often respected but rarely loved. He lacks subtlety and doesn't always know best how to relate to others. He's ruthless, too. He may glorify everything to do with tradition until it doesn't suit him any more. Then he will glorify something new and call it traditional.

I suppose your best way to deal with this unswervable, attractively active person is to start by being strong-minded – a Tiger, at least, or a Dragon, or an I don't give a damn Rooster – and to show your strength up front. Once in a while give your Fire Ox a start by turning his telescope right side up. It won't cure his short-sightedness but it might possibly jolt his ego enough to give him a hint about just how far he is off the mark. Otherwise, tickle the bottoms of his feet. He is certain to hate that and yet silliness, and purest, most innocent love are the best cure for those, like the Fire Oxen, who take themselves too seriously.

Despite his relentless activity, the Fire Ox is a family person: he is deeply responsible and committed to the well-being of his spouse and offspring. He will rule their domain, too, and refuses to take any backtalk from them. He is kindly and makes a generous parent. He may not be very receptive to kids who complain or tell him their troubles – feelings are not his strong suit. But if anyone should attack a member of his family – even his good-for-nothing brother-in-law who can't find a decent job and drinks too much – the Fire Ox will protect his own.

The Earth Ox

1709 Samuel Johnson
1769 Napoleon Bonaparte
1889 Charlie Chaplin, Sessue Hayakawa, Jean Cocteau
1949 Ivana Trump, Lindsay Wagner, Billy Joel, Sigourney Weaver, Paloma Picasso, Jessica Lange, Whoopi Goldberg, Richard Gere, John Belushi, Jeff Bridges, Sissy Spacek

The Earth Ox is the busybody Ox. He's curious to a fault, nosy and meddlesome. He thinks he knows best, and often does.

In general, Oxen think they are better than other people. Earth Oxen not only think they are better, they believe they were born to lead others, to teach the poor things how to live and to tell them what to do. What we have here is a very nature-oriented, earth-bound, power-mad megalomaniac whose nose for locating flies in life's various ointments is practically infallible.

A more self-possessed person you will rarely meet. This Ox is not only self-reliant, he is convinced that you are not. Ask the Earth Ox a silly question and you will receive a great sigh of impatience in return. 'How can you be so dense?' he may groan. 'I already told you that the mouse controls the arrow on the screen. Are you too stupid to learn to use a computer?'

Don't let this superior attitude put you off. Ox groans don't mean very much. All the tut-tutting and grousing the Earth Ox does serves as a defense mechanism, a method of humiliation, keeping you off balance so that you don't notice that he has got fat or has dyed his hair green by accident. I'm not trying to excuse his tyrannical teaching methods but his behavior is often so offensively pushy that it requires some explanation.

Earth Oxen firmly believe that the true goal in life is perfection in every area. They do not quail at the idea of intense hard work. They are horribly organized and can tolerate *no* spontaneity. Life and soul of the party the Earth Ox is not.

But he's brave. Temerity is his middle name. Think about it, Earth and Ox together: bulldozer. This person will caterpillar-tractor his way over any number of corpses to get into any board meeting, cabinet meeting or bedroom he feels he should be allowed to enter without compunction. As long as he needs something and feels he wants it, it's his. He takes it.

Now such a snatch-and-grab approach may seem horrendously cut-throat to you but the Earth Ox's suffering and inner woe is about as overwhelming as his exterior bulldozer act. Insecurity is the key to all bully behavior and Earth Oxen bullies are no exception.

This person secretly suffers from fear of being unloved, rejected and abandoned. He is never sure of his best friend or even his best bed partner because he knows that he is clumsy and unskilled at appreciating subtleties. To spare his own feelings he uses tactics which appear positively aggressive.

He doesn't know any better. The successful Earth Ox is a *klutz*, an awkward peasant in bourgeois clothing, who wishes he had never become so successful because now he has to hobnob with all these splendid people who only make him feel more like a hick. What the Earth Ox wanted to do when he decided to take over the world, was to *lead the people*.

If you wake up one day to face the responsibility of piloting the world, it might be less than easy to keep your lid on. Since the Earth Ox was born with this leadership certainty and is a sincere person, when he accedes to his massive job as shepherd to the world he wants everything to go perfectly. So, when he assumes his role as Captain Universe, the outcome of all human endeavor rests with him. Inside his swelled head, if things go well he feels he is doing his job right and he's probably in a good mood. If the works gum up, which they invariably do, this poor over-responsible creature believes it is all his fault.

Does he get depressed and sulk? Will he explode and knock over tables and chairs? Or might he take to drink or drugs? No. The Earth Ox who notices that his subjects have been flagrantly breaking his rules drops leader for dictator. He is convinced that because he defines the limits he need not hesitate to overstep them – all the time.

He's too zealous. Inside he's tender, good-hearted and loving. But who has time to look inside?

One way to assist this over-bold person to feel better inside his own skin would be to show him how to put the brakes on his ego-enthusiastic exploits. But to do this you would have to get him to accept advice and he *hates* advice. He knows everything so why waste time on other people's prattle?

The one sure way to his heart is through his stomach. This person loves to eat. Drown him in thick, country-style soups. Woo her away from her chores with a plateful of lobster titbits. Then turn on a thirty-minute CD recording of applause – the Earth Ox's lullaby music.

To the Earth Ox, sex is a physical act. Romance may be cute but it is not their means of communication. The Earth Ox *has sex*; he does not make love. Don't expect an Earth Ox lover to confess to intricate fantasies or cook up fabulous scenarios to awaken your droopy appetite between the sheets. When you go on picnics with Earth Oxen leave your poetry at home. A good hearty meal, a glass of wine and a little sexercise will do them just fine.

Finally, although the Earth Ox is a meticulous rule maker and disciplined self-starter, he's often literary or artistic in some specialized area. He always finishes what he starts and can be counted on for promptness and trusted for his basic honesty. However, his blindness to his own fallibility may lead him to commit some awful errors and, as profound guilt and denial follow, he may lose confidence and become more and more defensive. If he doesn't lighten up by the age of forty, he can expect to live out a bitter old age, stiff and unyielding and without a sense of humor about his own flaws.

The Metal Ox

1841 Anton Dvořák, Edward VII
1901 Gary Cooper, Walt Disney, Clark Gable, Margaret Mead, André Malraux, Melvyn Douglas, Linus Pauling, William Paley, Lee Strasberg, Jeanette MacDonald
1961 Eddie Murphy, the Princess of Wales, Michael J. Fox

Metal Oxen have something that other Oxen cannot boast: charisma. There's a magical quality about them: an aura or halo surrounds their spirit and glows. People are automatically drawn to the Metal Ox's warm public personality. The charm which emanates from him is natural, artless – and winning. The Metal Ox is the most socially adept Ox.

In true Ox fashion, he has great personal ambitions, wants to achieve in the areas he chooses and sees no reason why he shouldn't become the best in his field. Take a few of the 1901 people: Walt Disney was talented, but there were lots of animators in Hollywood back then. If he hadn't had the crisp, wintry drive and determination of a Metal Ox, he probably wouldn't have created the mammoth industry that bears his name today. Or André Malraux – a giant of intellect. Had he been born a Dog or a Pig, he might have been content to write books and teach at university. Instead, he became a world traveller, art critic, cultural minister of France, public figure and a maker of strict laws about how the artistic patrimony of France should be preserved. Or take Eddie Murphy, born in 1961: he was already working on TV as a teenager, writing his own hilarious scripts and performing them in night clubs. By the age of twenty-two he was a star. Now he's a rich and famous man who can choose which roles he wants in movies.

This person is not your average stay-at-home pipe and slippers, beer and peanuts fellow. Metal Oxen do not usually moon about waiting for Godot or the Tooth Fairy to tell them they are loved. If you are the partner of a Metal Ox, remember that you are expected to be not only faithful, loyal and true, but also dutiful, jolly and up-tempo. We already know that the Metal Ox pushes hard to get to the top but because not every day brings sufficient victory, he will grow frustrated and often come home in a foul temper. At these times, he is unreachable, lost in a haze of blue smoke in a sulk.

As far as the Metal Ox is concerned, it is your job (or at least his family's responsibility) either to get him out of it or to get out yourself. You can argue, he will argue back. You can shout, he will do likewise. You can even reason, and he will engage you in a reasoning match. But your Metal Ox will not accept criticism. He cannot tolerate reassessment of his methods or approach by anyone but himself. This refusal to see your point of view may slow him down but he will not care – his pride gets in the way of his grey matter.

His denial of interference reveals another unfortunate side of this charming person's obstinate character. Metal Oxen tend to mistrust the judgement of those closest to them in favor of that of a perfect stranger – a dangerous attitude as strangers may attempt to dupe him.

This Ox is patriotic to a fault. He believes strongly that might is right and grows more conservative as he ages. He is neurotically nostalgic: in the old days, he believes, the world ran smoothly. He longs for things to be right, for people to be honest, for the rain to fall only at night. A Disneyland world of blond children and pretty music without the bad guys is the Metal Ox's dream-world ideal.

As life doesn't often happen like that, the Metal Ox is frequently in a state of semi-despair, carping and grumbling, and assuming that it's all the fault of everything from today's lazy youth to hippies or hooligans or the breakdown of the dress code in banking institutions. He finds fault with everybody except his own clan. Never criticize his work, his person or his family. Only he is allowed to tear them apart at home behind closed shutters. For the gallery, Mr and Mrs Metal Ox and all the little Metal Oxen are perfect.

The artistic side of the Metal Ox is his greatest saving grace. The real contributions he makes are through his creative efforts which are always imaginative and well intended. If the Metal Ox's at-home personality were as sweet and fun-loving as his deft, lyrical creations, he would not be perceived as such a gloomy guy by his family and close friends.

The Metal Ox is a more than serious soul whose affable public self belies the dour, grumpy one who blusters on the home front. He is as hard to live with as he is critical of almost everything and everybody he's close to. His sense of humor may be incisive on life's grand stage but his ability to laugh at himself is nil.

He is intuitive and will listen to your problems and advise you, but if you don't use his suggestions, he will take umbrage. The Metal Ox is reliable and monstrously hard-working. He is an excellent provider and will always keep a roof over the heads of his loved ones. If you have lots of easy-going patience, take up with a Metal Ox. If you have trouble accepting criticism, steer a wide berth around him and bag yourself a gentler bull.

The Water Ox

1913 Burt Lancaster, Vivien Leigh, Oleg Cassini, Albert Camus, Willy Brandt, Menachem Begin, Danny Kaye, Jean Marais, Alan Ladd, Hedy Lamarr, Stanley Kramer, Stewart Granger,

Tyrone Power, Lionel Hampton, Sonia Henie, Gerald Ford, Temple Fielding, Frankie Laine, Mary Martin, Jane Wyman, Danny Thomas, Sir Anthony Quayle, Irwin Shaw

Water endows the Ox with extra ponderousness. This person is a thinking, planning, plotting plodder who always takes the long view. A rice-paddy water buffalo, symbol of fertility and patience, service and strength, is the best description of this kindly, yet stern and unflinching soul.

No Water Ox begs for a living. He is clever and hard-working and will eventually dominate and thrive in every professional undertaking. He is strong and persistent, slow, accomplishing things in a deliberate fashion suitable to his temperament. Water Oxen make little noise and demand less frivolous attention. They move ahead. They start a task and labor at it with regularity and certainty. They don't need modern methods or technological wonders to put them over the top. Water Oxen are born knowing how to succeed.

Nobody should stand in the way of a Water Ox. As they are patient, they are slow to react. They simmer for a long while, going quietly about their business, saying nothing and waiting to see how things develop. The only time they move quickly is when they are just about to boil over. Suddenly, they pick up speed, their voices rise a few decibels and THWACK! They put an end to their embarrassing rage by annihilating the enemy.

Water Oxen are not in a hurry because they are not content with short-term solutions. For them, if something is worth doing, it has to be thought out, reflected and ruminated on until all sides have been examined through a microscope – no hasty risk-taking here. They have all the time in the world to muse, waiting for the jumpy enemy to show a weakness or make a tactical error.

The Water Ox is at his happiest in the countryside. Deep down, he is a farmer, usually a rich one, but he is also a leader. He will take up the causes of less fortunate farmers or lead the Rotary Club orchestra. The Water Ox is not lazy, but as his pace is unhurried, he can be construed as laid back. From an outsider's perspective, the Water Ox does not appear busy: he doesn't gallop about trying to accomplish sixty things at once nor does he sit back and let life live him.

Outwardly, the Water Ox is never frenzied or pressed yet he gets tons more done than others who race ahead and slur over hundreds of daily activities. The Water Ox likes routine, reveres punctuality and enjoys doing things when they 'should' be done. He wants to get up and retire to bed at the same hour every day. It makes him feel secure to know that lunch is at 12.20 and dinner at 7.15.

The Water Ox is profoundly family-orientated. He cannot live without his kin surrounding him. He is possessive and jealous of their affections and always wants them to conform. The Water Ox is the sort of parent who has five children and nominates each for a profession at birth – Charlie will be a lawyer, Arielle a doctor and so on. No arguments, no substitutions.

The unwavering resolve of the Water Ox should be bottled and sold to flaky people. Add to that a lucid grasp of reality. He knows the pitfalls of human interaction so well that, if he so desired, he could be president of the universe. But this rustic soul wants no part of politics. He feels clumsy at smart parties and is inhibited in small talk. He's happiest when ensconced in his solid stone house in his comfortable drawing-room with old friends and family around him. Traditional feasts exalt his taste for ritual. He loves to cook and eat the food he grows, preserves and prepares with loving care. He's a country man with the bank account of a bank president.

The Water Ox is a loving, sensitive soul and will gladly listen to and sympathize with other people's woes. He will take time to ponder a complex situation and will give a sound reply. Neither egotistical nor self-centered, he does, however, like things run his way. He is generous to those he loves, always giving them the benefit of the doubt and a leg-up when they're in trouble.

It's rare that a Water Ox backs off from an opinion. He is stubborn and intransigent, believing firmly that *he* possesses the only truth. He never openly questions his methods or asks, 'Am I doing the right thing?' But he is secretly sentimental and can be swayed when his feelings are appealed to. The Water Ox finds affection irresistible and may astonish you by suddenly opening his ears and his heart to your desires.

Finally, Water confers a hefty dose of vengefulness on this wise anti-sophisticate. A person who betrays or wrongs a Water Ox will rue the day. The Water Ox could give an elephant lessons in remembering every detail of pain that was ever inflicted on him. Water Oxen wait, think, ruminate, connive, plot and KILL. Stay downwind of their rancor.

Ox health

Of all the Chinese signs, this one is blessed with the greatest longevity. Providing they don't overdo it and learn to pace themselves, Oxen statistically live longer. Not that they don't fall ill, because they frequently do – they are even hypochondriacal. But the amazing long-term resistance of the sturdily built, close to the ground, tight, muscular body of the Ox is well known in China.

Ox people are subject to stomach troubles, partly because they love to eat and are forever ordering or preparing food too heavy with fat or sauces or too acid for their fragile digestions. Bouts of gastroenteritis, cramps, diarrhea, and vomiting may plague them, interrupting their precious work and disrupting their private lives. I know Oxen who are hooked on Alka Seltzer.

But I firmly believe that these tummy troubles are also due to the Ox's pent-up nature. Ulcers and gall-bladder problems, intestinal lesions, colitis and other nervous tummy ills may be the obvious wages of over-indulgence, but they are also the direct result of too much self-restraint. The old Ox, in his unshakeable determination to play the waiting game, glimpses light at the end of the longest tunnel as a beacon. He is patient, long-suffering and capable of biding his time to wait out almost any conflict or upset. This approach affords him a greater chance of winning through holding out longer than anyone else. But his stomach pays the price. The Ox's exterior anxiety level is so low as to make you think he's dead half the time. But trust me, in the gut where it really hurts, the Ox is burning alive.

Oxen are commonly overweight and may also be troubled by a reddish tinge on their face and upper body. Ox women's cheeks go bright red as soon as they sit in the sun, eat strong foods or drink wine. The Ox male, also, may have an unsightly reddish, peeling condition that is not psoriasis but is caused by over-indulgence in rich sauces or acid foods. Oxen are also subject to hemorrhoids, and, from the age of fifty, ought to learn to control their diets, eating little meat and concentrating on vegetables and fish. Otherwise, they may even fall victim to strokes.

The Ox is a nibbler. Although he may seem to prefer hearty meals and feasts to snacks, he should not be allowed peanuts and chips or pretzels. Nervous noshing between meals can contribute to the breakdown of even the most cautious Ox's basic good health. And yet, no matter how many ulcers the Ox cultivates or how red his face may become, or how this forceful, obstinate person behaves, basically he has a strong constitution. They may be mortally ill but through sheer single-mindedness will return to a full, active life.

City life is no picnic for Oxen. They should live in the country, eat fresh foods in season, avoid starches and sugars, Ox's *péché mignon*, and be encouraged to follow the rhythms of nature. Exercise is a must if the Ox wants to maintain good health. He is naturally sluggish but swimming, yoga and – although the Ox *hates* the very idea – meditation will help him learn to relax, which is the secret to learning how to live a healthy life.

As I have already said, Oxen work insanely hard. Work is to the Ox what playing is to Monkeys and activity to Rats. Work is the area in which the Ox excels and feels most comfortable. But I have seen several Oxen work themselves to death. In 1979, while we were living in the States, our dear ex-nanny Anne-Marie died, aged sixty-five. That's too young and she seemed so strong. She was overweight, had arthritis in her knees and didn't exercise enough. But she was our tough old Anne-Marie. Why did she die?

She wouldn't stop working. I couldn't get her to sit down. For years I could see she was exhausted and begged her to take a break when the kids were at school. But she wouldn't listen.

One day, when she was so tired she could hardly keep her eyes open, I suggested that I look after the kids for a week or two so she could rest. 'Oh, *non*!' she replied. 'Every time you take them for weekends I end up having to keep them in bed all week.' I knew Anne-Marie so well I understood that her criticism was her Ox-like way of pleading 'Please don't take the kids away from me: I would be lonely without them to love and care for.'

I said, 'All right, the kids can stay. But you must promise to sit down after lunch for at least half an hour and take a nap.'

Anne-Marie looked at me with tears in her eyes and said, 'Please don't ask me to do that. If I stop I'll die.'

And that's what happened. It was finally the doctor who made Anne-Marie stop and rest because he had decided to operate on her stiff knee. She took a month off, stayed home and rested in preparation for the operation. In the hospital, they didn't get her up right after the operation and when she did get up next day she had an embolism and died on the spot.

Ox futures

What the Ox should expect from the next twelve Chinese animal years

2008, the Earth Rat year – Rats covet power and they often get it. Whether in relationships, in government positions or in business dealings, Rats seek dominion and get it. Once they do, they often handle it well. This year fairly reeks of the Rat's powerful influence. But that smell doesn't bother you Oxen too much as you were born with a fine sense of your own strength and haven't had to struggle, as the Rat does, to gain control. In your case, control comes with the territory. Because the Rat's drive for supremacy doesn't threaten you Ox people, you usually cruise right through Rat years without missing a beat. Rats move quickly, however. You tend to advance more slowly and march to the steady cadence of your own inner drummer. You will be left alone to accumulate wealth, nurture your crops and tend to your family's harmony this year. In the autumn, tension threatens your professional life. It will no doubt come from a person born in a Dragon or Cat year. Keep your ears pricked up for signs of nasty backbiting and subterfuge in the wings at work. Someone would like to unseat you. Even if you must use force, take explicit action to discourage that person's desire to do you in.

2009, the Earth Ox year – Finally! Steady plodding really does win the race. At last you find yourself here in your own very own year. This year offers a major chance to make a big difference in your life now and for the next dozen years. The year itself usually runs relatively sedately along without too many political or social hitches. But in your case, if in an Ox year you don't jump at the chance to implement adjustments in your point of view and lifestyle, you may end up suffocating under a mudslide of majestic proportion. You're not one to unduly upset apple carts. Normally, your job is to pull them. This year, it's time to give that cart a good shove and let all the apples roll into the road. Then take a good look at which are the choicest picks, gather them and split with the booty. Build a house.

Take a trip around the world. Buy an island or an abandoned hamlet in Croatia. The message? In Ox years, take charge of your existence and make it different from what has gone before. You are sometimes reluctant to grab change by the throat and run with it. This year, either you do so or you will be condemned to slog and drudge for twelve more years without making any real progress.

2010, the Metal Tiger year – Lie low, Oxen. Avoid the fray. Don't get caught up in the Tiger's frenetic pace, or you may lose your sense of direction and feel your brain turning to cooked cabbage. Tigers move far too quickly for your taste. Tiger years pick up speed right from the jump. By this time, with the stability of the Ox year behind it, the world itself feels the need to go thrashing about seeking novelty and excitement. Thrashing and hunting are not at all what you Oxen are about. You like to till and toil and build and improve. And you like to do it all at your own sweet deliberate pace. Tigers? They get a lot done too. But in a very short time so they can move on to newer, more instantly satisfying chores. Not your style. Stay at home by the fire in your lovely new castle with that kindly ally of yours – the significant other of your dreams who will stick by you no matter how slowly you progress. Take time to concentrate on gaining the advantage over your enemies this year. Be wise. Strategize.

2011, the Metal Cat year – A bumper year for the canniest of Oxen. And a bummer year for those of you who lumber clumsily along, divulging trade secrets or loaning out keys to your safe deposit boxes. First of all, Cats long for security and almost always make good investments. Often, they very stealthily acquire great wealth. Normally their stealth doesn't get in the Ox's way because Oxen don't feel jealous about other people's success as long as that same success in no way threatens him or her. If Jack Nicholson (Ox) got upset every time some little whipper snapper hotshot pretty boy/girl Cat actor or actress got a better role than his, made more money or won more Oscars, he wouldn't be Nicholson. Ditto Redford (Ox) and Hoffmann (more Ox) and many many others. The Ox is the strong, talented and unflummoxable presence. The Cat is also strong. But neither presence nor conflict characterize his or her strong points. So furtiveness must suffice. Cats like luxury, but are they willing to put their life on the line for it? Not by the hair of their chinny chin chins. Hence, if I were an Ox in a Cat year, I would remain as invisible as possible and as mute as a drum so as not to allow any of my secrets to be stolen or plagiarized. Work will be fruitful. Keep quiet about it.

2012, the Water Dragon year – The percussion level this year will no doubt be well above the Ox's tolerance point. Try and ignore the din and get on with being you. The Dragon's influence means you no harm. But Dragons do not fancy competition. So stay out of the way. May I suggest holing up in your country house with pair of hefty earmuffs to keep out the noise? Or perhaps you will want to rent out your house in town and move to China for an unparalleled study experience. Whatever you do, expect to be drowning in decibels. The love picture improves for you this year. That very handsome man or woman you have been dreaming of dating becomes available in 2012. Make it your business to mean business. Take the trouble to seduce this creature. Don't hang back or be shy about your approach. You may just have found the love of your life. Take your health in hand as well. Stave off illness by indulging in healthy diet and more exercise than you ever thought possible. I know. You do housework and mow the lawn and you think that's quite enough. It is not. Get thee to a gym.

2013, the Water Snake year – You and the Snake get along like a set of fraternal twins. You don't look anything alike – yet you are inseparable pals. Snakes always carry their weight in attraction and are not afraid of assuming power. The Snake's style never interferes with yours. You plod. Snakes slither. But you are both rather slow and deep-thinking. Hence, the wave lengths match and you truly appreciate each other. You each enjoy a quiet, yet stolid, presence. You will be granted all manner of successes in this year. Kudos, prizes and honors will come your way because the Snake admires you Ox people and the feeling is mutual. Eat more fiber, take vitamins and learn to accept the benefits of alternative medicine. If you have children or have the opportunity to borrow or rent some, you will find that you enjoy their company most in this Snake year. You (deliberate Ox that you are) may even find you can have fun at the theme park. An Ox on a roller coaster is not a common sight. But in a Snake year such a sight is all too plausible.

2014, the Wood Horse year – Because of the general ambience of diligent labor which characterizes all Horse years, this year will be fortuitous for Oxen. It's no secret. You Oxen love to work and work hard. You enjoy an exceptional capacity for exertion – both physical and mental. Work energizes you. Why? Because you live for results and are not too fussy about how you get those results – even if you have to struggle uphill with a thousand-pound boulder on your weary shoulders – reaching the destination is always worth the effort. So when Horse years come around, you are favored and applauded and praised for your unparalleled work ethic. When the Japanese took Koreans as slaves in a darker period of their history, it was commonly said: 'We worked them like horses and oxen.' Nobody works harder than you two. So in this Horse year you may be working your buns off, but the results will be precisely what you were after because the Horse's influence protects and preserves the Ox. It may not prove to be the most jovial year in your life . . . but then when you have rich and tangible rewards from your work, who needs fun?

2015, the Wood Goat year – Goats get your goat. There is friction between you and the Goat because the Goat puts more emphasis on the lighter side of life, wants to depend on a stronger being or institution and is frequently not a self-starter. Goats may be geniuses. But they don't have the kind of kick-ass presence and plodding spirit that you have. Goats often work in spurts. Three or four nights at the computer without sleep and then a week's snooze is fine with them. Their sense of time is other. You, determined, pre-programmed and steady at the helm, cannot abide this lurching rhythm and tweaking of schedules. You want more equilibrium in your day-to-day. So in this Goat year, I suggest you take to the hills. Buy that chateau in the south of France, watch your grapes grow, harvest them and turn them into wine; but don't try to compete for prizes or honours. Give all contests a wide berth. Enjoy your love life now. It can be a number one priority because, in this frivolous Goat year, you won't need to spend all your time working. When you're not busy making love, why not plan your next business coup? Next year, your Monkey chum comes around. Monkeys let Oxen get away with a lot.

2016, the Fire Monkey year – This year bodes plenty of activity and a speeding-up of the pace for you Oxen. I know you don't adore hurrying and hate to be told to go faster. But Monkeys have no time to waste standing around tapping their feet whilst you Oxen ponder and plod through mountains of what Monkeys consider useless details, paperwork and administrative BS. Monkeys see a problem and get right to the core of it, solve it and move on to the next one. So you will have to drop the spreadsheets, abandon your precious red tape and learn to hurry. And (because you are hell-bent on getting ahead no matter what) you *will* pick up speed. This hectic cadence, however, may take its toll on your health. Be sure, during this Monkey year, to get regular check-ups and tests for everything that can go wrong with Oxen (especially digestion-related ills). Bottom line? You will thrive in a Monkey year because the Monkey is cleverer than all of us and knows when he has found a sane, safe ally. That, my dear Ox friend, is you. This year will be fruitful and you will not be sabotaged or refused much of anything. You will, however, have to pick up those clodhoppers of yours and get a move on.

2017, the Fire Rooster year – Rooster years are always salutary for hard-working people and you Oxen are no exception. However, as the recent Monkey year really took it out of you and wore down your capacity for tolerance of someone else's pace, you will tend this year to be reluctant to cooperate. Joint projects, group efforts, associations and partnerships will suffer because you want to have a year off from being a frenetic someone's ally and crony. You just want to be your own person and move once again at your own sweet (slow) pace. For this year, then, I suggest you go it alone. Stay working at whatever you enjoy and are sure will bring you success. But don't sign any contracts wherein you are obliged to participate in meetings or agree to indigestible clauses. You are just not in the proper frame of mind for joint ventures. Your love life suffered a bit from the general tumult of last year. Take some time to bill and coo with your sweetheart or spouse this year. The Rooster enjoys your company and doesn't really mind if you sneak away for a few sexy weekends. You always give your all when you return – and you are usually in a far better frame of mind as well. This sign is not called Rooster for nothing. Roosters appreciate the necessity for lust in the lives of their subjects. After all, isn't sex what Roosters are so famous for?

2018, the Earth Dog year – The Dog is no threat to you Oxen. A Dog can yap and growl and snarl at a stolid Ox for as long and as loudly as he wants. And you just sort of stand there, silent and Ox-like, waiting for his tantrum to be spent. However, wisdom has it that in Dog years, the Ox should keep out of the public eye. Why?

Because the criticisms and outcries against injustice and demands for fair play in government for which the Dog is so famous don't appeal to you. And if you joined in, you might be noticed. You are not the type to carry a placard in the street or bandy slogans in front of government buildings to get what you want. You are a slow-burning-ember person who waits and watches and acts only when he or she is certain of a positive result. You might be clumsy. But you are not stupid enough to be upfront about how you would change things. You would rather die than go to jail for a night because you participated in some riot over health care. Instead, you push that rock up that hill ever so slowly, marking all the paths with your name, and then you overthrow the entire government by rolling that huge boulder lickety-split from the top of the mountain on to the offenders' heads. That's what I mean by keeping a low profile.

2019, the Earth Pig year – Oxen usually thrive in the early part of Pig Years. This year will be no exception. You will surely find both adventure and fun aplenty in the first months. But round about June, just before summer sets in, you will need to keep a closer eye on your budget than you have been doing. Rather suddenly, it will seem as though your bank account has sprung a leak. Do verify all banking and investment statements, as computers tend to make more mistakes in Pig years. Overly generous to those they love, Oxen also frequently fall prey to oversight or miscalculation. The Pig and the Ox are generally complicit in their pursuit of affluence for its own sake. You are equally gifted for gathering not only money, but precious possessions – art and antiques or vintage cars and outrageously expensive wines and caviar. So in a luxury-loving Pig year, you will be tempted to purchase major works or cases of rare Bordeaux or champagne. This may be one clue as to why that bank account is leaking. Another possibility is the presence of a loved one who is draining you of resources he or she has not earned. Check with your accountant more often, count those pennies and keep a weather eye out for chicanery coming from those closest to you.

The Terrible Tiger

Honorable Tiger,

Noble and fearless, you are respected for your courage and dreaded for your ferocity and incessant intemperance. Like a raging torrent, you constantly overflow your banks. Where are you going in such a hurry? Can't you take just one teensy peek before you pounce? Try to slow down, practise a little moderation. Stop going around being so heartbreakingly attractive. It's exhausting.

Of course, some people find you so dashing and plucky that they want to climb aboard and go along for the ride. But you, Tiger dear, are a swashbuckling loner. The top is the only place you want to be. You court danger. The fiercer the enemy, the more dramatic and calamitous the situation, the broader grows your Tigerish grin. Your changeability, disdain for rules, self-sufficiency and devil-may-care jauntiness could be your undoing.

In matters of the heart you are too demanding. But you certainly aren't boring. You get on best with devoted Dogs who espouse your causes. Independent Horses and complicitous Dragons love you, too. Monkeys admire you, but remember, Monkeys can be tricky. Whatever you do, don't take up with a tempestuous Tiger like yourself. You are lucky, but not that lucky.

You'll breeze through your youth. But by the age of thirty-five, half a lifetime's excesses may start to catch up with you. Call yourself to order by forty and by the time you reach fifty you'll be young again, ready for a productive old age.

A piece of advice? Go ahead and take the job as a five-star general, but choose your lieutenants wisely – you'll be needing lots of loyal counsel.

Recklessly yours,

Suzanne White

In the twentieth and twenty-first century all Tigers were born between the following dates:

8 February	1902	and	28	January	1903
26 January	1914	and	13	February	1915
13 February	1926	and	1	February	1927
31 January	1938	and	18	February	1939
17 February	1950	and	5	February	1951
5 February	1962	and	24	January	1963
23 January	1974	and	10	February	1975
9 February	1986	and	28	January	1987
28 January	1998	and	15	February	1999
14 February	2010	and	2	February	2011

The Tiger ID card

Lasting symbols have special powers. Enhance your self-image by surrounding yourself with tangible signs of your own identity and make these symbols known to your friends and loved ones. Use them daily and they will bring you luck, security and a feeling of personal worth.

Your best
color is bright red
flower is carnation
fragrance is jasmin
tree is sycamore
flavor is sweet
birthstone is ruby
lucky number is 7

Your favorite
food is fruit pie
animal is tiger
drink is lemonade
spice is cinnamon
metal is gold
herb is thyme
musical instrument is trumpet

The Tiger is yang

The Tiger's motto is 'I win'

On their best behavior, Tigers are lovable, alluring, warm-hearted, altruistic, honorable, hard-working, pleasant, independent, engaging, dynamic, idealist sweetie pies.

When they act up (which is often) Tigers are rash, hot-headed, reckless, infatuate, quarrelsome, caustic, moody, predatory, rebellious, disobedient, irreverent rascals.

A Tiger by the tale

Consider the terrible Tiger – a doer, a mover, a shaker and an accomplisher of world-class projects. Because of this sign's unusual accessibility and ease of manner, we almost immediately love the Tiger. We are attracted by his magical aura, enthralled by his charm, enchanted and impressed by his fun-filled lifestyle. We drink it all in. The benevolent Tiger nature goes down like a wondrous potion, guaranteed to cheer us up, designed to make us believe in a better life and certain to involve us up to our necks in the most sensational methods of survival in the quicksand wilderness.

Hop aboard a Tiger's tawny back and you will never again need to board a roller-coaster or engage in any other thrill-seeking pursuit. Tigers are *les enfants terribles* of the Chinese zodiac. They are tempestuous yet calm, warm-hearted yet fearsome, courageous in the face of danger yet yielding and soft in mysterious, unexpected places.

When they don't get the full spotlight, Tigers, like the naughty children they are, act up. Tigers cause trouble or skulk away into the dark forest of their secret selves and stay away for a long, long time. Tigers are indefatigable self-promoters, willful but damnably lovable egomaniacs.

Tigers are unpredictable, which makes them exasperating and hard to read or pin down. They are notorious for stumping their friends and enemies by blinding them with gestures of kindness and hospitality followed with a cool denial of contact for weeks at a time. Tigers are ultra-social beings; but they are also mighty fine loners, prowling and stalking their prey in the dark night of the forest.

Afraid of nothing, the Tiger charges around the world at a pace and with a vigor better designed for re-entering satellite shrapnel than for a human being. No one can stop the Tiger and no one can ever get through to him. Tigers are almost never at home. They are peripatetic to a fault. They are erratic, sending out mixed messages that can drive their interlocutors mad with insecurity. 'Where were you? I called you fifty times on Sunday. You said you'd be home. Why weren't you there?' is the common plaint from members of the Tiger's entourage.

The Tiger merely studies his fingernails. No excuses: the Tiger is hard to find, difficult to confine to regulations – and he likes it that way. If you want to keep your Tiger friend, don't bring it up again. Try to see it his way: the Tiger feels that it is not his fault if he's not at home, it's your fault for expecting him to be. Tigers are strong, brave and sure to get things done, but they cannot be counted on to adhere to schedules meant for mere mortals. Tigers are pathologically independent.

Furthermore, they hate to be scolded. Hence, they flatly refuse to accept 'friendly' observations or allow for constructive criticism concerning their gadabout lifestyle. They fly off the handle at the slightest reproof or disapproval. Tiger disdain for hierarchies and status, snobbery and social strata is active. When in full rebellion against fusty systems and censorious rigidity, Tigers are at their harshest. Watch your ego because a threatened Tiger may fling some very muddy language around and will spare nobody's feelings.

Tigers are not quite as intangibly dramatic as Dragons, but they are just as fierce and twice as vengeful. Nor are Tigers as tricky as Monkeys, nor as stolidly obstinate as Oxen, but they are three times the strategist of either and at times almost as unreasonable as the worst Ox. Tigers are not muscle-man Schwarzenegger or Rambo strong, or tough-guy gangster dangerous. No. The Tiger is strong because he *feels* strong. He's close-to-the-ground muscular yet streamlined and linear. He's always on the *qui vive*, taut, ready to spring and pounce at a split second's notice. Underneath that luxuriant striped coat, the Tiger is all sinew and power, gristle and brawn. Inside his bones and behind his jocund smile, the Tiger is as ruthless and deceptive as Satan.

But Tigers are nice guys. Despite their sharpened claws and razor fangs, Tigers are noble. They don't like evil. They are anti-nasty. Tigers are ghost flushers, natural-born exorcists and undoers of evil spirits. The Chinese claim that having a Tiger in your house keeps you for ever safe from fire, thieves and ghosts. Would it be wise, then, to resist the Tiger's tireless insistence on coming to live in your heart? With such foolproof references who wouldn't take him on?

Lots of people. Firstly, Tigers are not easy-going lightweights. No matter their size, shape or persuasion, they take up acres of emotional space. Even the gentlest of Tigers is neither house pet nor casual acquaintance. Nobody who has more than a howdedo acquaintance with one is ever able to slough him off with an indifferent shrug. Tigers need attention, lots of it. They want to work, play, make love, converse and interact with you in all sorts of ways. You cannot tune them out. They don't even talk a lot. But Tigers are just plain *there*. Nobody says, 'Go and lie down on your blanket!' to a pet Tiger and lives to tell the tale. By nature, they do not remain in the background, so you have to love them adoringly or hate and reject them. But you won't get off by being apathetic, so don't try.

Secondly, Tigers are spiritually invasive. They demand our unflinching devotion to their endless causes and sympathy for their countless woes. Sometimes it seems as though Tigers were put on Earth to force us to make choices, pass judgements, take sides and prove or disprove our loyalties.

Tigers are God's all-or-nothing people: there is no middle ground. Intensity is a word that might have been invented to describe the Tiger's state of mind. Tigers are constantly involved in stormy litigations or giant power struggles in which they involve themselves without reserve or good sense. If you have opted to be their friend, they want you to take their side against the bad guys, and, because the Tiger is so winning and adorable, you often do. Then you find yourself being invited to bear witness at a trial where your pet Tiger friend is the plaintiff and wish you had never let him cross your threshold.

Thirdly, nobody loves having a Tiger around all the time because Tigers are territorial. A Tiger's house is *his* domain and – like the rest of his life – his lair is usually a minefield of dispute, breaches of contract and stormy legal battles. What's worse, the Tiger nearly always stands his ground. Faced with his adversaries' draconian claims and accusations and even the threat of disrepute or eviction, the Tiger stays put. He doesn't seem to care what people think of him. No long-term, Ox-like, wait-and-see solutions for him. The Tiger acts on impulse to protect his cover. His actions are directly connected to his emotions. Yell at him and he replies in kind. Attack his geraniums and he'll brain you with the flowerpot.

Fourthly, Tigers disregard jeopardy and have an unhealthy penchant for risk-taking. They get involved in zany schemes and major humanitarian or world-scale projects that nobody in his right mind would try to accomplish in two lifetimes. A Tiger might buy a ruined hamlet in the south of Romania and decide to turn this sleepy village into a new vacation spot. Or he might embroil himself in a business scheme involving heavy artillery price wars or dicey takeovers. If you have the stomach to be a long-term friend to this derring-do addict, don't be surprised when he unabashedly asks not only for your undying moral support in his risky new venture, but perhaps even for a loan or a long-term investment. Never fear – he'll pay it back. But when?

The Tiger has no fear of the results of his recklessness. He'll enter battle on a hunch, fight like a Tiger and sometimes even lose. But if the world crumbles around him, he will be crushed. But not for long. Soon he will bound from his bed, leap into the car and race off to blaze a new trail.

The Tiger is capable of enormous sacrifice in return for the special attention he needs to survive. If the Tiger loves you and feels that his love is aptly reciprocated, he will crawl on chilblained knees through the snows of Siberia to reach your prison bedside and then he'll pry you out with a can opener; he will dare the demons of hell to save you from drink or drugs. Tigers know no bounds anywhere. And that's just the trouble.

Befriending this engaging character is a breeze. But it's an endurance test to remain his friend. You must be not only sympathetic to the Tiger's goals but join him in achieving them and be thoroughly compassionate (and even get involved with your fists) when he is thwarted.

Partly because of their inability to see a flying peril until it hits them squarely in the solar plexus, Tigers have a reputation for being uncommonly brave, which they are. The Tiger will rise to any challenge he feels worthy of his august attention, probably because he doesn't see danger for what it really is. Tigers will toy with a grenade the way cats play with a half-dead mouse – they prowl around it, pretend to ignore it, walk away, come back, tease it with their paw, give it a nudge with their snout and finally stick their noses right in it, touching and prodding it insistently. But the grenade doesn't explode. No wonder the Chinese teach us that the Tiger is a very lucky sign.

Sometimes this streak of good fortune abandons the Tiger. Occasionally, when the Tiger courts danger just a bit too off-handedly, he falls down dead. (Remember Marilyn Monroe, Natalie Wood, Oscar Wilde, Isadora Duncan and Buddy Holly?)

For Tigers, the word 'danger' can also mean excess. Every Tiger is a potential burn-out case. Tigers are eagerness and excitement addicts. They love to find out about obscure laws, uncover new centers of activity and cultivate freaky or exceptional people. Then they chase their new-found prey with the spontaneous speed of a pot of milk boiling over. Tigers are always in a hurry and can often be found swimming around in spilt milk.

As my brother Peter the Dog repeats almost daily when I'm near him, 'The trouble with you, Suzie, is that you don't *do* anything. You *overdo* everything.'

Poor Peter has three siblings: one is a Rooster – hardly a restful case – and the other two are Tigers. As the Dog is the Tiger's chief advisor and watcher, Peter inherited a rather large share of responsibility in John and myself, twelve years apart and as reckless and driving as each other. We Tigers need Peter the Dog and appreciate his sound reasoning, but we pretend that we don't want his advice. We claim that we know better and that we can manage alone. But we agree that we only *pretend* not to need Peter the Dog's meddling and also that we wish he would shut up about healthy diets, that we should stop working so hard and quit running around in such eager pursuit of our own early deaths. Pete usually sighs and gives up.

I trust you won't divulge our Tigerish family secret but later on, after the ferry boats have disappeared from the San Francisco horizon and the clean-living Dog has trotted home to his sensible early bed, then my Tiger brother John and I agree that we might be better off taking Pete's advice. One day soon, we promise each other, we will learn to value peaceful free time over resounding profane victory. We sagely agree to give up our addiction to excitement.

By the time the alarm rings next day these sound reasonings have vanished. John and I head off at breakneck speed into the jungle of new experience, acquaintance and adventure that we renounced only hours before.

Tigers are incorrigibly contrary. The only way they ever learn is the hard way. They have to be at death's door before they accept moderation. Tell a Tiger to get a haircut and the next time you see him he'll be walking on his flowing locks. Defiance is his middle name.

My earliest memory of my own Tigerish contrariness must be when I was three years old. We were having lunch in my grandmother's kitchen. Granny served homemade tomato soup in bowls and placed one on the tray of my high chair, warning gently, 'Don't touch that, honey, it's very hot.'

I surreptitiously raised my right hand, letting it hover over the bowl for a second, then plunged its little pink palm into the scalding liquid. I don't recall crying. I got into deep soup for being naughty. But I was confused. I didn't consider my gesture particularly naughty – it was an experiment, a chance to get close to danger, a challenge.

Besides, what my granny didn't then know is that sometimes Don't can mean I dare you, especially to a card-carrying Tiger.

Tigers re-invent their lives every single day. Because of their low boredom threshold, they strive to escape sameness and avoid routine by any means. Count on the Tiger to move house at least five times in his adult life and any self-respecting Tiger will change jobs about twice that often. His messy divorces are not necessarily countable on one hand, either. Tigers get a kick out of change and crave upheaval. They won't own a house for two minutes before they're knocking down walls to make room for the new lifestyle they've just dreamed up.

Take my friend Ana Monroe, my Earth Tiger twin born on the same day in the same year and latitude as I was. Ana is an intellectual – Harvard, good family, history, obscure languages, the works. She moves around a lot: New York, France, Cambridge, Massachusetts, Oxford, England, Cape Cod, Martha's Vineyard and back to New York again. 'For a change of scene,' says Ana with a wink.

In Ana's many houses, you will always find winter and summer arrangements of furniture. Once in a while, when she's feeling particularly energetic, she puts on special spring and autumn furniture displays, too. Ana's architect husband, a sedate, scholarly British gentleman, whose Chinese sign is a secret carefully guarded from me, tries to explain to his wife, 'I conceived the spaces and volumes in this room for their symmetry and handsome good taste, my dear. Why must you constantly change everything?'

To me, Ana's mutable decorating schemes seem utterly reasonable. I'm a flexible Tiger. But Cuthbert likes his surroundings to remain constant and in infallibly good taste. (Maybe he's an Ox.)

Cuthbert has more supporters than Ana in this couple's lifelong furniture-geography battle. Once it is established, most people prefer to retain their floor plan. But not Tigers. Claude Lamorisse in the South of France has a lovely old house in the grounds of her children's *château* which nobody ever sees. It is always under tarpaulins because it's being built. One doesn't even see her much because while she is waiting for her house to be finished, she moves around. She stays in her *palazzo* in Venice or with friends in Paris.

Then there's Jean-Paul Biron, the Tiger whizz-kid editorial sales genius. Jean-Paul's Monkey wife won't let him move the furniture so Jean-Paul flexes his restless Tiger muscles by flying around Europe buying old houses – just for fun. Martha Shulman, a young Tigress writer friend who lives in sumptuous digs in Paris and throws elegant *salon*/dinner parties every month, has never held her *salon* in the same room of her vast apartment for twice in a row. I've sat on that red velvet settee in at least three different major rooms. Martha claims it's because she needs more or less space, depending on her guest list. But sometimes she takes a small room for the *salon* and uses the hugest one for the dining-room. It really depends on her mood.

But finally, the best example of Tiger *vagabondage* is Drifter Nancy from Ibiza, who carries her home in a single basket with shoulder straps plus one small suitcase. In the twenty-five years I have known her, she has lived exclusively in other people's houses – once, in Ibiza, she rented an apartment with a boyfriend for a few months, but that was over by 1970. In Paris, she spent six or seven years at Ellen's, whose daughter she babysat in exchange for a room. Then, in London, Nancy lived at Penny's, whose child she took on outings in exchange for lodging. Then back in Paris she stayed with Zinnia, a five-year-old blonde girl who Nancy took up with for the purposes of living in her parents' flat. When Zinnia's mum had a second baby and had to use Nancy's room, Nancy went back to New York. There she lived with other friends for a few months while she buried her father and sorted out the details of her new private income. After that, she came back to London where she stayed with some old rock star friends till she decided what to do next. And what was that? Teaching English in Thailand. Nancy has now been miraculously settled in Bangkok for two years. There she lives full time – in a converted trolley car!

The Tiger's delight in change can be an asset. In a wink, she can make up her mind to enter a Carmelite convent and the next day can have completely forgotten the name of the order. An old yellowed newspaper clipping can set him off on a telephonic goose chase across the earth to find the five Rembrandts advertised for sale in the *International Herald Tribune* last February.

These hasty Tigerish pounces on ideas and arcane notions can be amusing. No Tiger can ever be accused of being stodgy or conservative. But as a result of his taste for haste, the Tiger has trouble concentrating. I remember wondering whether the novelist John Steinbeck was born a Tiger when his widow Elaine told a story about the day she presided at the opening of a writers' room in her husband's name at the college where I used to teach in Southampton, Long Island. 'John had a terrible time finding a place to work,' she told us. 'Something was always disturbing him. He would complain about noise from the kids but he was also bothered by traffic passing three streets away or could even be unsettled by a buzzing fly in the kitchen when he was two rooms away in his study.' She explained how she had decided to donate a sound-proofed room to the college library, with separate desks for each person working there, for writers who needed a quiet work space and couldn't find it in their homes.

As soon as I got home that evening I looked up Steinbeck's birth year. 1902. A free-floating Water Tiger if ever there was one.

In Tigers (who ultimately *do* get things done) this habit of easy distraction creates an intensive work pattern I like to call the 'Blitz Effect'. Tigers prefer not to take up anything that has to be accomplished over a long stretch of time. Ask a Tiger to paint your fence, cook you a meal, take you on a hike or write you a letter. The job will be undertaken and accomplished with enthusiasm and efficiency. Tigers need to feel the pulse, to sense that the goal is not too far ahead. Pressure makes Tigers perform at their best but as soon as it eases the Tiger flounders, loses interest and forgets what he was about. The Tiger is also easily sidetracked. Because he can't forget those five Rembrandts he saw advertised six months ago, he drops whatever he is doing and begins calling around the world again to locate those non-existent masterpieces. He is sure he can make a killing if he can only track them down.

The Tiger's decision-making sometimes has an annoying hippity-hop quality, too. People even accuse Tigers of procrastination. But the odd way they have of holding off until the 'right moment' when acting on major decisions is strategy. A Tiger may seem to hesitate, even shilly-shally about buying that house, getting married or signing the big contract but he is only cautious or stand-offish because he's waiting for the most propitious instant before pouncing. He knows that once he has made the fatal leap, he will never turn back. When the stakes are highest, the Tiger may let his partners or adversaries 'stew in their own juice' until he considers the time is ripe.

Because Tigers are urgent people and always in a hurry to get things done right, they commonly choose to operate alone. Associations and group or team projects are ill-advised. Tigers have a low tolerance for inertia, weakness, laziness, bossiness, lack of focus or hierarchy in their associates. In their impatience, they simply wrench the helm from the unsuspecting hands of a partner and decide willy-nilly to go it alone.

But let's go back to spilt milk. Tigers are past masters of rash moves, hasty decisions, ill-advised marriages and collectors of bad debt. When the Tiger takes hasty steps he frequently finds himself in piranha-infested hot water. Tigers are too altruistic and specialize in rescuing sinking ships, bankrupt businesses, frightened battered wives and mistreated children. There's a hero streak in the Tiger character. No Tiger can resist getting involved where someone is struggling against unjust odds. A Tiger child will want to rescue the poor spider that's about to drown in his bath water, or send his brother's pet turtle back into the sea. Tiger adults never lose this habit. My friend Gloria worked in fashion-related jobs but has become an accomplished and successful painter. Her life is every bit as frenzied as before because she has turned three rooms of her Parisian flat into a unique sort of youth hostel. Some years back, she began letting foreign students crash in her spare bedroom, much to the disapproval of her neighbors.

'Damned French bourgeois and their stupid Cartesian categorizing!' rails Gloria when questioned on the subject. 'Of course they look scruffy – they're students!'

Racism in all its forms, unfair business practices that promise non-existent sweepstake prizes, overbearing merchants and clerks who snub underdressed customers from behind their shiny countertops, fat-bellied insurance companies who won't pay for necessary operations or treatment for their unsuspecting subscribers, mean-spirited killjoy neighbors – beware! The Tiger is watching you. Don't step out of line or a huge and tawny hero may leap from the decorative jungle scene on your office wallpaper and pummel you into submission.

Mediocrity is another Tiger pet peeve. Tigers can be nearly always found hobnobbing with people from either end of the social spectrum. But you will not find many Tigers lurking around middle-class, middle-ground, or middle-aged cocktail parties. It's part of his all or nothing attitude. He will happily invite a bum to lunch or, with reckless abandon, charge into a reception at the White House, looking for his crony Georges the waiter from the old days in Montmartre who is now the President's *maître d'hôtel*. Tigers don't understand artificial boundaries between human beings. Titles and position, labels and rank pass right by the Tiger's twitching snout. They are not even curious about the inner workings of social class and they certainly couldn't care less if your illustrious father-in-law makes the fabric that NASA uses for astronauts' gloves and socks. If the Tiger meets *you*, he is interested in *you*. What do you do? If you reply, 'Oh, nothing much,' the Tiger will scratch you off his list. But if you even hint that you do something interesting or adventurous, the Tiger may take you home with him.

Never trifle with a Tiger's confidence. Let's suppose that he agrees to sponsor you or assists you in getting ahead. He lends you money or steps in on your behalf with a superior. You get your promotion or pass your exam and the Tiger is delighted for you. Tigers are able to share in other people's happiness. They do not expect any recompense for their efforts other than your continued loyalty and friendship. But once they have got you out of your jam, if you dare to rub shoulders with those unjust people the Tiger was born to hate, he will avenge your betrayal.

Unlike the Monkey, who is immune to the effects of treachery and can walk through a crowd of killers with a smile, the Tiger is ripe prey to danger and often falls victim to it. There is something mysterious or magical about the Tiger that causes unstable people to fixate on him, become obsessed with him and find reasons to be jealous or envious of him. Jodie Foster unwittingly became the reason for somebody to shoot at a president. Tigers are not easily duped, because they are quite suspicious by nature. But when they believe in something or someone they are not often discouraged from following it or them over a cliff.

The list is long of Tiger lives tinged with disappointment. Look at Christina Onassis who married a number of ne'er-do-wells before giving up all hope of happiness and making herself disappear, or the sad end of Groucho Marx who, it is said, gave his fortune to a younger woman who claimed to love him when nobody else did, or Marilyn Monroe, misused by smarty-pants politicians and big-time operators. The Tiger longs for allies. He needs trustworthy cohorts and partners-in-crime for when he pulls off his daring capers. He often places too much belief in his allies, blurting out the details of every campaign, entrusting them with his secrets. When the Tiger trusts too much, he sometimes finds his best-laid plans undermined by those in whom he had the most faith.

Tigers make money. Although the world's richest billionaires are not often Tiger-born, the Tiger is not one to slack off when it comes to putting his shoulder to the wheel and so earns plenty. Tigers also invest cleverly but are more likely to build a fortune from nothing after following through a brand new concept they have devised. Quick-tempered and hot-headed, the Tiger usually chooses to improvise and invent creative new ways of making money rather than taking workaday jobs that only require his presence, say, on a production line. Boredom, remember, is the Tiger's arch enemy.

However, although he usually ranks on the high side of middle-income, the Tiger has little or no respect for money. His financial picture is fraught with devil-may-care spending, perpetual overdrafts, a general irreverence towards money. Lots of Tigers keep their cash scattered around in the bottom of their purses (or in their cars) rather than in their wallets and never know how much they have. A wise Tiger (a contradiction in terms) lets his trusty mate do the household accounts and takes an allowance to live on. As for savings – forget it. The Chinese say that the Tiger need never worry about money: just when he fears it's all gone, more seems to arrive – as if by magic.

For most of his life the concept of different, to the Tiger, means better. But if he stays alive until middle age, the real challenge for the Tiger is to grasp the true meaning of moderation. Rather than rushing headlong into thicket after thicket and coming up with little more than burrs on his snout, the mature, sensible Tiger will accept that calculated preparation is the key to fine-tuning his plans of attack. In this way he will bring not only his intelligence, optimism and energy to each new project, but will eventually become the engineer of his own designs. Sooner or later (despite his fear of boredom and distaste for sameness), the discriminating Tiger will swop his virtuoso juggling of time, money and energy for a disciplined personal management program. It is only by learning to cope with routine and accepting to sink his eager fangs into the chewy day-to-day that the Tiger can hope to achieve a healthy and harmonious existence.

The lady is a Tiger

Do Tiger women have more fun? Well, speaking from experience, I would say they do. But fun is not everything, and being a Tiger woman is not all fun. It's wild and woolly and downright dangerous. Tiger women inherit more brushes with death and more knock-down struggles against evil than the women of most other signs. And, what's worse, despite all their best intentions, harmonious, long-term love relations elude them.

Tiger women are frequently single. They are just as frequently married – but they don't often stay married long. If they are married, much of the time it is not to the same person. The Tigress has a strong personality, a no-nonsense approach to life and doesn't suffer fools gladly. Being her partner, especially her mate, is a life-threatening challenge. No man who has ever survived as full-time spouse of a Tiger will tell you it has been a bed of roses. But, then, no Tiger mate will ever complain of having been bored.

There is nothing humdrum about the Tiger woman's existence. Tiger women are 100 per cent non-conformist. You won't find one of these feisty creatures living quietly in a tranquil setting in the suburbs. She doesn't know how to do things half-way or how to measure out her life in sensible portions. It's all or nothing. And no lukewarm emotions: to Tiger women, caution was invented for throwing to the winds.

The Tiger woman is feared and even reviled by the philosophers and wise men who rule Chinese astrology. No bearded sage advises any reasonable man to rush into a marriage with a gorgeous Tiger woman – unless she's very rich and he isn't. In China, where the Tiger woman is considered a natural feminist, a man-hater, the feminine equivalent of a male chauvinist pig is the female chauvinist Tiger.

The Tiger woman cannot allow any limitations on her independence. She doesn't know the meaning of restriction and is downright disdainful at any hint that she might need help with something. Enthusiastically gallant men must be careful around proud Tiger women. Don't ever walk up to a Tiger woman who is busy installing new gutters on her garage, grab the soldering iron out of her hand and indulgently suggest, 'Here, baby, let me do that for you.' She'll brand you with that hot iron as soon as look at you. Tiger women don't like interference from people whose credentials consist purely of extra muscle or brawn. They are not being stoical about trying their hands at everything traditionally reserved for males: they want to do things on their own and are gifted for doing just that. They are not shy or retiring and almost always come out with what is on their minds. If they need help, Tiger women will, thank you very much, ask for it.

Tiger women don't hate men. They are often accused of liking men a tad too much. But the Tiger woman champs at the bit of her own femininity. Deep down, she sincerely believes that her life would be better if she had been born a man. She wants to do great things. She hates taking petty little jobs that don't challenge her true abilities and she vigorously resists riding in the back seat with Auntie Ethel or having to drive hubby's old car to the supermarket so he can zoom to the office in a new convertible. Tiger woman wants that convertible and all the mobility and pizazz that goes with it. She wants to be first and categorically refuses to live in the shadow of anyone else. The Tiger woman wants to run the world, so why should she settle for less?

I dare say you won't find a single Tiger woman who has not been fired from at least one job in her life. In the male-dominated world, the Tiger woman struggles harder, and more vocally, than most women to be heard, promoted, respected and to receive equal pay for equal work. She's a toughie, a scrapper and a ready-for-anything warrior for what she thinks is right.

The Tiger woman is no slouch in seduction. She considers her feminine wiles part of her natural weaponry. A good-looking body, healthy hair and teeth and a fine eye for sexy yet sober fashion are but some of the heavy artillery that the Tiger woman is never afraid to flash in times of serious negotiation or battle with the enemy. Her motives are always honorable and her goals respectable. She is not an evil person nor is she tempted to commit a crime or get involved in chicanery for its own sake. The Tiger woman is neither tricky nor devious. She practically always knows ahead of time what she wants to achieve and goes about it directly and with strength of purpose. Though she is not consistent in much, she is almost always head-strong, artless and chronically ingenuous: when confronted with a thorny issue or complex problem, the pure-hearted Tiger woman tumbles into even the clumsiest traps.

Because of her lack of guile and refusal to have recourse to circuitous means, the Tiger woman is not subtle. When a crucial business meeting reaches its zenith of tension, when the male members of the steering committee are silently tearing at each other's throats, the unstoppable, pounce-happy Tiger lady might just plop her forepaws loudly on the conference table, and intone, 'Come on, you guys, cut this petty wrangling and make some decisions. You've been pussy-footing around the real issues for days now. Are we going to do something about these problems or not?'

The blatantly honest Tiger woman soon has everybody cowering and burying their heads in their briefcases. They are in dire fear that something might happen. What next? Do they promote her? Aren't they relieved that finally somebody came out with it? Of course not. They fire her.

These outbursts can make a loser of the Tiger woman. She has *no* patience with what she considers time-wasting, water-treading. She wants action, and she wants it *now*. The Tiger lady wants everybody to accept change because she sincerely feels that there is salvation in a fresh outlook but her cohorts (and especially her superiors) don't necessarily take kindly to her brutal approach. So, Tiger woman is sacrificed. But there is a happy ending: because our bold-faced Tiger lady almost always knows too much, she is often asked to leave quietly by the back door with a nice packet of hush money under her belt.

Tiger women exhibit talent, sexual attraction, exciting or unusual destinies, but they are also ready targets for early burn-out. Too much excitement and hurrying around, seduction and ceaseless racing with the moon can make a Tigress very dead very young. She must be wary of many dangers – especially the self-destructive one that throbs beneath her pretty striped coat.

The arch enemy of Tigress beauty is her hyperintensive approach to life and her inability to perform even the least significant of her duties without engaging her emotions. She is passionate, involved so profoundly in her pursuits that she sometimes cannot see the forest for the trees. Both overwork and over-emoting wear her out. She is just as forceful as she appears but she is not so psychically strong. Her nerves grow quickly ragged with fatigue. She gives herself little quarter when it comes to exhaustion, working far beyond her physical capacity. Sooner or later, the effects – lines around the mouth, puffiness, wrinkled brow and nervous tics – start to show and can destroy her girlish looks.

Superficially, Tiger women are vigorous, healthy types. They are usually tallish and often angular and muscular rather than round or soft-featured. They stand erect and have a proud manner. Because of her elegant stature, the Tiger woman appears tall even in old age. She stands straight and looks you in the eye when she speaks. Her forehead is high, her cheekbones prominent and her mouth small. The chin is set resolutely, and the lips are thin and well bowed, not severe. She has a look of disarming candor in her eyes and appeals largely by virtue of her vibrant youthfulness. She emanates a girlish quality which she never loses, walking tall in graceful strides and dashing everywhere at once without artificial poise, pose or aforethought. The Tiger woman doesn't wear much make-up and cannot hide her emotions as her innocent eyes give her away. She is slim and wears trousers or sober suits without frills or furbelows. This Tiger woman is neither classically beautiful nor even pretty, but there is a quality of mystery in her manner that makes her a *femme fatale* to beat all others. The Tiger woman's beauty is fragile as she is far from frail or delicate. I can best describe her looks as kaleidoscopic. The next time you look at a Tiger woman, watch her face as she talks. Notice her chameleonic expression.

Her face does not show humor or satire such as we see with the Monkey woman. Rather, the Tiger woman is buoyant and optimistic. She is dynamic and communicates hope. Like a tall, strong sunflower waving alone in a field of wheat, the Tiger Queen salutes her subjects. Her solid, stately energy and pugnacious punch are contagious.

Tiger women are not exclusive or jealous. Their romantic goal is to have a go at love with a lot of different men. Tiger women love fiercely, with passion and intense loyalty. But they are easily distracted. A Tiger woman cannot imagine going to the grave without having shared at least a few intimate moments with everyone to whom she has ever been attracted. She is voracious and yet oddly faithful and apple pie 'normal'. She is not a perverse or kinky sex object. Tiger woman is strictly a missionary type with a little taste for fantasy thrown in for excitement – eager, lusty and accommodating, but never the siren.

The Tiger is given to loving friendships. She can have a long, serious love affair with a happily married man or be content as the secret mistress of a powerful fellow who is too busy to spend all his time with her. Or she might choose to love a fragile or weak man on whom she has no long-term design other than shared sensitivity. The Tigress can love one or all three of these men equally and/or simultaneously without ever wanting to live with, marry, or even take them home to Mum.

Possessiveness confounds the Tiger woman. She neither understands possessing nor being possessed by a lover. For this reason it is difficult to break a Tiger woman's heart. Her pride may be hurt if she is jilted or spurned, but she is not one to snivel over the loss of one lover when she knows there are fifty more out there to be seduced and conquered.

Neither is she sexually jealous. She can empathize with a man's desire to solicit, beguile and win over another woman because *she* is never quite satisfied with the affections of just one man. Again, the

Tiger woman behaves in love the way she perceives most men do. She is quite capable of picking up a man, taking him home and making love to him and then giving him the taxi fare so she won't have to see him in the morning. She is sexy but she is not adoring, or obedient to the object of her affections. Her independence comes first.

Like everybody else, Tiger women can be crushed or broken by rejection. Her friends and acquaintances are everything to this versatile creature. If one of these should drop her, she may pine for years over the loss. As the Tiger often leaves her parents' home young, she creates a new family with which she interacts during her adult life, often in preference to her parents and siblings. The woman Tiger is a curious character who learns only from experience and depends on her friends both for advice and for those loyalties for which she is so famous. If her select few friends ever let her down, she dies.

Tiger women make wonderful sales people. They enjoy all jobs where the challenge is immediate, the strategies quick and bone-slicingly efficient and the results out by morning. They are happiest when they win a contract or gain a customer, but even if they lose, Tiger women are always ready to try again. They constantly test their strength against unheard-of odds. They will try anything once and are for ever on the lookout for hot new experiences.

I have just spoken to one of my favorite Tiger ladies, Céline, head of the foreign rights department at a publishing house. Céline is as Tigerish as they come. She's buoyant and lithe, tough as a smoking gun and just as chill-inspiring. Her life is her work and yet she has two young sons. One lives in Austria with his father; Céline sees him in the summer. The other lives with her in Paris and spends lots of time with *his* father. Céline runs her career first and her love life second. Both are busy. She just doesn't have time for coddling anybody – even her kids.

Once last year, I asked Céline if her French son enjoyed his summer camp. She answered in her flippant girlish way with a quicksilver giggle and a wave of her hand, 'I never thought to ask him.'

As mothers, Tiger women are devoted and responsible. To them mothering is about protection, teaching and setting examples. However, the Tiger mother is not very cozy or tender. She would gladly commit multiple murder to hang on to her kids or keep them from harm but she is not the smothering earth mother of Woody Allen movies. Nor does she demand her kids' unfailing attention: she wants them to be safe, attractive and to do her proud. If they fail, she buoys them up. If they succeed, she applauds. All the Tiger mums I know work outside the home and make arrangements for childcare. They love ferociously but are neither exclusive nor possessive. They believe that their children – like their men – belong only to themselves.

Because of their disdain for imposed schedules, traditions and rules, Tiger women, especially single ones, are often perceived as eccentric. They are not 'normal' nor are they dangerous or destructive. They simply need to live *their* way. I've already mentioned Nancy who lives in a trolley car in Bangkok but there's also Riva, who paints huge paintings in her high-rise apartment living room. The neighbors are always trying to get these oddball people erased from their area or their luxury high rises – not that our Tigers cause trouble or make noise, but Riva does trundle her giant paintings into the lift on the way to the gallery downtown and occasionally some snooty tenant's mink gets brushed with a smudge of burnt sienna. Nancy's trolley house is – even for Bangkok – considered an eyesore and her neighbors complain that she should turn it into a real house. But Nancy likes living in her trolley car.

I live in the middle of Paris – in a tiny, dilapidated cabin that looks as if it was transported board by board from Mill Valley or Woodstock. It is not on the street. It's inside the courtyard garden of a staid middle-class block of flats. My Parisian neighbors think I am weird. They cannot understand how I keep warm. (There are hardly any wooden houses in France except in the mountains where chalets with stone or cement foundations rise out of the snow.) It's simple. I heat it with a wood stove. 'But doesn't the heat just seep out the sides?' they ask me.

'No,' I assure them. 'Wood is a good insulating material.'

Still, many remain sceptical and some of the die-hards believe I am very strange. Bad enough to be an American *and* artistic, but to live in that fur trapper's cabin in the back garden . . . They wonder if I might not be dangerous.

My own irreverent behavior in Paris is pale by comparison to the classic Tiger rule-flouting story about Kerry Kelly and her Bobtail, Old English Sheepdog, Kleps. Kerry loved Kleps more than anybody else in the world. She lived alone and Kleps made her feel safe. One day she was invited to France – her boyfriend wanted her to accompany him to a conference. Kerry was delighted but didn't want to leave Kleps behind and asked her lover to pay for her dog to come too. He agreed.

Next day, Kerry set about organizing her own and Kleps's departure. Air France said she could take the dog, but explained that he would travel in a cage in the hold.

Kerry called other airlines – same story everywhere. She was furious. She would not have her clean, upstanding American dog freeze and be traumatized by a dreadful travel experience, bumping around with a lot of suitcases. She offered to pay any amount extra, but no. No dogs in plane cabins. Kerry was discouraged and annoyed, but she was not licked yet.

To try to forget her woes, Kerry sat back and watched a sentimental TV movie about Helen Keller. By 8.30 p.m. she had worked out a plan.

Next day Kerry bought a pair of dark glasses for herself and a special harness and leash for guide dogs. She donned the shades, harnessed up Kleps and they practiced all weekend, boarding buses and getting on and off Métros. On Tuesday, when they arrived at the airport, the taxi driver took her bags to the desk. Air France ground personnel went mad trying to assist her in every way. They gave her preferred boarding and, once inside the plane, made a portly gentleman give up his double seat, put her up to first class and settled her and Kleps for the long journey to Paris.

Tiger man

Tiger men never take the easy way out, or choose compromise over action. The Chinese say that Tiger men like difficulty. I agree: they are challenged by adversity. They thrive on cracking the hardest nuts with their bare hands and then gloating about it.

Unlike the Ox male, who gets his kicks from pushing a boulder up a mountain over thirty years, the Tiger prefers to dive into a roiling pit of poisonous snakes and walk out victorious after thirty seconds. He basks in the applause, takes pride and pleasure in surviving against all odds and instantly goes hunting for another pit. The Tiger man enjoys the immediacy of his accomplishment. He gains self-esteem by being able to turn the tide in the shortest possible time. He's a mover and a shaker – and with that, he is controversial, always moving ahead by leaps and bounds, armed with new ways of doing old tasks. The Tiger man is an innovator and a ruthless perpetrator of his own original schemes. He wouldn't have the patience to roll a boulder up a hill of beans.

Yet the Tiger man knows how to persevere. He craves challenge and change, assumes responsibility with ease and takes on leadership with gusto. Once he gets hold of an idea or project – even one of his apparently hare-brained schemes – the Tiger man hangs on like a terrier until he wins the prize. But if he does not get it quickly, he'll drop the whole thing in the waste-paper basket and invent a different plan of attack. Watching a Tiger man in action is enough to give you a lifetime of neck problems.

Because these fellows have the advantage of being the stronger sex, they don't need to be as overtly aggressive as their female counterparts. A man is *expected* to have a strong personality and be decisive and effective in the big bad world. The Tiger man is all of these – and more. He is comfortable in his skin and relaxes into any role where he can lead.

When Sir Ralph Halpern lost his job after thirty years it was front-page news in the British press. He had been director of a failing chain of men's fashion shops that he had practically single-handedly turned into a multimillion-pound empire.

When I found his age noted in an article, I realized that Sir Ralph Halpern is a Tiger.

Novelties and gadgetry abound in the lives of Tiger men and they love fitting out their grand houses with things that spout, light up, dazzle and play music. Remember Hugh Hefner and his Chicago Playboy mansion? A Tiger. Maybe not a five-times-a-night Tiger but pretty close. The whole picture: the cars, the ladies and the gadgets, the success and failure syndrome, the happy, loving employees who receive handsome salaries and the unhappy top dogs who are plainly jealous of the company head who not only gets all the glory but beds the girls to boot.

Sir Ralph Halpern's exit is also a typical Tiger man story. This hugely successful man left the thriving company he built, taking with him a severance pay arrangement that gives him a stipend of $25,000 per week for the rest of his life!

Tiger men are driven to achieve. They need the security of money, social position and the fine trappings that go with a high standard of living. They are self-starters and in their quest for success can be both ruthless and cunning, but the Tiger boss is beloved by those who work for him. He is exacting and demands top performances but he knows how to share his toys. Tiger man likes to see his head foreman drive up in a prestige car.

All Tigers are blind to racial, class and social distinctions when choosing their friends and acquaintances. To Tiger men, the most important aspect of anybody's curriculum vitae is whether or not he or she can get the job done. They want to know whether the person has good personal standards and a good track record. The main concern of the Tiger man is personal merit: integrity, loyalty, creativity and spunk.

The Tiger man is a benevolent tyrant. He often neglects both his own and other people's feelings. He forgets to care if he's offended someone by ignoring them.

Charles de Gaulle was a Tiger man *par excellence*, an arrogant but effective leader who was unable to accept either defeat or compromise. He arrived in England in June 1940 with $1000 from the French secret fund, a change of trousers and three or four shirts. He rented a house for £14 a month and was given an office in London where a barrel of wine stood to welcome any new recruits. Many other Frenchmen in England wanted nothing to do with this obscure maverick who had been a general less than three weeks. But slowly people were attracted to his side. By the end of July de Gaulle had a following of 7000 Free French. He was furious with Winston Churchill for not finding him a Free French flag to carry in a parade. He explained, 'If I must, I will even be rude to show French independence.'

Churchill rejoined, 'Well, I must say you are very perseverant at that.'

In 1943 de Gaulle left England for Algeria and didn't come back. He paid the bill footed by His Majesty's Treasury for his sojourn in Britain before the end of the war and never mentioned it again. No public praise sessions after the war about how England had bravely sequestered him . . . Nothing but bravura and snoot.

It's all typical Tiger man stuff. Hotshot, pushy, chauvinistic, and an even fanatical belief in ideals with a total disregard for anybody's feelings but his own. Open shows of emotion disconcert the stiff-upper-lipped Tiger hero. He has nothing but contempt for self-pity and, if he isn't checked, kicks weak people in the butt, hiding his tenderness under a gruff exterior. The Tiger man's armor is sturdily constructed of self-confidence and hope. His self-assurance is contagious and irresistible, his integrity unquestionable. How is it that he sometimes fails?

Pride, haste, insufficient planning, over-confidence, recklessness and indiscretion are some of the minor flaws of the tough Tiger man but worst of all, is his intemperance. This man will go to *any* lengths to win, to have fun, to make money, locate an old girlfriend, shelter his family or to hide his peccadilloes. Whatever he does, he gets carried away with it, even with some fool notion that he *knows* is crazy. He cares so little for what people think of him that he commits the worst *faux pas*, forgets to listen to his lieutenants or worse, he tells them, 'Shut up, will you? I know what I'm doing.' When the ship starts to sink, the Tiger is left gazing into the distance, planning yet another victory. By the time he notices that his boat has sprung a leak, his fellow sailors have manned the lifeboats and Captain Tiger's paws are getting very wet.

He is quite a charmer, is this Tiger man. Because of his virile appearance, women usually go mad over him. He has an expressive face, long legs and a trim figure, which he takes care of. The Tiger man has good hair, often dark and tightly curly, usually staying put well past the age of fifty. Tiger men have a pronounced facial structure: firm jawline, well-shaped nose, prominent forehead and high cheekbones. Their ears may be large but are well shaped and don't stick out. The Tiger man's eyes sparkle behind a hard glare and the corners of his eyes crinkle when he talks or smiles. He has a lovely clear, resonant voice and laughs uproariously. His speech is glib and rapid. When he talks to you, he looks you in the eye, and leaps so quickly from subject to subject that he often interrupts others. He strides around briskly as though he had been enrolled in a walking tournament at birth.

Love and the Tiger male bring up a whole spectrum of interesting Tiger trouble possibilities. Tiger men hate to be owned but they can't stand not to be married. As most wives like to think they have exclusivity on their husbands' sexual fidelity, many Tiger men's marriages end in a huff.

The secret of staying happily married to a Tiger man is learning how to wait. Tiger men are so easily infatuated and just as quickly uninfatuated that any tolerant wife who can wait it out whilst her Tiger hubby is 'fooling around' will usually maintain her inviolable spouse position. Her Tiger husband may often 'work late' and perhaps seem to be having an affair – but he doesn't have many affairs and even if he tries, he's such a rabbit both in bed and in the head, that they are usually of no lasting importance.

A wise wife will give her Tiger husband the impression that he can be as free as he likes. This is the best way to keep him at home as he is very jealous, too. If you let him think he's totally free, your Tiger mate is sure to think *you*'re having an affair while he's out gallivanting. This reverse psychology is a bit tricky, but I highly recommend it as a method of keeping the Tiger by the tail.

The paths of Tiger bachelors are strewn with multiple precipitate engagements and a like number of hasty retreats. If he doesn't find the ideal partner while he's young, this impulsive, passion-propelled gentleman can find himself embroiled in one imprudent union after the other. Marriage and stability should come early in his wild oats period, otherwise the Tiger will flounder, either unattached or sequentially (and often miserably) attached, for the years when he could be building a home and rearing a family. If he finds himself still floundering at forty he will almost certainly marry straightaway, if only to give the appearance of being substantial. And, as he makes a wonderful father, the Tiger man really misses out (and so do his kids) if he doesn't start a family while he's still young.

The Tiger man is misogynous. He loves to chase, make love and show off with women. But deep down he can't stand Woman. If he can dominate or keep them at arm's length, he can admire their grit, but frequently women co-workers irritate the Tiger. Women, he feels, should be kept in their place, protected, gorgeous and enticing. He is not one to cultivate their company or to get a charge out of going clothes shopping with an old girlfriend.

The Tiger man's career possibilities are endless. He is probably the world's most employable man. There are few jobs he would not be able to do but certain professions truly suit him. Because of his taste for danger, the Tiger makes a terrific hard-line journalist, private detective, smuggler, policeman or secret agent. His humanitarian-adventurer side gives him access to leadership posts in areas such as aid missions, anti-hunger campaigns in Africa, world health organizations and other UNESCO-related areas. Office work kills him. The Tiger is meant to be out and about, accomplishing, doing, and seeing that things get done. He makes a good colonel or general. His acute sense of justice makes the law attractive to him. He's just sadistic enough to like being a dentist. Above all, the Tiger is successful at business – particularly in sales-related jobs. He can charm and sweet talk the tuxedo off a penguin.

Since he is as good a leader as he is a salesman, the best job for a Tiger male is sales manager of a large company. The terrific Tiger will manage his sales force in an orderly and equable fashion, be liked and respected by everyone and, through his shrewd powers of conviction, can be counted on to sell everything in sight fast. The Tiger has an innate sense of marketing tactics and will seek the same high-level performance from his sales reps as from himself.

He is unafraid of the rejection a salesman often finds discouraging and continues to charge ahead even when his prospective client has barricaded himself behind his door. Undeterred, the Tiger sticks around in the corridor playing nice and easy-going until his quarry cannot resist any longer, opens the door and invites the engaging Tiger in for tea.

The main thing to remember about the Tiger man, when next you meet one, is that Tiger men don't *look* dangerous, don't *seem* hard-nosed or tough-minded. They are always polite and easy to talk to. They are usually good-looking and well dressed. Butter wouldn't melt in the mouth of the innocent-looking Tiger man.

My advice? Enjoy his company. Accept his charming ways and spend some good times with this adorable feline monster. But if you're after permanence and security to be happy, unless you're prepared to keep the home fires burning well past midnight almost every day for the rest of your life, don't get too involved. One more thing . . . watch your back.

The five Chinese elements and how they influence the Tiger

The Wood Tiger

1854 Oscar Wilde, Arthur Rimbaud
1914 Richard Widmark, Alec Guinness, Peter Townshend, Romain Gary, Pierre Balmain, Marguerite Duras, Dylan Thomas, Sarah Churchill, Dorothy Lamour, Arthur Kennedy

Energetic beyond belief, the Wood Tiger is a hypercreative innovator and bounds around like a chicken with its head cut off, getting into monumental vats of piping hot water. This Tiger lacks the guile and stealth of gentler Tigers. He's sociable, up-front and constantly yearns to undertake the most grandiose projects and make public his extraordinary views.

There is a positive side to the Wood Tiger's hasty behavior. With so many irons in the fire at once, he is always busy juggling, plotting and strategizing. He is never bored. The Wood Tiger is delighted when his alarm rings in the morning as he can almost taste the variety of possibilities for expansion and instant involvement in new deals that he stands to get out of each new day.

All Tigers like change but this one is addicted to it. The very idea of buying a loaf of bread in a new shop or taking a different route to the hardware store sends ripples of anticipation down his striped spine. You will never catch him philosophizing or daydreaming languorously. The Wood Tiger has a dickens of a time sitting still. He's affable, too, and quite easy to get along with but he is proud and rankles when others attempt to direct or counsel him.

This person is not an intellectual but he thinks brilliantly on his feet. He's impatient with high-flown idealism and theorizing. He prefers to get down to the job in hand and get it over with, the faster the better.

He thinks he can do it all and likes to see it done well. What's more, he thinks you should not only follow him and believe in him but, to prove your loyalty, you should not hesitate to invest your money in his schemes. The Wood Tiger is a world-beater but often feels thwarted because he can't find allies as dauntless as he. His vision of the world is very personal, sometimes incisive and often witty. Part of the charm of this magnetic Tiger resides in his never taking himself or anyone else very seriously.

The Wood Tiger's devil-take-the-hindmost approach doesn't go with his earnest desire to find a life's work or a true vocation that *really* suits him. He's always torn between settling down and rampaging about, turning on the seduction machine and handing out free advice to his court of adoring admirers. The Wood Tiger cannot resist even the hint of an opportunity to shine, to woo and to convince others that he is right.

He's quick to anger and just as fast to cool off. He's a charming, lucky person who can be taken anywhere at all levels of society without embarrassment. He loves all types of people and is tolerant and democratic in his choice of friends and partners, a smashing addition to any social gathering. He always has plenty of clever things to say and tons of arcane notions to add to any conversation. The Wood Tiger is generous and will shower his loved ones with comforts. But he is also selfish and, in all human interaction, demands the role of Top Tiger.

What this Tiger needs is a strong, interesting and stable mate who can hold his attention and force his nose to the grindstone. If the home life of the Wood Tiger is sufficiently loving, cozy – and disciplined – he can accomplish *great* things.

The best way of dealing with this strong-minded yet lovable will-o'-the-wisp is, sadly, to manipulate him. Telling a Wood Tiger flat out what you think of his delusions of grandeur or criticizing his hare-brained designs head-on may get you little more than a black eye or, at best, a wounded ego.

Flatter this daring character and he'll follow you anywhere – at least until something more alluring comes along.

The Fire Tiger

1926 Queen Elizabeth II, Hugh Hefner, Edouard Leclerc, Miles Davis, Marilyn Monroe, Marc Bohan, Mel Brooks, Martin Gray, Norman Jewison, Jerry Lewis, Klaus Kinski, John Derek, Roger Corman, John Schlesinger, Sydney Chaplin, Andrzej Wajda, Allen Ginsberg, John Fowles, Andy Griffith, Colleen Dewhurst, Aldo Ray, Chuck Berry, Garret Fitzgerald

The Fire Tiger is a charismatic, highly dramatic and sensual leader. Fire gives the vibrantly impressive Tiger even more pizazz and oomph than he might normally possess. He's as energetic, if not more so, than his Tiger brothers and sisters. But his power gets ahead of his good sense. He's recklessly spendthrift with his strengths and overdoes and over-achieves everything he undertakes. The Fire Tiger simply refuses to husband his own vitality. He pushes and strains and forces himself through the tightest knotholes for the sake of his brave ideals, wearing himself to a frazzle to give shape to projects in which he believes almost too fervently.

Sleepless nights are the norm rather than the exception. Erratic dietary habits and exorbitant sexual exploits are the fuel that fires this powerhouse's constantly revving engine.

From fifty onwards (if he lives that long), the Fire Tiger would be well advised to slow down, take it easy, stabilize his private life, engage in a steady program of healthy diet and exercise or yoga. After fifty, he should content himself to delegate authority and run his huge empires from the wings. He should cultivate hobbies and/or take up meditation. To lead a full and healthy life in his later years, he must narrow his field of action and find ways to cool his overworked mind. Otherwise he will be taking a great risk: his nerves may suddenly give out, his heart may attack or a stroke cripple him. I don't even want to think about the extravagant crankiness quotient of a bed-ridden Fire Tiger.

The Fire Tiger is a revolutionary, too. He wants change and is not afraid to initiate it, manage it and sell it to the people. Look at what Hugh Hefner did in America with the Playboy philosophy. Not only did he build a magazine, he changed people's views about many aspects of their sex lives. Same goes for someone like Edouard Leclerc in France. He built a supermarket empire, defied government rules and regulations, undercut and undersold everyone else and never ceased to be outspoken about it. Then there's Martin Gray, the man who survived the Warsaw Ghetto and wrote a book about it. Afterwards he lost his wife and three kids in a forest fire in the South of France and started a foundation to preserve forests. Nowadays, at sixty-four, Martin Gray heads a foundation for global preservation and unity. The Fire Tiger expresses himself freely and openly and is unmoved by tight-lipped scolds who would see him sanctioned for his outrageous ideas. The Fire Tiger is a tough cookie. He devises grand plans effortlessly and can carry them through better than almost any other Tiger. Fire Tigers either make a world class difference or die trying.

Imprudent as this Fire Tiger may be and often as he finds himself embroiled in scrapes, he is remarkably resilient. It's almost as though adversity charged the Fire Tiger's batteries. Not only does he want to be the first and the best, he is always ready to go back into the ring after he's been knocked down repeatedly. The Fire Tiger has guts.

The home life of the Fire Tiger will be compromised by his constant movement. These people don't usually marry young. For the sensuous, passionate Fire Tiger lover, marriage is an inevitable part of plan B – the slowing-down period. His sexually libertine youth represents an immature approach to sex and the conquest element stays with the Fire Tiger longer than most. Perhaps in youth, he is too preoccupied with world-class projects to devote sufficient time to long-lasting and profound emotional exchange, or maybe he is a classic late bloomer. Whatever it is, don't be surprised if you meet a sixty-year-old Fire Tiger with a couple of kids still going to school.

The Fire Tiger esteems honesty and wants to be valued as fair and just. However, if pushed, he is capable of chicanery and, even, outright ruthlessness. He does not suffer fools and will briskly leave any detractors in the dust without a backward glance. Ends, he feels, invariably justify means. The Fire Tiger knows that his schemes and ideas will improve humanity's lot and never questions his motives or allows self-doubt to put on the brakes.

The Earth Tiger

1878 André Citroën, Lionel Barrymore, Isadora Duncan, Arletty
1938 Germaine Greer, Evil Knievel, Susan Strasberg, Daniel Hechter, Bernadette Lafont, Elliot Gould, Oliver Reed, Romy Schneider, Jean Seberg, Jon Voight, Roberta Flack, Natalie Wood, Buddy Holly, Diana Rigg, George Carlin, Richard Benjamin, Nicol Williamson, Tina Turner

We twentieth-century Earth Tigers have a gruesome history of early death resulting from sudden and tragic events – suicides, accidents and even murder.

In China the Earth Tiger has a reputation as the thinking man's Tiger. He is thought to be less restless, more determined and sagacious than his counterparts. Earth Tigers make superior political chiefs or top business executives. The desire to lead is strong and so is the desire to occupy a respected position in society. The spirit here is autonomous, self-reliant and fiercely individualistic.

Despite the calming influence of the Earth element, this Tiger is still impetuous and headstrong. He concocts scheme after scheme and rushes around flashing his complicitous smile and charming the wits out of the world. However, he doesn't get himself into such cans of worms as the other Tigers because he asks advice before he acts on his rash impulses: he consults his pals, his lawyer, doctor and even the neighbors before he makes big decisions.

Another special thing about this Tiger is his non-Tigerish ability to lie about and do nothing. Most Tigers have trouble sitting still but Earth Tigers can stare into the distance for hours, musing and dreaming of greater moments. They are the most laid-back and temperate of Tigers.

The Earth Tiger enjoys learning new disciplines and putting together logical plans for the betterment of his own and other people's lives. Because of this, he is sometimes thought to be meddlesome and over-interfering in the lives of those he loves.

Earth Tigers are monuments of strength and purveyors of justice. They cannot tolerate unfair practices and will fight against social injustice and combat ethical wrong-doing fiercely. Like a combination terrier and elephant, the Earth Tiger takes an idea between his teeth and hangs on for ever if necessary because he *never* forgets: revenge is common practice for Earth Tigers. Nothing makes the Earth Tiger happier than demanding and receiving payment for a long overdue moral debt.

The Earth Tiger is wildly passionate in love. He adores both seducing and being seduced. He's a playful person who knows how to indulge his mate in fanciful love games. He's relatively faithful and true and prefers not to be informed of his mate's infidelities but does not like to be made a fool of. An Earth Tiger can bound away from a bad relationship without so much as a shudder of regret. Unless he is certain of total reciprocity in love, he never allows his heart to rule his head. Unrequited love seems like a shameful waste of his precious time.

The health pattern of most Earth Tigers is sketchy and uneven but they are essentially strong. Though danger befalls them in surprising and fearsome ways, they can survive amazing ordeals and often land safely on all four paws. They take the lead with ease, love having a good time and don't give much quarter to self-pity or snivelling. The Earth Tiger is dutiful and will pay dearly to stand by his beliefs and ideals. But, when wronged, he can also be ruthless and callously cruel. He is purposeful and unyieldingly independent. This last quality can indeed be a fault, as in his resolute way the Earth Tiger often ends up standing stubbornly by his views and feelings without giving space to others whose fervent desire to love him can never be as grand as his desire to remain aloof.

The Metal Tiger

1890 Charles de Gaulle, Fritz Lang, Man Ray, Rose Kennedy, Stan Laurel, Dwight D. Eisenhower, Vaclav Nijinski, Helen Hayes

1950 Princess Anne, Phil Collins, Fanny Ardant, Peter Frampton, David Cassidy, Jay Lenno, Christina Onassis, Gregory Harrison, Mel Gibson, William Hurt

The Metal Tiger is principled, straight-arrow, conservative and energetic, yet all Tiger charm and propulsion. He's a powerhouse of energy and a doer of grand deeds but more serious than most Tigers. He is not one to leave projects unfinished. He's a bulldozer with the engine of a tank and the scope of at least sixteen aircraft carriers.

The Metal Tiger has a reputation for making the right decisions at the right time and will hang about waiting for the precise moment to pounce. This behavior can sometimes seem like procrastination but his hesitation is a form of strategy. He lies in wait, raising an eyelid from time to time to check out the scene. Then he gets up, yawns, stretches his limbs, tenses his muscles and POW!

On the other hand, if the Metal Tiger has to wait for someone to show up or for something to happen, he goes berserk. He wants what he wants when he wants it and has difficulty understanding why others might not want to adhere to his schedule. He hates to obey and insists on obedience from others.

This Tiger is afflicted with a somber penchant. From a young age he may be fascinated by weapons and intrigued with death and death symbols. He faces a lifelong struggle to squelch this tendency. The Metal Tiger needs to surround himself with *up* people who keep his mind on the positive aspects of life. Otherwise, a bent for self-destruction, blind heroism and a taste for danger can lead him into serious – even fatal – accidents.

The Metal-born Tiger child should be raised in harmonious surroundings and taught to love peace and cherish his fellows. Wise adult choices should lead to harmony and a close-knit family life. Tensions within the family or a rocky marriage could upset his mental stability. Divorce would be preferable to a stressful marriage.

On the surface, the Metal Tiger appears optimistic, buoyant and full of humanity. And, on a grand scale, he is. Yet he is not always compassionate in one-to-one situations. You cannot get him to sit down and spill his thoughts or hash out feelings. Other people's needs and the ramifications of complex emotional situations seem to escape this Tiger's notice. He can be callous and heartless in love and in family relations. Yet if his cold-heartedness is remarked on or criticized, he simply laughs it off, pretending it does not exist. There is no cure for the Metal Tiger's emotional shortcomings. My advice is work around it. Don't take his sharp comments and absence of empathy too seriously and the Metal Tiger will never ask for your commiseration – he doesn't see the use of it.

This Tiger is a creature of legendary magnetism – not classically handsome or even sexy but more like a charismatic Pied Piper who knows instinctively how to convince his audience and recruit the minds of others in his quest for superiority. It's no surprise that de Gaulle was a Metal Tiger. This is a tough leader type who stops at nothing to reach his ends, knows precisely where to strike for the jugular.

The Metal Tiger wants to make the world a better place. He will not take advice or listen to condemnation of his often unreasonable means to his ends. For the Metal Tiger, any subterfuge or machination is fair game when it comes to winning the war. And for him the war is always going on, right versus wrong, good versus evil, them versus him. *He* is right and *they* are wrong.

The Water Tiger

1902 Sir Ralph Richardson, Leni Reifenstahl, Richard Rodgers, David Selznick, Darryl Zanuck, William Wyler, Leland Hayward, John Steinbeck, Max Ophuls, Louise de Vilmorin
1962 Jody Foster, Tom Cruise, Tracy Austin, Elizabeth McGovern, Lew Diamond Phillips, Matthew Broderick

Water Tigers exhibit smooth, creamy manners and seem to lead a charmed life. Great personal (and often early) success characterizes their lives. This Tiger is a lovable and loving creature, whose strength of will and determination to gain both respect and power are admirable. People honor and esteem the Water Tiger.

The Water Tiger is more stable and leads a more balanced life than many of his fellow Tigers. He is often artistic and able to perform in public with ease. Water Tigers tend to be musical and know how to imitate accents and speech patterns with remarkable accuracy. Having a good ear makes them natural linguists. Travel appeals to their taste for easy adventure: they prefer to go first class.

Discipline is not always a Tiger's strong suit but the Water Tiger is capable of protracted diligence in the accomplishment of work projects. He also boasts a socially pleasing personality and loves being with groups, making jokes and displaying his seductive talents. As this Tiger loves company, he will be a happy family person. He is reliable and takes responsibility for his kin and his home.

The Water Tiger is known for his sense of fairness. Unlike some Tigers who cannot tolerate advice or criticism, he is able to view his own shortcomings objectively. His open-minded approach to thorny issues might make him choose to study law. He would make an excellent magistrate: his judgements would be unbiased and humane.

Water Tigers are not so drivingly vain or ambitious as other Tigers. Scholarly pursuits such as philosophy, languages and comparative literature are possible but it's the entertainment professions – especially those concerned with music and communication – which will ensure both the Water Tiger's career stability and his joy. Barring success on the stage or screen, he might choose to be a professor, a literary agent or even a promoter of concerts or other spectacles.

Although they make excellent performers, these Tigers don't ache to appear bathed in spotlight every waking second of their lives. They can work contentedly behind the scenes, creating, inventing and planning. An eager, clear-thinking Water Tiger is a welcome addition to any group effort.

He is mostly a virtuous creature whose greatest fault is his rare but frightening rage. The Tiger cannot abide betrayal and will react rashly when he falls victim to it. But, as my mother used to say, 'Still waters run deep'. The Water Tiger appears calm and unruffled, affects a slick, jaunty exterior. He is everybody's pal – until he is wronged. The bitter anger which ensues is bloodthirsty and long-term vengeance-seeking dangerous.

Cultivate the friendship of this Tiger. Enjoy his love and bask in his charming company. Take him up on his proposal to collaborate. But don't try to do him in or he'll make Tiger baby food of you and slurp you up for breakfast.

Tiger health

The average Tiger believes that he is immortal and will always remain in excellent fettle. He is not one to hie himself to the doctor at every wince or stitch. Nor is he prudent. He is often run down from overexcitement and his highly strung nerves teeter on the edge of a permanent precipice.

The Tiger is always tense, never on time, constantly behind schedule and racing to keep up. Tigers *like* to be in a hurry. The Tiger is often in a rage over some injustice and freely engages in psyche-rattling debates. He hardly ever admits or even recognizes it, but he is almost always dead tired.

Tigers are born with a very sketchy, all up or all down health pattern. They are often imprecise and scornful of routine and they *hate* performing any task for the sake of mere maintenance.

By now we all know and accept that, to a large degree, our state of health depends on how we take care of our bodies. But even though they know better, Tigers don't take very good care of themselves – except in spurts. A Tiger woman may decide that she is going to lose twenty pounds in a month but if it takes longer, she loses interest instead of weight – the old instant victory syndrome again.

Blitz methods and quick results are all the Tiger knows. If he is obliged to calculate his food intake over a period of months to lose weight cautiously and definitively, he won't do it.

The Tiger is effective, fast and efficient – but he's not disciplined. He wants to have beautiful straight teeth all his life but if that means he has to brush them three times a day, use dental floss too and go to the dentist every six months, '*Bor*ing!' says the Tiger. He frequently has serious dental problems after forty.

A few Tigers manage to work out alone in gyms, showing tenacity, perseverance and demonstrating amazing personal strength. They are self-starting independent workers, too, and will use those various torture machines until their muscles are burning and their heads aswim. But don't ask Tigers to work out in a class or join a team – they hate groups (unless they are the head honcho) and being in one might mean getting to the gym at a certain hour on a certain day and Tigers don't like routine.

Hastiness and leaping before you look can mean that the Tiger life is full of accidents. I know a Tiger who dived into an empty swimming pool and, because Tigers are so lucky, survived with a few scrapes, bruises and concussion. You know those people on the road who ride your bumper? I bet more than half were born Tigers. Tigers like big fast cars, are born daredevils and have no time to waste.

Slowness in others and in life frustrates Tigers. Deliberate, painstaking cohorts thwart the Tiger's *élan*. He always feels he must blaze the trail. But the Tiger does a lot of navigating by the seat of his pants. He may miss the target and cause himself excruciating frustration, which leads to aggression – and here comes the unhealthy part. Sooner or later Tigers may have to slow down or be obliged to contain their enthusiasm. Frenzied activity is followed by total collapse which can cause the Tiger to become depressive and even to succumb to serious diseases such as heart attack or cancer. He can also fall into the trap of swallowing speed-up drugs or resorting to alcohol to pep himself up. Then he may have to turn to sedatives to slow him down. The Tiger often thrives on coffee and cigarettes until, one day, he finds himself flat on his back.

To avert the danger of this frantic pattern, the Tiger should practice a sport every day. Running, windsurfing, walking, biking and swimming are excellent because they force the highly strung Tiger to let off steam and relax his muscles. Yoga and meditation also do wonders for the tense Tiger spirit and body. He should only eat meat twice a week and stay away from carbonated soft drinks and canned foods. Fresh fruit encourages the Tiger's sluggish intestine to perform more regularly and should be eaten either half an hour before meals, three hours after a meal or just before going to bed.

The Chinese say that Tigers are given to sick headache, tic douloureux, fever, allergy and (because of their highly charged emotions) convulsions, sometimes even epilepsy. All are nerve-related disorders and stem from over-stimulation.

To avoid aggravating these complaints, the Tiger who wakes up tired even after a good night's sleep should start to recognize his limitations. If he is smart he will cultivate the art of spending a whole day in bed. A Tiger's bedside table should be well equipped with unread books and papers he's been wanting to catch up on. He should keep a ready supply of unfinished projects around the bedroom – things he can do in bed – so that his day of rest will not seem unfruitful (the Tiger hates sloth). A well-occupied, cozy day of recess will set the average Tiger back on all fours for a good month or so of chronic overdoing.

Although he frequently prefers the city, the Tiger should often get away to the country. Country people are gentler than city folk and the tone of rural life won't twang at the Tiger's exposed nerves. Also, country air and hardy physical jobs will fit the Tiger's excess energy bill to a 'T'.

Most of all, the Tiger must go to the doctor. Telling a Tiger to do this is about as effective as telling a housefly to turn into a 747 and fly you to Africa. Doctors irritate the independent Tiger, who thinks they are mostly overpaid pill pushers and admires only those who care for the poor or the suffering hungry masses. The Tiger may even consider that people who go to doctors are nothing but hypochondriacs or sissies. The Tiger, you will recall, is Mr Individualist.

You may also recall that lots of Tigers die young. They are stubbornly excessive, daredevils, undertake too much at once, don't want any interference and hate maintenance. Symptoms, lumps, bumps, odd bleedings, coughings, aches, pains or dizzy spells often go ignored. The Tiger does not want to appear weak and hasn't got time to be ill. Last summer, I suggested to a nervous, run-down Tiger that he might try vitamin therapy.

'Shut up,' was the answer to my kind suggestion.

I tried another tack. I have been a *very* sick little Tiger and I learned moderation the hard way. Now I try to maintain my good health. As my Tiger friend looked so tired, I thought I'd put him on to the homeopathic doctor who helped me regain my own equilibrium.

'Maybe you can just stay out of my business,' snapped the tired Tiger. 'Don't mother me. When I get round to it, I'll get some sleep.'

My Tiger friend chose to fall asleep at the wheel of his BMW on the way home from work one night. He got about three months' enforced rest but doesn't have circles under his eyes any more. So much for sharing health secrets with fearless fellow Tigers.

Tiger futures

What the Tiger should expect from the next twelve Chinese animal years

2008, the Earth Rat year – As you no doubt already know, the Rat always wants power. In relationships, in business or government, the Rat wants to dominate. Now for you Tigers, this peculiar Rat character trait is both unnerving and irritating in the extreme. You don't necessarily want to be in control of much of anything. Answering phone calls and e-mails in an office all day long, waiting for people to come to boring meetings, would bore you to extinction. But the Rat does not necessarily know this about you. You appear so strong and so sure of yourself that the nervous Rat feels threatened. Hence your life in the Rat year can prove to be less than delightful. The Rat may try to thwart even your most innocent desires for leadership, belittle your cleverest ideas and sabotage your plans. You see, the Rat not only wants power. He or she wants security and is a hoarder and a saver. You are a spender, a devil-may-care guy or woman who believes that money grows on trees and if you keep changing forests, there will always be more there for you. Conflict between your splurging spirit and the Rat's desire to stash will arise. Advice? Plan to travel this year and stay out of public view. If you don't menace the Rat in any way, he will do you the favor of ignoring you completely.

2009, the Earth Ox year – I must warn you off trying to make a lot of money or landing the prime job you long for in an Ox year. Why? Well, it is not only because the Ox doesn't want you to succeed. But also your speedy, catch-as-catch-can methods drive the Ox to distraction. As a long-term planner, he or she gets dizzy just watching you rev up and zip about. Ox people have a great talent for leading. They often become dictators. But they are not terribly quick on their feet and they are even slower in the *cabeza* department. Their brains function in an unhurried manner. Do they dawdle and take a leisurely approach to running their year or their empire? Not on your life they don't. But they churn and you pounce. Hence in an Ox year you are well advised in advance to remove at least one of your jet engines so as not to appear threatening or to confuse the ponderous drudgery-loving Ox. You won't have to bow and scrape to get ahead. But . . . you will need to do some 'yessing' to those in power. As you despise being anyone's 'yes-man' or woman, you may suffer digestive problems, migraines and other stress-related complaints as a result. Keep your romantic life in good fettle by making a special effort to commit loving acts of kindness and servility towards your sweetheart or spouse (or both) in this rather dicey, unfriendly Ox year. You need all the approval and affection you can garner from those who love and admire your saucy style.

2010, the Metal Tiger year – After a couple of slow but not disastrous years, you will take wing and soar over all you survey. I have mentioned several times that Oxen often become dictators. But curious as it may seem, so do Tigers. The style is different, but the aim is the same. Tigers like to imagine themselves the saviours of a people for a cause (Ho Chi Minh, Ayatollah Khomeini, Castro), whereas Oxen might just take over because they want to take over (Idi Amin, Saddam Hussein, Napoleon). So this is your year to rule. You will no doubt adore the power, but you probably will not abuse it as you will be using your superior position to further an ideal – something you are proud of and wish to impart to others. If, however, you let the notion of power for its own sake take over, you will have a dreadful Tiger year. Do also remember that this year you must plan the next twelve years of your existence. Don't let the months slip by without sitting down with yourself somewhere quiet (countryside, retreat, mountain top, etc.) and thinking hard about where you want to be in twelve years. Then decide how you want and need to behave in order to reach that goal. A dozen years may seem like a long time. But life is shorter than we think, and those who plan well ahead and stick to their timetables are those who live longest happiest.

2011, the Metal Cat year – Cat years are rife with elegance, keen on security and skittish about conflict. Your naturally hurried style and incorrigible taste for change doesn't always sit well with the Cat's love of refinement, which can mean you will meet with opposition if you attempt to bully your way into anything at all. My advice? In the Cat year, keep your elbows to yourself. Don't plunge ahead into new adventures without doing some serious planning and plotting beforehand. Even your best-laid plans must be laced with a good deal of strategy and cunning as the Cat may try to slow you down in all manner of clever (and possibly even underhanded) ways. If you fail at something in this sticky year, do not despair. Pick yourself up and start over. Diligence counts in Cat years. Romance with a capital 'R' will present itself a few times this year. The one thing the Cat cannot take from you is that inimitable Tiger charm. Love will bloom in unexpected places and times. No matter how hard you try to remain cool and collected, that old Tiger blood will rush and all four knees will buckle somewhere, sometime – a few times – during this (for you) rather bland Cat year.

2012, the Water Dragon year – Not the Tiger's year to shine. Rather, you should take a back seat during this chaotic and festive twelve months. Let the Dragon take the wheel and don't get any fancy ideas about back-seat driving. Dragons are lovingly egomaniacal. They want the floor, and if you don't concede the spotlight, they will simply douse the electricity and keep on keeping on by candlelight. Tigers are beloved by Dragons and are even perceived as allies and cronies. But both of you always want to take the lead. My advice?

Stay out of sight. Don't compete. Ponder your next coup. Think up new and amazing schemes to put into practice next year when the slinky Snake is in charge. Snakes never need to grab the limelight. It shines on them no matter what. Late in the Dragon year, you may lose something important – a document or a piece of jewelry or even a dear friend. Don't fret or sweat the disappearance of this element in your life. As time passes, you will note that it was not so vital as you imagined. Take advantage of the Dragon's willingness to run the show whilst you rest your weary bones at some exotic spa or peaceful retreat.

2013, the Water Snake year – A year of love and romance is ahead for Tigers when the luscious Snake is in charge. Better for you, Tiger, to be snuggled under the quilt with some sexy character you adore than to be racing about at your usual breakneck pace. Snakes hate to hurry. And they are not amused by your natural penchant for living life in the fast lane. Money will not avalanche into your bank account this year. But you will have tons more time and good luck when implementing projects and concocting business deals. Everything to do with luxury is favored now. Take stock of your own treasures and heed the sage advice of your lieutenants as to how best to dispose of them. There is much to be learned and advantage to be taken from the Snake's wisdom. Stop. Look. And listen to the lessons that this year has in store for you. If you can, slow to a crawl and don't look too busy. Snakes work hard. Then they lie down in some warm place and ponder the universe. Imitate them this year . . . especially when your new passion partner is in town.

2014, the Wood Horse year – In Horse years, Tigers are not always as lucky as usual. The Horse truly loves you and approves of your zany energy. But sometimes – only sometimes – misfortune befalls Tigers in Horse years. Don't panic. This bad luck is not life-threatening. But it does mean you will have to labor harder under somewhat adverse conditions in order to reach the kinds of summits of success for which you are so famous. I don't mean to imply that you won't have enough money or that you or some beloved family member will fall ill and die. But small events will arise as obstacles and may cause you grievances. More specifically, this Horse year can impinge on your natural good health. Here, because luck is not always on tap in Horse years, you will have to work harder to keep fit, avoid sugars and starches to stay thin and double up on the workouts at the gym. If you happen to be married or in a long-term relationship now, take your loved one on an exciting journey somewhere new and instructive. In Horse years, you will enjoy entering a whole new culture together, bringing back souvenirs, taking photos and maybe even making new friends. The mood will be jolly this year. But the work may prove difficult.

2015, the Wood Goat year – Tigers generally fare better under the Goat's influence this year, but they also have to fight harder to get what they want. The Goat and you do not view life in the same manner. Basically, Goats enjoy being tethered in fertile fields where they can work their creative magic without worrying about having to slog away on their own. You are quite the opposite. You are a born independent. You don't enjoy being tethered anywhere. Ever. As a result of this major difference in approach, in Goat years, you often feel disapproved of. Not that you give a single whisker whether or not you are liked or accepted by the Goat. But you do wish he wouldn't try to cramp your style. Ideally, in these years, you will do more traveling for business and pleasure. You will enjoy the roaming about. Meeting some new like-minded folks will help keep your furnaces stoked for the twelve rather languid months ahead. The money gods are on your side in Goat years. This may not mean millions will be showered on your tawny head, but it does signify that you are doing something right, i.e. itinerating!

2016, the Fire Monkey year – No monkeying around! This next twelve months will offer you a spree of activity just the way you like it. Multi-tasking and multi-meetings and multi-proposals for work, cultural and sports experiences. Take the Monkey up on all of these propositions. You, more than any other sign, can surely multi-manage such a variety of goings-on. Where other people might feel they have been bushwhacked by such a plethora of fresh things to learn and do, you revel in the newness of it all. A change in your work environment is in the offing this year too. You are a person whose enthusiasms need changing about as often as you change your shirt. So get cracking on finding that unusual job straightaway this year. You will not be sorry you did. Love life? Medium rare. I say that because the love situation you have been in for so long is well done by this time. Overdone, in fact. Hence, time to make big changes. Pounce a bit now from prey to prey. See how it feels to enjoy seduction again. Change is what the Monkey year is all about for Tigers. PS – Your current partner will more than likely be overjoyed to see your tawny rump slink out the door.

2017, the Fire Rooster year – Let the Rooster run the show. Or at least give him or her the impression they are in a position of leadership. Roosters like to move quickly into action, have their fun and (unlike yourself) prefer not to leave a trail of dead bodies behind. As you probably have a new love interest under your belt by this time, you will be busy thinking up new tactics to hang on to this prize. However, your nose needs some application to the grindstone this year. Roosters want to see people busy at work on their various projects and are not amused by stragglers. So keep a high profile. When you are laboring in the hot sun or mining coal deep underground, groan a lot and sweat profusely to let your superiors know just how tough Tiger life can be. Otherwise, if you are not stealing his fire, the Rooster will leave you to your myriad own devices. Travel and visits to relatives in distant cities is favored now. There is a family member that you have been avoiding. Make it your business to pay them homage. It is in your financial interest to be kind to them now and make amends for any past neglect.

2018, the Earth Dog year – Phew! There is relatively little that can go plumb wrong for a Tiger in Dog years. You and Dogs get on well together because you have similar beliefs and take a world view of even the most minor events. Differences of opinion arise when you sense the Dog's innate paranoia rising to the surface out of nowhere. Dogs possess a unique understanding of Murphy's Law; they know instinctively that something that can go wrong will go wrong, and they are more than willing to announce it ahead of time. Hence, in Dog years an ambience of free-floating anxiety hovers about which drives Tigers round the proverbial bend. My advice to Tigers in this otherwise somewhat thorny year is to enjoy the goodwill that the Dog offers you as his protective companion. Bask a bit. Let up on the accelerator at work. Spend some enriching down time just hanging out with friends or family – or both. In Dog years you can also enjoy engaging in cultural jaunts. Take tours of exotic lands where you have always promised yourself that one day you would go. Go see the Pyramids or visit Niagara Falls. Do something wonderful for yourself, but leave the Dog and his paranoia at home.

2019, the Earth Pig year – Pigs confess to a certain gaping awe when confronted by you gadabout Tiger people. Pigs are strong, knowledgeable and culturally adept folks. But they do not understand your exaggerated need for change. You are forever buzzing about, never lighting long enough to accumulate capital or amass riches or collect art or luxurious homes or whatever it is that the Pig sees as wealth. Nevertheless, the Pig and you can be bosom buddies. You admire the Pig's purity and authenticity of spirit. What he doesn't understand about you is what will get in your way this year. The air of plenty will lead you to assume you can spend and give and squander your money, and so – in a word or two – you overspend. If you are not more careful about where your money is going in the first part of this Pig year, by September you will find yourself behind a financial eight ball. So tighten your stripes, Tiger. Contain your desire to be too generous to those you love or those you feel are in need. Hang on to your war chest and do not sell the family jewels in order to acquire a fancy new car to impress your sweetie. Put yourself on a budget. Give wantonly of your love but take fewer fiscal risks. Slow down. Sit still. Read. Knit. Go to the countryside. Sit under a tree and think.

The Cat Out of the Bag

Ah Virtuous Cat!

You seek harmony. You are careful and practice discretion in all things. When you sense a conflict lurching your way, you skitter off and hide. Distinguished, diplomatic and well-mannered, you are also as nervous as a cat. Culture and refinement comfort you. You don't hate money either: you know instinctively how to earn and keep your fortune without flash or flaunt. You favor traditional antique furnishings over chrome and glass contemporary. You're a soft-stepping go-getter . . . ambitious but never aggressive, strong but never rough. Your brand of wisdom says that 'He who fights and runs away lives to fight another day.'

You are hypersensitive – squeamish, even. You are a bit of a hypochondriac: an innocent hangnail on your big toe alarms you. 'Call an ambulance, Get me to the emergency room!' Chronic illnesses – migraine, asthma, hayfever, lower back pain, warts, hives – you've tried them all.

Buy yourself a big house in the country, then fill it with brilliant, well-behaved kids. Choose a partner from among gentle Goats, scrupulous Pigs or loyal Dogs. If you're feeling lavish, remember that Snakes are delighted to languish on

Cats' velvet divans. Avoid Tigers, Roosters and Dragons. Their unrelenting panache threatens your tranquil existence. You plan your life to run smoothly. And usually it does. But should spontaneity enter the picture and events go awry – you freak out. Take my advice and lighten up. Not only on yourself but, more especially, on the rest of us.

With all due respect,

Suzanne White

In the twentieth and twenty-first century all Cats were born between the following dates:

29	January	1903	and	15	February	1904
14	February	1915	and	2	February	1916
2	February	1927	and	22	January	1928
19	February	1939	and	7	February	1940
6	February	1951	and	26	January	1952
25	January	1963	and	12	February	1964
11	February	1975	and	30	January	1976
29	January	1987	and	16	February	1988
16	February	1999	and	4	February	2000
3	February	2011	and	22	January	2012

The Cat ID card

Lasting symbols have special powers. Enhance your self-image by surrounding yourself with tangible signs of your own identity and make these symbols known to your friends and loved ones. Use them daily and they will bring you luck, security and a feeling of personal worth.

Your best
color is grey
flower is rose
fragrance is shalimar
tree is poplar
flavor is tangy
musical instrument is piano
birthstone is sapphire
lucky number is 4

Your favorite
food is fish
animal is squirrel
drink is bordeaux
spice is pepper
metal is bronze
herb is tarragon

The Cat is yin ***The Cat's motto is: 'I retreat'***

In pussycat mode, the Cat person is sensitive, tactful, home-loving, refined, prudent, discreet, long-living, ambitious, cultured, well-mannered, artistic, considerate, scholarly, suave, graciously hospitable, modest and unimpeachably virtuous.

But rub his fur the wrong way and he becomes snobbish, secretive, pedantic, complicated, haughtily indifferent, self-indulgent, hypochondriacal, punctilious, judgemental, self-righteous, deceptive, self-centered and terminally condescending.

The Cat personality

For years, I stubbornly clung to the idea of using Cat as the name of this fourth Chinese sign. I learned Asian astrology from the Vietnamese in Paris, and they use Cat. For a few years, I received mail from Chinese people protesting: in China, it seems, they resolutely use Rabbit instead. So I went through a period where I called this sign Cat/Rabbit. Then, more recently, I received a letter from a Chinese person asking me to go back to Cat because the only reason that the Chinese do use Rabbit is that the powers that were in olden times considered that the Cat slept too much to serve as a good role model for the peasants. Hence they turned to the eager jumpy bunny Rabbit and made him the symbol for this fourth sign of the Chinese Zodiac. Basically, I confess, I never got their Rabbit idea. What sort of personality does a Rabbit have? I don't really know. But I do know that Cats have personality. Lots of it. Result? I am going back to Cat. It works for me. It worked for most of my readers for twenty years, until I tried to accommodate everybody and invented Cat/Rabbit. That was pretty silly. The moral: you can please some of the people some of the time but you cannot please all of the people all of time.

Cats are discretion incarnate. They live quietly, in refined surroundings, prefer to ask very little of others and are not keen on entertaining just any old company. Cats observe the world from their place on the hearth, meticulously scrutinizing their own and others' behavior. No matter how successful or socially respectable they are, Cats often feel unsure of themselves, worrying about the impression they make, wondering if their gestures and actions are acceptable and decorous enough to pass muster with higher-ups.

Although he always claims to be ready to learn new things, the Cat is not a willing traveller or changer of address. Ideally, he lives in a harmonious relationship in a lovely home with close friends and family nearby. Despite his native curiosity and dreams of touring exotic lands, home is still the best place for a Cat. He feels safe and secure, comfortable and cozy in his own home and would prefer never to spend so much as a night elsewhere.

Nothing gets under the Cat's sensitive skin more irritatingly than disorder. He is fastidious about structure. He hates chaos, deplores anarchy and refuses to have anything much to do with liberalism. Although he might claim to adhere to the principles and espouse some of its more humane aspects, the sternly traditional Cat does not see any better way to run the world than to maintain a rigid social structure – even at the cost of justice and, if necessary, under the yoke of tyranny.

Therefore, he possesses an odd combination of conflicted characteristics. He sincerely believes in justice, yet, he is mostly unwilling to stick out his delicate neck to make certain that it gets done. He will speak at length about his pet theories and share his rigid opinions on many issues, but when it comes to defending them, debating openly or standing up for issues he claims to hold dear, the Cat disappears.

Cats cling to old-fashioned tenets and are virtually cemented in their ways. They feel that dissension should be kept out of life altogether, preferring to ignore discord and pretend that violence never existed. Cats like books that don't upset or frighten them, rigorously avoid seeing disturbing movies or TV shows and steer a wide berth around truth-revealing confrontations.

The Cat constantly seeks protection from reality. You will rarely find one of these vulnerable creatures beating a path to the scene of an accident. Cats are afraid of their own shadows and do not want to live in or deal with tumult or upheaval. They also hate tardiness and have no patience with procrastination. For the Cat, all aspects of life should be clear-cut, well thought-out, on schedule and up front. If Cats had their way, all human beings would be preordained, by birth, social status and degree of civilization to fit neatly into 'life slots', do their respective jobs well, marry, procreate, die and get buried in the local churchyard.

Messiness and confusion are the Cat's worst enemies but should he encounter either, the Cat rolls up his sleeves and dives in to put it to rights. Cats will take charge of de-mildewizing your fridge, untangling three hundred feet of garden hose or clearing weeds out of a vegetable patch in a trice. Cats so dislike anything they feel is opposed to the natural order that they often jump self-righteously at the chance to make order out of chaos. Some call it meddling.

In recent years, I have been living in a pretty tile-roofed cottage in a village in the countryside, one hour outside Paris. Across the road lives my Cat friend, Madame Léa, who is the respected doyenne of our community. Léa resides quietly in her own small house with a neatly tended garden that she cultivates with loving, expert care. Her windows face mine.

For the first year I noticed Léa and the neighbors observing me. They were friendly, but when I passed, they spoke behind their hands. It appeared I didn't have any fixed hours: I didn't eat lunch at noon and dinner at 8 p.m. Why did I leave the shutters closed in the day and only open them at 4 o'clock in the afternoon? Was I a night watchwoman? A dancer in a night club up in Paris? Maybe even a drug dealer?

One day, I stopped to chat with perky white-haired Madame Léa. She asked me to step into her cozy salon. She repaired to her usual chair and bade me sit. 'People are talking,' she explained. 'They don't understand.'

'About what?' I asked.

'They don't see why you don't open and close your shutters,' she said shyly.

'But I do,' I protested. 'Whenever I use a room, I open those shutters. But if I'm not in there, I leave them shut.'

'Why?' she inquired.

As I had no answer, I decided to embroider a little story which might make sense to village people. 'I have a rare eye disease,' I invented, 'that requires me to live practically all the time in the dark. I chose this leafy forested village and my house's northern exposure so I wouldn't have sun.'

Madame Léa was more than understanding. But a couple of weeks later, she came to my door, slipped herself Cat-like inside and whispered, 'I don't want a sou for this. It's a favor.'

Was she offering to cook me a meal or volunteering to sew some curtains? 'What favor?' I asked suspiciously.

'From now on, I will open and shut your shutters for you,' she said. I stared at her agape. I had lived in France for thirty years but I had never heard of this sort of service before. 'Oh, it's an easy job,' said Madame Léa, reassuringly. 'Of course, I am not as strong as I was but I can still take care of shutters.'

Nothing made sense in her proposition, so I declined. I thought it a little invasive of Léa to suggest that I needed a person to do what I didn't want done.

A few days later, she came tap-tapping again. She entered, sat and exposed her case. 'The villagers don't see why you won't let me take care of your shutters.' There was a sob in her voice.

At first, I took umbrage. How could anyone decide for another when to open and shut shutters? The very concept was difficult for a private Tiger like me to grasp. 'Why can't I just leave my shutters alone if I want to?' I asked.

'In these parts, shutters are opened in the morning and closed at dusk,' she explained. 'The mayor prefers it that way.'

How had this salient village detail escaped me? The way Léa presented the situation, it seemed my shutter whimsy was affecting the mayor's aesthetic sense.

She went on. 'The village looks more uniform like that. Less gloomy. In the daytime, when the shutters are open, it looks like everybody's home.'

'Why must they be shut at dusk?' I asked.

'So people don't see you,' she told me, 'or come in and kill you.'

I suddenly remembered that Léa was born in 1903 and that Cats hate disorder. I didn't want to relinquish my shutter freedom but knowing that, to Léa, a Cat woman *par excellence*, my shutter pattern signified that Mother Nature's very digestive system was in turmoil, I agreed to make her shutter-patrol captain of my house.

Cat people are masters of self-pity. Their experiences are always more traumatic than yours, their family history more tragic. I know a superbly talented musician Cat in Paris named Jeff, who blames the world for everything that has ever gone wrong in his life. When he was in his twenties, trying to make it in New York as a young composer, he complained about his mother, that he was generous with her, but she was stingy with him, had never given him enough affection and had always criticized his work.

By the time he was in his thirties, Jeff claimed that his young wife, Lucia, to whom he had only ever been adorable and giving, had become selfish and insensitive. At the age of forty-two, he divorced her. By forty-five, he lamented that his ruin was being caused by his former partner, Steve Stern, now a famous rock star, who had pirated Jeff's melodies and elbowed him out of all the important deals.

A couple of years ago I saw him in a café in central Paris. 'Hey, Jeff,' I shook his hand, 'You look great. How are things?'

'I've met the most wonderful woman. We are going to make a record together. Sylvie is the best thing that ever happened to me. She's kind and generous, and easy-going as hell. This relationship is going to change my life.'

I was pleased. Jeff writes the best songs around yet, partly because he always felt sorry for himself and couldn't accept even constructive criticism, he had never made it. Maybe at last he had met a real soul mate who wouldn't try to use him like all the others he'd got close to in the past.

Last year I ran into Jeff in Montparnasse. Now in his early fifties, he looked sixty-five, grey-faced and miserable. 'Hi there, Jeff,' I said tentatively. 'How's it going?'

'Terrible,' he replied, gesturing for me to sit down. 'My girl left me.'

'Oh, I am sorry,' I said, and ordered a *café au lait*.

'Don't be,' said Jeff. 'She was no damned good, anyway. She was selfish, stingy and pig-headed.'

'What about that record you made together?'

'Nah,' said Jeff with a shrug. 'The record didn't sell because Sylvie always wanted center stage. She stole all my songs and then took off.'

'Just like Steve did ten years ago, huh?' I said.

Jeff perked up. 'Yeah.'

'I never saw Sylvie,' said I. 'Was she pretty?'

'Looked just like my mother,' said Jeff. 'And you know, she had a big mouth, like my first wife, Lucia. And she had that same critical personality.'

I finished my coffee, commiserated a bit more with Jeff about how tough his life had always been and excused myself.

As I strolled up the Boulevard Raspail towards my house, it struck me that Jeff was about my age – but not quite. He was born in 1939 – a Cat year. I should have known.

One reason for this is that Cats worry about being perfect: they always strive to be liked, to be acceptable company and to do the right thing. Cats need to appear virtuous in the eyes of others. Yet they don't always manage to maintain their virtue – which drives them a little mad, skewing their judgement.

It's logical – if you need to be considered wonderful by others and you know that you are not always perfectly wonderful, rather than admit it to yourself you simply declare that others are flawed, which allows you to rise in your own estimation.

If you know any Cats who are given to self-pity, don't tell them about their flaws. It only reinforces their belief that you are trying to reduce them to apple sauce. Cats need encouragement, lots of security and indulgence. Detractors abstain.

Cats are proud of their honesty. In their quest for nice-guy status, they make every effort to be trustworthy. Where money and deals are concerned, they are as wide open as Montana. 'Hi. Come on in. Do sit down. So good to see you. What'll it be? How's your wife?'

When you begin dealing with a Cat, you think you've stumbled into goody-goody heaven. On the surface, he is nice, good, straightforward and hospitable. Everything is overwhelmingly pleasant. You drink in the welcome and willingly absorb the warmth. After a few of these friendly encounters, you are ready to give the old Cat your shirt. He seems so reliable, always on time, never makes promises he doesn't keep . . . you are convinced that this guy is A-OK.

Soon, after extending a few of his special small favors, the Cat offers to let you use his daughter's old car while yours is in the garage.

You protest. Thanks very much, but you can just as easily rent one.

The Cat urges you not to be ridiculous, 'Lisa's away at college. The car is just sitting out there.'

You sputter a bit more about how you don't want to put him out and what if the kid comes home unexpectedly and can't go anywhere?

He answers with a laugh, implying you shouldn't be so silly. It's no imposition: 'Just to get that old Fiat going, you'll have to put in a new battery. And it probably wouldn't hurt to have the fan belt replaced. But as soon as you do that the old clunker will be fine for a while.'

You realize that you are being asked to pay to fix Lisa's car. Then you get to use it for two weeks while yours is being repaired and next month when Lisa comes home from college, her car will be in good running fettle. In the Cat, what appears to be largesse or *noblesse oblige* may not always be without ulterior motive. What appears to be hospitality may be something quite different. Twelve years ago, when I was trying to get well after a debilitating illness, I had decided to return to France. A young French Cat friend, la Princesse Charlotte de la Rochequitombe, wrote to me from Paris inviting me to live at her mother's house with my kids while I recuperated. 'Maman is inviting you. As long as you need,' said Charlotte's note.

I resisted vigorously.

'But Maman knows your whole story. She says you can stay as long as you like. There's plenty of room. Marianne's apartment is free now. Besides,' Charlotte added, 'Maman is lonely since Marianne got married. It will do her good to have you nearby and to be with the children. Please accept our hospitality.'

I was desperate. And very tempted. The kids were twelve and thirteen. Charlotte's mother's village was close to the international school where I wanted to send them. I needed a place to live. Also, a few years previous, Charlotte had lived with me for a particularly rocky university term: she had some extravagantly gauche political views and was not getting along with Maman. The offer was appealing: I had been gravely ill, I was weak, had green skin, no hair, oodles of medical bills and no money. I finally accepted, thinking that when I was feeling stronger and had made some money, I would find something to rent.

A month later, we arrived. Charlotte was there to greet us and Maman was away on a short trip. The accommodation was a lovely duplex apartment built into an old stone, beamed barn with two bedrooms, a loft bed-sitting room and a second bath upstairs. The kids and I embraced Charlotte, so grateful to be safe in such pleasant surroundings.

In a day or so, Charlotte's mother, a dark-haired, well-preserved beauty, returned. A Duchess or a Marquise or whatever. First morning back, she came a-calling at the apartment. I opened the door, gushed greetings and gratitude and bade her sit.

'No, thank you,' she said sternly. 'I have much work to do this morning.' She opened an exquisite large oak Louis XV *armoire* into which she had built a series of shelves for dishes. I watched while she fingered the cups on the first shelf. She turned to look at me. 'Do you put cups away like this in America?' she asked in perfect British English.

'Yes,' I said meekly. 'I suppose I do. I'm left-handed.'

'We don't put our cups away like this here. Why didn't Charlotte tell you this?' demanded Maman.

'Perhaps she forgot,' I said. 'But if it makes you more comfortable, I'll put them back the right-handed way. I had no idea . . .'

'Do you have the money?' she said, closing the *armoire* and locking it. 'I prefer cash.'

'I'm sorry but I don't understand,' I said.

'Surely Charlotte told you the amount of the rental,' she said with a smile of superior indulgence that could have slashed through the huge diamond on her finger.

My old pal, Charlotte-the-Cat, had forgotten to tell me that I was not to be her mother's guest but rather . . . her new star tenant. Of course! I said to myself, mentally slapping my forehead with the heel of my hand. Cats are chronically neurotic about leaving out sections of information which might elicit conflict or cause them discomfort. I should have known better: Cats had proffered me loaded gifts before: the offer of an excellent deal on a Cat's house where the taxes turned out to be astronomically high. 'But,' says the Cat, 'If *you* go to the tax office, I know you can get those taxes down. Then you'll have a great bargain.' *He* is not going to the tax office. *You* do it. You're braver. You tell the lawyer. You ring up the doctor. You ask the boss. It's the Cat's chicken way of facing facts. He'll applaud while you risk your neck.

Not only do Cats bob, weave and dodge direct collisions, they also retreat. They stealthily back out of what you might naïvely consider done deals. My good Cat friend, Adam, is brilliant. His manners are impeccable, his style irreproachable. He is a fountain of wisdom. Just to be in his pleasant company for a meal or a movie defines the word cordiality. But . . . after knowing him for almost ten years, I have become circumspect about the inescapable aspect of his Cat character. Adam, like so many Cats, wants to please. Conviviality is like a drug to him. He needs to make each of his friends feel that he or she is the single most important person in his life at any given moment, which is never to be lost because you are both going to perpetuate it soonest. Adam's goodbyes are always chock-a-block with plans for the next meeting. So far Adam and I have planned to take the Orient Express, drive across the United States in his sports car, tour Poland on foot, walk across Hannibal's route in the Alps and then collaborate on a book about it.

Adam-the-Cat always wants you to feel that all he craves is more time with you in a more intense way. When the time for execution of the plan comes round you ring him up: 'Hi kid. Have you bought your gear for the big Polish walk?' you ask jauntily.

Adam has forgotten. He is sorry but he can't. He meant to get back to you on that but he's met this ballet dancer and she's invited him to Moscow for her début. Don't make far-reaching plans with skittish Cats unless you simultaneously confiscate their passports.

Meanwhile, back at the *château*, when Charlotte came home from her office that fateful evening, I charged right over to confront her with the drama which had occurred in her absence. 'Charlotte, I cannot pay your mother five hundred dollars a month. I am broke. My publisher owes me money but I won't have that till April. Why didn't you tell me? We could have stayed in a cheaper place until we get back on our feet.'

'I did not want to hurt you,' she shrugged. 'And also, I did not want to upset Maman.'

Most of all, Charlotte didn't want to hurt Charlotte. Lesson number one in dealing with Cat people is *'Delve.'* Don't take anything at face value. Cats deplore and despise anything antagonistic. They *always* pussyfoot.

The children and I survived the incident at the Château de la Rochequitombe. Within days I found us a tiny flat in our old Paris neighborhood and we moved away from Hospitalityville. Hard feelings? You bet. Charlotte and I have not spoken since.

Pedantry is another little Cat fault. Cats like to be qualified as intellectuals. They read voraciously and spend much of their time cultivating their minds. Many gain an encyclopedic knowledge of a variety of subjects. In conversation, should you touch on one of the areas where the Cat feels knowledgeable you may never voice a further word. Cats are notorious holders-forth. When they decide to wax eloquent, you can forget about their reputation for modesty and prudence. They detest being contradicted. If you dare to interrupt, Cats won't shush you or order you to let them finish, they filibuster. They talk right through your protestations, out-shout you and hold the floor so tightly that you cannot get a claw in edgewise.

Despite their general affability and air of constant goodwill, Cats are not really hail-fellows-well-met. There is nothing easy-going about them. They are essentially stand-offish, snobbish, bourgeois and maniacal about petty details.

They are also sentimental and maudlin. Cats cry at the drop of an onion. They are moved to tears by the passing thought of a dead ladybird. They are forever 'shuddering to think' of one icky thing or another. Yet, oddly, they are as fascinated as they are horrified by the gruesome bits of human interest stories. Sometimes I wonder if Cats don't revel in sorrow. They seek out melodrama, stalking the pages of local newspapers to uncover even the tiniest shred of tragedy, then announcing, 'Have you heard what happened over in Bunkersville?' The Cat moves along in his practiced horror-show tone, 'A man was washing his spinach in four changes of water. He forgot to close his waste disposal unit. All at once tons of the spinach flew down the sink, he tried to catch it and . . .'

You can guess what happened.

But the Cat barrels recklessly on. 'The poor man stuck his hand down there to save his spinach and . . .'

Yuck.

The Cat tells us all his second-hand sadness stories and regales us with the goriest of woeful events because, as long as they aren't happening under his nose, he feels both safe and a tiny bit naughty. However, this fascination with other people's dire circumstances can be a dangerous game for Cats. First of all, it's downright catty – pure gossip. But secondly – and more dangerously – the Cat's preoccupation with doom, gloom, hopelessness and misfortune can undermine whatever intestinal fortitude he ever had. It's as though he were trying to deflect from the central issue by captivating himself and us with mawkish drivel. All Cats should beware of this tendency as it threatens to diminish their image in the eyes of those whom they think count.

Cats are squeamish and shy of contact with the seamy side of life. To protect himself from it, the Cat will take refuge in his cozy, luxurious, safe home life. Great wars or famines may occur yet the Cat will show only a mild interest, tutting and wiggling his whiskers in disgust. He is 'upset' about the Ethiopian famine and the Mexican earthquake, may even be visibly moved but he'd rather not discuss it. He's a regular *revolutionaire de salon*, always claiming to be ready to fight the big battle – from the safety of his favorite antique armchair. You are not likely to find many Cats down in the flood plains bailing water out of ditches, carrying babies to safety under mortar fire or manning the front lines in anybody's war. The Cat prefers to stay out of the fray.

Cats feel it their duty or mission to maintain decorum and social respectability. Think of Queen Victoria, a Cat if ever there was one. She practically invented etiquette. Generations have been touched by her idea of good form. Cats not only like to think they know how to behave but they also work hard at demonstrating good taste. His discriminating interior decoration alone denotes the Cat's penchant for favoring refinement and tradition above all else. Cats invariably choose to live in gracious, well-decorated surroundings. Their furniture is usually traditional. The colors they choose are neutral: beiges, greys and subtle or natural shades. If his budget allows, the Cat will opt for high ceilings, carved moldings, heavily curtained french windows and elegant oriental carpets. If not, he may settle for the inclusion of one gorgeous antique highlighted against a sober, modern backdrop.

The Cat's wardrobe is sedate. He enjoys the feel of luxurious cashmere but will rarely be caught in a bright yellow or fuchsia sweater. Buff, bone colors, russet and sometimes navy blue accessorized by plain-cut shoes of finest leather mark the style of most Cats I have known and loved. I know a Cat woman doctor in the South of

France who sports Burberry tweed suits, plain leather pumps and heavy twill raincoats in summer. As a professional, she feels compelled to maintain a certain dress code. Although she has a lovely figure, this woman wouldn't think of wearing anything but the dumpiest of classics. Her colleagues may allow themselves the luxury of smart little summer frocks but to my friend the Cat, they don't look properly dressed: a doctor wears suits, preferably tweed and Burberry.

Finally, the Cat is the aristocrat of the Chinese zodiac. He is content to live outside the swarm, in ease, to direct operations from the wings, give orders to underlings, delegate authority and accept an honored social position without making any hands-on effort. He is bright, charming, witty and friendly. People enjoy his company and admire his polished manner and dignified lifestyle. The Cat will never be a fist fighter but he does uphold definite ideals. He will do anything to keep his distance from personal conflict, bloodshed, social unrest or any potential clash. It is not surprising that, to the Chinese, this character is known as 'the Happy Rabbit'. He is *determined* to protect his comfort, a pleasant well-bred person devoted to self-preservation and often devoid of altruism, conscience or humanity. The moral struggle between good and evil does not unreasonably trouble the extenuated Cat's soul.

To ensure the survival of his snug way of life or keep his psyche's integrity intact, the Cat is capable of elaborate subterfuge. This underhand behavior can range from ignoring pleading letters to recording phone conversations unbeknown to the caller, blackmail, or the concocting of dissimulations so baroque as to make hair grow on your ear drums. Worst of all, cornered Cats, apprehensive of confrontation, are capable of self-delusion bordering on madness.

Mother Cat

What sets the Cat woman apart and gives her the reputation of being a cut above the rest of us is her distinguished air of refinement. She often appears shy and retiring. Her quiet charm may be accompanied by an air of pale melancholy or hurt. The lady Cat has a wistful look that makes one want to cuddle her and reassure her that everything will be all right. Men, of course, adore her.

Cat women are meticulous about their *toilettes*. They attach the utmost importance to the elements of their wardrobes as well as to their *ensembles*. Everything must harmonize. Colors must blend and tones complement one another. With her exaggerated concern for propriety, she will never appear dishevelled before others. She is the sort of woman who puts on make-up to run to the store for a loaf of bread, answers the postman's ring dressed in her best silk morning coat and appears before her lover or husband in a sedate satin gown covering a bridally prim négligé every night of her life. She works hard at staying thin and takes excellent care of skin and nails.

Cat girls are generally blessed with a perfectly oval face. Their features are fine, the forehead smooth, the nose straight and the mouth small and surrounded by thinnish lips. Her teeth are usually straight and pearly white. The Cat woman's eyes are soft, large and moist, lending a seductive, long-suffering air to an already sweet face. Her creamy complexion and pinkish cheeks add luster and give her a translucent, youthful glow.

As a rule, Cat women are not tall or long-legged. Their young bodies are taut and move with a certain grace. Trousers and jeans suit their well-rounded *derrières*, discreetly setting off their slim waists. As they get older, the Cat's delicate skin sometimes loses elasticity and she may grow thick in the middle well before the age of sixty. As she is very cautious about maintaining the proper weight and attentive to grooming, daily exercise would help her keep her girlish figure. Unfortunately, the Cat woman is rarely athletic, preferring a sedentary evening's purring with a book to performing rigorous, repetitive physical feats on a hard unfriendly floor.

Her body language is never blatant or outrageous. She moves in a modest, unassuming way. The Cat woman is not comfortable with her adult sexuality and often displays adolescent clumsiness, which serves to enhance her demure girlish charm.

By contrast to her male counterpart, the female Cat is stronger-minded and more sure of foot. Classical Cat characteristics such as hypersensitivity and sentimentality, gushing emotions and chronic 'weepies' are somehow more seemly in women than in men and the Cat woman is not as frequently obliged as her Tomcat brothers to camouflage her sensitive nature.

All Cat women are fearful. Even when they live, as they almost always try to, in a safe, secure environment Cat women routinely double lock every entrance and exit and have more alarm systems than Manhattan. Cat women are secretive about their habits, ultra cautious about when and where they use public transport and shrink in horror when faced with any danger.

Health matters unduly concern the Cat woman. She is anxious about everything. She complains continually about her symptoms: endless headaches, joint pain, lower back trouble, asthma, hayfever, tightness in the chest, knots in the stomach, weariness and general fatigue to name but a smattering.

Yet she is far from a simpering layabout: she is hardy, hardworking, never afraid to dig right into the toughest labor, always pulls her weight in group projects and takes pains to prove her worth at all times. What can be annoying is that her own herculean efforts impress her – a lot!

Where a Dragon lady might tear into a task, pull it apart and throw it back together without a second thought, or an Ox might decide overnight to get up early and single-handedly move Manchester or Buffalo to another location, then lope off into the fields and hatch a calf, a Cat woman will accomplish feats of labor worthy of the most rugged men. Then she'll never stop talking about it: 'I'm so exhausted. Do you know what I did today? Have you any idea the amount of work I got through this morning?' Cat women are capable but not stoical. They are able-bodied and willing but do not bear pain or adversity in silence. They are thin-skinned and unafraid to show it.

A marvellous quality native to the Cat woman which somehow escapes her more egocentric male brothers is altruism. She is one woman you can always call on in a pinch. She'll pop right over and help you move the furniture before hubby gets home to stop you. She'll take your kids to dance class so you can tryst with your lover at three. She's amiable, and happy to be of assistance. She loves animals and will adopt slews of orphaned cats and even form or join organizations to rescue whales or penguins or stray bison.

The Cat woman offers a reliable shoulder to cry on. Her sympathies are always with her friends and she will defend their interests in discussions and disputes with much more mettle and might than she could ever defend her own. As she is not forceful about looking out for her own whiskers, perhaps she finds strength in fending for others. But the Cat woman is notorious for beating a retreat soon after she has made a foray into altruistic endeavor. She would like to be eternally kind but if she delves too deeply and truly gets 'involved', she's afraid of reprisals.

Feminism does not tempt the Cat woman: she is anything but militant and feels no need to struggle against the system for rights she does not think she needs – some might accuse her of smugness or self-satisfaction. But the Cat woman is a rank and file traditionalist who believes in building on what is already there. She is horrified by revolution and frightened of gender confrontation: men, she feels, will be men. She cannot trouble herself to imagine how they might be persuaded to be different.

The Cat woman gives the impression of thoughtfulness – maybe it stems solely from her desire to display good manners but she never fails to bring a gift or a bottle of wine to a dinner party. She remembers to cut your favorite flowers from her garden and calls you on your birthday. Couple this with her gift for listening to sob stories and you discover that the Cat woman has remarkable talent for long-term friendships. She possesses true generosity of spirit. Underneath the arch decorum lives a caring person who is brilliantly able to uphold her end of a relationship.

Despite her marked tendency to weep and wail at the slightest provocation, the female Cat is not soft-hearted. Rather, she is level-headed and coldly logical. She may have an excellent grasp of cerebral matters but where the heart is concerned, the female Cat is a dunce. Although she openly makes mistakes and has glaring flaws, she rarely, if ever, indulges weakness in others. She tends to be judgemental and critical and will employ any amount of ruse or guile to get what she wants.

Zelda, born in a Cat year, began her association with me by lying about her age. She told me she was born in 1937. Although she looked a bit older, I believed her. She approached me once to ask if she might live in my French house while I went to America for a few months. Zelda was an American who had spent the last twenty years travelling and living in Europe, and painting abstracts. Her sob stories were legion. Everybody Zelda had known had tried to do her in. Her art career had gone nowhere because she had had to move all the time. She was a dedicated artist but people just didn't take her seriously. They criticized her unjustly. To Zelda, all that mattered was her work. She would be so happy to have a nice house to hang her paintings in but she had never been able to afford it because, you understand, she was a true artist.

When Zelda arrived at my house for our first meeting, she was driving a large red school bus with 1984 Tennessee licence plates tacked on both ends. 'This is my travelling studio,' she said, with an engaging grin. 'I can live in there all summer but in the winter it gets too cold, even in Greece or the South of France, so I need a house.'

Zelda also exposed the story of her life as a poor young woman from San Francisco whose painting career had been thwarted by her husband's many unreasonable demands. She explained how he had died, leaving her a little money. Ever since, she had been gypsying around Europe, painting pictures. In winter, she usually used Americans' houses in various countries in exchange for caretaking and paying the utilities.

On the strength of an evening's intense conversation, I agreed to allow her to use my house for three months while I went to the States. I did not know Zelda's Chinese sign: because she insisted she had been born in 1937 I was under the false impression that she was an Ox. Oxen are homebodies, householders and straight dealers in business.

My business dealings and in-house experience with Cats has always been less than straightforward. Cats love to weave intricate tales designed to keep them out of the line of fire. Also, they nearly always need to think they are fooling someone. I would never have lent a strange Cat my house, my utilities and my telephone.

For security's sake, Zelda had given me a modest check for the first month's utility bills. I accepted it, put it in my purse and didn't think about it until about two months later when a friend who lives in the same village rang me in New York to say, 'Suzanne, I went yesterday to see your friend Zelda and your furniture has all been moved out of the living room and front bedroom.'

'I'm coming home soon for some business in Paris,' I said. 'I'll go down there right away and have it out with her.'

I tried to ring Zelda the next day but there was no answer. I rang my friend, who told me 'She's gone to Greece. To have an exhibition.'

To cut a long story short, I got home and found, to my horror, the living room and guest bedroom empty – except that, attached to the multiple beams throughout the two rooms, were about twenty-five gigantic mean-looking abstract scrawlings in lightning-bolt patterns and shades of red, yellow and black, hung out like tawdry laundry – I presume, to dry. There were volcanoes of dishes around the kitchen and the sheets on the bed hadn't been changed since I'd left for America two months earlier.

I did not go mad. I simply wrote Zelda a note asking her to be ready to leave by the time I got back from the business trip I had to go on to the South of France.

When Zelda returned the next week she didn't contact me. I called my friend who told me Zelda had refused to accept or read the note. I rang Zelda, informed her verbally of the note's contents and said I would be showing up next Thursday so please be there to settle up for the phone and electricity.

Three days before my arrival, another neighbor rang me. 'Suzanne, Zelda just left.'

She piled all her stuff into that bus of hers and threw the key on my doorstep.

'I think she went to avoid you.'

I confess I was bewildered. But when I got back to my little cottage and found that everything was still there, I was relieved. The planned chaos persisted but Zelda, the Ox, had not stolen anything. No-nonsense dealing was true-to-form Ox behavior. But I was baffled that Zelda had twice left town when she knew I was arriving. Was it so she wouldn't have to pay the bills? That was not Ox-like behavior. An Ox might rob you blind but he would never wriggle away over a few hundred dollars' worth of phone bills. To an Ox – fair is fair.

Next day I stumbled on some old papers that Zelda had left behind. Among them was a wrinkled, out-dated health insurance form on which her birthdate, 12 October 1927, was clearly marked. Zelda's evasiveness, subterfuge and oddball penchant for valuing her own sense of order over mine all made purrfect sense.

I had to chuckle at my naïvete. Tigers like me love to play hero. Who better to buy Zelda's tale of woe about how living in the bus was so cold in the winter? Zelda was a Cat and a half: devious and self-serving, polite but determined to stay out of the line of fire. It cost me plenty to find out Zelda's little birthdate secret: just a shade over a thousand dollars in phone bills to start with and the check she had given me bounced all the way from her Boston bank back to my little village bank. I repeat, if ever you choose to do business with Cats, DELVE.

Cat women can and do engage in a variety of careers. They make competent, responsible employees, ever willing to learn and enthusiastic about new projects. They have a built-in sense of self-confidence about professional pursuits and are clever at sorting out muddles. Give a female Cat a department to run, a project to engineer or a schoolroom to manage and she will always come through with shining colors.

Cat women are thoughtful and solicitous of both bosses' and employees' needs. They would usually rather not be in administrative positions but choose to remain safely ensconced at managerial level where they can count on both hands-on experience and security. The diversity of her responsibilities never flummoxes the Cat. She is content to be in charge of everything in an office, shop or lab, from cleaning the john to decorating the windows. She knows how to render herself indispensable to an employer and still be looked up to by her subordinates. Her dignity and bearing appeal to the boss and her thoughtfulness and easy-to-cry-on-shoulder please those she rules.

One thing Cat women are particularly gifted for is running a restaurant or hotel; they are superlative decorators, good money managers, hospitable and know how to run a decorous tight ship with both guests and employees. They are also well suited to shop owning and selling, especially home-decorating shops, pharmacies and art galleries. They should, however, always take care to preserve their peace of mind. In choosing the items they want to sell, they ought to consider up-market goods that are sold in gracious atmospheres: expensive property, books or paintings and sculpture, to name but a few. The more caring Cat woman might investigate jobs involving nurturing kids or the elderly. Tourism is another favorite. Cats are not major travellers as a rule, but they love dreaming about exotic places while planning trips for others. They make excellent editors and journalists: their ability to recall detail is invaluable in reportage. Cats can be terrific teachers but they must be protected from difficult disciplinary situations.

Because of her heightened sense of aesthetics, the Cat woman can also become a competent artist or writer. If she doesn't marry a high-powered man while still young, she may couple her cold logic with her inordinate social ambition and try her velvet paw at medicine or law.

As a wife, the Cat woman is much sought after by men of public importance. No matter how successful a Cat may be in her own profession, if you quiz her with perspicacity you will discover that she would almost always prefer the role of woman in the home. She wants luxury and needs refinement and if her husband cannot provide it, she will. But many Cat women marry sports champions, movie stars, politicians or prominent executives. They are instinctively gifted at flower-arranging, hostessing, decorating and rearing well-bred children. As a snob, the Cat woman is crucially aware of the importance of social and professional contacts; what's more she is a razor-sharp networker whose assistance can become invaluable to a busy husband who is after power.

Cat women abhor the idea of ending up single. Yet their romantic demands are stringent. Cat woman envisions herself comfortably ensconced in a grand home with gilded antique furnishings and oodles of leisure time. She adores dawdling about with books and magazines. She enjoys listening to music. She is addicted to shopping. She also has time to brood. Her marital daydream consists of loping about the baronial mansion being lovely and contemplative. She does not want to be overly sought after in the bedroom and, within the confines of her daydream, will never lose anything of her privacy, dignity or independence. With her frequently soggy will to win and her tendency to flee the slightest vexation, Cat woman must be wary not to get caught in the web of her own outrageous fantasy. She must stay clear-minded. The female Cat needs to be married, or at least nominally attached. She hardly ever goes out on a date without first sizing up the security and companionship her suitor might offer. She never lets things go too far physically unless she sees a glimmer of a matrimonial prospect. She is a hunter and a clever one at that.

Cat woman's notion of love combines ambition and social advancement with sentimentality and reason. She is determined to catch a man she respects. If she considers him worthy of her admiration, then he is also worthy of her love and devotion. The rest, she hopes, will fall into place on its own. In some ways, any man the female Cat chooses to hang on to will be lucky: his home life will tick along smoothly, his family environment will be harmonious, and conflict will mostly be averted in favor of peace and quiet.

Her habit with the opposite sex, even as early as adolescence, is to charm with gentility, entice without force or overt displays of sexuality, or lure them discreetly to her side. She is never slow to use feminine wiles and stratagems to land the gentleman of her choice. She gets up to all sorts of seductive tricks involving her appearance – hairpieces, facial tucks, and cosmetic appurtenances. She is also ruthless about fibbing – appropriately – to get her man. She may embroider pitiful tales of her unhappy childhood, her poor father's fatal illness and her mother scrubbing floors to put her through law school, or she will concoct high-falutin' stories about her elegant background, glibly inventing servants, summer at Newport and winter sports in Gstaad. Cat women will marry for social position and their imagination is heavily armed to deal with the preliminaries.

Do not be misled, however. The female Cat's talent for improvisational wooing tactics is all part of her design for better living. She wants her existence organized. She tries to smooth out roads before they get bumpy and would rather leave nothing to chance. She prefers to maintain her distance from excessive emotional involvement as she needs room to maneuver.

This woman will make a top-drawer wife: she cooks, sews and gardens with skill and taste, decorates and housekeeps with flair, is cultivated and intelligent, loves her home and rears her children well. Her sexual fidelity is unfailing and her willingness to please superlative. She is, however, reputedly not a wonderful lover. She can never quite understand what everybody's panting and fainting about when it comes to sexual attraction and physical pleasure.

Cat women are rigorously faithful to their husbands. Their husbands do not enjoy the same reputation . . .

Tom Cat

You will not find many hippies among Cat men. Little matter how Bohemian they seem, Cat men want to appear as low profile people. They are always well turned-out. They like to dress differently for each occasion and are fond of owning many clothes. Not usually foppish in manner, they do have a casual style of gesturing, sitting and standing, which could be interpreted as effete, sedate, patrician, aristocratic or – at the very least – supremely gentlemanly.

I once knew a hugely attractive French male Cat who, although sorely impoverished, came from one of the oldest noble families in all of 'France and Navarre'. We'll call him Xavier de Laigle Fourchu.

In 1962, Xavier was twenty-three and a student at the central Paris law university. His parents had raised eight previous de Laigle Fourchu children and were poverty-stricken and elderly. Xavier lived at home and received daily spending money for buses, the métro and lunch. He did not have a part-time job because 'it wasn't done' in his family. Students were gentlemen. They studied and did not soil their hands with work.

Xavier's Chinese sign suited him. Even physically, he matched the portrait of Cat man to a T. Slight of build, tall but somewhat frail of limb, high forehead, straight aquiline nose, handsome, smart but not swashbuckling. Despite his impecuniousness, he always managed to be dressed to the nines. His shoes were shiny black, much-repaired wing-tipped Oxfords, from the best men's shop in Paris. He wore lush crumpled pigskin gloves. Even in summer, Xavier always looked the picture of the destitute aristocrat, trying to keep up appearances.

What finally suggested to me that Xavier was even more Cat-like than he was aristocratic was a recent flash memory of him, shivering in the worst wintry weather, striding bravely about Paris wearing little more than those gloves to keep him warm. He was forever hunched inside his two-button, leather-elbowed Harris tweed jacket, with grey flannel trousers, strict silk tie and white dress shirt. He never wore an overcoat or raincoat.

One day I realized to my surprise that Xavier wore *three* superimposed dress shirts. 'To keep warm,' he explained.

'Can't you wear a coat?' I wondered.

'Don't have one,' he said, embarrassed by my question. 'Except my brother's old one and he's much taller and broader than me. I can't wear that, it doesn't look chic.'

'But it will keep you warm,' protested practical me.

Xavier sighed and tried to explain. He cleared his noble throat. 'When I take the bus in the morning, other passengers will misjudge me. At the university, the other students will laugh and point at a de Laigle Fourchu who wears old clothes. Policemen won't be obliged to respect me,' he said, approaching a mild rage. 'People of my class cannot risk being frowned upon. It's a question of reputation.'

Xavier would have been more accurate had he said, 'People of my *Chinese astrological sign* cannot risk being frowned upon,' because soon thereafter I met seven of his equally noble brothers and sisters who wore ordinary sporty indifferently old and new clothing. They were all de Laigle Fourchus, but they didn't give a damn who thought what about them. This 'stay chic and look good' approach is a further indication of the Cat man's need to appear superior.

The male Cat's voice is unusually mellow and he has an innate ability to use it to good effect for speaking, singing or elocution. His mouth tends to be small, his lips thin. His eyes are bright with intelligence and curiosity. The Cat man is slender, lithe and moves well. His joints are supple and he walks briskly. He is a nimble creature whose gift for dancing is undeniable. Before the age of forty, his muscles are firm and his limbs sinewy. Because he is so rigidly non-athletic, middle age sometimes slows him down and allows an ugly spread to thicken his mid-section. Naturally, the tone in his muscles tends to slacken with the passage of time. If he does go to fat in middle age he will more closely resemble a pot-bellied professor than a manual laborer with a paunch.

In company, public places or at work, the Cat male is always careful about his demeanor. He wants to fit in, but not to stand out. He is easily put off by sloppiness in others and will often snap-judge new people on the basis of their looks and bearing. A carelessly dressed person may be dubbed untrustworthy by the male Cat employer. He likes to choose his friends among those who have 'made it', prefers to live only at the 'best' addresses and tries to remain a cut above what he considers 'the common people'. At times, this policy of exclusion borders on racism and is a form of unfortunate snobbery that Cat men should, at all costs, correct.

As the male Cat adores his independence, he often chooses to run his own enterprise. He doesn't like to work in crowded places and is not relaxed about sharing professional quarters with people he deems his social inferiors. A solo operation suits his snobbishness and fits his character well. As his main aim in life is financial and mental security, a good home and a harmonious lifestyle, it behooves the Cat to play it safe, stay away from jobs which require daring feats of individual creativity and/or long periods of impecuniousness before reaching success.

Cat men are well suited to professions requiring method and punctiliousness. Some even accuse the Tom Cat of being a nit-picking fusspot whose over-developed sense of precision is enough to drive normal folk to drink. These fine people make wonderful accountants, businessmen, pharmacists and paramedics, librarians, researchers, archivists, scholars and scientists. They are conscientious, discerning and possess much native ingenuity. Cat males are also gifted for providing art expertise, curating museums, dealing in *objets d'art* and even restoration. If their manual skills are well honed, they can make excellent craftsmen working in traditional fields such as cabinetry and fine gold or silversmithing. Security magnetizes him while he is young and still feeling his way in the big bad world; he may be tempted early in his career by a stint as a civil servant or bank employee, a commodities trading firm or a stock brokerage house. If he does take a job with built-in security, he will quickly tire of it unless it allows him freedom of movement and plenty of decision-making. Cats seem easy enough to get along with, but the Cat man is never anybody's 'yes' man and will bolt if he's feeling hemmed in by a stiff taskmaster.

Probably due to his constant need to head trouble off at the pass, the Cat male knows instinctively how to reach to the heart of thorny situations. He is especially endowed with the ability to see potential catastrophe. He is also clever at uncovering hidden meanings and ferreting out concealed information. All of these talents point to a career as a detective, a psychologist or psychiatrist, a private investigator or spy.

All Cats, most particularly males, benefit from a sound sense of judgement. Justice and respectability are two of the Cat's bywords. He believes in the system and wants it to work; Cats frequently enter law. Although he prefers never to confront others or fight about issues concerning him, the male Cat argues well and will stand up, within the confines of the judicial system, for what he deems fair. In the light of his talent for discerning truth and the heart of a problem, the Cat could occupy a position in the magistrature. Both male and female Cats make seemly, unbiased judges.

We do not often find the Cat in jobs where the well-being of others comes first. Male Cats are mainly concerned with their comfort and security paying close attention to their own surroundings and welfare. They are not likely to choose medicine or social work because they don't like taking care of others and cleaning up their messes. If a Cat man became a doctor, he might opt for research or the development of pharmaceuticals.

The Chinese say that Cats make canny gamblers. They are lucky at games and shrewd at speculation. Pure commerce also attracts the devious Cat man. At first, he may be timid about collaring clients and talking them into buying his products but once he overcomes his shyness and applies his sixth sense in sniffing a bargain a mile off, the male Cat can turn a handsome profit.

Cat men write well, too. Their fine sensitivities and desire for clarity in expression pair up to give them a distinguished style. More non-fiction orientated than literary, the Cat male works well in jobs where he is asked to draw up detailed reports, write briefs or draft book-length manuscripts on specific subjects. He documents every detail and deftly handles each paragraph. He may also be drawn to writing for theater and film, and particularly to melodrama – he could make a terrific soap opera or 'bodice-ripper' novelist. His bent is to give his readers a sentimental thrill. The Cat is a competent commercial writer whose texts please the public and usually sell like hot cakes.

Diplomacy appeals to the male Cat. He enjoys entertaining royally and hobnobbing with the 'right' people. His skills at gently prodding high-ranking officials in directions they never expected to move are well appreciated by government officials who need the aid of soft-treading Cats.

I cannot imagine how male Cats perceive love. In romantic situations, they are notoriously reasonable, sensible and correct. They rarely get swept off their feet or fall madly in love with the wrong person. The very idea of love at first sight makes Cat men feel ill. These discreet fellows mistrust their own sentimentality and are suspicious of everyone else's motives. They fear irrational acts and are circumspect about where they place their furry paws in marriage.

Cat men often choose bachelorhood or even a non-involved homosexual relationship rather than become embroiled in conflict-ridden marriages. If and when he decides to marry, the Cat prefers a woman whose pedigree and manners, appearance and behavior border on perfection. The Cat man feels that everything his wife does reflects upon him, colors other people's image of him and may make or break him in life. Many a Cat man would rather be married to a princess in a tower whom he never gets to touch or romp with – simply because she comes from a good family and, as she's sequestered up there in that tower, her presence and moods would pose no threat to his household harmony. This attitude not only demonstrates the Cat's pristine approach to love, but also gives us a clear idea of how *many* times this poor fellow must be disappointed by the bevies of imperfect ladies he might have loved.

Cat men like to feel that they have initiated their relationships. They are so dignified that they would never stoop to be seduced by a siren or shamelessly tumbled by some gorgeous movie star or model. What's more, Cat men are skittish, sniffing around life, fearing that every new event might prove a major snag. They tiptoe warily around the fields of love as though land mines were everywhere. They never embark on the search for a new love without first making up rules about how she should be or what she should want out of life. I have a Cat friend in France who deliberately chose his current wife because she was ambitious and he wanted someone who would work alongside him in business. He had lived some years before with an English woman he claimed he loved whose ambition was insufficient to his needs. He chucked her. 'She did not suit my plan for life,' said he. 'But Andrée is devoted to her own work and will also help with my success.' He was right. She does.

Xavier, of tattered overcoat fame, came to see me in hospital when I had my second child. He was now apprenticed at a small law office. I suppose he'd made a little money – he wore a navy blue double-breasted blazer which had replaced his Harris tweed jacket. Same grey trousers and white shirt with tie and shiny black shoes. A soberly cut newish navy overcoat appeared to have belonged only to him.

He came in, doffed his coat, glanced politely at the baby, congratulated me and sat down. 'I have been wanting to tell you,' he announced sedately, cigarette poised daintily between his thumb and forefinger, 'I am engaged.'

'Oh, X,' I said gaily. 'How nice! Who is she?'

'Her father has a large house in the Avenue Foch,' said Xavier, smiling smugly. 'Her mother has a grand *château* in Switzerland. Her father is the Duke of Castilane and her mother is from an old Swiss family. Rich watchmakers,' he added. 'Her sister is married to the Marquis de Salernes and her brother has married into the exiled royal family of Yugoslavia. He is a diplomat.'

'And the girl? Your fiancée? For God's sake, Xavier, *what is she like?*' I felt like shaking him.

'Oh,' he looked at me to comment drily, 'she's all right.'

In true Cat fashion, Xavier married the 'right' wife whose background and lifestyle would never put his own reputation in question.

Cat men are paranoid about women's designs. They never quite take them seriously and always think they are being duped. They almost always refuse to share their innermost thoughts and secrets with their lady friends. If you love a Cat man, you may grow frustrated and even fed up with the wall of chronic silence concerning emotions that he erects between you. If you suggest counselling or psychiatry as a way to find each other, he will most certainly balk and run the other way. Mr Cat doesn't want any third parties or strangers prying into his private life. Fortunately, he may mellow with age. Meanwhile, I suppose you could take a nice open-hearted Rat or Dragon lover to tide you over till your Tom Cat grows up. Even though the male Cat is known for being selfish and too reserved, he always comes to the fore when he is asked to come to the rescue of someone he loves. Cat men love to play hero. An ailing or despondent wife will receive all of his gentlest attentions. The Cat is generally faithful to his mate as well and if he ever cheats on her it will be in very unusual circumstances.

Perhaps because he lacks the gift of easy intimacy, the Cat male is rather inhibited in the bedroom. He likes things to be too pleasant, requires an excess of perfection and has an exaggerated, puritanical sense of decency. As a result, although he boasts a hearty sexual appetite, his creativity in lovemaking leaves much to be desired. He goes through the ritual motions with alacrity and skill but remains stonily silent, leaving his partner out of his sexual sphere and often chilling her to the bone. I was never comfortable with my Cat lover's insistence on wearing his tie in bed. But if you are a patient and nurturing sexual partner, the reticent male Cat lover may present just the challenge you have been waiting for. Teach him how to turn himself on and he will follow you anywhere.

The five Chinese elements and how they influence the Cat

The Wood Cat

1795 John Keats
1915 Ann Sheridan, Saul Bellow, Ingrid Bergman, Cornel Wilde, Yul Brynner, Frank Sinatra, Anthony Quinn, Edith Piaf, George Guetary, Edmond O'Brien, Eli Wallach, Orson Welles, Ring Lardner, Moshe Dayan, Memphis Slim, Billie Holiday

The Cat sign is already governed by the Wood element so a Wood year birth confers extra stability, sagacity, generosity and altruism on the already solid-citizen Cat. He can work his little paws to the bone and never show a second's fatigue or nervousness. This steadiness and strength of purpose is often evidenced by his uncanny endurance and *sang-froid* when helping care for old or sick people. The Wood Cat is that well-recognized good Samaritan whom everybody praises, saying, 'He was such a brick during his mother's long illness.'

He is also self-centered, and meticulous about having things done his way. He can be demanding and even hard-hearted – especially if he is contradicted. He cannot take any teasing or even gentle criticism. He is hard to get along with when harmony is disrupted, which poses a real challenge for those who live with him. Creating full-time fair weather around the house is no mean task and yet that is what the Wood Cat wants and even insists upon.

His sexual motivation cannot be defined as passionate but this character can be moved to a high degree of sexuality if he is properly stimulated by an enticing, sensual partner. As for romance, he is neither gifted nor interested in Valentine's Day hearts and flowers. He would rather take a civilized, rational approach to love so that he can remain in control.

Largely, this Cat will do almost anything to maintain equilibrium, keep the peace or avoid making waves. He is hampered in his dealings with others. He cannot be perfectly honest for fear of disrupting the prevailing serenity. Though not dishonest, the Wood Cat *is* devious and shrewd about camouflaging feelings.

This flexible person will be accepted almost anywhere he goes because of his open-handed and easy-to-get-along-with nature. These traits may not always work to his advantage as others may misconstrue his kindness as weakness. If he is wise, he will choose a strong lifetime mate who will serve as his permanent shield against the harshness and rough edges. Then he can take it easy and get on with his many artistic and literary pursuits.

The Fire Cat

1867 Pierre Bonnard

1927 Harry Belafonte, Sir Stanley Baker, Bill Haley, Gina Lollobrigida, Jerry Schatzberg, George C. Scott, Simone Weil, Gilbert Bécaud, Maurice Béjart, George Plimpton, Mort Sahl, Neil Simon, Doc Severinson, Fidel Castro, Peter Falk, Emmanuelle Riva, Ken Russell, Christopher Plummer, Edward Albee, Ivry Gitlis, Coretta Scott King, Estelle Parsons, Alan King

Fire often brings instability to the staid Cat yet also adds verve to his prissy, over-correct nature. He cannot be called aggressive, but the Fire Cat is generally somewhat feistier than his fellow felines.

Genius thrives in this Cat. Many great writers and musicians, painters and poets were born in Fire Cat years. Emotionally intuitive, he can pick up extra-sensory messages in others and frequently knows how to transform them into poignant works of art. This Cat will also have an incisive sense of humor and knows how to charm people with it. Others usually enjoy his company and find his wit intelligent and easily applicable to real-life situations. The Fire Cat is the least shy of all Cats. He can handle fame and deal competently with the public without needing to flee the spotlight.

He is no altruist, however. He is supremely self-centered and wants his way in most relationships. He can be strong in the face of opposition – if he needs to, he will bare his claws and hiss loudly to warn off attackers – but he would prefer to play a waiting game, using devious tactics to avoid confrontation and skirting most thorny issues. The anguish the Fire Cat experiences during a waiting period can cause him serious health problems. He is not naturally well equipped for dealing with inner conflict. Yet he creates it by holding his real feelings in while waiting for the moment to strike. If he could learn to be more humane, put his ego in his pocket, acquire a knowledge of how to care for others and exchange his feelings more readily, he could avoid engendering complex chronic health problems such as depression and neuroses later on.

People accuse Fire Cats of arrogance. He may at first seem reserved and aloof. Mostly he attempts to present an affable façade but sensitive people are not fooled. He is over-confident and full of himself when it comes to matters of the mind.

The Fire Cat reads a lot. His memory is vast and its information well organized. In discussion he can be arch and pedantic, causing his friends and family to spend many a yawnful evening hearing him out on subjects of arcane interest to nobody. Others, again, don't count for much – and their opinions, frankly, bore him.

Government jobs and administrative posts attract and suit the Fire Cat. He will be at home in the snobbish, gilded atmospheres of embassies and diplomatic missions around the world. He also makes a wonderful business executive. Not only is he capable of brilliant management, but the Fire Cat has a way of infusing his workplace with that special Cat flair and elegance and he can spot problems before they happen. No budget-conscious, caution-loving, self-respecting, hotshot Fire Cat would ever allow a small financial deficit to grow into a looming red figure on the bottom line.

The Earth Cat

1519 Catherine de Medici
1819 George Eliot, Queen Victoria, Jacques Offenbach
1879 Paul Klee, Ethel Barrymore, Albert Einstein
1939 Vince Taylor, Alexandra Stewart, Pete Bogdanovich, Peter Fonda, David Frost, Judy Collins, Paul Morrissey, Sal Mineo, James Caan, Volker Schoendorf, Mort Shuman, Francis Ford Coppola, Sam Cook, George Hamilton, Rex Reed, Jane Alexander, Liv Ullmann, Fránk Langella, John Hurt

Observation and a keen sense of style characterize the Earth Cat's nature. He is inventive, too, capable of impressive creative feats and often responsible for the planning and execution of aesthetic projects of vast scope. The keenest intelligence lives in this person and he always knows how to use his sharp brain to good advantage. He is a leader whose style is passive and laid back but who rules with an iron paw.

The Earth Cat is too critical and conservative. His nit-picking attitude towards his surroundings and his entourage often make him feel out of place. He therefore carries a weighty mental baggage of social inadaptation with him. Because of this misfit complex, he also tends to enjoy travel and even to expatriate himself. The average Earth Cat is always seeking to transplant his existence into a location or society more suitable to his tastes and needs. He imagines life will improve if only he can live somewhere he feels he belongs, is understood and less pressed to maintain an inordinately high degree of social decorum.

The Earth Cat depends for his equilibrium on maintaining a realistic approach to life. He doesn't enjoy any pursuit which is not clear-cut. He is candid in speech and action, not mincing his words the way many other Cats will.

Earth Cats exhibit a deep interest in the meaning of death. Somehow, he is convinced, we do not terminate when we die. He sincerely believes in an after life. Reading up on after-death experience, reincarnation theories and the like is his favorite pastime. He is also intrigued by the esoteric and perhaps metaphysics and extra-sensory perception in midlife.

The Earth Cat is the sexiest of all Cats. He obviously doesn't have the capacious sex drive of Goats or the round, sweet sensuality of

Pigs. But the Earth Cat is reputedly a voracious indulger in sexual activity. His style may be superficial as he doesn't like to get too involved in the funkier side of sex. He's not one to give in to total self abandon but the list of his conquests is impressively long.

On the positive side, the Earth Cat is always willing to listen and learn about his shortcomings. He would fare better in life if he sought professional help from an early age and ironed out some of his more glaring neuroses before making any big mistaken choices in his adult life.

The Metal Cat

1471 Albrecht Dürer
1891 Henry Miller, Ronald Colman, Sergei Prokofiev
1951 Kate Nelligan, Cheryl Ladd, Lucy Arnaz, Patrick Sabatier, Dominique Sanda, Treat Williams, Jane Seymour, Tony Danza, Richard Thomas, Joe Piscopo, Michael Keaton, Anjelica Huston, Sting, Marvin Gaye

This character is stronger willed than most other Cats. Metal confers a steely strength of purpose and more courage than we normally see in Cat behavior. He's no world beater in the confrontation department but, unlike some less feisty Cats who flee, he can hold his ground if and when he meets with an obstacle. Due to this ability to defend his point of view, he is more optimistic than other Cats. One could say he is even a tad aggressive.

Metal Cats are hypercautious, though. They never take risks. They never act on impulse, thinking everything through, combing the details as though searching for fleas. Rather than find themselves in fuzzy situations where each element is not crystal clear, Metal Cats will avoid investment, commitment, marriage and even family closeness. They need their lives to be orderly and prefer to stay out of the muddy waters of indecision.

If his projects don't work out, the Metal Cat may not only stumble and fall but face ruin. This person is a great believer in sticking to his ideals. Unfortunately, he is rarely able to do so because he holds very precarious positions and is easily shot down by ruthless adversaries. His downfall often comes in the form of a permanent depressive attitude towards getting ahead and a fatal loss of self-confidence. Sometimes the Metal Cat races ahead of his failures: he might deliberately undertake a project he knows is above his capacities so that he can foresee and therefore deflect the pain of the inevitable failure. This auto-immunization against suffering may endow him with a defeatist personality.

The Metal Cat's word is as good as gold. He makes a point of always honoring his statements and backs them up with sound informational data. He considers disloyal people and unfaithful friends or relatives to be banishable from the kingdom. He is impatient with all messy human endeavor and insists on clarity and a hundred fail-safe clauses and procedures before signing any document.

This creature may well possess special gifts which allow him to read other people's minds. He tends always to live inside of his own head. Although he can be deliberately charming, the Metal Cat is never quite as affable and outgoing as he may want us to believe. The dark underbelly of his nature resides in grey areas of thought, nether regions where ghosts and spirits play. He is more than occasionally involved in séances where the tables turn and people return to claim communication with their loved ones still on Earth.

The Metal Cat has good taste. He may well become famous in some profession such as decoration or architecture, art history or even painting or drawing. He is an avid collector of *objets d'art* and rarely, if ever, falls into traps such as being duped by crooked antique dealers. His canny sixth sense perceives dishonesty through almost any disguise. At an auction, he picks up on authenticity instantly, his velvet paw heads straight for his checkbook and buys all the bargains he comes across.

Finally, this finely honed aesthete doesn't have masses of friends or cronies. He is hardly someone to hang out with or have over just to shoot the breeze. The Metal Cat is a serious fellow with serious intentions and goals. He lets practically no one into his private life and rarely shares intimate information with anyone – even his spouse or partner.

The Water Cat

1483 Martin Luther
1843 Henry James, Edvard Grieg
1903 Benjamin Spock, James Beard, Bob Hope, Bruno Bettelheim, Vladimir Horowitz, Cecil Beaton, Cary Grant, George

Balanchine, John Dillinger, Edgar Bergen, Malcolm Muggeridge
1963 Tatum O'Neal, Nicolas Cage

The Water Cat is a more 'female' sort than most other Cats. His sense of taste and love of refinement for its own sake is exaggerated by the gentling water's influence. He is also more squeamish than other Cats and will shy and turn his head away from all physical illness, disability, emotional and mental instability. He cannot tolerate the sight of blood and indeed nearly passes out at the idea of an injection.

This Cat, no matter how he may protest his preference for the joys of living on the edge, lives solely for security. Despite a penchant for taking up with the odd weirdo or dating a nutty art student or dancer, the Water Cat doesn't conceive of himself as departing from the norm to live any type of Bohemian or even freelance life. Not only does he like to make money, the Water Cat requires luxury to survive. He cannot bear squalor, prefers to control and discipline all his food intake carefully and must have the right bath and toilet facilities complete with all the properly appointed cupboards and shelves to keep his finery safely housed. Otherwise, without a well-established plan and a rigorous infrastructure, the Water Cat grows afraid. Besides fearing impecuniousness, he worries that he may grow lazy, be in constant danger of attack from outsiders and even face premature death. More than almost anything, this delicate person fears losing his way, and perhaps even his mind, if he doesn't maintain clarity and a rational point of view.

True love and commitment often escape this character's clutches too. He falls in love easily and is enthralled by romance. Yet the Water Cat won't fight for his rightful position in relationships, rarely speaks of his innermost feelings and keeps his own counsel when confronted by the threat of conflict. His dream love is so idealized and vague that he often makes grave errors when seeking a mate, so carried away with the ideal that he forgets how difficult it is to live out one's dreams.

The Water Cat is a daydreamer too. Aloof and seemingly above it all, he frequently abides in a dream kingdom wherein he is master and monarch of the realm. He longs for excitement but doesn't dare indulge in outlandish experience. He muses about being brave enough to escape the drudgery of a nine-to-five lifestyle. He would love to be a spy, an international whizz kid or a philosopher, but underneath he prefers the safety of material gain to the danger and adventure of passionate or romantic endeavor.

This person will have a showplace for a home. He spends much time there, in elegant rooms surrounded by collections of antiques, first edition books, and classical music. This Cat reads voraciously, cares little for gourmet foods, drinks only the best wines in moderation and imagines his next coup on the stockmarket. The Water Cat is attracted by all that is ethereal and vaporous yet he will always remain maniacally attached to his creature comforts. The Water Cat never dashes off, scornful of convention, disconnected from society for the pure joy of participating in some exciting fling. He is too staid and 'fraidy-cat for that.

Charming and amiable, he has many acquaintances and few real friends. The Water Cat is also known for his intellectual prowess. He is usually highly educated or would like to be considered both cultured and profoundly wise. He often cultivates people for their social worth, is attracted to those whom he feels come from the 'right' families but may also have some pals from literary or artistic circles. He has a tendency to exploit these marginal friends, impose his whims on them and sometimes even leave them in the lurch when it takes his fancy.

This person is a great conversationalist and a good raconteur. He is well respected in his work as he is undaunted by decision-making and can out-think and -maneuver practically anyone. He is a terrific strategist and a keen plotter of schemes for getting ahead. Water Cats are always employed in the most lucrative careers and, due to their guile and caution, almost always live to a ripe old age in the very lap of elegance and plenty.

Cat health

Cats are conscientious. When the doctor or practitioner advises them to avoid certain foods they heed the advice. They are capable of great personal discipline and will go to any lengths to preserve their health and physique. They care about the prevention of illness and the maintenance of a sound body and mind, and will spend much time and no end of money in such pursuits. Cats always get themselves vaccinated, ingest endless vitamins and drink biological concoctions to improve their resistance to disease.

The Cat person spends more time thinking and worrying about his health than other average people. He is forever suffering: a bad back, a pain in his shoulder, a trick knee or migraines, a recurrent ache in his upper right chest or a burning in his esophagus. Cats are just about never symptom-free.

For the purposes of combating ill health, the Cat is always going on diets. He may stop eating salad and begin living on boiled meats. He can go vegetarian, refusing to eat eggs or dairy products too. Or he may undertake an entire regime of nothing but eggs and red meat. You never know what a Cat is up to in his dietary restrictions but you can always be sure he maintains several taboos. One word of warning: Cats are easily influenced by quacks, faddish diets, purge cures or weirdo exercise programs. They would do well to see a psychologist simultaneously as they may get waylaid on a mistaken path to heavy disappointment if they don't remain objective.

Cats live quite a long life. It is true that he is often ailing and indisposed, but he is more than able to snap out of it and go back to work in a jiffy after a short rest. Not only are they cautious and circumspect about their health, but Cats are endowed with good health from birth. As they grow older, their tension diminishes and, with it, their pettiness. Elderly Cats are usually jollier and less persnickety than younger ones.

The Cat's weak spot is his digestion. As he is susceptible to emotional strain, his digestive tract reacts like a barometer to bad weather. Any disturbance or hitch in the harmony of his life may cause the poor Cat's tummy to attack him viciously, resulting in loss of appetite, gas pains, nervous constipation, muscular contractions or diarrhea. Relieve the tension, take the pressure off and the resilient Cat's digestive system springs right back to normal.

Unless the Cat is diagnosed as having a serious irreversible illness, he should avoid all classical medical treatment. Instead, because he leads a quiet, organized life and doesn't mind following instructions, he should avail himself of homeopathic remedies. Remembering to take small exact doses of homeopathic granules and drops several times a day doesn't flummox this detail-prone person. Such draconian disciplines appeal to his sense of order and give him the impression he is *doing* something about his sorry state.

His interest in eating the 'right' foods will help him to avoid many of the above-mentioned symptoms. If he is wise, the Cat will never become a pure vegetarian. His nervous colitic intestine doesn't have an easy time digesting salads, raw or half-cooked vegetables and fruits. Starch, fats and barbecued meats are also hard to digest and the chronically dyspeptic Cat should avoid them. He is always better off on a diet of citrus fruit, grapes, cereals, wheatgerm, yeast, eggs and fresh milk. He should avoid foods with a high fermentation rate such as vinegar, yeast products and brewed drinks. He can add some meat and fish to his diet and remember to cook vegetables well and poach fruit. This way he will enjoy a well-balanced food intake which won't make him miserable for hours after a meal. Yoghurt is another must in the Cat's diet: its antibiotic properties will protect him from bacterial infection. Despite nervous constipation, the Cat is advised never to overdose on cellulose or bran. Better he should ingest yoghurt, a few prunes, grape juice and chicory tea along with his daily food intake. Mineral oil – 2 teaspoons per day – might help as well. Above all, he ought to drink at least 2 quarts of water daily.

Cat women suffer from gynecological problems between the ages of puberty and menopause. After that, the dysmenorrhea, cramps, bad moods and sieges of hypersensitivity and tears will even out. It is often said in Chinese astrology that the Cat woman suffers from a faulty endocrine system. Her doctor should routinely monitor the performance of all hormonal aspects of her health. If they are not checked, metabolic problems, slow digestion and weight gain after the age of forty-five can contribute to depression in her later life.

Cats *must* learn to pace themselves. As perfectionists, they have a tendency to attack a job and persevere right on through till it's done – positively dangerous for the delicate Cat. His nervous system is fragile. From an early age, this person should be told to make peace with his basic need for equilibrium. The Cat is gifted for neither war nor strife. Forcing himself to live or work in stressful situations will not only shorten but make his life perfectly miserable. Unless they must go there to work, Cats should stay out of cities. A quiet country home where he evolves with the rhythms of nature, keeps a few pets and adheres to a strict routine would be ideal.

Cat futures

What Cats should expect from the next twelve Chinese animal years

2008, the Earth Rat year – Not the most encouraging of years for you Cat people. Why? Because the Rat is jealous of your settled, secure lifestyle and would not in the least mind turning it on its head. Rats love drama and excitement. You prefer safety and time for quiet pursuits in the countryside. Of course, you are the wiser of the two signs. But you prefer not to have to fight to get what you want. Rats seek power. They want to dominate and are not afraid of confrontation. Don't perform any public stunts which will attract attention to you during this sharp-edged year. It's not the time to run for mayor of your town or even to seek the presidency of your French conversation class. Nor is it the year to splurge on frivolity, showy vehicles or mansions in high-end neighborhoods. Your finances could come under some scrutiny from the tax authorities. Better to lie low and while away weekends listening to classical music, reading history books or polishing your antique clocks. You might enjoy a fling or two with someone charming and frankly, openly sexy. Take pains to protect your reputation for refinement and good taste.

2009, the Earth Ox year – In Ox years you Cat people tend to feel out of place. They are hardly keen on slaving. You despise the very notion of toting barges down muddy riverbanks or lifting bales of cotton all the livelong day in the blazing sun or the spitting cold. You are an indoor sort of person who, for sport and adventure, might take to her garden for a stroll among the beds of hydrangea and heliotrope. The Ox is a bull. He willingly activates himself in any weather whatsoever in the name of 'hard work'. Exertion and everything to do with industriousness and labor are part and parcel of his belief system. That you might not want to soil your hands or muss your finery in the name of toil, rather gets on the Ox's nerves. So this year you will have to hide from the taskmaster and expect to be heavily criticized for any unnecessary expressions of snobbism or couth. Your home life (unless you have married an Ox) should not be seriously affected by the adverse atmosphere. Stay close to family. Potter in your wood shed. Teach yourself to knit or tat or do needlepoint. Whatever you do, don't attempt to compete with the powerful Ox in any project where brute force is a deciding factor.

2010, the Metal Tiger year – Tiger years are full of hasty rash moves and risky changes of direction. In the early part of the year, you might still be reeling from what the last couple of adverse years have done to your gentle spirit. Once you are back up on your feet and feeling tip top, you will be pleasantly surprised at how clement, easygoing and devil-may-care the atmosphere is in this Tiger year. Many of the major events happening this year will affect you directly. A person or people whom you didn't know till now will approach you at several different times for your assistance or engagement in their projects. Remember. You work best with Pigs and Goats. Whatever you do, don't take up with a headstrong Horse or a daring Dragon. Their very style abrades your delicate nervous system. By year's end you should be feeling terrific and perhaps even a bit sentimental. Why not spend some quality time with old friends from school or grab your mom or dad and hie them off somewhere exotic where you can stroll along a beach and learn more about your childhood? Health looks relatively good this year for Cat people. Keep to your diet and exercise routine or you will spend the better part of next year getting rid of excess weight.

2011, the Metal Cat year – Some details of your romantic life need dealing with. Either you are or your significant other is unhappy with certain aspects of your relationship. Are you bored? Is he or she too busy to be available when you are? Is one of you suspicious of the other's extra-curricular activities? More than likely you have let too many issues be swept under the carpet and now they are oozing out around the fringes and filling the air with tension. Nothing worse than silent mealtimes and unspoken differences of opinion. If you (who hate confrontation) cannot discuss the problems at hand, get thee to a counselor and take your sweetheart along for the ride. Financially, you are in better shape than you have been in eons. This is your very own year in which to plan the next dozen years of your life. Ask yourself seriously, 'Where do I want to be in 2023?' Then draw up a plan of action to get yourself to that place, one year at a time, over the next ten or twelve years. You would be much happier if you lived outside of the city. Should you find yourself in an urban environment, the acquisition of a secondary residence in the countryside might not be a bad place to begin your plan. You need birdsong and antiques, refinement and natural surroundings to keep your hypochrondria at bay.

2012, the Water Dragon year – The Dragon atmosphere of rambunctious parties and spirited conversation doesn't do much for you discreet Cat folks. You are always better off in the quiet of your own comfortable home or at a cultural event or concert in the park. The Dragon harbors no grudges against the Cat species, but his demands are not few. Dragons want everybody to pay attention to them, to follow their rules and applaud their antics. Generally, you Cat people are too busy thinking up quiet ways to take over a giant corporation or buy a winery in Bordeaux to bother attending all the Dragonesque festivities on tap in this noisy celebratory year. The Dragon year is yet another good reason to have bought yourself that country retreat. Go there as often as you can. Travel when there is no traffic and return to town when the others are already back. Or better still, hole up all year in your manor house in remotest Bavaria and write that book you have been meaning to get cracking on. Dragons, frankly, are not your most rewarding companions. If you choose to stay in the fray, they will do everything in their power to drag you into their dashing lifestyle where you will be tempted to overindulge, drink too much and party till you drop. Where will your twelve year plan be then? One year behind schedule.

2013, the Water Snake year – This is a fine year for Cat to gain ground. The Snake admires your quiet charm and has identical taste in finest luxuries. You, of course, may prefer castles on the Loire and the Snake will fancy diamond necklaces from Cartier. But the similarity is there. Snakes are philosophical as well and can work quietly behind the scenes to make a great deal happen in a very short time. You enjoy quiet and are comfortable with the brand of enduring beauty that belongs solely to the Snake. Hence the atmosphere of this year doesn't tread on your aesthetic. You will have time in the Snake year to take stock of what has been going on in your own personal hard drive as well. Meditate or write poems. Some emotional crisis will arise before the summer that threatens disappointment in somebody you care deeply about – a relative or an old friend. The event will shock you. It has to do with foolish comments or remarks made concerning your character. Try not to take it too seriously or allow it to ruin your friendship or mar the harmony in your family. Sometimes thoughtless people make terrible mistakes. But they don't realize how damaging those blunders can be for their nearest and dearest.

2014, the Wood Horse year – Horse years are notorious for their galloping rhythm and amazing speed. Some might term these years 'dynamic'. I tend to think of them as wild and wooly. There is a lot going on and it's usually about work. Unlike the sedate, rather langourous Snake, the Horse is a large, nervous, muscular beast whose capacity for labor is legendary. Horses can raise their own food and build their own houses and bake their own bread and raise kids and pets – all the while juggling three plates on sticks in the air over their heads. They are stunningly talented and beaver-busy all the time. This, of course, is quite the opposite of you Cat people who enjoy quietude and (as long as there is someone to do the gardening and muck out the stables) seek the tranquility of the countryside. So you will no doubt find the pace of the Horse year irksome. You may be surprised – even shocked and frightened – by the degree of headlong interference which occurs in your backyard during this Horse year. You might be reading a book under a tree in the park and suddenly be turned upside down by someone 'working' there. Or you could be sunning on the beach and out of nowhere be instructed to 'move along' by the life guard. Horse years are famous for invading people's peace and quiet. Don't be alarmed. Be careful. And if you don't want your life meddled with in some aggressive manner, don't make any waves.

2015, the Wood Goat year – The Goat is one of your most fervent allies. Not that Goats are as refined or highly strung as you, but your characters complement each other – the way beige goes with tones of brown or sage green. The atmosphere in the Goat year suits you. And even the most successful, rich or famous of Goats longs to have the practical side of their life taken care of. Cats make excellent caretakers who look after their own and other people's goods and chattel with a cautious eye. Hence, the Goat feels safe in your company and is willing more or less to fall into your lap and let you do the organizing so that he or she may gambol through a work day safe in the knowledge that his financial picture is being overseen by someone competent. You tend to complain a bit and suffer physical ills more imaginary than real. The Goat understands you, listens to your wailings and even takes you seriously when others won't. You should spend this year accruing not only interest from your precious offshore bank accounts, but also gaining ground in your personal life. The issues and unresolved problems that you were encountering early in the Goat year will dissolve as though by magic after the month of March. Things quieten down in your home life because you can breathe easier and feel less fraught and defensive than you did last year.

2016, the Fire Monkey year – One of the most salient aspects of Monkeys (and hence of the years in which they govern us all) is that deep down, they really don't give a damn. You Cats give much more than a damn – about everything. So sometimes during Monkey years, you feel frustrated. You wish people would do something about the chaos, shore up the bridges, repair the roads, improve the schools and create some sort of public transport system that functions properly. As you are a bit of a fusspot when things don't work as they should, you are a sitting duck for living this year in a state of aggravated agitation. This will be a year of social disruption for a medley of different reasons. One of those is the fact that Monkeys can solve most problems for others, but rarely for themselves. So when it's their turn to govern and the problems become theirs, they want no part of it. Too complex. Too difficult. Too much visibility. Monkeys hate all that. They just want to be free to be entertaining and smart. The Monkey prefers to get on with his jolly life on his own with his loved ones and wants no part of the authority that comes with the territory of reigning over skejillions of people. Needless to say, the Monkey's jaunty laissez-faire attitude toward governance irritates you Cats. Yet because you never do conflict, you remain in the background, stewing. To palliate this general feeling of irritation, I suggest twelve months of bed rest, hot-water bottles, silken sheets and a soft loving companion.

2017, the Fire Rooster year – Your luxury-loving streak will have to be curtailed this year. Roosters want us to behave thriftily and stick close to our budgets. As a general rule, Cats don't strew money carelessly about as though it were autumn leaves, but they do tend to part with great sums at one time for major purchases such as expensive antiques, sterling silver tableware, porcelain dinner services, paintings by old masters and castles in Spain. This year you should not buy any of the above. Just coast on what you already own. Clean up your stock portfolio and make certain your bank has not made accounting errors whilst you were abed with your soft companion from last year's time out. Use the time you aren't spending at auctions and antique shops to chat with your family. Find out what they have been thinking about you and perhaps even about what monies of yours they have had their eye on. You always have enough. They just about never do. Do be cautious. Don't let anyone's sob stories crack open your safety deposit box. See to any physical symptoms that you can't seem to get rid of with your ritual dietary supplements, homeopathic remedies and/or general *woo woo* cures. Sometimes – only sometimes – doctors can be useful.

2018, the Earth Dog year – Traditionally, in the West, Dogs and Cats are seen to be enemies. In Chinese astrology, however, this is not the case. You Cat people love the dutiful, disquiet Doggie and he, in turn, admires your calm, quiet and mostly gentle nature. The only aspect of the Dog year which might adversely affect you Cats is the aura of liberalism and near-revolution which clouds the political scene in almost every country on the planet. Dog years are messy with dissent. Cats hate dissension and flee dispute. Hence, the highly charged atmosphere afoot in this Dog year may leave you with a bad case of the jitters. You fear upheaval and revolution because you generally comply with the system and enjoy the benefits of its privileges. Should the government be overthrown, you might well lose some of these advantages. The very thought of having to hand wash your table linens from Porthault or award the household staff a rise gives you gooseflesh. You will enjoy this Dog year only if you can abstract the fear of loss and accept that social change is necessary for the good of all. Besides, you hardly ever give those lavish dinner parties for twelve any more because they are simply passé.

2019, the Earth Pig year – The Pig admires your discretion and tact. Nonetheless, the year may bring emotional upsets. These will have to do with family and (of course) money. In late spring, there will be either an inheritance or a gift bestowed on a single family member. If you are the recipient of this good fortune, keep it under your mustache. Boasting by someone less discreet will engender serious fireworks. You hate scenes and will no doubt suffer a panic attack. Excuse yourself and stay gone until tempers have cooled. This year is one of plenty so you will feel like investing some money. Any real estate you purchase must be sound on the ground and not require too much renovation, as in Pig years, the work tends to cost more than the actual house does. Beware of crooked financial counsel. This year there are many underhanded stock schemes about. In matters of the heart, the Pig will bless you with a highly charged, passionate romance with someone you have always known. Your health is generally sound in Pig years. All in all, this will be a quiet, prosperous year for the careful Cat – as long as you remember to scat when family crises arise.

龍

The Dauntless Dragon

Magnificent Dragon,

Sure of yourself, dynamic and noisy, you are a born master of ceremonies. Fireworks, parties, festivals, holidays, rallies, you get things started and keep them moving. You're feisty and gifted with power and luck. People look up to you. You can be a braggart and you don't trust easily. When you know you are right you are inflexible. In business you appear tough. But even you, dauntless Dragon, are not invincible. All those flames are mere camouflage. Underneath, you are a soft touch. A pushover. You faint at the sight of a weeping willow. Sentimentality stalks your every step: you cannot resist its maudlin tug.

Faithful to friends and family, you are less so in matters of the heart. You are devastatingly attractive. And romantic too. You long to crawl into cave after cave with a series of passionate lovers who tickle and hurt and thrill all at once. You dream of a lifelong moment of ecstasy. Dally with a hard-driving Rat or a clever Monkey. But when you choose a mate, pick a solid citizen Rooster or a Tiger (your accomplice). Don't bother with taciturn Oxen or outspoken Dogs. Not your style.

A regulated, disciplined family and school life in childhood may frustrate your need for applause and undeserved attention but it may also set you on a more realistic path than one you would have chosen yourself. Your mid-life crisis will be a humdinger! But if you're still alive at age fifty, your real work will begin to pay off. You know how to learn from your mistakes. Dare I give you advice? Don't let your ego get the jump on your brain. Practice laughing at yourself in the mirror. Lower your profile.

In all humility,

Suzanne White

In the twentieth and twenty-first century all Dragons were born between the following dates:

16 February 1904	and	3 February 1905
3 February 1916	and	22 January 1917
23 January 1928	and	9 February 1929
8 February 1940	and	26 January 1941
27 January 1952	and	13 February 1953
13 February 1964	and	1 February 1965
31 January 1976	and	17 February 1977
17 February 1988	and	5 February 1989
5 February 2000	and	23 January 2001
23 January 2012	and	9 February 2013

The Dragon ID card

Lasting symbols have special powers. Enhance your self-image by surrounding yourself with tangible signs of your own identity and make these symbols known to your friends and loved ones. Use them daily and they will bring you luck, security and a feeling of personal worth.

Your best	***Your favorite***
color is gold	food is steak au poivre
flower is rose	animal is monkey
fragrance is Eau Verte	drink is bloody mary
tree is sequoia	spice is cardamom
flavor is pungent	metal is hammered silver
birthstone is ruby	herb is dill
lucky number is 2	musical instrument is clarinet

The Dragon is yang ***The Dragon's motto is: 'I reign'***

The awesome demeanor of Dragons leaves no doubt as to how vibrant, magnanimous, charismatic, principled, self-sufficient, discriminating, compelling, sentimental, accomplished, noble-hearted, healthy and prodigiously shrewd this creature can be.

But one tiny glimpse of the Dragon's scaly underbelly gives us a less enchanting image of our mythical hero. In their worst moments Dragons are bombastic, dissatisfied, ruthless, demanding, opinionated, mawkish, egocentric, defensive, power-mad, foolhardy, willful and pompous.

Me and my Dragons

When a Dragon enters a gathering, the room starts to simmer, heads turn, people frown or smile and sniff the air suspiciously. A whisper passes through the company: '*Who* is that mysterious-looking woman in the shocking pink mini dress? *She* looks interesting . . .'

Or 'Who brought that guy over there in the white silk shirt? Why doesn't somebody tell him to button his lip?'

Nobody can tell a Dragon to button anything. He carries a self-assurance so impressive, an inflated ego so visible and a mouth so loud that it is useless to try to *tell* him anything. Even suggesting that a Dragon 'cool it' or openly observing the boldness of his comments is apt to net you multiple third-degree burns. Trying to talk sense to an excitable Dragon is like trying to tame an oil-well fire with a watering can.

Dragons are born monarchs. As far as they can see, their power is indisputable, their charm absolute. Nothing dampens their tungsten spirit. Nothing scares them. No whisper of doubt intrudes to cloud the Dragon's crystal clear self-image. Dragons are born thinking they are perfect.

Dragons are human giants whose magnificence defies life, challenges both good and evil and carries off amazing feats of prestidigitation which leave us all reeling. There are no more grandiose folk in the Chinese zodiac than the dashing, dauntless draconian Dragon.

Naturally, Dragons cannot always live up to their impressive reputation. Still, one can't help but admire their limitless ambition. When a Dragon feels the seed of a monumental idea bouncing around inside his head, he goes right ahead with its execution. He starts by trying to get everybody into the act and his excitement is contagious. He sits you down and exuberantly expounds on his crazy notion, exposing all the details with flair and conviction.

Dragons never hestitate or shilly-shally. They get a notion, pick right up and dig in. Going after what they want is second nature to Dragons. They never waver, get cold feet or waffle. Dragons just *do* it. Happily, Dragon charisma is not just hot air. The formidable projects and enterprises of Dragons often come off. Success is never just a dream: unreliable or vaporous schemes don't interest the Dragon. Dragons are momentous performers: not only will they achieve on a personal level, but they are incomparable leaders who know instinctively how to engage the participation and willing complicity of partners and associates.

In the interest of accomplishing their extravagant projects, Dragons have masses of preposterous adventures. They are forever dashing off to exotic places. As though propelled by some weird outside force, Dragons leap in or out of private planes in barren wintry cornfields and career wildly through quicksand-infested bogs in prehistoric-looking vehicles. They cannot resist challenge, will not back away from breathtaking experience or brush off the possibility of some dramatic escapade.

Although the Dragon is often an intellectual, his true place is definitely in society. There is no such thing as an unprepossessing Dragon. This person cannot hope to make it as a wild-eyed hermit philosopher. You won't find many Dragons in soup kitchens either. Dragons are born winners, tough guys who love to take risks and will walk over any number of dead bodies to get where they feel they need to go.

Yet, nobody is more oblivious to his own abrasive bravado than an unsuspecting Dragon. 'Who me? You're insinuating that I was not pleasant to that horrid little man? Are you crazy? I was *adorable* to him.' Never mind that he was the chairman of the company with which Dragon was trying to collaborate.

The Dragon does not see himself as others do. He may deport himself arrogantly, pompously and aggressively and insist that he cannot fathom how or why he lost such and such an account or was summarily jilted by a lover. Although he may be devastated by his loss or failure and cannot sleep for weeks afterwards, the Dragon has no idea what an obnoxious effect his boastful, superior attitudes and noisy habits can have on outsiders.

The innocent ruthlessness of a classic Dragon is well illustrated in a person I knew called Charles Little, an American writer and professor of French literature. A consummate Dragon, Charles is an organizational genius. He is invariably chosen to be the head man, department chairman or editor-in-chief. He is perspicacious, knowledgeable and discriminating. He is an excellent cook and gourmet diner *par excellence*. He is a miraculous linguist. Charles is a competent, capable driver, a wonderfully interesting travelling companion and a personal counsellor of the first water. He is also a warm-hearted friend, whose generosity of spirit and contagious enthusiasm about his work are legendary. He looks like a combination of Woody Allen and Dustin Hoffman with glasses and a rather fetching paunch.

I got to know Charles Little when he and his first wife came to Paris in 1973 on one of his lucky sabbatical leaves and we stayed friends, with periods of more or less intensity depending on whether or not Charlie was in France or California. A few years ago, Charlie came back to Paris to research some complex subject in modern literature. I was happy to have him around again: his observations were fascinating, his enthusiasms pyrotechnical and his lust for life so delightful that I found him irresistible. We spent lots of time hanging out together.

At that time, Charles Little was between lady friends. He was divorced for the second time. One day as we were lunching on some gorgeous *foie gras*, Charlie confided that he was lonely. 'What the hell is wrong with these French women? They're so uppity. They turn away and act as though with my American accent I might just whip out my chain-saw and hack through their torsos. Suzanne, don't you have any friends?'

I was pleased to help. Luckily, I had about five pretty French girlfriends aged from forty to fifty, fine for Charlie. Caroline was the owner of a chain of department stores, Florence directed feature-length movies, Francine ran the most archly chic paper shop in France, Lydia was editor-in-chief of a small feminist newspaper and Elise owned a prosperous advertising agency.

These five busy glamorous (rich and single) women agreed to meet Charlie and have dinner with him. They fell shamelessly in love with him. He was so *bright*, said one. So *sexy*, said another. So *understanding*, said a third. So *romantic*, claimed a fourth. So *funny*, said the last. On top of which, they all thought that sleeping with an authentic American professor the most exotic activity on earth.

Charles Little had never known French women before. Now he had five of the most elegant attractive *parisiennes* clamoring for his time and affections. He looked younger. A luster glowed from his heavily lashed dark eyes. He was a happy, spoiled brat of a man.

Then, little by little, over the next few months, as each of my women friends got to know my friend Charlie more intimately, they began to pull away from him, to make excuses for not being able to see him any more, to change the locks on their doors. Just as rapidly as they had fallen in love with him, they were bowing out. They didn't explain. They just moved off, like chic rats deserting a sinking yacht.

Dragon Charlie knew that *he* could not be at fault. In typical Dragon fashion, he found reasons to hate them all in succession. Francine was too fat, Florence was pre-menopausal and hysterical, Lydia had cheated on Charlie with her own ex-husband (an act of betrayal which Charlie found totally unacceptable), and Caroline, *the bitch*, was too busy with business to be a good partner for such an emotional, lusty man as himself.

According to the girls, Charlie was a fabricator of delectable pretty lies who instantly lost their favor when he started making noises about moving into their flats and being supported by them while he wrote books about Flaubert's potted palms.

Charlie bad-mouthed them all – except Elise, and told me he had decided to remain with her. She was his favorite, a real person, not a phoney French sophisticate with airs and graces. Initially, Elise was delighted to have Charlie all to herself. She recognized his faults: 'Sharlee eez arrogahnt. I sink eee eez also a beeg liar. Of corrrse, eee eez compleeettely crayzee.' But as she confided over dinner one night, 'Eee eez soooo adorahble. Sooo funnnneee!' Elise could not resist Charlie's Dragonly charms. Even though she knew he was unfaithful and never told her the truth, Elise loved Charlie. After six blissful months, when he left Paris for California, Elise the Pig paid Charlie's way on Concorde so they could fly to the States together for she had business in New York. They shared her suite at the Plaza. Charlie was in heaven. 'At last,' he divulged to a mutual friend, 'I am a kept man. This is what I really deserve.' He smiled wryly. 'I am worth it.'

Elise returned to Paris that summer and phoned me. Everything between them, she said, was still fabulous. There were some minor *normal* couple problems, but she had them under control. She had gone to Charlie's tiny house near the university and found it quaint but shabby. She was having it repainted, skylights put in to let in more light and a new bathroom installed for Charlie's convenience on the second floor. And, she said, 'I went into Sharlie's closets. I srew away all heez dumb American clothes and I bought heem all new ones. Some Saint Laurent shirts and good tight jeanz.' She sighed. 'Eee looks sooooo cute.'

Elise was besotted. She was round the bend over this Dragon lover and had totally succumbed to his mythical charm. I could not help her, so I put my phone on remote 'nobody's home' mode and went to spend the summer in the country.

Late in the following September I got a call from my friend Carole in Santa Barbara. She rang to say she was coming to Paris on business soon and wanted to get together. She had some great news. She had fallen in love. With Charlie!

In the previous year, under pressure from Charlie's whinings about never meeting any women, I had also introduced him to Carole. She had come to Paris, they had had a brief affair and Carole had gone home. Trust Charlie: as soon as he returned to California, he looked up Carole to tell her she was the only woman he had ever loved and would she agree to see him?

I was furious. Charlie should have known better than to take up with *all* of my friends at the same time. I felt he had been disloyal even to me. How dare he! But with Carole. Carole is married, to Ben, one of *my* best friends, who knew nothing of any of this.

And Charlie was still very much with Elise, who was still renovating his house and buying him tickets on supersonic jets. She was also still calling me in Paris to keep me abreast of her (their) plans about her meeting his parents and him meeting her widowed mother.

I could have skinned Charlie alive. I knew how much he was revelling in this gigantic transatlantic ruse he had created. Yet I had reservations about spilling the beans. He was being a perfect cad but he was still my good friend and so I kept my mouth shut. Carole, who was now concocting a plan to divorce Ben, went back to Santa Barbara whence she flew to and from Charlie's place when Elise wasn't there. Elise blithely came and went, supervising the ever more opulent renovations and wallowing in Charlie.

I finally spoke to Charlie just before Christmas. He was coming to Paris to spend the long winter academic holiday with Elise. She worked all day so he would be able to hang out at her place and work on his book.

Mid-conversation, I piped up. 'Charlie, what about Carole? I talked to her yesterday and she's very much in love with you. She's about to divorce Ben for you.'

'That's her problem,' replied Charlie. 'She's a big girl. It's over and she knows the ropes.'

The ropes! What kind of criminally minded person would say such a thing? Carole is a sweet, loving wife and mother. This man is a monster. Aloud, I said, 'Charlie, you have to call Carole and tell her you don't love her. She might be about to ruin her life. Think of her children.'

'Sorry, Suze, but I really don't have time.'

Furious, I didn't ring him back during the whole holiday. In early January I heard that Charlie was living in a small cheap hotel near the Montparnasse cemetery – alone.

I rang Elise, who said that she had had enough of his jealousy over her correspondence with a male cousin she'd known all her life. 'But eet was not onleee zat,' Elise added. 'I found out eee was cheating on me. Wiss one of *your* friends.'

Good, I thought. At least Elise is out of the woods.

As for Carole, I finally called her to say that Charlie was in Paris. I was surprised to hear that she already knew that. In fact, she had discovered more about Charlie's romantic antics. On his final visit to her Santa Barbara beach house, Charlie had left a packet of steaming love letters from one of his undergraduate students. 'How could I have been such a fool? I actually entertained the thought of a divorce,' she exclaimed. 'While Charlie, the bastard, is having an affair with a child in his class who happens to be *my daughter*!'

So much for the romances of Charlie Little. After that fateful Christmas, he went back to his college, I stayed in Paris, Carole's daughter Alex changed universities, Elise married a Belgian.

As for Charlie and me, our paths did not cross again until two years later when I heard from mutual friends that Charlie had been awarded another sabbatical in Paris. After a few weeks when he hadn't phoned me, I rang him. His voice was non-committal. He said he was busy. He'd get back to me. He never did. So, after another few weeks, I wrote him a note: 'Dear Charlie, I miss you. Please call. Let's have lunch. Love, Suze.'

Two days later, I received this note from Charlie:

> *Dear Suzanne,*
>
> *I would rather not see you again. In my mind, you are intimately connected to the pain I suffered two years ago over the loss of Elise and Carole. Seeing you again would only bring back the whole terrible ordeal that I went through during that time. I cannot risk any more anguish. Please don't try to contact me any more.*
>
> *Yours sincerely,*
>
> *Charlie*

Believe it or don't. At first I could not. How could Charlie Little implicate me as instigator of his own crimes? Because the Dragon must always be right. No matter what shenanigans he gets up to, you must forgive him because he always forgives himself first. Dragons are worse than arrogant. They cannot accept their own errors because, as far as they can see, they never commit any. They categorically blame their lowly subjects (everybody else alive) for their foolishness and go on blithely believing that they were perfectly correct in their assessment of the situation.

Their pompous personalities and lack of humility will not permit them to reassess anything. It is up to us to forgive them their follies. Dragons are innocent because they are unable to see their guilt.

The Chinese say that the Dragon has two roles in society. When things are moving along smoothly, governments are governing and everybody is more or less content, the Dragon is often perceived as an intellectual crank. In times of plenty, he spends much of his time engaged in abstract and unfathomable thinking. In his perpetually agitated state of dissatisfaction and arch, impenetrable philosophizing, the Dragon sometimes seems to have gone mad. However, when the mud hits the revolving door, society may suddenly find it needs the dotty old Dragon. When times are hard, his subjects call on King Dragon, begging him to lead them out of the wilderness. I have not yet needed to call upon Charlie Little to lead me out of the forest, but the day I do, I'll learn how to tiptoe.

Dragons are tyrannical. They hate orders except when they are giving them. Unlike the Tiger, who imposes his will seriously and firmly, the Ox, whose authority is implied in his very stern demeanor, or the Rat, who thrusts his dominion over others, the Dragon knows innately how to exert authority yet be gentle with his slaves. He has no problem with taking over, fearlessly grabbing the reins from any competitor. Yet, he never rules in a mean or cruel manner. The Dragon is a kindly despot. He never forgets to call his servants by their pet names, send their kids a birthday present or hand out a bonus at holiday time.

Dragons are terrible snobs, too. From an early age, they plot means of climbing the social ladder. Although money is not always the object, they are slavishly impressed by wealth, prestige, rank and splendour, which leads Dragons of modest backgrounds to marry people more educated or of a higher social caliber. If he is not to the manor born, the Dragon will the manor storm. In his rush to acquire superior social rank and, through this upgrading, assume more power, the Dragon often meets with emotional ruin.

An outgrowth of the Dragon's snobbery is a dreadful habit of name-dropping and socialite hobnobbing. Hanging out with big shots makes Dragons feel secure. I am forever meeting Dragons who are proud to inform me of how they flew to Tokyo seated next to Tony Curtis or how lucky they were to get on an elevator with Sting or sit across the dining-room from Kathleen Turner. Dragons really get off on the 'who do you know?' game. They forever blow a vicarious trumpet. 'I cannot tell you what a kick I got out of eating in the same McDonald's where Jacqueline Kennedy's maid always eats,' they may swoon at you.

Dragons feel that recounting a simple gesture of human interaction with a celebrity will enhance their image, make them appear cool, improve your opinion of them. To the Dragon, proximity to fame increases his own extraordinariness. He naïvely imagines that some of the luster of notoriety will rub off on him.

As far as I'm concerned, the Dragon can act up all he wants. Whatever he gets up to, no matter how much pain he causes, a Dragon friend or family member is always there when we need him most. He is unerringly faithful and sentimental in both friendship and family matters. I recall with aching nostalgia that crucial occasion – when Charlie Little and I were still speaking – that he stood patiently at the foot of my hospital bed while I took my good old time groping my way out of an anesthetic. I recollect with tenderness that Robert Laffont, my trusty Dragon publisher, bailed me out of debt when my kids were small, my ageing mother ill with cancer and my coffers as empty as tin cans on a wedding vehicle. Dragons are born crisis interveners. They may behave in a bumptiously daunting fashion, they may be snobs and social climb their way to hell, but when life's voyage is at its roughest, you can always count on your Dragon cohorts to see you safely home.

Dragons are inveterate show-offs. But the Dragon's outward personality – he who belcheth great fire and poureth forth acrid smoke – is entirely made up of hot air. Underneath it, the fiery Dragon is not only tender-hearted, he is endowed with the highest of moral standards. However, unlike some people's, his flamboyant appearance, boastful noisiness and vocal snobbery are not designed to cover up a basic shyness. The Dragon is not in the least timid or duplicitous: he's straightforwardly pushy, proud and overbearing.

Dragons are intelligent, curious and analytical to a fault. They carry a prodigious memory between their ears and know instinctively how to glean lessons from past events. A powerful ability to synthesize information and translate it into action gives Dragons an edge in politics and bumps them straight into leadership. Dragons are also sharp and witty. They make very amusing and informative conversationalists. Also, they don't usually feel the need to parade their knowledge and are neither pedantic nor didactic.

Petty people drive the Dragon crazy. He doesn't mind being confronted head on by outspoken tough guys who tell him exactly what they think of him. If someone is honest with him he will return the compliment. But he hates mean-spirited folk who try to con or fool him into reacting.

Although he is not above committing a crime or two before he dies, the Dragon is a sincere and honorable person. Though he can tolerate the idea of wrong-doing, he resists resorting to shady deals or engaging in small-time chicanery. His public style is noble and magnanimous. Even when strategizing, he employs high-minded tactics and attempts to steer clear of the tawdry.

One of the major drawbacks to being a Dragon is that Dragons are not well suited to growing old. Though they are usually in high spirits for most of their lives, laughing off major setbacks and maintaining equilibrium in toughest times, they do not handle the ageing process with grace. The prospect of losing power, the helpless feeling of youthful strength ebbing away is unbearable to this superbly healthy creature. Also, the possibility of dependency on others, whom they have always deemed weaker than themselves, is patently unacceptable. Many Dragons would prefer to end it all than to endure the final insult of creeping old age.

The Dragon lady

Personal magnetism is what sets the woman born in Dragon years apart from her more subtly attractive or merely physically beautiful sisters. The female Dragon, by virtue of her exalted place among her peers, lives a charmed life. From childhood through marriage, career and children, straight on through middle and old age, almost everything goes well for her. Dragon women never go unnoticed by good fortune either: whether they admit it or not, they always manage to attract a hearty portion of the world's wealth and creature comforts.

Usually the physique of a Dragon woman is highlighted by a single unforgettable show-stopping feature. She may have flaming red hair, a regal bearing, a ballerina-graceful gait or a heart-stoppingly creamy cleavage. Often, she is not classically pretty. It's her air of distinction, her carriage and manner that set her apart and makes her appearance so special. She benefits from excellent health, too, and remains young-looking much longer than some of her less fortunate sisters. Wrinkles don't creep in early. And if she gains weight, it only makes her more sensual to behold. Usually, Dragon women are quite tall. They have an ample but not excessive bosom, a flat abdomen and broad shoulders. The arch of her long back is graceful. In short, she gives the impression of a sturdy, well-proportioned plant.

Her interesting facial features are enhanced by a glowing complexion. Her teeth show snow-white when she smiles her broad smile and crinkles her lovely deep-set eyes. The package is rarely standard issue. Dragon females look exotic. Their well-shaped triangular faces contain a promise of excitement no man can resist.

The Dragon lady has enormous personal charisma to blend with her physical beauty. She may not charm with ineffable mystery like the irresistible Snake woman does. Nor will she melt the hearts of giants with her accepting goodness like the gentle Goat and the giving Pig. The Dragon woman's singular attraction results from her careful dosage of a bewitching appearance with an extravagant personality.

The Dragon woman is never self-effacing. She cannot be accused of timidity as she has no talent for soft-pedalling or discretion. She is, however, remarkably discerning. Her mind is so acute that she can quickly grasp the pith of an issue, analyze its components and synthesize it in a wink. She becomes vocally opinionated on any subject whenever the mood takes her, sometimes holding the floor for hours while others patiently await their turn.

The Dragon woman's powers of reasoning are exceptional too. She has an innate sense of how to grade the importance of issues as they present themselves. Her mind functions with rigor and logic, coming up with original views and sound ideas. Her thinking on most subjects is considered both valid and valuable as she recognizes the pertinence of even the most abstract concepts to their practical applications.

Dragon women are highly respected by their peers. Even the most prejudiced man will one day find himself admiring the steel-trap thinking of a Dragon female. He cannot help but marvel at her ability to see both sides, to abstract emotion and finely balance her conclusions.

As long as her ego is not threatened, the female Dragon's wits remain about her but, when she feels attacked below the belt, when her pride is scratched or her private self invaded, she may grow too verbose, yammering in self-defense, losing all logic and attacking in a 'damn the torpedoes' manner, hence losing credibility. These outbursts may demolish the sterling image we once had of her. The Dragon lady's worst failing is her inability to see herself as she is seen by others. For this reason, she cannot take criticism. Even polite suggestions rile her and bring out her thorniest side.

Dragon women usually get married although they continue to cherish their independence and, to maintain her social freedom, a married Dragon will often choose to work outside the home. But Dragon women believe that marriage, and its attendant trappings such as home, children, security and social clout, oils the stubborn creaky gears of life. They make supportive wives and indulgent adoring mothers. At home, Dragon ladies are capable at sheltering, feeding, petting and caring for animals and kids, relatives and even hangers on. Lucky is the child born to a Dragon woman as he will be able to share his mother's lavish hospitality with all of his cousins and cronies for the rest of his life.

Although she is happiest when attached to a man, the Dragon lady is hardly a clinging vine. She has absolutely no patience with soppy snivelling women who hang on to their husband's coat tails and his every word, agreeing with the most outrageous or conservative views. She can always be counted on to speak up and expose her most cogent thoughts. The Dragon woman is neither petty nor hypocritical: you won't find her a good gossip partner or a loyal ally when she feels you have acted unwisely.

This is a scrupulously fair woman whose intellectual integrity matters immensely to her own opinion of herself. She needs to be seen as fair and just. Also, she is flattered when others consult her for advice about their personal, financial or emotional problems. She is a wise and serious counsellor and can be counted on to give candid, considered opinions.

Pithy brevity is the stock in trade of the Dragon lady: the only time they talk a lot is in relaxed intimate company when they usually talk about themselves, their kids and their friends – in that order. Business for the Dragon lady, is *strictly* business and does not warrant wasting time exchanging drivel. She gets right to the point, offering sound advice. No matter how hurried or busy she is, the Dragon lady invariably takes time to slow down at the end of her conversation, lower her voice from a shout to a normal tone and say, 'Don't hesitate to call when you need me,' or 'Take care of yourself.' Tenderness and affection are worn close to the surface in the most forbidding of Dragon ladies.

A Dragon woman practically never thinks ill of others unless she has been sorely misused by them. Her instinct tells her to give each person the benefit of the doubt. She is profoundly philanthropic and will make real sacrifices of both personal time and finance to aid an important cause. Because she stubbornly maintains a firm belief in the basic goodness of humankind she can sometimes be duped and sometimes she trusts too much. When and if she discovers she has been betrayed, the Dragon lady will go up in smoke and come right back down again on the culprit's head. Dragon lady anger is horrible to behold: her recriminations wound deeply. Her enemies are justly afraid of her volcanic temper.

Luckily, she knows how to forgive. No matter how wronged she is, the Dragon lady will not hold a grudge. She may learn not to trust someone a second time but a single bad experience will never sour her on the rest of humanity. Head high, dreams intact, the Dragon lady goes on helping out those who need her, comforting those less fortunate and inviting the whole lot to dinner into the bargain.

Her professional talents are, of course, centered in leadership. Management positions and enterpreneurship suit her perfectly. But she will also make a great secretary or personal assistant to someone she admires. The Dragon lady's faith in herself is unshakeable. Whatever she undertakes, be it a personal project or a duty connected to her job, she will always see that it is accomplished correctly and will follow it through to its conclusion.

She does, however, need a lot of attention. Whether the Dragon lady is president of her own company or head clerk in a typing pool, she must have the assurance that she is receiving most other people's unceasing consideration and is noticed at all times. She may give stormy speeches about how *she* feels things ought to be done or she may content herself with rattling papers loudly on her desk and sighing heavy sighs. One way or the other, the Dragon lady employee keeps a high profile.

Dragon women are determined to have it all: comfort, love, children, professional success and even total freedom. But, unlike many other women, they usually carry out their duties to their close family and friends before setting off on fancy adventures. They are courageous, burning with fervent idealism. They want only the best of life and are not afraid to give as much as they demand.

One drawback may be the Dragon lady's 'attitude problem'. Even though she may carry an ideal of true sentiment and humility inside her heart and head, her outward carriage and demeanor is brashly imperious – and frankly annoying to outsiders. She is smug, haughty and aloof in her dealings with strangers. Often, the Dragon woman behaves as though she owned the world and was only allowing you to sit on it so long as your presence pleased her. She is vain too, always primping and tossing her hair about ostentatiously. And domineering – my, does she have to rule! At home, as in the workplace, she acts as though the universe revolves around her whims and needs. Her family defers to her orders, scuttling along the walls so as not to be scolded or told to shape up. Her co-workers watch their words with her and, although they love her, know better than to rile her. Her husband brings her breakfast in bed in the hope that she will get up on the bright side and not demolish household harmony. From birth, the Dragon lady makes it her business to be treated as the spoiled princess. If she doesn't get her way, she freaks out till she gets what she wants. She is rarely devious or duplicitous. She confronts with ease, laying out an impressive array of demands and rarely settling for one iota less than the lot.

Fate has a way of twisting us all around her fickle little finger and Mother Nature doesn't always give in to the Dragon lady's exacting temperament. Her seductive force tactics may not work on everybody: some people are eventually turned off by her incessant truculence. When all doesn't go according to her plan, watch out. Ms Dragon blows the lid off, creating scenes that Cecil B. De Mille would kill to have invented.

Marlene, a beautiful buxom provincial French woman from a town near Lyon, is a freak-out Dragon woman. She fell in love with a scientist named Jacques in the early eighties. After about a month of being in love with him, Marlene informed him that she was quitting her job and moving to Paris to live with him. He loved her but at first, he advocated getting her own flat and seeing each other only in the evenings and at weekends. But Marlene insisted on cohabiting. Jacques gave in and Marlene moved into his sedate domain, a tastefully decorated apartment in a quiet Montparnasse street.

Now Jacques was a private man who had always cherished his antique furniture and peace of mind. He had known many women in his fifty-three years but, he often joked, to preserve his sanity he had never married. Hurricane Marlene whooshed into his placid existence and blew away his resolve.

But after a couple of weeks of Marlene's demanding to be taken out nightly, inviting herself along on his solitary walks and even showing up spontaneously at his research lab, Jacques gently suggested to her that their live-in arrangement did not seem to be working. He offered to help her find an apartment and even to bankroll the first few months' rent.

Marlene reacted volcanically. She wept and recriminated and mocked him pitilessly. She made such a fuss that Jacques relented, allowing her to remain – on one condition: she would have to get involved in her own evening activities so that he could have a few hours of peace. Marlene agreed.

Despite a few half-hearted attempts at classes in watercolor and some very distracting (to Jacques) piano lessons, Marlene remained dissatisfied. She wanted Jacques's attention. She insisted he come out and play with her, pay attention to her, admire her spirit, applaud her body and watch her live. She had found life horribly boring just doing quiet things.

Getting Jacques to come out of his self-made shell proved impossible. Their arguments became more and more heated, the live-in life was pure hell. Marlene kept intruding on Jacques's privacy, pushing and worming her way into his every waking thought. So, one night when they had stayed up until three o'clock waging one more long row, Jacques informed Marlene that it was definitely over between them. He apologized for hurting her feelings but admitted he could not stand her omnipresent presence any longer. Then he went to bed and drifted off to Sleeping Pill Land.

But Marlene stayed up. In a fuming rage she concocted a demonstrative plan to prove to Jacques that, no matter what he had decided, she was not going to let him go.

When she was sure that Jacques was soundly anesthetized,

Marlene unearthed a long, strong rope. Then she crept into the bedroom and commenced to tie up the bedroom and Jacques with it. From Louis XIV wardrobe doorknob to Louis XV bathroom doorknob and on to Louis XIV second wardrobe doorknob, she tied knot after knot. After making sure that no opening in the room would open, she moved to the center of the room, creeping carefully towards the bed where Jacques lay in a drugged sleep and proceeded to lay the rope several times over the covers atop her sleeping lover. On Jacques slept, further and deeper imprisoned in his sleep and in his own bed, until Marlene gave the whole thing a good hard tug, snap-tightening the rope around Jacques's body and woke him up.

He flailed. Then he laughed. He wriggled. 'Marlene!' he ordered in a cranky sleepy voice. 'Let me up.'

It took about two hours for Jacques to convince Marlene that she had to release him so he could go to the loo. Meanwhile, she had two full hours of his undivided attention. 'I made him miss his laboratory, didn't I?' she asked me the next day, triumphantly tooting her horn.

You might think Marlene is insane but I can assure you she is not. She is a sober school teacher in a girls' school where her work is highly respected. But Dragon women always go to extremes. Attention, theatrics, fireworks, ballrooms with chandeliers and fancy dancers are part and parcel of their everyday and their dream world.

More than their male counterparts, Dragon women are appalling snobs. They drop names and social status, inform you of how many 'servants' their parents had when they were small and constantly fill you in on the high and mighty friends and neighbors they have the honor of knowing intimately. To a Dragon woman, the mere acquisition of power and money are never enough. Dragon women need to be able to boast that their friends live in luxury palaces in ritzy towns or elegant neighborhoods. Their top-drawer friends must belong to the 'right' country clubs and send their children to the 'best' schools so they, too, will grow up glamorous and eventually live in high-flown circumstances so then their Dragon mothers can boast about *their* social status. It's like a disease. Dragon women must impress.

Dragon women are not above ruse when it comes to dealing with men. For starters, love does not figure in first place on her list of priorities. She's more interested in improving her social class, maintaining a high level of comfort and acquiring jewels than she is in love for its own sake. Passionate love comes second in importance to her ambitious drive for glory. Loving someone is pleasant enough but loving someone rich, famous or socially prominent is much more sensible to this rapaciously aspiring woman. So eager is the Dragon lady to get and stay in the spotlight that she might even take up with some worthless do-nothing layabout lord just to be able to emblazon her title on her stationery. She very often gives her all to the advancement of her partner but her intentions are not always selfless. The Dragon lady doesn't mind being a passenger, even a parasite – she will even take second billing – as long as the publicity quotient is top quality and constant.

No Dragon woman is ever without male companionship for long. No matter how she looks, this woman is fascinating to men. Men meet her and instantly fall in love *kaboom!* with her captivating charm. It's odd, too, because Dragon women come on very strong. Most women would be embarrassed to behave so outrageously; Dragons meet men and start wriggling, squirming and batting eyelashes. You will even see them giggling at nothing, laughing uproariously at the guy's dumbest jokes. The Dragon woman is a shameless seductress, a courtesan born. Yet she never acts the shy violet, shrinking from expressing an opinion and it is not that she's masculine or macho. Without being aggressive, Dragon lady is lovingly pushy and fetchingly forceful. She usually gets her man.

All of her men don't get her – yet they continue to pursue her relentlessly. And she continues unabashedly to flirt with them. For her it's a game. Many's the man who carries a lifelong torch for a Dragon woman and lives in a perpetual state of disappointment. In her youth, she will probably take up with several different lovers but as she gets older, the Dragon woman's interest narrows. By the age of thirty she is interested only in her future and that of her chosen partner, who will certainly be someone with both position and money to recommend him. Dragon women prefer spinsterhood to poverty and ignominy. Because she is so practical about passion, it is practically impossible to break her heart. If relationships come apart, she will make it her business to be the heartbreaker. She sees no reason for undue pain and is never the victim of unrequited love. If she isn't getting positive feedback from someone she fancies, she drops them and moves on to the next.

Her sexual prowess is legendary. Dragon women may seem hard-nosed, calculating and can be cold fish in public – for effect. But between the sheets, a Dragon woman doesn't fool around. She wants no backseat or backstreet loving either. Her lovemaking has to take place in a well-appointed bedchamber where she feels comfortable and at ease. In bed, she is said to be submissive, giving and voluptuous. Come daybreak, she's up and out and right back to her fire-spewing quarrelsome Dragoness self.

The Dragon prince

Having once been madly in love with a classic Dragon Prince and coming out of it breathless and barely alive, I can personally testify that all of what you are about to read is true. Dragon men are hedonistic, volatile, dramatic and persuasive. They're selfish, too. Yet, they are dreamboat sexy, hilariously funny and delightfully entertaining partners. With a Dragon man around the house, there is never a dull moment.

Dragon men want to be thought to have class. They often demonstrate their so-called good breeding by affecting a haughty, aristocratic bearing which may give them the distinct impression of pulling social rank but nearly always gives observers the clear idea that the Dragon man is putting on an act.

Dragon men are usually tall, erect and slender. Their bodies are muscular, taut and topped with powerful shoulders. Their gait is lithe and steady. He is never in a hurry. Nonchalance becomes him. He leans jauntily on a car radiator while chatting with a pretty woman or pulls up alongside a lady in a miniskirt and gently talks her into accompanying him. Smooth charm and a delectable line of pretty lies make him a dangerous enchanter. His own self-assuredness inspires confidence in his prey. Until middle age when it thins slightly on top and goes salt and peppery, the male Dragon's hair is abundant, thick and of a frank color, blond, brown or black, depending on ethnicity.

The Dragon man is positive. He always knows where he is going and how he wants to get there. Interference from outside is not welcome. He hates taking advice but never stops giving it. He is independent to a fault, striving in his own way, at his own speed, to arrive at the goal he has set for himself. He demands to be acknowledged as the leader of every game, the inventor of every scheme and the planner of every event. Being both generous and hospitable, the Dragon invites everyone and his brother to come to the game, take part in the scheme and enjoy the event. But he needs to know that these guests are there at his behest and wants them to express just how appreciative they are of his generosity.

The narcissism of Dragon men can prove tiresome. On first encounter, one may be impressed with his aura of splendor and perhaps even grateful for his munificence. By the second, he will undoubtedly inform you of how hard he worked to make all this happen, fishing for compliments and lighting up like a beacon for any and all stray kudos. The third time, he will probably tell you a story or two about how he was awarded a medal for bravery in some obscure war. Then he will drag out his uniform and perhaps even don it to inspire your further admiration. No matter that the uniform doesn't fit any more or has moth holes the size of ping-pong balls. Dragon men cannot resist making a spectacle of themselves. They seem to have no sense of the ridiculous. The primary goals of a male Dragon often appear dead simple: make noise, be seen and get attention.

However, the male Dragon is truly sensitive and honestly emotional. It is he who suffers most when his puffed-up behavior loses him friends and costs him loyalties. But Dragon men take a long time to trust others and understand that sharing feelings will not hurt them or mar their macho image. They are also given to pretension. A Dragon male's wish to climb the social ladder will sometimes cause him to behave in a smug or snooty fashion. As he is naturally given to excess and braggadocio, his remarks quickly grow into ostentatious displays. If he learns to lower his profile and keep out of the line of fire, he is almost always assured of success. A more intelligent and competent person hardly exists anywhere, but conceited Dragon males too often insist on playing the know-it-all game and, in the process, lose the respect of their peers.

Goals inspire the Dragon male: the achievement of an objective can make his day. He deplores mediocrity and will not tolerate laziness. The energy level in Dragons is higher than in almost any other sign. Dragon men are at their best when they are moving through life at their own speed, accomplishing what they set out to do and not meeting with too much resistance. They are determined without being stubborn, they are thoughtful and make up their minds which road to take, long before embarking on any new venture.

The Dragon needs his successes to be admired and looked up to. He has no time for selfless struggles or expending years of personal sacrifice. He wants what he wants when he wants it and is not afraid to go after his booty full tilt until he gets it. People who choose to remain anonymous and cultivate their domains in the country quietly both baffle and annoy the daring Dragon. He must be seen and admired, approved of and adored – or he shrivels and dies.

The Dragon man should take care to choose a career which gets him seen: he is often brilliant at performing in both theater and cinema. His charm captivates audiences as he is a person of grand scope with universal appeal. Politics suit him and his desire for success, public life and applause. He knows how to galvanize audiences, persuade people and inspire his public in a clear mellifluous voice: votes fly towards him like moths to a flame. However, in politics lies a grave danger for the Dragon male, who is so eager for success that he may be tempted to transgress the boundaries of morality. Nowhere is shady activity more prevalent than in political life. If he has a strong backbone and solid principles, the Dragon can serve his constituents admirably. If not, he will be setting himself up for a Humpty Dumpty scenario in which he could lose everything he has worked for.

This man is an old-fashioned 'man's man' and would make a tough trade union chief or top flight business executive. He might manage a sports team or head up an entire army. As a leader, he is always willing to do more than the job requires to set a good example for his subordinates and/or beat competitive co-workers to promotion. Those who work for Dragon bosses are often devoted to them and will work longer hours because they respect the Dragon's methods and original ideas.

This man has a strong, creative appetite and a great sense of taste. Literature will make him a fine profession. He might write anything from novels to songs or short stories as he is versatile as well as intelligent. Along with his flair for spotting a fine piece of art work, the male Dragon is a born merchant: he can do well as a gallery owner, art book publisher or even as an auctioneer of fine objects or property. With his gift for communication he could also be a journalist, create advertising campaigns or engage in public relations. Law makes a good career for Dragons too. Their ability to plead effectively for their clients' rights before a judge or jury is an obvious asset. All careers which offer power and authority over people who need convincing will suit the Dragon down to the ground.

Menial tasks, however, repel him. My friend Charlie Little, the Dragon professor, is a gourmet chef of immense talent. When he finishes cooking, his kitchen floor is awash in a slippery mélange of olive oil, soap suds and vegetable parings. Magically, Charlie always has someone in the kitchen cleaning up after him.

Once the male Dragon gets home, extinguishes his fire-breathing mechanism and removes the heavy armor of scales from his tender skin, the menial chore embargo ceases to exist. His pride and preoccupation with what others think of him, means that the male Dragon must always flash a neon KING. In private, however, it is different. Whenever Charlie Little visited my house, he always offered to cook – *and* clear up!

Male Dragon love behavior is epic. This high-handed yet loving man has a preconceived notion of the mate who will grace his life. She must be breathtakingly beautiful, with a perfect figure and a compliant, easygoing nature. His wife must be stunningly intelligent in private to keep him amused but in public she must play the clam. She must be modest, too, and, most importantly, should admire and revere the very ground he treads. As he is never half-hearted, when the Dragon man finds his dream girl he pursues her relentlessly, exhorting her tirelessly and interminably to be his wife, bear his children, clean his house, take care of his paperwork and . . . wind the applause meter every night before they retire. In return, she will have the honor of being the partner of Monsieur Dragon the Magnificent.

With a Dragon lover, rows and arguments are part of one's daily bread. Dragon men make scenes over everything from what time the news comes on TV to who gets to read the color section of the newspaper first. They are attentive, forever bringing presents and cooking up surprises but they are also vociferously jealous. A woman involved with one of these haughty fellows cannot speak to the family doctor without him suspecting something's going on. Dragon males imagine their mates to be as inconstant as they tend to be. Even if their heart is dedicated to the ideal of a happily monogamous marriage, male Dragons cannot remain faithful. Remember, they are dependent for their self-confidence on admiration and applause from others and *no* spouse has time to go around ooohing and aahing all day and all night about how fabulous her husband is. When would she get anything done? Dragon husbands fool around. Little can be done about this: Dragon men need adulation from lots of women. Disconcertingly, they sometimes flaunt their peccadilloes, courting marital disaster. I knew a Dragon who asked his *wife's brother* to find him a date for a business trip and another who brought his mistress home to the marital bed while his wife was in hospital having a baby.

Chinese scholars excuse the Dragon's faithlessness, calling it a search for the goddess who matches his own exalted opinion of himself. I say hogwash: Dragons are horny. Flatter them and they fall at your feet. Weep and they beg your forgiveness. But never mother a Dragon. As he must not be made to feel he is inadequate, mothering does not rejuvenate this gargantuan ego. He considers mothering an attempt to smother his fire and will flee at the idea of being pampered. He wants to do the caring, lead the household, make the rules and be the unmitigated hero.

Despite this, the Dragon male aspires to being a good husband and father. He frequently succeeds because, underneath all the fire-spewing and tom-tom beating, the Dragon is smart. He instinctively knows whom to marry so that his kids will be safely brought up. He chooses his life partner wisely, favoring a gentle, yielding woman to someone fiery and dangerous. The former, he trusts, will put up with his difficult nature, appreciate and encourage his talents, whereas the latter may be exciting but will never wash his socks.

To stay married to a Dragon male, his mate needs a sense of humor plus perseverance and devotion to the idea of living in the shadow of a great (or pseudo great) man for a lifetime.

The Dragon man's sex drive is powerful. He makes love the way other men paint pictures or write music or poetry. To him, the act of love is an important creative expression. Not only is his sexuality hardy, he is able to prolong lovemaking for hours. He is tenderly passionate and deeply involved in capturing the essence of his partner's pleasure. As he is generous, he takes great joy in pleasing his lover and will find the subtlest messages where she didn't know they existed. His virile self-image must remain intact and his tendency to stray grows more intense as he ages and fears the loss of his sexual prowess.

The Dragon male as father is a benevolent despot. He wants his kids to conform to his ideals, behave in a prescribed manner and want for themselves what he so generously (and condescendingly) wants for them. The drama and theatrics he creates at home don't make for a particularly stable environment in which to nurture kids but his heart is in the right place. He dearly loves his children and would kill for their welfare and survival. But he's egocentric and often bossy – especially with boys of whom he is envious because they are young, virile and sexier than he. He is likely to disapprove of a teenage daughter dating boys he doesn't choose. The Dragon father wishes that his kids were as wonderful as he imagines he is. When they don't measure up to his ambitions for them, he is disappointed.

The male Dragon's strongest suit lies in his boundless energy and goodwill. He suffers from excessive vanity and allows his ego to block the way to his brain too often. But he is not unwilling to hear criticism nor to try to modify his often pompous behavior. He can be vituperative and will often rave when he could speak normally. He likes parties and cannot live without festivity and gaiety. He's finicky about how he wants things done and he has the necessary authority to ensure that they are done his way. People like Dragon men upon meeting them because they are sympathetic and kindly, reacting ebulliently to each newcomer and treating him as though he were very special. The Dragon man gives the impression of being fearless and even a mite dangerous but he is sentimental, easily moved to tears and hugely loving when he feels his emotions reciprocated.

The five Chinese elements and how they affect the Dragon

The Wood Dragon

1844 Sarah Bernhardt, Paul Verlaine, Henri Rousseau, Nietzche
1904 Irene Dunne, John Gielgud, Jean Gabin, Joan Crawford, B. F. Skinner, Pablo Neruda, James Cagney, Justice Sirica, Sam Spiegel, Salvador Dali, Dick Powell, Count Basie, Ralph Bellamy, Graham Greene, Hans Hartung, Peter Lorre, Bing Crosby

The Wood Dragon is the warmest, most sociable of all Dragons. He's a sunshine of goodwill and helpfulness, giving free advice and assisting his friends whenever called upon. He is a devoted partner, never backing off from duty or responsibility once accepted.

This Dragon also has a special capacity for philosophical deep-thinking. His ability to deal with abstract concepts and synthesize ideas from them is well known and highly thought of among his peers.

The Wood Dragon is a peacemaker, too. He can turn around a potentially explosive situation in a flash with his clever tongue, infusing humor and light-hearted logic into stressful situations. His counsel is often requested by people in high places as he has an uncanny talent for peering through hazy circumstances and coming up with the truth. Although he does not consciously attempt to cause pain, his incisive comments often hit close to the bone.

Wood Dragons are so perspicacious and open-minded that they could become soothsayers or spiritual leaders. Notions from realms outside our world seem to reach this character and the Wood Dragon often knows what will happen before it occurs. This gift makes it possible for him to take up astrology, study metaphysics or become a prophet or healer. A Wood Dragon could also enter the medical and religious professions or even politics and government. Because he is multi-talented he might choose painting, sculpting, writing or acting, but whatever his choice, the Wood Dragon will never be bored or boring. His life is full of activities and hobbies. As long as he can sew and build, plant and pot, paint and decorate after work, the Wood Dragon is happy.

This artistic bent removes some of the stigma of meticulous pickiness which characterizes so many other Dragons. Wood Dragons have a Bohemian streak which allows them the freedom to live in a relaxed way, to forget to put the cover back on the barbecue or to resist the urge to straighten every painting in someone else's house.

All Dragons are fun-loving and festive but the Wood Dragon is the king of dramatic parties. Wherever he finds himself, the Wood Dragon sees to it that he is the center of attention. Salvador Dali was a Wood Dragon – remember his taste for spectacle. No recluse was he. A true Wood Dragon, Dali longed for company, lived for theatre and showed off shamelessly. From his outlandish costumes to his appallingly wild sweeping statements, Dali was the perfect Wood Dragon.

This Dragon is not very courageous or long-suffering. Adversity throws him off course, upsets his tender center and causes him to back away. As the Wood Dragon is not aggressive – one might even call him a reluctant Dragon – he shies from conflict, preferring diplomacy to aggression and love to hate. Because he is a philosopher and wishes to be thought of as the instrument of harmony, the Wood

Dragon gets involved in the most convoluted discussions over a simple issue. The important thing for him is to appear to know what he's talking about: don't hesitate to suggest he shut up if he distracts you from the business at hand. He'll be furious – but it won't last long.

The Fire Dragon

1856 Sigmund Freud
1916 Peter Finch, Kirk Douglas, Betty Grable, Glenn Ford, Luigi Commencini, Olivia de Havilland, Walter Cronkite, Sterling Hayden, Irving Wallace, Harold Robbins, Robert Laffont, Madeleine Robinson, Alice Sapritch, Raf Vallone, Charles Vanel, Jean-Christophe Averty, Gregory Peck, Trevor Howard, François Mitterrand, Yehudi Menuhin, Walker Percy, Martha Raye, Margaret Lockwood

Fire is the Dragon's currency so this is the most dragonesque Dragon. He's certain of his superiority, blatant about his lofty ambitions and is totally self-propelled. Fire Dragons rarely need assistance or beg a loan because . . . when they want something, they take it.

This energetic, feisty, dynamic person is *always* someone to be reckoned with. Whether a Fire Dragon is born starving in the humblest cave or comes into the world with a giant silver spoon melting in his jaws, he stands out above the crowd. He makes a name for himself and causes buckets of trouble for anyone in the immediate neighborhood who doesn't feel like going along with his plans.

He is also extremely generous. Devoted family members and favored friends praise his loyalty and open-handedness. He is intelligent, quick of wit and gregarious. A droll smile often accompanies his brisk remarks as he sees the irony in everything. An innate natural authority lends him an air of grandeur and permits him to behave in an irritatingly condescending fashion. He puffs himself up like the worst sort of dictating monarch, seeming simultaneously to be peering down his nose and inspecting you for fleas.

Even so, the Fire Dragon is the most attractive, charismatic creature in the Chinese zodiac. His personal magnetism is such that people cannot leave him alone. He is bafflingly contradictory. He's rampantly sexy and full of wisdom. He's constantly giving out sound advice, yet is not afraid of taking major risks or embarking on oddball campaigns to effect the impossible. He can be warm-hearted and giving but, when crossed, he is ruthlessly vindictive.

The Fire Dragon is impressive. Upon meeting him, we are initially taken aback. He presents an image of courtesy coupled with masterful hospitality, a kind of *noblesse oblige*. But make no mistake: he may be fabulous to behold and imposing to encounter, but he is also vulnerable. The Fire Dragon's ardor to achieve and succeed is viscous with passion.

Likewise his sentimentality: despite his apparent armor, the Fire Dragon's feelings are easily hurt. His skin is thinner than those green scales would have you believe. And, like many great people, he is a victim of emotional highs and lows which keep him in a dangerous state of nervous tension. He must be wary of over-extending himself, of diluting his cohesive forces by having his finger in too many pies and of being toppled by a craftier, less generous soul than himself.

One of the greatest strengths of the Fire Dragon is his ability to accept his mistakes. Although he is always making sweeping gestures, involving himself in grandiose schemes and craving attention, he is not afraid of the criticism his behavior often affords him – it seems to fuel his ardor. His determination to dominate frequently places him in the public eye. And his earth-shaking decisions often put him on the public firing line. But the Fire Dragon can handle flak. His ego (unlike many Dragon egos) never gets in the way of his desire to be king. A cool customer, he understands the necessity of diplomacy and knows how to withdraw gracefully from untenable positions to smooth the way for a comeback at a more propitious time. Obviously, politics suit this Dragon to perfection.

The Fire Dragon adores engaging in vast projects. He is enterprising and will not involve himself in anything piddling or which is not guaranteed to reward his efforts with world-renown. Although he truly wishes to be effective and use his intelligence wisely, he is not interested in thankless behind-the-scenes work which might not lead him to leadership and celebrity.

Does the Fire Dragon want a better world? Yes, he does. But he also wishes to invent it himself, call it by his own name and rule over its kowtowing subjects.

The Earth Dragon

1928 James Garner, James Brown, Edward Albee, Bo Diddley, James Coburn, Che Guevara, Martin Luther King, Stanley Kubrick, Cannonball Adderley, Alan Pakula, Hardy Kruger, Roddy McDowell, Tony Richardson, Roger Vadim, Frank Borman, Ethel Kennedy, Eddie Fisher, Fred Rogers, Roger Moore, Eartha Kitt, Jeanne Moreau, George Peppard, Fred (Mr) Rogers, Shirley Temple (Black), Grace Kelly, Jean Simmons, Ruth Westheimer

The Earth Dragon is the most ego-driven of all Dragons. He needs flattery, applause and the brightest spotlight under which to evolve his magic. When his ego is stroked his mind comes alive. Tell him how gorgeous he is and he will preen and puff up to bigger than life size and be able to effect amazing feats. Compliments and approval are the fuel of his daily life and without them he is lost, desperate, and subject to depression and even addiction.

Earth Dragons have oodles of charm. They attract, without trying, more members of the opposite sex than they can handle. Their arresting physical presence commands every eye. People never ignore an Earth Dragon, who shines like a beacon in any crowd, attracting hordes of admirers.

The Earth Dragon wishes to help. He is always willing to involve himself in the problems of others, giving aid and assistance to friends, family and even those he does not know well. The Earth confers an uncommon gentleness on the feisty Dragon nature and this Dragon is easily affected by the pain and struggles of others. He offers sympathy and even money to those he feels need his helping hand. As he is completely ego-driven, he will also give his shirt to anyone who pays him tribute.

I would not advise anyone to confront this Dragon over personal policy or ideals. The Earth Dragon is not only serious about his convictions but he can become passionate and even dangerous if crossed – especially by people he considers his friends. Friends are his lifeline: family is necessary and business acquaintances are pleasant, but what really counts are friends. The Earth Dragon coddles and caters to them. He invites them to dinner, takes them to lunch and drags them along on his mammoth fishing trips. Wherever there is an Earth Dragon you will find a bevy of fine, well-aged, true blue cronies on whom he can count and for whom the feeling is mutual.

Career choices for this Dragon should always take into account the necessity of the spotlight. Money alone would never be enough to drive this Dragon to work: no Earth Dragon will be happy doing accounts in an office somewhere out of sight. Even if he decides to be a philosopher or a poet, he must be given top billing and loads of visibility.

This Dragon will never be solitary. He will always choose to be married or at least hitched to someone he loves. He will probably not be capable of sexual fidelity as he is so fetching and so outrageously winning that people fall at his feet for the potential treat of a one-night stand or an afternoon of stolen bliss. But his faithlessness is not treason. He will never abandon his family as no matter how naughty he knows he is, he knows better that his family reveres him most and will provide him with more adulation than a thousand flings. The Earth Dragon has his head screwed on tight and will never surrender security for froth.

This Dragon is a Bohemian. Although he requires constant attention and depends on his public's applause for his sanity, he would prefer to live as an outsider, a rebel, a non-conformist. He delights in eccentricity: no Earth Dragon is happy as a middle-class bourgeois living in the suburbs. He wants pizazz, seeking out the marginal and hunting down the rare. Sometimes he leans towards laxity, forgets discipline in favor of wallowing in wacky pastimes such as hanging out with ne'er-do-wells, drinking, gambling, or taking drugs. This can be his undoing and he should monitor his bad habits from an early age to enjoy a long healthy life.

The Metal Dragon

1820 Florence Nightingale
1880 Lytton Strachey, Guillaume Apollinaire
1940 David Carradine, Ringo Starr, Anita Bryant, John Lennon, Faye Dunaway, Placido Domingo, Raquel Welch, Rex Reed, Richard Pryor, Bernardo Bertolucci, Thomas Harris, Joan Baez, Cliff Richard, Frank Zappa, Julian Bond, Bob Mackie, Rick Nelson, Bruce Lee, Tom Jones, James Brolin, Martin Sheen, Valerie Harper, Brian De Palma, Al Pacino

This Dragon lets nothing stand in the way of his work. He is a Doer. Projects abound – the more difficult and exacting the better. Metal Dragons do not like to be idle: they always choose busyness over inertia. No sitting on the sidelines for this Dragon, who never accepts the role of wallflower. Like time, Metal Dragons wait for no man.

Astrologers say that, of all Dragons, the Metal influenced are the least favored by the gods. They often fall into situations where the vibes (and the company) are unsavory, and are then drawn into intrigue and, ultimately, misfortune. Perversion and even sadistic tendencies are common among Metal Dragons. Their type puzzles even the craftiest of psychoanalysts as they seem so strong, stable, affable and gentle. Even the politest, nicest Metal Dragon often finds joy in deviant behavior. His salvation is to be clever enough to know how to use this taste positively – otherwise he may fall victim to his own (real or imagined) demons.

The Metal Dragon is tough and believes in mind over matter. Thanks to his power, he need not be afraid or shrink from storm-trooping his way out of ugly circumstances. He's both knowledgeable and determined where his work and ideals are concerned, and will always know how to wriggle out and rise to the top – even if he chooses not to.

This Dragon is ambitious beyond all our dreams. He wants to be *somebody* and he devoutly wishes everyone else to notice. He's happiest when he is involved in some lofty cause. Anything from orphans to orchestras will do but the Metal Dragon ought always to have a favorite charity cause which keeps him absorbed and interested enough to stay out of trouble.

He needs to travel to faraway lands. Jobs in public relations or international banking or politics will suit his peripatetic nature. He is very observant and gifted with a prodigious memory. Journalism or scholarship suit his passion for collecting facts and extrapolating knowledge from them. Travelling out of his normal element is just the challenge the Metal Dragon needs to feel that he is being kept on his mental toes. Also, he is attracted by cult religions, which allow him to depart from his childhood ethic and study new ways of solving philosophical problems. The Metal Dragon might make a pilgrimage to the highest regions of Tibet where he sups with monks in rarefied atmospheres and comes back acting all quiet and calm. You might say he goes looking for new ways to skin old cats.

The Metal Dragon is responsible and makes an excellent parent. He will always be married or hitched – even though he strays occasionally, if only for novelty and perhaps the odd learning experience.

Metal Dragons usually earn lots of money at solid, sane jobs. They can take over management posts and make order out of the worst corporate messes. They can handle the thorniest issues and perk up any group with their wise and humanitarian leadership policies. Elect him president, yes, but don't hand over the purse-strings: the Metal Dragon spends money like a drunken lottery winner. And he doesn't like being told to be more economical. He wants no backchat or flak from his underlings and will display his superiority – even at the expense of his composure.

His temper control switch is very sensitive. The Metal Dragon flies into wild fits of anger and will visit them on whomever happens to be brave or foolish enough to confront him. These tantrums don't last long yet they are so impressive that more sober people may doubt the perpetrator's sanity or at least find it hard to forgive him. He should be warned against perpetrating these outbursts when he is not among friends.

Above all, the Metal Dragon loves money. His work is important to him and so are his family and friends but, most of all, he wants to live lavishly, be waited on and deferred to, cooked for and looked after, to laugh and make jokes with his adored friends, to gaze at pulchritude and curl up in the motherly lap of luxury. He will be happy to work towards this goal. But he will also be mighty annoyed if he doesn't reach it. The failed Metal Dragon would be capable of marrying for money, living as a courtesan or settling down in a posh nunnery for the rest of his days.

The Water Dragon

1892 Oliver Hardy, Eddie Cantor, Marcel Dassault, Haile Selassie, Margaret Rutherford, Iphigene Sulzberger, Cole Porter

1952 Dan Aykroyd, Gelsey Kirkland, Jimmy Connors, Robin Williams, Sylvia Kristel, Christopher Reeves, Daniel Balavoine, Roseanne Barr, Carol Kane, David Byrne, Jeff Goldblum, Mandy Patinkin, Chrissie Hynde, Pee-Wee Herman, Jenny Agutter

How about these Water Dragons? Fire and Water don't seem compatible. How does it work? Are Water Dragons contradictory? And contrary? You bet they are! But even when water-soaked and cooled out, the Dragon is extra sensual and an inveterate show-off for life. His behavior is a tad more moderate and his verve is tempered by the influence of Water. He does not present like other feisty, noisy, sometimes bumptious or bombastic Dragons. Instead he gives the impression of high-born gentility, of being well mannered, likeable and, well, scholarly and informed.

You can count on this creature: friendship is his extra strong point. When he takes a liking to someone, and the feeling is mutual, the Water Dragon vows to involve himself for ever in that person's welfare and well-being. He's thoughtful, rings his friends weekly, cheers them when they're down and gives them a boost or even a loan in a tight spot. The Water Dragon is home-loving, adores having a big house, a helpful mate and lots of progeny, pets and other trappings. He revels in inviting cronies round for drinks and dinners, games of cards, a round of badminton or simply a long pleasant chat. He's proprietary, too, showing off his terrain, boasting about the new trees he's planted and the flaming yellow lilies' special blossoms.

He is a curious person, too – like all Dragons, but worse. The Water Dragon is nosy: he cannot glimpse a slip of paper lying on a table or desk without aching to know what's on it. 'Where'd you get this letter? Who wrote it? Are you going to answer? What will you say?' are only a few of the questions that Water Dragons can think up to insinuate themselves into every cranny of your private life.

The Water Dragon's contradictory nature often makes him unsure of his ambition. On the surface he seems directed with clear aims for success, but, underneath, he is not so energetically involved in 'getting there' as he appears. If having money and achieving success means conformity, you can count this Dragon out. If being a star depends on kowtowing to a bunch of witless cigar-smoking producers, the Water Dragon will back out before he begins. Either success comes because of his talent, his unusual gifts and his remarkable brilliance, or he simply cannot be bothered. He'd rather go and live in the country and raise goats.

This Dragon is intuitive, and can advise you on almost any thing. If he does not know an answer to a direct question he will say so. But he will always have an opinion and will probably know where to look for any facts he is missing. He has the capacity to be a real soothsayer. He can sense coming events that will occur in the future for others.

Love is his main objective. Even though he has affairs and flings galore, and seduces and bewitches lovers far into his old age, what really counts for the Water Dragon is *love*. Family, children and long friendships are the mainstay of his emotional stability. He lives for improving the structure of his family and thrives on the approval and gratitude he receives from them.

Most of all, the Water Dragon is creative. His ideas are innovative. He knows how to marry the new with the established and come up with plans which surprise us by their improvisational yet solid sturdiness. He's economical, too – even penny-pinching. He likes to be careful with money so he doesn't have to work at that dratted office where conformity threatens to spoil his fun.

The greatest quandary facing any Water Dragon is caused by his multitude of talents: he finds it difficult to eliminate any in favor of one single pursuit. Most Water Dragons can paint, write, invent, dance and even sing. They are amusing, attractive and easy to like. Early on, when it becomes obvious to the young Water Dragon that he will be forced to choose one discipline over another, he may balk. He wants to imagine, because of his vast stores of energy, that he can one day do it all, have it all and be everything to every man. If he doesn't make some definite choice before the age of twenty, undertake a course of study which offers him a solid future or profession, he had better inherit a lot of money from his rich uncle Harry. A clever Water Dragon can happily while away the oats-sowing years as a professional creative genius or even as a bum. But thirty arrives bringing with it responsibility, children and the desire for security and an under-educated or -employed Water Dragon whose finances don't measure up to his self-image may end up dissatisfied indeed.

My advice? Structure. Discipline. Focus.

Dragon health

If ever I was certain of one Chinese astrological fact it is this: *Dragons are healthy.* They are famous for their vitality and renowned for their physical strength and longevity. As history has proved, it is not all that easy to kill a Dragon.

Now, there is longevity and longevity. Living a long time can be wonderful fun. It definitely postpones death. But living to be a hundred if bedridden and/or senile is hardly worth it. Dragons are lucky: they enjoy old age in the finest of fettles. Even at ninety-five the elderly Dragon is still bossing his children and grandchildren around, commanding both attention and respect. Dragons never give up.

Almost everybody finds the Dragon sexy. He finds himself irresistible so there's no use advising him to curb his enthusiasm or his forays into excessive dalliance. Vitality and pep are two of life's most attractive qualities, especially when they apply to a person of the opposite sex to whom we are attracted. The Dragon's robust physical vigor and basic liveliness of spirit are his main seduction weapon. When he blends his vitality with that warm sentimentality of his, the result is enchanting.

But Dragons *must* curb indulgence and excess. They are outrageously sensitive and enjoy fine food and the best in wines and spirits. They adore a good cigar and many smoke cigarettes to excess. They often enjoy heavily sauced or spicy cooking too. The activity besides sex that Dragons like best is entertaining. No anniversary or birthday goes by without the Dragon concocting a special dish or exotic new drink to celebrate it. The result of all this carousing is a tendency to gain weight. In later life overweight begins to compete against the Dragon's driving ambition to maintain good looks and still operate at full energy. The Dragon's terminal excessiveness may have a disastrous effect on his longevity. Yet the Dragon is a strong-minded soul and able to discipline himself to stop overeating and drinking. From time to time, he abruptly goes on a crash diet and ends the frenzied intake for a while. He may undertake a programme of exercise as well. In a few weeks he will be thin, but, rather than adopting his regime permanently, the silly Dragon goes back to over-indulging and soon finds himself fat and breathless again.

This foolish elastic-band dieting and fasting is damaging to the Dragon's already fragile heart and arterial system. Too much pressure exerted first by over-indulgence then crash dieting will weaken the Dragon and a downward spiral will set in. If you are a Dragon, take up yoga, study meditation, find a way to relax and moderate your favorite pastime – eating and drinking – instead of making yourself sick by repeated deprivation and binges.

Hypertension is another of the Dragon's weak points. As he is naturally short-tempered and preoccupied with achieving the impossible *NOW*, the Dragon is impatient. He can often be heard to snap and carp at colleagues because he perceives them as slow or lacking in spirit. Because of his hot temper the Dragon may also be subject to tachycardia, cardiac spasms and even mild symptoms of angina pectoris, which are not necessarily dangerous on their own but may herald other more serious complaints. Again, the remedy is found in relaxation, exercise and a diet composed mainly of vegetables, fish and grains. Vitamin B complexes have been known to assist the Dragon in lowering high blood pressure as well as improving circulation, which, in his case, is sometimes sluggish.

After the age of thirty, the Dragon often suffers from a 'bad back'. Although he doesn't enjoy physical labor, he is always eager to shine and may attempt to prove himself by lifting and carting heavy things, offering to carry an old lady across the street or picking up heavy loads for effect. Repeated abuse of the backbone's flexible good nature will cause slipped discs or at least a nagging sciatica attack. The remedy? Restraint and moderation. Or, if he is lucky enough to find a good chiropractor, the Dragon should take a life subscription and listen to the practitioner's advice.

If you have a sick Dragon friend, send a get well card when you first hear about his illness. He may have a few bouts of ill health but, with his marvellous recuperative powers, he can pop back into action after only a matter of days.

To maintain his strength and powers at their zenith, he must take care to survey the state of his health, have check-ups regularly and listen to the wisdom of his own body. If he's tired, he must rest. When he's nervous he should do breathing exercises or meditate. The cure for anxiety or frustration is not found in a medicine (or other) bottle. 'Cooling off', by going fishing or taking a long walk, is by far the best way for the Dragon to handle stress.

The best foods to encourage the Dragon's sluggish circulatory system are shellfish, offal, algae, citrus fruits and pineapple juice. If he suffers from anxiety or depression, stimulants such as alcohol, coffee, cola, tobacco and tea should be rigorously avoided in favor of fruit juice, especially apple or grape. He can eat all he wants of dried fruits such as dates, raisins, bananas, plums and figs. Appetite-stimulating spices are all right so long as they are not used in excessive amounts. Garlic pills or garlic cooked with food will ease his chronic hypertension.

Finally, the Dragon's most delicate health problems often stem from the difficulty his mind has in coping with reality. Frustrations crop up and cause him great anxiety – either he cannot get this or that accomplished his way fast enough or else he's not getting the co-operation he needs from associates. Or perhaps he cannot choose one subject to pursue as there seem too many available.

The best therapy for Dragons in trouble is one-to-one exchange of information, where he feels he is being taken seriously and can use self-help methods to effect an improvement or cure. He must never be made to feel helpless or powerless: such feelings only drive him deeper into his illness, making him violent and intractable.

Dragon futures

What the Dragon should expect from the next twelve Chinese animal years

2008, the Earth Rat year – Here comes a bonanza year for you Dragon people. Nobody admires your dashing self more than the canny Rat. And the feeling is often mutual. You will be awash in propositions for new projects and called upon to direct (one activity you simply adore!) everything from the village orchestra to the Neighborhood Watch. You are a star in this Rat year – and what's more you can feel it. A rush of approval and freewheeling comes over you about mid-March and won't leave until the end of January. Take wise advantage of the opportunities presented to you, because they are almost all excellent chances for the betterment of both your financial and personal life. A love interest appears about halfway through the year. If you are attached, beware of temptation. This person is most attractive and is drawn to your charismatic personality. If you are not hitched, go for it. Family members' needs may impinge on your time in the Rat year. Give some to those in need of your moral support, but don't be tempted to shower them with your new-found wealth. You have better things to do with your money than bail people out of gambling debt or lend your new BMW to your shiftless brother-in-law who lost his license for drink-driving.

2009, the Earth Ox year – Providing you keep the lid on your notoriously flamboyant nature, the Ox will not interfere with your progress this year. What gets under the Ox's thick hide most is your tendency to concoct disorder and create chaotic celebrations out of everything from the dog's wedding anniversary to your wife's sister-in-law's menopause. Ox years are about hard work and order. Oxen are not always fond of anything or anyone who colors outside the lines in life's big coloring book. They love tradition and social structure. You do too. But you need to make a brouhaha about it and the Ox does not. Oxen, too, are bullies. They enjoy giving orders and don't take them very graciously. As you are a more natural leader type – a beloved despot – you may find clashes cropping up where you least expect them. I am not suggesting this will be a difficult year for you – unless of course you forget to lower your voice and keep your vociferous opinions to yourself. Because of the conservative atmosphere in this Ox year, let me suggest that you take a closer look at your accounting strategies. Pay off your credit cards. Wild spending sprees occasioned by last year's elation are not favored in Ox years. Take a more conventional approach to budgeting, or you are in for some timber-shivering surprises.

2010, the Metal Tiger year – There are a number of things about your character which irk the tawny Tiger. First of all, he abhors snobbism and name-dropping. The Tiger is irritated by your causal boastfulness about the famous *Who's Who* person you saw at the fancy restaurant, or which celebrated author gave you her estimable autograph, or who you sat next to at the Academy Awards. Big talkers' words fall on his deafest ear. Tigers don't care much about *Who's Who*, and they deplore pretensions of all variety. So no matter if the Pope comes to your funeral, don't do any bragging or trying to impress during this Tiger year. Same holds true for your famous maudlin displays of sentimentality and that tendency of yours to want to steal every show. Basically, this can be a bang-up year for you financially. All new and unusual projects are favored. The Tiger is your ally. He admires your spunky spirit and your words of sane advice are always welcome. So long as you don't spout any flames through her bedroom window or steal his sweetheart with those seductive swishings of your scaly tail this year, the Tiger will encourage all of your pursuits and applaud most vigorously when you succeed. Be as subtle as you know how. And don't show off. Tigers hate braggarts.

2011, the Metal Cat year – Never your favorite years, these tranquility-seeking Cat years frankly get on your nerves. You are forever prospecting for excitement, seeking sources of joy and lighting your own fireworks displays. The Cat intuits this rambunctious Dragon-esque behavior as rowdy and disruptive. Face it. You Dragons are a noisy lot! Cats are quiet and even secretive. So the overall atmosphere in this current year will want to tone down your life. Frustration is then in store because you really are sad when the fireworks go out and the last of the Roman candles lies sizzling at your feet. How to handle it all? Reflection is not your strong suit. But you can do it when pushed. This year you will not be pushed. Rather, you will summarily be given the hook from offstage and find yourself in the quiet backstage of most of the action (which in Cat years usually happens in banks and other such august institutions). So why not learn to meditate or join a Dragon support group wherein you might learn to button your lip and do some deep deep thinking? Why? Because you need a plan. Make lists. Set up goals. Build new dreams. Next year is the *Dragon* year. You better be ready to roll!

2012, the Water Dragon year – The year is all yours! For Dragons, the words 'all mine' are particularly meaningful. You like to have control of your own existence and are not disinclined to taking control of a few other lives along the way. You have just had eleven long years to complete your previous twelve year cycle and now you are off on a new one! But of course you are in the rebirthing stage of the cycle – the very first year indeed. So you may find yourself uncharacteristically childlike again. Louder than ever. More flamboy-ant and mouthy. Increasingly self-important and just a shade on the rambunctious side. Never mind. Go ahead and cavort and enjoy the party. But, when you wake up each morning, do remember to add something solid to your list of the accomplishments you want to be proud of over the next dozen years. Ask yourself: 'Where do I want to be in two years? Five years? Nine or ten years?' How do you intend to live out your dreams and with whom by your side? All of these considerations are key to a person's success as a significant human being. Do not plan to fritter away a couple of years in sabbatical mode. You cannot afford to miss a single opportunity to shine. A Dragon's life is always a barrel of monkeys. Make the best of it.

2013, the Water Snake year – You will be obliged to cease the romps and quell those party instincts this year. The Snake is not a slave-driver. But he/she needs *all* the attention. You also fall smack dab into the attention-getter category. But you are not fond of competition. You like floodlights and marching bands. The Snake prefers soft Debussy and fragrant bathtubs surrounded by flickering colored candles. One may be as attractive as the other. However, this is not *your* year. It belongs to the quiet, unobtrusive, philosophical but powerful Snake. So what will occur between you and the Snake year is a clash of styles. Your turn to don a bushel basket to cover your head and scuttle along walls so as not to be noticed. This may cause you some degree of indigestion because when the limelight blacks out, you grow blue and sometimes even pity yourself. *Poor me* is unbecoming to dauntless creatures like you. So check yourself before you sink into your own home-made oblivion. Keep in mind this is the second year of your twelve-year cycle and you need to have a plan. Where did you put that list I suggested you write last year? Find it. Add to it. And implement each step one by one so as to stay on track.

2014, the Wood Horse year – Dragons can easily find themselves flummoxed by Horse years. First of all, these years are notoriously fraught with tension. The Horse is often a strong yet troubled soul whose sense of self can be easily disrupted by the slightest setback. You, Dragon, might just be part of one of those setbacks as you are not daunted by the prospect of conflict with anyone – least of all a Horse. You sense the Horse's force. But sometimes you don't intuit the Horse's skittish fragility. Horses are powerhouses of talent. But they don't always seek to shine. They are not so interested in hogging the stage as you are. But they do want and need and actively seek recognition. This year I suggest you chill. Hang back a bit. Look around in your own life and wonder to yourself just how much progress you have been making over the past couple of years. Then, on tiptoe, return to the fray without making waves or awakening the Horse's aggression. You will be able to make enormous progress in Horse years and enjoy loads more time with your family . . . if only you can keep the lid on that your flamboyance. Horses need understanding. Sentimental people like you are capable of largesse and compassion. Use those talents this year and you will float right through unbridled.

2015, the Wood Goat year – You are a star with Goats. Why? Because they need your power and are willing to go to almost any lengths to be able to depend on it. Goats are all about creativity and zany, wigged-out notions. They love ease and long for comfort. They dream of languishing in plenty. But they are not always able to secure those dreamed-of luxuries by themselves. So when a big, strong, capable Dragon comes sashaying along, Goats prick up their ears and keep their eyes peeled for inroads so they might benefit from the Dragon's willingness to lead them forward. Goats have many more good ideas per second than a Dragon can keep inside his proud scaly head. Goats don't mind being humble and even modest. But they do not ever want to have to compete or impose their wills in the big bad world. They prefer to feed the strong leaders. So your job in a Goat year as one of those same strong leaders is to take the reins without appearing to. Run the show from the wings and let the Goat have his day. He or she will thank you for ever after and shower you will love and devotion for a lifetime.

2016, the Fire Monkey year – Monkeys are some of the most unpredictable characters in the Chinese Zodiac. Hence, we are never very certain of outcomes in Monkey years. Dragons don't usually fear change. Nor do they need to be reassured at every bump in the road. But the danger for Dragons in Monkey years is risk. Dragons rarely shrink from the precarious. They feel that they know how to handle it. If something goes wrong, they always think they know how to fix it. But in Monkey years, we cannot be so sure. You, Dragon, may be inclined in these testy years to embark on one or two big, chancy ventures and then watch them slowly but surely disintegrate before your big, glaucous eyeballs. So the message for Dragons in Monkey years is to hold off from embarking on gigantic, revolutionary projects. Remain in the realm of safe and sound investment. Put some money into further schooling or travel to places where you can learn something new that you will be able to use next year when the more predictable Rooster comes along and tries to hamper everybody's progress – except his own.

2017, the Fire Rooster year – Marriage, for Dragons, is one of the most important states of being they know. Dragons (like Rats) tend to be marriers. They may marry many more times than once. But they like to know that their main squeeze or significant other is securely hitched to their tail. Now in Rooster years, Dragon marriages tend not to fare well. Ditto for long-term live-in relationships. There is something about the rigidity and firmness of mind of the Rooster which impedes the Dragon's normally sane emotional grip. This phenomenon gets under the Dragon's scaly skin and itches. The

Dragon grows cranky and irritable and his significant other frequently chooses a Rooster year to tell her Dragon to go get scratched elsewhere. Romance, then, is not favored for Dragons in this stodgy Rooster year. Moreover, as the Rooster always wants to prance and crow and be on top, Dragons feel competed with for the spotlight. My advice? This year should serve as a wake-up call. Work on your relationships. Delve into the depths of your partner's emotions. Figure out what is really troubling your business associates. Ask frank and open questions of family members that you cannot seem to get on with. The fault is not necessarily yours. But it's likely that you haven't been listening.

2018, the Earth Dog year – You shine and can breathe freely in Dog years! There is a harmonious energy between you and Dog people. You admire their grit and determination and, although they would never dare imitate such extravagant behavior, they like your style. They are also fond of the fact that you speak up and express your opinions about matters they find urgently important, such as politics and humanitarian endeavors. This year, you will be called upon to assist the Dog with his causes and crusades. These efforts may of course involve extensive travel to not-always-savory environments. But no matter. What's a little indigestion when you are serving humanity? You will be well served by your philanthropies. Your family is still riled about that delicate matter too long left untreated. Let them dig out on their own, but lend moral support to those you feel are doing the best job managing. You have been quite sentimental enough and given your all. Now, it's their turn to take care of their problems; your turn to applaud when they succeed and share their disappointment when they fail. Do not give away money. Right now, you need all the cash you can muster to carry on your good works.

2019, the Earth Pig year – Glory and Jubilation! The Pig and you get along like two pigs in the proverbial *merde.* The Pig approves of you wholeheartedly and even admires your trumpeting manners and overweening pride. For the rather retiring, self-effacing (but tough and ambitious) Pig person, you are tantamount to a god or a prophet. And what is even better, you are beloved by Pigs. They truly like you and enjoy your raucous company and invite you to their dinner parties because you are so brilliant and entertaining and witty and alive. Under this benevolent influence, the upheavals of your personal life will iron out as well. You do need to show some indulgence and improve your listening skills. But the mere ambience of munificence inherent in all Pig years for Dragons will supply any slack in your intimate relationship with just the jump-start you need to gain momentum. Your money picture improves in this Pig year too. Somehow you have finally got the hang of the job or profession or project you have been working towards. With all the fun you are having this year, you might be tempted to coast a bit now. I wouldn't advise it. There's a Rat year ahead for all of us and no matter how much they like us, Rats can be stern taskmasters.

The Tantalizing Snake

Oh Tempting Snake,

How does it feel to be irresistible? It must be super to know that the whole world is intoxicated by you with your bewitching perfume, your silken scarves and your glamorous accessories. Everybody is in awe of your appearance. And you, in turn, are in awe of how adoring your admirers are. You do so love to please. Some think of you as the silent type. But you can be very talkative when there is something important to say. People cherish your sagacious advice. Those seeking peace of mind are drawn to consult you for counselling and wisdom. You can always tell what's about to happen before it does. One wonders if you receive messages from other realms. If you do, don't fight it. Listen to the spirits and learn. With money, you are both a miser and a spendthrift. Rather than pushing up the thermostat a few degrees, you'll wrap yourself in sable and curl up with a good lover. You are famous for demanding exclusive rights on your mate while blithely maintaining your own busy private life on the side. Security is your all time favorite happiness-provider. Marry up with a resourceful Rooster or a stabilizing Ox. The first two parts of your life will be hectic and nerve-racking. But old age becomes you. Enjoy it.

Some advice? Be generous with your glory. Try to decline the spotlight when someone who needs it more than you is around.

Fetchingly yours,

Suzanne White

In the twentieth and twenty-first century all Snakes were born between the following dates:

4	February	1905	and	24	January	1906
23	January	1917	and	10	February	1918
10	February	1929	and	29	January	1930
27	January	1941	and	14	February	1942
14	February	1953	and	2	February	1954
21	February	1965	and	20	January	1966
18	February	1977	and	6	February	1978
6	February	1989	and	26	January	1990
24	January	2001	and	11	February	2002
10	February	2013	and	30	January	2014

The Snake ID card

Lasting symbols have special powers. Enhance your self-image by surrounding yourself with tangible signs of your own identity and make these symbols known to your friends and loved ones. Use them daily and they will bring you luck, security and a feeling of personal worth.

Your best	***Your favorite***
color is ice blue	food is caviar
flower is camellia	animal is turtle dove
fragrance is musk	drink is champagne
tree is palm	spice is curry
flavor is bittersweet	metal is platinum
birthstone is opal	herb is fennel
lucky number is 3	musical instrument is violin

The Snake is yang ***The Snake's motto is 'I feel'***

When a Snake is at his most appealing he can be amiable, compromising, fun-loving, altruistic, honorable, sympathetic, philosophical, charitable, a paragon of fashion, intuitive, discreet, diplomatic, amusing and sexy.

But when a Snake decides to be a pill he becomes self-righteous, imperious, judgemental, conniving, mendacious, grabby, clinging, pessimistic, fickle, haughty, ostentatious and a very sore loser.

I slink therefore I am

Snakes were charming men long before men charmed snakes. A profound stillness of spirit inhabits every Snake. This quality is silent yet never sombre or sullen. The Snake's quiet is icy *coooool*. Compound this unruffled dignity with exceptional physical beauty and you get a fair sketch of Snakes. Their sinuous manner and graceful gait inspire more than just admiration: people don't gape curiously at Snakes or even ogle them. They fall madly, passionately and irrevocably in love with them.

Any learned Chinese will tell you that Snakes have always been the mainline seducers of the human race. Once you get to know the difference between Snakes and the rest of us, you will concur.

Masses of people are secretly or hopelessly in love with Snakes. Feature those frustrated folk you know who have been lusting after a gorgeous, unattainable creature, blubbering into their pillows and wondering why. They are probably in love with a Snake. Or take those people who sulk and snivel all the time because their spouse or mate 'plays around'. Those poor unsuspecting persons are probably married to, living with or in love with Snakes. Snakes are either the cause or the effect of so many love affairs that I could write a thirty-year TV soap opera about them.

Snakes are spotlight magnets, too. The Snake will not be ignored. Peer group attention and public recognition are the least of what he expects. Yet Snakes are never noisy or deliberately outspoken. They have little but wisdom to dispense. They rarely behave blatantly or show off. They are always correctly attired in subtly elegant clothing. They have excellent manners.

Why, then, do we feel so drawn to them? Why do grown men weep rivers through their shaving cream over these creatures? Why do sane women chew their false fingernails to the elbow waiting for a phone call from a missing Snake lover?

Because the Snake is the tempter, the universal symbol of sexuality and faithless passion, the emblem of wanton ardor and romance. The Snake invented naughtiness when he seduced Eve into sin. But the astrological Snake, the one we all adore, is not a devil, not even a little demon. The Snake is a nice, oversexed normal human being.

Snakes don't perform their enticement routine with malice aforethought. They simply don't know how not to enchant unawares the victims who fall at their expensively shod feet.

I have a Snake daughter named Daisy. When she was a baby Daisy was a blue-eyed, bald butterball of perfection. At three she got some fine white-blonde hair which at six was pageboy length and she had become a photogenic monster of kid beauty. By ten her golden tresses had thickened and her waist begun to slim. She looked so gorgeous I was afraid to let her go to school on her own because clumsy adoring hordes of boys attacked her. In the sixth year, during a stampede to be the one to tread off the back of Daisy's sneaker and give her what little boys called a 'flat tire', one pre-teen lunkhead broke poor Daisy's ankle. For love.

Daisy the Snake was *such* a beautiful child I felt guilty about teaching her to wash dishes. I came to my senses and continued to insist she did it but, from time to time, even I fell under Daisy's serpentine spell. Everybody did.

Once, when Daisy was twelve, we were invited to dinner by the novelist, Irwin Shaw. In those days, he took people to a well-known restaurant we all liked. Irwin had never met my kids before. Daisy strolled into the restaurant ahead of me and Irwin, who was a big man with an even bigger voice, zeroed in on the ravishing blonde, tanned Daisy, pointed and said, 'Good God, will you look at that creature!' Wolf whistles came from somewhere and made me feel, suddenly, very protective.

I looked quickly at Daisy to see how she was faring. *Everyone* was looking at her. If I had been in her shorts, I'd have died of embarrassment. But not Daisy: she was beaming, maintaining perfect dignity and moving along until she paused beside Irwin Shaw, looked him in the eye and said coolly, 'Excuse me, sir, but I am only twelve years old,' then continued, with perfect composure, to her seat.

Irwin cleared his throat uncomfortably. As I passed him, he said, loudly enough for all to hear, 'Suzanne, you really ought to put a sign on that kid. Something like: "Hands off, I'm only twelve."'

Contrary to most people's notions, it is possible to be too beautiful: it can even be a handicap. For Daisy, having close, loyal girlfriends has always been a problem because of jealousy. She has a terrible time if she has to work for unattractive women, too. She once had an old-maidish drama teacher who tormented her by warning that she might be too beautiful to become a successful actress: Daisy's beauty was bound to be a distraction to the audience. Being too good-looking has prevented my unbelievably handsome Snake doctor friend, Yvan, from getting patients. He's a gynecologist and husbands don't want him around their wives.

But beauty is only the half of it. With Snakes, the sorcery doesn't stop at the physical. It is in the allure that surrounds them. Snakes do not get dressed in the morning the way the rest of us do. They prepare meticulously to meet their public. They may only don jeans and an old sweater but they are always careful to accessorize, to smell right for the clothes they wear. On a Snake, rags would look chic.

Are Snakes narcissistic? Yes, I daresay they are. They don't just accept their faces, bodies, limbs, ears, hair, teeth, skin, fingernails and toenails, they *love* and take special care of them. They are impeccably groomed inside and out. Coiffeurs, barbers, beauty parlors and plastic surgeons would go broke tomorrow if some well-meaning Irish saint came along and rid the world of Snakes.

Snakes also keep designers and couturiers afloat. They all feel that they look best in expensively cut, perfectly fitting, made-to-order clothes. Worse . . . Snakes cannot take a bath without the proper accessories. Without Snakes, the Louis Vuitton luggage company would go out of business and so would Hermès, Cartier, and Bulgari. Go into the best apparel or designer accessory shop in any major city, on a busy Saturday, take a survey of customers' birthdays and I guarantee more than half turn out to be Snakes.

Snakes *really* splurge on accessories. Baubles, trinkets and adornments seem to cry out from their locked glass cases at Tiffany's directly into the ears of the marauding Snakes in all the poshest shopping areas of the world. Snakes get others to buy them fancy accessories and buy them for themselves. They wear gold chains around their necks and never go anywhere without the cuff-links which match the tie-pin, or the tortoiseshell hair-clip to go with the glasses' frame, which matches the clasp on the handbag which picks up the tone of the necklace and matching earrings.

The Snake's preoccupation with appearance may lead one to believe that Snakes are superficial. Nothing could be further from the truth. Despite their narcissism and ostentatious dress habits, Snakes are among the most profoundly thoughtful and philosophical members of our race.

Take Gustave Flaubert. If Flaubert had not been such an incredible Snake, he would never have been able to create Madame Bovary, the perfect Snake, victorious through marriage in satisfying her desire for luxury and social acceptance, yet unable to curb her sexual appetites sufficiently to keep up appearances. Madame Bovary lost everything she had ever wanted – security, propriety and the love of a good husband – because of her fickleness and wanton flaunting of moral convention. Oh, the transparent autobiography of it all! Flaubert should have called his novel: *Madame Serpent*.

Another annoying habit of Snakes, which goes along with their addiction to seduction, is the skillful telling of lies. To some Snakes lying is essential and takes the form of a true pathology. To others, lying is for fun, a way to liven up a story, or even a tool which assists them to slalom their way to the top. In China, Snakes are reputed to be out and out liars.

I find this judgement harsh. The Snake prevaricates more than many but I like to see this as a kind of prestidigitation. The Snake knows how to mislead, to misrepresent, to work magic on the psyche of his interlocutors by seeming to be what he or she is not. Such a gift is hardly simple lying.

For Snakes, evasion and omission are the preferred methods of dissimulation. Any Snake worth his skin would rather embellish a terrible truth than hit you over the head with it. Or, when these tactics don't work, the Snake will use another: he invents a second truth which he hopes will throw powder in the eyes of the first or real one.

At my country house in France, I have a Snake neighbor. A year ago, in the interest of building a fence along the edge of my property, I had surveyors come in and stake out my land. When they were through it came out that my neighbor, who had lived there for a year, had paved over part of my land to use as her driveway. It was a simple miscalculation, I thought. I knew that she had not had her land properly surveyed before installing the drive but I thought her paving on my side was an honest mistake. She had also planted sixteen trees along her driveway – on my land. She was not pleased at the result of my survey. I apologized for the inconvenience and called in a man to see how much a fence might cost. He strung a rope between the surveyor's stakes along my property line and hung pretty blue flags on his line so we could see clearly where it ran. He said he could install a fence in a couple of weeks' time. His price was quite high. I said I would think about it. The next weekend I went away to Paris.

I returned on Monday. My ropes, flags and surveyor's stakes were gone. I called my neighbor to ask if she'd taken them away,

'... perhaps by accident while you were gardening,' I suggested diplomatically.

'Oh no,' she replied in a voice cool enough to freeze the phone wires. 'I didn't even know they were missing. But now that you mention it, on Saturday night I heard a noise at about two a.m. I thought it was an animal. But maybe it was someone who——'

'A marauding stake puller-upper?' I said sarcastically. 'I strongly doubt it.'

She went on, 'Well, next morning when I got up, I saw a footprint in the bank across from my back door.'

I said, 'I have a sneaky feeling that if I go on a hunt for those stakes and flags and ropes I'll find them.'

I heard a gasp. 'Where would you look?'

'Right behind that muddy bank in the woods.'

'Wait!' cried the Snake. 'I'll go with you.'

'No, thanks. I think I can handle it.' I hung up. Skirt and all, I clambered to the summit of that bank in my best suede sandals. Once on top, I sat down, shaded my eyes with my hand and surveyed the woods like Pocahontas. At first I saw nothing. Then my X-ray eyes detected seven wooden surveyor's stakes, scores of little blue flags and snippets of rope strewn casually in the weeds. I ruined my skirt and muddied my feet but I picked up my lost goods and scrambled back up the bank victorious.

If you have dealings with Snakes remember that they are capable of *biggie* lies. Also, they frequently suffer from working their own magic on themselves. They are almost too clever at bamboozling and will tell little stories to their psyche that can get them into terrible trouble. If they pursue self-delusion, they can easily begin believing that they are better than other people because they are more handsome or beautiful or sexy. They may fool themselves into imagining they deserve more attention and consideration than their peers, that favors should be dealt them simply because they deign to grace the world with their presence.

A dangerous business is this shamming of the self: it is loaded with possible disappointment. There is nothing more intransigent than a Snake who does not feel he's getting his due out of life. He may grow sad, self-pitying and embittered. He may even fall ill or become addicted to drugs or alcohol, turn into a philanderer who makes a fool of himself, having sex with anyone he can lay hands on just for the thrill of being accepted, appreciated and desired.

Sometimes Snakes embroider on their woes. As they are given to self-aggrandizement, requiring a personal mythology to find self-confidence, they view themselves, self-defeatingly, as misunderstood or rejected by those they deem should love and appreciate them more. This is a bad habit and should be discouraged early on as it feeds into the Snake's neurotic pattern of constantly seeking approval and attention.

Money and Snakes is a hot issue. Although they adore opulence and lust after luxury, Snakes deplore utilitarian spending. They may throw money away on loot such as gold trinkets or platinum earrings, the right finish on the antique desk they picked up at Christie's or Sotheby's – but *hate* having to cough up for the electricity bill. They are greedy for money, stingy with it in specific circumstances and lavish with it in others. Generally, Snakes are careful but generous with friends and family. They know how to count pennies when necessary and are almost never in danger of declaring bankruptcy.

Emotional stability is of paramount importance to the Snake's well-being. Rejection is the worst blow his delicate ego can suffer. The Snake must be received, welcomed, accepted and approved by those with whom he comes in contact. Only when he is certain he is liked does he feel safe and able to progress. To ensure both his financial and mental security, he acts prudently and is rarely confrontational. He gives the impression of being even-tempered and conciliatory. One often perceives him as a person who adheres to the least line of resistance, takes life easy, doesn't make waves.

But these apparently pacifistic habits are but a defense strategy. He remains beguilingly cool to avoid disrupting his precious security and thus his progress. He cannot function in chaos. Routine appeals to the Snake. Tradition and sameness are his friends. He likes to evolve in an atmosphere of predictability with people he can be sure of, even if those people are not the most exciting he will meet. Snakes often compromise the pursuit of thrills or knowledge – and sometimes even passion – for the sake of remaining part of a continuum in which they feel safe.

Snakes have been known to stay on in failed marriages where nothing works any more, where passion is long dead and where quiet desperation is the order of the day – just for security.

I know a beautiful French Snake named Mireille who, at the age of fifty, still lives with her mother. She is married and has even had a child but Mireille never felt that her husband was capable of providing her with the same cozy, predictable security that her mother, a widow who raised her as an only child, had always given her. Her mother makes the rules and the decisions and Mireille has always worked side by side with her in Maman's restaurant bar. The husband lives in, too, but has long since turned to hunting and card-playing for outside company. Mireille's son is grown and married and Mireille is still contentedly living with and obeying her mother, who has just decided to retire.

Last time I saw her I asked Mireille when she was going to take over running the restaurant. My question surprised her. 'Me? Run this restaurant all alone? Without my mother?' She gaped at me. 'Never!'

Her mother sold the restaurant and Mireille retired too. Maman still does the cooking and makes the decisions. Just last year Mireille became a grandmother. Maman made the arrangements for the baptism, chose the invitations and even Mireille's dress. As a result of this kind of sacrifice for security, certain Snakes become inhibited and frustrated. They know that they are over-dependent on others for their survival and happiness. But they just can't help it.

The Snake tends to exhibit almost obsequious gratitude for gestures of kindness or generosity as he is always currying favor, playing up to his audience and hoping he will be loved as much as he needs. When and if he does find someone to provide him with unconditional love, he may sit back, breathe easy and grow placid and lazy. Which, any Snake's long-time mate will tell you, is precisely what he does if he isn't pushed or sufficiently challenged. The Snake seduces until he doesn't need to any more. Professionally, he throws himself into tailspins to get ahead in his work until, when he gets the big promotion or makes enough money, he sits down and does nothing.

Remember Greta Garbo? Her life story began with beauty and continued in fame. Then, in the thick of the glory, her career screeched to a halt. Garbo's life continued sedately and comfortably in seclusion and relative idleness until she died at a ripe old age. A legend in her time.

The Snake woman

When people tell me that their mistress, wife, sister, daughter, friend or acquaintance was born in a Snake year, I know without seeing her that she must be very beautiful. *All* Snake women are wonderful to look at. They know instinctively how to carry themselves, how to behave and how to enchant everyone they meet. To say that Snake women are seductive would be understatement of the lowest sort. Snake women are positively bewitching!

Yet they are not intentionally provocative. Unlike the powerful, compelling Dragon woman or the perky, mischievous Monkey, Snake women rarely wear garish clothing or buzz fetchingly about at parties poured into fluorescent or diamond-studded gowns. A Snake woman doesn't speak loudly or make flashy statements to get attention. Yet eyes light on her like bees on a radiant flower. Nobody ignores a Snake woman's presence. Is it the grace of her gestures or the feminine way she holds her glass or tea-cup? Are we drawn to her because of her serene, soothing manner? Or is it something spiritual and glowing that seems to rise from within and belie her glacial, intelligent exterior?

As an admirer of Snake women and their uncanny talent for wooing the public, for entertaining us without trying, I vote for the latter: there is a mysterious 'something' about Snake women – an ability to spin heads without uttering so much as a peep. Snake women have simply got 'it' and 'it' (as all of us thinking women well know) is all it takes.

Not only can the Snake woman charm the pants off the world, she also gets to carry her physical gifts into a ripe old age. Be she long and willowy or shortish, pillowy and dimpled, the Snake woman is always distinguished and dignified. She is never cute or bouncy. Her body usually boasts strongly muscled legs and arms which keep their tone long after the menopause. She is supple and undulates subtly when she walks. The Snake woman is naturally gifted for dancing, especially ballroom dancing. Executing deft steps in the arms of a gallant gentleman is the romantic Snake woman's idea of heaven. Even though she can be wraith-thin, she never appears skinny or unappetizing. Her well-shaped bones are coated in soft curves. She has the kind of caressable shoulders that men long to stroke, so frocks with a plunging neckline or off-the-shoulder *décolletages* suit her beautifully. She is sexy, sensual and desirable. The Snake woman is rarely big-busted or buxom: her breasts are usually smallish and high on her chest. Her hips are well shaped and her waist narrow. But her body never screams *sex*. She is neither Marilyn Monroe (a Tiger) nor Madonna (a Pig). Rather she is *gorgeous*!

The Snake woman is blessed with a fair, satiny complexion and a perfect oval face which wears a permanent expression of childlike innocence. Her voice is pleasant, too – but it can be irresistibly velvety or cold and hard. Her almond-shaped eyes are often misty and carry a promise of tenderness and unfathomable sensuality which turns on even the hardest-hearted of men. Her lips are always pronounced, seeming to have a natural outline as though she were wearing lipstick even when she is not. Her smile might be likened to the knowing grin of an enigmatic Mona Lisa. It expresses candor, wisdom, generosity and a beguiling hint of cynicism.

The Snake woman, although vain and fashion-conscious, limits herself to expensive, well-designed clothing, well-cut furs and sumptuous jewels. She doesn't feel comfortable going anywhere unless she is richly adorned and will spend much of her earnings (and those of her admirers) on garments suitable for draping her gorgeousness. (PS Imelda Marcos is a Snake.)

I don't know a single Snake woman who is not well groomed. Although these delicious creatures are famous for their languor, they take rigorous care of their physical selves, with regular exercise, rigid diets, taking off make-up and weight, and religiously applying creams and lotions to soften their rough dry skin. It's as though they know instinctively that their appearance is the strongest arm they will ever have in the battle for a good life.

Settling down to married or at least 'live-in' life at an early age is highly recommended for Snake women, to satisfy their deep need for security and predictability. There are several reasons for this advice: first, Snake women have precarious, uneven health. Their physical constitution is anything but robust and they easily contract ailments which leave others alone (see health section p. 255). Second, Snake women often have several children, but enjoy working outside the home. They have remarkable intellectual and professional endurance but can be guilty of driving themselves physically to breaking point. For all the elements of her life to operate in harmony, they need to establish a sound social structure – marriage and a home – before going on with building a career and family. Third, Snake women are highly susceptible to psychosomatic and stress-related illness. The physical symptoms are very real but aggravated by stress and more so by unstable environments. A solid family base, a home and a well-functioning support system will serve as a haven for the Snake woman's tired mind and body.

The Snake woman's physical lot is not comfortable and is complicated with contradictions and caveats. Snake women are naturally indolent and feel the need to lie for hours immobile in the sun. But strong sunlight is dangerous to both their health and beauty. The sun dries their already fragile skin, making it brittle, flaky and crackly-looking and can cause sunstroke (to which fragile Snake women are particularly susceptible), cancer, or encourage the engorgement of varicose veins. A little sun is all right but too much is dangerous and destructive.

To maintain a balance of good health, the Snake woman should eat only the things that her body tolerates well and nibble at those she cannot assimilate without painful after-effects. She should avoid draconian slimming diets and maintain instead a sound, structured nutritional balance which suits her physical make-up. She should *always* take mild daily exercise. If anybody needs a daily *constitutional* walk it's our lovely Madame Snake. As a rule she does not perspire much so exercise helps her body eliminate toxins by forcing it to sweat. Violent exercise is out: swimming, gymnastics, dancing, slow walking or muscle training will suffice to keep her metabolism and sluggish plumbing system stimulated. I also recommend seeing a vitamin and nutritional therapist regularly to help maintain the immune system. It wouldn't hurt either to go for frequent relaxing massages.

Strict maintenance is essential to the Snake's welfare. She must take care of herself or she will fall into a state of languid disrepair and possibly waste away. Hence the need for more than a little disposable income. Thanks to her incredible attractiveness she may land a rich, generous fellow who will take care of her for the rest of her life.

But although the Snake woman requires an inordinate amount of rest and spends much of her leisure time in bed, she is not usually the type to lie about doing nothing and growing neurotic over her woes. She is not busy-bee industrious but she is ambitious, wants to be involved in a career and 'make something' of herself.

Snake women are also notoriously brilliant. They make excellent students at school and, once given their head in any intellectual pursuit, will usually outshine the competition in endurance and brains. The Snake woman is an avid reader and learns everything easily because of her powers of concentration.

Culturally, as in other areas of her life, she will not settle for the mediocre. In literature, art, music, ballet or theater, she is only interested in the best – and usually gets it. She rarely says anything vapid or silly and is much sought after among her friends for her wise advice and sound philosophy.

Those careers for which the Snake woman is gifted depend on appearance and include fashion model, performer, diplomat, saleswoman, actress, negotiator, public-relations expert or dancer. In these professions she may succeed by enchanting her opponents or seducing her public rather than using her mind. If she prefers to be out of the limelight, she could make a wonderful doctor, psychologist or investigator. She would be a first-rate philosopher or theoretician. Because of her natural gift for clairvoyance and her uncanny intuition, the Snake woman might well choose a career in extra-sensory areas such as fortune-telling or astrology.

She is an especially creative person and can engage in all professions which touch on the world of art and culture. As she is a wizard with money, she might aspire to be an art dealer or painter, a writer or publisher, a sculptor or even a museum curator. The arts fascinate the Snake woman and she knows instinctively what is good art and how to make it work for her. She could be a top decorator, a designer of anything from clothes to gardens. She might become a caterer, decorator or professional home entertainment specialist (she gives great parties). She could edit a magazine devoted to any of the above subjects, using her rich husband's (or lover's) money to start it up and making a go of it through her talent and delight in amassing more capital than she started with.

The Snake woman's strength in the workplace is manifest because of her special attitude towards being paid handsomely for what she does. Despite her reluctance to deal squarely with reality and her natural torpor of soul, she knows what she wants from life and does not bother trifling with details (such as guilt) which might impede her progress. The Snake woman believes that she should be paid to advance her own cause and will not work solely to advance the causes of others. It is impossible to under-pay a Snake woman. She simply will not allow it. Often (except in health) she is luckier than other people and stumbles on just the patron she needs to finance her next project or send her to study. She is a woman born to have great wealth, either by marriage or inheritance.

Earlier I mentioned the Snake woman's emotional make-up as the cause of some of her physical ills. She is physically and mentally hypersensitive: proportion must be guarded, harmony in line, color and shape impeccable. To function properly, the Snake woman should be surrounded with peace, stillness, safety and attentive, loving people who drown her in affection and understanding. She cannot stand to be jostled or hurried. Ugliness, untidiness, disorder, noise, pollution, vulgarity and disrupted schedules make her crazy, miserable and depressed. Her sensitivity to her environment is like a radar which goes haywire when it meets with any displeasing interruption.

Because of her penchant for the predictable, the Snake woman cleaves to ritual. She loves tradition, history and even religion because its well-established shapes and structures comfort her.

The Snake woman functions most with her heart, which creates a vulnerability which is often her undoing or at least a source of perpetual perplexity. She is constantly disappointed by the evil in the world, troubled by imperfection and laid low by instability or disruption. Her intellectual capacity is forged of hardened steel, but is often shrouded in dreamy romantic idealism. If she keeps the lights on in her head, she knows that her mind is her savior. All she has to do is remember to call upon logic for answers to what troubles her and the clever Snake woman will always find the solution.

Unfortunately, the need for affection, warmth, approval and acceptance is paramount in Ms Snake's life. She is always stepping gingerly over mines in conversation so that she doesn't ruffle anyone whose approval she may need to survive. Her vulnerability makes her prudent. The good news is that her stand-back attitude enables the Snake woman to see both sides of human behavior. She tries to be fair as she abhors injustice. Her instinct votes for tact and thoughtfulness.

She would like to be a better person and sometimes perceives her grasping need for attention as selfish. Her perceptions are keen and she excels at intuiting what others are feeling. She readily admits her mistakes and never holds grudges. If she feels any aggression, she usually chooses to conceal it to show her best side. The Snake woman maintains an admirable and exquisite affection for those she loves, and because she depends on their approval defends them to the death.

This person is a dreamer and brooder. She cannot help it – she doesn't want to face reality. Her other-worldliness is a large part of her charm but it can be a hindrance to her advancement. She needs urging and loving tugs on her sleeve to remind her that she must put all her imagination into seducing her way through life, hence forcing the competition to surrender to her superiority. This is a tall order and takes nearly all this fragile yet fiercely determined person's strength. Yet she can (and will) win.

The Snake woman can be a bit of a snob. She likes her comforts, friends and associates to be of the highest calibre. She finds people of wealth, fame, rank, prestige and superior intellectual ability appealing and is drawn to the sense of security it gives her to be included in their circle. The Snake woman wants life to treat her like a fairy princess. She doesn't like menial or manual chores, is not attracted to roughneck activities such as camping or mountain climbing, always preferring to sprawl in the satiny lap of luxury.

I went to a book fair some years ago where I was invited to stay in a plush hotel suite if I agreed to share a room with a Snake woman editor from my French publishing house. The arrangement was fine with me. We both spoke French so communication was no problem. After the first gruelling day at the fair, I invited her to unwind with me over a drink in the city where the fair was being held.

She looked at me sorrowfully and said with true regret, 'Thank you, Suzanne, but I just want to go back to our hotel now. It's so warm and beautiful there.'

I acquiesced and returned to our hotel with her. I planned on going straight to the pool for a little exercise before dinner. When I'm exhausted I must keep moving. But not Ms Snake.

When I came back from swimming, she was sitting there, wide awake, dreamy-eyed, just *be*ing. I ordered her dinner in the room where, for four whole days, she spent every hour that she wasn't at the book fair, luxuriating and loving every inert minute of it.

Lastly, I must tell you about the Snake woman's immensely interesting love life. This woman is a born *femme fatale*. Her voluptuousness is vividly obvious and men are spellbound from the moment she meets them until she leaves their presence (she never leaves their minds). Her problem will rarely be one of how to find a mate. Rather, the Snake woman has too many admirers, lovers and Prince Charmings falling all over their swords just to breathe the air she breathes, which often confuses her. She sincerely wants to please them all and yet – except for security – she secretly doesn't want to settle down with one man for ever. But the prospect of loneliness is the Snake woman's biggest fear. She cannot live without the company, attention and companionship of a man. Her identity depends on being part of a couple and a family, belonging to a group, adhering to a social structure. Whatever logic may dictate or reason may try to tell her, the Snake woman believes that loving and being loved is the most vital business in life. To live without love, for the Snake woman, is tantamount to being dead.

But how does she love? With intensity, passion and romanticism. Her commitment to love is so great that she demands her love be honored in return with the same profound exclusivity. She has no time for half-way measures or lukewarm sentiments.

Her lovemaking is reputed to be wantonly abandoned, but she deplores vulgarity or coarseness and will shrink from rough sex or sadism. Her sexuality is ethereal yet she can be down-to-earth too. She has the reputation for wrapping her sexual self around the loins of her gentlemen conquests and never letting go – even after it's all over between them. The melody lingers on. She is both possessive and avidly jealous of any attention paid her mate by others. Snake women cannot stand competition in any area, particularly in the sexual arena, and will suffocate competition rather than allow it to surpass them.

The Snake woman's love comes at a high price. Men who wish to enjoy her favors for extended periods must be able to bankroll a luxurious lifestyle. She is not an easy person to live with because she needs constant reassurance and will falter and balk at the least hint of her mate's inattention. She is never boring as her mind is active and bright, and she has a great sense of humor.

Her own fidelity is relative. Because she cannot help but be attracted to the effects of her own attractiveness, the Snake woman tends to stray. Yet if her lover or husband should be caught with *his* pants down, the Snake woman will be unforgiving. She may ask for a divorce but usually she doesn't mean it unless the defecting husband can make it worth her while financially. Even if she is furious with him for betraying her, she considers her husband the pillar of her security and will not let him go easily. She fears loneliness and loss of face almost as much as she hates his adultery.

There is a certain hypocrisy, too, in the Snake woman's behavior towards her children. She is wont to declare that her kids are her whole life. Yet she knows full well that she is more a lover than a mother. There is not the faintest trace of maternal instinct in her personality. For all kinds of reasons – especially those relating to her figure – she is afraid of childbearing. She doesn't really like babies either, and her rapport with children grows as they reach adolescence and early adulthood and become both adoring and reasonable.

But the Snake woman is kind and charitable: she loves animals and is an attentive, earnest friend to anyone suffering or in pain. She often does voluntary work and is always willing to give her time (and sometimes her husband's money) for humanitarian causes.

The Snake woman wants it all ways. She would like it if all the men in the world were hers to love. Yet she needs desperately to be loved by one man and be kept in the utmost security and luxury. She longs to be rich but cannot stand to see anyone go hungry or suffer from want. She believes firmly that life should be spent in pursuit of the philosophical truth – yet she finds herself guilty of dissimulation and prevarication. She knows that the early bird gets the worm, but she lies abed till all hours unable to force herself to rise and shine. Hers is a sometimes trying and always contradictory existence, rife with complexity and questing for answers.

Monsieur Snake

The male of this species is equally as adorable as his female counterpart. He is handsome – oh, so good-looking – and, although not usually of heroic physical proportions, sexily built, boasting a muscular frame and a nice flat tummy. His hips are usually slim and his bottom firm and attractive. The Snake male's bearing is sylphlike and elegant. He walks lightly and is inordinately supple. He has long legs, yet is not tall. Snake men are born distinguished. They are smooth-talking, dignified and mannerly, rarely raising their voices or stooping to exhibit aggressive or vulgar behavior.

Facially, the Snake male boasts a refined, delicate bone structure. Regular features without any outstanding flaws are the rule. His eyes are heavily lashed, adding to the air of dreaminess and unreality for which he is famous. His mouth is heart-shaped and his forehead both broad and smooth. Usually, his hair is long and silky and sticks to his scalp all his life. He has an aquiline nose, a true sign of nobility, but his rounded chin shows that his will is weak.

Although he does it subtly, the Snake man loves to show off his body. Frequently, that gorgeous guy on the beach that you can't take your eyes off – the one with the teeny trunks and the lanky legs – was born in a Snake year. He adores being looked at and willingly exhibits his physical endowments in intimate – and even not so intimate – gatherings.

He is very fastidious about his appearance. Being by nature narcissistic, he maintains a dignified, well-groomed manner and is nattily dressed. He goes in for affectation, too: it is not unusual to see him wearing gloves or sporting exaggerated refinements such as silk handkerchiefs, custom-made designer spectacle frames or sunglasses, elegant ties from exotic shops, antique brass buttons and signature scarves, forever adding foppish details to his outfits. He doesn't hesitate to use gallons of toilet water and daubs perfume where he thinks it will have the most captivating effect.

The Snake man benefits from a sunny personality and pleasing manner. He readily engages in idle chit-chat which, among his many other attributes, has a special appeal for women. He always has time for the latest gossip, comment on the fabric of your skirt or notice the way you have changed your hair.

He is just as sensitive as he is affable. He requires harmony and seeks pacific environments wherein no rudeness or vulgarity exists. He hates disruption, haste, abrupt change and hostility. His inner peace depends on how much security he can create around his person. He seeks a life of calm with space inside the tranquillity for him to remain free yet be certain of the loyalty of his companions and far-reaching support systems. He is essentially a family man and, because of that, no matter what crazy complications arise, the Snake man always slides back to normal.

The male Snake's need for psychological well-being to be created for him by others – never by himself – makes him vulnerable to negative influences. He learns early that to maintain his security, he must force himself to appear non-confrontational, compliant, and meek, and adapts a *modus vivendi* wherein he exercises caution and vigilance at all times. He is circumspect and prudent, scrutinizing every situation for tension or danger to his quietude. Whenever he senses tension, he attempts to smooth things over, settle quarrels and get his life back on an even keel.

These elaborate tactics amount to a strategy wherein caution takes precedence over almost everything else: the male Snake, too, often adopts the line of least resistance. This over-prudent attitude, although it usually keeps him safe, may paralyze him and inhibit his progress in the world. Initiative becomes a serious risk to a person whose defences are always up and whose main goal is to stay out of harm's way. Any gift he might have for entrepreneurship is hampered because he is so often afraid to make a false move.

Some people call him cowardly or lazy. He is certainly too compromising and easy to manipulate. He is also an inveterate fib teller. He lies his way in and out of conflict until he no longer knows what the truth is. Perhaps out of frustration or maybe in an effort to counteract his toyings with truth, he frequently cleaves to hidebound traditions and becomes a conformist or moralizer where others are concerned.

In all of this our Snake man is only trying to secure the necessary goodwill he needs from others to survive. He treats everybody with gentle consideration and rarely affronts anyone directly, because he is afraid to lose their love. He never raises his voice or loses his temper, swallowing his real feelings and concealing his pain (1) to spare other people's feelings (2) to keep their affection (3) to maintain his dignity. He is not a fighter or a bully. He is never vengeful or reproaching of those he loves and he rarely defends himself openly – even against patently violent aggressors.

The Snake man is an intellectual, a man who works with his head. Whether educated or not, he is intensely curious and seeks to be informed about life and is intimately aware of the complexity and profundity of the human condition. He is patient, showing indulgence for the follies and vicissitudes of those who call on him for his intelligent advice. A casual Snake friend or acquaintance can quickly become a mentor as his decisions and considerations, although never hasty or even spontaneous, are nearly always creative, workable and wise. He has a natural sense of equity and fair play, makes honest efforts to weigh all sides of a question.

The down side of this talent for giving good, level-headed advice is that male Snakes take for ever to make up their minds. Their lives are fraught with deliberation and hesitation. They lack for ready decision-making and agonizingly resist committing to a firm point of view. The Snake man is so resistant to taking a new stand on contentious matters that he may seem stubborn and intransigent when he is only being careful not to make waves. When he balks at changing his mind, it is usually because he is afraid of the consequences of adopting a new platform.

Unless you know him well, you might never guess that the Snake man's mind is a veritable mosaic composed of ephemeral spiritual depths and poetic, romantic considerations. He's a strong, silent type, a dyed-in-the-wool visionary whose exacerbated sensitivity makes him able to grasp the subtlest nuance of feeling, guessing accurately at the innermost thoughts of his enemies as well as his friends. He is susceptible to the tiniest shift in emotion and will react to events before they happen, as though he were gifted with extrasensory perception.

The Snake man, like his female counterpart, believes in the basic virtue of humankind. He trusts in the essential power of good over evil and of reason over folly. He longs for altruism to triumph over violence and hatred, and will spend large portions of his time hunting for solutions to the inequities he so strongly desires to see eliminated.

It is said that the male Snake is the sexiest of all the Chinese zodiac signs. He cannot resist the temptation to seduce *every* woman he meets. Although his aim is to get them into bed, he doesn't despair if he does not at first succeed. As far as the male Snake is concerned, there will always be a next time.

The Snake man is incurably romantic. He sees his role as a professional lover, Lothario and tender-loving-care giver as a mission. His love of his fellow (men and women alike) is so great and his ability to love them so enormous that he can never leave them alone. He always wants to help people in trouble, to raise someone's spirits or lift a bum out of the gutter. He is princely in his desire to take the failing masses under his tutelage and care or to lend a helping hand to a chum. When he takes on a 'case' his motives are pure and noble. He is driven by real compassion for the victim's sad situation.

But . . . God help the downtrodden wretch who improves his lot. If those the Snake man was so selflessly assisting no longer need him, he sags and feels unwanted. He sincerely wants to help but he'd rather his charges did not become independent of him and fly away.

I know a woman whose philandering Snake husband metamorphosed into a faithful stay-at-home as soon as she broke her leg. He found her the best surgeons and spent hours reading up on physical therapy. He took her everywhere in the car, hauling the wheelchair to the finest restaurants and practically spoon-feeding her while she was laid up with a cast. Yet as soon as she was better, her dutiful Snake husband returned to his parties and re-entered the role of Romeo, complete with intermittent and sometimes severe spates of ladykilling.

Snake men see their flirtatious, libertine behavior as charity or a cure for what ails society. They are in love with love and lovemaking. They have no time for uptight, narrow-minded people who denounce their good works. Love, the Snake gentleman feels, is supposed to be free for everybody, a simple human pleasure or commodity laid on by God. He deplores sexclusivity – except, of course, for his own mate whom he knows could never stray from his attractive side.

In this area, the male Snake's lucidity is dim. He cannot see how easy it is for some women to up and leave his irresistible company. Usually, he chooses a partner who adores him absolutely so that he is fairly certain never to feel the crushing rejection he so abhors.

Once in a while, though, a Snake man will meet, fall in love with and even marry a woman who can be equally infatuate as he. If he does, the Snake man falls apart. It is inconceivable to him that any member of his family might defect. No matter how inconstant he is or how numerous and blatant his infidelities, he would never divorce unless he was divorced first. But, then, he would probably never marry either, unless he was coerced into it. His lack of will, his insatiable desire to please and his unwillingness to say no to possessive ladies who long to bear both his name and his children are the only reasons he ever got married in the first place. Some Snake men's wives believe that they can reform them, keep them out of the beds of all the other ladies they love. Miraculously, once in a while, Mr Snake does stay physically faithful, swearing off his addiction to conjugal infidelity, but it would be over-idealistic to imagine that this lover of love and the thrills it procures him could stay on the wagon for ever.

Love represents the Snake man's sustenance. For him to live without it in profusion is to die. Any woman who wants him as a mate will be unhappy if she allows his dalliances to cause her anxiety or jealousy. She should not take it personally. Infidelity is just his way.

The clever-minded Snake man can choose from many different careers. He is intelligent, lucid and wise about all affairs except his own, creative and sensitive to all that is artistic and harmonious, and eminently capable of assuming a post of authority and handling high official or executive positions. At work, he is responsible and operates out of deep conviction. But whatever brilliance he possesses, whatever talents he may exhibit from an early age, or whatever superlative contacts he makes, he should *never* be called upon solely to perform manual labor. Not only is he clumsy at such jobs, but he is at risk of accident. He can cook, sew or do tapestry or upholstery – craft-related work – but don't ask the Snake to become a plumber, mason, carpenter or even a surgeon. He will find manual jobs dull, unaesthetic, and, if he doesn't die of boredom, will probably be killed in some accident caused by inattention, daydreaming or attempting the impossible.

I once employed a Snake plumber in Paris. Jean-Jacques was the best plumber because he was *there*. But he was ever so slow – and *far* too creative ever to be a plain old plumber. His copper pipe hook-ups always twisted and turned into funny places such as up over the back of the sink because he thought it less unattractive that way. Our plumber/employer relationship became so impractical that I settled for staying good friends with Jean-Jacques and used another plumber. Snakes don't hold grudges so there are no hard feelings between us. As a pal, Jean-Jacques advises me about everything from finances to emotional planning. I wondered why he became a plumber. He said his father had been a plumber. Like so many improperly disciplined Snakes, he had opted for the path of least resistance, deciding not to struggle uphill in a demanding career which might force him to get out of bed when he preferred to lie there and muse.

Their creative abilities coupled with their good looks make Snake men naturally prepared to engage in all artistic professions such as painting or decorating, designing, hairdressing, *haute couture*, dancing, acting, singing or performing as an entertainer. As he is both altruistic and deep-thinking, he can be successful as a philosopher, psychologist, detective, physician, researcher, scholar or scientist. His business acumen is excellent. He makes a willing team member – even if he is the leader – as he prefers to work in groups rather than operate alone. When properly surrounded, he is capable of managing large sums of money and making wise investments. He could be a banker, an estate planner, an administrator, an investment counsellor or a behind-the-scenes property developer. He can be a highly successful art or antique dealer, too.

Diplomacy is an art and the Snake man knows how to manipulate others skilfully. He wriggles his way in and out of tight spots all the time and might choose jobs in journalism, the foreign service, agenting (travel and other) or even espionage.

The Snake man needs good associates to help him make prompt decisions, but with them he can become a rich and powerful entrepreneur, especially if he teams up with a Rat or a Dragon. Money comes easily to the Snake and he is articulate so law as a profession might work. His remarkable ability to invent and present emotional pleas for the welfare of his downtrodden victim clients will surely persuade judges and juries alike. He would also make an excellent judge.

The male Snake is potentially lazy and should be firmly disciplined as he is growing up. It may be hard going at first, but if, finally, he learns self-control and concentration, he may be able to take over the world. His capacity for abstract thinking is exceptional. It should be encouraged. His talents are many but his will to fight is weak. Good parental and educational guidance will help him to develop determination. Without it, he may surrender early on and take the path of least resistance.

Returning to the romantic life of the Snake male, his popularity with women is not entirely of his own making. The Snake man is tremendously attractive, not only physically winning, but his gentle heart is like an open rose, fresh and full of promise. Ladies simply fall at his feet. They sense his willingness to love them just as they are. He adores them. And they adore him.

The Snake male happily accepts the opacity of male/female intimacy and is undaunted by its tangles. He's a smashing lover, fearless and expert at giving pleasure to his partner. Sometimes, he gets so enthralled by *l'amour* that he falls in love with several women at once and is at a loss to refuse their blandishments because he feels strongly for each. He is always kind and not vicious or meretricious in love.

Of course the complexities this behavior produces are scary and fraught with jealousy and rage. But the Snake man isn't frightened. He spends his time involved in endless emotional snarl-ups, sexual traffic jams and endless discussions and recriminations which would paralyze an ordinary soul – I *don't* wholly approve of his messy sex life – but there's something mildly heroic about his wild, spendthrift attitude to love.

The five Chinese elements and how they affect the Snake

The Wood Snake

1845 Gabriel Fauré, Mary Cassatt
1905 Robert Penn Warren, Henry Fonda, Myrna Loy, Greta Garbo, Howard Hughes, Munro Leaf, Clara Bow, Leo Campion, Raymond Aron, Jean Arthur, Mischa Auer, Claudette Colbert, Joel MacCrea, Ashley Montagu
1965 Brooke Shields, Charlie Sheen, Robert Downey Jr

This Snake is the public speaker, the actor, the skillful communicator and presenter of grand-scale ideas. His exquisite laying out of information guarantees him success. He knows instinctively what place in society he wants to carve out for himself.

Although the Wood Snake suffers from more than his share of reversals, he will make a million comebacks, returning valiantly to the front lines to begin again, perhaps in another way, to climb the golden ladder of success. The Wood Snake, like all Snakes, has to fight a tendency to laziness and an exaggerated love of luxury for its own sake but because of his intense will to reap applause, renown and great wealth, he will always overcome his negative penchant for sloth.

He is a dreamer and often has to force himself to be practical. But, unlike some Snakes who are incapable of disciplining themselves, when it comes to making money, the Wood Snake can be downright pragmatic. If he can't make it as a painter, he'll try illustrating children's books and if that doesn't work he'll go into advertising or commercial design. The point is to get there. Any means to the end is valid. The Wood Snake may be vain but he is not proud. He is always able to discern winning from just getting by – and he knows that what he wants most is to win.

As a bona fide Snake, he is conscious of a deep-seated sneaking desire to enjoy all the pleasures of life. He is not one to refuse the joys of the palate, the eye, the ear and whatever else he can get his body round. No matter how immense his projects or public his image, the Wood Snake is always furiously involved in seeking new ways to enjoy himself.

The Wood Snake's drive to achieve fame and fortune is powered by his ambition to please, to win approval and to get his persona across to his audience or public. He loves kudos and being admired is his drug. He is a perfectionist in his work and stops at nothing to learn more, ever challenging his intellect to break through new territory and find novel means of transporting both his charismatic image and powerhouse ideas to the world.

All Wood Snakes suffer from rejection. It is difficult for them to accept flaws in others. They want their partners to be wholly attentive to and responsible for their well-being. They require constant attention and big doses of compassion and understanding to survive. They also need security and a calm environment to thrive. If the object of their affection cannot provide these or doesn't measure up to the draconian criteria set forth by this demanding lover, the Wood Snake's heart may be broken.

Although he demands intellectual freedom for himself and is scandalously flirtatious – even patently unfaithful – he is jealous, exclusive and monopolistic when it comes to love. He will never take a back seat or allow total freedom to the other person. For the sake of his love for another, the Wood Snake is not above dissembling and committing emotional blackmail. He will make his loved one feel guilty until they either conform to his ideal or give up and leave. Emotional involvement with the Wood Snake is anything but simple: the rules are hard to follow for anyone who has outside interests. Extricating oneself is even harder. The unsticking of the Wood Snake's stubborn tentacles of unconditional love and devotion from someone he loves is a horrible, painful process to observe.

As being left alone is exactly what this Snake fears most, the loss of a loved one can mean physical as well as nervous collapse. Serious illness and depression may overcome the poor bereft creature. The road back will be long and arduous but he does come back and, once restored in body and mind, he enjoys renewed stability, rekindled ardor and belief in the all-powerful emotion for which he truly lives – love.

People adore this charming character. His presence is always desirable as he talks easily and has a quick sense of humor. The Wood Snake really likes social intercourse: he's happiest when surrounded and adored. He's friendliest when he knows he is liked and is a wonderful friend whose wise advice is invaluable to his many cronies. He's a fervent advocate of the arts. He spends much time and money promoting cultural activities. His homes are showplaces of precious works of art and antiques. He entertains with generosity and style. His manner is obliging and, as long as his own advancement and personal interests are in no way compromised, he will go far out of his way to accommodate those he cares for.

The Fire Snake

1797 Franz Schubert
1857 Joseph Conrad
1917 Raymond Burr, John Fitzgerald Kennedy, Robert Mitchum, Cleveland Amory, Robert Lowell, Frederick Brissom, Mel Ferrer, Dean Martin, Sidney Sheldon, Anthony Burgess, Dinah Shore, Lena Horne, Joan Fontaine

The deep-thinking Fire Snake is not only brilliant, he is power hungry. When he wants to succeed, he is capable of gigantic masterful strokes which will propel him into the public eye, wipe out the competition and, with a swish of his tail, confer on him a title he can be proud of. This Snake means business.

The Fire Snake's will is stronger than that of his fellow Snakes. He can glide in and out of social gatherings with panache. He sidles up to important people and turns them to putty with his inimitably slippery charm. He makes contacts and uses them to his own benefit, leaving, if necessary, the contact in the dust. Fire Snakes are ruthless, glamorous and profoundly learned. They are unafraid of scholarship, know how to concentrate and assimilate knowledge like other people soak up sunshine.

Friends and acquaintances play a significant role in the Fire Snake's life. He makes friends easily and keeps them interested because of his charm and willingness to participate in their lives. He will always help out a pal or even give a leg up to a person he has just met, because the Fire Snake believes avidly in the goodness of humankind and in its ability to right its own wrongs. To this essentially altruistic person, nobody is altogether a fool or a criminal.

Unlike their somewhat reticent counterparts, Fire Snakes have strong opinions that they are not afraid to express with vehemence and clarity. This gift makes them keen politicians, actors, singers, writers, poets and film-makers, professions that give them the chance to put their strong ideals into action.

One drawback to the Fire Snake's charm is his unquenchable thirst for sex. His overactive sensuality is so forceful and directive that he is almost handicapped by it. Sex is omnipresent in his everyday thoughts. His propensity for promiscuity is so great as to constitute a danger for his personal safety. He so needs to be found attractive, to make love, to be courted, admired, hugged, kissed, wooed and smothered in love that he can forget his usually excellent manners and commit acts of foolishness which threaten his reputation and even his personal safety. He usually curtails his murky private involvements sufficiently not to besmirch his public persona. But if he isn't careful, he may be blackmailed or attract nasty newspaper coverage. Scandal sheets seem to sense the vulnerability of the Fire Snake.

Although he usually marries for love, the Fire Snake will not remain physically faithful for any reasonable length of time. He is incapable of resisting the tug of sexuality which keeps him constantly on the *qui vive*, prowling and hunting for new blood. His mate, however, should not interpret this as disloyalty. The Fire Snake is fiercely devoted to his family. He spends lots of time with them, nurtures his children and fawns on his partner. He depends on his family to anchor his fickle heart and keep it from drifting off into uncharted territory for ever.

The Fire Snake likes to travel and is at ease in all social gatherings. His manner is sardonically subtle and secretive. Although he is a deep thinker, when it comes to relationships he is not profound. He can, however, be counted on to keep a confidence or to hold up his end of a bargain. He's sometimes too judgemental and not indulgent enough with those he feels less socially responsible than he is but the Fire Snake is a gentle sort. His sterling integrity informs his every act – except, of course, in the bedroom, where no holds are barred and the sky's the limit.

The Earth Snake

1809 Felix Mendelssohn
1869 André Gide
1929 Milan Kundera, Beverly Sills, Anne Frank, Imelda Marcos, Jacqueline Onassis, Bob Newhart, Ed Asner, John Cassavetes,

Buzz Aldrin, Irene Papas, Régine, Audrey Hepburn, Jacques Brel, Max Van Sydow, Yasser Arafat, Larry Collins, Hughes Aufray, Bruno Crémer, Peter Maas, Lee Grant, Dick Clark

Here, in the Earth Snake, is the very lightest of Snakes. The Earth element lends frivolity to the already delicately constructed Snake and gives him an extra dose of feminine charm.

More than any other, this Snake feeds on dreams. He is often lost in reverie and seems to be floating above the clouds. The baser parts of life, such as violence, raw sex, dirt and poverty, upset the Earth Snake so much that, to survive, he must always remain at a safe remove. His cozy swarm of illusion serves as a cocoon for this fragile creature's sensitivities and protects him from reality.

The Earth Snake is, nevertheless, an intelligent person, full of wild ideas and heady plans. But, no matter how he works, he is not always able to carry through with his plans because of his curious, defeating habit of self-deception. He is a potentially marvellous magician who knows how to twist and turn facts and create his own version of the truth but he fails to apply this talent to the outside world where he might need it to make a deal or slither through some difficult stage. Instead, he tells himself that everything will be all right so long as he believes his own trumped-up version of what's really afoot. This Snake ends up with a reputation for lacking perseverance and stability. He's forever joining forces with people who are even better at duping than he is and finding himself lost and without an anchor for the duration.

To counteract this tendency, the Earth Snake is a marvellous seeker (and finder) of rock-like mates to shelter him from the big bad world and who know how to appreciate (and perhaps even exploit) the Earth Snake's brilliant lies.

I renovated a ruined house in a Provençal village some years back. My mason was a fantastically inventive Spanish craftsman named Juan who built me a fabulous four-bedroomed house out of a ten-room dump. Juan always told me the truth – *his* truth. But sometimes his truths were just fantasies about how it could be so much more beautiful if I had a mezzanine here or a terrace there.

'I prefer to work on a house,' he explained, 'that I create myself than just execute some foolish plan made by a mere architect!'

As long as this Snake is well married or still in the safe cradle of his parents' home, he will not encounter too many disasters. At home, he is a kind of genius: he's tender-hearted and makes an excellent family person who always listens and understands the miseries of other members. He's an excellent parent and a superior host. His warm welcomes and pleasantries infuse his guests with joy and a feeling of warmth from the moment they cross the threshold. He's generous and spontaneous, giving of his goods and himself for the sake of friendship or loyalty to his clan.

The Earth Snake is more dependent than the other Snakes. He is very hard-working and clever at sorting out thorny issues. Ideally, he should be employed by a large corporation or at least a solid small company or even the government. An insecure job where money and stability are not part of the package would cause him too much inner turmoil and lead to his departure or failure to uphold his end of the responsibility. He is not hard-hearted enough to boss others around but because he's so damned creative he has plenty of trouble following orders.

The nature of this gentle soul is so pleasing and his temperament so even and jolly that people with selfish motives, who berate him for his lily-liveredness, his love of luxury, his easy-going attitudes and his pure joy in living, often take advantage of him. He must be careful not to attach himself to those who don't have his best interests at heart. Those who associate with him must know how to appreciate his easy charm and be able to leave it at that. He cannot be hurried or pressured or changed.

If alerted to the dangers surrounding him, the Earth Snake can usually sort out the predators who seek to tame and torture him. He is more than wise. He is wily and *ever* so clever at understanding reality. He may become cynical and crudely aware of what *is*. But he is oblivious: he prefers to dream, plot and scheme than to get up every morning and tussle with the truths of the hard life ahead.

Aware of his frivolous nature, this Snake is often attracted to conservative types. Somehow, he's able to discern, through his haze of fantasy, that the best way to survive is by locating folk more down-to-earth than he and cultivating their friendship and love. He will often seem very creative and even silly by comparison to his plodding mate. You might wonder why he chooses to live in a backwater when he seems more Bohemian. Truth is, he's happier among the middle class who demand only that he gossip or shop, cook or dispense love. And ... he is happiest in a natural setting where trees, woods and flowers provide a constant refuge from aggression. By staying out of the way, he isn't obliged to leave his cozy nest of fantasy and can roll about with his dreams all day in complete safety.

The wise Earth Snake knows what he needs to survive and uses his innate charm and merry manner to get it. Perhaps in the context of suburban bourgeois security, or as a country gentleman, he will energetically fund-raise for museums or restore a lovely old mansion, feed the starving millions from his brocade armchair, or even adopt unfortunate third-world babies. But don't count on the sensitive Earth Snake's willing participation in any projects requiring scrambling in the rough. Even though his governing element is Earth, this Snake will fade and be miserable if he has to dip so much as his dainty big toe in the mud.

The Metal Snake

1821 Fyodor Dostoevsky, Gustave Flaubert
1881 James Joyce, Bela Bartok, Picasso, Franklin Delano Roosevelt, John Barrymore, Cecil B. De Mille
1941 Michael Moriarty, Julie Christie, Bob Dylan, Beau Bridges, Carole King, Aretha Franklin, Art Garfunkel, Otis Redding, Paul Anka, Muhammad Ali, Yuri Andropov, Dionne Warwick, Chubby Checker, Sarah Miles, Ryan O'Neal, Stacey Keach

This brand of Snake lusts after a grand life and an even grander wealth. He is a big time person with grandiose ideas – you might even say, *delusions* of grandeur. He is ambitious and wants notoriety. He seeks to show off his talents to get the attention of the entire world. Because of his searing need for public acclaim, he often succeeds at becoming something of a star, wherever he may live or ply his trade.

The life of the hyper-talented Metal Snake is marked by difficulty. He often suffers giant reversals, losing fortunes or loved ones, falling into drug excesses or cultivating religious foolishness, both of which lead to disaster and cause him to lose precious time in his quest for fame and fortune. But he always pulls himself together and starts his quest again.

Like all Snakes, because of his deep desire to please and be accepted, the Metal Snake is vulnerable, but he is even more so because he doesn't hesitate to wear his heart on his sleeve, to shout his opinions and throw open the door of his heart to the general public. He melts with joy at the thunderous applause. But he is unwary of the fickleness behind the applause of a public quick to lose interest, to grow critical and unkind towards the unprotected Snake whom they have admired. Bad press or an unappreciative audience can defeat this unguarded genius and render him suicidal.

Although he is insufficiently wary of his public, this Snake is usually suspicious in his private life. He doesn't trust easily and will search for a long while before committing to marriage or family life. He wants to be sure he is not played for a fool. He needs to know that his partner will be faithful and uphold his ideals. He must be assured of security before accepting to wear the yoke of family. Of all Snakes he is the most naïve and believing in the basic goodness of man. He tries to be a good person, to emulate those he admires, to speak out for humanitarian causes. Because the Metal Snake is disingenuous, he is easily taken in by unscrupulous characters who do not have his best interests at heart, accept his favors, use him and dump him. I would not go so far as to say he is attracted by low-lifes – but perhaps he is.

The Metal Snake knows that he has a taste for adultery and cannot remain faithful for ever to a sexual partner. He also knows that one day he will break the covenant of good faith that marriage demands. He feels this as a chink in his armor, which somehow, somewhere, breaks his callow little Metal Snake heart.

When he becomes aware of his imperfections, conflicts arise inside the Metal Snake's responsible, solid citizen head and he is not always comfortable in his skin. He may experience a difficult period of self-doubt. Or, more likely, he may do what he is so gifted for: rationalize. He will tell himself that he needs freedom to be creative, or that he must be at liberty to roam so that he can help mankind, or that a few infidelities will ultimately do the marriage good. This Snake lies like a rug but he means no harm.

Ironically, Metal Snakes are chronic truth-seekers. They may be superficially sociable and want to make it in the world but they dream secretly of solitude, of living on cloud nine with an unlisted phone number. In their daily life they sometimes simulate a desert-island anonymity by choosing not to answer personal questions, evading reality to maintain an aura of mystery about and for themselves.

There is none so opportunistic as this incisive and intuitive person whose creative genius usually finds a lucky star on which to ride to the top. The Metal Snake can see a chance for success in everyone he meets. He cultivates contacts the way other people grow cabbages. His method of operation begins with charm and ends with seduction. One day, he will hitch a ride with the perfect sponsor and before you know it you'll be reading about his superstar status in everything from the tabloids upwards.

Despite his vulnerability and desire for fame and positive cash flow, this Snake is somewhat of an intellectual. He is curious and interested in the inner working of the mind and will spend much of his spare time reading and studying, listening or finding out about things. He may choose to specialize in history or even devolve into obscure fields of philosophy and exotic Eastern religions. He keeps his own counsel, is superbly self-confident and manages to remain remarkably independent – for a Snake.

The Water Snake

1713 Thomas Jefferson, Denis Diderot
1833 Johannes Brahms
1893 Karl Menninger, Mao Tse-Tung, Dorothy Parker, Mary Pickford, Edward G. Robinson, Clifton Webb, Leslie Howard, Ben Hecht
1953 Tom Hulce, Kim Basinger, John Malkovich, Oprah Winfrey

Great minds run in the family for these eminent Water Snakes. Their advantage over other, less logical and more thoroughly sensory, Snakes is that they are meticulous planners. Before embarking on any far-reaching project or money-making schemes, the intuitive Water Snake designs himself a sound, well-thought-out schedule with specific parameters and follows it to the letter. He's a world-beater, a force to be reckoned with.

The Water Snake is wildly imaginative. He spends much of his time meditating on new ways to solve old problems or speculating on inventing new ones. He is devoted to childhood's fairy-tale world and cannot ever climb completely out of the comfortable cradle of infantile fancy. An active imagination can be a marvellous asset but the fertile mind of the Water Snake may explode events out of proportion, interpret them too vividly and muddle reality. If this trait runs away with him and he falls victim to exaggerated mental meanderings, the Water Snake may become paranoid and suspicious, fearing aggression or threats which aren't really there.

This person can be gainfully employed as an astrologer, soothsayer or psychologist. His psychic abilities are appreciated by friends and clients alike, who don't hesitate to call on him for advice. His cool, reserved personality inspires confidence and his soothing voice calms the shattered nerves of many who consult him. He can make even the most afflicted person feel better because he knows so well how to soften harsh realities.

The Water Snake is always fresh and young-looking. He preserves his good looks long into middle age. He takes care of his body and his diet. Vanity plays a part in this but so does common sense, of which, despite his penchant for the fantastic, he possesses a good measure.

The Water Snake is socially responsible and cares deeply for the outcome of human events. He worries a great deal and is anxious by nature. Unfortunately he suffers from a mini martyr complex too and would rather play the victim than be the aggressor in his partnerships. This attitude may lead to self-pity, which, again, borders on paranoia. With luck, his tendency to snivel and feel sorry for himself will always be discouraged and managed by the good sense with which he was born.

The Water Snake can never be accused of maliciousness. He is kindly and tries to comprehend the legitimate motives of people who hurt him. He is never unnecessarily judgemental or cruel. He boasts bevies of friends who enjoy his sweet nature and approve of his methodical approach. He is generous – except when he has to pay for necessities – and can be a lavish spender. He is often an excellent cook, too, and lays on feasts at the drop of a hat.

He is drawn to professions where music and art play an important role. Beyond that, anything from architecture to advertising or telecommunications would suit him. Like other Snakes, he is after power and money but, unlike them, he is not conniving. He knows how to go about achieving his goals in a reasonable and honest fashion. He usually studies hard at school and leaves with decent grades. He's able to conform to the norm sufficiently to make himself liked by his classmates as well as respected by his teachers.

The Water Snake is an active, serious person who lives life to the hilt, yet stays more than most other Snakes on the marital straight and narrow. He might enjoy the odd dalliance with a stranger but knows that such a peccadillo might jeopardize his overall plan and confuse his already heady psyche. He convinces himself that such dangerous toys are not for him and takes comfort in his fantasy world, drawing, painting or listening to music while reinventing the wheel.

Because he is dreamy, the Water Snake exposes himself to huge disappointments. He often overvalues a person or gives too much credit to an event and then finds out he was wrong. His views are clouded by his desire to improve on reality. This sets him up for emotional or sentimental decision-making, which can be disastrous.

Snake health

The health complaints which manifest themselves most often in Snakes begin to show in early childhood. In tense circumstances, the Snake child's health often crumbles, causing him to suffer adult ailments such as kidney stones, digestive and urinary tract infections as well as unpleasant and painful inflammatory diseases of the mucous membranes.

Stressful events can cause his ability to eliminate toxins to seize up. As he is generally externally calm, handles his nerves and doesn't give in to hysteria, these complaints will not always show up immediately. The Snake child may maintain a cool head for a month or so, thereby creating (unbeknown to him and his parents) a storm of bacterial conflict in the digestive or urinary tract.

To add insult to injury, the Snake doesn't recover quickly and often finds himself laid low for long periods. Invalidity causes him no little anxiety and can sometimes even compound the illnesses, establishing a vicious circle which only increases the stress.

To combat kidney and digestive sluggishness, the Snake should get into the habit of drinking water every two hours, ingesting at least two quarts per day, which encourages liver and kidney function and assists in scouring the urinary tract and bladder of poisons otherwise dangerous not only to the mucous membranes but to the organism.

Snakes should stick to purest mineral waters without bubbles and never drink white or rosé wines. Champagne, although they adore it for its festive and luxurious qualities, is a definite no-no. A glass here and there might not hurt but Snakes should be forewarned of its harmful long-term effect if imbibed in excess. Bladder irritants such as spinach, asparagus, sorrel, vinegar, unripe fruits, spices, alcohol and tobacco should be all but deleted from the Snake's diet. Cranberry juice has been found to aid in discouraging the bacteria which causes urinary tract infections in women and can be tried as a substitute for citrus products, which may prove too acid for the Snake's delicate system to tolerate.

Gynecologically, the Snake woman often has to bear more than her share of miseries. She may have trouble with her ovaries. Cysts and infectious or allergic inflammations will plague her all her reproductive life. To combat and monitor their evolution, she should establish a good relationship with a compassionate gynecologist early. Her ability to give birth to children is reputedly good.

Allergies also afflict the poor Snake who may present symptoms of hay fever, post-nasal drip, painful sinus problems, reddish swellings and spotty hives on the skin and redness around the neck. Snake allergies may also cause chronic painful muscular contractions, particularly in the lower back.

Snakes are often cold. Their bones feel tiny inside their taut skin which is often cold to the touch. Medical experts may advise them of poor circulation but I reckon Snakes are cold-blooded, hence requiring warmth, the sun, affection, security and cozy luscious sexy love. A Snake who loves animals often uses a cat or dog as a lap rug. Snakes need body heat.

Weather variations can affect this delicate creature's nerves. Hurricanes, floods, earthquakes and even a cloudy or muggy day can set him back. If possible, the Snake should be cared for by a homeopathic doctor who can attempt, with remedies, vitamins, minerals and diet, to establish a harmonious balance in the Snake patient's body to assist him in riding out crises. His organism is so hypersensitive, leaving him very little room to maneuver and recover his equilibrium, that he must guard against excess, both dietary and emotional.

Peace and quiet, moderation and safety in everything are as indispensable to him as the air he breathes. The Snake should avoid fats and eat digestible, ultra fresh foods, take meals at regular hours and never go to bed on a full stomach – a walk after dinner will be a boon to his digestion. All mild exercise is good for Snakes: dancing, gardening, hiking, jogging, table tennis, lawn tennis, swimming and even slow walking in town will do him good. He must, however, rest between exercise sessions, stay away from violent physical exertion and resist the temptation to join in games that over-exert him. The Snake is not built to be a football player or to wrestle or box. Even tennis is a sport he should practice only in moderation.

Snakes are built for love and romance, for poetry, dancing and deep-thinking. They should never attempt physical heroism. Over-exertion will only exhaust them and set them back for another period of frustrating recuperation which may, due to the anxiety it produces, cause them to fall ill again.

Rest and relaxation are paramount to the Snake's well-being. Without empty mental spaces in which to float free, the Snake's drowsy mind has no room to evolve its reveries into plans and action. If he is forced to adhere to rushed schedules and abrupt changes imposed on him either by himself or by outsiders and is not granted enough time and space in which to rest and retrench, he will be likely to fall ill. His malady may take the form of a purely physical disease or he may become depressed. At the very least, to conform and please he may adopt a defensive strategy which will ultimately detract from his body's stability.

Snake futures

What the Snake should expect from the next twelve Chinese animal years

2008, the Earth Rat year – Your health and well-being are in fine fettle this year. All the ills you were suffering last year will dissipate in the salutary ambience of the protective Rat. Trouble may be afoot, however, in your financial sector. Although you will start the year with a sense of plenty and even continue it in ample sufficiency, you may stumble on some unexpected cracks in the sidewalk towards the end of the year. You should begin putting money away for the future and stop the buying frenzies. Shopping may be tranquilizing for you while it's happening. But when those hair-raising credit card bills and excessive mortgage payments start avalanching into your mail-box, it will be *bye-bye* to serenity and *hello* to stress and late-night nail-biting sessions. Much emphasis has been put on your family situation for the past twelve months. Now it's time to attack career goals and make them happen for you and your family's benefit. The Rat is a nervy sort and that sizzling atmosphere which emanates from inside the very vector of this year causes you anxiety. Secure those purse strings more tightly and stock up on security. Invest only in what you can actually afford. Otherwise you will be paddling against the current for twelve long, frazzled months.

2009, the Earth Ox year – Snakes are the Ox's best friends and vice versa. You are both slow and deliberate and your energies are similar in character. So this coming Ox year for Snakes will be beneficial, productive and personally valuable. You will be back in your native groove and enjoying the type of languid mood in which you always concoct your best schemes and are able to carry off projects that needed finishing or topping up. Last year really slowed your progress to a slithery crawl. But the Ox appreciates your quiet sense of esthetics and is always there to help you realize your dreams. Love is back, too. You'll be feeling more romantically intense than you have been in a while. Reason? Your money and health troubles are behind you. Do remember, though, that the Ox is a demanding old character and does not tolerate a lazybones. One has to show a willingness and an ability to labor under duress in Ox years, and even though the Ox favors you and considers you his pet, you will still have to put your pretty little nose to the grindstone and get cracking on projects and problems left undone in previous (less benevolent) years.

2010, the Metal Tiger year – The Tiger wishes you only the best. His influence, however, is another pair of socks altogether. Tigers have a reputation for prowling low in the jungles of the world late at night stalking their prey. This animal portrait does not quite fit the profile of the restless Tiger person. Tiger people are active in the extreme. They leap and bound and careen about searching for new and different experiences. They adore change and prefer that it happen in a hurry. You Snakes prefer to languish in silken repose on *chaises longues* reading novels with dense, sinuous plots, expansive detailed geographies and complex *dramatis personae*. Let's just say your styles are different. And your goals are not the same either. You want to reflect and philosophize. Tigers act first and think second. Because of their immense charm, Tigers are frequently chosen to lead. But they rarely lead far without the sage advice of someone like you. How could they? They have change for brains – loose change at that. So this Tiger year will be a challenge for Snakes. You will be called upon to counsel friends and foes alike. You will be in charge of wisdom. Small accidents and tiny setbacks will annoy you. But you are not in danger. In the hands of a Tiger, a Snake can feel a certain thrill. But don't look for security this year, cos there isn't any to spare.

2011, the Metal Cat year – A bonanza year for ambitious Snakes. You will meet up with very little opposition to your own projects and plans. Your quiet manner appeals to the Cat's sense of proper behavior and you thrive in his aura of peace and refinement. There is not a great deal of upheaval or mishap for Snakes this year. You will be free to be yourself and not obliged to work extra hard or to hoard or save. On the other hand, you won't feel much like staying close to home this year. Vast journeys and even round-the-world tours are in order for Snakes, whose taste for culture and history suits the Cat's preference for the traditional down to the ground. Should you be interested in seeking your fortune in far-flung territories, this will also be a bumper year. Whatever you do when the Cat is in charge, be sure to keep the din to a minimum. These tranquil creatures confer kudos on the strong, silent types. You may find yourself preoccupied with your health. Minor aches and pains turn into major complaints. Seek the advice of the best specialists. Steer clear of alternative medicine and newfangled methods. Your problem is something purely allopathic. Luckily, in these years, money is plentiful for Snake people. Don't go on wild spending sprees. But don't stay awake nights worrying about paying the rent, either.

2012, the Water Dragon year – Dragon years bring good health and loads of new challenges your way. Although the Dragon adores Snakes, he cannot take time to look after your well-being. He is totally preoccupied with his own self-importance and is busy making his reign a memorable one, planning celebrations and festivals galore for his subjects' pleasure. You will be busier than you like to be with multiple projects and commitments away from home. For some reason, in Dragon years, Snakes devote giant chunks of time to kindly and charitable efforts. You may simply be called upon to look after someone's children when they're ill, or perhaps you will decide to help distribute food after a tsunami in some exotic land. But whatever you decide to do, it will necessarily steal time from your regular domestic routine. If you are planning to be away much of the time, do install an alarm system or get a house-sitter or a neighbor to look in on your precious possessions. Dragon years sometimes encourage robberies and household disasters. It is also possible that your love life will be disrupted this year. Nothing terminal. But rather more drama and recrimination than you care to put up with. Remain your usual calm, collected self through it all. The rough spots will soon smooth out of their own accord.

2013, the Water Snake year – As you will be in the driver's seat this year, you can expect to be supercharged and cheerful most of the time – except when events accelerate and too many demands are made on your time. You prefer to live your life at your own pace. This year you will be obliged to follow the hectic cadence of the world and its drastic politics. In Snake years, the planet's geopolitical climate generally heats up to full tilt by about July and doesn't simmer down until well after the following January. I know that being a member of the ruling class sounds terrific in theory. But in practice, it's another kettle of crabs all clawing each other for top-of-the-heap status. You will need scads of rest and relaxation this year if you want to survive in good fettle. Best would be to take one day off a week. But of course just about nobody – not even you languid Snake people – can do that in good conscience. Instead, tune out. Wear earphones and blinkers. Turn off the house phone, the mobile, the TV and your computer so you can check out for a few cat-naps here and there. If you are still without a life partner (rare for the irresistible Snake), this year will present you with a couple of serious options. Stick to Roosters and Oxen if you can. If not, dare to marry a Tiger. Or . . . why not hitch your wagon to a Dragon?

2014, the Wood Horse year – Many people think Horses and Snakes don't harmonize. Many people are right. This year will be choppy at best for Snakes, as the Horse is not even-tempered and doesn't much care one way or the other about his subjects' well-being. Horses are rankly pragmatic. They just want to do things their way. They are talented and savvy. And they are artistic. But not necessarily altruistic. You Snakes are motivated by compassion and philanthropy. You sincerely believe in your ability to contribute to the betterment of mankind. So Snake dissatisfaction is common in the ego-centered Horse year environment. You will feel as though you just can't get going on any project and keep at it without obstacle after obstacle being thrown up and roadblocks appearing at every turn. You might, moreover, be entangled in a legal battle over a contract or real property. As the climate in Horse years is unfavorable to positive outcome for Snakes, you will not stand much of a chance of winning. Better try some tricky tactic to get the lawsuit delayed until next year when the gentle Goat will rule – a more clement climate for Snakes involved in legal tussles. Obviously, this year will not be your favorite. Take your frustration on a long holiday somewhere warm and tropical with your main squeeze in tow. Should your significant other be (for some weird reason) a Horse, I advise that you leave him or her at home. Maybe you should think about seducing someone more philosophically inclined.

2015, the Wood Goat year – Goats usually find you Snakes alluring. But in another way they can't stand to be near you. Why? Because you are so quietly strong, capable and attractive. And Goats are so dependent and pessimistic. Deep inside, they sincerely wish that you would take care of them. You, of course, are not very willing to take care of anybody except your good looks, your favorite charities and your beloved family. So the atmosphere in this Goat year is lukewarm for Snakes. And if there is one thing Snake people don't like it's tepid love. Snakes like it hot. Goats like it comfy. So watch out for the possibility of somebody younger or weaker than you who will try to crawl into your life, eat from your fridge, soak up your central heating and generally just nestle there until you chuck them out. It might be a relative or an ex, a niece or just a nice person you feel sorry for. You invite them to come and stay until they get back on their feet. After only a few months, they now live with you and your family, and the entanglements are many. Take advice from your significant other or a wise close friend who will show you how (diplomatically) to get rid of the interloping guest without having to either make scenes or watch a very unpleasant house-guest tantrum unfold.

2016, the Fire Monkey year – You will need your indomitable strength this year to withstand the onslaught of the Monkey's fiddly antics. Monkeys need attention and will perform almost any type of outrageous act to get it. Perhaps you won't be drawn in by the Monkey's neurotic charm. But if you are – beware! You provide an excellent audience because you simply *love* spectacle. This characteristic puts you in no little danger in Monkey years. Because you find entertainment so attractive, you can be duped. Monkeys are tricksters who don't much care who they are singing to as long as the public throws coins their way. So in this year of the Monkey, Snakes must watch their wallets, tie their purse strings tightly and stay out of the way of temptation. Don't even think about entering a casino or going near a card game. Remain above it all by undertaking a major creative project that keeps you grounded and in one place. Your love life may also supply a safe haven – provided, of course, that you aren't married to a Monkey. Should this be the case, see a Dog or Ox psychiatrist – or else move to Tibet – alone!

2017, the Fire Rooster year – Snakes and Roosters make excellent bedfellows. You appreciate one another's energies and can both easily see the other's point of view. Being naturally able to peek into the behind-the-scenes life of almost anybody, you Snakes do have a distinct advantage over us mere mortals. Roosters live their lives and play their cards very close to the chest. Hence, to be capable of sneaking a peek at those cards (as all self-respecting Snakes can) constitutes a huge advantage for you in Rooster years. As the Rooster is so comfortable in your presence, you can also count on this year to provide you with the financial security you so long for and deserve. What's more, this Rooster year gives you the opportunity to soar to new and more honorific heights in your professional life. All doors seem to open at once. Executives who till now refused to receive you suddenly ring you up to find out if they can make an appointment. Promotions come your way when you least expect them. It's a great year for Snakes to make progress in every area of their existence. The ups and downs created by this new hubbub will surely land you at the doctor's surgery once or twice during this twelve-month period. But never mind. The rewards will be worth any anxieties or upsets you may suffer because of the Rooster's harrowing pace.

2018, the Earth Dog year – The Dog protects his charming Snake companion and, like all dogs, loves you unconditionally. Both Snake and Dog people have humanitarian goals. The Dog is feistier and noisier about wanting justice for all. But you do see eye to eye when it comes to believing that something can and ought to be done about the innumerable examples of man's inhumanity to man afoot in the world today. You may not make a terrific team, however, as you and the Dog both prefer to be boss. But each in his or her own way is constantly on watch for signs of bias and unfairness. The Dog is slightly more paranoid about evil being perpetrated on his own person. You are cool-headed and sure of your own ability to right wrongs. But no matter. You will be appreciated for who you are and of course admired and adulated for your natural beauty. In this clement climate, you should dare to undertake new projects, create your own business or build yourself a dream house. Whatever you create will be solid and well received. Dogs emanate anxiety vibes. As the year goes by, this fretfulness will most likely get to you, as it is contagious and can undermine your peace of mind. Take time out. Do yoga, tai chi or meditate to quell the disquiet.

2019, the Earth Pig year – Take advantage of the Pig's abject adoration of you to make headway this year. Nothing is more attractive to a chubby, credulous Pig person than a willowy worldly wise Snake who (for Pigs) seems to have all the answers. Pigs are sweet, innocent and tough. Snakes are not so sweet, never innocent and . . . they are far tougher than Pigs. Pigs, however, have something that all Snakes want. It's called money. For some queer reason, Pigs attract wealth. They moreover covet and acquire everything authentic in sight – from rococo antique tables to old masters' paintings and gilded Louis XV sconces and castles and palaces and gold. Snakes certainly do not turn up their noses at that sort of asset and will sometimes vigorously pursue and even conquer the poor, unsuspecting sitting duck of a Pig. But that's another story. This year Snakes thrive. You can count on everything from passion to a reprieve from your allergies and skin ailments. The only dark corner of this year's forecast will show itself if you try to make rapid decisions. Stay away from people who ask you to participate in their schemes. Stick to your own work ethic and don't partner with anyone except your good self.

The Headstrong Horse

Distinguished Horse,

High style is *your* style. Self-possessed and proud, you dream of cutting a swath through life, moving mountains and changing the shape of things. You are active and energetic. Yet, unless you feel like it, you may stubbornly refuse to do anything at all. Nobody can make you budge an inch. You're not lazy. You simply do precisely as you please. None the less, Horse people *are* doers. You are a resolute achiever who cherishes his goals. You fear failure and will slave to save your career. Money is important to you. And you never let sentimentality get in your way. You are even willing to prance over a few cadavers to get what you want out of life.

Passion is the only emotion that can turn your ruthlessness to mush – may even cause you to give up the keys to your innermost soul, turn your back on family, desert friends and eradicate your past for the sake of pursuing an idyllic future with the object of your affection. Beware! Such exclusive devotion can be the ruination of an otherwise hardy and practical Horse.

Underneath a façade of near dandyism, you are oddly conservative. Your regulation striped ties may boast a shocking pink background but they are still regulation striped ties. Your basic black dress may sport a sexy off-the-shoulder neckline, but it is still basic black. You may think of yourself as a solid-citizen straight-arrow person. But verbally you are outrageous, outspoken and often out of line. To belong (and despite your rebellious streak, you long to belong) you will spend much of your life learning to control your outbursts. You're snappish and arrogant when riled – and you are invariably riled.

Childhood is easy for you. Kids are expected to be feisty and turbulent. Young adulthood will be a stormy foot-dragging period. Although fitting in attracts you, responsibility dampens your high spirits. Maturity comes late to Horses. Once common sense is second nature, the Horse progresses smoothly. Here's a piece of advice: don't break rules. Crime is not your strong suit. Your happiness is in your work.

Diligently yours,

Suzanne White

In the twentieth and twenty-first century all Horses were born between the following dates:

24	January	1906	and	12	February	1907
11	February	1918	and	31	January	1919
30	January	1942	and	4	February	1943
3	February	1954	and	23	January	1955
23	January	1966	and	8	February	1967
7	February	1978	and	27	January	1979
27	January	1990	and	14	February	1991
12	February	2002	and	31	January	2003
31	January	2014	and	18	February	2015

The Horse ID card

Lasting symbols have special powers. Enhance your self-image by surrounding yourself with tangible signs of your own identity and make these symbols known to your friends and loved ones. Use them daily and they will bring you luck, security and a feeling of personal worth.

Your best
color is ebony
flower is narcissus
fragrance is wildflowers
tree is white birch
flavor is sweet and sour
birthstone is topaz
lucky number is 8

Your favorite
food is vegetables
animal is wildcat
drink is red wine
spice is cloves
metal is silver
herb is parsley
musical instrument is the human voice

The Horse is yang ***The Horse motto is: 'I control'***

The handsome Horse is at his most attractive when he manages to be productive, enthusiastic, amusing, warm-hearted, talented, agreeable, industrious, generous, sociable, autonomous, strong-minded, sexy, curious, persuasive and logical.

But . . . when he fails to control himself, even the most delectable of Horses becomes defiant, condescending, unscrupulous, anxious, moody, excessively pragmatic, opportunistic, hard-nosed, self-serving and so obtuse as to seem to have gone both blind and deaf at once.

The headstrong Horse

The old saying, 'You can lead a Horse to water but you cannot make him drink', suits our astrological subject. Horses cannot be *forced* into action. All the prodding and cajoling in the world won't spur these devotees of self-determination to advance, retreat, sidestep or jump hurdles. Horses are exasperatingly self-contained creatures whose sense of what is most practical for them always comes first.

Although they are capable people, Horses must be left to their own devices, allowed freedom of movement, without interference or criticism. Except when they fall hopelessly in love, Horses remain entirely self-motivated, self-centered and self-propelled.

Horses are so fiercely autonomous, that in many Asian societies where the family's welfare is a crucial priority, Horse babies are considered undesirable. Sometimes prospective Asian mothers refuse to carry them to term because of the far-reaching consequences to the family circle. In 1966 there was an upsurge of abortions in Japan, apparently to avoid hatching children in the year of the Fire Horse, which traditionally produces the stormiest of Horse babies. This year only comes every sixty years but when it does, it drops millions of the most passionately self-minded of all Horses into society's lap. In the West nobody takes any notice of Fire Horse years, but Asian cultures fear the Fire Horse's presence, claiming it to be violent, intractable and disruptive. In Western cultures where the individual is highly regarded, spirited individualistic children are prized. Docility and obedience are not necessarily qualities sought by occidental parents.

Chinese astrology tells us that all Horses invariably leave home young. As soon as they are old enough to work most Horses bolt, abandoning their parents and siblings without a backward glance, leaving behind a trail of sorrowful memories. In Asia, a child who deserts his home selfishly to pursue his personal destiny is a curse.

It would be folly to say that all Horse children are born home wreckers. But, no matter how integrated he seems to be, a Horse child's inner self remains powerfully rebellious, unusually sensitive to criticism and independent to a fault. The Horse despises being pressured to act for the good of the group or made to feel guilty. He has no time for recriminations, nor to display contrition for his wrongdoing. His motto? 'Stay out of my way and I'll stay out of yours.'

Although they have boundless energy and ambition, appear ebullient and optimistic and usually succeed at almost everything they do, Horses have a hard time belonging. They deplore the bounds of convention, feeling it limits their scope. They eschew the support of family and close ties in favor of what they see as freedom. In the process, they often lose what they most desire and need – the loving mirror of familiar folk who might afford them a clearer view of themselves. Yet – they cannot help it – they see all family intervention as undermining criticism. Even brotherly or sisterly love is often interpreted as sibling bullying or condescension.

Outside their disdain for the rigors of home and family, Horses willingly enter almost every race they come across and often win. Adventure delights them as they enjoy evolving in an exciting whirlwind atmosphere where new things are always happening to keep them amused and titillated. They enjoy challenge and have a unique talent for undertaking arcane or unusual hobbies such as cataloguing jazz musicians who played golf in the thirties or embroidering puppies on stationery for sale to ASPCA members.

Horses are thunderous. They almost never know exactly how or when to keep their own counsel. They are not noisy and fire-breathing like Dragons: Horses appear dignified. Yet they are forever laughing too loudly in the wrong places or whispering loudly in company, making rude remarks about someone sitting next to them. This talent to guffaw in the holiest parts of a church service could be called spontaneity. Nothing wrong with being irrepressible and uncontrived – who wants to be thought of as stuffy, rigid and predictable? And the sudden, impassioned outbursts native to Horse behavior serve as a healthy overflow valve for the Horse's notoriously pent-up emotions.

Horses are wizards at speaking in public and influencing others. They can persuade a Laplander to buy a reconditioned air conditioner, eloquently defend a hopeless case in court and even get themselves brilliantly elected to public office. But, sadly, a Horse can hardly ever say what's buried in his heart. He cannot express his inner feelings so his strongest emotions can cause him awful pain.

The Horse is emotionally hamstrung. In an attempt to communicate, when he goes to the theatre, he may burst into a patriotic folk song or leap up from a spellbound crowd of spectators and harangue the performer. He may fly at a loved one during a

Christmas party, letting go with a strident verbal volley of wholly inappropriate proportion.

Having had an exuberant Fire Horse child of my own for the past twenty-six fun-filled years, my observations come from long experience. My daughter Autumn Lee, was almost always a *model child*. She was not only a pretty, intelligent little girl, she was that delightful variety of kid who spends a lot of time just playing alone with her toys and enjoying life. Of my two daughters, Autumn was the one who chose never to make waves. Yet when the atmosphere became charged with emotion Autie would suddenly manifest her presence in some unexpected way.

Autumn was four. It was Christmas time and I had taken the kids to see *Peter Pan*. During the first part of the show, she sat in silence, transfixed by the action, the costumes, the characters and the suspense. Her nut-brown eyes gleamed. Her soul was up there being pushed and pulled about by Peter and the crocodile and the evil Captain Hook. When Peter found Wendy, relief entered the theater and Peter triumphantly led the boys off the stage to prance through the audience. It was a lovely surprising moment. I looked down to my right to assess the reaction of daughter number one, Daisy, the five-year-old Snake. Ever the perfect spectator, she sat there riveted with tears of relief running down her cheeks.

When I looked to my left to behold the response of my stoical four-year-old Fire Horse, what did I see?

Nothing. Autumn was gone.

Panic! A huge theater. People everywhere. She could have been kidnapped. I looked under the seat. Nobody. I crept down two seats to where my mother was sitting, and gasped, 'Mom! Autie's gone!'

'No, she's not!' smiled the proud grandmother. 'She's up there!' and she pointed on stage to the front row where a familiar long-haired elf stood holding hands with Peter Pan, singing her little heart out.

Later, when I asked her why she had gone up there she said, 'I just felt like it.' That's about the best explanation of an emotional reason for doing something rash that you can ever expect to glean from the Horse's mouth. He is mostly discreet, and well behaved in nearly all social circumstances – except when he does something wildly adventurous.

The Horse is uncompromising. He has no patience for subtleties of meaning, hazy inferences, intentions or vapid nuance. As far as he is concerned, in this world it is every man for himself and he is not about to let himself be trampled by detractors. This may sound selfish. It is, and Horses are also opinionated and think they know best. They attack each new experience with vigor and exercise a rare brashness when faced with counter-attacks or adversity. The Horse believes in his own mettle and is convinced that victory requires only perseverance and strength of mind. He will not allow himself to be undermined by those who would see him fail. Nor is he discouraged by failure.

This hardy creature is as impatient with his own as he is with other people's weaknesses. To him, all solutions are practical. Any action must necessarily propel him from square one to square two – if not, it should be scrapped in favor of something that *works.*

My friend Sheila Lukins is a famous American cook. She has published three best-selling cookbooks, and recently replaced the great Julia Child at a foodwriters' conference in Washington. Sheila is a Horse *par excellence.* She left home young, spent a few years at art school in New York, living in rebellion against her family. Later she returned heroically to the family fold. But on *her* terms. That's the only way Horses know how to operate.

One day, in the form of an attractive bachelor named Richard, Sheila found the key to the door of her new life. She married him and bore him two adorable daughters.

In the typical Horse tradition, Sheila was born multi-talented. She could have been a painter, designer, decorator or an illustrator. For the first seven years of her marriage, she was active in just about all those artistic professions. No area of visual art daunted her. Yet nothing really 'clicked' as well as the joy of preparing and hostessing elegant, festive dinner parties.

In the early seventies, Sheila went to Paris to study the French language and cuisine. When she came back to New York after Paris, her dinner parties became even more famous among her acquaintances. She began receiving requests from friends, especially single male friends, to cater for them.

'Poor Geoffrey can't tell the difference between a can of ravioli and a can of cat food,' Sheila once confided as we sat across the dinner table from one of her customers. 'But he is rich and he has lots of posh friends to entertain. I could serve his guests burnt toast and he'd probably think it was a French delicacy,' she giggled naughtily. 'But I think I'd better stick to salmon mousse, don't you?'

I laughed too. Sheila's sarcasm is part of her charm and it is also typical of the Horse's ability to see straight through everything and everyone they ever meet. Horses are amusing and never hesitate to poke fun. (Autumn was so good at zeroing in on other people's flaws that we used to call her the Voice of Truth.)

In the beginning, Sheila cooked for George. Then she cooked for Bill and Harry and Walter and shortly after her second daughter was born she started a catering business. 'I'm going to call it The Other Woman,' she said. 'I'll cater exclusively to single males.'

For a time, Sheila did just that. It was horribly hard work and the pay was terrible. But Sheila was doing something of her own that she had thought up and she adored it. The rest is history. Her success as a roving caterer led her into starting a *charcuterie*, which took her into writing and designing cookbooks and now into writing a weekly food column in a national magazine and lecturing all over the world on food. She stayed happily married and, although she had plenty of hired help, took her kids to school every morning and spent time with them in the evening.

Although Sheila's success story represents a rare individual triumph, it is typical of a Horse. The Horse starts out rebellious, usually staying reactive until shortly after he reaches thirty. Then he decides to grow up. And with that maturity he often becomes a world beater.

Among my own Horse clients and friends, I see this slow growth as natural and know to expect a twenty-five-year-old Horse to be intelligent yet insurgent, wild-headed and mutinous. When they look back on their youth, my adult Horse friends tell me, 'I was such a difficult young adult. I always resisted authority and bucked the system. I couldn't stand any competition from my brothers or sisters.' Then they tell me how they *suddenly* grew up and decided to *go* somewhere and *do* something great.

Horses are often found living in places foreign to where they were born. They like breaking ground and are not afraid to cross both real and fictional borders. Leaving tired routines and weighty emotional hindrances behind provides a Horse with a clean slate on which he can draw his own plan.

Regrets? He has none. The Horse's only aim is to progress and the past does not exist. The present is an eternal starting line which he finds rather boring and constraining. The present leaves him champing at the bit. But in the future is the race, the challenge of being in motion for a purpose. The Horse isn't keen on destinations: getting to the goal will mean he has to stop running. The mature Horse wants, more than anything else, to stay in the race.

With all his incessant activity, you might assume that the Horse does not have much of an inner self or is content to gloss over serious issues. This is false. The Horse desperately needs to be active but also has to believe strongly in what he is doing. Horses are idealistic: lofty causes and noble goals appeal to them and infuse their fervent action with passion. Horses cannot accept lazy-mindedness in others. They will throw themselves into helping someone who shows verve and goes after what he wants but will turn their backs on people who let life wash over them.

Horses hate wimps. They prefer tough people of solid integrity and strong feelings. As they are resolutely loyal, stand by their friends and are sincerely interested in their welfare, they demand as much of them as of themselves. They are good listeners and will sit patiently while a friend expounds his troubles. But the Horse has only practical advice to offer and either you do as he says or you don't ask advice again. The Horse is always convinced he is right.

A Horse rarely lies, preferring to be seen to act openly and without guile. Although he knows that this inveterate candor may be his undoing, the Horse nearly always says what he is about to do. He would prefer to be betrayed by disloyal dissenters than have to resort to cheating or lying to get ahead.

My Fire Horse daughter, Autumn Lee, has never been able to lie either to please or get through a bad patch. She is a true Horse in that she never fakes anything, blasts her most distressing truths in stentorian tones to whoever is in her path. Autumn was fourteen when she came home one evening after school with a sore ankle. She was crying.

'Honey, what happened?' I raced to meet her as she limped through the door. Images of monster trucks running her over or of giant dogs knocking her down and chewing her leg off barged through my mind.

She sat down and cried harder. 'I was riding this girl's bike,' – *sob* – 'in the courtyard of her farm down the road' – *sob* – 'and I caught my ankle in the chain' – *sob* – 'and I fell off and' – *sob* – 'it hurts.'

I finally got her patched up and sitting at the table. The ankle had swollen but I encouraged her to eat her dinner and try to forget the pain.

She had quietened down and seemed to be almost enjoying herself when suddenly she began to howl. I was sure her foot had fallen off. I begged her to stop shrieking and tell me what had happened.

She banged down her spoon and looked at me through tear-filled eyes. Then she came to my side of the table, threw her arms around my neck and wept even harder. 'Mommeeee,' she wailed, 'I lied to you. Oh, Mommy, I'm so sorry.' She sobbed out, 'I lied!' about thirty more times. 'You made us promise never to go on a motorcycle,' snuffled my sweetly honest love bug. 'I did it. I went on Delphine's Mobylette and I fell off and hurt my ankle so I came home and then I lied. Oh, Mommy, I'm sorry I lied to you.'

The poor child was more upset over lying to me than she was over nearly breaking her leg. I was a fairly advanced wimp so I didn't punish her although I did thank her for telling the truth. Her leg was not broken but she had to stay off school for a few days. All the time she was convalescing, Autumn apologized for lying but never for disobeying me. For the non-conforming, self-legislating Horse, disobedience is not a serious crime.

Courage, too, is part of the Horse's natural baggage – and stoicism. There is no more courageous sign in the Chinese zodiac than the Horse – except perhaps the Tiger who is often more courageous than smart. Difficulties and obstacles spur his energies, adversity gives him incentive and risk makes him salivate with enthusiasm. The Horse is an adventurer first and never hesitates to gamble for big stakes. Of course, Horses are pragmatic and don't indulge in dream-style heroics but they do go in for *tours de force* wherein they can prove their mettle, impress their loved ones and make off with the biggest prizes.

Although the Horse's activities are rarely glamorous, he is endowed with the ability to be unusual within the confines of the ordinary. Because of his practical nature, he will almost invariably prefer a sedate career image to an exotic or Bohemian one. Horses like to be well thought of by their peers. As they have an exaggerated fear of looking ridiculous, they often choose to be doctors, lawyers, architects or engineers rather than rock musicians, actors, trapeze artists or private detectives.

The expression to 'work like a Horse' is right on target, for Horses can stick to a routine job without becoming impatient in the role of employee. They are able to appear to respect the boss and hierarchies, and button their lip to progress within the structure. Horses are not afraid of starting out small to rise to the top. And they know how to get there fast! They are notorious for learning their trade or craft by being there, working harder than everyone else and making themselves indispensable to those in command. Once they know how to do everything perfectly, Horses don't hesitate to ask for a raise and promotion. They are self-motivated and believe that their efforts should be compensated. Employers find it difficult to refuse such diligence its just reward. You often find Horses in responsible positions at a young age because of their willingness to accept a low starting salary and rapidly work their way up through the ranks. Horses, unlike other forceful signs such as Tiger, Dragon, Ox and Rat, neither require nor even desire instant power, recognition or acclaim. The Horse's secret weapon is his steady-as-you-go perseverance. It always serves him well.

I know several serious thirty-five- and forty-year-old Horse executives who have steadily worked their way up through the perilous complexities and ruthless politics of executive ladder-climbing, gaining stronger professional ground every year by getting on with their jobs in a disciplined fashion. Bosses quickly come to trust their balanced determination and award Horses ever bigger salaries and titles. Both women and men Horses alike achieve favor with superiors for their reliability and unwavering purpose.

The Horse is vulnerable to rejection and coldness. He wants to be liked, to fit in and belong: to this end, even if he doesn't really care for the policies of a group whose favor he covets, he can be charming but will not, however, agree to anyone's opinions just to gain their companionship. Horses make great conversationalists and will join almost any chat session. They are often super-intelligent and frequently find themselves in the public eye because of some novel theory they have stumbled on while experimenting with something else.

Although this character gets on well in most social situations, he prefers to stay clear of the limelight. His fragile nerves do not easily handle the excessive pressure, tension and criticism of the fickle public. The Horse needs respect and to belong: stardom means belonging for only a time, which could never fill the space in the long-term-stability-seeking Horse's heart.

Some call Horses hard-nosed, and they are controlling and strong-minded. Underneath their ability to say the right thing to get where they want to go, Horses are opinionated and uncompromising. Some call them stubborn. When a Horse is proven wrong a hundred times over he will not budge. He has his way of looking at issues and that, my friends, is that.

Which brings me to one of the least charming aspects of the Horse character: Horses always want things run their way. The Horse is always boss. My Horse friend Michèle, who runs a serene French country household for her family, has the softest iron hand I have ever encountered. She seems the incarnation of femininity. When I first knew her I did not believe that this gentle woman could be a tough-minded Horse. But one day as a guest in her home gave me all the proof I needed. 'Get me that towel!' 'Run me a bucket of water.' 'Julien! Call your grandmother. Right now!' 'I have an appointment in town at three o'clock and you, Suzanne, will have to put the dishes in the dishwasher.' Everybody in Michèle's house marches to Michèle's drum. It's not unpleasant – she has a happy family. But even if a Horse seems passive on the surface, he or she still runs the show.

Although they can be surgically critical of those around them, Horses are not intolerant or judgemental. If somebody wants to spend his time at the racetrack gambling away his family's fortune, the Horse mate or parent will not try to stop him. Rather, when the weary gambler drags in broke and contrite, the Horse will read him the riot act and institute a severe no-nonsense anti-gaming rule. Horses are essentially loving and forgiving. They give of themselves in almost all human situations, calling for compassion and understanding. But they demand love and obedience in return. Ironically, in large families, it is often the runaway Horse child who ends up, at forty or forty-five, caring for his old parents.

Being born a Horse is not an easy destiny. There are many contradictions in this person's character. Horses are proud yet sweet-natured, arrogant yet oddly modest in their approach to love, envious but tolerant, conceited yet humble. They want to belong, yet they are burdened by their need for independence. Like everybody else, Horses need love and crave intimacy yet often feel cornered, pressured and that others are judging them unfairly. Such confinement makes them feel vulnerable, weak and confused. His quick temper lets him down: he over-reacts and lets forth with hateful remarks. To others, this explosive behavior is unacceptable but his friends and loved ones know that the Horse uses flare-ups to keep them at bay. So, despite his desire to be accepted and his will to belong in social situations, the Horse is often hoist with his own petard because he can't accept the constraints imposed by intimate relationships.

He is proud to a fault – but his practicality overrides it for the purpose of advancement. Wherever he can, he will demonstrate his power to persuade others, rule them and organize their lives. Underneath a jaunty or even cheery façade, the Horse takes himself too seriously, secretly deems himself superior and cannot let down the barriers to his emotions without becoming harsh, rude, angry or depressed. A successful sort who refuses dishonesty as a method of advancement, the Horse is, above all, an individual, his own man, dependent only on his wits and his labor to get what he wants – and insists on – out of life.

Maresy dotes

These fascinating women are rarely classically beautiful but Horses of the fair sex always boast a certain physical *something* which sets them apart from their sisters. The Horse lady's special gift is a natural self-assurance and social accessibility which can be much more fetching than the cold-featured good looks of your standard *Playboy* centerfold. She is not mysterious or charismatic. Rather, the female Horse has the unmistakable sureness of the thoroughbred filly. She instinctively knows how to carry her head high as she walks elegantly through a room. She often distinguishes herself by a marked flamboyance in dress and manner. She is an arresting creature who rarely accepts to be overlooked. Her behavior is sometimes over-emphatic and she may even be accused of insolence. But the Horse woman's outrageousness is not an attention-seeking device: eccentricity is her way of establishing herself as unusual, exceptional, and independent of what she considers stultifying convention.

The Horse woman is incapable of concealing the state of her soul. Her face is expressive and even when she tries to hide her feelings they tend to seep out of the sides of her darkened countenance. She can become melancholy under stress and has a reputation in China for being unstable, nervous and excitable.

Her eyes are usually clear, lively and mobile with a provocative twinkle. She has a frank stare which she often accompanies with a knowing grin, using this redoubtable combination to tame adversaries, convince clients or even persuade a political constituency. The Horse woman's mouth is large with full lips which grow thinner as she ages. Her teeth are long and very white, her smile winning and her voice mellifluous, resonant and cheerful.

You may be able to recognize the Horse women in your own entourage by their straight, wiry build. They carry themselves bolt upright and often have broad shoulders and a short torso with longish arms and thighs. Her build is not exactly what we think of today as feminine, as she is neither delicate nor voluptuous. Yet Horse women have an active, lusty sex life and are attractive to men.

Love, for the Horse woman, is rarely peaceful. There is something tormented about her approach to love which robs her of the pure joy of letting herself go. The Chinese say that she is more attracted to the erotic aspects of sex than to the emotional. The way she often insists on odd or novel positions and is attracted to arcanely adventurous escapades such as making love in an airplane lavatory remind one of the classical male approach to sex which, by virtue of its emphasis on technique, is often accused of lacking romance and warmth.

In her secret heart, the Horse woman longs for a Prince Charming who will whisk her off to some mythical sex dreamland whence she will never have to return to punch a time-clock. In reality she is often attracted to weak-willed, ethereal men whom she can *handle* and even squash. She likes to feel stronger than her mate but feels she can help him to be happier in her company and care.

She is usually faithful in marriage but sometimes, because of a difficult chapter in her relationship or a nagging sense of inadequacy in sex and love, she will throw herself indiscriminately into one or even a few mad affairs. Not everyone feels as profoundly as Ms Horse about marriage and family and she may find herself in the arms of philanderers before she realizes that men of easy virtue couldn't care less about her. Sadly, because she is so essentially serious about sex, these hastily terminated marital asides often cause her great sadness and may only increase her sense of failure. She should be careful not to leap before she takes a good look over the precipice of any apparently irresistible *aventure sexuelle*.

In intimate situations this woman is frequently thought to be cold or stand-offish. The properly stimulated Horse woman, however, will prove a sensual, gentle and even submissive lover and will know how to please even the most complicated partner. But she needs an understanding lover. She is skittish about being touched or intruded upon and must be cajoled and caressed skilfully before becoming aroused. Once a lover has learned the secrets of this woman's complex sexuality, she can be his for ever as she is not one to flit about looking for cheap thrills.

The Horse woman is usually ebullient and vital. She exudes energy and enthusiasm for all that is new and exotic, for adventure and fun. Mostly we perceive her as self-confident, at ease and glad to be alive.

She is always on the move, restless and raring to get up and go – sometimes she grows neurotic and paranoid because she cannot find enough to *do*.

Idleness is her enemy. Even bedridden, the Horse woman stays busy. The idea of sitting in a room without doing something causes the Horse woman unbearable moral pain.

Concerned first with the material in life, the Horse woman is rarely preoccupied with spirituality. Religion only interests her for its social value. She feels that the church is a good place for the family to go once a week or a convenient outlet for her energy, perhaps volunteering to arrange the flowers or to organize Sunday school picnics. The Horse woman does not seek to penetrate far beyond the surface: she likes to deal in the concrete. She may be said to lack subtlety in her approach to life but this is the 'deficiency' which serves her practical needs so perfectly. Horse women are not solely interested in gain, ownership and wealth, but they would prefer to be comfortably secure than entrust their survival to chance, God, or even the goodwill of another human being. They invariably choose the solid-citizen tangible long-term solution over the temporal pleasures of any fly-by-night scheme or the thrill of a fleeting moment of joy.

Once the Horse woman has made up her mind, she sticks with it. She's a rugged individual, a self-starter and finisher. She has unusual strength and a strong, almost virile character, knowing exactly what she wants out of a given situation and going after it in her own inimitable fashion. Beyond the normal courage of meeting everyday life head-on, the Horse woman is capable of unflinching confidence in the face of impossible odds. She is frequently over-optimistic and may even think she can do more than is humanly possible.

When Autumn was small she used to tell me not to worry about being poor because she was going to win a sewing contest where the prize for the best-designed dress was a million dollars. 'And I'll give all the money to you, Mom.'

'But, honey,' I had to tell her, 'you don't know how to sew!'

'I'll learn,' she said gaily.

And she did learn. She didn't win the nationwide contest, and was sharply disappointed, but she so believed in her own talent that she did not let a detail like not knowing how to sew stand in her way.

Autumn's optimism was not entirely unfounded: female Horses are gifted in crafts, arts and skills involving the hands and the head. It's not unusual for a Horse wife and mother to make all her family's clothes, preserve vegetables from her garden, entertain in high style, decorate her home intricately and find time to be a lawyer or a doctor.

Like her male counterpart, the female Horse has impressive intellectual capacities and can choose almost any profession where she will be challenged and guaranteed to keep busy. She also needs freedom and cannot be confined to a small office, or a tiny desk in a typing pool. She takes up a lot of social room and will always set herself apart by exhibiting her desire to take charge and organize the time and efficiency of others. She has little patience for waiting out long-term goals and prefers immediate satisfaction. She loves excitement, challenge and risk. She's addicted to novelty and prefers surprises to predictability, in her work as well as in her colleagues.

Providing she finds the right trainer to emulate, the Horse female could be a professional athlete, musician or dancer. She is combative and persuasive as well as socially correct and could do well in politics. As she is an effective reformer and rabble-rouser, any career choice involving teaching, social work, the law, medicine, journalism or psychology will involve struggling against worn-out, established traditions in favor of practical, up-to-date methods. As she likes meeting the public, she might choose to be a travelling saleswoman or product demonstrator, or, in keeping with her craving for excitement, she might be a success as a spy or a private detective, a thriller writer or an international commodities broker.

The Horse woman despises convention and cannot abide snobbery. She chooses her friends from every walk of life and takes pride in her ability to alter her thinking, shift her ideas or make sweeping life changes at a moment's notice. Always confident that things will work out for her, she's a true survivor, who instinctively knows how to bend society's rules and get away with it – without losing her solid social reputation.

A few unappealing character traits may cloud this dashingly interesting woman's personality portrait. She is excessively emotional and controlling her impetuous outbursts is almost a full-time job for her. Also, she is an exacerbated egotist. She is completely insensitive and indifferent to the world's ills. No matter how apparently involved she seems in family or friends, love or money, the Horse woman lives solely for herself and is interested only in serving her own interests. Even the most persuasive and reasonable pleas for humanitarian causes go right over her head. Yet she is usually immensely kind to her friends and immediate family, going out of her way to be hospitable and caring because she feels that she has either chosen, given birth to or inherited these folk and therefore enjoys helping them as an extension of herself.

But outsiders beware: the Horse woman can be ruthless and is entirely self-serving when her own interests (or ego) are at stake. She is a harsh judge of those whom she deems weak or too sensitive to criticism and will often taunt them with hurtful remarks and provocative behavior. Like her male counterparts, she thinks she is always right and speaks presumptuously on subjects about which she knows nothing. She can be argumentative and outspoken but if suddenly proved wrong or finding herself cornered by a better debater, the Horse woman will cease communication in a flash and disappear into an impressive silent snit that could shroud Russia in darkness for several months.

It is at this point that her emotional vulnerability shows most vividly. The Horse woman can 'dish it out but she cannot take it'. The smallest slight may cause her to retreat into one of her tomb states. An unintentionally wounding remark can put the Horse woman off her feed for days. When rejected or humiliated, she pouts and sulks. Joshing and jollying usually don't help – better leave her alone to ease out of her black periods. She lacks the ability to laugh at herself, a sense of cynicism or fun, a security valve that lets off steam slowly, allowing her to play it cool when she is attacked or overpowered. But the Horse woman stubbornly perceives herself as alone, aloof and unafraid. Ordinarily, she relates to society and loved ones through solid, pragmatic acts. She believes in honesty and forthrightness and is undone by the irrational or supernatural. When she's befuddled by an intangible, she will scrub the floor or wash all the windows in her house. She is a doer, a thinker, but not an effective layabout who sorts out problems through rumination. Meditation might do her good but she would never go near it for fear of the idleness it involves.

At work, the Horse woman can be both vengeful and vindictive. She is often a die-hard feminist who means to turn the world around and see it run the proper way – her way! The man's world is an abomination. She would like nothing more than to show them all how to do it better, more efficiently and without violence. But because she is profoundly vulnerable and emotionally unstable, Ms Horse sometimes lacks persistence in her vendettas. She knows that she needs to focus on her prey, yet she is hounded by a million angry-hunting-dog distractions nipping at her heels and throwing her off her target. Her energies are diluted, time runs out and she sometimes misses her goal, suffering enormously for the failure she perceives as her own damn fault. She may become depressed and despondent. Her biggest enemy is self-doubt, which throws her off course whenever she confronts it.

She never blames others for her mistakes but she is neither circumspect nor perceptive enough to work around self-doubt by cajoling herself, taking a do-nothing holiday and being gentle with her fragile nervous system. Her fear of inactivity coupled with the lack of self-confidence will usually send her into spasms of anxiety followed by surges of empty motion which only serve to tire and lead her ever closer to the abyss of total nervous collapse.

How can the Horse woman improve her life? Professionally, she is not unlike the Tiger woman and should learn early on to curb her impulsiveness and temper her passion for independence.

Whatever she does, whether she stays at home raising dogs and kids and making a comfortable nest for her family, or becomes a world-beating women's rights attorney the Horse woman will do it well. From birth she is bound for an exciting – and unusual – lifestyle that she will create for herself and her loved ones in her own far from uncomplicated fashion.

Sylvester Stallion

As I write this, I am living in the French countryside. My old Horse crony John Laupheimer just rang me on the telephone from London. 'I left a message on your machine in Paris about half an hour ago. Did you get it?' was his opening gambit. 'I called you earlier in the country too,' he said accusingly. 'You weren't there.' John hates it when he calls and you are not *there*. 'Where were you earlier?' he asked.

John is not my boyfriend. I don't owe him any whereabouts explanations. 'I was working. I can't hear the phone from my office.' Then I wondered, 'What's up, John? Why are you ringing me all over the map of France?'

'Just to talk,' he said.

I laughed. My dear old friend John is the archetypical male Horse phone addict. I didn't need John to remind me, the species is everywhere, worming its way through miles of fiber-optic cables, interrupting our most intimate moments *just to talk*. The Horse male cannot help himself. The moment your name or image pops into his mind, he starts hitting those buttons or twisting that dial.

I have a theory about this behavior in Horse males: it goes along with their need for intimacy which is constantly at battle with their disdain for being needy. Phones are technical devices which do not allow for touching or cuddling, fisticuffs or nose-punching, providing plenty of distance between the communicators. With it, the male Horse can exchange ideas and even shout without risking involvement. I hate to think what Horse phonatics can do with fax machines.

There exists an ambivalence in the Horse male's character. He is never quite sure how to behave: he is constantly at war with himself over whether or not to display his true feelings or to maintain his serious, elegant public image without which, he fears, he would be a social dodo whom nobody would love, accept, or hire.

His way of working out this permanent dilemma is to control his ardor for life, sit on his *élan* and quash his high-spirited nature by creating and displaying a persona of sedate rectitude for the world to see. He confines his native fervor and allows himself to be ridden by social convention to maintain his rank and position in the accepted social group to which he so yearns to belong.

You will notice that the male Horse illustrates this tactic through the important choices in his life. His wife is usually socially acceptable and intelligent. She is informed, has good ideas and can exchange them with him. The Horse male requires a mate who can be taken anywhere and who will not drool at important dinner parties. His home is always built and furnished traditionally and located in an upwardly mobile or top-drawer neighborhood. His kids go to the best schools. His clothes (and theirs) come from the right shops and bear the right signature labels. He belongs to the best associations and clubs. He likes to be noticed and considered a winner in his own social group, yet he will only excel if it doesn't cause him to be in competition with someone whose territory he ought to be wary of treading on.

On the surface, the male Horse is a traditional darling. Unlike his sister, whose iconoclastic habits he rarely copies, the male Horse is a flat-footed solid-citizen guy. He works harder than anyone else, often makes good money and, despite a tiny penchant for philandering, usually keeps a sterling reputation among his peers as a stand-up fellow on whom anybody can count. One thing is certain: the Horse male is one of the world's most able men. He knows how to apply himself and is clever at thinking up novel ways to attack difficult problems. Horse men are particularly happy when their work obliges them to move about. As they must keep a strict public image alive while involved in their daily lives, travelling gives them a chance to let down some of the constraining social barriers to which they are so wedded, and the time just to lie back and think. Horse men are gifted in exchanging ideas and making deals in foreign lands. They find it easy to understand the ropes in new cultures and enjoy the opportunity of contact with exotic peoples. All forms of import/export businesses suit the male Horse. He makes a terrific sales, travel or estate agent, too.

All sports and outdoor activities delight the male Horse. Competition and remaining fit are two of his major preoccupations and he takes them both seriously. He could choose to be a tennis or football coach, a jockey or even a professional athlete as he adores participating in races of all sorts – especially when he wins, which is often.

Most of all, the professional Mr Horse is an incurable independent. He prefers to make rules rather than follow them. He loves to hold forth and make pronouncements which affect and influence other people. He does not like to take a back seat or relinquish the limelight in favor of someone he sees as less worthy than himself. He has a healthy ego and doesn't want to share the podium with fools. He is at his best when he has the luxury of being his own boss, but if he must be subjugated in either civil or military service he will gracefully buckle under, if only for the sake of rising quickly through the hierarchy to bear the honors he feels he has won by the sweat of his brow.

I wouldn't advise the outspoken Horse man to take up a career as a diplomat. He doesn't have the necessary subtlety and tends to be too fixed in his attitudes. Neither would I counsel him to go into philosophy, theology or even psychology. The Horse is not a speculative person and doesn't usually deal well with metaphysics (except, perhaps, the Metal Horse, see page 297). *Fuzzy* new age thinking confuses the practical Horse.

Chicanery and shady get-rich-quick schemes definitely do not suit this earthbound workaholic. Male Horses make poor liars as they are far too direct and straightforward to enjoy the game of duping others for the sake of making a buck. Horse men are born wedded to the normal. They function well as bourgeois and make wonderful yuppies as they are truly talented for conforming to established patterns.

In love, the Horse man can be said to be the master of passionate, short-lived affairs. At some point, however, he almost always gets married and, unless his spouse leaves him, stays that way. Horses are too pragmatic to risk instigating divorce proceedings. Yet, in this marriage he so clings to, the Horse man is not seeking stability but rather social correctness. He needs to be seen to do *the right thing* – no matter how much it hurts.

As a parent, the Horse father can most closely be compared to the male Ox. He imposes his authority on everyone living under his roof, regardless of their age and rank. He means to be obeyed and respected – never challenged. He finds nothing degrading or subservient in helping around the house and is always willing to dry a dish or dress a toddler. He loves to be surrounded by family and takes willingly to the added responsibility that children bring to a marriage. I remember when my Horse lawyer friend Gene Dye's baby son, Seth, refused to take milk from a bottle and wanted a cup. He-man Gene stood, pressed against the edge of the sink, bottle in one hand, teat in the other, eyes cast down. Emotion was palpable. He showed me the bottle and said, 'I guess this is the last baby bottle that will ever come into my household.' Tears ran down his cheeks. 'Seth's growing up,' he said, sighing painfully as he searched for a trainer cup.

In spite of his outwardly stodgy, staid appearance, the male Horse is not sexually conservative. He can frequently be found clandestinely visiting elegant brothels or showgirls and gogo dancers – but, entirely in character, observing the rules of safe sex. He is drawn to the underbelly of life, the tawdry side of sex and is usually active in earthy, funky, extra-marital horsing around.

As long as he can keep it to himself, none of this hanky-panky need really threaten his marriage. His image as family man and provider comes first. Too often, though, the guilt-ridden Mr Horse spills the oats about his one-night stands – which is both indiscreet and stupid. But Horses don't deal well with guilt and, when plagued by the memory of their own infidelities, are tempted to ask forgiveness of the person they cuckolded. I strongly advise Horse men against this: it's positively cruel to be unfaithful and then ask absolution of the person you cheated.

The capacity for great, humungous love which blinds and

paralyzes, is at its zenith in the male Horse. Marriage and affairs may cease to count when the Horse's romantic heart is struck by Cupid's arrow. He becomes a total fool. If Horses are difficult to budge and independent-minded, watch them when they suddenly fall hopelessly in love. They can't think straight and talk about nothing but the person they adore until you feel like throwing up.

'Come on, Jim,' I said to my stockbroker friend last month. 'Let's talk about the stock market or prices of blue jeans, huh? I know how much you love Jane. It's too bad she's married.'

'Yes,' said Jim sadly. 'But she and her husband are in therapy,' he added hopefully. 'Right now they're at the Hôtel du Cap in the South of France,' he said. 'They're trying to work things out.'

'What? They're together on holiday and you call that therapy?' I gaped.

'Her doctor said she always ran away from emotional attachments and this would be the test to see if she could stay with her husband. I know she won't be able to. He's a creep,' Jim said confidently.

'So why did she marry him and why is she at Cap d'Antibes with him and not with you?'

'Because she doesn't love him but she has to let him down easy,' he told me candidly. 'She's trying to give him a last chance because the shrinks think she should.'

'Jim,' I began, 'how long have you been in love with Jane?' I'd been hearing Jane's name for well over ten years but Jim was never with her.

'I met her twenty years ago,' Jim confessed, 'and I have always loved her.'

'And Jane?' I interjected.

'She says she only loves me,' he explained.

'Why don't you just zoom down to Cap d'Antibes and whisk her away?' I asked incredulously.

'I'm afraid. If I lose this round it's the end between Jane and me. I'm almost sixty. This is my last chance,' Jim said morosely.

Talk about carrying a torch! I felt that Jim was in for such a mammoth fall that he might do something foolish if he didn't win her. The thought of never having her permanently might break his spirit. I said, 'You should ask her to see a therapist with you, too.'

'Good idea,' said Jim. 'But she's pretty caught up in this therapy with her husband and I guess I'd have to wait my turn . . .' His voice was humility itself.

Jim Flint is a handsome man who swashbuckles through the world of international finance, sails every kind of boat, knows the best restaurants from Bangkok to Bangor and comes from a mainline Philadelphia family. Normally, he is anything but humble. How can he be so self-sacrificing? Answer? He's a Horse in love. Blind love collapses this character's starchy nature and handicaps him for as long as it lasts – which is sometimes for ever.

While he doesn't have the Snake's finesse and talent for romance, deep down, the male Horse is a hearts-and-flowers romance seeker. He likes to remain free, able to wander away from his family and spouse. He wants to know they are always there, tending the home fires, while he has adventures but he gets bored in routine emotional situations and needs the sexual challenge and excitement of affairs. If you are married to one of these attractive studs, don't despair if he philanders. He will always love you most and first. He's a good provider and an excellent father, but like every self-respecting Horse, he needs to run free and feel the wind in his mane.

If you fear your Horse husband is straying and want to try to keep him at home, you might try using glamor tactics. Horse men like aggressively gorgeous women. They find sophistication irresistible: they are turned on by painted fingernails and lots of long, bushy, well-coiffed hair. They especially look for those thin women who look as though they spend half their lives on tennis courts or in beauty spas. And the Horse man also wants his ideal woman constantly to reinforce his highest opinion of himself, to be a challenge to him intellectually and . . . to be completely understanding of all his sexual and emotional needs.

He is a clever lover. The Horse male likes to think himself supersensual and is affectionate, delicate and warm as a sex partner. He is, however, modest, shy, even, about showing his body and may need coaxing. His emotional hang-ups and problems don't follow him into bed. Once involved in lovemaking he is as far away from the world as he will ever be – perhaps this is the reason he needs to remain passionate about sex. He has remarkable sexual endurance: the male Horse uses sexual intercourse as an escape valve to keep himself calm and moderate. He is a dominant lover and will nearly always take sexual initiatives. He acts fast, too. If you go out to dinner or to the theater with a new Horse boyfriend, don't be surprised when you find yourself in his bed next morning. Horse men are seductive and insistent.

As former girlfriend to a few beautiful Horse men I would warn you not to be disappointed that yours won't talk to you. All men can be mute about feelings but Horse men simply *never* say what they feel. If pressed, they go all shy and stubborn and claim that they cannot tell you what's bothering them. They shrivel and become morose. You give up trying because it just won't happen.

Years ago, I had a Horse boyfriend named Nathaniel, a doctor in a town far away from where I lived. We only saw each other occasionally but it was always fabulous – a meeting of mind and soul. Then I met someone new who lived near me and felt I was falling in love with him, which frightened me. I loved Nathaniel, he was my best friend as well as my lover. I needed to discuss it with him. I broached the subject thus: 'Nat, I have met this guy I really like. He works with me at the university. And it worries me. How would you feel about my falling in love with someone else when you aren't here?'

'I can't really do anything about it, can I?' said Nat. 'Let's go downtown and buy some clothes.'

I didn't know how to act or what would happen if I let myself love this new person. I certainly didn't want to give up Nat. But I found myself reacting positively to the blandishments of this other guy. Talking it through with Nat would have helped me to find my own position as well as define his.

I did fall in love with guy number two and felt guilty about still seeing Nat. Finally I rang him and said, 'I think you ought not to visit me this weekend because I have met this other guy and I don't feel right two-timing him – or you.'

Typically Horse, Nat didn't get angry or sad, he acted infuriatingly normally. Then he wrote me a letter wherein he said he had no idea that I had met anybody else, that I might have mentioned it before. But he did not say how *he* felt.

I called him and tried to get him to talk about us. He was cheerful: he told me about his practice, his mother's arthritis, his tennis. I asked him if this new development between us bothered him. He said he was making dinner for about five people and he was happy to be using the new garlic press I'd given him last time he visited me. I never stopped loving Nat but I had to stop seeing him because I couldn't live without discussing things in detail. If you're in love with a Horse man, I'm sure you understand. And I don't know what to tell you to do – except, perhaps, to fall in love with your French teacher.

The five Chinese elements and how they influence the Horse

The Wood Horse

1834 James Whistler, Edgar Degas
1894 Jack Benny, e. e. Cummings, the Duke of Windsor, Nikita Krushchev, Aldous Huxley, Walter Brennan, Martha Graham, Jacques Lartigues, Jean Renoir
1954 Kathleen Turner, John Travolta, Dennis Quaid, Harvey Feinstein, Patrick Swayze, Shari Belafonte, Kevin Costner

Perhaps the most opinionated of all Horses, the Wood Horse, although a sociable, convivial person, gives little quarter to weakness, either in others or in himself. This Horse, governed by the verdant Wood element, has a tendency to judge others by his own standards, making him intolerant, harsh and, at times, impossible to get along with.

Although he can hardly be considered a Mother Theresa or Albert Schweitzer, the Wood Horse is capable of great altruism. He is often known for his generosity towards those less fortunate – but only those – he deems worthy of his gifts. He thrives on influencing others and enjoys watching people pull themselves up by their bootstraps finally to take charge of their lives. The Wood Horse will gladly help the strong grow stronger but is not apt to endow fragile souls who will always depend on others. You might say the Wood Horse is not truly charitable as he is exasperated by those who never show progress no matter how much help he proffers.

Wood Horses may suffer from the blinding light of their own brilliance. From birth, they feel different and special. At home and then at school, they are applauded for their fine intelligence and hailed by teachers as more willing to take chances than the other kids. Once out in the world, the Wood Horse, a sociable and likeable person, is again encouraged by the praise of bosses and superiors. He seems to know instinctively how to rise to the top without trying.

As a born over-achiever the Wood Horse may arrive at the age of thirty holding three doctorates and a master's degree in four different subjects. Being the type to try anything once, he may suddenly decide that what he really wants is to become a writer, singer, actor, painter or dancer! He may set aside the job offers, close his ears to the kudos and take up residence in a freezing cold garret where he will sculpt until he gets really good at it, then grow bored and decide to further his study of nuclear medicine.

If he is not careful to husband his talents, zero in on his aims at an early age and find his social niche before he reaches thirty-five, this Horse may find himself, at forty, a burnt-out case, a jack of all trades and master of none. There are worse fates than being forty and knowing how to fly airplanes, do brain surgery and tap dance, but it is wise to have some idea of who one is and where one is going before the onset of middle age. This is the Wood Horse's toughest challenge. Not only is he so good at everything, so adventurous and such a hearty risk-taker that he feels tempted to have it all, but he is so highly susceptible to praise and so greedy for the thunderous applause all this achievement brings him that he can't get off the roller-coaster of his own design.

Wood Horses hate authority and refuse to buckle under to those who claim to rule them from a position of hierarchy. If the Wood Horse feels that the person telling him what to do is not equal to him in brains and brawn, he will walk away, leaving the boss to listen to his own rantings. He is bold and, at times, foolhardy. Important jobs will be awarded to him because of his excellent academic record and affable personality but sometimes he loses them or is demoted because he refuses to be dominated by those he considers fools.

The Wood Horse is an excellent self-promoter. He knows every string to pull to get himself noticed. He usually sports a very pleasant demeanor and, as he is superlatively gifted in holding the attention of an audience, often has good luck in careers where public speaking or performing are prerequisites. Wood Horses can excel at politics as they are both bright and persuasive. They are also very funny with a sharp, biting sense of humor. Unfortunately, they don't usually know how to laugh at themselves. Their jokes almost always poke fun at others and they can be extremely hurtful.

The Wood Horse is not only intolerant of those he considers less clever than himself, he is envious of those who are better set up or more successful. Jealousy is a terrible curse and its presence in the life of this otherwise sunny soul gnaws away at his nervous system, eats at his equilibrium and causes him both emotional and physical distress. Ordinarily he looks before he leaps but in an attempt to eliminate anguish, the envious Wood Horse is capable of making rash moves and committing foolish warlike errors which may cause him to lose both ground and face with those who hitherto respected him for his wisdom.

On the surface, the Wood Horse is easy to get along with, charming and friendly. He loves novelty and is attracted by new ways of approaching old problems. He is a jolly companion who likes to be the center of attention. In love, Wood Horses make fun-loving sex partners who enjoy the game of seduction. They are good-looking, innovative and never boring in bed. Wood Horses tend to be a shade on the selfish side. They may seek their pleasure first and, if there's time, will then consider that of their partner.

In general, Wood Horses try to be co-operative. They may be head and shoulders above the crowd, but they still want to fit in. Yet compromise is not their strongest suit. They bridle at the notion of keeping their opinions quiet as they like to think of themselves as authorities on lots of matters. If consulted they may swell with pride, make grandiose pronouncements, give untimely or overbearing advice and even become meddlesome with friends and family.

There exists in this creature a lack of intuitive perception. If you have dealings with a Wood Horse, no matter how his aura of genius impresses you, remember that exceptional intelligence does not make up for lack of feeling and insight. He is smart, elegant, glib and fun-loving. He is witty and multi-talented. He can talk the pants off anybody and is afraid of nothing. But he has about as much second sight as an earthworm. If the Wood Horse is wise he will try to learn the trick of true human understanding by listening through the gentler hearts of those he trusts to feel and intuit in his stead.

The Fire Horse

1606 Rembrandt, Pierre Corneille

1846 Carrie Nation, Thomas Edison

1906 Adolph Eichmann, Henny Youngman, Abe Beame, Samuel Beckett, Josephine Baker, Count Basie, Leonid Brezhnev, Agnes Moorehead, John Huston, Aimé Maeght, Lou Costello, Luchino Visconti, John Carradine, Billy Wilder, Mary Astor,

Roberto Rosselini, George Sanders, Sir Carol Reed, Otto Preminger, Marcel Bleustein-Blanchet, Marcel Carné, Leopold Senghor
1966 Laura Dern

Oh, la la! The hardest sign of all to define. Before I attempt to describe the Fire Horse's character, let me say that whatever I have previously said about Horses in general (brilliant, rebellious, attractive, hard-headed, self-centered, socially obsessed, etc.) can now be multiplied tenfold in strength and applied directly to this mystifyingly irascible and lovable personality.

Fire Horses don't do anything by halves. Every Fire Horse is a walking magnifying-glass for ordinary experience. In the mind's eye of a Fire Horse every tiny gesture is a world-class event, every sigh a howl, every friendly kiss a meaningful experience. Fire Horses turn every tear into an ocean of sorrow and transform every titter into an uproarious belly laugh.

In getting along with Fire Horses, you can't win for losing. If you make any attempt to get close to this adorable monster of temperamental behavior, you will end up confused and bewildered, wondering what you have said or done that could cause such an unmanageably inappropriate reaction in what, two minutes before, seemed a normally balanced human being.

When it comes to talking about himself, the Fire Horse is a sealed tomb. He is a past master at putting off interlocutors with sullen glares and arch remarks. He places sticks in the spokes of all probing intercourse to stop the wheel before it gets started. The Fire Horse is unable to engage in normal discussion or argument, dares not pass a few sociable remarks back and forth or indulge in verbal jousting with friends. Life itself is amplified for the Fire Horse. Whatever happens, he almost always over-reacts. He knows he might get so angry that he could hurt somebody.

Wise Fire Horses learn early how to stop the battle before the first shot is fired. They simply take the initiative and chop off their enemy's head. Conversing with these volatile Fire people is dangerous to the self-image. So, if you are planning an affair with a fascinating Fire Horse, prepare for a constant volley of rapid-fire put downs – and don't say I didn't warn you. Fire Horses are tough customers.

Yet even at their most smouldering, Fire Horses are among the most endearingly genuine souls on earth. All of their shenanigans and hyperbolic behavior make them extraordinarily interesting to be around. They are oddly naïve and, at the same time, amazingly sophisticated. They can kiss you one minute and try to annihilate you the next. They may taunt or tease you into striking out at them and then be deeply sorry and claim that they wish they were dead because they hurt your feelings. They are deliciously funny and playful, too. Their incisiveness is remarkable and their talents myriad. To know a Fire Horse is to love a Fire Horse – or else!

But, like the fickle element that governs them, Fire Horses get so swiftly out of control as to be in constant danger of setting their own precarious world on fire. These are rebellious, difficult, hard-working people. It is impossible for most normal mortals to comprehend what Fire Horses are really up to because: (1) they are not natural sharers of private or emotional information; (2) they prefer only to emanate vibes about what pertains directly to them and their own ambitions, hopes and dreams; (3) they have practically no capacity for compassion; (4) they have little sense of family or loyalty to it; (5) they are excessive and unstable; (6) they are ruthless, selfish and proud.

Fire Horses have some dreadful faults but they also have multitudes of good qualities: (1) Fire Horses are splendid; (2) they are exciting; (3) they are creative geniuses; (4) they have limitless energy for work and achievement; (5) they are solid citizens; (6) they are ingenious; (7) they are too clever by half; (8) they love with burning intensity.

The basic character problem stems from an overdose of native fire. The Fire Horse lives with a volcano inside him, which threatens to erupt if he opens his mouth a crack. At an early age he becomes aware that his reactions are considered excessive. He cries louder than other babies, laughs harder and eats more. Soon, his parents begin to perceive him as a perilous pot of simmering milk about to boil over. They handle him gingerly, as though he might explode. Yet, despite the inner volcano, our subject is, first and foremost, a Horse. He wants to fit in to a group or social unit. He wants popular acceptance and needs to be cared for and about by his peers and family. The Fire Horse becomes an early victim of misunderstanding, out-of-phaseness, ambiguity, confusion and even fear.

The young Fire Horse's life is a series of attempts by himself, his peers and entourage to control the flames, to stay close to the warmth without being scorched and to keep the home fires burning without having to call on the fire department. This touchy lifestyle is hardly conducive to stability. In this atmosphere, the young Fire Horse often grows more and more remote, rigid and unapproachable. His own family feels left out. His friends find him impenetrably sulky and removed. But the Fire Horse suffers most from his unbreakable spirit. He encounters immeasurable difficulty controlling his own rage and tempering his fervor. He finds normal expression pale and even dull when compared to what he really feels inside. He thinks he is a misfit.

Usually, feeling ill-at-ease among his wary friends and kowtowing relatives, he rebels and leaves home early to make his own way in his own time. As a result of this defection, the Fire Horse meets head-on with his extravagant self in the big real world of work and money-making, spending and responsibility. The new challenge is gigantic and more to his liking. He may feel importuned when asked about his headaches in the confining intimacy of his home; but competing to become a first-rate opera singer in New York doesn't deter him for a second. He believes in his own capacity for greatness.

Fire Horses try to bring about change through sheer force of will. They push hard until the wall gives or walk away in a huff and go it alone. They don't have patience with long-term solutions or power games, refusing to enter into either unless the choice is left up to them.

The life of a Fire Horse is never simple. He struggles uphill against his own interior resistance, suffers from envy and seeks revenge against his enemies. He is enormously talented and his gifts are usually recognized early by teachers and specialists alike. But he lacks perseverance, refuses authority and often gives up a brilliant future in favor of his solitude and independence.

Virtually all Fire Horses have difficulty with personal relationships. They want to believe that others are perfect and when things don't turn out as they hope, they are stricken with disappointment and despair. Many Fire Horses suffer from depression and may have nervous breakdowns. They grieve over losses which less hyperbolic souls would term moderate, languish in netherworlds of silent rage where they feel lost and scared but whence they are unable (and sometimes unwilling) to escape. Then again, they may suddenly feel wonderful, get out of the right side of the bed for years at a stretch and dwell for a period in euphoric Hahaland. During these good spells, Fire Horses often make positive things happen. Genius is not too strong a word to describe their creative talent. Even in love, Fire Horses are rapacious and abstinent, greedy and generous, selfless and selfish. Hitch yourself to one of these volatile characters and you won't be bored for a millisecond.

The Earth Horse

1918 Rita Hayworth, Pearl Bailey, Jack Parr, Leonard Bernstein, Jerome Robbins, Spiro Agnew, Alexander Solzhenitsyn, Robert Stack, Ingmar Bergman, Alan Jay Lerner, Susan Hayward, Dorothy Macguire, Jeff Chandler, Ella Fitzgerald, Art Carney, Pierre Desgraupes

In the Horse born in an Earth year, we encounter a better-natured and easier-going Horse than the rest. The Earth gives a solid base to this otherwise skittish and nervous creature. He is less impetuous, less hot-headed and also less over-imaginative than his brothers. The Earth Horse is a straight-arrow person with sound ideas that he puts into practice either alone or under the guidance of some serious higher-ups. He works well in groups and is able to add an aspect of fantasy to even the most mundane work situations.

For a Horse, he accepts authority graciously. As an employee he knows instinctively how to be innovative and competitive without committing juvenile acts of insubordination. Although he may be excitable, and even inconsistent, generally his work deportment is positive.

Just as he is good at taking orders, he is also able to give them. He handles people well, is never too bossy or critical and, as he has a congenial and sociable nature, he is usually well liked. The Earth Horse has fewer problems with relationships than his fellow Horses: he is perhaps the most compassionate and altruistic of them. He sincerely cares about caring for others.

The Earth Horse is usually a talented person whose attraction to the arts precludes his accepting routine jobs. He would much prefer to be a film director than vice president of a bank. He'd rather do cabaret than work in an office, and he is far more gifted for singing the blues than he is for practicing medicine or reading law. The Earth Horse knows how to take a back seat and put his ego in his pocket. Compromise and diplomacy come easily to him. His financial picture is generally healthy too. Thanks to his reputation as a competent budget manager, the Earth-born Horse is frequently called upon to put failing businesses back in the black, to clean up messes made by incompetents in the building trade or even to trouble-shoot in the military.

Although he can be excitable and may get carried away, the Earth Horse is just as capable of toning down his extravagance. He is a fighter and will go to the front for what he believes in. But he is a born advocate of the adage, 'He who fights and runs away, lives to fight another day.' The Earth Horse will only struggle up to a certain point: if he can foresee that a battle might deplete his resources, he will turn tail and race back to the safety of the stable. The Earth Horse doesn't mind losing face by losing a single battle as his aim is to win the war.

Less selfish than other Horses, the Earth Horse often engages in activities which cure society's ills. He may be involved in anything from feminist politics to adopting orphans or helping the elderly to claim their rights.

Even though he rarely appears timid or acts the shrinking violet, the Earth Horse is reputedly hypersensitive. He may weep at the slightest provocation – at a stranger's wedding or through an entire movie. If he sometimes appears grouchy, it is often because of this hypersensitivity. He usually loves flowers and animals, involving himself in gardening and husbandry with gusto and true sweetness. The Earth Horse cannot tolerate petty annoyances. He is easily aroused to anger by details and, when crossed, he can be vengeful and unforgiving.

The Earth Horse loves the countryside. His mood is often deeply affected by feeling confined in the city. He needs to be able to run wild and breathe fresh air or else he and his artistic bent may be choked and smothered. His best choices for a career are in art or art-related fields. Painting or any graphic art will suit the Earth Horse and allow him the freedom he needs to interpret nature's beauty. He can be outstandingly successful in all areas involving the theater and cinema. He is a truly creative person whose ideas are not merely new and exciting but, because he is a Horse, practical – *and*, as an *Earth* Horse, his projects are always down to the ground, sane and safe.

Writing is a less obvious profession for this Horse because he doesn't enjoy sitting still for long – he needs activity and movement to be happy. If he likes to write he might want to try journalism or copywriting where he can stay active. This talented character can also flourish in music. He can become a maestro in almost any field where a musical bent is required. He might be a producer or an instrumentalist, a singer, conductor or composer. The Earth Horse has a special gift and even if he doesn't opt for it as a profession, he should stay close to music, using it as a hobby or a second career.

The Earth Horse, like all the other Horses, falls in love like a ton of bricks. Once he has found the person he feels is right for him, he is likely to stay where he landed for the rest of his life. The Earth Horse is faithful and traditional: he enjoys family life – especially if he is the parent who rules everything – and insists on well-behaved happy children. He has intense and long-lasting friendships which he cultivates as carefully as his garden. If, however, he feels betrayed by someone he cares about and trusts, he will seek revenge and demand retribution. He can be vindictive and blind to his own faults. He's a saner, more reflective and certainly more common-sensical Horse than most.

The Metal Horse

1930 Joanne Woodward, Ornette Coleman, Silvana Mangano, John Barth, Clint Eastwood, Charles Conrad, George Steinbrenner, Polly Bergen, Neil Armstrong, Jimmy Breslin, Alvin Ailey, Robert Duvall, Clifford Irving, Antony Armstrong-Jones, Claire Bloom, Vera Miles, Sean Connery, Nestor Almendros, Sir Peter Hall, Gene Hackman, Steve McQueen, Robert Wagner, Claude Bolling, John Frankenheimer, Paul Mazursky, James Earl Jones.

Outstanding talent and a knack for basking in the spotlight without developing a swelled head are two of the Metal Horse's special qualities. He is adroit, forceful and combative in his driving ambition to *get somewhere* in life. People usually think of this person as a real 'scrapper', someone who is definitely out there, fists up, armed with a strong personal sense of faith in self. Though not truly a pugnacious sort who goes out looking for trouble, the Metal Horse likes to remain on the *qui vive*, rarely letting down his guard. Metal Horses walk tall, which discourages others who might try to get in their way.

Maybe such bravura is just a defense to hide sensitivity or lack of confidence? Not really. The Metal Horse has a tight rein on his emotions: he must hold himself in check to maintain a dignified and respectable public and private image. He's always well dressed in a conservative, tasteful manner. He lives in the 'right' neighborhoods, buying or renting in the most proper of suburbs or keeping a swish *pied-à-terre* in the snootier quarters of all the best cities worldwide. The Metal Horse is careful to engage in acceptable, noble, sports activities: tennis, golf, sailing or fencing. He usually marries people from 'good' families, joins up-market clubs, sends his kids to the right schools and eats at the 'in' restaurants recommended by the 'best' critics.

The Metal Horse is a bit of a snob but he has a solid reason to look down his nose at poor fare and proletarian sports. The Metal Horse feeds on material comfort, which he knows he can only ensure for himself and his family if he travels in the right circles, goes after the cushiest jobs and is seen to be better mannered, educated and dressed than his rivals. The Metal Horse is more ambitious than intelligent, more self-driven than a scud missile . . . and tougher than tungsten.

It is not quite fair or correct to condemn this eager-beaver figure so hurriedly, slotting him recklessly into the empty-headed category of the blindly ambitious go-getter. The Metal Horse is nobody's fool. He is unusually quick-witted, bright and fleet of foot. He likes to stay within the boundaries set for him by society, pays his taxes on time and never cheats. He is always punctual, looks nice and, what's worse, has perfect teeth. His kids never take drugs and his dog doesn't bite the postman. You must know at least one Metal Horse: he is that infuriatingly well-turned-out person who lives in the lovely flat on the second floor of your building, about whom nobody ever knows anything except that he does everything right.

Obviously, the Metal Horse is far from perfect. He has faults but he hides them. He has troubles but keeps them to himself. He has a heart but it's kept under wraps. The Metal Horse keeps it all to himself because he fears both pain and the guilt of shame. He's skittish of messy emotional situations and flees every intimate discussion because he hates to hurt. His cupboards are in perfect order and his kitchen sink shines because he is worried what others may think. His dinner parties are timed to the last toothpick and his car never breaks down because he's determined to appear to be in control in the eyes of his guests. The Metal Horse is terrified of disorder and an excess of spontaneity because something might go *wrong* if it isn't planned in advance. Life scares the Metal Horse less when everything is planned ahead. When the dishes are washed and the sink is scrubbed and the fire's laid then (and only then) the Metal Horse will allow his compulsive little head to lay itself upon the pillow for a well-earned snooze.

This Horse is a bungler. He is always tripping over things and half drowning in his own bathtub. From an early age he starts polishing his image, planning his time slots and setting up sedate covers to hide his inadequacies. He's a walking time-bomb of potential mistakes but you will never have to deal directly with them because he is a master of camouflage.

He is a rather rough-and-tumble lover. Though his technical skills may be excellent, he never seems to be doing much more than performing a job well. He's not cold or without physical passion, but he never lets go. I suppose, as his sensitivities must remain hidden, tenderness and gentle stroking can hardly be his strong suit. If you love one of these effective and ambitious creatures, you will be forced to employ ruse and chicanery to keep him in bed after lovemaking. A Metal Horse is likely to make love and leap up to do the laundry, make a phone call or turn on the TV.

Of course, he is a serious worker. All professions requiring good social skills, group dynamics and team integration are custom-made for the Metal Horse. He can be an efficient boss or a junior employee, but the Metal Horse will not stay an underling for long. He loves hierarchies and thrives on the vicissitudes of climbing the sturdy ladder to success. He adores material wealth and has an obsession with acquisition. Good things with pedigrees and historical references line the walls of his house. You never eat from cheap dishes in the Metal Horse's home and the flowers are always fresh too.

The Metal Horse, however, deplores routine and dislikes confinement. He is a peripatetic soul who requires change and movement. I do not advise him to get a desk job which doesn't involve travel. Action is his best friend and the more he has the healthier and happier the Metal Horse will be. His need for motion sometimes hinders the Metal Horse from enjoying a sound family life. He can make a commitment – but not to anything which doesn't evolve. If he feels trapped in a static relationship or family situation where he feels there's no room for improvement or modification, he may bolt. The Metal Horse would prefer to live alone than feel trapped in a no-win marriage or love affair. Some turn to drink when strangling in bad marriages or relationships and divorce is preferable to drugs, gambling or lifelong depression.

The wise Metal Horse will try yoga and meditation to temper his fever-pitch existence. Otherwise, the stress he engenders by living through one of his chock-a-block days might push his delicate nervous system over the edge. Nervous collapse is not uncommon in the Metal Horse. Vitamins and a steady diet of grains and vegetables are recommended to aid his sometimes acid and sluggish digestion. He usually chooses to remain fit as he adores sport and exercises obsessively.

When at his best, this Horse is productive and active. He is even thrilled by adversity, considering setbacks mere hurdles. Then, when the moment is just right and the multiple irons in his myriad fires are all meltingly hot, the Metal Horse will leap any obstacle with grace and style. Watch him as he lands smoothly and emerges from his herculean effort, looking smashingly elegant and almost always winning by at least a nose.

Lastly, this Horse is very kind and charitable, giving his time and money for communal and group events. Often these activities are Church-orientated but they might also have to do with philanthropic or philosophical movements. Unusually for a Horse, the Metal Horse is a spiritual soul, who is attracted not only to religion but capable of expanding his mind in search of philosophical truth. He can succeed in even the most obscure abstract metaphysical realms as writer, teacher or physician.

The Water Horse

1942 Aretha Franklin, Paul McCartney, Karen Black, Bob Hoskins, Jimi Hendrix, Linda Evans, Madeline Kahn, Erica Jong, Paul Simon, Harry Nilsson, Jim Croce, Janis Joplin, Sharon Tate, Chris Evert, Patti Hearst, Werner Herzog, Taj Mahal, Brian Jones, Martin Scorsese, Michael Crichton, Daniel Barenboim, Barbra Streisand, Leon Russell, Harrison Ford, Nick Nolte, Michael York, Marsha Mason, Roger Ebert, Michele Lee, Stephanie Powers, Marilyn Horne

Here we have the most generous of Horses who dotes unconditionally, doles out fabulous gifts and smothers loved ones with old-fashioned practical favors. He's hospitable, full of good Horse-sensical advice and bubbling with energetic attention. He is superbly intelligent and acutely talented, as are his Horse brothers and sisters. But the Water Horse is different – mellower, cooler and more truly socially inclined than the others. He likes to belong, but he doesn't care if he belongs to the country club and can settle for belonging to his family, or to a group of good friends. Because his days are madly busy he has neither time nor talent for mulling or analysis and the Water Horse is not as neurotic, self-involved and angry as other Horses.

This Horse is a winner. In every Horse's life there is a beacon of ambition. He also knows he needs to stand out while living among strangers. Such early awareness usually spurs him to leave his family to make his own way and with the Water Horse this is only slightly modified.

Like other Horses, Water Horses usually leave home early but they always return before the age of thirty, bearing the fruits of their forays and desirous of sharing their good fortune with the family they left behind. A Water Horse may always need to keep a safe distance from his home turf because he doesn't function well when encumbered by standards which are not his own. But he is always there for his parents, ready to pick up the pieces for siblings or take in a stray cousin. Water Horses feel the suffering of others intensely and are not afraid to show their devotion in practical ways.

The Water Horse is gregarious and loves to be surrounded. He likes having litters of kids, enjoys working in groups and having admirers who watch and clap while he performs his wondrous tricks of bravura and brilliance. Whether his trick consists in getting together a tasty dinner for a troop of tired girl scouts, piling everybody into the car for a swim in the nearest waterfall or belting out a few jazz ditties on stage at Carnegie Hall, he is happiest when performing for his adoring audience who make him feel wanted and loved which is what he is really all about. APPLAUSE. APPROVAL. ADORATION.

It would be pleasant if these Horses were duly rewarded for their generosity and compensated for their glad-handing but that is often not the case. Mostly, the Water Horse goes on giving while his entourage receives but does not completely return the favors. People do not rush about telling each other how selfless their Water Horse friends, parents or colleagues are. They may be impressed that a Water Horse took on the baking so twelve hundred schoolchildren could have cake on their picnic. But they are usually baffled when it comes to knowing how to approach the Water Horse with gratitude.

Why? The Water Horse emanates a hard-edged aura of competence and self-confidence which inadvertently puts people off. Once we have watched him in action and applauded, we would like to throw our arms around the Water Horse's neck and kiss him to death. But something about his demeanor discourages us. Is he too uppity? Does he make us feel small? Are we afraid of him? Does he give us an inferiority complex? Would he rather we applaud and then go home and leave him alone?

All of the above. As kind, giving and generous as the Water Horse can be, he is also stand-offish and non-receptive to gushing gestures of affection or tenderness. He is afraid of intimacy. He wants to be admired but hates admitting it. He craves adulation but doesn't believe he deserves it. He goes out of his way to do giant love favors for people and has difficulty accepting a hug for his trouble. He needs to maintain distance from those he helps out. I suspect that the Water Horse is locked inside himself in puritanical pulled-up Horse-like fashion and cannot allow himself the luxury of receiving his share of tenderness. He fears he might look silly.

If you love a Water Horse, this aloofness may throw you off your feed. You may feel rejected, unloved and have to perform some tricks to get close to this character. Not to worry. The seduction, the ruses and emotional slaloming that the Water Horse demands are worth any self-doubt you may feel: once you are allowed into the cosy sweet heart of a big old Water Horse, you will feel safely loved back for ever ... plus, you will have gained the best friend you could want – for life.

The Water Horse is not introspective. He is practical and is not drawn to the metaphysical – he hates abstraction. He thinks intellectuals are doodlers who get paid for doing nothing. He cannot abide laziness – either in himself or in others. He likes his life (and the lives of those who surround him) to be lived on the surface. He enjoys material things and is happy working with his hands, making curtains or re-covering a sofa, building an attic room or driving around the countryside hunting down antique glass or ceramic figurines in obscure little shops. He doesn't require luxury but he likes his comforts to be more than adequate.

The Water Horse is funny too: his jokes are always acute and, when it comes to sarcasm and satire, his comments are right on the button. He has usually mastered the art of seeing through artifice: if you want an opinion on good taste or authenticity, whether with regard to a person or an object you found at a flea market, consult a Water Horse. These folk have impeccable taste and a flair for everything visual from decorating to evaluating old paintings.

Water Horses were born to be bosses. Holding down mundane jobs is a problem for the over-achieving Water Horse. He cannot be subjugated to anyone for long and is especially sensitive to taking orders from fools. He simply cannot tolerate idiots and phoneys. As he comes off beautifully in the interview, he gets the job right away, but although he may remain polite and answer dumb requests courteously for the first few weeks, he will soon commit an act of blatant insubordination which usually ends in his early resignation. Job choices for this creature are simple – he can be the boss of anything. Independent careers are what he excels at and he is good at everything from medicine to cuisine, from real estate to accounting, from law to photography, acting, singing or film-making. Musicians abound among Water Horses, as do graphic artists and writers. He will certainly be artistic and might even be a genius.

Luckily for him, the Water Horse is among the most adaptable of the zodiac's creatures. When he's down he doesn't lie there for long before getting up and starting to run again towards goals of his own making, leaping hurdle after hurdle and finally making it. Project after project may fail but, one day, because of his strong belief in self and remarkable ability to zero in on his goals and stick to routine, the Water Horse will triumph. Because he likes change and rarely uses the same tactic more than once, he may be exhausted by the time he reaches his goal but whatever gain or joy he derives from his major success will be richly deserved.

Horse health

Horses are disgustingly healthy. They are born with a robust constitution, seem immune from childhood diseases and carry this resistance into a hardy adulthood. Good health, for the Horse, is a way of life.

The Horse doesn't have to work at staying in good health. He is a natural as he loves movement, is interested in sport and sincerely enjoys athletic self-improvement from muscle-building to aerobics. Exercise calms his nerves and keeps him in shape so he can handle his heavy schedule without collapsing from fatigue. Take a survey of the joggers in your neighborhood and you'll find a preponderance of Horses out there.

Horses, however, have weak livers and a sluggish digestion which may prevent them living to a healthy ripe old age. They also have excellent palates and greedy gullets. Horses love to eat meals composed of *foie gras* and comforting stews simmered in sauces, and to accompany them with good wine followed by cognac and tobacco. Horses are also inveterate snack-food junkies. They like to crunch French fries and slurp ices and dessert creams between meals or even at dead of night.

You've heard the expression 'hungry as a horse'? Well, it's true. Horses really are hungrier than others. They need to eat more, more often. However, they cannot persist in this gluttony or they will fall ill at a young age and become grumpy old invalids. No Horse in his right mind wants to be confined to a wheelchair for so much as a day. The Horse's angry liver will not resign its functions but it will, none the less, take its revenge: any one or a medley of the following complaints may set in: gout, acnea rosacea, obesity, high cholesterol, heart disease, arteriosclerosis, shortness of breath, hypertension and/or impotence.

On the emotional side, the Horse is not a comfortable sharer of emotional information. He keeps things in. When he is sad, he is morose and silent. From time to time he erupts and blurts out some anger, joy, excitement or pleasure, but then he clams up again. He is never expressive of his feelings for long. He tends to let things build up until he cannot control himself and then some tiny event will set him off like a Roman candle. This build-up of rage is like a mineral deposit or a sleeping volcano and while it is dormant, it can cause the Horse some serious mental as well as physical disorders. Some are both classical and chronic such as acid indigestion, ulcers, colitis, constipation, muscular tension, cramps, back pain, bursitis, gallstones and bloating. The less obvious (and perhaps more disturbing) mental illnesses run the gamut from melancholia to schizophrenia and serial nervous breakdowns.

The Horse must learn to manage his precarious emotional structure. He can help himself by eating right. Simple grilled fish or meat, lots of fruit and vegetables, grains and legumes cooked simply and as little wine as is tolerable to this confirmed *bon vivant*. Bread should be wholegrain and butter and all animal fats are to be avoided or used in minuscule quantities. Then, too, the Horse must avoid excessive ingestion of alcohol, drugs and tobacco. His system is hypersensitive to stimulants – even coffee, which jump-starts the Horse's already overloaded nervous system. Avoid, also, spinach, sorrel and asparagus as they are rich in oxalic acid which is harmful to the Horse's system.

The Horse should sleep long hours regularly (not escape sleeping). Infusions of thyme, verbena, camomile or orange blossom drunk before bedtime ought to ensure a sound sleep.

Regular exercise is *de rigueur*. Tennis, equitation, golf, bicycling, jogging, walking and cross-country skiing are recommended. He should also consider engaging in an artistic pursuit. Painting, singing or dancing, playing a musical instrument, writing songs or stories, amateur theatricals, drawing cartoons, photography could all suit the Horse.

Horses, especially women, are markedly more emotionally unstable than they appear. Perhaps it is the added element of possible hormonal imbalance which often causes the Horse woman to be, by turns and without warning, joyful then tearful, calm then suddenly anxious, affable, then, within a split second, furious and sharp-tongued.

Once again, to control this weathercock temperament, the Horse woman ought to keep a close watch on her hormonal and gynecological health. She should make certain she is cared for by an understanding and sensitive gynecologist who knows how to discern psychological from purely physical states. For both women and men, these problems of uncontrolled changeability can sometimes be handled by an endocrinologist. Psychiatry might be considered in extreme cases but these tempestuous Horse mood swings are inborn and often can be best handled with alteration of lifestyle and dietary surveillance.

Lastly, the Horse should learn how to smooth out the angles of his emotional life. He has to try to understand the uses of relaxation, rest and leisure. Rather than wash the car, he might discipline himself to sit still for an hour in a quiet room and read a book. He might paint instead of doing his accounts so compulsively often. He could learn how to meditate, and do yoga instead of engaging exclusively in violent or competitive sports which may help him spend his energy but also over-stimulate him. This person is so excitable that the last thing he should be looking for is another adrenaline rush. The more he forces himself to relax, the more he will get used to appreciating leisure. It may take years of practice to change his bad habits but Horses have plenty of time to modify their lifestyle as they are among those who live longest.

Horse futures

What the Horse should expect from the next twelve Chinese animal years

2008, the Earth Rat year – Don't expect any miracles to waft down the trail to meet you this year. Rats and Horses are notorious enemies. There will be an initial attraction, a brief honeymoon period, and then a swift slide into bickering and eventual divorce. Rats like power. You hate to be told what to do. Get the picture? Rats need to surround themselves with people they can feel protective of, look after and give direction to. There is nothing worse for Horses than to feel smothered by some meddling outsider who sticks his or her nose into everything the Horse does. Horses like freedom and independence. They do not wish to render accounts. So in this Rat year you Horse people had better chill. Remain in the wings. Don't attempt any great stunts or public displays of your talents. Of course, you probably won't follow my advice any more than you would follow the Rat's instructions. Horses can be led to water but we cannot make them take even a tiny sip if they don't want to. No amount of coaxing or blackmail or guilt trips will make them ingest a drop. So, Horses . . . this Rat year will be a trudge. You will be better off retiring to the countryside for the duration. But as you will not heed my good counsel . . . as they say for good luck in the theater, 'Break a leg.'

2009, the Earth Ox year – Things are looking up. Oxen admire your stamina and ability to undertake hard labor without a whimper or a whinge. This, then, should be a terrific year for Horses. No interference. No meddling in your business. No directives. However, Ox years are not brilliant for the Horse's romantic life. You may indeed fall in love this year. And when you fall, you crash. Thunderously. But this year, the more passion you throw at your chosen significant other, the less the person seems to want to cozy up to you. You can avoid being disappointed in love by simply leaving your hormones at the gate and running the race alone. Your professional picture bodes nothing but success. So long as you apply perpetual elbow grease and show persistence, the Ox will not only stay out of your way, but will applaud you, encourage you, and when he can, will recommend you highly to any influential people you may need to know in order to advance your career. Health? Nothing serious or life-threatening in the offing. But you really ought to look after yourself better. Horses tend to think they are invincible and rarely, if ever, bother going to doctors or visiting other health practitioners. Avoiding the symptoms you have been living with now for far too long without a medical opinion or two could lead to a chronic illness which will stay with you for at least the next dozen Chinese years.

2010, the Metal Tiger year – You are in for some major alterations in everything from the romantic picture to your actual lifestyle. Tigers require change. It's in their genes. Horses and Tigers are the best of cronies. In the Tiger year, you will feel free to be entirely yourself. The real you. The headstrong, feisty, talented, outspoken you. You see, Tigers don't mind your playfulness and strong will. They, in fact, approve of how Horses manage their lives and are themselves terminally independent and free-spirited. What you do have to look out for in Tiger years is being drawn into crazy schemes, urged to take zany jaunts to far-out destinations or dragged into nutty real estate projects without a backward (or forward) glance. Be cautious of feeling too free. Avoid taking off for some cloud cuckoo land whence you will not be welcomed upon your return. You might instead be severely criticized for being irresponsible, as Tigers tend to encourage loonies to be loonier. Snoop around in your own garden this year. If you do, you will be pleasantly surprised to find that in your immediate surroundings lurks a surprise love interest. Someone you have known for a while will suddenly take a shine to you. Don't back away. This could be The One.

2011, the Metal Cat year – You are favored by the Cat who never wants to get in your way. You are all action and brisk movement, always careening headlong into projects both new and old. The Cat is a more ponderous, reflective sort who, unlike you, does little to draw attention to him or herself. Providing you show your usual ability for hard work and dedication to same, the Cat will stay right out of your way. This is a good year for you to expand your business, open some franchises, buy land, refurbish or renovate a property or two. Devote some of your free time to your art as well. Drawing and painting, singing and dancing. Film-making or photography or sculpture or ceramics . . . any and all artistic pursuits will thrive under the influence of the refined Cat. One small pimple on the otherwise pristine face of this Cat year . . . you may lose confidence in yourself. This sudden slide into melancholy or self-doubt could be caused by boredom. This is not an exciting year. No great new romance. No terminal illnesses. Not much high living. Just work and art. But consider yourself lucky, because those are the two things you do best.

2012, the Water Dragon year – Here is yet another year in which the ruler keeps a hands-off policy in your regard. Dragons don't meddle much with Horses. If you have the good sense never to attempt to steal the spotlight this year, you will be surprised how positive this twelve-month period will turn out to be. First of all, there is a whiff of marriage – or at least a live-in long term relationship – in the offing for Horses. You are not usually much on living full-time with anyone. But when you fall for somebody, you tumble hard and this year is favorable for just that kind of passionate abandon. Dragon years are famous for celebrations and festivities. One of those shindigs might just be your wedding or at the very least, your engagement party. Before you get too involved, however, I must warn you that part of the Horse's problem with intimacy stems from the fact that you cannot be happily corralled for long. Make absolutely certain that your significant other or future spouse is aware of your penchant for trotting off from time to time into your own realm or even into the ether. Marry someone whose independence quotient harmonizes with your own: A Tiger or a Dog would be best. Second best? Who wants second best?

2013, the Water Snake year – Not the easiest year to come along for Horses. Your new family (read, in-laws) wants a lot more from you than you are willing to give. Their needs will create dissension and, if you are not careful, could lead to a nasty break-up of your couple. The Snake's influence can be laden with half-truths and even fantasies which don't quite wash in the real world. The Snake longs to believe only his or her vision of a given situation and is often loath to surrender to reality. So you may come up against some real obstacles this year in your attempt to get your marriage or long term live-in relationship off the ground. New brooms usually sweep clean, but as they get older, some of the dirt begins to be swept under the rug or even altogether neglected. Same holds true for a new relationship. Whatever messes are troubling you or your partner must be cleaned up. And first they have to be brought out into the open. Sit yourselves down – alone or with a marriage counselor or shrink – and talk things through. You will both need to decide where your loyalties lie this year. And it had better not be with the in-laws. A couple is a couple is a couple. No intruders necessary, thank you.

2014, the Wood Horse year – According to Chinese legend, the Horse year is not an excellent one for Horses. Almost all other signs benefit from their own years. But not the Horse. This will be a troubled and sometimes even dangerous year for you Horse people. The perils are not your fault. They are simply there . . . like bad luck. The best way for you to handle this situation, of course, is to exercise caution in all your activities. Opt out of chancy business deals. Don't go trekking in the Himalayas. Cancel your subscription to the Bungee Cord Club and renege on all plans for ski holidays in avalanche season in the Andes. In other words, keep it simple. Stay around home a lot. Busy yourself with homey projects like baking Christmas cookies or working in the garden – and even then watch out for domestic accidents. You could pierce your palm with a tomato stake or dent someone's car on the way to the market to buy the flour and chocolate for cookies. Just be careful. You are walking on eggs this year. Now, please don't go sulk somewhere and not come out till the year is over. Do understand that the reason for such a difficult time in your life is so you will learn new lessons. It's all about helping you to see what it's like to be a Horse of a different color.

2015, the Wood Goat year – It is about time you got a break from learning new ways to behave and stopped having to be so cautious all the time. Goat years are a breeze for Horses. They bring sunshine into your previously dreary life and cheer you along to ever more arcane acts and ambitious endeavors. Goats don't want anything much from Horses – except that you be strong enough to provide them with a generous back to ride on. You don't mind holding up two ends. You can handle being depended upon by someone vapidly artistic or too brilliant not to be just plain idle. The Goat spends his or her life seeking a pot of gold at the end of the rainbow. He or she knows that you might just be the vehicle to carry him there. This is your chance to go to extremes again. Time to go on that hike in the Himalayas. Or why not try out several different gambling casinos around the world? Or marry up with your cousin Charlie? Do something outrageous. One way or the other, under the Goat's Horse-friendly influence, everything will work out for the best. Even your health will be excellent – so long as you keep up your fitness routine and stick to lean meats, fish, vegetables and, of course . . . oats.

2016, the Fire Monkey year – Being of a pragmatic nature, you are not often drawn into shady schemes or led down sinuous paths where outcomes are not clearly visible. But Monkeys are agile folks. They are nimble of foot and mind. If you are ever tempted to get involved in anything that deviates from the straight and narrow, it is likely to happen this year. Watch your step. Horses need to work hard in order to make progress and earn success. Horses usually don't cotton to short cuts. Therefore, should you be tempted away from your usual strict adherence to the rules of striving and toil, you may indeed fail – miserably. When presented with attractive 'quick fix' plans to avoid taxes by sheltering your yacht in Panama or opening an offshore bank account, just say no. There are no free lunches for the hard-driving Horse. Monkey years also threaten your waistline. These nimble-minded creatures cannot keep their hands off food, and if you are not extra careful about watching your diet, this year could expand your girth to twice its normal size. In fact, the general message for Horses in Monkey years is: Stick to routine and keep your nose clean.

2017, the Fire Rooster year – If there is one thing you hate more than anything, it's being held back or restrained in any way. You are a do-er, an active person with more irons in the fire than a roomful of blacksmiths. You are a runner, a worker and a striver. Nobody should ever attempt to hold you down. Yet you do have to live through this Rooster year where we all feel somewhat constrained by the Rooster's firm grip on his pocketbook and his disapproval of our wildest dreams. Roosters are serious, single-minded folks. They cling to conservative ideas and prefer the traditional to the far-out freaky in life. The atmosphere this year, then, inclines us all to adhere to rules, be thrifty and stick to tried and true methods. You might, however, be tempted this Rooster year to travel afar to visit tombs and museums, churches, temples and monuments. The Rooster doesn't usually disapprove of travel – especially if the journey leads to somewhere instructional and is not just for 'fun'. I wouldn't advise you to make any major purchases this year (houses, cars, boats, buildings, farms, etc.), because money will be generally tight and interest rates quite high. All your favorite outspoken and outrageous extreme behavior should be curbed. Don't try dabbling in clandestine love affairs, either. Hanky-panky is simply not on for Horse people in Rooster years.

2018, the Earth Dog year – Horses and Dogs belong together. You gad gaily about the countryside along with scads of children and cats and chickens and ducks. You two have a natural affinity, and although of different breeds and species, you could easily be thought siblings. This year, then, will be a gracious year for Horses. You will however be called upon to demonstrate a side of yourself that we do not frequently see. The Dog requires that we involve ourselves in world issues. Dogs want justice and will do almost anything to see that justice is done. They care about the future of the human race. As being engaged in political goings-on has never appealed to the Horse's free wheeling, outspoken character, you Horse people will be hard put to show that you care who gets to be president – or, for that matter, leader of the entire planet. Why? Because you don't give a fig. You know in your heart that all politics is corrupt and you want no part of corrupt anywhere in your straight-arrow existence. My advice for you this year is to attempt to care. Just do it for your pal the Dog's sake. Be more generous of heart, more giving and loving to others. Remember. You get out what you put in. That's the rule in the benevolent Dog year.

2019, the Earth Pig year – Pig years are not among your favorites. Horses insist on working long and hard and being visible about it. You want to be seen to be industrious. You need us to know what a good person you are – and how honest and forthright as well. Pigs are not slovenly or lazy. They also work and sometimes they work extremely hard. But Pigs like a good time. They enjoy inviting people in for a meal, drinking a bit too much and eating slurpy delicious culinary concoctions (often of their own making). You don't mind a good time. But you are not one to waste hours lolling about at table over a final glass of wine or two and some scrumptious cheeses or dessert. The ambience of conviviality afoot in the Pig year, then, might get on your itchy nerves. You want action. Doing, going, working and being busy keeps your mind off more ponderous, irritating, soulful matters. So this year you need to slow down and kick back. Take a lengthy journey in your new sailboat or buy yourself an old barn to renovate in the country. Be busy. But be relaxed as well. Watch out this year for symptoms of depression or other illnesses caused by stress. You have needed to let up on the accelerator for too long. Take a break and enjoy some of the good clean fun connected with all Pig years.

The Gentle Goat

Oh, Gracious Goat,

Your sign is the most creative. You are truly gifted, have a flair for the aesthetic and enjoy being in tune with nature. You're so artlessly intuitive that you could give 'take it easy' courses. But first, before you try to do anything, you must be provided with security. You need to feel loved, protected and be grazing safely in a fertile field. Without structure, you're helpless.

You are an eccentric, and something of a winner, too. You don't mind struggling and straining in an effort to reach a noble or tangible goal, but you hate adhering to schedules or performing repetitive, routine chores. You need lots of ready cash, yet you scorn budgets.

A formidable ambivalence divides your basic need for security and your longing for total freedom from stressful limits. Goats are generally very delicate. Your good manners, wiles and charm will go a long way towards finding that person, group or profession that offers you maximum protection and allows your talent to thrive. Try your hand at poetry, research or, better still, just lie back, relax and wax Bohemian. You would make a perfect hippie.

Try courting an eloquent Horse. Horses know best how to work hard for others. Bat your eyelashes at a refined, home-loving Cat or – better still – grab yourself a scrupulous, competent (and often rich) Pig to lean on and love for life. Avoid Tigers and Oxen. They don't approve of your capriciousness.

You don't mind the role of dependant so you'll probably enjoy a peaceful childhood. As an amorous and fanciful young adult you may experience some devastating romantic disappointments. But luck shines in the third part of your life, bringing love and security to coddle your tender soul. A bit of practical advice: find your 'fertile field' at a young age and force yourself to graze patiently. Your fortune will most likely be found in somebody else's bank account.

Fondly,

Suzanne White

In the twentieth and twenty-first century all Goats were born between the following dates:

13 February 1907	and	1 February 1908
1 February 1919	and	19 February 1920
17 February 1931	and	5 February 1932
5 February 1943	and	24 January 1944
24 January 1955	and	11 February 1956
9 February 1967	and	29 January 1968
28 January 1979	and	15 February 1980
15 February 1991	and	3 February 1992
1 February 2003	and	21 January 2004
19 February 2015	and	7 February 2016

The Goat ID card

Lasting symbols have special powers. Enhance your self-image by surrounding yourself with tangible signs of your own identity; make these symbols known to your friends and loved ones; use them daily and they will bring you luck, security and a feeling of personal worth.

Your best
color is light green
flower is narcissus
fragrance is apple blossom
tree is dogwood
flavor is bland
birthstone is sapphire
lucky number is 12

Your favorite
food is raw vegetables
animal is nightingale
drink is mineral water
spice is saffron
metal is aluminum
herb is mint
musical instrument is harp

The Goat is yang ***The Goat's motto is 'I depend'***

On good days, Goats are appealing, altruistic, creative, empathetic, intuitive, generous, artless, gentle, romantic, sensitive, compliant, candid, self-effacing darlings.

But when the going gets rough Goats become self-pitying, pessimistic, fugitive, parasitic, vengeful, lazy, indecisive, contentious, violent, capricious, irresponsible, tardy, careless, bigoted, nasty little pieces of work.

Getting my Goat

Goats are the dreamers of the Chinese zodiac. They are languid creatures whose aim in life shifts about with ease and grace, following no particular pattern and confounding all and sundry. The Goat person is a thoroughgoing maverick. His brain rarely obeys his feet. He seems content to be blown along by the wind. Then, suddenly, he alights in some uncharacteristic place without having given or taken notice. Before the Goat knows it or bothers to resist, he often finds himself embroiled in some unlikely plot, surrounded by people with whom he has nothing in common, accomplishing precious little and going nowhere fast.

Because of this tendency to give in to will-o'-the-wisp behavior and the obvious strains which all that whimsy and sudden change place on his gentle but pessimistic nature, the average Goat worships inertia. He dreams of being able to sit still somewhere pleasant and not move for fear of finding himself up a tree or down a well, victimized once again by circumstances over which he is convinced he has no control.

In this last assessment, the Goat may be right. Of all the signs of the Chinese system, Goats are the most pliable, gentle and willing to please. Their natures are fluid and their hearts full of sympathy for those involved in dilemmas with which they can closely identify. If they dare to engage with the world at large, Goats are easily drawn into complex predicaments. This being so, they usually shy from confrontation, pull back when faced with heavy decision-making and blatantly refuse to take an unpopular stand in a conflict.

Frequently Goats willingly take a back seat to a shrewish wife or bossy husband who provides security. They adore being putty in the hands of an exacting boss or superior authority. They thrive on deadlines – the more demanding and urgent the better. Other people's draconian demands constitute a refuge from the ever-present tug of escapism to which all Goats at one time or another fall prey.

Although the Goat symbol is Yang, every person born in a Goat year comes into the world literally drowning in Yin. Not exactly effeminate, there is, however, in this character a hypersensitivity and talent for tender compassion that ill prepares him for the drudgery, tribulation and hard angles of real life. The Goat is too gentle, too gracious for the crushing pressures of day-to-day reality, and not equipped to function in our climb-the-ladder-to-success, Dog-eat-Goat world. If pushed to conform to the mold of the self-starting, aggressive business person, the Goat may suffer a nervous breakdown or else simply take to his *chaise-longue* and plunge head first into his mental safety net, entering a personal nether world where real psychological detachment and terminal daydreaming are the private symbols of his Goatly success.

The best way that these flaky Goats have found to navigate the perilous trip through life's jungle safely is quite simple: Goats depend on the kindness of strangers for their survival. If you take the often puzzling, non-committal attitude of the Goat in this light, it will help you understand why he so exasperatingly resists making decisions.

This is not to suggest that Goats don't have reserves of force or that they are unable to exert their will. The clever but yielding Goat is a powerhouse of passive resistance. No Goat worth his salt wins anything through humiliation or aggression – Goats are much more imaginative than that. They know how to employ the strength of the weak. They are past masters at clandestine manipulation. When angered they are capable of concocting life-consuming pain-inflicting vendettas or achieving their own ends through patient and painful picking at the scabs on an enemy's body. If you have a Goat for an adversary, you'd better hire a battalion of brilliant and wily advisors because there is practically nothing you can do to put a dent in this creature's sluggish ego or confound his determination to beat you at your own game through endurance and behind-the-scenes machination.

The other-worldly side of the Goat nature lends itself to the study of the esoteric. It is not unusual to find Goats employed as astrologers, soothsayers or fortune-tellers. Like Snakes, they have a sixth sense about what may happen next and often enter professions where prediction is useful, such as fashion or design, decorating or the stock market. Armed, then, with a master talent for back-room intrigue as well as foreknowledge of future events, the Goat can be a treacherous foe.

The sense of time with which most of us are born, the need for tidy spaces in our days and nights for each activity is almost totally foreign to Goats. A Goat can stay up for three days and nights to work on a project or exhibit uncanny powers of endurance in stressful moments. Yet most Goats have difficulty rising each morning to get to work or an eight o'clock class on time. They hate schedules and routine. You will meet Goats who seem so relentlessly organized and fanatically neat that it belies everything you thought you knew about Goats. This is what I call a 'reverse reaction': if a Goat can adhere to a schedule about his morning toilette, he feels he has won a victory. The well-organized Goat is fighting the constant temptation to disappear into rumination, or even be brought down by incursions of schizophrenia or manic depression. It's a tough Goat indeed who always does his shopping in the same supermarket at the same time each week. For the Goat, the idéa of accomplishing habitual chores is distasteful and dull. He would always prefer to dream, wish, hope and wait for Godot. When you meet up with an orderly Goat, stop and make his acquaintance. The combination of self-discipline and natural creativity is an unbeatable force for innovation and even genius.

It has long been my habit to indulge in a naughty bit of Goat bashing in my books. In self-defence I confess that my father was a gentle but organized Goat and my first (and only) husband was/is a superlatively disorganized Goat. After having experienced unchecked Goatliness in the two most imposing male figures in my life, I gave up on Goats. Every time I met a Goat man, or woman, in the years following my animated childhood and my hilariously disastrous marriage, no matter how attractive they were, I climbed the nearest baobab tree and sat there shaking until I was certain the said Goat had passed me by.

Later on, after the age of forty, I dared once again to rub shoulders with a Goat and soon I found I had a few Goat friends and was able to accept their flights of fancy as adorable quirks of personality. Nevertheless, I have deep reservations about the possibility of a Tiger/Goat entente and am always on tenterhooks, waiting for disaster.

In an attempt to redeem my earlier reluctance to hobnob with Goats, let me tell you about my Goat friend Birdie Trundle.

She is not beautiful, but she's a Goat girl – witty and intelligent, fragile, tender, warm-hearted, eager, compassionate, smartly dressed and sensitive beyond belief. Just like many security-conscious young Goats, Birdie Trundle met and married her husband directly out of school. A young lawyer from a sound New England family, Roger Trundle was Birdie's idea of the perfect man. She wanted security and Roger offered oodles of that. He was also dull, non-communicative and domineering.

Roger and Birdie had two sons. Soon, Roger got busier at the office and Birdie got bored and lonely staying at home with the turbulent boys. After a while, when Roger didn't come home until 10 or 11 p.m., Birdie realized he was up to some hanky-panky. As is frequently the Goat's wont, young Birdie became interested in a junior colleague of Roger's who, in his turn, became crazy about Birdie.

Birdie got pregnant. It turned out that the young man and cause of the pregnancy was so bowled over by Birdie's wondrous self that he proposed. Once she was divorced, he would carry her, their child and Roger's two rambunctious rascals off to a new and perfect world.

Birdie thought it over. It would be lovely to marry this young lawyer and run away to a new, non-boring life with him. Roger was a pill and Birdie deemed her young life was worth more than just a home, kids and the errant husband in the suburbs routine. She's a Goat – hates routine, deplores sameness.

Paul, the young lawyer father of the unborn heir and my oldest male friend phoned me to ask if his new-found lady love Birdie can come and visit me for a while. Why? I wondered.

'She needs an abortion,' he informed me.

'What?' I shriek. 'You got her pregnant? You should know better!'

Birdie came to stay and had her awful abortion. When she was feeling a bit better we got to chatting. 'Are you in love with Paul?' I asked her openly.

'Oh yes,' she said emphatically. 'He's the most wonderful man I have ever met.'

I envisaged Birdie and Paul hand in hand striding off into the sunset. 'Will you get a divorce right away, then?' I asked her outright.

She gaped at me in utter horror. '*Me*? Get a divorce from Roger? To marry *Paul*?'

Something didn't seem right. Birdie was not in love with her husband and she had just said that she adored Paul. Wasn't it logical to get divorced and marry the man she loved?

Not for a Goat. Birdie broke into my churning thoughts with, 'Suzanne, Paul is a rookie lawyer. He doesn't even have a proper job yet. You can't imagine I could go back to living as the wife of a junior lawyer?'

But Goats are security junkies. Their priorities begin and end there. They care most about being well sheltered and living in a peaceful environment – even if it is outrageously demanding of their time and nervous system. Birdie Trundle, twenty years later, is still married to

Roger Trundle, bored out of her mind and often complains of her 'dead marriage'.

The single most important flaw in the Goat personality is his talent for acting inconsequentially. Some call it creativity or spontaneity. I call it caprice. They shilly-shally over the decision to buy either Wheaties or cornflakes as though they were deciding whether or not to use nuclear weapons. Having gone out to buy cereal, they impulsively buy a bottle of cranberry-flavored wine vinegar instead – Lucas and Eddy can eat something else for breakfast.

There was the nice Goat locksmith who started installing a lock on the gate of my Paris garden one day and decided that the galvanized lock I'd bought looked too ordinary. He hied off to an elegant hardwear specialist and bought me a $200 brass alarm lock, installed it and then presented me with the astronomical bill, saying how he just thought it was more *handsome*. I could have killed him, but the lock was pretty and he looked so crestfallen. Besides, it was very cleverly installed. I kept it.

I cannot say the same about my ex-husband, Todd, who taught me all about astrology in the first place. He was handsome, too. I did not keep him because he could have won the 1931 Goat-of-the-Year award. His flight-of-fancy character so closely fits the Chinese astrological Goat description that it's eerie.

When we were married I used to ask Todd to pick up some small item on his way home from work. I remember once having flu and being in bed for a weekend. By Sunday afternoon I was bored. Todd was on his way out to buy some milk for the babies so I requested he get me two magazines as well. That was at three o'clock in the afternoon. It was snowing.

At 8 p.m. I finally went and borrowed some skimmed milk from my dieting neighbor, who commiserated with me about the mysterious absence of my husband. Todd's capriciousness and total lack of a sense of time was legendary around the block of flats where we lived. If I recall correctly, I phoned my sister at about 11 p.m. She said not to worry. You know how he is.

Todd came back at seven o'clock next morning without the milk. But he was laden with dozens of magazines. I was livid. Where the hell had he been?

'Sweetie, I met the nicest guy,' Todd countered in his inimitably gentle and infuriating fashion. 'There was this neat guy with a pointed beard in the grocery store. He said hi to me so I struck up a conversation with him. Our grocer didn't have any more milk so this guy says, "Why not come over to my neighborhood? There's an all-night store where the guy always has milk." So I got in his car and drove with him over to Jefferson Street where he lives in this tiny two-room flat with his wife and their four kids. They're all musicians,' Todd said proudly as though he'd discovered the Ink Spots. 'So his wife gets out some food and we start drinking beer and then we start playing music and before I know it it's three o'clock in the morning . . .'

'And now it's seven twenty in the morning,' said I snidely, plumping up the chubby little cushion I had just dressed with a kiss or two on her button nose. 'And this little cherub and her sister have to go to the babysitter so I can go to work.'

'I didn't want to wake you so I slept over there.'

'I'm very glad they didn't murder you,' I commented coldly. 'Now go and take the children to the babysitter.'

'But you're sick,' he protested. 'I thought you'd still be in bed. I brought you all these magazines. Look, I got *Fortune* and *US News* and *Connoisseur* and *Maison et Jardin* and *Vogue* and . . .'

This scene was representative of the very nature of our Tiger/Goat marriage. Todd got the role of happy bumbling fool who forgot the milk and brought home fifty dollars' worth of magazines, while I played his straight man.

In retrospect, it was quite amusing. I never had time to be either bored or lazy while Todd was my husband. Being married to a Goat kept me on my Tiger toes. But later on, after we were no longer locked in wed, there were a few times when Todd was supposed to take the kids for a day or two at weekends to give me a break. One of these visits sticks in my memory because Todd's Goatly scorn for time and method nearly killed me.

He was to take the kids on Friday at three. I had them ready and they were excited. They loved spending time with their daddy. But Todd neither showed nor called. Next afternoon at about two, he rang up asking if he could come over to pick up the kids. 'What happened yesterday?' I demanded.

'I've bought you some oysters and a bottle of champagne,' he said eagerly. 'I'd hate to see them go to waste.'

This sort of off-the-wall gesture of Todd's had always appealed to me. I couldn't resist his oysters. Along he came and we sat in the kitchen while the kids played in their rooms, sharing the oysters with my mum. We were laughing and chatting – when suddenly I knew – the smell, the slushy feeling of too gooey, spoiled fiber – I had swallowed a bad oyster. I became instantly and violently ill. Then a headache slammed into my brain and settled over the whole surrounding area. It was positively frightening. The kids became crazy with worry and started to cry.

Todd was lost. He felt bad. I accused him of attempted murder. 'Todd.' I finally lost control. 'Please take the kids out and buy them some toys,' I begged in a breathy sob. 'I'm in such pain,' I wept. 'I have to cry.' Todd bundled the kids off to a local shop where I guess he remembered which floor the toy department was on.

They returned with three big boxes. Daisy, aged seven, had a batik tie-dyeing kit. I could feel the boiling water spilling on her silken skin. The package warned, 'Ages fourteen to twenty'. Autumn, aged six, had an ice-making machine. She liked dollies and colouring books. I could see her pudgy little fingers shredded by the blades of this complex kitchen item. Then came my present. 'There must be a mistake. Surely this present is for Autumn and . . .'

'No, no,' said Todd excitedly. 'I chose this one especially for you. Didn't I, kids?'

They nodded.

I opened the box. Inside was exactly what had been depicted on the outside: a Tiny Tears doll. 'Because you were crying,' he said.

Your average Goat does not work well without supervision. Although they make wonderful employees because they don't mind being bossed around and told what to do, you cannot trust a Goat to carry on while you aren't there. He may or may not do things the way you said you wanted them done. The Goat's feet are activated solely by whimsy and impromptu brain waves.

Fortunately, most Goats know themselves well. They understand and accept their basic need for outside support and protection and have little difficulty in accepting the sometimes dreadful facts of life which can accompany that support.

I used to live next door to a great big grown-up Goat named Larry who has lived in his vehemently disapproving mother's tiny studio flat for over twenty years. The place is minuscule and dilapidated, an appalling mess. Larry's mother is a well-to-do harridan who lives luxuriously nearby, comes round every other day and commences shrieking at Larry about everything from the cottage-cheese walls to his ne'er-do-wellness. But she supports him and gives him somewhere to live.

Larry spends his nights hunched over a computer, smoking packets of Gauloise, hammering out never to be published novels. He sleeps all day and emerges to buy a loaf of bread or a pint of milk. He never washes or cleans his teeth.

To me, Larry's life is hellishly deprived. Yet he never complains. His mother takes care of him in her own Dragon-like way and that's enough for gentle, good-natured Larry. Larry is jaunty, charming and helpful in a crisis. He once saved my life when an imposing Gertrude-Steinesque neighbor tried to brain me with a huge flowerpot because she didn't like the bourgeois way I had planted my garden. I yelled, '*Larrrry!*' and my sweet hippie neighbor hopped out of his ground-floor window and came to my rescue. He didn't ask why. He just acted fast as all Goats know how to in a crisis.

As I'm forever crusading to extricate people from their own petards, I often asked Larry why he didn't try to get something published. 'I think about it sometimes,' he said, 'but I don't think I could go to a publisher myself. I'd need somebody to go for me, somebody who could pull some strings.'

In response to this typically Goatish plea, I gave him some money to get a manuscript ready. Then I took it to a couple of publishers for consideration. The replies? The book was brilliant in spots but it needed work: tightening; changing; moving things. Larry was irate. After all the trouble he'd gone to to get the manuscript cleaned up and photocopied, how dare they? Not long after that his mother phoned to say that she would thank me not to exploit her son any more.

As any Goat knows, his best arm in the big bad world lies in the hands of those who like and champion him. For this reason, he usually keeps a low profile and doesn't rock the boat. A Goat is rarely someone to take a vigorous public stand or demonstrate for an unpopular issue. Being on the bad side of authority is not the Goat's idea of a peaceful existence: peace and quiet is what the Goat is all about. Except, of course, when he blurts out a *faux pas* or tells an off-color joke in politest company.

Goats so often enter a new situation from their cloud nine reverie that they haven't always been following what came before. This makes them seem bumptious and feel clumsy in certain situations. Which brings me to the Goat's famous contentiousness. Goats are basically pessimistic: except during their periods of escapism, they suffer from free-floating anxiety. Goats are easy prey for depression and self-destruction. They tend to accentuate the negative and can be hypercritical over details, especially if they are feeling inferior or insecure. So, to make themselves feel more 'with it', they get into rows with loved ones. Out of nowhere you may suddenly hear, 'Now you listen to me, young lady . . .'

Goats butt vehemently into discussions and because they may not have been paying attention or don't know anything about the subject, their vehemence seems misplaced or out of synch. But they diatribe away, yelling and frothing at the mouth in defense of some arcane premise. It's best to let them down easily, and to surrender your point of view because Goats can and will hold a nasty grudge if they feel they have been made a public fool.

The Goat must be allowed to live at least part of the time in his own dream world. He cannot tolerate intrusion into this fantasy realm. If crossed or asked about his shortcomings, he may become enraged and even violent. He finds it difficult to accept anyone else's accusations or assessment of his behavior as he truly feels that no one but himself can possibly know where he's coming from (outer space).

Goats are narcissistic. Their appearance and image play an enormous part in their sense of personal stability. If they don't look their best, they may be afraid to go as far as the corner shop. Much of the time, they choose to stay at home where it's safer, have the groceries delivered and tinker or potter.

What role does a creature of such frail sensitivities play in this stiff-upper-lip world of ours? Goats are decorative. They are also highly creative and compassionate. They adore nature and thrive on being with animals and children. They are pleasant company and often know how to make people laugh. They make grippingly interesting small talk. Goats are empathetic and will sit through sob story after sob story. They take a vivid interest in improving society and care deeply for preserving beauty. They make excellent abstract thinkers. Goats are enormously talented at working with their hands. When lovingly handled and appreciated for their efforts, Goats know better than anybody how to be productive and put in endless long hours. Goats so want to please that they take pains to add joy and fantasy to life's humdrum nature. Most Goats display a modest social image and, unless pushed or frustrated, rarely make waves.

Unless it has a perceptible purpose, the Goat *hates* physical exertion. You won't find many famous Goat weight lifters or sports heroes. Most Goats don't go out of their way to swim the English Channel just to prove it can be done.

In summing up, I will remind you that, despite his unwillingness to participate in real life and his penchant for excessive rumination, the Goat can be a thoroughgoing genius. But for the prodigy to emerge from childhood into productive adulthood and know how to put his gifts to work, ongoing and continuing security and, most of all, personal discipline must be encouraged.

Unfortunately, the average Goat child is not only charming, delightful and artistically talented, but also easy to spoil. Little Goats co-operate in a secure family environment. They are eager to please and to make others happy; sharing is no problem for the Goat, who will prove generous to a fault so long as he benefits from sufficient stability and love. Goat offspring never forget a birthday and are usually good-looking, too, and irresistibly affectionate.

But, indulgent parents, be warned. You are not doing your Goat child a favor by encouraging daydreaming and not emphasizing constructive thought. You are right that this youngster needs torrents of love and approval, but he must be taught to build on his talents and put them to use. Provide him with a structured environment. Insist on schedules and teach him to budget both time and resources. Encourage him to speak up in turn in public. Teach him good communication skills. Help him grasp the importance of measure, reserve and good manners. Otherwise, your mastermind child may grow up dependent on the kindness of strangers and his genius may be handicapped for ever.

Nanny Goat

For the female of this species, Goatliness is next to godliness. For women, the Chinese Goat sign is a blessing. Being born a female Goat allows a girl shamelessly to display enhanced femininity, plot, plan and connive all she wants and even to lean lusciously and profitably on a big strong he-man without so much as a twinge of feminist regret.

Goat women are often successful. Being intuitive and sympathetic, reacting hysterically or excitedly, appearing delicate and sporting eccentric, up-to-the-minute fashions are all socially acceptable *womanly* attributes. Peer acceptance, coupled with the Goat's remarkable artistic talent, plus her essential gift for creativity and lightning-streak perception pave even the roughest road towards a fruitful, productive life for the intelligent she-Goat.

I say 'intelligent' because the Goat woman should know how best to use her exceptional attractiveness. An elegant yet childlike accessibility and susceptibility are the first things that strike one about Goat females. Then, their eyes appear almost misty and their gaze distant, which adds to an aura of mystery that many members of the opposite sex find irresistible. Like their male counterparts, Goat women move well, gliding smoothly across a room. Goat girls exude helplessness, charm and vulnerability.

The Goat girl presents a leaf-in-the-wind quality that sets her apart from more pedestrian females. This ephemeral aura endows her with an other-worldly tentativeness which makes people trip over each other to try to take care of her. One brief conversation with this beauty and you instantly feel you can share your knowledge with her and give her a leg-up towards her goals. Little matter if she doesn't always finish what she starts. You feel flattered just knowing that you can rescue her. She's so perceptive that you cannot help but be 100 per cent on her side. The Goat lady is always open to suggestion, more than willing to change horses mid-stream, eager to learn new methods and, oh, so glad you came along just in time to save her from her own poor judgement.

The Goat woman is so accessible to interference and apathetic about self-aggrandizement that she'll generously allow you to finish her sentences, advise her on how to decorate her house or raise her kid. Her acquiescence is an enviable trait. Her heart – and her ego – are both squarely in the right place.

However, Goat women are not known solely for their compliant, willing natures. They are also frequently as sharp as needles and successful in what we think of as a 'man's world'. Something about the way they appear so non-threatening and open-minded encourages bosses to hire Goat women. Then, too, a Goat lady's willingness to perform menial tasks is reassuring to a superior who fears the shrill wrath and resistance of your average gum-snapping siren or hard-edged feminist office manager. Goat women generally maintain a sweet countenance and are always fashionably dressed.

Let me tell you about my neighbour and friend in Paris, Armelle Jeanneau, the most self-disciplined of Goat females. Losses and setbacks have led to many disappointments and even once to a nervous breakdown, but Armelle is a wise and, by now, cautious Goat woman who has taught herself how to control her own destiny.

As is common with Goat women, Armelle fell madly in love, left her home in the countryside of northern France and married young. Her handsome husband, Jean-Paul, worked in the post office in Paris. He was from the Pyrenees and had always been a near-champion skier. Shortly after their marriage, they went on a skiing holiday. Without waking his bride, Jean-Paul tiptoed out one morning to ski a glacier and never came back. His body was not found until months later when the snows melted.

Goats are fragile and require secure environments. Pulling out a stable affection-source-cum-security-blanket from under a gentle Goat woman is both cruel and dangerous. Armelle had only been married a little over a year, but the time she had spent with Jean-Paul had been easy, loving, harmonious, productive – and secure. He held a safe civil service job with a future and they had dreamed of a home in the country, some animals and raising vegetables and a family.

The loss of Jean-Paul devastated Armelle. Six months of grief led her to a major nervous collapse that wasted well over a year of her life.

'It was hell,' says she. 'I would wake up some days and I just wouldn't be there. There would be someone else in my skin and in my head, a strange person I didn't even know. I had visions and voices and I couldn't keep any of them straight.'

Of course, such a loss is enough to make anyone fall apart, but the loss of a personality and incursion of a new one is common in Goat women. Goat women have built-in antennae: even when in repose, their minds work as finely tuned receptors – they are frequently involved in extrasensory perception, making excellent fortune-tellers, mediums, tarot card readers and astrologers. But when they are thrown off balance, this sensory gift can become their worst enemy. Keeping her head straight is not always the Goat woman's strongest suit.

These days, Armelle is as steady and sturdy as Notre Dame. She has never had a recurrence of her depression, perhaps because she keeps her life on a steady keel, rarely taking risks and surrounding herself with cozy comforts. I asked her how she did it.

'I noticed that my depression always got worse when I was idle or bored. So when I'm sinking or out of sorts, I plunge into a pail of elbow grease and work hard.'

Armelle's receptors are so acute that she cannot stand even to imagine the window-cleaner at work while she is not at home. She fears she might visualize him having an accident and thereby cause him to fall. She constantly and accurately predicts events without knowing the people involved and, astonishingly, wears this hypersensitivity under the conservative yet feminine façade of the business woman she has become.

A good career is often the best refuge for the clever Goat woman. She doesn't encounter as much resistance to success as her male counterpart. Her attributes give her easy access to workplace environments where, as soon as the boss realizes what a jewel he has hired, her diligence, devotion and intuition come to light and she is often rapidly promoted.

In love relationships, Goat females are noted for their penchant for flirting and even 'fooling around' on the side. It could be that, like Snake women, Goat ladies need the attention of many male admirers. Or maybe it is simply impossible for the beguiling Goat woman to resist the onslaught of suitors who curry her favors. But I believe that this naughty she-Goat habit of taking several lovers at once evolves benignly from her innate Goatly desire to make other people happy. Although not glaringly indiscreet, I haven't known many Goat women who sneak around in back alleys to conceal their peccadilloes. Their live-and-let-live approach, accompanied by a grin and a wink, seems to suit them just fine.

As for their sexual habits, I would venture that Goat women are rather innocent in bed, and like to be 'taken' by their man. Initiating sex may not be their idea of sexual nirvana but they are not against some kinky game-playing and may indulge in a little S&M if it pleases the gentleman in question. The Goat woman is both pliable and shy. Her entire resistance artillery amounts to the odd verbal rebuttal or sharp rejoinder, usually followed by a giggle, a sigh and surrender.

Even though Goat women can accomplish hard work, they abhor physical exertion for the sake of itself. You will not find many Goat women at aerobics classes or signing up for the volleyball or squash courts. If there was a sport best played from a supine position, Goat women would enroll in droves.

Her beauty is Madame Goat's best asset. Her face is oval and finely drawn. She often has healthy-looking rosy cheeks. Her nose is never too big, harmonizing with the rest of her features. Her mouth, however, is often too small. Her voice is mellow but sometimes she talks too much and its pitch rises and takes on a grating shrillness bordering on squeakiness, which she would be well advised to modulate. The Goat woman's best feature is her beautiful eyes. There is something spellbinding about her candid girlishness which helps Ms Goat to charm even the most blasé of gentlemen.

In marriage, the Goat woman is at her best and most serene. Matrimony (especially if it provides material security) affords her a solid identity of which she is proud. The Goat is at his or her happiest when tethered in a fertile field.

Of course, the odd spree of jolly extra-curricular lovemaking can get this lady into hot water with hubby, who has a tantrum, snips the tether and turns her out of the field. On the loose again, the she-Goat grows morose and miserable. She is constantly out of sorts until she lands herself another awe-struck hubby and the game starts again. Many Goat women marry several times, and few are single for long.

Goat women stay maddeningly friendly with all of their ex-lovers. It's a secure husband who can tolerate meeting up with old Pierre or Steve sitting at his kitchen table having a coffee with the wife. But if he wants peace and quiet, he will have to learn to accept his Goat wife's old boyfriends as part of the domestic landscape. She is probably not sleeping with all of them but she likes to stay close to those adorable fellows she once loved.

Although she certainly keeps busy and does her job well, the average Goat woman doesn't think of herself as a slave – not at all! The goal for women born in this sign is retirement, time off, and leisure. Of all her gifts the greatest is for living without constraints. Her ideal life would consist of activities which involved decorating for a party, re-covering a sofa, planning meals, redefining the lighting plan in her sitting room, gardening (lots of that), making music, writing poems and really just *being*. She likes keeping her hands busy but she is nobody's drudge. Given the right amount of security, a happier householding wife and mother there will never be.

Goat women must beware of the temptations of drugs and especially of alcohol addiction, which provides a false sense of security and confers a kind of 'Dutch courage' on habitual imbibers. Sometimes, because Goat women are neither tough nor disciplined and cannot, physically or emotionally, resist the mad pace imposed on them, they drink until they collapse and have to disappear to rest for a while until they can regain a healthy sure footing.

If you are a Goat lady, don't get depressed just reading this and rush to the kitchen to pour yourself a drink. Relax. So what if you never finished that novel you started ten years ago but still so fervently believe in? What does it matter if you've been in the same marital rut for fifteen years and sometimes feel there is no excitement in your life? Is it so bad that you're happy just sitting around playing wife to your darling mate? The centrally important factor in your life which counts for your health and emotional peace of mind is *security*. If you've got it, *don't* knock it.

Billy Goat

Unlike the rigorous, driving, steady-as-you-go Capricorn (which means Goat) male in the Western zodiac, the Chinese Goat sign indicates a languid, dreamy man whose kooky, unpredictable behavior almost defies definition. Sometimes, the Goat man may wax ambitious and seem to have the get-up-and-go necessary to achieve grandeur. Then again, he may change his mind, drop everything and drift to some realm where he no longer has a visible goal, cannot be reached for questioning, and couldn't care less.

The Chinese sometimes say that Goat men are feminine. Knowing as well as I do the capacity for mettle, intense perseverance and striving of most of the women of today, I can hardly agree with that. Perhaps in dubbing the Goat male 'feminine' they mean that his methods do not include strong-arming. Rather, in a less aggressive (hence more classically woman-like) way, Goat men contrive to get where they want to be by hatching plots and schemes and manipulating others in their own interests.

Goat men are often reedily built. They glide about in an attractive, graceful, dancer-like way as though not to disturb or raise dust. They pride themselves on sporting garish, unusual outfits, appearing eccentric and outlandish. A wild pink bow tie with a pale blue and white checked shirt under a black velvet smoking jacket might seem conservative to the male Goat's eye. They are fey creatures whose aura is definitely not that of football player or muscle-builder.

Goat men's cheeks are frequently full, their noses thin and their mouths small. Their beards are not usually bushy but rather pointily shaped, like their chins, and sparse. They often go bald early in adult life. The Goat male's teeth are widely spaced, his smile crooked and his forehead broad and flattish. Unconventionally attractive, Goat men can be extremely sexy and make desirable and unusually sensual love partners.

The overall look of a Goat man is that of a gangly, long-limbed, astonished child who stares out at the world through large, somewhat protruding eyes, seeing nothing but the great beyond. The delicate outward image of the Goat man might lead one to believe that he has little strength, cannot defend himself and is almost to be pitied for his gentle, ineffectual and non-aggressive manner.

Don't be fooled. The Goat man is master of the art of passive, enduring resistance. To get his way, he can outwait an ice age. He'll just sit there hatching plots until his adversary's back is turned, when the Goat man will strike. He won't attack with violent or obvious aggression, oh no. The Goat man is no fool. His tactics are always subterranean. Added to which, they are remarkably ruthless and unexpectedly brilliant.

Behind the Goat man's childlike grin and air of innocence lies a ruthless enemy who has no regard for the Geneva Convention or even old times' sake. Undermining and insidious, his quiet scheming has been the undoing of some of the world's most clever, classically forceful creatures. His enemy never knows his strength until he attempts to break him. The male Goat is cunning. He bobs and weaves and changes his identity and address. He crawls under rocks and hides in unlikely alleyways, aided and abetted by formidable allies. This silent resistance and gift for long-term machination so common in Goat men is what I like to call the strength of the weak.

Goat men love to spend money, even money they don't have, and especially other people's money. Beware the wolf in Goat's clothing. As they are born philanderers and ultra-talented at the game of seduction, Goats have an adorable, profligate way of stalking their prey. They give outrageous gifts to their sweeties, wine, dine, theater and vacation their potential mistresses and lovers, pummelling them with affections and tokens to the point of exhaustion and, ultimately, delectable submission.

Goat men never forget birthdays and Valentine's or any other festive day. And watch out for Christmas! Goat men are positively daft about preparing for and experiencing the joy of Christmas.

Animal lovers one and all, Goat men need a dog or cat – preferably both and preferably a few other species, too. Of all the signs, the Goat male understands animals best. And there is no lack of tenderness in this peace-loving man. He will spend hours stroking his dog's ears or cuddling a child. If all life asked of men was to be at one with nature, provide compassion and affection, the Goat man would be king.

Goat men make imaginative lovers. They are the type who always want to make love in the shower or in the laundry chute – just to see what it feels like. We must remember that Goats are born eccentrics, which makes them naturally kinky. You will often find Goat men who can't make up their minds between AC and DC and who prefer a bit of both. Sexually, they are human joysticks, more than willing to give as well as take pleasure. Although I have frequently heard women complain of the ineffectualness, irresponsibility and general inertia of their Goat lovers or husbands, I have never heard a whimper about poor-quality lovemaking.

As for professions, Goat men are best employed where they can be part of a team or totally on their own. They don't like to boss others around and if they must, they often do it too gently and get walked on. Because of their unique sense of time – which is no sense at all – Goat men make excellent artists, film editors, writers, independent workers such as plumbers, electricians, architects, decorators or even surgeons, or dentists or astrologers. The intuitive Goat can also be a whiz at predicting stockmarket trends and, providing he is previously grounded in both knowledge and security, could make an excellent psychologist, psychiatrist, social worker or – as he is an excellent abstract thinker – physicist.

One of my favorite geniuses alive is the French plastic surgeon Michel Soussaline. His life is a total success. He carves and remodels, shapes, molds and innovates all day long and always achieves fabulous results. In the evenings and at weekends he sculpts, paints and gardens, again shaping, forming, building and creating. His wife of twenty years is a strong-minded Rooster on whom he can depend entirely for solidity and a sound home base. Michel has turned the Goat's deft genius into a successful career. He always works with the same team of assistants in the same hospitals and within the same professional framework. His unique strength is in knowing how to manage his Goatly genius. And, believe me, that is the hardest part of being a Goat male.

Luckily, Goat men often inherit wealth or find professions wherein the System or an institution protects them. They also have few compunctions about marrying for money, playing gigolo to an older woman or house husband while the wife is out working. Don't count on a Goat man to watch the kids, though. You'll need a nanny for that and a good laundress and cleaner. The Goat male makes a better courtesan than housekeeper.

If you are a strong, independent woman and enjoy being out in the world rather than at home in the kitchen, you can count on a Goat to assume all the gentle sides of homemaking – even the cooking at which he will probably be competent. If you can plough through the debris in the kitchen, your dinner will be both tasty and unusual. It may not be served promptly but the table setting will be gorgeous and the ambience restful and fun.

The trick of getting along with a Goat male is a willingness on his wife's part to ignore stereotypes. She must accept her man as a delightful love object, who may not be rigorously or regularly productive in a financial sense. If she can live with this shift in roles, she will have a good life as her Goat mate will always be malleable, easy to have around, undemanding of her time and willing to create or share in having fun.

Placing heavy financial or emotional burdens on the Goat's shoulders doesn't often work. The Goat must feel free yet be applauded for the competence he shows in the areas in which he feels proficient. If you are the right partner for this innovative creature, your life can be both fun and profitable. But you must actively admire him, look up to him and show appreciation at his arrival on the scene.

Although the Goat man is frequently AWOL in the concrete real world department, he cannot tolerate being ignored when he is there. 'Doesn't anybody around here care that I'm home?' was my dear departed father's way of saying, 'Hi, honey, I'm home,' when no one came racing out to wave hello to him half-way down the driveway.

It seems as if all I can find to describe this adorable love-bug of a man are faults. But everything is relative. Of course, what I see as faults may well be interpreted by another, less scrutinizingly critical woman as tremendous strengths.

The Goat is a born remittance man. I know at least three Goat gentlemen who live in Spain or the South of France on small family incomes in modest but comfortable digs where they do nothing much and are happy as Hannah.

Take Nathan, a painter, whose parents bought him a flat in Ibiza in the sixties, ostensibly to use as a studio. His work was terrific, full of sunlight and flowers – people always wanted to buy it. Gallery owners made a point of snapping up each canvas as it came off the easel. Nathan was living very well but soon the gallery owners realized that demand was exceeding supply. They questioned Nathan about his slow-down in production, urging him to speed up. He told them he had stopped painting to become a musician.

When I lived in Ibiza I often invited him to dinner. He was great company, handsome and full of fun. One evening he told me he was flat broke, which was indeed unusual as he had always earned so much from his paintings. He explained he wanted to do music now and no longer had time to paint. 'The parents,' he explained. 'They'll stake me to it.'

In those days, Nathan was twenty-five and getting support for his new career from Mom and Dad seemed almost normal. But last year I went back to Ibiza to visit an old friend and, in the Montesol café, spotted a still handsome, white-haired Nathan, aged fifty-five. I ran up and said hello.

He stood up gallantly and found me a chair. 'I live here,' he said. 'I never left. I'm into mime now and I work with a troupe of young Spanish kids twice a week.'

'Where do you live?' I wondered. 'And how?'

'Still in the little flat in Figueretes and still living off good old Mom and Pop,' said Nathan, grinning. 'They're in their eighties and still running the family business,' he said proudly.

I did not comment. It's his life after all. And (thank heaven) he's no relation of mine. Goats don't take kindly to criticism and hate hearing the truth. I once had an argument with my ex-husband Todd where I clearly recall saying, 'But it's the truth, darling. You can't deny that you're scatty. This week alone you forgot to pick the kids up from the babysitter twice in a row.'

Todd answered me calmly, simply reminding me what I should have understood by now. 'Certain people don't want to hear the *truth* and prefer to live without it being stuffed down their throats.'

Of course. How could I be so foolish?

Reversals throw these fellows for a lifelong loop. My daddy had a severe financial upset at fifty and felt so devastated about it that he moved the whole family out of the city of his birth to another, far more hostile town where he had to start all over again. He died young of that effort and the loneliness and frustration he felt so far away from his beloved home town.

And I've seen it happen with many other Goat men. For them to settle down and get anywhere in life, they must struggle harder, concentrate more and go against a peace-loving, retiring nature to learn to care about striving, pushing and aggression. When (and if) they take the bull by the horns, and failure hits them, they collapse into their initial position, which was, 'Why bother?'

Aberrant sexual and social behavior, drugs and drinking threaten the male Goat's stability. He is often pessimistic, misunderstood, easily swayed and not always able to resist the temptation to veer into untrodden territory. He may be a near-genius in one area but otherwise feels himself a social misfit easily falling into deviant behavior.

Goat men are hypersensitive, strong but not classically forceful or macho. They are gifted, intuitive and discriminating. But their raw sensitivities make them vulnerable and may even lead them to dangerous, suicidal behavior.

The five Chinese elements and how they influence the Goat

The Wood Goat

1775 Jane Austen
1895 Carl Orff, George Burns, Lewis Mumford, Arthur Murray, Bud Abbot, Busby Berkeley, Rudolph Valentino, George Raft, John Ford, King George VI, Marcel Pagnol, Buster Keaton, Groucho Marx, Babe Ruth
1955 Maria Shriver, Debra Winger, Bo Derek, Isabelle Huppert, Isabelle Adjani, Bruce Willis

The influence of Wood on the Goat's whimsical behavior is definitely salutary. Here we see a shored-up and buttressed Goat person. Instead of indulging in capriciousness, this Goat manages to maintain a healthy balance between frivolity and stability. Of all Goats, this type is most likely to be able to surmount harsh setbacks and carry on valiantly as though nothing untoward had occurred. This Goat is equally creative yet more ambitious than many of his counterparts.

The necessity for security and moral support from the immediate entourage is still very much present in this Goat's life. Take just a few of the above-mentioned famous men as examples. Arthur Murray, the celebrated dance instructor who gave his name to thousands of ballroom dance studios throughout the world, was typically Goatly: tall, graceful and willowy. Dancing is a perfect career for a Goat; and Arthur Murray was an excellent, innovative teacher. He was not, however, a manager. He always said that his wife Katherine was the brains behind the expansion and management of the Arthur Murray operation. Without her, he claimed, 'I would still be swirling around a summer pavilion dance floor looking gorgeous.' Knowing his Chinese sign, I believe him.

Another such example is Groucho Marx, who was at his best as one of the Marx Brothers, only functioning alone when he was given a team-run television show in the fifties. The structure of the Marx Brothers team allowed Groucho's genius to shine through.

The Wood Goat is young at heart. Even under duress, he manages to keep a smile or a joke on his lips. Because of this gift for optimism, he confronts adversity more readily and extricates himself more graciously than most Goats who are likely, in their frustration, either to crumble and surrender or strike out violently.

Given to mood swings, the Wood Goat gets depressed from time to time. These sinking spells or periods of gloom are often caused by the hormonal fluctuations common to all Goats but particularly severe in this Goat. Careful monitoring of endocrine gland function is advised.

The Wood Goat lives in a permanent state of moral dilemma. He is, like all his Goat counterparts, a hedonist, a potential lifetime lotus eater. However, the Wood Goat wants to achieve. He does not choose to remain in the herd and he knows that to reach the lofty goals he imagines, he might have to commit himself to a life of both hard work and protracted routine effort. This prospect, for any Goat, is daunting.

To satisfy his desire for success, the Wood Goat, in his inimitable resourcefulness, learns young how to choose effective friends and associates. First he cultivates their affections, then trusts them implicitly to assist him in getting where he wants to go. I would not go so far as to call this Goat a 'taker' who uses people to his own ends. Rather, the Wood Goat is a jolly parasite. He is easy to have around – a joy and an inspiration to those who will generously surround him with essential comforts, calm and sustenance.

The Fire Goat

1907 John Wayne, Laurence Olivier, Cesar Romero, Barbara Stanwyck, James Michener, Peggy Ashcroft, Robert Bresson, Tino Rossi, Anna Magnani, Robert Young, Alberto Moravia, W. H. Auden, Anthony Blunt

1967 Boris Becker, Keifer Sutherland, Julia Roberts

The Fire Goat is a walking emotional holocaust. Passion rules his existence. No matter how he tries, he cannot react collectedly to stimuli, remain cool in the face of insult, appear aloof when provoked. Mind you, this Goat is no pouncing Tiger who chews the head off his adversaries before they have a chance to finish their sentences. His methods are more akin to histrionics. He is given to theatrics and flies into rages or succumbs to nervous prostration. The Fire Goat is too sensitive by half and needs a heavier lid than most to keep his volcanic sentiments in check. A steady partner can make all the difference to the success or failure of the Fire Goat's life.

This character is renowned for his charm and ability to affect others through a quality we might call refinement. His is an epidermal sensitivity which raises the very hairs on forearms. People warm to him and instantly admire his edifying style. The Fire Goat's ability to reach masses of people with his words or to touch their emotions with his talent for seizing the moment or interpreting a role is legendary. He is talented in the extreme but requires top-notch guidance to ensure his perseverance.

This subject must not be obliged to handle his own finances. The idea of balancing a checkbook is enough to give the Fire Goat one of his attacks of the vapors. If success knocks at his door, he is well advised not to open up until he has summoned his resident accountant to stand by. The Fire Goat is a reckless squanderer of money – his own and other people's. If you know and love one of these fey creatures, you are hereby warned to keep a tight rein on the joint account and hide the credit cards. The Fire Goat is not dishonest, but he is both thoughtless and inconsequential about spending. Fortunately, he is also incredibly lucky. I certainly don't advise gambling, but the occasional raffle ticket couldn't hurt, could it?

This Goat can enjoy some degree of superiority in a hierarchy but must not assume too grand a role as excess responsibility can lead to the onset of chronic ills such as migraine or ulcers. A Fire Goat has a short fuse. When angered, he doesn't know how to keep his antagonistic feelings under his horns.

Charisma is the Fire Goat's strong suit. His gentle manner and aura of mystery attract others. The best professions this person can choose will have to do with mysticism, philosophy, the subconscious, occult science or perhaps physics or other mind-liberating sciences.

It follows, then, that the Fire Goat is drawn to causes that seek to improve the quality of our inner as well as our outer lives. Fire Goats can take the lead in such areas as ecology, health professions, nutrition or alternative medicines. A smart Fire Goat can make a handsome fortune in these and other New Age pursuits. But he must surround himself with honorable and sympathetic associates who will never give him the key to the safe.

The Earth Goat

1859 Arthur Conan Doyle, Billy the Kid
1919 Red Buttons, Margot Fonteyn, Malcolm Forbes, Zsa Zsa Gabor, Anita O'Day, McGeorge Bundy, Hugh Carey, Art Blakey, Dino di Laurentiis, Pete Seeger, Veronica Lake, Jack Palance, Michel Deon, Louis Feraud, Jennifer Jones, Louis Jourdan, Celeste Holm, Lana Turner, John Cardinal O'Connor

There is genius in the Earth Goat's make-up. Given the proper circumstances, skill and business may combine to help this Goat to create a superlative and luxurious (just the way he likes it) lifestyle.

But the Earth Goat is terminally erratic. Half the time he cannot decide what he wants to do and the other half he suddenly waxes determined and goes after a difficult-to-achieve goal. Sometimes he gets there and things go swimmingly, providing he is well protected and insured against his own worst enemy – himself.

This Goat is very argumentative. His talent for talking things out is more pronounced than that of other, less naturally verbal Goats. But he often bases his arguments on illogical premises or flighty dreams which just happen to be zooming around his psyche and catch his fancy. As he doesn't always think things through to their logical conclusion, the tone of these discussions is often chaotic. If he is not careful, eventually people grow to mistrust his judgement and he becomes the subject of some ridicule among his peers. Studying logic in college and participating in school debating teams would provide a sound basis for the Earth Goat to spare himself taunts in later life.

Despite his tendency to bicker over the inconsequential at every turn, the Earth Goat has one of the easiest Goat natures to put up with because he knows very well that his survival depends on the goodwill he can muster among those who surround him. He hardly ever pushes his spats too far, causing rifts or break-ups. He displays almost no follow-through urge to stick up for his rights, demand his due or seek reparations if he feels he has been wronged. Consequently, life with the Earth Goat is suffused with a spirit of co-operation and gentility.

His lack of objectivity gets him into scrapes, however, particularly in the work hierarchy. Because of his native passivity and gift for concession and compromise, the Earth Goat is sometimes blamed for wrongs he didn't commit. More ambitious, ruthless cohorts will happily take advantage of his laid-back unresponsive nature to leap over his desk in pursuit of their own selfish ends.

Ultimately, the biggest challenge to the Earth Goat is simply to abide, but not necessarily to prevail. More than anything, he wishes to be left to his own devices to follow his lucky stars and dream his impossible dreams without interference from more down-to-earth folk who feel that they are doing him a favor by bringing truth into his life.

It's a tricky and perilous management challenge both to remain dependent on the support of others and still maintain intact one's integrity and dreams. The tightrope he walks may cause a feeling of imbalance in the Earth Goat's inner self. Physical symptoms may result which are solely manifestations of this lack of equilibrium. Epileptic seizures, spells of weakness and dark, gloomy depressions may crop up. When this happens, a good lover or lifelong crony needs to be right there for his Earth Goat friend. Nothing short of sitting him down with some old-fashioned straight talk and reassurance about his security will clear up the messy muddles into which this Goat's fugitive psyche can lead him. When properly handled, the Earth Goat's startling talents can afford him the highest kudos. His imagination knows no bounds. He is sympathetic and understands even the most incomprehensible human behavior. He is a brilliant and sympathetic soul. But he has to watch out for his own scattiness. If not, he may well ruin his image in the eyes of those who respect him.

The Metal Goat

1811 Franz Liszt
1931 James Dean, Donald Bartheleme, Anne Bancroft, Monica Vitti, Ettore Scola, Angie Dickinson, Lonnie Donegan, Diana Dors, Anita Ekberg, Mike Nichols, Barbara Walters, Tom Wolfe, Annie Girardot, Nelly Kaplan, Hal Linden, Leonard Nimoy, Olympia Dukakis, Leslie Caron, Shel Silverstein, Dan Rather, Rita Moreno

On the surface, the Metal Goat seems, to the uninformed outsider, a gentle pushover. His unprepossessing, dishevelled, casual style bespeaks only simplicity and innocence. But beware: although the influence of Metal does enhance the gentle Goat's resolve, it also hardens his heart, causing him to become unnecessarily combative when dealing with others.

Goats are non-confrontational and are known to have to depend on the kindness of strangers for their survival. At all costs, they must appear to be compromising, easy-going. This is as true of the Metal Goat: he cannot and does not risk open conflict. Yet, as he is temperamental, he often feels interfered with and put upon. To avoid being visible and therefore doubly vulnerable, the combativeness in this subject goes underground. Metal Goats delight in secret manipulation and subterfuge, and perform their most skillful string-pulling from behind the scenes.

For this reason, the Metal Goat makes an easy-going friend but is a daunting adversary. He will never speak his mind in any controversy. He categorically refuses to deal one to one in open conflict. He will not take stands on any controversial subject nor will he brave danger for the sake of a good cause. The Metal Goat favors underhand means and is quite capable of lying and justifying even the most amoral behavior to himself if he does not get his way. The wronged Metal Goat is ridden with the need for revenge and will stop at nothing to gain ground against his (real or imagined) enemies.

At home in the nether regions of the collective unconscious, the Metal Goat can readily pursue careers where knowledge of the inner workings of the human mind are a prerequisite. He will make an excellent forecaster and interpreter of human behavior: a soothsayer or psychiatrist, an incisively charismatic actor or film director, a brilliant writer or singer or, more simply, a willing courtesan. Alternatively, he might choose to stay at home and become an inventor, trying to concoct a gourmet elixir of youth, to make gold from aluminium foil or improve on some secret eavesdropping device.

Of all the Goat types, this one is perhaps the most elementally lacking in a sense of urgency. He will not hurry. He insists on living in a leisurely way and hasn't got a clue how his lackadaisical behavior affects others.

This Goat can rise to great heights by advancing square by square at his own languid pace. But because the subterranean is always pulling at him he often falls victim to self-duping bad habits, such as drug, alcohol or diabolical religious addictions.

A well-nurtured Metal Goat's talent can bring him enormous rewards but he must watch out for a dangerous tendency to self-congratulatory horn-blowing. Metal Goats suffer from an excess of pride. Sometimes their vanity gets in the way of their common sense and scotches the possibility of reaching a desirable goal.

Remedy? Lots of tough love and no-nonsense nurturing may help to bring reality out of the basement of the Metal Goat's mind and put his thoughts into better perspective.

The Water Goat

1883 Lon Chaney, Douglas Fairbanks, Franz Kafka, Kahlil Gibran
1943 Ben Kingsley, Arthur Ashe, Sharon Tate, Georgie Fame, Catherine Deneuve, Mike Leigh, Joe Frazier, Jim Morrison, George Harrison, Joni Mitchell, Mick Jagger, Billie Jean King, Johnny Hallyday, Jean Claude Killy, Sally Jesse Raphael, Lynn Redgrave, John Major, Leslie Uggams, Robert DeNiro, Chevy Chase, Sam Shepard, Lech Walesa

The Water Goat's claim to fame is his intuition. Of course, all Goats are sensitive and pick up easily on feelings but Water confers a special talent for intuiting the flavor and tone of even the most subtle of life's situations on this liquid variety of Goat. Where hints of danger, twinges of fear or suggestions of sexuality or extra-terrestrial activity may pass unnoticed under the noses of less perceptive folk, every nuance is picked up by the supremely impressionable Water Goat. He seems able to understand without learning and to know certain things instinctively without necessarily having first understood them.

Although compassion is the emotion that could be most profoundly felt by him, the Water Goat is oddly egocentric and quite unable to escape from his golden bubble of preoccupation with himself long enough to relate to those he might feel sorry for. He is neither a natural care provider nor is he very altruistic. Rather, the Water Goat senses the way things are moving, then zigzags through the loaded minefields of life, relying solely on his inner radar to guide him. He seeks more to stave off danger and predict events for himself than to warn others of potential harm.

Water Goats are intensely charming and sensual. They love being needed and adore having an audience. Adulation and applause provide approval and help to keep them moving. Appreciation serves to push them to heights they might not aspire to without outside urging. Their inner emotional structure is somewhat shaky so being encouraged, cheered and inspired by friends and family is of great assistance to them in making decisions, accomplishing tasks on time and leaping hurdles without the usual Goatly hesitation.

There is a kinky side to this Water Goat's sexual character. The male of the species is amorous and romantic and requires physical attention from females. In her geisha-like way, the sensuous woman Water Goat also comes on very strong. Although quiet and unassuming, the Water Goat lady is a true siren whose amiable sexual prowess is never a well-kept secret. In fact, ne'er a day goes by that this Goat does not engage in sexual activity or fantasy. There is a strong propensity among Water Goats to engage in group sex and other forms of aberrant and even promiscuous activity.

When you get to know this Goat well, you rapidly understand why this has often been known as the sign of the hippie or Bohemian. Water Goats don't care to heed the rules and regulations of the standard social system. They prefer to remain outside, looking in, enjoying a certain remove from the mainstream and managing to hover about three feet over their own and others' heads.

Water Goats, like their brothers and sisters of the other Goat signs, frequently have genius. When they put this to practical use, the road ahead may quickly lead to stardom because, of all Goats, this one knows best how to use his elbows to make contacts, open doors with his sexual charms and leap wantonly into the arms of opportunity. He knows instinctively how to travel in the right circles, get himself known to the right people and find ways to be noticed by influential types who can get him where he wants to be. This Goat is never too pushy or boastful but, rather, plays his hand deftly by maintaining tight relations with influential people who can put him where he thinks he ought to be.

Although he doesn't usually make his will felt aggressively, the Water Goat does not fancy being thwarted or interfered with. If he doesn't get his way, or feels he has been shunted aside, his well-developed sense of martyrdom rises straight to the surface. His whining can be heard for miles. The 'Poor me' side of the ultrasensitive Water Goat is absolutely his worst fault. Without it, he is a true charmer, a love of a well-mannered fellow and a terrifically amusing friend. But when that 'Why me?' refrain rises from the depths of the silken *chaise longue*, I advise you to head for the hills and hide under an anonymous rock until the snivelling is over. And don't feel guilty. If you don't take care of poor little Water Goat in his deepest chagrin, he will make it his business to see that somebody else does.

Goat health

The Goat's health can be best defined as precarious. Although, in spurts, Goats can stand up to endurance tests and sweat out ordeals of superhuman dimension, their foundations are shaky, timbers friable and delicately shaped ankles weak.

The Goat's health pattern is irregular. His demeanor is so listless and his spirit so hazy that sometimes he doesn't know if he's feeling ill or simply in a state of stratospheric suspension from which he finds it painful to emerge.

But the Goat is not a hypochondriac. His jaunts into the nether regions of the mind and frequent disconnection from the real world are not mere avoidance tactics or psychic voyages fraught with anxiety and panic about being stricken with cancer, multiple sclerosis or migraines.

Yet he is vulnerable, hence easily overcome and invaded by all manner of unexpected illnesses. This creature is no model of physical force: Goats are ethereal. Characteristically they tread lightly and float around in a constant state of semi-remove from reality. The delicate Goat soul lives in an equally delicate and finely wired body, an obvious target for sudden onsets of infection, attacks of acute illness or pain and often falls victim to the ravages of anarchic living and weirdo eating habits.

The Goat doesn't always complain and when he does his symptoms are rarely specific. He may just feel 'all in' and take to the couch where he seems to vegetate. You feel his brow for fever, look at his tongue and examine his eyes but standard first-aid methods don't reveal anything and the 'How do you feel now?' question gets a fleeting, sketchy answer. 'Mmmhh? I'm just sort of tired. I think I'll lie down for a while.'

You won't get straight answers about headaches and joint pains or sore throats or throbbing muscles. The Goat is not given to identifying gory details. Instead, without a word, he'll drift over to the *chaise longue* and sprawl attractively there in a state of advanced lethargy which, although it is pretty alarming to behold, usually means that your Goat is just plain *tired* – tired of fighting all day to pull himself back from the twilight zone, tired of keeping business hours when he'd really rather work all night and sleep all day, tired of coping with the impenetrable rigors of survival.

Goat children almost always fall prey to the full battery of childhood diseases. Parents of Goats should always have them immunized. When they do get sick coddle them and keep them extra warm. Teach them how to protect themselves from infection. In China it is well-accepted that the earlier a Goat acquires good personal hygiene and healthy eating habits, the better the chance he has of achieving a sturdy, ripe old age.

Puberty is always wearisome and strenuous for youngsters but especially traumatic for the growing Goat. Both sexes of Goat suffer from slow development and lazy metabolism but the male Goat is particularly susceptible to sluggish hormones, a condition which sometimes delays the appearance of secondary sex characteristics such as a beard and voice change. This pubescent hormonal imbalance, for which young Goat boys are so famous, may severely hinder their physical growth. Nothing is more traumatic for a sixteen-year-old boy than to find himself elected Midget of the Year by his classmates who not only tower over him and jeer at him in their taunting, deep, male voices, but are also on all the varsity teams and seduce all the girls. If these slow-growth tendencies are detected early on by the discerning parent or pediatrician, they can be medically corrected. If not, the young man may begin his adulthood with very little self-confidence.

What this all boils down to once more is that Goats, whether in the workplace, on the sports field or in the kitchen, enjoy being constantly monitored. With few exceptions, they will not take responsibility for their own well-being. They don't scorn healthy notions or find routine work or eating habits contemptible – they just cannot police their own behavior. They know that a forgotten jacket on a bitterly cold day can lead to a cold which may turn into pneumonia and even end in death, but your average Goat doesn't stop to find out if it's cold or warm out. He leaves his coat in the hall and goes out without it. He will not have forgotten to dress in a very chic color-co-ordinated outfit. But as for the temperature: well, is it really so important?

Goats are often allergic. Hay fever, asthma, nagging dry coughs, chronic stuffy noses and sinus headaches often plague them. For best results Goats should try to avoid allopathic medicine which often treats only symptoms and doesn't go to the root of the disorder. Allergies are essentially caused by an energy imbalance, and attacks are often at least partially precipitated by the emotional state of the sufferer, with symptoms that are diffuse, changeable and elusive. The Chinese believe in treating these functional disorders with natural medicines, homeopathy and acupuncture. For the intangible Goat, these highly refined subtle methods invariably work best.

Mental illness may lurk in the befuddled psyche of the gentle Goat. Autism, paranoia, schizophrenia and mental black-outs are common entries in a Goat's medical history. Remember that Goats are particularly susceptible to the effects of drugs and alcohol and must cultivate a disciplined, almost militant, attitude against the use of mind-altering chemicals at a young age.

Goats should eat lots of greens, fruit and grains and avoid sweet and starchy foods. Lean meat, fish and legumes will provide the necessary proteins and should be consumed regularly. The Goat benefits from drinking lots of fruit juice and mineral water. Broth is good, too. And, despite my earlier caveat about ingesting alcohol, the Goat can use good wine, tea and coffee in moderation as these last three beverages tend to spur him out of his chronic physical lethargy.

The best sports for the Goat are gentle water sports or easy walking and jogging. Violent activity does not suit his temperament. He feels zingiest in iodized seaside air which may stimulate his recalcitrant thyroid gland. He also craves the deep green of temperate climates and their gently rolling countrysides. Mountain air may make him uneasy and enervated. A quiet, non-stressful life is best for the health of the Goat. All city rat races and polluted places undermine the delicate balance with which the Goat is born: a Goat in city traffic is a very unhappy Goat.

The Goat's quirky digestion, especially bloating and pain in the intestinal tract, can cause him discomfort. As he is frequently tempted to live by fits and starts, spurts of frenzied activity followed by long sedentary periods, the Goat often suffers a week of constipation followed by a few miserable days of diarrhea, spasms and painful wind, heartburn and especially hemorrhoids. More whole grains and vegetables in the diet help to regulate these problems, but you know Goats: they usually eat whatever's there and will always gobble something they *love* rather than bother to prepare a complicated recipe or learn how to use an unfamiliar foodstuff. The road to rack and ruin for the Goat's health is the self-same path for which he must be ever on the alert – that of least resistance.

One further thing can assist the Goat to maintain a healthy equilibrium: the pursuit of peace of mind through yoga, meditation, relaxation techniques, vitamin therapy and osteopathy. Without release from the tension that daily life places on the Goat's incessantly fugitive psyche, the important balance of Yin and Yang will never be re-established. When this happens, his resistance is lowered and he undergoes a shockwave attack of some unexpected malady which nails him to his bed for months.

One more aspect of the Goat character which has to do with health and medicine is an irksome preoccupation with plastic surgery. Although this obsession doesn't usually come to light until later in life, the average Goat is so immersed in the physical appearance of things and their beauty that they cannot stand to see so much as a pimple left unturned by the scalpel of their favorite hatchet man or woman.

So picky are Goats about other people's physical shortcomings that they often miss some of their own. I know a chubby Goat lady who constantly decries the obesity among her compatriots. The typically unevolved Goat tends to criticize others for his own faults.

This hypercritical Goat lady is long past pleasingly plump, but she feels her excess pounds are different – a luxury item. She has undergone thigh and hip liposuctions, stomach-fat removals, cheek replacements, upper lip silicone injections and boob transformations, but if any other major structural beauty-enhancing operations were available, this Goat gal would save up her husband's pennies and get herself sliced some more.

Finally, the longevity of the Goat is almost solely dependent on his lifestyle. My gentle Goat father died at sixty-two after a lifetime of ignoring warnings about eating too much meat and smoking cigarettes and working insanely long hours and drinking too many cocktails. His arteries clogged up, his incipient stroke struck and his heart finally gave out from blitzkrieg overwork and cholesterolically anarchic living patterns.

Goats, you'd better get cracking now on your longer-life plan. Clean up your act. Get more regular sleep instead of snoozing in the living room half the evening and then roaming around all night. Put yourself on a schedule or get someone meaner than you to do it for you. Eat the right things at the right time. You are a person of fragile constitution. Try to get your sense of time together and, most of all, *do* something besides lying down to learn how to relax.

Goat futures

What the Goat should expect from the next twelve Chinese animal years

2008, the Earth Rat year – As the Rat seeks power and wants to protect and push people around, Goats are hard put to make much a of personal statement in this year. Being hustled or crowded doesn't have the desired effect on you devil-may-care creatures. You are always willing to cooperate and be pleasant when asked to perform. But when someone literally kicks you in the rump and orders you to get a move on, you back away in fear and loathing. You may feel misunderstood and sulk, but you definitely don't feel like painting the *Mona Lisa* or reinventing pizza. Moreover, when you feel lousy, you often spend money like there was no tomorrow. Not at all a healthy way to react, but a typically Goatly method of 'dealing' with pain. You can be creative this year. Work away at your pet projects in a protected environment where you feel safe and cared for. But Rat years are no time for building up your reputation as the genius you often are. Love will come along to spare you too much misery this year. Someone sweet and strong (a Pig perhaps) who will love and admire you, who will truly appreciate how exceptional you are and encourage you in your artistic and inventive projects.

This love interest will appear out of nowhere . . . a restaurant, a public beach or even on an escalator going in the other direction. Don't miss out. When the first look proves interesting, leap at the chance to team up with this cutie.

2009, the Earth Ox year – While the Rat tried to urge you to perform under the guise of trying to protect you, the Ox takes a different tack. The Ox dictates. No guise necessary. You work alongside him and get the job done his way, or you are out on your chinny chin chin. Goats usually complain loudest in Ox years that they are being misunderstood by the powers-that-be. And they are. Goats don't like to be told what to do any more than anyone else does. But they might go with the flow if the Ox were saying, "Gambol on over there and graze on the fresh green grass and I'll call you when we're finished working here." Ox years mean hard work. And that work can take many forms. It might be ditch-digging, or it might be something involving big changes in the Goat's plans. Something like: 'You are going to buckle down and finish university and get straight As this year'. Or the Goat might be called upon to serve in the armed forces of his or her country. Or ordered to help clean up after a tsunami. Bottom line? There is hard work for Goats wherever they look this year, and wherever they try to hide they will be discovered and pressed into service. Luckily, while under all this duress, your love life is moving ahead swimmingly. You have found someone (or he or she has discovered you) on whom you can depend to defend and protect you without bossing or tyrannizing. Hang on to this person. You need security in order to carry on your actively inventive existence.

2010, the Metal Tiger year – Keeping pace with Tigers is nobody's favorite sport. Tigers leap and bound and pounce and nomad about like so many grasshoppers on crystal methamphetamine – and they always come up smelling like a rose. If it were only the pace that the Goat can't keep up, that would be one thing. But fact is, the Tiger also has outlandish ambition and drive to succeed. Goats cannot – and will not – try to keep up. So when it's the Tiger's turn to rule the world, the Goat pretty much goes into hibernation or else pretends to admire the hectic chaos and applauds the innumerable curtain calls without much conviction. Either way, Goats and Tigers often clash. They not only don't have the same way of going about things, they disagree on what outcomes they want to achieve. These disagreements don't mean that the Tiger doesn't want you to succeed. Basically, Tigers don't care if you make it or you don't – as long as you are not holding them up. So in Tiger years, I suggest that Goats work and play as much as possible on their own. Go on solitary walks. Paint pictures. Write a book or sculpt a sculpture. But stay out of the Tiger mêlée. You were not made for coexistence with this hasty beast. Use this year to build your own career or your own house, or to learn to cook or to sew or knit or crochet or do judo or yoga. But do not try to compete in the big bad world in the Tiger year.

2011, the Metal Cat year – Having had two rather difficult years, you can finally can let go and lighten up in the kindly refined atmosphere of the Cat year. Not only will you feel more alive and be open to meeting new people, but your social life will vastly improve. You might only be invited to tea or to an intimate cocktail party. But those are just the sorts of get-togethers that appeal to you. There, you get to hold forth and exhibit some of that Goatly charm for which you are so famous. This year is auspicious for you to meet an important new someone. Perhaps a love interest, but not for certain. It could be someone you will work with on a new project or somebody who knows somebody who is able to lend you just what you need (money or influence) to start your business or buy yourself a country place. If you have things to get done and want to do them at your own speed, this Cat year is the one you have been waiting for. There will be no outside influences forcing you to intensify your efforts or beating you up about how long it takes you to thread a needle. You are not comfortable with other peoples' deadlines. A project may take you a few days or it may take weeks of concentrated application. And most of that time you will get no sleep, not eat regularly or talk to many people. But the job will be done right. You have no sense of time. It's your way. The Cat will not interfere.

2012, the Water Dragon year – Before I forget to remind you, start now to save up a few months' salary during this Dragon year. You will be needing it. In Dragon years, the pace grows more hectic, but the goodwill towards Goats continues apace. You will not only feel free and unhampered by meddlesome influences; you will be entertained by the general feeling of celebration and festivity which pervades every nook and cranny of our lives in Dragon years. You

Goats often need that extra spark of energy (or kick in the rump) in order to take on the vicissitudes of daily life. You can be both pessimistic and defeatist. The Dragon wants no part of your negative attitude and will do all in his power to keep your spirits buoyant. All year long you will be able to claim little victories over adversity. You won't get that flu that's going around. And you will win the lottery and be able to find just the curtains you wanted for your TV room. Nothing earth-shaking. But the triumphs will be sufficiently frequent to keep you prancing towards the future with your head held high. Toward the end of the year you will probably experience a financial reversal. Take pains not to panic. Instead, be comforted to know that you stashed away enough money to see you through till next year, when your fortunes will definitely increase.

2013, the Water Snake year – Still zipping along in a freewheeling mood, you will be enjoying a new found sense of luxury and social acceptance by the end of this Snake year. Snake people are not the most outgoing people alive. But they often choose the gentle, artistic company of Goats. You are on your own wave length now, doing your thing at a fairly leisurely pace. That unhurried manner of yours appeals to the Snake, who prefers to move through life smoothly and without haste. Your easy-going companionship warms the tootsies of the otherwise chilly-toed Snake. Plan on being invited to a raft of elegant dinner parties and events in exotic venues and even on yachts and/or chateaux in France or Spain. Tune up your fanciest car, spruce up your wardrobe and don't forget to douse yourself with the best French colognes and other glamorous cosmetics. Of course, all this primping and partying will afford you a plethora of romantic adventures. You'll be courted by so many new and different types that you will scarcely be able to keep track. Enjoy these adventures while they last, as by year's end things amorous will slow to a screeching halt. If you're thinking of marrying one of your conquests, think again. Matrimony is not on the cards . . . yet.

2014, the Wood Horse year – Goats are fairly comfortable in Horse years because the industrious aura surrounding the Horse keeps you feeling secure and safe. You would do well this year to ensure your position in the structure where you find yourself currently ensconced. Now, you may claim that you are not part of any structure, that you are a freelance magician, a self-employed dog-walker or a famous plastic surgeon who operates alone. But if you do work on your own,

I'll bet that you are very married to a solid citizen type who either pays the bills or keeps the books – or both! If you aren't married, then you probably live at home where you can be sure of three square meals and a warm coverlet. Goats do not go it alone very often. Which brings us back to the Horse year. You enjoy the atmosphere of this year because it cradles your need for dependency. You can count on the Horse. We can all count on Horses. They are consistent and solid and practical beings. So in this year, you will continue to sail ahead with Lady Luck by your side. Invest some money in property. Get yourself a cottage or a bungalow to restore. You work very well with your hands, and this year, handiwork is on everybody's docket.

2015, the Wood Goat year – At last you are in charge! Not exactly your style, however, as you would prefer to be named Chancellor of the Exchequer or perform as the king or queen's jester. You feel more secure when safely employed and protected by the society in which you find yourself. But never mind. You have the throne this year, and you will handle it – your way. As providence is with you, this year will give you all that you have dreamed of in the way of freedom, and the means to create and do and invent and put into production all the wondrous notions you have been able to cook up over the past three years. This is, as well, the year when you must make a plan for the next twelve years. It should go something like: '2015, Innovate. You're the leader. 2016, Get the production line moving. Hire new people. Make changes, but keep away from spotlights. 2017, Tighten your belt', etc. . . . until you come to 2027, when your year comes around again. The Chinese divide time by sixty-year cycles of twelve-year periods. This is the beginning of yours. By 2019, you should have decided either to get or to stay married. Decide now where you want to be in twelve years: what do you want to be doing and with whom? Aside from running the world this year, you must get busy drafting a twelve-year plan.

2016, the Fire Monkey year – This year is a bit on the chaotic side for your taste. Monkeys are forever dashing about hatching circuitous schemes and plotting ways to entertain the world whilst solving all of its problems. Fact is, Monkeys are rather discombobulated folks in the guise of orderly people. You don't get that much-needed rush of security from Monkeys. And with good reason. They are neurotic as hell and are always imagining people might be out to get them. They strategize and wangle. You are just about never guilty of either. You prefer to face problems head-on – even if you fail at sorting them out. The Monkey's planned chaos sets your teeth on edge and makes you doubt yourself. As you don't have all that much self-confidence to start with, this muddle-headed year makes you extra anxious, brings out your pessimistic side and more than once puts you in the corner with a dunce cap on. Why? Because you insist on being direct and open about what you are up to. Monkeys don't get that. They prefer labyrinths to freeways. If I were you, in this Fire Monkey year, I would seriously consider a complete change of *métier*. Ask a rich friend to to buy you a restaurant. Or get the bank to sponsor your career as an opera singer. Remember, you prefer security. Do not self-finance. If you fail, let someone else take the fall.

2017, the Fire Rooster year – Here, you find yourself in a year when you get the impression the sluices are closed up tight and nothing much is flowing smoothly. Roosters are tough customers who are just about never as flexible as we wish they were. And that lack of flexibility is only part of the problem. Roosters do not fancy giving up their own independence for the sake of someone else. They enjoy being the bosses of their own lives and the lives of those dear to them. But their charity stops right there. Moreover, they cannot tolerate anyone unless they are fully pulling their own weight. You need to be coddled and understood. You long to be made to feel secure. This year you can forget all those wishes and dreams. Maybe you should take a sabbatical or hitch a ride on a rich lover's yacht. Your health picture is sound. Those symptoms you were feeling last year have abated. Maybe they were stress- and anxiety-related. Monkey madness can do that to Goats. Romance will be sketchy in the Rooster year. There won't be much commitment to spare, but there should be plenty of passion on the agenda. Ample sex is small compensation for the fact that you won't be raking in gold ingots, either. The Rooster is cautious about spending and doesn't encourage squandering or waste. As your favorite sport is buying lavish futilities, you may be disappointed. This year does not bode any Christian Lacroix frocks or Rolex watches for gentle Goat people.

2018, the Earth Dog year – The Dog herds Goats. Goats, however, do not adore being herded or made to participate in any activity that is not of their own choosing. Yet, in Dog years, we are all more or less obliged to join the fight for justice for all, to pull hard for the good of the order and raise our voices in protest against all that is cruel and inhuman in this big bad world of ours. Luckily, for you, Dogs have a soft spot in their heart for Goat people. Why? Because Dogs are partial to all forms of companionship. Goat people make excellent companions. When they are not working thirty-hour days without eating or catnapping, Goats are very present. You can always count on a Goat friend to call and chat, spend an evening watching TV with you or accompany you to a movie or a bistro. So this is a good year for your social life. You will be asked to go on dates and attend community functions. You may even be invited to take an active role in the local political scene. What may appeal to you least about this Dog year is the Dog's tendency to criticize your methods and sometimes even say hurtful things to you. At times, you will feel scrutinized. Try not to take these inspections too seriously. The Dog cares a lot for you and worries that you can't take care of yourself. Be patient. You are loved.

2019, the Earth Pig year – You may relax. Goats are the Pig's favorites among all the varieties of men and women alive. This year you will be spoiled and cosseted and made to feel ever so good in your skin. You wanted security? You have it. A full calendar year of safety and admiration is on tap for Goats in the Pig year. What should you do about this sudden sense of well-being? Get out there and perform. Make your voice heard. Show the world your myriad talents. Make movies or write books or poetry, or sculpt or invent or act or dance . . . but do something about your career and your future now. In this benevolent year, you can make enormous strides towards success in the discipline of your choice. Don't be shy about presenting your innovative ideas to bosses or showing your work to galleries or sending out multiple manuscripts. You will be making all sorts of deals and contracts and signing agreements in the munificent atmosphere abroad in this Pig year. You may also get married. Yes. And/ or you may indeed have a baby (or even two!), because this is the year in which things just plain work for Goats. Take full advantage. Next year is not quite so promising.

猴

The Merry Monkey

Merry Monkey,

You're a delightful person who never misses a trick and who, despite an undeniable tendency to cunning and chicanery, rarely jumps a red light. Contradictory? Yes, indeed. And more. Monkeys are astute and like to be in on everything. You catch on long before the punch line, but you never laugh till you're good and ready. You're a plotter and a planner. When confronted with a seemingly impervious miasma of human complexity, you, nimble-spirited Monkey, will always find the means to restore order.

You are an invaluable aide-de-camp, employee and helpmate. You'd make a super vice-president. Titles and position mean nothing to you as you instinctively recognize that, no matter how high up you are seated, you will still only be sitting on your *derrière*. Without fanfare you manage to run the show quite deftly from the wings. You refuse to grow old. If you have the funds you will be first to leap on to that old operating table for a face lift, nose job, hair transplant – or all three!

In choosing a partner, treat yourself to a magnificent Dragon, a go-getting Rat or even an impetuous Tiger, who will keep your problem-solving talents busy. The first and last phases of your life will pass smoothly. At around thirty-seven or thirty-eight you may experience a sudden loss of confidence from a major mid-life love crisis. This sinking spell will pass after the age of forty-five.

My advice? It's not enough to be cleverer than the rest. Knowing when to bet and when to pass is the secret of winning at those games you so enjoy. Refine your sense of timing through careful, patient observation. You will live longer and better on less if you learn to save your precious energy (and your money) for the big stakes.

Playfully yours,

Suzanne White

In the twentieth and twenty-first century all Monkeys were born between the following dates:

2	February	1908	and	22	January	1909
20	February	1920	and	8	February	1921
6	February	1932	and	26	January	1933
25	January	1944	and	13	February	1945
12	February	1956	and	31	January	1957
29	January	1968	and	16	February	1969
16	February	1980	and	4	February	1981
4	February	1992	and	22	January	1993
22	January	2004	and	8	February	2005
8	February	2016	and	27	January	2017

The Monkey ID card

Lasting symbols have special powers. Enhance your self-image by surrounding yourself with tangible signs of your own identity and make these symbols known to your friends and loved ones. Use them daily and they will bring you luck, security and a feeling of personal worth.

Your best	*Your favorite*
color is yellow	food is fruit pie
flower is dandelion	animal is tiger
fragrance is jasmine	drink is lemonade
tree is sycamore	spice is cinnamon
flavor is sweet	metal is gold
birthstone is tiger-eye	herb is thyme
lucky number is 10	musical instrument is guitar

The Monkey is yin ***The Monkey's motto is 'I entertain'***

On the happy-go-lucky surface, Monkeys are reasonable, faithful, autonomous, candid, altruistic, successful, inventive, co-operative, loving, intelligent, individualistic and generous entertainers.

But behind the scenes, Monkeys are hyperemotional, capricious, guileful, self-indulgent, immature, insecure, indifferent, careless, gullible, petty, grabby scene-stealers.

My life among the Monkeys

Monkeys are fun but they hate confinement. Their need for freedom and craving for motion, their insatiable thirst for the novel and outrageous, their hunger for mental challenge and passion for full-swing elbow-room latitude plus their remarkable ability to adapt to any new circumstance in seconds (and often only for seconds) makes Monkeys both incapable and unwilling to accept restriction. They refuse to be caged.

Not that Monkeys are greedy for space – nor do they demand lavish or vast homes – but they must be independent. A word of advice: if you tie a Monkey down, don't expect to remain friends with him.

Whatever havoc this canny creature may wreak on his fellows, one thing is certain: Monkey does *not* rhyme with Donkey. These wily, clever people are renowned for their extraordinary problem-solving talents. Give a Monkey a baffling issue to settle, a negotiation to handle or a filthy hundred-year-old attic to clean and (providing you don't hold him to a deadline or attempt to force him) he'll set straight to work, heaving things and ideas here and there, darting his attention everywhere at once and applying his nimble intelligence to every nuance of the issue. Then he comes up with the single most ingenious answer ever.

'It's obvious,' says the Monkey. 'The shortest distance between your mother-in-law and your peace of mind is a trip to Romania.' Not so obvious to the plain-brained rest of us, but if a Monkey says so – nay, *because* he says so – we should run out and buy her a one-way ticket to Bucharest. Wherever you are, whoever you may be, if you've got a problem pick up the phone and dial-a-Monkey. Advice and good counsel are his strong suit. He knows how to listen closely and work out solutions at the same time. You'll be amazed at the originality he applies in formulating answers to your weightiest problems. Monkeys always come out the winners, especially if the fight is hard.

Take my Monkey friend, Kathryn Weissberger. Kathryn is my favorite Jewish saint. With all she has done to help me since I've known her, she's probably also qualified as my best girlfriend. I don't know anyone so gifted for sorting out messes. And as I am a past master at getting myself into scrapes sending me Kathryn was undoubtedly God's way of protecting me from early oblivion.

She used to be my secretary. Actually she wasn't, she was James Jones's (author of *From Here To Eternity*) secretary in Paris in the sixties and seventies. Then Jim moved back to the States and Kathryn took other jobs such as typing and editing my manuscripts. In the mid-seventies I was so busy writing books and raising kids that I invited Kathryn to move with me and the kids to Connecticut. Although she, the kids and I only cohabited for about a year, enough happened during those twelve months to cement a lifelong inter-dependency.

Anecdotes about Kathryn would fill a whole book but they don't all illustrate her Monkeyness as well as this one. Kathryn is single. She has never had kids. Her skills at dealing with children in that giant pink house in snowy Cornwall, Connecticut back in 1975 were unsharpened. We shared household responsibilities but part of Kathryn's saintliness as my live-in friend was to look after the girls when I wasn't there.

During that year I went off on tour to promote a book and, apart from the usual chores of typing, cooking, shopping, laundering and washing up, Kathryn had to take responsibility for everything from damming up the drafty house's cracks to nurturing two newly transplanted little Franco-American girls.

Trouble was afoot from the moment I left. Daisy, the eldest, had decided that if she made Kathryn's life miserable enough, then Kathryn would panic, phone me and I'd come straight home. Not only did neither child eat the healthy food that Kathryn cooked, they refused to go to bed and to get up for school. They wouldn't change their clothes, do their homework or come in on time for supper. They acted as though they hated Kathryn. For three days, there were scenes, fights, tears and brawls. Kathryn, kind and indulgent Monkey, was patient and tolerant. Our daily long-distance phone conversations were full of trying to reason with the kids and trying to cool down anxious Kathryn, who had begun seriously to doubt that she deserved the title of Jewish saint. 'I'm so frustrated with Daisy,' she admitted late one night. 'She just won't do anything I tell her. And she hit me . . . I was awfully tempted to give her a shake – but I didn't. I went to my room to cool off.'

I replied anxiously, 'If you can't control them just tell me. I'll come right back.'

The challenge to control them and herself caused the Monkey Kathryn to take over from the Jewish Saint Kathryn. She gave me one of her characteristic 'in-no-uncertain-terms' replies, 'Don't worry, I'll figure it out.'

And I knew she would. Hadn't she kept me from murdering my ex-husband several times over by removing all the knives from the kitchen whenever he came to dine? Hadn't she invented a neat pulley system to get wood up the steps and into the house without breaking our fragile female backs? This resourceful woman was no slouch: when it came to problem-solving Kathryn was a Monkey's Monkey.

Following that tense phone call, she cooked up a foolproof scheme. She chucked out the rules. As a true Monkey, Kathryn avoids rules anyway. Like all Monkeys, she flees discipline. She shies from either buckling under to or enforcing repression and, like most Monkeys, would prefer to be condemned to chaos rather than adhere to constraining regulations.

Next morning, when the time came to get the girls up for school, Kathryn the Monkey took over. She didn't call up to the children or try to rouse them with any of my routine (and useless) Tigerish tyrannical threats. Kathryn, the Monkey problem-solver and entertainer *par excellence,* went up the stairs at six thirty and sat at the top singing. The kids wondered what the heck was going on and got up to find out.

Once they were up she danced them downstairs, served them a radically new type of breakfast consisting of hot chocolate and pancakes with marshmallow and syrup, next to the cozy woodstove, all the while performing clown antics to make them laugh. The kids didn't know what had hit them. As they ate with kiddy gusto, Kathryn announced that everything was going to be fun from now on. 'While Mummy's gone, you only have to come home at six every night to eat. Otherwise you have no chores. If you don't do your homework I don't care. You'll do it when Mum gets home. We'll only have two kinds of dinners while Mummy's away: either hamburgers with chips and chocolate ice cream for dessert or hot dogs with chips and chocolate ice cream for dessert.'

'Hooray!' said the little girls.

For the next three weeks, Kathryn woke her charges every morning with a new song, filled the fridge with their favorite drinks, bought forbidden comics, roasted marshmallows and sat with them while they watched endless hours of the worst programs on TV.

By the time I came home, exhausted, my kids were happy, comforted and relaxed.

Not bad, thought I admiringly. Not bad at all for a woman without children who had felt like shaking one only a few weeks ago. A discipline-happy Ox would have failed miserably, a Jekyll and Hyde nice-guy Pig would have flown into a rage and stayed there, and a high-handed Horse would have become the children's secret laughing stock. But no rules at all, full-time entertainment and fun is only normal for a Monkey.

Aside from and along with their problem-solving gifts, Monkeys are enthralled by the sound of their own chatter. They talk – a lot. They are never boring but they can be unnecessarily long-winded. If a Monkey parent is telling a child why he or she should make a bed, the little speech may become a lecture on 'The Art of Bed-making in the Twentieth Century'.

As natural teachers, Monkeys have opinions on everything from politics to lawn sprinklers. Yet, as they are essentially tolerant, they are unusually respectful of the opinions of others. Monkeys adore a spirited conversation and worship background noise – they're noise junkies. Just for company they'll turn on a portable radio in church, flip a few TV channels during their own weddings, switch on the news at the most solemn point in a love spat. And in planes, trains or even bomb shelters, count on the Monkey to engage strangers in spontaneous chit-chat. A Monkey could chat up a corpse.

The Monkey has a joke, an anecdote, or a yarn to share with any audiences he can corner for long enough to tell it. He is not as eloquent as the Ox, and less persuasive than the Horse, but the Monkey needs to be amusing and instructive and, most of all, to please his public – which makes him one of the Chinese zodiac's best hosts.

Here's a perfect example of Monkey problem-solving, entertaining and hospitality. My friend Yves Decroix, a genius cancer specialist to whom I owe at least one of my lives, is a Monkey. He's also a Gemini which enhances both the comedic and resourceful sides of his Monkey character. Not long ago, he kindly invited five of us to dine in a restaurant near Notre Dame in Paris. It was to be one of those difficult visiting-foreign-doctor dinners where two of the party spoke only American English and two spoke only French. I speak both but only have one mouth. From the outset, I was worried that this dinner was doomed. I didn't see how I could possibly talk and translate fast enough to keep everyone apprised of both food and conversation.

We all sat down, dutifully dumb, politely expecting the worst. Wanting to be of some use, I translated the menu into English while watching the visitors blanch at the idea of having to look at, much less eat, stewed tripe and jellied calf's head or pig's knuckle salad. The more I read the more the atmosphere grew grey with dread. I sensed that the nice Americans didn't want to offend their host by refusing to eat whatever was placed in front of them, but sautéed thymus glands just doesn't sound good in English. As I hunted for something tasty but *normal* to mention to the tourist contingent, Dr Decroix ordered champagne kir for everyone.

'Excuse me, Suzanne.' He interrupted me to inquire of his guests, 'Do you prefer to royale kir wiss berry juice black ones or kir wiss berry juice red ones wiss ze bumps?'

Did they understand? Had they ever even heard of kir before tonight? I butted in to explain. 'Would you like blackberry or raspberry kir?'

They looked beseechingly at me. 'Help!' said their silent plea. 'What's kir?'

Not to worry. Our Monkey host, whose bumbling attempts at English are legendary in medical lecture circles worldwide, went on. 'Do you know ze champagne tra la la?' He wiggled his fingers in this bubbly fashion he has. They could *see* the champagne.

'Yes.' They nodded and smiled.

'You take ze champagne tra la la and you put ze berry one inside, zing zing, and you make ze kir.'

Who could resist such a delectable description? Certainly not our Yankee friends to whom lovely long-stemmed glasses of delicate pink and black raspberry flavored champagne were soon served. They found it deliciously different and also soon found themselves roaring with laughter at their Monkey host's jokes in a language he does not speak. But does he know how to act!

Thanks to Yves's zany attempts at speaking English, the dinner zipped uproariously by like a chimpanzee on a motor-bike. By the end of the meal he had transformed himself into a veritable comic tour guide. In no uncertain terms, he instructed his American guests that the best way to get around Paris was to take 'the suburbs'.

In response to this suggestion, they shot him a blank look and turned to me for elucidation. I hadn't the foggiest.

'You know, zat small choo choo who goes to the city basement,' he explained.

'The subway!' said Phyllis.

When the Americans complained that they would have no room left for dessert he suggested they order a 'baby dog' . . . doggy bag.

By the end of the evening we had all decided it would be best for the future of international oncology if Yves Decroix never learned to speak English.

Give a Monkey a potentially dull situation and he'll turn it into a Broadway production. And better yet, he'll pay for it. Monkeys are notoriously generous when it comes to spending money on others. They can't resist watching your eyes light up when they give you a present or find you a special treat or locate just the right holiday spot for you. Challenge a Monkey to please you and he will lead you into some rich temptations.

Because of his curiosity, the Monkey deems everything worth knowing about. For one so active and mobile, he has remarkable perseverance when it comes to study and gathering information. He can plough through tomes for fact-finding purposes or sit for hours poring over charts, tables and relief maps. Many learned geniuses were born a Monkey.

Monkeys are hard to describe. They nearly always present us with a strangely harmonious mixture of contradictory strengths and faults. They are sometimes exasperatingly childlike, yet surprisingly sophisticated, adult and practically unshockable.

As friends, Monkeys are both loyal and devoted, yet as lovers they can be flighty and faithless. Sometimes they gossip, meddle and pry, yet at others a safecracker can't get them to spill so much as one bean.

Monkeys have no time for prejudice or out-dated social custom. Snobbery bores Monkeys and the word racism doesn't exist for them. They are truly fair and equitable people yet if a Monkey feels trapped or cornered – or even personally justified – he can surprise even himself by committing an isolated survivalist act of unreason and injustice.

Although he doesn't take kindly to repression, the Monkey has no time for head-on conflict with authority. He rarely gets nabbed for bending laws: parking tickets flee from him; summonses leap away from his doorstep. He is supple of mind and body, and good at moving through the minefields of life without ever feeling so much as an aftershock. As much as true disaster stalks the very paw prints of Tigers and tracks the wake of the Dragon's fire, it eludes the Monkey.

Monkeys are good at ruse and hypocrisy. Call it diplomacy if you will, it's still a form of deception. They owe much of their social success to their ability to nod and smile while fools spew inanities into their ears. Monkeys don't always respect the opinions of others but they enjoy a rare talent for maintaining an agreeable countenance in the face of discord. Because they can fool their audience into thinking they are truly involved in some drivel, Monkey people often prevail. Unafraid of subterfuge and not burdened by petty moralities, the Monkey is a canny piece of work. He's clever and sometimes unscrupulously cagy. But it's more than that: he's not a rebel or a renegade. The Monkey is satisfied to be a true marginal. Society doesn't interest him. Frankly, he couldn't care less. He is oblivious, self-motivated and damnably free-spirited.

Remember those little bronze statues that school mistresses used to keep on their bookshelves? Three monkeys, one with a paw over his eyes, one with both paws over his ears and one with a paw clamped over his mouth. Underneath were etched the words 'See no evil, hear no evil, speak no evil'. A better material portrait of the facetious Monkey character I have yet to see.

Monkey women

The contradictory character of all Monkeys is dramatically emphasized in the female of the species. It's maddening. Just when you think you have Ms Monkey figured out, she ups and does something totally out of character which sends you back to the drawing-board. But once you have it all down, once you comprehend and fully appreciate the truly unpremeditated, genuine good nature of the frantic female of the Monkey species, you will have fallen in love.

Although Monkey women prefer not to conform to type, there are some Monkey traits that they cannot deny. For starters, they are ever youthful. Their limbs are usually thin and muscular. Their heads are small and well shaped. They have neatly proportioned upper bodies, small breasts and sturdy shoulders. It is unusual for a Monkey woman to be overweight, but if she is, her plumpness ordinarily shows during childhood and early adulthood. By middle age the Monkey woman has started to thin down and the older she gets the more sinew and muscle she shows. Elderly Monkey women don't have many heart attacks.

The Monkey woman's face is often sharply defined about the jawline and boasts high or at least prominent cheekbones. Her forehead tends to jut out over the eyes which are sunken rather than protruding. The lips are clear-cut and well drawn. Her nose is short and unobtrusive. Teeth are a prominent feature in a strong but never heavy jawline.

There is nothing grand or regal about the Monkey woman's features and the word 'pretty' doesn't do justice to her simian good looks. Madame Monkey is not just lovely to look at. She's well turned out, carries a singular air of competence and a fetching, mischievous twinkle.

The attractive Monkey lady doesn't have trouble finding love partners as men are drawn to her spirited manner. Although she is not the most constant of mistresses or wives, Madame Monkey can be counted on to amuse her lovers, diverting them with funny stories or a finely honed wit. Her jokes are light-hearted and rarely cutting or hurtful. She seems able to pick out the silliness in any situation. Monkey women don't want to appear grumpy, stubborn or mean. They have no time for anything that impinges on fun. The Monkey woman's main objective is to remain young at heart, active and open-minded, to observe and poke fun, to entertain and sort out others' problems.

Ms Monkey is creative in bed. She never lets her partner get bored and is careful to maintain an atmosphere of humor and good cheer in the face of almost any wild behavior her lover thinks up. If her husband minces into the bedroom wearing high heels and a pale pink taffeta skirt, she will not shrink away in horror. Instead, she will carry on regardless and when it's over, she'll nestle down and comment wryly, 'Pale pink is definitely your color, darling,' before dozing off.

In both home and workplace, the Monkey woman is a good sport and an excellent organizer. No matter how badly she is offended, she doesn't hold a grudge or harbor resentments. Also she can be counted on to smooth over her own and other people's differences and remain even-tempered. Ever the versatile problem-solver, Madame Monkey has a talent for dashing off ten thank-you letters to friends while polishing her nails and phoning her boss's wife to explain his sudden need to work late.

The Monkey woman's foibles are curious. Here, too, paradox reigns. She's as hysterical about her own problems as she is practical about other people's. Madame Monkey tends to be neurotic. She often has difficulty separating emotions from facts. She frets and panics over what others might see as the least little thing. If she thinks it's directed at her, she can work herself into a terrible lather over a passing remark or a whisper dropped in her presence.

Years ago, when the greatest Monkey woman on earth, Kathryn Weissberger, was working for James Jones in Paris, she was distraught over a bad love affair. She dragged herself into work one morning and moaned, 'Oh, Jim, I think I'll just commit suicide.'

'Oh, no you won't, Kathryn,' he said without looking up from his manuscript. 'You're far too neurotic for suicide.'

'And he was right,' Kathryn agrees whenever she tells this story. 'I get so crazy and hysterical at the slightest provocation that it's impossible for me to distinguish a serious nervous collapse from a normal every day crack-up over a broken cup or a mildewed dishcloth. I could never kill myself because it might turn out that I had slit my throat over nothing and then I would really feel like a fool.' And no Monkey, male or female, likes to appear foolish.

Which brings me to another tiny female Monkey flaw. Monkey women have to be right. Because of their outrageous capacity for accuracy, amazing visual memory and need to seem at all times to be doing the right thing, Monkey women make excellent editors, private secretaries, script girls, bookkeepers and fact checkers. Proficiency is their middle name.

One of my favorite, and most proficient, Monkey women friends is the editor-in-chief of a famous magazine in Paris. She's all of the things I mentioned above, beautiful, lithe, sexy, unpredictable, spontaneous and deadly serious about her work. Yet this calm, collected, serious woman of the world is apt to go mad over a tiny detail with the left side of her brain while the right side is busily putting a huge magazine to bed without a hitch or driving safely and steadily twelve hours each way to the South of France to check on her ageing mother.

Working for and with this Monkey editor has always been pure pleasure. She taught me how to write in French. Whenever I submitted an article, she would patiently and painstakingly pass her intelligent pencil over my manuscripts, always advising, reminding and adding just the right touches thoroughly and efficiently.

One day last year, in New York, I was involved in a complex, long-winded lawsuit against a giant American insurance company.

Suddenly in the midst of all this, I needed some important documents, which were locked up inside my country house in France near Orléans. Unfortunately, in the small village where my house is situated, my neighbors are solid, honest country folk: nobody has the haziest notion of what a filing cabinet might look like.

My Monkey editor friend won't want me to tell you her name so I'll call her Juliette. She has a country house about ten miles from mine in another even more agricultural village. I called Juliette on a Saturday afternoon from my lawyer's offices. 'Juliette, I'm in New York doing that trial thing I told you about and I need some papers from my house.'

'Sure, which papers?' she said immediately – no hedging, no stalling or excuses. Monkeys are loyalty itself in friendship.

I described the file and said where I thought it was. A few hours later I rang her back.

'Sorry, Suzanne, but the file you were looking for wasn't where you said, but I know where it is.'

This woman had been at my house twice. How *could* she know better than I where things were?

'You know that locked room off the garage you showed me last year, where you put a lot of old furniture? I'm sure I saw your insurance file in there.'

'Mmm,' I answered. That room was used to store junk. 'I don't usually put important papers in there, Juliette,' I replied.

'Believe me, your documents are in there,' she said. 'But I don't have the key.'

I told Juliette where to find it and hung up saying, 'I think we can forget about using those papers at the trial on Monday,' to my attorneys.

On Monday morning, thanks to the Monkey's thoroughness and prodigious memory, the papers were delivered into my astonished lawyer's hand.

This attention to detail can be positive as I have just demonstrated with Juliette but it can also translate into an exasperating stubborn eccentricity that bends to no persuasion and resists even the most compelling reasoning. This tale is typical of the oddball things that Monkey women get up to in their heads – screwy, far-out antics that can baffle even the most baroque minds.

Years ago, Kathryn Weissberger was shifting the remains of her household in Paris back to New York where she had finally moved after her year-long stint with me in Connecticut. As she needed space for her furniture and a large luggage allowance, she had flown to Paris but was planning to go home on the *Queen Elizabeth II*. Some of Kathryn's household goods had been stored in a moldy Paris basement for over a year when the moving men came to take them to Le Havre for loading into the ship's hold and many of the cartons were soggy on the bottom. Kathryn was directing the moving men, watching to see that they handled everything with care. At one point, one of them lifted a carton and the paper came away from the bottom to reveal, as he stood up, a neat, carton-sized pile of bricks. He asked reasonably, 'Don't you have bricks in America?'

'*Pas encore, Monsieur, pas encore*,' (Not yet, sir, not yet,) said Kathryn, who claims not to speak French well (remember that another Monkey trait is difficulty with foreign languages) with her little Monkey smirk.

The men moved her bricks and her planks, too, from Paris to New York and today they sit in her New York flat twelve years later – the bookcases she slapped together back in the old days in Paris. Monkey women are obstinately eccentric.

Monkey men

The girlfriends of Monkey men have more fun. All Monkeys give lots of presents, but Monkey men give more. Not only do they wine and dine their loved ones but they heap them with luxuries. They offer exotic trips, diamonds and fashionable furbelows to their lady loves, houses, cars and allowances to their families, and freebies to their friends.

Our old friend Yves Decroix, the famous linguist/tumor specialist, stuck his grandmother's diamond ring into a glass of champagne and handed it to his girlfriend when she came home after work. Anne kissed him, carried the glass into the kitchen and began cooking dinner. Without even sipping it, she put it down and started chopping onions and browning meat.

Decroix didn't flinch but sat placidly in the living room petting his dog and watching the news.

'What if she had decided not to drink it and dumped it down the drain?'

'Call the plumber,' said Yves with a grin.

'Luckily,' Anne later told me, 'I did find it. But not until I'd almost choked on the damned thing!'

Monkey men are so profligate that they might give away the shirts off their backs. But no matter how much they love, adore or care about another person, Monkey men *never* give up their freedom. They eschew marriage and its dull routines. They prefer live-in arrangements and will stay in a relationship longer if not called upon to commit themselves on paper to any legal contracts. Monkeys need room to move around so if you love a Monkey male and wish to entice him to hang around on your branch for a long stay, don't mention marriage and keep pretending you don't give a fig if he goes away and stays away for a hundred years of solitude.

Where money's concerned, Monkey men are more than just attracted to playing the spending game. My old friend Dan, the first big Monkey romance of my life, used to wake up some days, look me benevolently in the eye and confess, 'I think I've come down with another bad case of the Buys. Get dressed, honey. We're going into town to throw some money away.'

Into the car we would jump and off we would drive to Manhattan to wipe out Bloomingdale's. We'd buy towels, sheets, rings for my fingers and boots for my toes, lunch at a three-star restaurant and then get to the decorating department for wallpapers and paints. These were not mere shopping sprees. Those days freewheeling gold and silver credit cards were buying binges, financial freak-outs, especially since they were – and this is typical of male Monkeys – invariably followed by weeks of long, nervous evenings spent totting up figures and racking brains to figure out how to be more economical and to invest wisely.

Although Monkey men often spontaneously lend hefty sums to 'iffy' friends and unload cash as if they had just bought Kuwait, they are clandestine bookkeepers who, deep down, deplore their profligacy. These same male Monkey spendthrifts, who swagger around lavishing their fortunes in public, can become overnight boy wonders in accounting, private penny-pinchers who fret away their nights over where the fodder for their next squander attack will come from.

Another of my Monkey ex-male friends, a South American, Peter Vannetti, is a professional poker player or, as my father used to say, 'Pete runs a card game in the back room.' Monkey men love the thrill of gambling and are well equipped for it. They know how to bluff better than most people, have no time for petty moralities and don't get hung up on society's opinion of them.

But when the chips are down, you won't see Peter Vannetti for months! Why? Well, he's broke and when he's broke he is sitting anxiously at home, calculating how he is going to pay his debts and, who owes him what and how long before they pay him back so he can start all over again.

And, typically, Peter Vannetti, like the rest of the male Monkey population, will not accept charity. Try to lend money to a Monkey man and he'll pretend he doesn't really need it or give it back if you leave it on the table. He can dish it out but he cannot take it.

As a true connoisseur of Monkey men, I can also attest that they are charming, intensely warm-hearted and caring, self-sacrificingly and playfully sensual and incisively sharp-witted, funny and smart!

Men born in Monkey years are physically similar, in my mind's eye, to those silver-grey BMWs that they all either drive or aspire to own. I know six Monkey males very well and five of them own those tough little motors. (The other one takes the train.) My Monkeys like the feel of a quality car. It must remind them of how they themselves are built, sinewy and tight.

Monkey men are muscular but not obviously simian. They have slender limbs and are finely featured. You might not find them classically handsome but Monkey men are sparklingly attractive. Their foreheads are high and their features clear and fine. A ready, sardonic smile is always on their nicely shaped lips and in their sharp eyes lives a flashing neon sign that reads, 'Hi! I'm a nice person.'

Women always feel comfortable in the company of male Monkeys. This infuriates other men but watch: at parties male Monkeys attract women, especially the stronger, more independent or mysterious woman: they have no preconceived notions or prejudices about women. They are infinitely approachable and open to discussion: they'll talk about everything from nightmares to nightgowns and be sure to show a keen interest.

The single most important trait that makes Monkey men so delightful to women is that they tend to think with their brains yet act with their hearts. They give easily of themselves, enjoy helping others and warm to the tenderness in each situation. Despite what some women may regard as the male Monkey's enraging tendency to gallivant and flit about, he redeems himself by unashamedly laying open his emotions and putting the needs of his heart before the deeds of his head.

Most of all (and I saved the best for last) Monkey men are not jealous. They care whether or not you love them and even worry that maybe you'll leave in a huff one day, but Monkey men (and women) have the capacity to abstract their emotions. They can remove themselves from whatever emotional fray is in the offing and hover at two or three feet above themselves, watching the action. (Hence switching on the TV during their own wedding.) Monkey men know better than anybody how to poke fun at themselves. They do not take themselves (or anybody else) very seriously.

The five Chinese elements and how they influence the Monkey

The Wood Monkey

1884 Harry Langdon, Walter Huston, Amadeo Modigliani, Eleanor Roosevelt, Harry Truman

1944 Angela Davis, Helmut Berger, Jacqueline Bisset, Françoise Hardy, Brenda Lee, Rod Stewart, Geraldine Chaplin, Joe Cocker, Diana Ross, Charlotte Rampling, Sally Kirkland, Tom Selleck, Tim Reade, Danny De Vito, Swoozie Kurtz, Frank Alamo, George Lucas, Julio Iglesias, Carl Bernstein, Jill Clayburgh

Belief in the future is the key characteristic of the Wood Monkey's personality. He's always out and about, into everything, doing something. He is forever building and making, plotting and scheming to increase his output, improve his own environment or make the world a more pleasant place to live.

Wood Monkeys are social creatures. They respond brightly to interaction with their peers and are always looking for new ways and places to find different friends, make acquaintances and widen the scope of their social lives. The Wood Monkey is a creative partygoer. He is the smily one who cuts a smooth path through any chattering company, meeting and greeting folk with a cheery 'Hi' and 'How d'you do?' as though swinging blithely from tree to tree in a squawking jungle. When it comes to getting along on a purely sociable, superficial level, the Wood Monkey is definitely tops.

The less positive side of the Wood Monkey's high affability quotient is that he often cannot (or does not) maintain long-term, high-quality friendships. Somehow, the good-natured charm which this Monkey exudes in public just doesn't carry enough weight to support and intensify lasting relationships. He suffers from a profound lack of intimacy, wondering why people find him so seductive and alluring and yet cease to be his friend after knowing him only a short time. He is certain his intentions are honorable. He tries to be helpful and generous. Where, then, does the Wood Monkey go wrong?

Perhaps he doesn't try to get to know his friends and cronies well enough. Though he means to be charitable and care about the other fellow's welfare, the Wood Monkey cannot sit still for long. He aims to be of use in the world and he really means to cultivate many friends but he doesn't take time to sit down and *be* with friends, to listen to their woes. He hates to wait for things to develop naturally, always thinking he knows better. He's jumpy and talks too much. He's always in a rush and has little compassion for people he considers weaklings. If devoted friendship is what he's after, the communicative Wood Monkey is missing the point. Either he doesn't internalize what he hears or he never listens in the first place.

The Wood Monkey bridles when he realizes that others cannot always keep pace with his hectic lifestyle. He is compulsively impulsive and is bitingly critical of slow-moving, single-minded types and those who prefer to take life as it comes. Although he reveres efficiency, he fails to see that this slow, methodical approach may be just as efficacious as rapidfire action.

This type of Monkey is a social climber. A name-dropper, he feels secure when surrounded by people of status who offer him both social rank and means. He is apt to seek lovers from among people he feels are socially superior as he fears being ostracized if he is not acceptable to equals or betters. This gregarious soul needs lots of outside assurance that he will be included, loved and, above all, allowed to hang around his peers for a good long time.

A fine quality which always saves the day for this impetuous creature is his good nature. This resilient person knows how to be the brunt of jokes and still come up smiling. He gets teased because of his obvious desire to be liked but he's got a strong grip on his own self-image. It is difficult to bruise this amiable fellow's ego. He doesn't mind criticism as long as there is plenty of love to go with it.

Wood Monkeys are achievers. They need and want to get ahead. They dream of ending up far above where they started off in life. To accomplish their ambitious ends, Wood Monkeys never stop studying the competition for flaws and strategizing to win in the most socially acceptable fashion.

If the Wood Monkey is really to succeed, he must learn to relax, to slow down and, most of all, to revel in friendship and intimate human love. Unless he can accept the idea of learning to listen, all the chit-chat and back-slapping in the universe will not get him where he wants to go. If he applies himself, the Wood Monkey *can* learn to share and exchange his deepest thoughts and ideals rather than just dropping them, like a bunch of hot bananas, in the laps of everyone he meets and continuing on his merry but solitary way.

The Fire Monkey

1896 Lilian Gish, F. Scott Fitzgerald, Virgil Thompson, Howard Hawkes

1956 Mel Gibson, Carrie Fisher, Björn Borg, Caroline of Monaco, Timothy Daley, Geena Davis, Eric Roberts, Tom Hanks

Fire Monkeys enjoy being dominant in all their undertakings. Unlike most Monkeys, these types keep a low profile and stay very much focused on their personal goals, creating and molding their enterprises as they go along. Fire Monkeys are driving and ambitious. They want results and are not afraid to look for the means to achieve them. The Fire Monkey is a self-starter whose enormous energy, although sometimes inconsistent and uneven, propels him speedily through life.

As the Fire Monkey's mind is fertile – his imagination is crawling with projects and innovative plans – he is doubly blessed. His capacity for hard work, coupled with his gift for invention, should make him a professional wizard. This Monkey will start trends, set a fashion in clothing or food, invent a new literary style or initiate a novel film project. But even with his myriad talents and dynamic personality, if he isn't careful, he may exhaust himself before he is half-way to his goal.

Although Fire Monkeys have all the punch, drive and authority necessary for high achievement, they also crave the baser thrills of 'having a good time'. Over-indulgence in gambling, late nights in clubs, and making whoopee may drain their strength, indeed may take precedence over their initial high-flown ambitions. Though not excessive by nature, Fire Monkeys are driven by the promise of excitement. They also have a dangerous taste for perversion. Some accuse them of being downright corrupt. If not curbed, Fire Monkeys can easily overload their systems and ruin their lives.

Fire Monkeys are deeply passionate, driven people. They respond to every experience with lightning speed and emotion. They struggle bravely with the complexities of getting things done and are even inspired by setbacks and stimulated by adversity. To the agile-minded Fire Monkey nothing is impossible. He looks for and finds solutions to the thorniest problems. He's wily and wiry, flexible and sharp. The Fire Monkey is always willing to take a chance or jump on a new bandwagon.

Though supple of spirit and freewheeling, Fire Monkeys enjoy controlling others. You will often find them drawn to or living with partners of lesser willpower who need them for sustenance or who look to them for emotional stability. Fire Monkeys may choose their lovers because of their own need to dominate someone less forceful. Yet the tables often turn on this would-be dominator and, through an odd system of emotional blackmail and unavoidable entanglement, the Fire Monkey dominator becomes the one dominated by the mate he imagined was the weakling.

Fire Monkeys are born cynics, too. In youth, they carry a disarming air of candor but as they mature, they grow wiser, less credulous and sometimes even embittered. They have a hard time trusting anyone, especially their colleagues and associates. Little by little, they lose their respect for morality and begin to wear a jaundiced, knowing smile. Raw ambition is not much of a cushion against disappointment, but once he has lost his youthful charm and earnest beliefs, ambition is frequently all this Monkey has left.

The Fire Monkey doesn't take kindly to being made to look a fool or suffering one-upmanship. He is jealous in both his love and work lives. He is competitive and can be vindictive, vengeful even. Speculation is his favorite game. He may take on many partners, form corporations or assemble groups for projects, but no matter how equitable the terms of any agreement, the Fire Monkey will always insist on remaining the boss.

This Monkey is far and away the most power-hungry of all Monkeys, yet he may not always be the most visible. Much of his real pith remains buried or hovers in the wings. Outwardly, the Fire Monkey is scornful of callow dreams and loudly dismisses ideals as corny, puerile and vapid. But the tough Fire Monkey longs for a better world, too, and would go to even greater lengths than all other Monkeys if only he believed that his wonderful dream could come true.

The Earth Monkey

1908 Bette Davis, James Stewart, Rex Harrison, Herbert von Karajan, Victor Borge, Fred MacMurray, Jacques Tati, Henri Cartier-Bresson, Michael Redgrave, Douglas Fairbanks Jr, David Lean, Joshua Logan, Carole Lombard, Robert Morley, Eddie Albert, Salvador Allende, Balthus, Simone de Beauvoir, Robert Cummings, Lew Ayres, John Kenneth Galbraith, Alistair Cooke, Amy Vanderbilt, William Saroyan, Milton Berle

This Monkey is calmer, more sentimental and deep thinking than most. Altruism is well developed in his character and he is markedly less devil-may-care than his fellows. He truly ponders both the past and future of mankind and attempts to comprehend the shape of things to come. Earth Monkeys love all types of people and can assume the problems of others as if they were their own.

The Earth element endows the Monkey with solid natural wisdom and insight. Because he is so perceptive, he is painfully aware of certain dark truths about life at an early age. He may speak out in family or school situations, shocking adults with unnaturally astute comments. Although silence is not his strong suit, study is. He will be capable of reaching lofty social positions through education, even though most Monkeys pretend to scorn all social climbing. In China, the Earth Monkey is known as the teacher Monkey. Not only is he learned, but he is also able to impart knowledge and exercise devotion in the pursuit of a professorial career. His students will be faithful admirers. They will adore his jaunty manner and are instructed and amused by the Earth Monkey's imaginative presentation of inherently difficult or dull material.

This Monkey's best attribute lies in his ability to interact with his peers: people like him immediately. He is affable and jolly, optimistic and inspirational. He's bright and witty, and so smart and intuitive that he seems to see around corners. Better yet, the Earth Monkey knows how to make us laugh. He won't waste time on gloomy reruns of his bad childhood or tedious school exploits. He is fun, spontaneous and full of life. He is strong without being overpowering and yet he remains a serious, even ponderous, thinker.

The biggest flaw in the Earth Monkey's character is his desire for perfection. This hail-fellow-well-met seems to be so easy-going and fun-loving that we sometimes wonder if he can truly be taken seriously but this Monkey is worse than serious – he's a nit-picking perfection-crazed maniac. He longs for a home that runs like a well-oiled machine, a family to be nothing but proud of, a place for everything and everything in its place.

But the family life of the average Earth Monkey is never nirvana. His need for order in the essentially disorderly atmosphere of home and kids leads to trouble for him and his poor subjugated offspring. Either the kids and spouse become terrorized by all the maniacal fussing or as time goes by, the meticulous Earth Monkey parent becomes a subject of family ridicule and has to take refuge in the basement or is forced out of the nest.

This Monkey is extremely attracted to the opposite sex. An imaginative lover, he cannot resist the urge to play at love. He adores the intrigue, the chase, the seduction. Extra-marital affairs are common in the life of this extra-sensual Monkey. Usually, fear of scandal (the spectre of imperfection again) prevents him from confessing his peccadilloes to a passing newspaper reporter. He hates to recognize his own mistakes yet is quick to point out those of his family. Live-in loving with the Earth Monkey is not for amateurs: it takes more than patience – even a spirit of masochistic self-abnegation. Yet this Monkey is kind and can be reached through a large, tender guilt window. If reminded of how difficult he is, the Earth Monkey will rally. Underneath his difficult superficial nature, he is devoted to those he loves and can always be counted on to provide and maintain order.

The Earth Monkey is blessed with good health and a sturdy constitution. He will live to a ripe age. With his innate talents for study and concentration, he could work in scientific research, law enforcement or history. Because of his ability to go it alone, he can pursue a career in the arts as an independent film-maker, a literary scholar, a painter or sculptor.

If an Earth Monkey could improve one aspect of his character, it should definitely be his perfection-seeking. He could and should partake of some of life's more enlightening spiritual pursuits such as yoga, martial arts, the study of Eastern religions and even pure aerobic exercise. Earth Monkeys need to cool out their fuddy-duddy side, break down personal barriers which prevent them from enjoying a relaxed lifestyle, and rid themselves of the need to show off their brilliant achievements in public. Developing the spiritual side of this neurotically driven perfectionist is a sure way to loosen those inhibitions for something more lofty than clandestine extra-curricular sex.

The Metal Monkey

1860 Gustav Mahler, Annie Oakley
1920 Pope John Paul II, Gaston Le Notre, Roger Angell, Howard Cosell, Federico Fellini, Charlie Parker, Roberta Peters, Dirk Bogarde, Gene Tierney, Montgomery Clift, Ravi Shankar, Mickey Rooney, Clive Donner, Tony Randall, Viveca Lindfors, Maureen O'Hara, Anatole Broyard, Walter Matthau, Ricardo Montalban, Carol Channing, Arthur Hailey, Isaac Stern
1980 Macauley Culkin

The thinking side of this Monkey aids him in being a creative, self-made person. He usually prefers to make his way alone, working happily at a job which takes him into lofty realms.

This autonomous person will encounter miles of obstacles along the road to finding his independent niche. But find it he will – or die! This is the fighter Monkey. When in doubt he confronts issues, battles with demons, fiercely attacks adversaries. He often wins by means of persuasion, reason and logic. But, if the issue warrants it, he is unafraid to put up his fists and trounce his opponent. The Metal Monkey's muscle is not like the stormy, fiery bravura of a Dragon. Nor can he match the Ox or Rooster for perseverance and endurance. The Metal Monkey comes on wiry and hostile. He simply annihilates challengers through might of mind and twist of spirit. Then he drops the cadavers in the ditch and moves ahead, as feisty as ever, to challenge the next contender. He's tough – but he's nice tough.

The Metal Monkey's personal life is never a romantic novel. He's too bent on achieving a major place in his career, making his mark on society and forcing his creative ideas through the fusty system to make time for a family or emotional space. As a major difference-maker, he must have unusual ideas. He is neither obedient to norms nor blatantly revolutionary but he needs the thrill of achievement, advancement, and position. He wants to be where the action is and if his entourage doesn't understand, then that's too bad.

It *is* possible for this person to marry and maintain a semblance of family life. Metal Monkeys are usually financially secure and make good providers but may not be disposed to spending much time at home. This person needs an independent, loving and patient mate, unafraid to take responsibility for home, family and marriage alone.

Metal Monkeys have sociable, gregarious personalities. They talk a lot and (although they are Monkeys) are often able to learn foreign languages. They enjoy travel and are quite apt to expatriate early in adulthood, moving away to start again in a new place to slake their thirst for self-sovereignty. The Metal Monkey hates criticism, does not wish to be compared to siblings and/or cousins, and deplores the existence of relatives who insist on loading his kitbag with unwanted advice. The Metal Monkey wants to be separate, officially unallied – an individual. He makes his own way and refuses to credit his frequent successes and financial gains to anyone else.

The Metal Monkey is intelligent. He is argumentative and yet has a charming, winning manner. The close relative who has to live with this seductive person knows just how cranky and picky he can be, and resents all the extra hugging and kudos that the Metal Monkey receives from his multiple admirers. For the Metal Monkey, family situations are often tense and fraught with hatred. Metal Monkeys are the sort of people who try to wrench the family home away from sisters and brothers to turn it into an old folks' home which, of course, bears Metal Monkey's name.

The Metal Monkey can be melancholy. If this person, who would perform amateur open-heart surgery on friend and foe alike to get where he wants to go, does not succeed he may go under. All that push and shove and strategizing is so depleting and the stakes so all-or-nothing that the fatigued Metal Monkey sometimes can't drag himself up to begin all over again. His sin lies in his puffed-up self-image – his pride. He can take setbacks as long as he comes out of them victorious. Too many losses and he skulks away, dejected and hopeless. I wonder how many down-and-outs are Metal Monkeys who gave up?

When and if despair sets in, the Metal Monkey may blame his failures on his upbringing, his family, friends or associates who were jealous of him and tried to do him down. This 'poor me' attitude is that of an unevolved character who cannot accept his own shortcomings, who will not assume responsibility for breakdowns in communication, and who can only see himself as a victim. Truly, this attitude is dead-ended.

The remedy for despondency in Metal Monkeys is directive group therapy. Although I don't often recommend it, I see the Metal Monkey as so blind to his own errors and so unwilling from an early age to consult with or take advice from elders or peers that he cannot help but benefit from a group experience. Metal Monkeys do not realize that they cannot always be right. They need to learn early on to take hints from those around them.

This Monkey makes an excellent salesman or TV talk-show host, newscaster or disc jockey. He is so articulate and nimble-minded that he could sell fur coats to bears. Whatever the verbal challenge that arises, he meets it with equanimity and a smooth-talking manner. He makes strangers feel comfortable. He exudes confidence and competence even when he hasn't a clue what he's about.

Finally, don't expect anything but the best from the genius side of this person. Leonardo da Vinci was a Metal Monkey; Pope John Paul is a Metal Monkey. These Monkeys can be *hugely* individualistic. This is a sign of achievement and versatility and these people can learn how to do almost anything.

But if Metal Monkeys undergo too many failures their mental and physical health will give out. They are born afflicted with more pride than resilience. The breaking-up of this brittle surface will destroy their sunny demeanor and they will begin to crumble into oblivion.

The Water Monkey

1872 Aubrey Beardsley

1932 Elizabeth Taylor, Melvin van Peebles, Sylvia Plath, Halston, François Truffaut, Omar Sharif, Gene Shallit, Anthony Perkins, Joel Grey, Meir Kahan, Angie Dickinson, Debbie Reynolds, Little Richard, Miloš Forman, Max Gallo, Emmanuel de la Taille, Anouk Aimee, Michel Legrand, Ted Kennedy, Jean Cacharel, Ellen Burstyn, Louis Malle, John Updike, Gay Talese, Peter O'Toole

A sublime combination of co-operation and genius, the Water Monkey is a peach! Ask around. Everybody agrees. He is one of the world's most spirited people.

Although Water Monkeys can always be counted on to defend their own piece of pie, they are sharing people, willing to lend a hand, or distribute whatever bounty they have. Water Monkeys are never slapdash friends who tramp through your living room, grab a pear or an apple and scoot out by the back door without leaving more than a lingering trace of patchouli. They take friendship and love seriously. Not that they go over the top about how *much* they *love* you but from the moment they decide to pull a friend on board their ship, their affection is true, their willingness to be there when the other person needs a hand is ever ready and their loyalty unswerving.

Water Monkeys are clever and witty without being cynical. There is a sweetness to their affability and they are always seeking to assist others in realizing their dreams. They have an innate ability to care deeply without being maudlin. They do not mind relinquishing the spotlight in favor of someone they admire and except for a basic need to maintain a modicum of security, they are squanderously generous with everything from hospitality to money, kudos and affection.

The Water Monkey has an elfin or spritely quality. A whimsical energy pervades everything he does. He is forever sending out vibes of ironic gaiety, which couples neatly with his natural tenderness towards others. Look at the teasing cartoons of Sempe, the lyrical films of Miloš Forman or the mordant yet humane works of François Truffaut. There's something both socially worthy and sardonic about the way Water Monkeys look at life. They're cutting and caring at the same time. They don't mind pointing out the foibles of friends and relatives but they wouldn't hurt them for the world because they care so ardently about their welfare.

Water Monkeys don't always fare as well as their friends. They tend to be needlessly neurotic. They are easily beset by worry and become flummoxed when little things go wrong – they may get anxious when the hall porter forgets to say good morning. Perhaps the porter is having a bad day and forgot to greet him – but it will trouble the Water Monkey, who may not be able to let himself, or you, forget it for weeks. The insignificant scene is inflated out of all proportion and the Water Monkey suffers. It is always he who apologizes and makes it up.

Water Monkeys are ingenious problem-hunters and -solvers. They do not want to know the word 'impossible'. For a Water Monkey, getting through a thicket of thorns means thinking your way round it and the Water Monkey makes an excellent mediator, trouble-shooter or organizer. He is a great motivator – can spend his life urging, scolding, monitoring, finding and fixing flaws, and be contentedly fulfilled with that secondary role.

The Water Monkey is never a prima donna or egomaniac. The innovative talents of this warm, loving person would not suit end-to-end talk show appearances. The Water Monkey's ego is trapped in the clever mind of a giving soul. Even Elizabeth Taylor, with her astounding beauty, has never become a siren like Zsa Zsa Gabor or a delectably simpering Marilyn Monroe. She's always married to some giant ego of a man whom she's trying to cure of alcoholism (and maybe getting caught up herself) or helping to combat prejudice about Aids. Liz Taylor is a failure as a prima donna – she wasn't born selfish enough.

Gloom and depression can sink the Water Monkey's buoyant spirit. If his petty neuroses or others' demands close in on him and he's made to feel guilty, his high spirits may crash. The idea of being wrong jangles his nerves and as he blames himself for much that goes wrong anyway, he is ill-equipped to defend himself against accusations. Water Monkeys are easy targets for manipulative folk who ruthlessly play on their sympathies.

There is something of the merry meddler in the Water Monkey. Sometimes he becomes intrusive. Water Monkeys enjoy gossip, which contributes to their reputation as sociable mates and excellent companions. But once in a while, they spill someone else's beans when they might better opt for the 'speak no evil' position.

Water Monkeys are wildly sexy. They adore cavorting in the act of love. They glory in all the imaginative ways to play the oldest human game. Unfortunately, they are rarely cool-headed in their choice of lovers and cannot resist taking up with complex and difficult characters. Perhaps it is natural for the problem-solver to take on problem people. Water Monkeys always find implacable monster mates with testy tempers and precarious emotional infrastructures. People whom you or I might joyfully throw out of the house Water Monkeys adopt as house pets. They are irresistibly attracted to living out perplexing scenarios in the hope that they will get to play a key role in untying the most defiant knots.

Monkey health

Monkeys are exorbitantly grabby where food is concerned; they need to eat often and have an annoying tendency to reach for and hang on to whatever is sitting in the middle of the table and has caught their fancy. No use protesting loudly because, in a wink, the Monkey has carried the food to his or her mouth and devoured it, lickety-split-boom.

What is it about Monkeys and food? It's simple. Monkeys have food fetishes. If not urged or forced to seek variety in their diet, they will simply eat the same things all the time. My friend Kathryn Weissberger eats watermelon all the time, summer, autumn, winter and spring in all circumstances. Or, if she fancies a bag of popcorn just before the huge Christmas dinner you have been slaving over for four hours, she'll run out and buy a huge bagful and crack it open right under your out-of-joint nose.

Take my Monkey pal, Jean-Louis Besson. His fetish is vinegar and chili pepper. He puts vinegar and chili pepper on his toast and on his Roquefort and if he weren't so well mannered, he would surely squirt vinegar and sprinkle chili pepper on to his ice cream. Serving a subtly flavored dinner to Jean-Louis Besson is not doing him a favor.

Monkeys are not pigs. They don't stuff themselves at meals or drink too much and grow obese. They just have this odd snack-and-grab-it habit that can drive normal people mad.

The Chinese say that Monkey subjects are born fragile and get stronger as they grow older. Their bones and teeth need reinforcement while they are small. Give baby Monkeys plenty of milk and milk products, vitamins and calcium supplements. Yoghurts and cottage cheese should be flavored with fresh fruits and no sugar.

Most of the adult Monkeys I have known have at one time or another suffered from stomach problems. Ulcers and intestinal infections, painful cramps and diarrhea are common symptoms. Very early on, Monkeys must be encouraged to eat vegetables and fruit even in between meals and to steer clear of fatty meat. Pork and sausage are clearly not on and should be avoided. No fats are to be served with starches such as rice or potatoes or pasta. A Monkey's digestive tract needs each element of the diet to arrive as a separate item to be dealt with on its own. A plateful of toasted bread, preferably wholewheat, should not be slathered with butter or there will be trouble. He can eat cheese, yes, but not with bread or crackers; pasta if you will, but not with greasy sauces – fresh tomato sauce made with olive oil is safest.

Most Monkeys have long thin limbs and if these are not exercised or kept supple and in shape, they will become brittle. It is wise for Monkeys to engage in exercises to strengthen the muscles of the arms and legs – squash, tennis, hiking, skiing and fencing. Strenuous exercise, such as weight-lifting and mountaineering, is not advised.

The Monkey's skin is usually clear in childhood but later on allergies may plague him. Although most Monkeys are spared the ravages of adolescent acne, many adult Monkeys suffer from psoriasis and other nervous skin disorders such as shingles and, oddly, dandruff. Monkeys, we know, are nervous and anxiety often leads to unbecoming skin disorders. For psoriasis, the best remedy is lots of exercise in the sun – no basking immobility, please! – and plenty of vitamins A and D. Wheatgerm and whole grains, bean sprouts and cold-pressed oils – all foods containing the B vitamins – should be favored by the Monkey.

Circulatory troubles are not uncommon among Monkeys. As their blood doesn't always move around as quickly as it might, they are often ultrasensitive to cold in their extremities and may also suffer intermittent dips in their blood pressure. Vertigo, migraines, giddiness and even fainting spells can ensue. Poor circulation can also lead to hemorrhoids, varicose veins and sometimes arrhythmic heartbeat. Nosebleeds, gum disease and tooth loss may also besiege the Monkey.

Ideally, Monkeys should live in quiet country surroundings, vary their diet, eat three square meals including phosphorus-rich foods, such as oysters and fish, and avoid all stimulants. Above all, they should get a lot of sleep. But they hardly ever can: even when Monkeys do sleep they lurch nervously around all night and instead of riding out these insomniac episodes by getting out of bed and reading, writing or doing a crossword till they become sleepy again, the anxious Monkey lies there twitching and tossing about, chewing off his knuckles in the dark.

Monkeys love the pulse of city life. They adore being lively and ready for action. I reckon that all my motherly advice about sleeping in tranquil surroundings is about as useful as sending a stodgy old Ox to a crowded, sex-filled discothèque for a rest.

Monkey futures

What the Monkey should expect from the next twelve Chinese animal years

2008, the Earth Rat year – After wading through a couple of challenging years, you are finally in a space where you will be understood and hailed and admired for a whole year. Rats and Monkeys get on like a pair of matched socks. The Rat is an emotional sort who often has trouble making decisions. *Should I buy a red car or a blue car? Marry a Dragon or a Tiger? Take that new job offer or stay in my current position? How should I configure my life now that my parents are no longer around to bother me? What should I wear to the ball?* By now, we all know that any time one is in the throes of a dilemma big or small, the solution is to ask a Monkey for assistance. Monkeys cannot solve their own problems very rapidly, but they are masters at helping others to make quick, workable choices. So in a Rat year, you Monkey people will find yourselves being called upon to give advice, to sort out thorny issues or to untwist the knickers of someone whose temper has him or her in a state of advanced frenzy. You can always figure out how most gracefully to exit a dilemma. As you are not power hungry and never want to risk being in the forefront, you are not in competition with the authority-hungry Rat. In other words, for Monkeys in Rat years, it's all systems go.

2009, the Earth Ox year – Your taste for the new and untried can irritate the Ox. Oxen like things to stay (as much as possible) the way they were. So along you trot into the Ox year, having spent a satisfactory Rat year doing your own thing, and BLAM! you meet up with the immoveable Ox temperament. Not to worry. Oxen can use some of your twittery energy, so hop aboard the Ox's strong back and lumber through this year at his unhurried pace. For Monkeys, Ox years are restful. The Ox protects you from yourself and may even prevent heart attacks by slowing you down and causing you to take a good look at certain of the behind-the-scenes complaints you've been needing to examine. How is your couple faring? Where are you in your career? How is your overall health? Medical and dental check-ups are in order. Long talks and walks on the beach with your loved one (or ones) should clear up any outstanding grievances. Make sure your blood pressure is on target and get thee to a gym or take a t'ai chi class. With your anarchic eating habits, the enforced slowdown in an Ox year can see your body balloon in a matter of weeks. Walk, run, jump – but don't stand still.

2010, the Metal Tiger year – The Tiger always welcomes the appearance of a Monkey in his neighborhood. But not consistently and not for long. In Chinese astrology, Monkeys and Tigers are traditionally enemies. In practice, however, Tigers befriend Monkeys and vice versa. But, what Tigers don't tell us is that they often welcome the company of Monkeys because Monkeys can solve problems that they cannot. Tigers enjoy Monkey humor and are somewhat entertained by their antics. But the real reason that you Monkeys will not tread a bumpy path this year is that the Tiger finds you useful. A business question? A travel predicament? Lost luggage? Lost love? Lost jobs? Dial-a-Monkey . . . which is precisely what the Tiger year will do to you. You will be called upon to advise and counsel others throughout this busy year. People may wake you in the middle of the night just to check your position on their church picnic for next month. How should Tracey approach Nancy on the hard-boiled eggs question? Who should cook the hot dogs? What sort of games are safest for the children? Any old problem is fodder for the Monkey's agile brain. And people catch on fast that you can fix things for them. So you will be solicited and respected for your opinions in this Tiger year. But you may not get married, get rich or live out some great passion because there just isn't time.

2011, the Metal Cat year – Monkeys notoriously gain social or political influence in Cat years. The reason for this is quite simple when you consider that the Cat wants nothing very public to happen to him. He prefers to wait in the wings whilst others perform and gad about on stage. You don't mind performing. In fact, entertaining others is one of your favorite pastimes. So, once again, you are useful to the ruling sign, and what's more, you're amusing. Cats often concoct excellent schemes for earning money or investing it. But they need a Monkey – a sort of engineer to bring it to the attention of the powers that be. They also have the market cornered on refinement and comfortable living. You don't give a hoot about where you live and are about as refined as brown rice in a bin at the health food store. This gap in styles might cause a rift between you and the classy influences this year. But it doesn't. The Cat employs your native cheek to front for him, to be his mouthpiece, to venture into society and state his case. That much you can and will gladly do. So this year there is no tension present which will foil any of your own plans. Take the opportunity to reconfigure your life. Use your new contacts in high places to further your career, and take pleasure from the Cat's luxurious lifestyle.

2012, the Water Dragon year – A year made for ambitious Monkeys who want to advance their careers and shine up their credentials. Dragons receive Monkeys into their hearts and homes and businesses and schools in a spirit of sunny hospitality. Dragons love to laugh and have a good old giggle over something amusing or unusual. Monkeys can think up jokes and stunts in a second and perform pratfalls and zany sight gags without blinking an eye. Monkeys love to entertain their friends and brighten the atmosphere in any way they can. To those of us who prefer quiet to noise, repose to activity and always choose the serious over the silly, the Monkey's need to divert and amuse is downright annoying. But for Dragons, who adore celebration, invent reasons to throw parties when there are none and willingly join in all general merrymaking, the Monkey's shenanagins are a welcome relief from boredom. This year you will get the chance to make yourself a lot of money. Nobody and nothing will stand in your way. The dauntless Dragon protects and admires Monkeys. Take full advantage of this benevolence, and for once in your life bask in the footlights, grab that microphone and belt out a better life for yourself.

2013, the Water Snake year – Not exactly Monkey Nirvana, are Snake years. You will be doing some fancy footwork to adapt. The Snake is a cool, collected individual. No-nonsense and philosophical, Snakes don't need or want to be entertained 24/7. Of course they enjoy a good professional show or concert where they can dress appropriately in all their finery and appreciate the play or the music at a correct, socially acceptable pace. But Monkeys riding around on unicycles or playing trumpets in their bathrooms dressed as scarecrows or nuns? Very little, thank you, and in tiny little eye-dropper doses. Basically, the Snake disapproves of the Monkey's zany approach. So in this year ruled by the sober Snake, slow your slapstick. Rework your comic routines so that they exude a more serious tone, and cool it with the pratfalls. If you manage to quieten yourself down you will find the company of the wise Snake extremely propitious. Listen to the Snake's advice. Make the moves and shifts necessary to adapt to the tone of this year and you will be free to move speedily ahead in all of your endeavors. As you like to give presents the way others change their socks, gift away! Give wantonly this year – and especially choose beautiful accessories – handbags, jewelry, scarves, gloves, hats, ties, cuff links of the finest quality will go over big with the recipients. Snakes are mad for accessories.

2014, the Wood Horse year – The Monkey's basic problem-solving nature appeals strongly to the practical Horse. The Horse will not stand in the way of Monkey progress this year. On the contrary, Monkeys will be encouraged to ply their variety of trades and manage things in their own clever way. Do not interfere. Do not take the wheel. When the car starts sliding towards the ditch, shut your eyes and whistle a happy tune. Horses do not like to be helped or corralled, hemmed in or criticized. Obviously this is a tall order for Monkey people, who can see through almost any situation and always want to help out in a pinch. Horses get themselves into many a scrape. My advice, Monkeys? Stay out of it. Unless the Horse year begins reeling and staggering and threatening to bring down your very own house, stay the hell away from giving any advice or sticking your nose into complex situations (If you are an in-law, this advice is especially targeted to you.) Let this year sort out its own difficulties. Go to all the parties you are asked to. Entertain your head off. But don't steal any scenes or try to take over where others have got there first (deals, relationships, business projects, inventions, etc. as well). Your job this year is to ride in tandem at the hasty circuitous Horse year's hectic pace and not fall off the planet.

2015, the Wood Goat year – Your natural generosity must be curbed in the Goat year. You see someone in need and, when you can, you dip your hand into your pocket or purse. It's not that you are careless with money, but you have an open-handed attitude about what you have to spare. You give a lot of presents, and you like to treat your friends and family to lovely meals in charming restaurants or take them on trips to interesting new places. The Goat year may tug just a tad too strongly on your purse strings. You will see openings for charitable or altruistic acts and tumble headlong into their tempting maws. Hold off. Watch your pennies. Goats love Monkeys and are especially drawn to their ability to be creative in so many different areas. In this way, you two are quite similar. But caution is advised. Goats are forever looking for someone to lend them money, give them a leg up, house them and feed them and well . . . take care of their everyday needs so that they can get on with whatever it is they are embarked on. Monkeys simply cannot afford to take on Goats. So this year, be especially wily when you are asked by some baleful soul for a handout or a loan. Smile, cry poor and say no.

2016, the Fire Monkey year – In your travels this year, you will meet someone who will have a profound influence on your career. It could be an older person who takes a shine to one of your brilliant ideas. Or it might be a contemporary who is willing to partner with you either in business or in love. Take notice of this person's Chinese astrological sign and compare it with yours. If the match is harmonious, think seriously about pursuing a project or a marriage together. This is your year to shine and preen and prance and dance on the tables if you feel like it. But do climb back down to earth once in a while, because this is also your year to plan your next dozen years. The Chinese don't have decades of ten years; their calendar uses twelve-year periods. Each year has a particular significance for each sign. When your own year rolls around, you are obliged to sit down with pen and paper (or computer) and outline the next twelve years of your life. Where do you want to be in 2028? What can you see yourself doing? How might you plot the path to this goal, year by year, so you are more or less certain to attain that objective? Not an easy task? No. But a necessary exercise in order to build your own life. Take charge of your destiny in this propitious Monkey year. Do not just sit back and let life live you.

2017, the Fire Rooster year – Roosters always take a shine to Monkeys because they know that they are the most comical people around and they sincerely need to be entertained. Plus which, Roosters are hugely impressed by your ability to sort out the knottiest of problems. You are not in the least similar. Roosters tend to be dour, stiff and serious sorts. You Monkeys are nimble-witted and lithe of both body and spirit. Nonetheless, in this Rooster year, you will benefit from great goodwill. You can earn scads of money, buy plenty of toys for yourself (cars, restaurant ranges, boats, houses and – if you are so inclined – even the odd winery or ranch). Best of all in this oddly generous-to-Monkeys year, you will have enough disposable income to drown your loved ones (and even your not-so-loved ones) in oceans of presents. There will be days in this Rooster year when you come home laden with gifts for one and all. Father Christmas in July. Mother Christmas in September. Be on the lookout for a craftier-than-thou associate who (while you were on your buying spree in Mendoza, Napa or Burgundy) may have been putting his or her hand in the till. It could be your accountant. But it might also be your spouse or significant other. You will know how best to solve this problem. Why? Because you're a Monkey, silly!

2018, the Earth Dog year – Dogs are mistrustful and derisive. You Monkeys are wise to corruption and savvy about the scuzzy underbelly of the world. But you would prefer to ignore all that and just live for today and have something lovely to eat. The Dog year is not disastrous for Monkey people. But it is not a walk in the park, either. First, money problems. In Dog years, money is scarce. Dogs do not believe in waste and prefer not to live in lavish luxury or have to witness expressions of glut. Dogs are crusaders for justice and are eager to see things done right. They are also outrageously direct and critical, spouting disobliging remarks apace without realizing just how cutting and cruel they sound. You Monkeys want no part of this cynicism and do not care to join any movements to improve the lifestyles of homeless urchins in Brazil. It just isn't your thing. So in Dog years you will want to cut back on spending (you needed to anyway) and keep abreast of current events. You will no doubt be called upon several times to participate in rallies for the future of married gay priests or to parade for the right to life of all the litters of all the dogs in the thousands of animal shelters across your country. Don't be surprised. Be amusing. Don't get depressed. Work hard and change your phone number often to fend off the do-gooders who will clog your driveway if you let them.

2019, the Earth Pig year – The pure-of-heart Pig doesn't harbor much respect for you madcap Monkeys. Not that Pigs are killjoys or want to plop a bushel over your light. They don't. But Pigs would rather luxuriate before a wood fire with a glass of finest cognac, a Havana cigar and a saucy conversation than join a bunch of cavorting Monkeys on a dance floor somewhere noisy and smoky and wild. Hence, in this year, although you cannot count on the Pig's complicity, you can count on your own spirited nature to get out and make money and enjoy hobbies and sports and other savory activities. This would be a great year for you to join an amateur theater company or participate in some group therapy. You know how good you are at solving other people's problems? Well, you are not known for being able to sort out your own. Monkeys are congenitally neurotic. Somehow you are blind to your own forest and often just stand there weeping and staring dumbly at the trees. All variety of talk therapy is indicated. You need to hash things through in order to be able to get a global picture of what's troubling you. If you can see yourself as others do, you will have come a long way towards emotional health. The Pig is definitely on your side in this effort.

The Resilient Rooster

Jaunty Rooster Mine,

Uncommonly resilient, you were born to bounce back. Even though your whole life is a roller-coaster ride, a crazy quilt of successes and setbacks, high times and low, trials, tribulations and other emotionally exhausting or gut-wrenching experiences, you remain an irrepressibly staunch and plucky spirit. No matter the degree of despair, you simply pick yourself up, brush your feathers smooth and strut all over again. You emit enthusiasm rays. Your joy in experiencing new kicks is contagious. People clamor to hang out with you, to go to your places, see your sights, share your thrilling way of life. You will frequently occupy positions of authority. You are naturally bossy and excel at setting a good example. You work very hard.

Despite a sometimes cocky attitude and a tendency to be conceited, you cannot be accused of being either pushy or pedantic. You are a multi-talented, open-minded yet conservative person. In love, you flip for elegance and class. Try courting a glamorous Snake. Or take up with an encouraging Dog. Better still, for the sake of challenge, let yourself be seduced by a fiery Dragon. All of the above are able to ease the strain of your exhaustingly busy life. Listen to this and heed my advice: you are too frank for your own good. Take pains to be less candid. Your blatancy can do you in. Blow your own horn if you will but try not to blow the whistle on yourself in the bargain. Remember, a Rooster in hot water is nothing more than chicken soup.

Buoyantly yours,

Suzanne White

In the twentieth and twenty-first century all Roosters were born between the following dates:

22	January	1909	and	9	February	1910
8	February	1921	and	27	February	1922
26	January	1933	and	13	February	1934
13	February	1945	and	1	February	1946
31	January	1957	and	17	February	1958
17	February	1969	and	5	February	1970
5	February	1981	and	24	January	1982
23	January	1993	and	9	February	1994
9	February	2005	and	28	January	2006
28	January	2017	and	15	February	2018

The Rooster ID card

Lasting symbols have special powers. Enhance your self-image by surrounding yourself with tangible signs of your own identity and make these symbols known to your friends and loved ones. Use them daily and they will bring you luck, security and a feeling of personal worth.

Your best:
color is violet
flower is chrysanthemum
fragrance is myrrh
tree is oak
flavor is sweetish
birthstone is topaz
lucky number is 6

Your favorite:
food is barbecued meats
animal is wild deer
drink is cider
spice is white pepper
metal is zinc
herb is savory
musical instrument is oboe

The Rooster is yang

The Rooster's motto is: 'I know better'

In a comfortable barnyard setting where all the animals know who is boss, the cocky Rooster will usually be forthright, brave, enthusiastic, loyal, hardworking, tenacious, resilient, adventurous, meticulous, prompt, astute, well-dressed, proficient, down-to-earth, gregarious, communicative, sensible, generous, charming, ebullient and terminally witty.

But on bad days, when everyone ignores his presence, nobody cares a whit for his genius or seeks his favor, the Rooster grows cranky, fussy, vain, self-involved, blindly egotistical, over-zealous, pretentious, materialistic, grabby, high-handed, cynical, mercurial, self-absorbed and quixotic as hell.

Cock of the walk

Roosters worship and cultivate the visible. What is tangible excites them more than anything ethereal or metaphysical. They also cherish experience and float through adventure and vicissitude with panache. With Roosters, what you see is exactly what you get. There are no hidden depths to the Rooster's character: he is neither complicated, profound or esoteric. Rather, he is straightforward and direct, able to tell right from wrong in a wink and comfortable when skimming along the surface of his existence. Depth makes Roosters seasick.

Roosters are conspicuous. They always appear attractive and beautifully turned out. They are sociable and free-wheeling, wickedly magnetic and love to bask in the truckloads of attention they receive from any gathering with which they grace their irresistible presence.

There are more authentically fascinating people on this earth than Roosters but somehow one is always drawn to the scintillating personality, wit and verve, of the Rooster, and enchanted by his ever-present aura of chic and hip. The Rooster moves through life in the superlative mood. To him, every event is either 'great' or 'terrible'. Every piece of furniture or art, drink, flower, tree, is valued by the judgemental, decisive Rooster's personal love/hate barometer.

For him, nothing is lukewarm. Hot dogs light up the Rooster's taste buds or make him want to puke. Curvaceous blondes set him on fire or freeze his vital organs. Burnt orange is a color which turns his stomach or makes him swoon.

Roosters do nothing by halves. They may get married and divorced in the same week. They might suddenly come out of a lifelong incarceration in a monastery to manage a sex shop empire. They are forever changing careers at thirty, forty or fifty, deciding to become ballet dancers, brain surgeons or tight-rope walkers. Roosters have no sense of the impossible and will dare almost anything once.

Of course, all this chronic lurching about from pillar to post stems from the Rooster's certainty that, no matter how devastatingly low he may plummet or how high he may fly, nothing lasts for ever. Although catastrophe may try to flatten him to a barnyard pancake, he invariably proves uncrushable. Try to drown him – push as hard and as long as you wish. He will not go under for the third time.

Life, for the Rooster, is a never-ending roller-coaster ride. The hills are exhilaratingly high, the descents rapid and dizzying, the valleys well below sea level and life-threateningly arid. The Rooster always intuits the close presence of the coaster's helping-hand chain which unfailingly catches the front car and yanks it to ever greater heights before nose-diving once more to new and ever more horrendous oblivion.

Roosters are lucky. They are born with the foreknowledge that if setbacks occur and obstacles shoot up before them, they can always stage a handsome comeback. A Rooster will always find a way to invent a new project and begin the long trudge and grind to the pinnacle of success and honor he so longs to occupy.

Opinions and sentiments, actions and thoughts follow a similar pattern of absolutism with the Rooster character. His all-or-nothing approach carries over into every area of his life. Roosters have intense, clear-cut, principles. They prefer never to consider nuance, refuse subtlety and eschew subterfuge and diplomacy in favor of bluntness in human interchange. Roosters do not know how to pause and consider what they are about while they are about it. When a Rooster thinks he knows best, he will never hesitate to act. He can be cocky, willful, heedless, unreasonable, illogical and surer than sure that he is right.

The Rooster is stoically sure that he can make his own luck, call his own shots and paddle his own canoe – alone! If they should dare to interfere, friends, family and associates will be left standing on the river bank quaking at his antics, while jaunty old *Cockadoodle-doo* races happily through hair-raising rapids, confident that he's headed straight to paradise when he is in fact Up the Creek.

My dear Rooster friend Paul Pierrot, a handsome confirmed bachelor and Parisian lawyer, practiced in a large international firm in Paris, owned a lovely flat in a pleasant *arrondissement* and an old ruined house in the South of France. He was part of our old gang of ten expatriate Americans. We had known each other since the sixties when we emigrated to Paris. We treated each other like family, consulting each other, dishing out advice and lending our shoulders to cry on.

Paul always threw the annual Christmas party. One year, the day before the party, I went to help him cook. When I walked in, Paul was scrubbing at a scorched pot bottom.

'Bonjour, kiddo!' I saluted him. 'How goes it?'

'Terrible,' said Paul, scouring away. 'I feel miserable.'

'Do you want to talk about it?'

'Not really,' said Paul. 'Do you want to peel those potatoes?'

Roosters often hold emotions in. Experience has taught me that it's best not to push them. I started peeling spuds.

Next day, Christmas Eve, the elements of the gang, friends of Paul's from work, Paul's mom and dad and some of our own family members on visits from the US wafted up to me, kissed me and whispered, 'You've got to stop him from marrying Agnes Charleville,' in my unsuspecting ear.

At first, I was staggered by the news. My astounded mind kept repeating over and over: 'Paul is going to marry Agnes Charleville.' The notion was *so* far-fetched and foolhardy. I had loved Paul as a brother for over fifteen years. He had courted many a beautiful female, sown his share of wild oats and even been seriously in love with one or two great women. Almost all of the women in his past had seemed possible spouses for him. But Agnes Charleville? She had been married three times. She must have been something of a sorceress because she was a mouse, a translucent blur of a girl whose only noticeable physical feature, her platinum blonde hair, was colorless. Her personality matched it. The Christmas party atmosphere was heavy with the appalling new truth. We agreed that he probably planned to announce his betrothal at this party, at midnight.

Try as I might, I could not corner Paul before eleven thirty. Finally, I followed him to the WC and waited till he came out. 'Paul, I have to talk to you. Don't marry Agnes Charleville,' I blurted out hoarsely. 'You'll be unhappy.'

A throttled gurgle emanated from Paul's throat. He sagged against the wall. 'Suzanne,' he said. 'I do not love Agnes. I like her a lot. I hate to make love to her, but I said I'd marry her. I promised,' he said, almost in tears. 'I said I would and I *will*.'

He seemed so firm in his resolve that I said no more and returned to the party. The whole crowd was awaiting with trepidation the stroke of midnight – when we felt sure an announcement would be made.

Midnight came and went. No announcement. At about twelve fifteen, we all began searching for Paul and Agnes. But Agnes, it transpired, had run off. Paul was moping in his bedroom, deciding whether to slit his wrists or face the music. We were concerned but knowing our Rooster Paul and his rejection of intimate exchanges at difficult moments, we got out, pumped up the rock and roll and danced holes in our Christmas stockings.

The next day I had lunch with Paul and endeavored to find out what had changed his mind about his engagement.

'While we were chatting in the corridor last night, my mother told Agnes I was engaged to marry a rich girl in America. Agnes left here on her own. I had nothing to do with it,' said Paul, obviously not displeased with the turn of events.

'Did you disabuse Agnes of your mother's story?' I asked.

'No way,' said Paul. 'Let her believe what she wants to believe.'

Close calls are a Rooster speciality and when confronted with a tight situation, they can be ruthlessly expedient.

The Chinese call the Rooster's mental rigidity 'intellectual inflexibility'. Whatever you call it, Roosters have it bad. When dealing with them, you tiptoe, dare not suggest alternatives or attempt to put your point of view for fear of clamming them up further or suffering one of their retaliatory attacks, complete with machete-like sarcasm and insults designed to cut your heart out. The Rooster is the last of the redhot diehards. He can be both sectarian and fanatical about all he believes in. No matter how thoroughly you prove to him that his course of action is a paved road to ruin, the further inside his resolve he will burrow.

Roosters often display a covert resistance when confronted by their own privacies in other people's mouths, annoying evidence of their sometimes perverse delight in keeping secrets. Roosters really know how to keep a secret: whenever, I need a safe place to spill some beans, I confide in a Rooster – their beaks are sealed.

Thirteen years ago, I was asked by movie star Jane Russell, a Rooster woman of the first water, to ghost-write her autobiography. She came to my house in Sag Harbor, Long Island, to work with me for a week. We were to prepare vignettes about her life that I might insert into her life story at the proper moments.

As soon as she was comfortably installed at my place, I sat her down to chat. I think I asked all the right questions: Who gave you your first screen test? What did your mother think of your sexy role in *The Outlaw*? When did you meet Hughes? What about the story everyone knows of him making you a bra on the set of some movie? Did you love him?

Jane claimed to be willing to talk to me but when it came to specific questions, her divulging center went on strike. Pry as I might, she would let not one whisker of the cat out of the bag. At first, I reckoned she was hiding facts from me out of modesty or shame. But some time later, when I went to visit her, I realized she was neither a prude nor a Pollyanna: she was simply a Rooster. Shortly afterwards, I grew too ill to write the book. But I did wonder who *would* be able to extract the information from this steely personage.

Answer? Nobody. We will never know what role Howard Hughes played in Jane Russell's life because she has decided, Rooster fashion, that the secret will go with her to her grave.

Unfortunately, the unevolved Rooster may use stored secrets to manipulate others. As the Rooster trusts nobody and hardly ever confides in others, one is well advised to know one's Roosters very well before choosing which wing to cry on. Betrayal is rare among Roosters but when it happens it's big time treason.

The Rooster is not easily fooled. His intelligence is penetrating. His mind is cautious, sceptical. He is perspicacious and shrewd. His effectiveness stems from his ability to see through a cloudy issue with X-ray Rooster vision, bypassing emotional obstacles, quickly separating feeling from fact with razor-sharp skill. No matter the cleverness of his interlocutor, the Rooster will pierce his smokescreen and figure out exactly what the person is thinking behind all his talk. Due to this perceptive gift, Roosters make excellent trouble shooters, detectives, doctors, nurses, psychiatrists and can turn their hand to anything requiring acute insight and a probing mind.

Roosters are always up, out and doing. They rarely pause to sit and relax or slip into languid mode. As they are frequently multi-talented, they attempt to become accomplished in many different ways. Valentine Armani, a peripatetic Rooster born in 1945, cooks *grande cuisine*, speaks six languages, plays Chopin with one hand tied behind his back, teaches tap dancing, designs gardens and travels all the time. He has recently mastered Polish and written a novel in Catalan. He has bought several properties around the world and hand-rebuilt them stone by brick into palaces. He has married three times, written a successful cook book and learned how to throw pottery. In his spare time over the past fifteen years, he has co-authored a book with his ageing father on jogging for senior citizens, given two public recitals of classical guitar and become a recognized expert in the complex field of eighteenth-century European painting. He still holds down a full-time job as an eye surgeon and only complains when he is on Saturday surgery call and cannot escape to his weekend hang-gliding classes.

All Roosters are clothes conscious. They may appear conservative but are infinitely meticulous about how they look. They are never satisfied with their appearance and spend masses of time and trouble, money and effort trying to improve it. Rooster women spend hours in front of the mirror, making up their eyes, crimping their hair, examining their expensively crowned incisors and gold fillings. Rooster men are almost worse. They don't want to go out unless they are primped, matched and laundered to the hilt. They tend to judge others by the way they look and are painfully aware of outsiders' criticism.

Roosters view life unadorned: they never gild the lily nor sugar bitter pills. It's almost as though they prefer to face harsh truths rather than soften hard blows or facts. They cling to an image of themselves as being insuperably courageous, accepting all aspects of reality unblinkingly and unflappably.

The Rooster is rankly suspicious of idealism and wary of vapid dreams. He thinks poetry is frivolous. He's attracted to the concrete, the tangible. He believes most avidly in staying close to tried and true methods, always opting for middle-of-the-road politics and choosing safe, sane ways of living. He is rarely creative in a spontaneous, improvisational way. Rather, the Rooster's genius is to innovate within a given structure: improve on a classical pasta recipe, alter the hackneyed phrasing in a favorite old love song, add his own two cents to a faltering business deal and turn the whole kaboodle to his advantage. He's always sharp, practical and resourceful. And he is never guilty of building castles in the air.

Roosters are serious. Their demeanor is usually sober. They are demanding of themselves and those around them. They often enjoy positions of authority and never hesitate to accept a promotion – even if it requires them to work harder or change their habits.

Rooster organizational talents are legendary. At the age of thirty-three my niece Pamela ran a huge department store with 150 employees and 33 departments single-handedly. Just this year, after having brought that store's profits up 170 per cent from the 1991 figures, she was given the job of regional manager and now has five suburban stores to manage. Next winter, she will be promoted to divisional manager and, according to her latest letter, by 1995 she hopes to become managing director of the corporation's south-east sector of the United States.

Roosters prefer to run things rather than take orders. If they have to ask you more than once for help, they will do it themselves, promptly and without further fuss. They can be helpful to others, yet, when asked to do a favor, Roosters usually set limits before attacking the job. 'Sure I'll make your wedding dress but I won't sew the seed pearls on the lace because it makes me too nervous.' This way, the Rooster can fit your needs into his plan of action and handle your case in his logical, serious fashion. The Rooster is infuriated by tasks which have no apparent end and his pride is severely affronted by jobs that are beyond his capability. He hates to appear ridiculous.

You won't find silver spoons emerging from the eggs when Roosters are born. Their lives are a series of financial pickles. Money comes in and goes out but they know not to count on a steady flow. Careful budget planners and savers, the average Rooster, however, is bankruptcy prone. His luck doesn't lie in the area of fiscal success. The getting and keeping of wealth is a permanent challenge to him and he does not take it lightly. As money doesn't come easily to him, he is rarely moved to be profligate. He must strive all his life, constantly experience mammoth reversals of fortune and repeatedly pass through the fires of hell before reaching his goals.

As a result, Roosters are most impatient with people who have no ambition, grit or resources. They are exasperated by those who refuse to pick up their tools and start scratching elsewhere for food immediately after a depression, disappointment or slump. They have no time for slug-a-beds and cannot fathom those so-called creative types who languish without anguish, smiling beatifically, munching bonbons and letting life live them.

The Rooster often seeks to add glamor to his workaday existence. As he is tethered to his work ethic and married to a negative money mentality, his everyday life is tough and often colorless. Naturally, when he allows a smidgeon of romance to swim into his ken, he dreams of imitating the dazzling lifestyles of the rich and famous. Sometimes, Roosters become incorrigible snobs and name-droppers, bandying about the glistening titles of their hotshot acquaintances if only to add a *soupçon* of pizazz to their otherwise workaday lives. But no matter how many elegant houses they buy in lavish spas or how frequently they jet to Gstaad or play golf in Saint Tropez, true glamor consistently eludes them. Roosters are often drawn to what they mistakenly perceive as chic only to find out that their perception was skewed by their own *arriviste* desires.

Roosters make great hosts and adore entertaining as it gives them the opportunity to show off – not that they are likely to disrupt a dinner party with a spontaneous burst of crowing or even demand that their guests sit through their rendition of Beethoven's Ninth on the kazoo. They are not boors but they invite people round for the fun of showing off new furniture or subjecting them to a two-hour slide show of their recent trip to Yugoslavia's war-torn coast. Roosters feel a strong need to captivate a willing audience and will go all out for the treat of setting the stage for their own best performances.

The main virtue in the Rooster character is loyalty: they make devoted friends. They always speak well of their pals and make allowances for foibles and faults. Roosters never break promises and are always true to their word. When Roosters love and admire someone, they will move mountains to keep them happy, advance their personal causes and provide a willing shoulder for the loved one to cry on.

The Female Rooster

Even though 'Rooster Female' is a contradiction in terms, this feisty, energetic, courageous and irrepressible woman embodies all the characteristics of a bona fide Rooster – and then some!

Both physically and psychologically, the Rooster woman is a person of extremes, never average or mediocre. They are exceptional, handsome and compellingly attractive creatures.

All Rooster women possess an exciting, seductive charisma: wherever they go, they become famous for their magnetism. Formerly reasonable men have been known to bankrupt themselves over the vivid beauty of a striking Rooster, to abandon house and home for the thrill of sharing even a brief encounter with a sexy Rooster lady, to bequeath a fortune anonymously to an exotic one they have for ever adored from afar. No one remains indifferent to this fetching siren whose power to attract and captivate others is at once mysterious and disquieting.

The Rooster woman is usually thin. Her naturally slim body can be described as serpentine. No matter her dietary habits, she is usually able to maintain a willowy silhouette into middle and old age. She often has large capable hands. Her skin may be dry. The ends of her slender fingers are frequently tipped by long nails carefully buffed to an elegant sheen, or painted with dark red nail polishes. Even in the hottest weather, the Rooster woman wears stockings. Her hair is combed flat or carefully arranged in a neat coiffure designed to frame her triangular face. Her chin is usually pointed, her cheekbones wide set and prominent.

The Rooster female's eyes are slanted, elongated and – once again – snake-like. Her penetrating stare is loaded with lucid perspicacity. Her voice is low, throaty, sexy and, as she is endowed with a superior intelligence and is rapaciously eager to learn, what she says is often of great interest to those around her. Her hair is usually abundant and hardy. It is often red – or, if it is blonde or brunette, at least tinged with red highlights or gives off a reddish cast.

Rooster women are neither supple nor elastic of spirit. They are stubborn and frequently rigidly set in their ways. But, like her male counterpart, the female Rooster is both resilient and resistant. She can weather delays and setbacks, come through emotional and physical storms with all her sails flying and unharmed, unlike any other woman – except perhaps the dauntless Dragon.

The Rooster woman collides head-on with almost everything. She confronts; she attacks. Faced with a challenge, she invariably 'goes for it'. In a wink, she assesses and judges the situation. Then, without hesitation, she takes the bull by the horns and, because of her willingness to leap into the fray, very often ends up holding the Tiger by the tail.

Although she appears flinty and somewhat forbidding, the Rooster woman surprises us with unexpected gestures of kindliness. She has great feeling for others and sincerely wants them to thrive and be happy. She is a no-nonsense, plain-spoken, frank person and rarely minces words.

Recently, I had to move house and when the movers arrived to pack up my things I was surprised to find that they were a married couple – Monsieur and Madame Arnaud. They worked together as a perfectly balanced team, sharing the packing of cartons, the lifting and carrying of furniture and maneuvering the truck in and out of small French village streets. I had never met a lady mover before. Her odd choice of profession made me curious. Madame Arnaud turned out to be a 1945 Rooster. Tough and strong, fearless and quite bossy. Her husband, a devoted Dog with all the good-natured dogged grit native to the Dog character, heeded her commands, heaving, lifting and carting according to her well-thought-out plans. 'No! Claude!' she would holler up the stairs. 'Madame White doesn't want that couch up there. Bring it downstairs. We'll deal with that later. Go get that measuring tape I brought. It's in the front seat of the truck.'

Her sinewy Dog husband raced about like a busy puppy, happily following orders. Madame Rooster did most of the thinking – as well as participating in the lifting. It was a muggy day but she looked hale and dry all the time. Her hair was cropped short and curled coyly around her pleasant face, her nails were painted red. I marvelled at how neat and groomed she managed to look all day.

At one point on the first day of this giant two-day moving expedition, I had made a Tigerish snap decision about placing our large double bed on a small sleeping platform. With characteristic good-humored vigor, the Arnauds hefted it through a window and up two flights of narrow stairs. They had to measure, calculate, twist, lift, remove some doors, take up the stair carpet and put it back down twice.

A few days later, they arrived at my new house to deliver the rest of my furniture. Tired as they were, the pair set straight to work, carting masses of stuff about the house in a courageous attempt to make order out of the reigning chaos.

At one point, Madame Arnaud took a short breather while the men lifted the piano down from the truck. She leaned over and whispered, 'Has your husband slept in the bed up on the platform yet?'

'No,' I said. 'Why?'

'He's too tall to sleep in that bed up there. He will surely bump his head on the beam in the night. If he gets up in the night to go to the bathroom, he'll kill himself,' she said candidly.

She was right. I had been having visions of waking up one morning to find poor Richard in a leaden comatose state after sitting up in bed in the dark of night. But after what the Arnauds had been through to get it up there, I would not have dared ask them to reverse the painful process of a few days previous.

'Why don't you just move the bed off the platform and leave the mattress on the floor?' asked Madame. 'We'll do it. It's certainly better than letting your husband commit suicide, isn't it? Claude!' she called as her husband moved past us, pushing his end of the piano. 'We're going to take the bed base off the platform!'

Monsieur Arnaud stopped. 'Where are you going to put it?' he asked warily, knowing that I had no storage space for the bedstead. In true doubting Dog fashion he was going to find out *before* he bothered to move it what would happen to it next.

Before I could answer, Madame Rooster stepped in, cockily announcing, 'I can keep it till you need it again. Maybe you'll take it down to the South when you go in September.'

'Where in the name of God do you intend to *put* that —— bed?' barked Monsieur Arnaud at his Roosterish wife.

'No time to worry about that now, Claude,' she told him sharply. 'When you're finished with the piano, get your trusty screwdriver and start taking the —— bed apart.'

Monsieur Arnaud, growling, promptly did Madame Rooster's bidding.

Rooster women can be unexpectedly kindly. Yet they are not easy to live with. The Rooster woman's tongue is honed razor sharp to deliver acerbic remarks. She is authoritarian and exacting about getting things done – and done *her* way.

Flexibility is not her strongest suit. Even the gentlest and most gracious of lady Roosters maintains unshakeable principles and opinions. She believes absolutely in her own wisdom and never wavers from her ideals – unless her adversary has masterful authority over her or is adept at manipulating her through emotion or guilt. Otherwise, she is unpersuadable once she has made up her mind, and will never listen to constructive criticism or take advice.

Knowing how quickly she throws up barricades and imposes limits, most people retreat from confronting Rooster women. They sense instinctively that underneath her cool, yet fascinating exterior simmers a volcano which may suddenly erupt and damage their equilibrium. She is a genius at seeking out your most vulnerable sore spot and zinging you right where it hurts, with despatch. Weaklings abstain.

However she appears, it is well to remember that the Rooster woman lives to rule. She is not security conscious. She cares little for social acceptance and openly scorns snobbery involving approval by an inner circle or judgement by one's peers. She is a loner whose ambition propels her towards goals that only she knows or cares about. She doesn't share her intimate secrets easily. She is aggressive with newcomers and closely scrutinizes their every move as though each gesture were part of a plot to commit a serious crime. Discrepancies in character or behavior spark her morbid curiosity. Just to be sure that she is right about this or that person, she may engage them in piercing cross-examination. Sometimes, to test their reactions, she will make brutal remarks about one of their flaws. When pushed or cornered, the female Rooster can be unfairly harsh and humiliating, crushing her interlocutor sadistically, not caring what happens to him or her afterwards.

She can also be vindictive, pursuing her adversary for revenge long after a slight has occurred. She is ruthless with her enemies, talks frankly of their faults and gabbles readily about the wrongs they have done her. Usually, the Rooster woman is secretive and sly. She's a past master at fooling her entourage into accepting her attitude as gospel rather than delving beneath the surface to uncover her real feelings. She is impatient and quick to anger: if her detractors know her well enough, they can easily tease her into a lather, which is when she may make a fool of herself with errors of judgement and blurted-out truths or confidences that would have been better left unsaid.

The Rooster woman's ability to penetrate issues makes her capable of swift and accurate judgements. She senses the integrity or lack of it in a person from the first encounter. She is able to edit out any smokescreen of flowery language that may block others from seeing truths and goes right to the pith of the matter at hand. Nobody succeeds at pulling so much as a thread of wool over her eyes or making her swallow even a white lie.

Joie de vivre is often glaringly missing from the Rooster woman. As she requires truckloads of approval to feel good in her skin, she will often appear too solemn, rigid and agonizingly self-righteous. This is not a pose: Rooster women like every detail of their lives to be calculated to run smoothly. They want to exist within carefully thought-out parameters and, if possible, encounter few or, better still, no surprises in their daily life. The Rooster woman tends to take both life and herself too seriously, is frightened of disapproval from outsiders and unwilling (or unable) to let down her guard to laugh at her own follies.

Yesterday, at the hairdresser, I met a lovely Rooster woman. She had a beautiful sharply featured face, neat reddish-blonde hair and a flinty, almost dry, manner. When I asked her the year of her birth, she told me, 'I was born in 1921.' The ramrod straightness of her back, her ready tongue and the jaunty tilt of her head had kept her so perky and young-looking that she could have lied about her age by twelve years. 'You are a Rooster in Chinese astrology,' I told her.

'I know,' she said. 'I don't believe in astrology much but those Chinese character descriptions really work. I'm very stubborn. Nobody can tell me anything and . . . I'm aggressive. Everybody agrees. And I'm obstinate. Ask my daughter. She's coming in to pick me up later. She'll tell you how intractable I am.'

By the time her daughter came I knew enough. My Rooster friend had rapidly divulged that she was currently going through a painful depression after divorcing her 'impossible husband' of twenty-seven years. She lived alone because she couldn't stand anybody around her but she hated being alone. She couldn't stop eating fattening foods and she despised herself for it but she had to accept herself the way she was because she could not change. 'I've gained fifty pounds. I can't stand to look at myself. But I'll never stop. I could go on a diet but I won't. I go to the mental health center in my neighborhood for group therapy and it's very nice but I get there and I immediately need a bagel with cream cheese and sugared coffee. The group tell me what I'm doing wrong, that I'm destroying myself. But I won't listen and I don't listen to my psychiatrist. I may have made a failure of my life but I don't need anybody to tell me about it.'

The Rooster woman frequently appears outrageous and even kinky. She might dress garishly, wear fluorescent colors and sport sexy clothes. She doesn't hesitate to use fairly crude language to express herself. It is easy to mistake the Rooster for a loose woman 'on the make' whose intentions are to get whoever into bed as fast as she can. Nothing could be more wrong. And nobody is more surprised than the person who imagines the Roosterette to be a 'one night stand' girl. She may not slap the fellow who lands a frothy kiss on her heavily painted but unsuspecting mouth while dancing close in a disco but she will almost certainly decide that she doesn't want to pursue this character's dingy carcass one step further. The Rooster lady is not only traditional, she is an old-fashioned, marriage and family-oriented girl.

The professional capacities of the Rooster woman are remarkable. There is scarcely a job she cannot do well, hardly a career she cannot succeed at. She is amply gifted for leading a group or managing people and she makes a competent, effective boss. As she loves to show her mettle and prove her ability to endure fatigue, withstand rigors and survive setbacks, she also makes a devoted employee. Difficulties bring out the best in her and she often chooses the rockier path rather than the smooth one for the challenge.

As she is keen to maintain her independence and never be beholden to anyone – even her husband – the Rooster woman often places her career ahead of lover, husband, children and other family members. If a Rooster woman seeks to reach the highest position in her field, it is usually because elevated rank will afford her respect from her peers as well as insurance against want in old age. Autonomy is her middle name. She will always prefer to be self-sufficient rather than be told how to live her life by outsiders.

The Rooster woman can ferret out answers in some of the most mystifying situations. She seems to know instinctively how to locate truths where no one else can. This gift for uncovering secrets and then keeping them to herself makes her an excellent candidate for a job as an undercover agent, spy, detective or police inspector.

Because she can face almost any horror with equanimity and is constantly struggling against an unreliable health profile, the female Rooster is also at home with medicine. Paramedical careers, too, attract her and suit her talents well. She will do well as a family or specialist doctor, surgeon, dentist, pharmacist, nutritionist, or medical researcher. Knowledge of character and the inner workings of her own as well as other human beings' psyches also fascinate this dark-minded person. She could make a capable and motivated psychologist, psychiatrist or psychotherapist.

The Rooster woman could become a professional athlete. She is born with endurance and determination. As she is almost fearless, you may expect to find her climbing the world's most precipitous mountains, sky-diving in the most perilous landscapes and free-falling with an elastic band tied to her ankle off almost any high bridge or viaduct. A Rooster woman astronaut would not come as a surprise to a self-respecting Chinese astrologer.

Idealism and philosophy do not interest the Rooster woman. She will rarely, if ever, become an effete New Age dancer or a free-spirited poet. The metaphysical is about as useful to the Rooster woman as hair to a bald-headed eagle. She just cannot care about romance, or ask herself questions about the meaning of life.

The Rooster woman is practical, yet not particularly manual or attracted to arty-crafty pursuits such as building models or tackling the single-handed building of a house. She might become a fine decorator but she will design basic, bareish rooms as she deems that the concrete takes precedence over less tangible areas such as taste, color and beauty.

Anything agricultural suits this earth-bound woman. She usually has a green thumb and while her flowerbeds may not be the most convivial or relaxed you have ever beheld, you can be sure that even her flowers know deep down that they had better grow well – or else!

Men who enter relationships with Rooster females should sharpen both their wits and their wiles to be certain *never* to let her get the upper hand. As Madame Rooster believes only in what she sees and can touch, he should offer her jewels, yachts, houses and cars rather than love poetry and musical tributes. Of course, to be happy in love the tough-minded Rooster female ought to seek out a strong mate – someone who can stand up to her, challenge her fierce will and meet her eye to eye on her own level. Unfortunately, she usually attracts or is attracted to weaker men whom she may criticize out of existence. Her tendency to boss and lose respect for a man who 'yesses' her all the time can be the undoing of an otherwise happy marriage or meeting of two passions.

Although Dame Rooster wants to marry, her self-destructive controlling streak causes her to avoid appearing frail or vulnerable, to pretend that the tenderness she feels for a suitor is not serious, and that romance is a rather silly business. Don't be hoodwinked. The Rooster woman is as susceptible to romantic sentiment as the rest of us. But because she is so afraid of appearing foolish, she is both unable and unwilling to show her real feelings. She picks at and finds fault with her partner until he becomes embittered and perhaps leaves her in the lurch.

Lucky is the fellow who can finally daunt the rugged Rooster woman, though, as she makes the most vividly interesting of mates. She's usually an excellent conversationalist: people are attracted to her verve and compete to spend time in her exciting company. She is a marvellous householder as she knows instinctively how to organize and, if necessary, hire and manage the right personnel to keep the home in order. She's a hard worker and a loving, if a little harsh, mother whose pride in her children's accomplishments is a driving force in her life.

The Rooster woman loves and needs lots of sex and, when inspired, goes at it like two houses afire. The darkly complex side of her nature may prevent her from having a really rollicking time in bed until she is sure of her mate's good intentions. But as soon as he learns how to gain her trust and turn her on she will remain interested. If the Rooster woman's husband or lover takes pains to jolly her up with presents and soften her testiness with sweet attentions before attempting to make love, he will never be at a loss for a lusty bed partner.

Rooster man

There are two distinct physical types among Rooster men: the first is a stocky, thick-set fellow with generous amounts of body hair and heavy thighs. The second is slimmer, longer-limbed with less hair, apparent muscles and a thin waist. Both types have broad shoulders and big, well-formed hands.

The face of a Rooster man is often square-cut and displays a certain severity. He has a large skull and angular, well-defined features. He often has abundant hair which he likes to wear short. His perpetual half smile is evidence of the Rooster man's constant effort to appear jolly and control his natural aggression. He always has a pleasant voice and, although sometimes shy, can be remarkably eloquent when called upon to speak in public. His gaze is pitiless and penetrating, which keeps interlocutors on their toes. Nobody ever gets the impression he has put something over on the Rooster man.

From birth, Rooster men are endowed with intense intrinsic energy. Their punch and dynamism show through even the most sedate and calm of demeanors. A permanent ready-to-pounce state of mind lends them an air of nervousness or at least restlessness. Not only does this man *seem* to be going in twelve directions at once – he usually is. He has myriad interests: no stone is left unturned, no phone unanswered, no friend or family member left out on a limb.

The Rooster male lives in a state of exacerbated tension designed to keep him constantly in motion and on tap for anything that might occur at any moment of day or night. Unlike the watchful Dog who skulks about peering at the world through narrowed eyes with disquiet and unease, the Rooster male is up front and out front, strung tightly as a piano wire and, like a karate master, ready to spring into action to save himself and/or someone he loves from evil, ruin or both.

Because of his frankness, unscrupulous people can and do dupe the Rooster male. He is outspoken and believes in blurting out the truth where a measure of discretion might have been better. I know a jaunty Rooster ex-husband and father who decided to divulge his naughtiest private exploits to the judge at his own divorce trial. The shocked judge threw the book at this honest man who, years later, is still obliged to pay enormous sums each month to his remarried ex-wife and grown children. A Rooster always tells it like it is and takes the consequences without whining.

Rooster men are productive. They enjoy making things happen and often get involved in novel projects such as learning to roller skate in middle age or perfecting their knowledge of some little-used language such as Sanskrit. A Rooster is serious about his work and equally deeply involved in his hobbies or extra-mural pastimes. Capable and talented in many and varied ways, there is little he cannot do.

Curiously, on the under side of his honesty lies the Rooster male's fascination with secrecy and subterfuge: he will be good at all professions that call for piercing secret codes, peering around corners and seeing through appearances – detective work or diagnostic medicine, spying or investigative reporting are excellent possibilities for him. As he has a taste for power, he might also sign up as a revolutionary or become a professional insurgent with political ideals he holds dear. Because of his need to dedicate himself to his job and be useful and active all the time, the male Rooster also has the stamina and endurance for a full scale career in medicine, dentistry, police work of all kinds, research or psychiatry.

Sometimes, because they are innately attracted to cultivating their macho appearance and lust after stardom and a glamorous lifestyle, male Roosters become movie or stage actors, military officers or even firemen who wear dashing uniforms and swagger when they walk.

If he chooses to become a professional artist, the male Rooster is always daring and brash in his creations. His paintings will be vivid and large or his writing intricately complex and concerned with life's harsher aspects. If he sculpts, the work will be angular and make a strong statement. The soul of his art must become obvious, showing itself to us unequivocally. The Rooster wants his personal trademark on everything he does.

Yet the Rooster male cannot be called megalomaniacal. He'd rather have a good job than run the show. Independence is more important to him than stardom or the chance to shine. As he deplores the very word 'paperwork', it is plain that he will rarely pursue careers where he is called upon to plough through stacks of documents or pore over accounts till all hours of the night. Hand a Rooster man a simple tax or census form to fill out and watch the panoply of avoidance tactics which spring into action. If he has a terminal case of red-tape horrors, he is likely to stash the form under a pile of papers where he is sure never to come across it again. If he has managed to master his fear of papery monsters he will probably put the form safely into a file where he won't see it until the next time his conscience wakes up and shakes him by the shoulders. Or because he is a serious person he may take a different and surprising tack, one used flagrantly by my Rooster friend Val Armani . . .

Val receives a lot of mail. He's a doctor, so not only are there letters, bills, newspapers and magazines in his daily mailbox but reams of medical journals, shiny pamphlets advertising new miracle drugs, lush gold-leafed invitations to international conferences in exotic places and, of course, the ubiquitous offers for every silver, platinum and diamond credit card cast in plastic. This Rooster man loves to read – hates paperwork – and, like the rest of us, despises the drivel we call 'junk mail'. However, because Val is also a diehard Rooster, he is responsive, interested and curious. He cannot bear to throw one shred of his mail immediately away. He reads the lot from cover to cover. With pounds of paper coming through his door every day, he can't store it in the middle of his bed or on his desk. He needs those places to sleep, write and study Finnish. He uses an avoidance/confrontation tactic. Val forces himself to face *all* his mail *all* the time. Because (among all the other millions of talents) he is also a gourmet chef, Val spends hours in the kitchen waiting for things to boil or bake. Every day he pours his mail on the central counter in his kitchen and a stack of it sits on the marble-topped bar, visible and within easy reach. This way, he can always put his hand on something to read. His leaning tower of envelopes and papers doesn't look very attractive but it works.

'Did I tell you I got a card from Tim?' Val said to me recently when I went there to dine. 'If you look in the middle, about four stories down, you ought to find it.'

I looked and I found. Male Roosters are efficient in their own innovative way.

And they are also responsible where work, friendship, hobbies and earning a living are concerned. But love, with male Roosters, is quite another matter. Not only do they have a reputation for promiscuity to live down but do little to quell the fears of their peers on this peckish subject. Rooster men favor complexity in love. Haunted by a streak of sado-masochism, which frequently involves exaggerated game-playing in love situations, the male Rooster's conjugal bed resembles nothing if not a lumpy patchwork quilt. It rarely reaches the carefully smoothed counterpane stage. No routine sexual encounters for this fellow. He wants adventure – or nothing.

As rotten rungs are forever giving way under the male Rooster's ambitious feet, he does not benefit from an easy climb up the ladder of success: he is often frustrated and comes home in a steaming temper over how shabbily he feels life has treated him. His boss victimizes him and his children don't appreciate him. His parents never understood him and nobody in the world will ever fathom just what he wants out of life. He feels injustice has been dealt uniquely to him and he wants retribution. This *poor me* attitude creates a nervy brain state which, in turn, builds into an emotional thundercloud, which the male Rooster drops smack into the lap of his unsuspecting loved one. Love, it strikes him, is the one area of life where he might possibly take his true revenge, where wrongs done to him may be righted – even if only symbolically. In love games he can feel the rush, experience the consummate thrill of winning.

The male Rooster's romantic life becomes his playing field: strategies and games, abysmal separations and passionate reconciliations, tidal waves of contrition and forgiveness abound. The Rooster is an: 'I never want to speak to you again' person. In love he feels he can control his destiny. Though hardly ever physically sadistic, the Rooster man knows how to taunt and frighten his lover, inflict emotional injury – and then repent. It's almost as though he enjoys listening to sobs and pleas, witnessing the maudlin cinema engendered by his repeated rejections, recriminations and sudden reversals of affection. It may even please him to invent tales of his sexual infidelities, to boast about imaginary lady friends and hint at comely secretaries' attentions. By toying with their most fragile sentiments, the Rooster man pushes his helpless lovers to greater depths of misery, flaunting the power of his love over them. He is worse than provocative. He can be downright mean. Yet, when the fall-out clears and all the screaming and shouting dies down, this man makes for an ardent and faithful mate who secretly yearns only for the reassuring words and caresses of his adored partner.

Like his female counterpart, this chap needs plenty of sex. Rooster man also enjoys fantasizing about baroque and unusual sexual exploits, imagining how deftly he inflicts pain on his loved one and/or conjuring himself as a great romantic figure – which he is most decidedly not. His sexuality is both powerful and attractive. He loves to dress smartly and is careful to remain fit. He receives scads of attention and has much opportunity for getting involved in all manner of hanky-panky. Yet the Rooster experiences great difficulty in sharing his emotions. He cannot easily say, 'I love you, want you, need you,' to someone he loves – he would feel silly – so, no matter how sensitive or compassionate he is, the Rooster man never comes over as truly warm-hearted or loving. He is naturally reserved and afraid of expressing his innermost desires or what he actually *feels* (rather than what he *thinks*). Male Roosters are emotionally awkward. Hence the recourse to fantasy and the conjuring of romantic self-images to substitute for the real thing.

The important things to remember about the male Rooster are: (1) At first glance, he seems outrageously adventurous but he is really conservative. (2) He is a loyal and devoted friend but is usually too brutally frank and honest. (3) Appearance is everything to him and he bases almost all of his snap decisions on what he sees. (4) He is essentially rather misogynous but can be tamed into marriage by a patient and demonstratively loving female partner. (5) The rearing of children is not his first priority but if he begets them, he sincerely tries to be a responsible father.

With these five qualities in mind, we can begin to understand this flinty Rooster fellow whose exterior somehow never matches his actions, whose methods and means continually surprise us and whose unflinching friendship we covet all the more for the depths and mysteries it affords us.

The five Chinese elements and how they influence the Rooster

The Wood Rooster

1825 Thomas Huxley
1885 Eric Von Stroheim, Wallace Berry, Louis B. Mayer
1945 Bette Midler, Henry Winkler, Michael Douglas, Priscilla Presley, Rob Reiner, Bianca Jagger, John Lithgow, Carlye

Simon, Goldie Hawn, Eric Clapton, Bob Marley, Marthe Keller, Van Morrison, Diane Keaton, Dolly Parton, Gene Siskel

This Rooster is singularly able to persevere in areas where hard work is essential to results. His natural vigor, conscience and meticulousness give him the power to carry out complicated tasks which might daunt less organized 'picky' people. Don't ask the Wood Rooster, however, to agree to pore over a lifetime of yellowed texts in some dark attic room to hatch a volume of encyclopedic magnitude at the end of his life. Wood Roosters can only put forth enormous effort for short-term undertakings. This character is best employed as an efficiency expert, trouble-shooter or project manager whose job is to 'get the job done well – *now*'.

He is a sociable creature and loves to be in friendly company where he can hold forth, tell some of his best stories, recount his travels or listen, rapt, to the yarns spun by his cronies. Parties and festivals delight this naturally hospitable type who will often play host, do the cooking, buy the wine and (although he is anything but profligate with money) indulge his beloved guests in luxuries for the pleasure of showing them a good time.

Some deem the Wood Rooster a superficial person as appearance is of the utmost importance to him. It is well to understand that, on a personal level, he is preoccupied – obsessed – with youth and fascinated by the 'look' of things. Wood Roosters sincerely believe that how one looks is how one *is*. They cannot bear the idea of being old, crabby, wrinkly or left out of the mainstream of ideas. To a Wood Rooster, an old person is automatically a dead person. Even after middle age, the Wood Rooster is likely to continue to dress in youthful, skin-tight clothing and do everything in his power to remain reed thin and agile and stay cocky. He seeks the company and intimacy of people younger than himself, in an attempt to retain his verve. He often behaves in a manner not entirely in keeping with his age – taking up roller-skating at forty, buying rock music CDs at fifty, boogie-ing at sixty in clamorous discos where no other patron has yet reached his twentieth birthday.

As talkative and sociable as this creature is, the Wood Rooster has a real block about expressing his feelings. He can yammer on about anything he considers polite conversation. In private, on subjects dear to one's heart and soul, he's a tomb. If you love one of these wooden people you will have your work cut out trying to encourage him to learn how to say what is on his mind. Whether this Rooster is angry or sorry, sad, glad or madly, passionately in love, his exterior remains cool, sleek, well-turned-out, nervous and rather too sober. The Wood Rooster is the sort of emotionally turgid person to whom it is necessary to say one hundred times a day, 'Do you love me, darling?' or 'Honey, are you angry with me?' They need earth-shaking events and insistent, aggressive lovers to loosen them up. Unless the Wood Rooster learns to deal directly with his feelings, an unhealthy accumulation of anger and resentment will most certainly be with him and his intimates for the rest of his days.

The Fire Rooster

1897 Thornton Wilder, Frank Capra, William Faulkner, Walter Pidgeon, Nunnally Johnson, Paul Muni
1957 Amanda Plummer, Melanie Griffith

Complexity! And passion. Fire lights the Rooster in queer, exaggerated ways, causing him to be born tormented, difficult and yes . . . fiery! Fire Roosters are volatile, craving confrontation and rushing cockily about from head-on collision to head-on collision without sustaining so much as a tiny scratch.

This Rooster seems to thrive on exaltation. He is excited about and involved in everything. Sameness and lack of challenge bore and depress him. He wants to be right inside the action, on the front lines. No matter the toughness of the dare, he will gladly tackle it. His capacity for work is monumental. His endurance is legendary. His state-of-the-art brilliance at absorbing information is staggering. And, finally, his ability to organize others at work and still retain their respect and affection is top drawer. Fire Roosters were born to be world beaters but, unfortunately for them, Fate simultaneously cursed them with a built-in emotional egg whisk.

Fire Roosters should be more successful than they are. They are terminally ambitious, bright, competent people. They make superior lawyers, caring doctors, innovative scientists and competent business people. But because feelings play a primary role in the way these folk handle business, they often make a muddle of it. Whether they are in the thick of a conference, waxing eloquent about the facts in a court case or reciting crucial figures at a bankruptcy hearing, Fire Roosters remain vulnerable to emotional involvement. They can be swayed into submission if the boss's wife has had a miscarriage, feel sorry because the accountant is so fat, fudge their plea because the other lawyer's husband just lost his job – anything emotional which enters the Fire Rooster's mind during business hours is a potential danger to the outcome of his efforts. Objectivity eludes him.

This person is impulsive, headstrong and cannot be easily reasoned with. Conjugal life with a Fire Rooster is a monument to friction and very often becomes explosive to the point of being unbearable. He can be tyrannical and despotic, too, especially if his pride is offended. The Fire Rooster believes strongly in right over might and earnestly wants the truth to out. But if voicing the truth involves showing his own vulnerability or letting down his guard, the Fire Rooster may just balk and miss the point altogether: his promises are often little more than promises. He's emotionally fragile, needing to be liked as well as to enjoy the thrill of victory. He fails because he's conflicted: he doesn't want to apply the rules of ruthlessness to his own advancement yet because he is so intellectually gifted for clarity, he can see perfectly well what is needed to succeed.

On the bright side, the Fire Rooster is a fabulous friend, a garrulous and amusing companion and an honest, truthful colleague. In society, he enjoys his role as nonconformist and is sometimes even exhibitionistically Bohemian to prove a point. He has a sound sense of morality but will not go out of his way unless you go out of yours to espouse causes or perform good deeds. He is a tit-for-tat person whose love of honesty and talent for being brutally frank carries him blithely along on the crest of his own enthusiasm. He crashes when he confronts emotional imperatives with which he cannot reason. But, because he is a Rooster, even repeated failures and torrential setbacks don't daunt his courage or dampen his pluck. He was born to bounce back.

As he is easily dubbed puritanical in his approach to sex, this sorely fraught Rooster might be better off living in a cloister or taking up some ascetic course of action that doesn't demand much emotional involvement. Well invested, the Fire Rooster's richly hued emotional fortune can produce excellent creative results. But if he chooses to become an artist, he will require both insulation and protection from the outside world.

The Earth Rooster

1813 Richard Wagner, Giuseppe Verdi
1909 Kate Smith, Margaret Sullivan, Errol Flynn, Andrei Gromyko, James Reston, Jose Ferrer, Guy de Rothschild, Robert Ryan, James Mason, Elia Kazan, Joseph Mankiewicz, Germain Montero, Stavros Niarchos, David Niven, Douglas Fairbanks Jr

A powerful intellect coupled with a flair for the aesthetic, feminine side of life gives this Rooster a talent for nuance and creativity which surpasses that of his square-cut Rooster brothers and sisters. Because of his gift of the gab, some find the Earth Rooster exasperatingly vague and accuse him of not sticking to the point when he gives his meandering speeches. His ability to grapple with abstract concepts allows him great verbal latitude but for those who worship the concrete, his mental wanderings can seem incomprehensible. But not to worry: this Rooster has his finger on the fact button, too.

His thinking processes can best be termed 'penetrating' and his critical abilities, 'dead accurate'. When he has to hit the nail on the head, an Earth Rooster always goes straight to the point, remembering every single detail and date of what went before. He will never let his interlocutor get away with fudging so much as a single figure. It's almost as if, to counter his own tendency to vagueness, he feels obliged to be ruthlessly factual. Earth Roosters have elephantine memories, minds like steel traps and common sense enough to manage both Hungary and Yugoslavia single-handed.

This is an uncommonly elegant person of regal bearing whose sense of humor – a twinkle, wink or swift ambiguous glance – always shines through his slightly forbidding façade. It is his great luck to have excellent health and frequently to live to a great age. Not only does he live a long time in fine fettle, the Earth Rooster ages gracefully, retains his agile quick wit and rarely suffers symptoms of senility. I know three 1909 Roosters and am certain that today any one of them could tackle a battery of the taxing exams we set our eighteen-year-olds. Earth Roosters grow old with aplomb, remaining flinty and individualistic but losing the anxiety of their troubled youth to become serene and accepting.

The Earth Rooster only reaches his cruising speed once he has found true love. As he is somewhat timid, in youth he doesn't always dare to be forward with the opposite sex. An air of naïve embarrassment may deter others from attempting to seduce this reserved, conservative creature. He is unlikely to bring home some fly-by-night lover picked up at a singles bar, usually taking up with someone met through a cousin or at a family gathering or wedding. They often marry later than their peers and because they choose so carefully and wait for the right person they rarely get divorced.

Sexual passion is not the forte of this deeply loving person. No tender pats on the head, overt signs of affection, poetic *billets doux* or exotic love potions for this no-nonsense character. The Earth Rooster prefers to keep love pure and sane, never allowing his pristine image to become muddled with maudlin scenes or sticky with sentiment.

To get on well professionally, Earth Roosters need a support network. Working for a family concern or large corporation suits them as they always enjoy playing an integral part in a communal effort. These people make excellent accountants, bankers, doctors, architects and designers. They are careful with details and non-impulsive. Although they may have some rough financial patches, Earth Roosters don't usually go bankrupt or lose their fortunes through foolish investments.

The Metal Rooster

1921 Paul Scofield, Rodney Dangerfield, Charles Bronson, Joseph Papp, Dirk Bogarde, Gordon Macrae, Deborah Kerr, Hugh Downs, Sugar Ray Robinson, James Jones, Steve Allen, Deanna Durbin, Satyajit Ray, Simone Signoret, Jane Russell, Gower Champion, Giovanni Agnelli, Mario Lanza, Manitas de Plata

Here is a creature born to be on the stage, in the movies or just smack in the middle of his own living room, putting on a show for his family. The Metal Rooster is a performer, a life-and-soul-of-the-party type.

People either like this vehement person immensely or have trouble tolerating him. Metal Roosters are sometimes boastful: they like to blow their own trumpets, share their success stories and those of their family and generally let you know how terrific they are. Although this trait can be tiresome, the Metal Rooster's purpose is neither egotistical nor greedy. He doesn't want to impress anyone because he needs or wants something from them. Rather, it is part of his bombastic nature. Although some find it irritating others, because this person is usually funny and imaginative, adore being invited to witness the daily spectacle and manage to live happily ever after with this incorrigible entertainer.

If he doesn't learn to temper it while young, this brash, cocky person's tongue can get him into trouble throughout his life. He is incapable of diplomacy and has a way of blurting out indelicate truths at the most inopportune moments, finding failure and rejection where he might have encountered success and approval. When chided for being too candid, the Metal Rooster may fly into a short-lived fit of defensive rage. He isn't the type to bear a grudge. But, given his bent for speechmaking, his verbose spates of bad temper can be impressive enough to cloud an otherwise sunny afternoon.

The Metal Rooster loves organization: he needs to keep things neat and tidy – a place for everything and everything in its place. He doesn't like to be interrupted when conjuring new tricks or employed at his favorite hobby. He cannot stand having too much improvisation inflicted on him.

All of the above borderline old-maidish traits may cause a Metal Rooster to spend his adult life alone, without a full-time partner, children or pets to disrupt the life he has so meticulously planned for himself.

Metal Roosters have conservative political opinions. They make excellent policemen and, as they crave movement, thrive on travel and enjoy being expatriate, may find lucrative secure positions with such organizations as the FBI or Interpol. Of course, their inveterate verbal indiscretion might hamper their progress in jobs requiring top secret classifications. But the Metal Rooster is bright and, with a little help from his friends, can certainly learn how to keep his trap shut in life-or-death circumstances.

The Metal Rooster is tailor-made for jobs in theater, cinema and TV. If he does not choose to perform, he should try to become involved in production. When he makes it in this difficult profession, he will certainly have lots of fans and followers who will cheer him along and keep his career moving ahead. He is a natural for stand-up comedy routines, as a talk-show host and might make a superb newscaster, roving reporter and even war correspondent.

The Water Rooster

1813 Kierkegaard
1873 Sergei Rachmaninoff
1933 Zoë Caldwell, Joan Rivers, Willie Nelson, Carol Burnett, Rod McKuen, Flip Wilson, Michael Caine, Quincy Jones, Philip Roth, Joan Collins, Roman Polanski, Dorothy Loudon, George Segal, 'Jimmy' Goldsmith, Sacha Distel, Costa-Gavras, Jayne Mansfield, Kim Novak, Tammy Grimes, Shari Lewis

Here we encounter the multi-talented Rooster *par excellence.* With all of the most important Rooster strengths and failings united, the Water Rooster might be said to be the model for all other Roosters. He is serious. He is flinty and meticulous. He talks about himself a good bit. He pampers his appearance as well as his wardrobe. He is a willing traveller and adores adventure. He knows how to work long and hard to attain a goal. He suffers many setbacks yet, no matter how far he is put in arrears, this Rooster can *always* find a new way to make a living out of nothing.

There are, however, a few special points about the Water Rooster that set him apart. He is ultra adaptable. He's not rigid but he does have conservative views on almost everything – except his own rather sketchy pattern of fidelity – which he accepts as his right and privilege. Ironically, the Water Rooster is also jealous and possessive of his lovers and mistresses. For him, the double standard applies.

Why? Because he said so. Water Roosters either get to be the boss or else they pick up their bags and go home.

The Water Rooster loves to be surrounded. The more people who ring him up in any given day, the happier he is. He seeks out the company of friends and family and will go to great lengths to help them succeed. He entertains a lot and is often a fine cook and generous host. Possibly because he is so eager for companionship, he may, at times, lend a hand to someone less scrupulous than himself. If he is not careful, he may be used by ruthless folk who profit from his goodwill and give nothing in return.

The Water Rooster is thin-skinned. He cannot abide being criticized, advised, meddled with or – God forbid – reprimanded. Even if he knows he has made mistakes or is about to dive into a barrel of rattlesnakes, he does not wish to be reminded or warned of it. His reactions are not positive to even the mildest suggestion on how he might alter his approach or modify his thinking. If you don't want to lose his friendship, don't try to play truth games with the Water Rooster. If you dare to say one piercingly true thing in his presence, he'll become nasty and hostile. He may only pout for a time. But he may never call you again.

Essentially, the Water Rooster suffers from an inferiority complex. He often wishes that he were someone more fortunate whose parents had left him a fortune, a string of influential contacts in the business world or, better still, a chain of supermarkets to call his own. This Rooster often carries a chip on his shoulder about the wrongs he feels society has committed against him but, as he will not listen to the truth about himself nor look squarely at his real place in the world, he often has to face failure, which increases his inferiority complex. As he grows older, the circle of events becomes more and more vicious. If he cannot let down his guard and learn to accept advice, he may become so disgruntled that, by middle age, he may become terminally embittered, dropping out of society and ending his life as a happy hippie or homeless bum.

Despite his unflagging energy and industriousness, the Water Rooster would secretly like to be rich. He often imagines himself ensconced in a luxurious environment where satin sheets are the norm and silk pajamas *de rigueur*. He even dreams of plenty of leisure time to lie about reading novels and books on philosophy. Yet Water Roosters are not good at being lazy as they get bored easily by having too much time on their hands. Therefore, this dream of *far niente* usually remains just a dream.

It is not in the Water Rooster's destiny to strike it rich overnight. If he marries a wealthy woman whose father owns the biggest construction business in town, the old man will certainly go bankrupt the week after the wedding or die and leave all his money to some charity. If he enters into some get-rich-quick business deal where he feels certain to make a mint in a week, the Better Business Bureau may close him down or someone will report on TV that his products are defective. The Water Rooster is born to labor. He is both talented for and fated to scratch a living out of the most arid of ground and, above all, to stick with it day after day, building a solid nest egg until he has amassed a fortune. His lot may be laborious but it is nothing to be ashamed of.

Water Roosters have a seductive streak. Not only are they excellent talkers but they have a charming way with words which renders them irresistible as salespeople, lovers, advertisers, politicians and teachers.

Loving one of these masterful Water Roosters is a full-time job. They don't like to be left alone and cannot tolerate idleness. They have to be adulated and adored – but even if they get more than their ration of kudos, they still may not always be true to their mate.

Rooster health

The Rooster anxiety quotient is well above average. Because of this creature's excessive, constant and implacable nervousness, his permanent waking hour mode is full speed ahead. Tension is the Rooster's full-time companion. And enemy number one.

What's worse, the Rooster's private life is in a permanent tailspin. Take a day, any day: the Rooster is exhausted because his mother won't stop phoning him at two a.m. to complain that he doesn't take good enough care of himself. It is true that he has had serious chronic bronchitis for six weeks now but he cannot possibly take time to go to a doctor because he's been working so much overtime lately. And the Rooster's landlord has just announced that he's going to be evicted because the lovely old building he lives in will be demolished to make way for a housing project. Too bad. The Rooster has just invested a considerable sum in having the vintage chimneys restored. Never mind, this is a normal Rooster day. Crazy. Busy. Full of potential dangers and impending setbacks. Roosterish. How can a Rooster manage not to self-destruct? How does he keep from exploding or falling ill or having a heart attack?

Well, Roosters are tough, resilient, strong-minded and cocky as hell. When they feel sick, they refuse to think about it. Roosters don't take to their beds. You won't find them lying down to rest an aching head, sore feet or weary bones. The Rooster resists fatigue, fights off ill health and never malingers. He may complain, moan and even sigh about how overworked he is but he never gives up. Just when you think he's about to succumb to the effects of protracted effort, he suddenly perks up. 'Hey, fellows!' he cries. 'Let's tote that barge one more time.' He is always setting an example, urging his cohorts to dig in deeper and try harder.

Roosters are bricks – until, one day, they drop down dead. The healthy Rooster performs perfectly but he isn't nearly as resistant as he would like to think. His body always gives out before his will gives up.

The chronic ailments plaguing Roosters are systemic, internal. They will thus concern the homeopath, acupuncturist and osteopath as well as the psychologist and neuro-psychiatrist. With women Roosters all hormone-based functions are in danger of falling out of synch: stress, tension and pent-up nervousness create imbalances in the endocrine glands which play havoc with Madame Rooster's general health. She is more than prone to suffering all the standard gynecological troubles such as pre-menstrual syndrome (depression, tearfulness, rage and weakness) painful menstruation and hemorrhage. She will be subject to vaginitis, ovarian cysts, cystic breast disease and inflammation of the sexual organs. She may find it difficult to become pregnant and, if she does conceive, may have frequent miscarriages.

Not only is her hormonal picture fairly bleak, but Madame Rooster entertains morose thoughts about death and has a fascination with self-destruction. She often grapples with harrowing dreams or imagines violent situations where her life is in jeopardy. She knows that to be well and thrive, she must struggle to control the urge to follow her bent for self-punishment. Because she is mostly a responsible person (even though she often won't seek treatment until it's much too late) she takes pains to remain mentally on an even keel. But the effort it requires to steady herself day after day is taxing to the nervous system, which confers on this tight woman's poor cranium some of the world's most painful migraine headaches.

Alternative medicine is the friend of Rooster woman. Painkillers and tranquilizers do her very little long-term good as they may serve to palliate the symptom but do nothing for the cause. Her ailments are best handled homeopathically. Also, she ought not to hesitate to see a psychotherapist regularly and not infrequently take a few days' vacation far from her regular source of tension. She should take care to avoid people who pump her energy for their own purposes, steer clear of anxious souls who drain her of her strength and flee anyone in her entourage who has depressive or suicidal tendencies. The female Rooster must protect her fragile nervous system against both inner and exterior onslaughts or serious long-term debilitating illness may ensue.

Despite an appearance of flawless health, Rooster men are far from immune to illness and suffer chronic complaints. Of course, like his sister Rooster, the male of the species prefers to ignore symptoms, pretend he is not in pain and carry on until he drops. Mr Rooster is affected by ailments concerning the head: chronic sinusitis, allergic rhinitis, internal ear disorders, raging toothaches and (although less grave and penetrating than those of his female counterpart) monster tension headaches. His over-sensitive nervous system may also lead him to contract stomach ulcers, constipation, hemorrhoids, misplaced vertebrae, discs and other lower back problems.

Most of all, Rooster health problems are psychosomatically based. The anxiety, stress and tension which cause his physical ills result from feelings of self-doubt, a preoccupation with violence and destruction and a morbid need to live permanently on the edge of an abyss. To combat these feelings the Rooster needs to be able to talk them through, confront his fears and demons with professional help and learn how to ease up on himself. He can also find a way to channel his energies through relaxation techniques such as yoga. He should engage in some sport, especially one that tires him physically and demands so much concentration that the Rooster ceases to concentrate on himself – perhaps tennis, soccer, mountaineering, skin diving, car racing, wind surfing and competition swimming. Martial arts such as karate, kung fu, tai chi or judo might also provide an excellent outlet for his nervous tension.

Roosters are lucky. They are born with strong digestions and have an abstemious or ascetic streak: they are often careful to monitor their fat and sugar intake, only feasting at a party or holiday celebration. The daily ingestion of lecithin (eggs and sesame products), a substance which protects the nervous tissues, is recommended.

Rooster futures

What the Rooster should expect from the next twelve Chinese animal years

2008, the Earth Rat year – Cut back on extravagances. Stop thinking you can just blithely fly off any old where, spend a few days enjoying yourself in Paris or Marrakech or Bali and still come up smelling like a rose. You Roosters are not very flexible and tend to crowd yourselves into a corner. If you're working, then the job becomes the only thing you can think about or do. You obsess, overwork and burn out very quickly. Then, of course, you feel sorry for yourself and decide that you are owed a break. But once again, instead of just lying down and reading a fat novel for a couple of days at home, you must move about. So you jet off to just the *place* you fancy with just the *right* climate and the *tastiest* food and the *best* people. Then, as soon as you are there, you start shopping up all the money you earned whilst overworking and burning out. Is this beginning to sound like a pattern? Well, the Rat year is a good year for you Rooster people . . . but only if you break this madcap pattern of yours and espouse rest and relaxation in your own surroundings. Sit still, for heaven's sake. Take breaks during the day to go to yoga classes. Meditate. Do t'ai chi or take pilates courses. And instead of spending your hard-earned burnout cash on air travel and wine, put a bunch away in the bank and let it earn you some interest. Slow down or die.

2009, the Earth Ox year – The Ox is your biggest booster. In fact, if you have not yet got amorously entangled with one of these steadying creatures, you have been missing the last train to paradise. Oxen tone Roosters down. Their sedate influence chops the Rooster velocity in half and allows for introspection and self-realization. As you Roosters normally do not fancy soulful thought and are just about never after anything more profound than a new outfit, a showplace house or a gourmet meal, the presence of the Ox this year helps add depth to your excessively materialistic ruminations. This year you may find out that there is more to life than stuff. Love is in the air and in this relationship you are the 'lovee' – i.e. the other person is desperately fond of you. Because you are so certain of this unconditional affection, you tend to imagine that you can get away with all manner of capriciousness (affairs, flirting, weekends off, etc). Be more gentle. The lover in question is beginning to learn to set limits and you may lose him or her to someone far sweeter and more attentive. You would do well to order up some gorgeous flowers and tickets to a tropical island paradise for two, or your loved one may get itchy feet. Money will be plentiful. But stop buying things anyway. Hold off on all wardrobe purchases – not because it's wasteful – but because you really don't need to own thirty pairs of designer jeans.

2010, the Metal Tiger year – For Roosters, the Tiger can be a pal and even a chum. But Tigers move around a lot and they move rapidly. Roosters are hardly slowpokes, but they will have a devil of a time keeping up with Tiger cronies this year. Of course, you can't back out now, so the slickest tactic will be to put on your skates and speed up or else risk losses – both financial and personal. It isn't only the breakneck pace that befuddles Roosters in Tiger years. It's also the multiplicity of changes imposed on them by the unpredictable tawny beast. Roosters are schedule people who enjoy structure and cleave to order. Moreover, Roosters require a modicum of comfort. They may appear audacious and seem to be able to adapt quickly. But in fact, although they often love to journey to and tour distant lands, Rooster-born people are downright conservative in their travel choices. You won't find many Rooster people hiking with backpacks in Patagonia or riding a bicycle a thousand miles through rugged terrain to help stamp out poverty. But Tigers fancy adventures both elegant and rough and, if they get the bug for a cause, they can and will walk across the thousand miles of rock and river to help stamp out poverty. So this year Roosters should be prepared to accept changes in routine, upheaval at work and at home, and setbacks both big and small. Keep up the cadence and you win. Slow down, and you will be outrun by Tiger competitors of every stripe.

2011, the Metal Cat year – Relieved to be out of the lunatic Tiger year, all Roosters will be able to breathe more freely this year. The refined and squeamish Cat feels neither here nor there about you and will for the most part stay out of your way. As you are not one to upset apple carts or make unnecessary waves, you are welcome in this year to advance your own projects and will, if you apply yourself as diligently as you usually do, make great strides. As the ambience surrounding you is less frenzied than last year, you can actually think straight and are not in fear of slowing down lest you be ambushed by some unexpected disaster. Your love picture remains bland. But not to worry. Next year promises to bring you both passion and commitment from someone you can actually imagine living with. Meanwhile, you ought to use the calm of this Cat year to clear up loose ends in your finances and tackle the messier issues beleaguering your family. Intruders may seek to damage your property this year. Invest in an alarm system or get a giant-sized pooch to guard your home. It's also an outside possibility you may be cheated out of a sizeable chunk of money. If you take precautions with all the new people you meet, work with or employ (checking their background and testing their mettle in the workplace), you should be able to avert the danger.

2012, the Water Dragon year – The Dragon enthuses you. You find his turbo-charged energy inspiring. You are also an energetic type. But your force is flinty and your demeanor stonier. The Dragon is all flames and clamor. He's throwing a party a minute, dragging people in off the street to celebrate any old holiday. And if there isn't a holiday, he or she will invent one for the occasion. You will certainly be among the guests at most or all of these bashes. Enjoy! But do remember that there is work to be done. You might want to start a business or open a few branch offices of the business you already have. You will be earning more money too. New capital. New energy. New love in your life! He or she will probably be someone you never imagined meeting. Someone rather unlike your standard type. If you always loved short, stocky men with curly hair, this one will be a tall, thin, bald geezer. If you always went out with airhead blondes with long legs, you will fall madly in lust with a short, dark-haired beauty with brains. Whatever you were used to, this year will bring the reverse. This character will not only infuse your life with soulful passion – he or she might even constitute a possible life partner. Take it slow. No commitments until eighteen months have gone by. Promise?

2013, the Water Snake year – Generally speaking, for Roosters, the Snake is a piece of cake. You two understand each other – viscerally. It's not emotional or even psychological. Your harmony with Snakes is at the gut level. You are attracted to them and vice versa. So the sailing should be smooth this year in everything related to comfort and luxury, money and good vibes. However, there is a cloud on the horizon and it resides in your love sector. Things were almost too good to be true between you and your sweetie. Then, at the end of last year, there came a major row which, in hindsight, you know full well was based on a gross misunderstanding. Up to you to make amends. And begging people's pardon is not something you do with ease. You are both proud and cocky. And we like that about you. But when you make a huge social faux pas, you must accept the blame and do some serious backtracking in order to regain favor in the eyes of the victim. You probably forgot to listen for a few weeks and missed the gist of what was happening, which caused the rift in the first place. Then you were so surprised when taken to task, you flipped out and left the premises without a backward glance. Now you would love to apologize. But because you are a self-congratulatory Rooster person, you don't know how. Let me show you. Here. It's easy. Go ahead. Get down on your knees and say you are sorry. You won't be *sorry* you did.

2014, the Wood Horse year – By this time, with all that went down over the past few months, your love life ought to be back on its feet (and you up off your knees). One thing Roosters tend not to do is listen. You act and manage and run things efficiently. You remain alert and on schedule. But you sometimes miss out because you think you know it all and you don't want to hear any new stuff which might clutter up your synapses and/or cause you to have to change your ways. Listen up. The Horse year is a workaholic's dream. You are a labor-intensive person. Even if you were retired, you would be *doing* something. Cooking, reading three books at once, gardening, jogging, building or . . . shopping. You are a kind of Renaissance person who likes to have a finger in every pie and an iron in all the fires. Your active nature suits the Horse's temperament down to the ground. If you continue to forge so avidly ahead on all your projects, you will meet with no obstacles to progress this year. Family squabbles crop up here and there during Horse years. You can't sort them out, so don't tire yourself trying. Illness may strike a loved one. Go to his or her side. Hold hands and coo soothing words of comfort. Nothing like solid support from a sturdy Rooster pal to boost one's morale. Eat more protein. Cut back on sugar.

2015, the Wood Goat year – The Goat is more creative than you ever hope to be. Goats live perfectly well by guess and by golly. They like to be free to gambol and graze in fertile fields which (preferably) don't even belong to them. You Roosters are dead serious about most everything – particularly your finances. So the capricious nature and tone of this Goat year does not exactly enchant you. In fact, it prodigiously annoys you. Why is it so difficult to get anything done this year? How come nobody is on time? How come the schedules got altered and we have to work overtime without a break? *Who stole my routine?* You may grumble and grouse, mutter and moan. But trust me, it will not change a thing. The Goat is comfortable in chaos. Especially chaos of his own design. You freak out in chaotic situations and long for order to be restored *illico presto.* Unfortunately, you can't have it your way this year. And not getting your way tends to unnerve you. You may spend much of this Goat year in a tizzy. My advice? Slow yourself down. Take a mild tranquilizer. Get more sleep and stop fretting about what cannot be fixed. Your significant other will help you to relax and take it easier. And if he or she fails to calm your nerves, try psychiatry.

2016, the Fire Monkey year – This Monkey year may inflame your temper even more than did the Goat. Monkeys are fairly organized and do manage to keep to routine. But they are tricksters. Monkeys manipulate events and people in order to get what they want. You Rooster people prefer direct, uncomplicated communication and action. You get things done by doing them yourself. Not the Monkey. The Monkey gets things done and solves problems by circuitous and not always truthful methods. And if Monkeys can get other people to sort things out for them – they will. So during this Monkey year, you will still be griping. But you won't be cranky because the trains don't run on time and the schedules have been altered. You will simply deplore the fact that, in order to understand what's going on in this tumultuous year, you have to read between the lines. Instead of being able to sit down at a conference table and hash out a budget for the year, you will be obliged to watch for ulterior motives in your associates and partners. Even your private life will be clouded by this sense that something is not being told to you. Secrets are being kept. This mood of unexpressed chicanery gets on your nerves. Although your nerves were certainly run ragged last year, this year may be worse. You will feel somewhat lost, like a deer in the headlights.

Huh? What is going on here? you wonder. Keep wondering. But hang on. Next year life will improve – vastly.

2017, the Fire Rooster year – Yippee! Your very own year to rule, to boss people around, whip them into shape and enforce all the laws of the land. It was about time you got a little respite from the last two untidy years and were able to put things to rights. You will have to watch your money outlays this year, because Rooster years are like that. But you don't mind keeping detailed accounts and watching each penny as it slides from your purse. What you do mind is being forced to allow less competent souls to give you orders when you know perfectly well how best to control yourself. Do remember that this year you must sit down quietly somewhere to ponder and plot the next dozen years of your life. Every twelve years, we must make a plan. How do you intend to build the next part of your existence? How do you mean to live out the years ahead? What are your priorities? You have got to the age you are and have begun to wonder what you can do to improve your lot. The big question to ask yourself is, 'What do I want?' Then set about imagining where you want to be in twelve years. How will you live? With whom? Where? If it's money you are after, make a business plan and stick to it. If it's love you want, get cracking on finding the person to share your life with. If you want to be an artist, take steps to do just that. Year by year, make lists of goals, and then (because you are so good at routine) make the necessary adjustments in your current life to adapt to your future.

2018, the Earth Dog year – Rooster survival depends on enduring a series of hair-raising roller-coaster rides. You coast up and down every breathtaking hill and vale, kicking and screaming. But you always come out smiling, once again making money and living the good life. In Dog years, there is a lot of resistance to people who make money. The Dog represents justice for all. He wants his subjects to involve themselves in causes, take up cudgels and parade through the streets demanding reforms in all social programs. The Dog makes life more pleasant for those people who join him in demonstrations and agree with his schemes to improve the lot of one and all. You, of course, might join a protest march against war or against tax hikes. But I don't see too many Roosters at rallies about building shelters for the homeless or providing equal health care for everyone. You are too much of an individualist to go joining forces with a bunch of bleeding-heart liberals. You just want to have a quiet life where the dates on your calendar stay the same from year to year and don't have to mean poverty marches this year and immigration rallies the next. This year, I suggest you stay out of the line of fire. Don't let the Dog catch you raking in too many shekels, or he may force you to finance his campaign for educating all of Africa. The Rooster roller coaster is on the way up the first hill this year. Slow but sure progress is guaranteed.

2019, the Earth Pig year – Where the Dog might be proud to have 'plenty of nothin', the Pig is delighted to offer us plenty of plenty. You needed a break, and this year is exactly that for Roosters. Your to-do list will shrink as the year passes because there is absolutely no obstacle on the horizon. You will not only enjoy the sense of security and prosperity which characterizes this Pig year, but you will take pleasure in the bawdy side of things as well. Pigs are known for their virtue, good taste and purity of heart. But they are also given to expressions of excessive sensuality. Pigs frequently tell dirty jokes. Other people have paintings of landscapes in their bedrooms. Pigs have nudes. Pigs watch porn films and dial up erotica on the Internet. I agree that virtue juxtaposed on lasciviousness is an odd combo. But it's very real. Pigs are a little bit 'piggy' about things sexual. This does not shock or offend you Roosters. You might not be the type to recount a smutty joke. But if one is told in your company, you may just guffaw and beg for more. In light of the Pig's penchant for the sexy, you or your significant other may be tempted to stray this year. If your lover confesses a tiny infidelity, please don't feel you must retaliate by committing one of your own. Forgive. But don't forget.

The Disquiet Dog

Dear Doggie,

Man's best friend indeed: you are honest, faithful and sincere. You give real value in return for affection. You are an agreeable companion – when you're in a good mood. To know you is to love you, except when you let go with a brutish comment or snap sarcastic zingers at us poor unsuspecting bystanders. You have a bark on you, Doggie, that makes even your most ferocious bite seem painless.

But you selflessly redeem yourself. You believe in justice for all and willingly take up worthy causes and bear weighty crosses against unfair practices. You respect tradition and value honor. You take real pleasure in helping a senior citizen cross a busy street. In life's big Western movie, you definitely wear a white cowboy hat.

A finely honed critical sense allows you to sniff out deceit and track down fraud. Trouble is, this flair for truth is so keen that it sometimes causes you to become pessimistic. Terminal disappointment and even depression may ensue.

As a hedge against this tendency to hopelessness, try to surround yourself with amusing people whose optimism and *joie de vivre* help you maintain your own equilibrium. Marry up with a carefree Tiger, a fantasy-loving Horse or a cozy, reassuring Cat. At a tender age you will begin to notice that the world is a very unfair place. You'll get involved in crusades and seek to right basic wrongs.

My advice? Try not to be so painfully righteous. Accept compromise. Curl up here by the fire and dream of better days.

Doggedly yours,

Suzanne White

In the twentieth and twenty-first century all Dogs were born between the following dates

10	February	1910	and	29	January	1911
28	January	1922	and	15	February	1923
14	February	1934	and	3	February	1935
2	February	1946	and	21	January	1947
18	February	1958	and	7	February	1959
6	February	1970	and	26	January	1971
25	January	1982	and	12	February	1983
10	February	1994	and	30	January	1995
29	January	2006	and	17	February	2007
16	February	2018	and	4	February	2019

The Dog ID card

Lasting symbols have special powers. Enhance your self-image by surrounding yourself with tangible signs of your own identity and make these symbols known to your friends and loved ones. Use them daily and they will bring you luck, security and a feeling of personal worth.

Your best	*Your favorite*
color is turquoise	food is meat pie
flower is calendula	animal is dog or sheep
fragrance is balsam	drink is strong coffee
tree is cherry	spice is clove
flavor is meaty	metal is lead
birthstone is ruby	herb is marjoram
lucky number is 9	musical instrument is guitar

The Dog is yin ***The Dog's motto is 'I worry'***

When all is well and the sheep are safely in the barn, Dogs are attentive, well meaning, helpful, warm-hearted, altruistic, modest, devoted, philosophical, dutiful, discreet, intelligent and enthusiastic.

But when panic strikes (at least once a day) Dogs can turn nasty, mean-spirited, disagreeable, bad-tempered, self-righteous, judgemental, quarrelsome, accusing, nervous, anxious and impossible to live with.

Beware of the damned Dog

Dogs are born old and get younger as they age. A wrinkled brow is the Dog child's trademark. A scowl seems built into the taut features of the adolescent while young adult Dogs shake their heads a lot and tsk and cluck at the stupidity and grabbiness of those who run the systems of which they so disapprove. Middle-aged Dogs develop a curling sneer which enhances their acid commentary about everything from the depressing state of the world to wasted resources, drug abuse, war, corruption, ecological disarray and the utter selfishness and greed of humankind when it comes to dividing the spoils of the massive rape and pillaging we all like to call capitalism.

After the age of forty-five, Dogs begin to mellow. A fifty-year-old Dog may still complain that the trains don't run on time, about the filth and danger in bus stations and parks and trot out a tirade on almost any subject which touches on social reform. But the older he gets, the less the Dog takes his own snarls and criticisms seriously. When he's about to retire from his life's work, the weary Dog will usually cease tilting at windmills and chasing ways to solve the problems of the poor mindless world, and be satisfied to surrender his ideals. An older Dog is a happier, more contented Dog.

Dogs are the original radicals. They profess to care more about humankind than they do about money or power, comfort, success or intimacy or, more especially, themselves. Because of this streak of altruism, these devoted creatures spend much of their time either attempting to do something about injustice or railing because so little can *be* done.

As a social reformer and minor revolutionary, the well-meaning, innocent Dog is most vulnerable to disappointment. He wants to believe in the basic goodness of humankind, to champion the causes of the misunderstood and to help right all wrongs that he sets himself up for disaster. Norman Mailer (1922–3 Dog) slaved for years, to get a murderer, Jack Abbot, released from prison. Mailer persisted because he was stubbornly determined to see justice done. As he saw it, Abbot had paid his debt to society. He had reformed and had written eloquently about his pain. To the militantly caring Mailer, years of campaigning for justice are not too much to give.

Thanks to his champion's dogged purposefulness, Abbot was released. He was able to resume a normal life, have his writing published and make some honest money. Then, not so long after his release, Abbot had words with a waiter in a restaurant on the Upper East Side of New York, invited him to step outside on the sidewalk and stabbed him dead. So much for social reform.

The Dog's social life is often skimpy. As he doesn't trifle with primping and feels he must not waste essential time on romance, he will, when possible, skirt all vain activities such as partying and dancing and living it up, in favor of sitting at home scorning society's frivolity, attending to duty and assuming responsibility. He misses many a chance to meet people, to find himself a lover or to surround himself with friends. The Spartan-minded Dog hardly ever pampers himself or indulges in self-improvement plans. He'd be happy to limit himself to hair shirts and cold showers which he feels sufficiently hygienic for one and all. The Dog has no time for layabouts who wallow in opulence while millions are starving and dying in Third World countries.

To the Dog everything is serious. He is sober, thoughtful and sincere, his profoundest conviction that life is a purgatory wherein he will never find happiness nor be at peace. He is scorchingly aware that we are all but passing through this grave and ponderous place we like to call our existence. He can never quite figure out what everybody's getting so excited about when they go around demanding more joy and pleasure from life. He cannot help but find them foolish. Yet he loves them. In an indulgent big-brotherly (yet reproving) way the Dog adores his fellow man, especially the underdog.

Yet although much of his behavior may appear condescending and is frequently performed in a dry spirit, tinged with personal sacrifice, the sharpest criticism and self-abnegation, the Dog is truly the nicest person alive.

Curmudgeonly? Judgemental? Picky? Punctilious? Yes, all of those. But when you discover how to pet them just right and massage that little spot right behind their left ear, Dogs make absolutely the best and most honorable companions on earth. Their touching candor and devotion quite outshine the occasional irascible grouchiness and holier-than-thou self-righteousness.

Getting to know a Dog is not always easy. Dogs are very often impenetrably shy. Except for the occasional terse, caustic remark, for which they are well known and even feared, when confronted by strangers, Dogs tend to keep their own counsel. Once you know them, they may hold forth for hours, outlining past and future campaigns, providing justifications for attitudes or behavior. But if they haven't met you before and don't know your political views Dogs see no reason to bound into your lap. At a first meeting they rarely try to be charming, communicative or warm.

You'll never catch a wary Dog napping: everybody born a Dog is a watchdog. The Dog evolves his daily life in a perpetual state of defensive vigilance, always on the *qui vive*, for ever attentive, giving the impression of being alert, skittishly wary and so highly strung that he jumps when the phone rings, snaps to attention at the slightest rustle in the next room and nearly bites off your head if you startle him.

The Dog is a moralizer, too. He is not satisfied merely to observe the inequities afoot in the world; he must hold forth on them. 'Of course *they* are keeping it a dark secret, but I heard that there has been a shake-up in the Pentagon,' and 'Have you noticed that the traffic light at the corner has been hanging by a thread for two whole months? Somebody is going to get killed if *they* don't repair it.'

The implication is *always* that the powers that be are trying either to disinform, pull the wool over our eyes to misuse our good faith, extort more taxes from us and keep us from living the way we might choose. The Dog feels strongly that he is born a helpless victim and that organized society has nothing to offer him but chaos. Naturally, then, he assumes that it is his duty to tear the wool from our eyes, keep us apprised of our rights and warn us against believing in hollow promises made by official Santa Clauses. The Dog is our champion. We can always count on him to stay abreast of what *they* are trying to put over us, guarding our liberties and keeping the bigwigs honest. He listens and assesses, surveys and scrutinizes.

Oddly, in spite of his caring nature, the Dog hardly ever gets involved in revolution or perpetrates coups. He is often so disgusted with politics and politicians as to be apolitical. He may refuse to vote; he will find local government abysmally manipulative and shamefully tax-hungry. Will the Dog run for office or even volunteer to sit on the board? Practically never.

The Dog finds so many things wrong with society that he frequently decides at an early age to steer clear of the whole shebang. As he is incapable of hypocrisy and intolerant of lying, cheating, stealing or compromising his conscience, how can he be expected to join the milling masses, the success of whose lifestyle rests solely on how much sanctimonious pretense they can either dispense or swallow in a single day?

As a result of this unwillingness to join 'em if he can't lick 'em, the Dog nearly always opts to lead the life of a confirmed individualist. He despises the lukewarm attitudes necessary to fit in with his peers. He cannot bear the idea of surrendering his ideals and beliefs to the middle-class dream. This does not mean that people born in Dog years are lie-down-and-go-limp hippies. Dogs are *always* stiffly correct, solid citizens. But often, Dogs retreat from the conventional lifestyle, preferring to remain aloof, to hover and observe rather than sacrifice their uniqueness.

Take the example of my middle brother, Peter the Dog. Peter, more intimately known as Howard (after Hughes), was born in 1946. In our family, we are all fairly peculiar but Peter the Dog wins the weirdo contest hands down. He's convivial but a loner, mostly pleasant, loyal, prompt and attentive to duty. Except for his occasional sharp comments about how lazy, conformist, selfish or apathetic everyone else is, Peter the Dog is easy to get on with. He's never moody or self-pitying. But sometimes, when caught off guard or riding on the wings of some new discovery of social wrong-doing that he especially wants to share with you, Peter can be acerbic, sarcastic and bitingly hurtful even to those he loves most.

If only to afford you an idea of why my two other (meaner) brothers call Peter 'Howard', I'll let you in on the most exotic feature of Peter's eccentric lifestyle. Although he supposedly lives in Arizona, he spends most of his life driving round America in a shiny black, spotlessly clean, ultra-safe, air-conditioned, luxury Japanese saloon car with automatic everything. Peter works – he owns two successful companies – but so that he needn't interrupt his favorite pastime he has implemented an ingenious, portable phone system that can be operated both from his vehicle and from motel rooms, while back in Arizona, two long-standing, loyal, well-paid employees take care of daily business in the office.

While Peter the Dog is on the road, he is not making personal sales calls on customers or checking out locations for new offices. Nor is Peter the Dog a marauding Don Juan. Oh no. Dogs are clean freaks and Pete's so paranoid about germs that he'd be more likely to get caught wearing rubber gloves to eat a Big Mac.

Does he drive around to some practical end? Nope. Peter the Dog, alias Howard, is simply driving around watching things, taking stock of the state of the union, chatting with folk in cafés about the weather or the way they think things should be improved.

Last time he got home from one of his cross-country jaunts to visit relatives up in Buffalo, New York, Pete called me. 'The roads in this country are in a terrible state of disrepair,' he said before even saying hello. 'The Illinois Toll Road has craters in it but the worst are the federal roads. You'd think you were in the English Channel when you're only in Kansas or Iowa. It's a scandal!'

Speaking of the English Channel, let me tell you briefly about Peter's first trip to Europe. I insisted, 'Peter, you are forty-six years old. You travel all the time and you have never been to Europe. This has got to stop.' He agreed.

In February we got on a flight for London. Pete hates flying and I'm not exactly Amelia Erhardt. I white-knuckled it while Pete watched the movie. After about five minutes of heaves, swells and fuselage shudders, I was ready to jump out. The seatbelt signs were on and I figured I'd die without seeing my beloved brother again. But Peter the Dog is a born helper, a comforter of the sorrowful and a stand-up friend to the worried. Heeding my inner wails, he rose nervously from his seat, inched his way back and was thrown down next to me. He took my bloodless hand. 'Is this dangerous?' I gasped.

'Oh, yes,' he whispered. 'But he's a good pilot because he's trying to avoid the really big air pockets which could dump this whole crate on that tundra down there.' He leaned over me to point out the site of our impending death. 'He'll probably make it. He seems pretty competent.'

I unfroze my index finger from the seat arm, stroked his paw and said, 'Peter, honey, could you please stop talking?' I realized he had pushed his own nerve considerably to come back, but every word he said scared me more. Peter squeezed my finger and said, 'It's almost over now. At this rate, either we die within seconds or it stops.'

I'm trying to avoid accusing Dogs of pessimism but they often tend to give voice to the blacker side of the burnt toast. They are born uneasy, anxious and fearful of the unknown. They always think they can feel the bogey man around the next bend. They live in a state of perpetual red alert, apprehending every confrontation with the unfamiliar and worrying themselves silly over what usually turns out to be nothing. They bark out a steady stream of warnings to friends and acquaintances of real or imagined impending dangers.

My good friend Bill Burton, the bookselling Dog of the Hamptons, is a perfect example. We never leave the house together without 'Did you turn off the upstairs light? Do you have enough petrol? Where will you park once you get there?'

No matter his position, the Dog will tend to keep a low profile. His innate reserve is much appreciated by his friends, but among acquaintances or strangers he may awaken suspicions or raise doubts as to his intentions. 'Is he being distant just to snub me? Why does he avoid my eyes when I speak to him?' The Dog is not naturally garrulous or overtly enthusiastic but he means no harm. And he is certainly no snob. He is just so easily embarrassed that if someone picks him out of the crowd and chooses to pay him public attention or in any way points up his specialness, he automatically beats a retreat.

Incidentally, one of my favorite editors, Tom Dunne, was born in a Dog year (1946). Tom is an absolute darling, revered for his sound critical judgement and adored for his tenderness with authors. He is doggedly faithful, devoted and loyal to his friends and colleagues. Nobody dislikes this guy, which, in the gossip Mecca we call publishing, is a miracle.

However, before I began writing this book I determined to find out from some of Tom's other authors if they felt as I do that he had this one terrible, bad, impossible Doggish habit. I interviewed three or four and they all agreed. He has one fault: Tom only ever talks on the phone when *he* wants to. He's too shy. He'd rather remain incognito and communicate through professional phone-answerers, mouthpiece people who call themselves 'editorial assistants'. Call him up sometime and see for yourself. 'Tom Dunne's office,' they answer politely.

'Hi, this is Suzanne White. I'm one of your authors. May I speak to Tom Dunne?'

You know the rest. 'He's in a meeting. He hasn't got his shoes on. Got laryngitis. In a pickle. In London. In limbo.' 'InSANE,' I want to scream.

Believe me, in over six years of knowing this darling Doggie, I've tried everything: the long distance 'I'm calling from a Moscow phone booth in a blizzard' ploy; the 'I'm switching to another publishing house' ploy; the 'I'm burning my manuscript page by page until he picks up that phone' ploy. But nothing works. Tom's a Dog; he keeps a low profile and retreats when bidden to interact one to one with another human. Case closed.

Integrity is another area of Dog overkill that I should warn you about. Never do a Dog a favor unless you are ready to accept a giant return on your investment. Take a Dog to lunch and he may surprise you by taking you to Europe. Pay a Dog a compliment and he's liable to thank you with a year's supply of good French wine. Dogs never forget people who make them smile, cheer up their day or give them a warm feeling and they are almost self-sacrificingly generous. When going Dutch, they always pay more than their share. They never forget to bring flowers or return a favor. They would *not* show up at your door empty-handed. Dogs are not profligate gift-givers like Monkeys, nor are they dramatic gesture-makers like Dragons or Tigers. They just remember that all-important token.

Now, we *need* more generous people in the world, for sure, but sometimes this sense of fairness gets out of control. In 1975, when I had just sold my first book in the States, I heard of a friend very ill with cancer in Paris. She was too ill to work, her husband had lost almost all his money in the stock-market crash and they had a young child. These people had always lived well and I couldn't stand the idea of Claire being sick and broke to boot. She deserved to have fun. I wanted to do something so I wrote out a check for $100 and sent it as a gift with a note saying, 'Go to your favorite restaurant on me.'

Years went by. Poor Claire died. Her husband, Nick, (1922 Dog) in true Dog-like fashion, had nurtured, cared for and wept over his adored departed wife. When I went back to Paris in 1979, he was teaching English and dutifully raising his daughter alone.

One day, after I had been back in Paris a few months, Nick sent me a check for $160. I was mystified. I had forgotten the $100 gift. But not Nick. He was repaying what he saw as a debt – with six years' interest at ten per cent per year. I immediately sent his check back, insisting that I had never lent him money in my life. But it came back. Several times. Until one day he got really cranky and I took the money.

There is a side to the Dog which is so militantly selfless that it stops being fun. *His* sense of justice is the *only* sense of justice and sometimes he cannot understand where the other person is coming from.

The Dog is not masochistic. Although he is self-effacing and can be stupidly proud, he is still quite lucid and willingly sees himself objectively. He is also an unbeatably hard, steady worker, who has great powers of concentration and can turn out miles of work where you or I might only turn out an inch. The Chinese say that hard work is the Dog's salvation; work keeps him busy and helps divert him from his constant worries.

The loss of a loved one or rejection can really knock a Dog's composure. More than any other sign, this one requires heavy daily doses of tenderness, kindness, gentleness and love. Dogs do not like to make promises they cannot keep so they are loath to surrender to love in the first place, afraid to commit or to assume responsibility for someone else's feelings, hesitant about taking on moral duties they fear they might not be able to perform. When a Dog does give in to the temptation to love and be loved, he becomes skinned-alive sensitive and ultra-vulnerable to the possibility of failure. Although he may camouflage his feelings behind a ruggedly individualistic stance whence he jokingly protests that he doesn't want to be happily married, the reason that most Dogs do not settle down and raise large families is their fear of rejection.

When this fear becomes reality, Dogs go a little crazy. The Dog enters a relationship where he is the giver and the partner the taker. The couple muddles along, the Dog giving his all and the other feeling guilty at not being able to measure up to her mate's sense of integrity, his honesty, his endurance and belief in their future together. One day, the other has an affair or a dalliance – they are only human – the Dog finds out and has a nervous breakdown.

The mate may explain, plead, say it will never happen again and beg forgiveness but the Dog's inner mirror has been smashed. When he tries to find his life again, he sees only broken faith. He is not usually angry or vindictive, simply broken, crushed and saddened, and has to come to terms with the knowledge that the world is a terrible place full of dreadful, dangerous lies.

Dogs might be able to forgive but they cannot live with hypocrisy or duplicity or tolerate shades of grey. Everything must be clear cut. Standards should be high. Dogs never cheat, fudge or fiddle. Therefore, they cannot conceive of anyone else doing so. The danger here is that the Dog may isolate himself from reality, become embittered and spend the rest of his life in a puritanical state of righteous indignation. He may sacrifice people's feelings to his own sense of what is right. He often ends up alone.

Probably the cutest and yet most infuriating trait which a Dog has is his talent for putting his foot in it. The average Dog is that person who walks into the kitchen when you're cooking your most delicate Roquefort soufflé, wiggles his nose and blurts out, 'Something smells like dirty feet in here.' Or perhaps he reads something you wrote and later hands it back saying, 'You don't need a publisher, you need a psychiatrist.' That's the way Dogs talk. Sensitive and touchy they may be, but they simply aren't able to edit their own words before they let them fly.

How's this for tact? My dentist, Leon Fishel, the handsomest Dog in Paris, is all the things Dogs classically are: he's a worrier; he's cautious; he's conscientious to a fault; he's honest and generous. Like all Dogs, Leon is too good for his own good. One day, while excavating the cavernous furthest recesses of my stricken mouth, he suddenly stood back and gasped, '*Mon Dieu*, Suzanne! You must have been so beautiful when you were young.' That horrible remark was so damned Dog typical that I leaped from the chair, tore off my bib, grabbed a pencil from his desk and wrote it down. 'One day, Leon Fishel,' said I, menacingly, 'you will see your words in print.'

Lady Dog

'Workaholic' is the word which comes immediately to mind when I think of the Dog female. Her stamina, endurance, grit and determination make the world a better place for us all to live in.

The Dog woman always remains alert and lives to serve humanity and right wrongs. She has a sharp tongue and a marshmallow heart. As she's a woman, her style is softer, more gentle, her emotions more readily accessible than those of her biting Dog brothers. As a mother, she's a saintly type. As a lover, the Dog woman is nervous yet tender, warm and giving. As a friend, the Dog woman is for ever.

Attractive – beautiful even in a flinty way – the Dog woman usually has an elongated face, slanting eyes and a short snub nose. Her cheekbones are set attractively high, her forehead is likely to be broad and because, even as a child, the female Dog is often anxious, tiny wrinkles appear early around her mouth and eyes.

No matter how indifferent she tries to appear, the Dog woman almost never succeeds in concealing her emotions. Her sharpish features seem to have been set in perpetual motion at birth. Her bright eyes dart here, there and everywhere at once. Her mouth moves expressively when she talks – and can she talk! The Dog woman is among the most prolix of signs. When she is not speaking, she assumes an air of preoccupation or aloofness. This aura of perplexing mystery is not unattractive: many find it enchanting, intriguing. What, we wonder, can she be thinking? Lady Dog often lowers her glance to avoid head-on scrutiny because her eyes, if ever she deigns to raise them to meet ours, eloquently reveal her feelings.

When she tells a story, the Dog woman knows how to be precise, choose poignant details and use sarcastic humor. Sometimes her attempts to be funny can be a tiny bit on the 'heavy' side. She'll unconsciously overplay a joke or deliberately attempt to be downright slapstick or comical. Yet, as she is so watchful, she instinctively feels her audience's reaction and will shift her approach to please or charm them. The Dog woman likes to hold forth but she is not a true performer. She's a bit too retiring. Yet she is so sensitive to the needs of others and so able to empathize with outsiders that she is able to 'read' their reactions to her stories as she goes along.

Age has an interesting effect on the Dog woman. In her youth, she may appear physically fit, be beautifully turned out, have a flair for style and the ability to wear clothes well. But, no matter how lovely she is, the younger Dog woman doesn't really feel comfortable in her beauty or know how to use her sexuality. Although her fine intellectual capacities propel her through the toughest school curricula – she is frequently that excellent student who gets all the scholarships and does advanced graduate work – emotionally this woman is a late bloomer. Her inner make-up, her self-confidence and her feel for the power of sensuality usually won't emerge until she is at least forty. Maturity has a favorable effect on this worried female's countenance. The onset of the menopause may even improve the Dog woman's appearance, relaxing her striding gait, causing her posture to grow more erect, endowing her with the natural beauty and confidence of age. A Dog woman over sixty can be startlingly beautiful.

The female Dog is more of a nature lover than a show-off. She's not happy as a full-time city slicker. Her roots are in the earth. She prefers farms and streams, orchards and woods to the clangor and hubbub of crowds and urban life. The well-integrated Dog woman has a proud, dignified bearing and appeals to men who appreciate modesty and a certain prudishness. She is not one to apply much make-up as she shies from artifice.

Professionally, this character is a human dynamo. Providing she finds the right ambience to work in where she feels unencumbered by arrogant superiors, can set the parameters herself and make the schedules her way, the Dog woman could rebuild the most war-torn of countries in about half an hour. Once she sets about a task, she simply stays there until it's done. Her physical endurance is admirable, akin to the Ox's, yet quicker, more lithe. She may get aches and pains, and her legs hurt when she's been ironing or typing for five hours, but the control she has over her mind, the disciplined way she can continually kick herself to get going and stay going, her determination and grit are superhuman.

One thing greatly in her favor is that the Dog woman hates to be idle. A naturally nervous woman, she prefers to fill her time with activity and even feverish interaction with others rather than remain broodingly on her own. Black moods quickly overcome her in times of stress and she prefers to be too busy than not busy at all.

One of my all-time favorite Parisian Dogs was born in Portugal in 1946. Her name is Maria-José but her nickname is 'Zazine'. For ten efficient years, Zazine was the *concierge* of the Paris apartment building where I live and which she guarded to within an inch of its life.

A truer Dog was never born. Zazine was devoted, loyal, anxious to please, fretful and hard-working. She mopped the floors of the entrance and corridor at 6 a.m. before she rolled the three huge orange rubbish bins on to the pavement. Then she roused her husband and sons and by 8 a.m. she would have finished the dishes, made the beds and rolled the empty bins back into the courtyard.

Then Madame Muche would arrive to deliver her eight-month-old twins before racing off to work. At 8.05 came Madame Truc with Sandrine and JeanJean, and by 8.15, at least four other babies and pre-schoolers appeared. At 8.25 Zazine started refilling and piling up double pushchairs and buttoning snowsuits so that by 8.30 she stood at the ready to start off for the local primary school where she shed about four. Then she returned home with the rest whom she then put down for naps while she distributed the building's mail. At 9.30, she began the ironing that had been brought in by her customers and at 11.45, bundled everybody up again and went to fetch the lunchtime crowd.

Zazine also looked after seven over-eighty-year-old ladies living in our building. All day long people came and went, asking her for favors or tipping her for accepting a parcel or asking her to remember to let the plumber into an apartment at a certain hour or to watch that the painters on the fourth floor didn't leave before 6 p.m.

Zazine always had something caustic to say about folk of whom she disapproved but she did their dirty work anyway – willingly, faithfully and with a smile.

To make a little extra money, she also took in sewing. She made cushion covers and curtains and did alterations for the neighborhood while the babies slept or climbed, giggled and fought around her feet.

Government-sponsored family day-care centers are subject to rigorous inspection tours and surprise visits from the thin, bespectacled Madame Legrandchef, head of the neighborhood crèche system, were not rare. Zazine was nervous about them – she was afraid the supervisor might disapprove of her sewing. But no matter the interruption, Zazine never missed a single beat with one of those babies.

Although all the above behavior is common to many people who work hard and are conscientious, it is characteristic of the watchful Dog woman's career life. In her own dogged way, Zazine has successfully glued together all the aspects of her watchdog self into a sprawling, successful profession.

In some Dog women there runs a streak of moral rectitude bordering on piety. She doesn't lord it over others – Lady Dog is not usually an openly demonstrative type – but because she is an upstanding, honest person, she refuses to accept that others might fudge, fib or dissimulate. Deceit drives her crazy and desirous of severing relations with the perpetrator.

Worse still, should someone ever accuse *her* of lying, the Dog woman is capable of venting her rage in an impressively exhibitionistic fashion, turning pale, shaking and even fainting from the emotional storm. Such outbursts should be avoided as they may have a deleterious effect on the nervous Dog woman's mental health.

Unfortunately, brushes with unscrupulousness or perfidy cannot always be avoided. If the Dog woman encounters a surfeit of conniving people or is too often manipulated, betrayed or cheated by less honorable souls, she may become paranoid and so distrustful as to cease enjoying human interaction.

Dog women are not only thin-skinned but they are painfully sensitive to what others think of them. Too many unpleasant experiences can break their will to continue to participate. Lots of Dog women retire early, preferring to stay safely at home, leaving public appearances to thicker-skinned folk.

Examples of hypersensitive famous Dog women who have found solutions to the problem of being misused by the milieu and the media are easy to find. The luscious Brigitte Bardot gave up her career early to found an animal rescue foundation, while the fine-boned Sophia Loren married a powerful film director who protected her against the sharks of the film world.

Thanks to their gift for empathy, Dog women frequently devote their lives to taking care of others, heading charity ball committees, raising funds for abandoned drug babies, speaking out for human rights and generally taking care of people and creatures less fortunate or weaker than themselves.

All careers where social progress or comment can be made will attract and suit the Dog woman. She may want to practice law or medicine or enter a related field such as psychiatry or nursing or homeopathy. The earth is her base. She could do well in any profession connected to it, such as conservation, geology, farming, property development or even building. She could be a terrific political speech writer or teacher, a playwright or novelist, a journalist or even a nun or some form of church leader. These serious, talkative and incisively intelligent women are often among the vanguard of feminist causes. 'Rabid feminist' is not an accidental coinage. It is no accident that Mother Theresa was born a Dog in 1910.

Dryness, a hint of reserve, strict personal discipline, X-ray powers of observation and crackling commentary are native to all sensitive Dog women. Of course, the socially aware wit and naïve charm are there, too. A fair number of Dog women public personages have checked out early, either expiring or retiring before fifty because the stress and pressure were too demanding. Drugs, too, can be a real threat to the timid Dog who seeks a public career. Alcohol tends to give shy people a kind of Dutch courage and may at first even help Dog performers to overcome stage fright. But later on, as it becomes a crutch, alcohol (particularly when combined with drugs) can very easily kill these delicately balanced women – or at the very least ruin their careers. Self-discipline, however, will usually save Madame Dog from herself. She can take herself to task and drive her mind and body to commit almost any act of self-denial.

Although Dog women are naturally affectionate, they are almost totally non-demonstrative. Open display of tenderness goes against their shy, retiring nature. The Dog woman would sooner bake you a cake or find you a good cheap hotel than caress your face or even squeeze your hand under the tablecloth.

Frills – the Dog woman thinks of all demonstrations of affection as excessive frills – do not necessarily precede thrills. The Dog woman's approach to the act of love is often, like her other traits, cut and dried. Even in foreplay she tends to be stiffly deliberate. Just as she is stern and prudish in other areas she is strict about the rules of the game of romance, erring on the side of taking it all far too seriously.

Lady Dog is neither yielding nor supple in her gestures or feelings. It is not easy for her to surrender, let down her guard and just *be*. Her lovemaking often remains wooden and feels contrived, even to her!

It's a challenge indeed to fall in love with one of these fascinatingly difficult – yet very rewarding – creatures. Try to be patient with her reticence, indulge her shyness. Don't leap on her unawares or attempt to force her into any compromising positions. If pushed or in any way coerced, the Dog woman may bite.

Don't be afraid to take all the gentle initiatives. Lady Dog is hardly the lusty type who will invite you to a roll in the hay: she is a willing and loving sex partner but has her reservations about anything she deems kinky or strange. Save your fantasy acting-out for business trips.

As a lover or husband to this interesting woman your job is to provide reassurance, gentle her troubled spirit and calm her relentless doubts. It takes a soothing and self-contained person to make life with a Dog woman even half-way serene. From morning till night you must be willing and ready to apply peace-giving balms and smooth a furrowed brow.

The Dog woman is somewhat masochistic and may attempt unwittingly to break up any happy relationship she is involved in. Deep down, she fears being left and bereft. As love is a matter of such importance in her own soul and mind, she cannot believe that she can hang on to anybody; she isn't certain she deserves to be loved. How, she wonders, could anybody love me as much as I love them?

It is a tall order. She will undoubtedly be tempted to hold up your devotion to the mirror of her own brand of unflinching loyalty. And because her standards are so unreachably elevated, she may repeatedly be disappointed. In her disillusionment she may decide that true love, such as she wants and needs it to be, can never exist so she will pursue men whom she knows she can never truly possess – married men, transient strangers. This way, at the first crack in the surface of their love, she can move on to another cleaner yet still imperfect relationship.

Spinsters are common among Dog women. Divorce, too. They expect too much from love and marriage, get less than they bargained for and so decide to give it a lifetime pass. The metaphysical or psychic side of live doesn't appeal to their down-to-earth natures either so don't worry, they will not lose any sleep over their partner's reaction to aborted relationships.

Ms Doggie makes a wonderfully responsible parent. Devotion is an understatement and the Dog mother lives for nurturing and adores her role as caretaker, schedule-maker and educator. She even enjoys the policewoman role that a mother often has to play. Dogs don't mind waiting up with one eye open till Jason or Carrie gets home from the movies: the herding and tending of sheep is in their natures. She is often funny, too, and can help kids overcome their own shyness even though (and perhaps because) she herself is painfully timid. Helping is the Dog woman's mission in life, and kids need a lot of help. She can shoulder them in and out of experiences, patiently teach them skills she has learned. She can be critical but her intention is always kindly and not self-serving. Without being the noisy, invasive type of mother who imposes her will and yells her demands, the Dog mother will fervently yet discreetly pursue the assistance and raising of her children till death do them part.

What she lacks in flexibility, the Dog woman makes up in commitment. I have a wonderful Dog friend, a painter named Mady de la Giraudière. Mady spent most of her life becoming a spectacular painter so she never had time for more than a brief marriage. Nor did she ever have time for children. But now she has reached a mature age and her colorful, primitive paintings are known worldwide. She paints all manner of Dog-like things such as brightly lit fields and the daily life of villages in south-western France. Her glorious sunrises and little girls at work under flowering trees are idealistic and uplifting.

I hadn't seen Mady for quite some time when three years ago I received an invitation to one of her one-woman shows in a Right Bank Paris gallery. I entered discreetly and stood next to the door. It was great fun just watching Mady's sunny-faced smile. She was shaking hands and kissing and joyfully receiving her guests and admirers.

Suddenly, a pretty young Asiatic woman with long black hair came up with a tray of champagne glasses and offered me one. 'Hello,' she said in perfect French, 'are you one of *Maman*'s friends?'

'*Non*,' I answered. 'I'm an old friend of Mady's.'

'I'm Tchin,' she answered with a hint of a curtsy. 'Mady is my mother. I am adopted. I was an orphan from Cambodia. You know Khmer Rouge?'

My heart sank at the very idea of this angelic creature having been victimized by monsters. 'How long have you been here?'

'Oh, five years,' she explained. '*Maman* is just about to adopt my little sister who has been too long in a refugee camp. She's coming in about a month to join us here. She will go to high school.'

Tchin will graduate from art school soon and her sister is entering her last year of high school in the French countryside. They are beautiful and joyful young women. Mady has done everything to make them happy and secure. Adopting bruised grown girls from a war-battered foreign culture is not an easy task, especially for a single woman with a demanding career. Yet such a gesture is typical of the self-sacrificing and sincerely humanitarian Dog woman.

Boy Dogs

The Dog may be man's best friend. The Dog-man's choice of best friend, however, is not man but the earth. And the disapproving Dog considers man to be the earth's very worst enemy.

Hounded by what he feels is the perpetual imposition of societal invention in the form of vapid mores, empty laws and unjust justice, the male Dog lives out his life on this planet as though it were a sort of purgatory, a place for doing penance and committing acts of contrition, a mere pit stop on the way to the victory of death where, at last, repose and true justice will free him from intense daily anxiety.

Don't infer even a smidgeon of piety from this image: the male Dog is a sceptic. He doubts and suspects every tenet of every 'ism' known to man. The dogma of organized religion doesn't tempt his cynical nature. You won't meet many Dog priests and, if you do, they will have chosen to become missionaries, healers, teachers or reclusive monks who never look up from their breviaries for more than a sniff at the feet of a courtyard statue.

The male Dog holds an eternal and tiresome conviction that everything and everyone he meets in a day's struggle will be at least partly false, fake, ersatz, and that nothing is truly virtuous, not even himself. He is, at best, dubious of everything, at worst positively paranoid. To the male Dog, *everything* must be sniffed before it can be enjoyed. He ascribes rigorously to the theory of testing before tasting. Before partaking of any joy, he wants to probe and scrutinize, inspecting all life experiences for flaws.

The result of this stubborn sniffing-the-lamp-post attitude is near extinction of spontaneity. Dogs, especially male Dogs, do *not* like surprises. Startle a wary Dog with a quick, careless pat or a rapid caress and start counting what's left of your fingers.

The cynical Dog is wholly convinced that human civilization constitutes the rape of Mother Nature. No use trying to disabuse him of this. You can cajole and persuade, promise and demonstrate to him that there is a strong movement afoot to improve the quality of the environment, to make what we eat more real and to decrease rampant infant mortality but even if he appears to accept your information, nods and seems to believe you he does not believe. To him, nothing that society has invented can be good for nature. As far as the male Dog is concerned, man was put on this earth to destroy it.

At face value this seems a sorry testimony. Are all male Dogs so pessimistic and misanthropic? Yes. With varying degrees of severity, all male Dogs are contemptuous of what the rest of society sees as 'normal'.

Even the Dog man's physical appearance shows how uneasy he feels. His gait, for example, is bumptious and awkward. He stoops slightly, seeming to carry the burdens of the world on his bony shoulders. Although he purports to project a self-effacing, quiet man image, the male Dog's gestures, commentary and head movements are usually quick and nervous. His watchful eyes seem to dart everywhere at once. Half the time he acts as though he was being tailed by the FBI.

Although he deems this tentative manner and clumsy appearance unsatisfactory and is often truly uncomfortable in his own skin, the male Dog doesn't often know what to do about it. One day he espouses the tousled, dishevelled, stinky muscle-man look and the next he will try to clean up his act by donning a laundered shirt and carrying a fine leather briefcase. The male Dog is so unprepossessing that even if he is born gorgeous, he always errs on the side of oafishness. He may try to be gregarious but then he talks too much. Posturing never works for him. His shyness is just too pervasively tangible and he doesn't really know what to do about it.

The male Dog has a thin person's nature. He's often tall and rangy, but even if he is small of stature, he's likely to be bony and slight of build. Though in middle age he may grow slightly paunchy or for a period of months become denser and more solid due to overeating and lack of exercise – he eschews exercise, especially organized exercise – it is not in his make-up to become and remain fat. His hands are often gnarled, his shoulders narrow and his facial features pronounced and distinctive. There is a caricatural air about the male Dog. He is rarely forgettable.

Frequently he will present a droopy countenance. The longing and anxiety he feels inside his heart show on his face. The fears and doubts are visible in the wrinkles around the eyes, the furrowed brow, the tense mouth. His hair is often thick and luxurious in his youth but becomes thinner as he ages. A tendency to early balding is common among Dog men.

Dog men frown on frivolous overspending. They are far from stingy but have strong reservations about lavishing money on things of inferior quality. When they do spend, they insist on buying top-drawer, sturdy, well-designed, handsome items of impeccable authenticity which would outlast Methuselah. Male Dogs generally have sober, conservative tastes and instinctively know a good thing when they see one.

I know a lovely British Dog who renovated a house in Provence. Let's call him George. Eleven years ago, he and his wife decided they wanted a retirement house in the rural South of France. In true Dog fashion, George sniffed, tracked and sought, then found, scrutinized and finally bought the prettiest ruin in a remote Provençal village. The view was fabulous.

Having done up one of those old stone houses, I know that despite dogged determination, elbow grease and end-of-the-rainbow sized pots of money these stone monsters and the wily surrounding citizenry harbor many surprises for the foreigner who wishes to return such a quirky building to its 'authentic' state, which was George's firm intent. He bought books of the floor plans of historic Provençal houses, spent time in libraries poring over texts about how old-time masons mixed mortar and which stone they used. He spent almost a year in research.

Just as he was about to start work, he got a registered letter which announced that a remote branch of the family who had previously owned the house had decided not to sign over two rooms, which they considered theirs from an obscure birthright clause in an antiquated law book.

Suddenly, George owned a ten-roomed ruin minus two rooms – on the middle floor. He could not restore the original staircase without passing through these two rooms, any more than the relatives could access them other than through George's front door and up his half-built stairs.

Stalemate.

George started work. He restored the kitchen, using cupboards from old *châteaux* and medieval shutters, and the drawing-room, where he installed a stone fireplace he had found in a mountainous Provençal village. For ten years, he pursued the legal right to buy the two rooms. George is a Dog. He was going to see that justice was done.

Meanwhile, he and his wife used only the four authentically restored rooms to which they had access and left their top-floor rooms alone. Lesser men might have moved out or paid off these obscure cousins. But not George. Last year he finally won.

In early spring work started again. It was as though George had never been interrupted. Dogged determination ensured that in six months he had completed his stairway, put in almost authentic medieval bathtubs, hired a plasterer to refine the moldings upstairs and even found a local artisan to fashion an iron banister in the seventeenth-century style. Of course, things had become more expensive over ten years but when a Dog is after authenticity, money is no object.

Although they are sometimes abrasive and picky, Dog men are profoundly affectionate. They may not splash romantic Valentines around, but they can be counted on to provide that little bit of extra attention women are so fond of. Being expert critics, they unfailingly notice every detail of your new *toilette*. Sometimes their criticism is sharp but Dog men make up for it. They pat your shoulder as they walk past or wag their tails when you give them a kiss on the nose.

In certain love unions this critical trait is most appealing; in others, less so. Dogs don't like to lie, so if you ask, 'Is my hair too long?' they say, 'Yes, cut it,' or 'No, it's pretty that way.' Or they may zing you with, 'I've always thought your hair needed to be redder. It looks so dull.'

The male Dog is eager to please but not brilliant at gauging the degree of his enthusiasms. Think of a big yellow Labrador retriever greeting you when you get home every night. They slobber, jump up at you and bark and try to frenzy you to death. Lots of Dog men do this to women when they are least expecting it. Then, when the woman resists or cries, 'Hey, down, Rover!' the Dog may feel rejected and unloved. All over-eager Dogs should take love-calm drops in their morning tea so that they don't risk rejection by an overwhelmed mistress.

Dismissal is the arch enemy of the male Dog's virility. If he so much as senses a possible *no* lurking in the heart of the woman he covets, he will desist from his seduction and lie down on his own blanket. The Dog male mistrusts *everyone*. He sees ladies as dauntingly, impenetrably scary. He is fascinated by them, seeks only to enjoy their favors and wants to protect them – all of them. But the Dog male is chary of the capricious feminine nature, suspicious of female whims and is painfully unsure of himself in most intimate situations.

The result of this vulnerability is that the Dog man frequently ends up alone, settling for the state of bachelorhood rather than risk rejection. He will rationalize that he is better off on his own because he is so critical, hence hard to live with. He will accept defeat easily because he knows how many compromises marriage and family entail and the Dog male is against compromise. He doesn't want to dilute his ideals or muddy his strict beliefs with senseless concessions and half-way solutions.

If ever he does decide to surrender to the rigors of a long-term love relationship, the male Dog can be counted on 150 per cent. He is loyal and true, dutiful, protective, and aspires to being a good provider. His commitment to love is a pledge of the highest caliber.

What the Dog man lacks in imagination in bed, he makes up for in enduring affection. Tenderness and caring are second nature to this loving person. He may bring you presents or breakfast in bed but he probably won't deafen you with verbosities on your beauty. If you are looking for pretty prevarications and hanker after baroque blandishments, take up with a Goat or a Dragon and let sleeping Dogs lie.

I ought to warn you, too, that if you want a Dog to love you and he doesn't give you a tumble it is probably because you didn't try hard enough. Underneath that detached, hesitant exterior, beneath the reserve, beats the heart of a lusty young puppy. Courtship will be all yours but once you capture his love this creature will follow you anywhere. And he will demand the same constant loyal devotion in return. If you aren't ready to give up your freedom, don't take up with a Dog man. He is jealous and possessive and if you betray him, he may die of it.

Examples of male Dog loyalty and caring are rife. I know a Dog man named François whose wife, Denise, a famous painter, was twenty years older than he. They were blissfully happy until, at about fifty-five, Denise began losing her mind. François was then thirty-five. Today he is past retirement age. Denise is over eighty-five and her mind is almost completely gone. Yet François still gives Denise a birthday party every year and invites all of their cronies. He wouldn't put her in a home, preferring to hire someone to look after her while he worked. Now he stays at home. Every summer he takes her on holiday in the car and points out the sights as though she could still absorb the beauty of the countryside and infuse it into her paintings. François is a wonderful person, and, of course, he is a 1922 Dog.

A few years after I was ill myself a Dog doctor friend named Dan Elstein came to Paris with his wife, Phyllis, and we went out to dinner. Dan asked why I lived in France. I explained that in 1978 I had been sick and that the health insurance company I had been affiliated with had cancelled my contract. 'They wouldn't pay my bills and I needed chemotherapy . . .'

'Why didn't you sue them?' he wondered. 'What they did was morally wrong.'

'I was too afraid,' I said. 'I was just so happy to be alive. I guess I didn't want to push my luck.'

I didn't need to explain further. Dan took all my papers back to the States with him and started a lawsuit against the insurer for me. He wrote scathing letters to the insurer himself and signed them. He hired a lawyer. He did it all gratis. Twelve years later I won the case, but if it hadn't been for Dan's good old doggy bravery and his valiant gesture of human caring, my anger would still be festering.

Justice, justice, justice. Dog men make superb lawyers, extra-fair judges and marvellous political leaders. But public careers demand almost too much of the sensitive Dog man: he cannot abide the dishonesty or hypocrisy that make all forms of government life go round. The Dog male is best off in professions requiring humanity: fund raising, charity leadership, social work and alternative healing will suit him down to the ground. He can also be a writer or own a bookshop as he is attracted to literature, and he will make a dedicated teacher. Advertising and country property aside, he's not good at jobs which require duplicity or hype. A used-car salesman the male Dog is decidedly not. He should steer clear of all shady activities as the paranoia connected with having done something wrong might drive him to drink.

The Dog man knows how to take his time, keep his own counsel and get on quietly with his work. He can do almost anything but his remarkable ability to concentrate on one thing for a long time makes him good at research projects. As a born analyst, he will, of course, make a good critic of anything from theater to fashion. He might also try medicine or psychiatry; although he will be impatient with snivellers, he is basically kindly. His scientific capacities are excellent, too, and he understands philosophy. He is strongly attached to the earth and the past so anything to do with either will suit his needs perfectly. The Dog man could be a farmer, a hunter, a geologist, an anthropologist or even an archeologist, as long as he runs his own show.

Dog men work best alone. They like to make their own rules and follow them to the letter. A single partner would be fine but working in groups or on teams doesn't suit this individualistic person. Solitude doesn't worry the male Dog. He can amuse himself with a piece of string. This subject is neither a visionary nor a poet. But what he lacks in metaphysics, he makes up for in creative excellence at fields such as architecture or theater direction, design or sculpture. Dogs need a practical result as they are wedded to the concrete in life.

Dogs are not ambitious. They enjoy reaching a plateau and can usually achieve a healthy personal gain. Yet they don't really care about money. To them, money is all part of the conspiracy of social organization which they feel is essentially corrupt. Of course, Dog men use and like using money but they can also lose it. Either way it's all the same to them.

Living comfortably and protecting one's territory and family is important to the Dog. But if that same responsibility means being a lifelong slave to commerce, he's usually not interested. Dog men make good, nurturing parents. They are non-invasive, non-egotistical leader types. Their mission in life is to serve and protect, to watch and warn us of danger and perfidy. They love intensely and with respect for their partner's well-being. They are not grabby or warlike. They don't take what isn't theirs. They are kind and liberal. Occasionally they may cut someone to the quick with a razor-sharp remark but aside from that annoying little quirk, a Dog man wouldn't hurt a flea.

The five Chinese elements and how they influence the Dog

The Wood Dog

1874 Arnold Schoenberg, Winston Churchill, Harry Houdini, Robert Frost, Gertrude Stein
1934 Alan Bates, Sydney Pollack, Sophia Loren, Ralph Nader, Brigitte Bardot, Shirley Maclaine, Kate Millet, Alan Arkin, Leonard Cohen, Elvis Presley, Beryl Bainbridge, Donald Sutherland, Kenneth Baker, Shirley Jones, Bill Moyers

With a heart as big as his mouth, this Dog is profoundly affectionate, tender and gentle. Once others learn how to penetrate the Wood Dog's flinty exterior, they love him and, for once, the feeling is mutual. Wood Dogs have a taste for social interaction. They want to know all sorts of folk, cultivate different social gardens and be able to mingle with every type of character on earth. For *this* Dog, group activity, professional partnership and even teamwork are not only advisable but preferable.

The Wood Dog is often a 'self-made' person. A natural superiority comes from being both hyperconscientious and doggedly determined. The combination propels Wood Dogs to the top of almost any field they choose to enter. Also, they are past masters at controlling everything, themselves included. They have their eyes on every detail, follow each project with minute care and can't keep their noses off the grindstone for more than five minutes without being overcome by guilt. Such meticulousness affords the Wood Dog a serious edge in all areas of work requiring in-depth research, precision planning and sheer perseverance.

The Wood Dog can ferret out a fake, detect lies and uncover subterfuge. He's intelligent in an analytical way and has a stern temperament suitable to leadership. The Wood Dog has a gift for inspiring the masses to noble goals. This demanding person has very strong convictions, too. Somehow he is convinced he can change the world in a matter of days. He will not budge easily when challenged on an ideal or a belief. He gives no quarter to charlatans or hacks and instinctively knows how best to choose his aides when given a position of responsibility.

The best thing about the Wood Dog is his sense of integrity. This person can be relied on. If he tells you he'll do something, you can be certain it will be done, when he said so, without shirking or delay. Conversely, it would be better if you didn't try to force the Wood Dog to do anything he hasn't planned. Like most other Dogs, he doesn't like surprises. Worse than that, he hates being caught off guard. He is after perfection and really thinks he must control every aspect of his (and perhaps your) life to reach that state.

As this person finds it tough to tolerate imperfections, sometimes the Wood Dog gives up hope of creating heaven on earth and leaves professional life well before age dictates. Rather than put up with some half-right solution, the Dog will simply remove himself from the fray, move to the country, raise goats and forget about controlling the universe. He is not usually embittered, just resigned.

This Dog is witty, too. He has a keen eye for the ironic, a scathing sense of sarcasm and a talent for turning a pithy phrase. Sassy social satirists, like Alan Arkin, are often Wood Dogs. Their humor constitutes a particular mockery of the banality of the human condition. They poke fun at everyday life and know how to make us laugh at ourselves. If they choose poetry or songwriting as a medium, their verses are often acid, their meaning dense with social comment.

Reformers enjoy spotting artifice, too. Ralph Nader has made a life's work out of highlighting imperfections in consumer products. His is a perfect profession for a Wood Dog. He's independent yet surrounded by a group or staff. He is called upon daily to criticize and find fault. He is paid to be punctilious and incorruptible.

This Dog is so sensitive and fragile, so warm-hearted and affectionate that the only way he could avoid having a nervous breakdown is to rechannel the energy of his sorrow into a cause. Look at Shirley Maclaine's crusades and books about the occult. People said she was crazy but that didn't stop her from wagging her tail and barking and jumping up at people until she found an audience. Likewise Kate Millet, feminist crusader, or Brigitte Bardot who, although she has been retired from films for many years, expends all her time and money on the improvement of animal life in France. She sponsors animal shelters, does TV marathons for the SPCA and guests on talk shows to encourage humane treatment of animals and to militate against hunting.

Wood Dogs are sensitive, strong and sexy but because of a streak of conservatism, they are usually late bloomers, non-promiscuous and don't start having intensive sexual experiences until their mid-twenties or even their early thirties. With such an innate overdose of warmth to share, they feel they must be extra cautious about how and where they spend their vast stores of faithful love.

The Wood Dog is non-materialistic. In both work and play he is a true trudger and slogger. Yet money comes easily to this industrious character. He does work hard but normally he is not working for the gain but rather to salve his overactive conscience. He feels he should make his fellow man laugh and inspire his family to higher ideals by example. The Wood Dog, except for his penchant for judging others too harshly and his habit of meddling, is a very nice and competent person.

The Fire Dog

1886 David Ben-Gurion, Al Jolson
1946 Sally Field, Liza Minnelli, Patty Duke, Marianne Faithfull, Donovan, Rainer Fassbinder, Chantal Goya, Diane Keaton, Tyne Daley, Donald Trump, Ron Silver, Leslie Ann Warren, Gregory Hines, Timothy Dalton, Talia Shire, Cher, Freddie Mercury, Connie Chung, Oliver Stone, Susan Sarandon, Sylvester Stallone, Ben Vereen, Rock Brynner, Bill Clinton, David Lynch

Don't count on the Fire Dog to sit patiently on the hearth without uttering a word. All Fire Dogs are enthusiastic. Their native ebullience and ingenuousness lend an attractive, childlike quality to a high-spirited personality and make us like and trust them instantly.

Because this person is so sincere, earnest even, we cannot help but want to listen, to be drawn into his sweetness and entertained by his artlessness. 'The President is the leader of all the people. If all the people don't agree, how can he send some of the people to war?' is the sort of comment we might hear from his lips. Or, 'Women can't stand men switching TV channels all the time because women like to sit still and men like to move around.' That is one of my Fire Dog brother Peter's latest brilliant observations on the war between the sexes. It's a beguilingly simple approach. Fire Dog logic is so innocent and unsophisticated that you almost wish it could be right.

He is well meaning and feisty but often the Fire Dog is off-base, naíve, quixotic. His virtuous logic is full of holes. Fire Dogs have to be the most ardent supporters of their own dream worlds, becoming solitary crusaders for righteous but simplistic causes. Because their interlocutors are usually more cynical and resigned to the peregrinations of the real world, Fire Dogs have difficulty attracting disciples. Yet their idealism is what gets them out of bed in the morning. They hope and plan every day for a better world. The Fire Dog is a courageous idealist who will charge forth into the fray and fight hard for what he believes in.

Sometimes, before he has a chance to swim far upstream, the Lone Ranger Fire Dog is discouraged by the hard truths he has to face along the way. People let him down. Lovers reject his romantic ideals. Dirty politics blind him with rage. Passionate, the Fire Dog flails before he is defeated, throws up his paws and turns to drink, drugs, overeating or some other unsavory pursuit to dull the pain.

Although he indulges himself in his own faults, the Fire Dog hasn't much time for those of his cohorts. The Fire Dog has a hard time mastering his recalcitrant spirit or pulling his act together to discipline his own behavior and is a sitting duck for addictive bad habits and must keep a vigilant eye on his febrile state of mind. When he's angry with the world, the Fire Dog ceases to want to control himself and may sulk or find fault with everything and everyone around him. As he is a Dog he still wants to remain loyal to his friends and go on believing in their basic good faith so an atmosphere of passionate ambivalence creates conflict for the Fire Dog and sets him up for some self-indulgent pain-killing activity.

Fire Dogs make terrific critics, editors, trouble-shooters and advisors. They can pinpoint a flaw and find the chink in almost any armor. But no matter how hard they try, these volcanic people cannot look objectively at their own faults. They see 'fat' people all around them but when they look in the mirror, their own paunches or jodhpur thighs miraculously disappear. They admire the grace of a well-dressed person and want to appear attractive themselves but they are often clumsily dressed and cannot imagine how to emulate anything fashionable. They often feel awkward in modish clothes and may even disdain stylish dressing, arguing vociferously and puritanically against frivolity which pokes fun at refinement.

Sour grapes? Not really. It's more like a contrary 'I don't give a damn' attitude, resulting from the Fire Dog feeling, once again, left out, misunderstood and furious with the human race.

Although they often suffer from rabid bad temper and temporary despondency, Fire Dogs never seem depressed. They are ever cordial folk whose good manners issue directly from an honest sense of altruism and love of humanity.

Fire Dogs are ambitious self-starters and will work harder than most people to get and stay ahead of the pack. Their only real enemies are their boiling passion, their inability to control their reactions to what they think of as wrong-doing and their unfortunate tendency to sputter, bluster and grouch.

As the Fire Dog is essentially modest his public anger is short-lived. He is considerate of others and would be embarrassed to make endless dramatic scenes. None the less, rancor burrows deep into the Fire Dog's molten little heart and confounds his capacity for forgiveness.

His memory for detail is extraordinary. He can tell you what dress his mother was wearing the night she forgot to tuck him in and which cupboard the sweets were locked in at the summer cottage his family rented in Maine. Yet this person's memory, like so much of the rest of his make-up, is largely based on emotional response. He recalls the day he was not tucked in and remembers being deprived of sweets, but the good times may be forgotten.

As his hypersensitivity causes the Fire Dog to feel things so deeply, he frequently absorbs the darkest aspects of any experience. By adulthood, the pain may have become unbearable and the Fire Dog may emerge as a crackerjack pessimist and Gloomy Gus. He must, of course, combat this tendency to view everything negatively and should surround himself with peaceful, positive people whose sensitivities harmonize with his. He should live in pastoral surroundings so that gracious Mother Nature will always be available to soothe his fragile nervous system. Fire Dogs should steer clear of competitive, political or commercial activities. They are not gifted for diplomacy or tricky negotiation as they have difficulty with both cupidity and half-way measures. Fire Dogs are not compromisers.

Healthy professions for the Fire Dog are to be found in medicine or education, literature or music. Though the murky vicissitudes of showbusiness may test the Fire Dog's basic good nature, he is gifted for interpretive speech and can make an excellent career in the theater. Behind-the-scenes jobs suit this explosive character: he will make an excellent investigative journalist or private detective. Law or government, providing the vehement Fire Dog is not called on to argue cases or negotiate deals, gives him a fine opportunity to exercise his reforming talents.

Although he considers himself the dominant party in all his relationships, the Fire Dog is neither forward nor pushy in love situations. He likes to be teased and seduced. Once in bed, he is tender and sensual. His dour, childlike exterior doesn't even hint at uninhibited sexuality he can unleash when properly stimulated.

Vital, independent and loyal to the death, the perplexing nature of the oddly enterprising yet shy Fire Dog is guaranteed not to bore you.

The Earth Dog

1838 Georges Bizet, Henry Adams
1898 George Gershwin, Bertolt Brecht, Golda Meir, René Clair, Paul Robeson, Peggy Guggenheim, Alfred Eisenstadt, Irene Dunne, Armand Hammer
1958 Michael Jackson, Madonna, Jamie Lee Curtis, Kevin Bacon, Daley Thompson

Earth endows the Dog character with reserve. He may believe in causes and crusades for justice, may long for a better world, but the Earth Dog is no zealot. He's cooler and more laid back than his fellow Dogs, more circumspect and non-confrontational.

Because of his high sensitivity, the Earth Dog is easily affected by changes in the weather and cannot help but note the tiniest shift in the atmosphere around him. He is terminally squeamish. His radar-like sensibilities pick up on the merest criticism or sharp remark, causing him untold suffering and he goes around in a permanent state of flinch. He is *so* touchy and fragile that he prefers to remain out of the spotlight.

Earth Dogs are artistic and thin-skinned, born to live in the wildest of countryside, surrounded by greenery and pets. They need to be protected from harsh reality and respond best to being tenderly stroked and made to feel safe.

The Earth Dog is a creative person who works best in solitude. Again, because of his delicately-balanced nervous system, he has to build up stores of vitality which he does by contemplating nature, remaining aloof from crowds and staying out of the rat race. Take a look at Michael Jackson, a genius and a dynamo indeed, but brittle and vulnerable, too. He makes a record or video and slinks right back into his California sanctuary where he lives alone, with family and animals for his sole companions.

Notice, too, that the above list of famous Earth Dogs is rather short. Dogs influenced by the Earth element often remain in anonymous jobs for life. Yet they are definitely ambitious for material gain: they may stay out of the way but they are not shy. Rather, the Earth Dog is naturally calm and exorbitantly secretive. He wants his intimacies to remain intimate and his dirty laundry to stay in its basket. If a public career threatens his private life, an Earth Dog may withdraw for ever.

As Earth Dogs usually stay out of the general hubbub, they are able to hover, watching how others live their lives. This gives them an excellent natural springboard from which to forge a career as a writer or journalist, diplomat or lawmaker. I'd venture to say that not many Earth Dogs have dabbled in politics as they are neither attracted to nor tolerant of hypocrisy and palaver. The Earth Dog may become a fine architect or fashion designer, decorator or photographer. He understands the subtleties of human nature and, as he is naturally innovative, he will produce works of humanity and charm. Earth Dogs make excellent scientists, too. If they become doctors, they will probably be happiest in research laboratories.

This quiet, soulful subject is also well known for his charm. Though he may not always show it, the Earth Dog can seduce the leaves off the trees. He's diffident, composed and knows how to listen. He's kindly and understanding of other, more involved, complex and chatty people. The Earth Dog is very supple of mind and, for a stubborn Dog, remarkably willing to bend his ways to fit any given situation.

Like all Dogs, the Earth Dog has the capacity to issue biting remarks when least expected. Yet because of his sensitivity and basic altruism, his remarks are less markedly mean-spirited and harsh than those of his co-Dogs. If he snaps at all, the Earth Dog is likely to make his point gently, camouflaging his naturally acid tone by nuzzling your neck or licking your bare knees.

The Earth Dog is a family person. He gives ponderous thought and attention to the well-being of his flesh and blood. Always the champion of the kid who lost his bike or forgot to do his homework, this character makes an excellent educator. He instinctively knows how to marry generosity of spirit to a firm helping hand. He loves kids and is apt to be quite conservative in his views on contraception and abortion.

Finally, the Earth Dog is a skittish, nervous person. He's not often bad-tempered but when he is, what he needs is silence, solitude and sleep. His physical complaints often relate to his sluggish digestion as he is usually not a frisky Dog, living sedentarily in his quiet haven by himself. He ought to be encouraged to eat lots of fiber and vegetables, to drink large quantities of water and get lots of outdoor exercise. If he nurtures his sensitive nerves and remembers to eat properly, this subject can live to a ripe age.

The Metal Dog

1910 Joseph Alsop, Rod Cameron, Jacques Cousteau, Akira Kurosawa, Jean Genet, Hugh Casson, Vicente Minelli, Mother Theresa, Joan Bennet, E. G. Marshall, Eliot Roosevelt, Joe E. Adams

1970 Kirk Cameron, André Agassi

This is the Dog that wants to change the world. He's strong-minded as well as generous and self-sacrificing. He's a brave, gallant person whose sole reason for being on this earth is to stalk the holy grail of perfection. Metal Dogs live for their personal missions. They are logical, zealous, methodical and rigorous. They do not believe in violence or upheaval, feeling that gentler, more civilized methods can and do work. They strive for an ideal with a determination that boggles the minds of less eager, less determined folk. Curiously, although they sometimes seem unapproachable, Metal Dogs long more than anything else to be understood, loved and revered by their peers.

Metal Dogs are the kind of people most likely to win the Nobel Prize, climb Mount Everest, discover a cure for psoriasis or reform a country's constitution. They are not only relentless in their pursuit of a noble goal; they never give up even when carrying out a long-standing vendetta. They are people of extremes whose goals are rarely lowly or modest. When he seeks change, the Metal Dog won't settle for less than revolution.

Metal confers a rather self-centered character on this Dog. He can and will accomplish great things. He is generous and even kind but he wants the improvements he achieves through his own efforts to bear his name and speak for his beliefs. He is profoundly convinced that his ideals are more noble, his objectives more righteous and his methods more efficient than those of less able people.

Metal Dogs understand the necessity of teamwork. Most Dogs prefer to go it alone but the Metal Dog won't shrink from interpersonal relationships, especially those which may lead him closer to his goals sooner. He is not afraid to impose his will on others, and is able to create a working entity and keep it functioning as a team to advance his cause. He is born with superior intelligence and can find quick, brilliant solutions to almost any problem confronting him. He is egocentric and not above getting a real thrill from the admiration, approval and applause of his teamworkers.

He is often coveted as a friend, associate or dinner-party guest. When it comes to serious matters, the Metal Dog is almost too earnest a conversationalist. Yet he doesn't disdain to engage in small talk with *Madame La Comtesse* whose main preoccupation may be her poodle's bald spot. He's a nobly motivated, truly altruistic person, who can be counted on to lend a hand as he wishes only to do the right thing by everyone.

As a parent, the Metal Dog can do great work. He adheres to schedules and instinctively knows how to run a household well. He's self-centered without being selfish. Children will not only benefit from the generosity of his spirit and feel a centering influence from him, but will never doubt their own importance. The ego-centered Metal Dog neither doubts his own nor wishes to detract from his offspring's sense of self.

Despite a strong love of his fellow man, this person can be sharply critical and even cruel about character flaws he sees in outsiders. However, his self-righteousness fades as, with age, the Metal Dog becomes more tolerant and mellow. It is young Metal Dogs who are so strident and unforgiving of their peers, their families and 'the system'. School authorities often have trouble with Metal Dog kids as they are unafraid to criticize policy openly or disapprove of disciplinary acts. As they are usually excellent students the principal may be stymied by this outspoken child's defensive attitudes.

Once he grows up, however, personal discipline is a quality the Metal Dog finds easy to manage. He can study law or medicine or undertake any scientific career as he can concentrate for hours on thick, boring texts the rest of us might resent even having to lift down from our shelves.

To be able to pursue his goals, finish his studies and climb towards ever higher plateaux, this person must feel secure. He may live at home until a late age or set up house young with a friend or lover. His need for domestic order is paramount. The Metal Dog is a choosy but loyal lover and spouse. He refuses to be distracted from his faith or purpose by marital strife and drama. He wants a calm, serious lifestyle and will stop at nothing to secure it for himself and his family.

Sometimes the goals of this driven soul preclude a family. Take Mother Theresa, whose mission to care for the poor provides her with full-time responsibility. She wisely chose the safety and regularity of a religious life: family life for such a driven humanitarian would be impossible.

There are few 'famous' showbiz Metal Dogs, who are never satisfied with the hollow applause of money or fame for its own sake. Metal Dogs want to achieve *great* things. Some, such as Jacques Cousteau and Akira Kurosawa, have used the media to expose their plans and ideals, but Metal Dogs are not of the same ilk as those who dream of Hollywood (Lollipopland) swathed in furs and driving fancy cars.

Because of his tendency to go to extremes, the Metal Dog often suffers from emotional instability. He may be jolly and frisky one minute but the next will have sunk into an abyss of misery. He needs people to shore him up, encourage and admire him during setbacks as he may lose faith in his goal and require moral support before diving in again.

The Metal Dog has enormous curiosity and *must* get to the bottom of whatever he undertakes, testing every detail until he knows the truth. Nothing gets past this person's sprawling magnetic field of vision, which makes him a nitpicker, always ferreting about, hunting for clues and maniacally making order out of chaos. When you match the reforming altruist with the snoop, you will see that the Metal Dog makes a remarkable law-enforcement officer, detective, forensic specialist or researcher.

Although he is usually thin and rangy of stature, the Metal Dog is a hearty eater. He enjoys high quality cuisine and is often a meticulous cook himself. He's dedicated to high quality, yet cares little for material wealth or gain. If money is there he will know how to use it wisely, buying only the best merchandise, eating in the finest restaurants and wearing top quality, long-lasting clothes. If he hasn't any money, the Metal Dog can always find a way to live comfortably in a civilized manner. He may be sociable but he doesn't care a whit for what others think of him or the state of his front lawn.

The Metal Dog is often a great talker. He will embark on an explanation, adding details and fitting in sub-plots, chattering with puppylike enthusiasm through mires of digression. He very often (yawn) loses his audience in a sea of unrelated detail. The only remedy for this bad habit is to time his speeches, then let him know their excessive length. He likes precision and has a horror of appearing ridiculous. If you remind him that his talk on whitebait in the Middle Ages lasted sixteen minutes and thirty-five seconds, he'll soon catch on. If this doesn't work and your favorite Metal Dog refuses to cease droning, buy a book on debating rules and a stopwatch that clangs loudly when a debater's time is up. The Metal Dog loves order. He'll fall right into the debating gong's trap and you may gain some table talk that doesn't last from the appetizer through to the dessert. And if this doesn't work, write me a letter and I'll try to think of a more draconian solution.

The Water Dog

1802 Alexandre Dumas (*père*), Victor Hugo
1862 Claude Debussy, O. Henry, Gustav Klimt, Edith Wharton
1922 Gérard Philippe, Helen Gurley Brown, Judy Garland, Pierre Cardin, Norman Mailer, Kurt Vonnegut, Norman Lear, Jay Presson Allen, Kingsley Amis, Franco Zeffirelli, Iannis Xenakis, Ugo Tognazzi, Dora Doll, Pier Paolo Pasolini, Arthur Penn, Ava Gardner, Vittorio Gassman, Bobby Lapointe, Jonas Mekas, Alain Robbe-Grillet, George McGovern, Ray Goulding, Shelley Winters, Blake Edwards, Carl Reiner, Jason Robards, Audrey Meadows, Sid Caesar, Barbara Bel Geddes, Michael Bentine

There's an odd bunch for you. A large number of writers, a smattering of musicians, a few actors and actresses, a painter or two, a couple of film directors and even one or two politicians – geniuses one and all!

This breed of Dog is difficult to get to know. Not only do Water Dogs act stand-offish and aloof when they first meet you, but they may even growl and bare their teeth. Aggressive? Yes. Yet the Water-born Dog is also kindly. He assumes responsibility for those he feels have been badly treated by life, calming their wounded sensitivities and reassuring them of their own basic goodness. He is a 'feminine' type, gentler and softer than his fellow Dogs, able to express as well as comprehend even the most complex emotions.

The Water Dog's strength lies in his ability to analyse and synthesize information into artistic form. He possesses a natural talent for tidily sifting the ashes of human relations into a mixing bowl and baking them into a delectable, incisive and witty confection. He's a Dog so he's hypersensitive. Yet he remains realistic and sufficiently strong-minded to resist caving in under pressure or criticism. His job on this earth is to teach us to laugh, cry, feel, suffer or come alive under the spell of his poignant artistic endeavor.

The Water Dog never misses a trick. He is born with powers that enable him to see round corners, grasp ideas before they are expressed or pick out a sound long before it reaches our mediocre ears. Because of this sixth sense, he sometimes seems to drift off briefly during a conversation into his own secret realm.

If he were not so gifted as an artist we might never notice him. The Water Dog has a distant manner and appears indifferent to others. The semi-hostility we think we discern in him usually stems of excessive caution. Because he never feels confident of others and mistrusts strangers, the Water Dog may turn away out of fear. He doesn't want to start some clumsy conversation or engage in idle chit-chat, so he chooses to remain unknown. He does not lack self-confidence but he is born with a reticent, quiet nature.

Oddly, once you get to know the Water Dog and become his close friend, he never shuts up. All Dogs have remarkable memories for detail but this one is a fountain of minutiae. He doesn't *tell* the story of how he met his first lover, he *reports* it as an in-depth journalist might on a reproducing molecule's progress over twenty-four hours. He starts, 'There we were at the thirty-seventh parallel at fourteen minutes and thirty seconds past seven. He was wearing a fawn-colored vest over a heathery blue flannel shirt. His trousers were cavalry twill, the kind with the nubbly twists not the chevron variety. The air was sticky and hot and he was perspiring fetchingly at the temples. An airplane passed overhead. One engine didn't sound quite right. Maybe it was missing or sputtering . . .' Water Dog build-ups are fascinatingly intricate. It seems as if he'll never reach the dénouement.

As a pal, he is affable and warm, helpful and self-sacrificing. He interests himself in all that you do and never forgets a particle of your pettiest problem.

The Water Dog is a fair person whose fervent desire to see that justice is done sometimes causes him to meddle. You know how it is when a well-meaning person sticks out his neck for you when he feels it pertinent and nets himself a volley of retribution. The Water Dog often receives this kind of unfair reward. No matter how delicate the situation, the Water Dog cannot resist the temptation to indulge in friendly interference. Water Dogs make great, loyal friends, but they are not peace-makers, negotiators or diplomats.

These attractive creatures are extremely sexy. Lots of their time is spent seducing and bedding lovers. Because they are Dogs, they tend to be faithful but sometimes they cannot resist trying out their alluring ways with someone new. Infidelity causes the Water Dog terrible guilt, which only increases his pessimistic outlook. His best bet is to try not to succumb to the tug of seduction because his moral structure is more fragile than he thinks. In his case, even a shred of pessimism can lead to bleak depression.

The Water Dog is never malevolent or vicious. Though he occasionally acts out his frustration with other people mildly aggressively, he rarely commits crimes. He doesn't look for excuses for his own misbehavior either. He's a straight shooter, accepting responsibility for his sins and dutifully atoning for them by creating sublime art, performing good works, always carrying his share of the burden connected to the social contract.

The outstanding characteristic here is beauty. We cannot help but notice it. Male Water Dogs are handsome and elegant. Their female counterparts are strikingly lovely, combining a fetchingly sharp bone structure with a touching air of suffering. Water Dogs try to live genteelly, surrounding themselves with beautiful things and enjoying nature's bounty.

Water Dogs are contemplative, rarely leaping up before they look. They work hard and achieve great deeds without false bravado or self-applause. Water Dogs will spend a long, adventurous youth seeking a life partner and are likely to marry people much older than themselves.

Dog health

'I'm very sedentary. I don't do any exercise yet I am in very good condition,' said my brother Peter the Dog when I approached him on the subject of his health. 'Actually I'm lazy. I really don't deserve such good health. But it just seems to be there for me. I'm lucky.'

My answer remained discreetly inside my mouth. So far, thought I, so far, so good.

Dogs are lucky physically. They tend not to be ill very often and rarely suffer from the severely debilitating chronic diseases of youth such as asthma or sinus disorders, diabetes, epilepsy or migraine. And although the Dog is apt to appear older than he is by the age of forty, he acts youthful longer, has more pep than his middle-aged peers and is likely to become more physically active as he ages.

Arthritis is the Dog's emblematic disease. They all have rheumatism in some form and will suffer all their adult lives from varying degrees of joint pain and its accompanying weaknesses. Dogs are those people whose backs lock when they bend over, whose knees buckle and send them flying, whose ankles are always being sprained and then swelling when it's damp outside. The remedy for this unfortunate chronic condition is, of course, regular physical exercise performed under the supervision of professionals. The Dog is best advised to visit a chiropractor or osteopath, have deep massages, see acupuncturists and follow the prescriptions of a homeopathic doctor. Chemical medicines and non-natural products upset the Dog's fragile system and should be resorted to only in extreme cases where naturopathic organic remedies have failed.

Of course, being as anti-social as they are, Dogs don't take kindly to the necessity of consulting doctors or going for regular dental check-ups. The Dog resists having tests or submitting to scientific examinations because he has so little respect for the concept of science tinkering with nature and also because he is so fearful and apprehensive about almost everything, he is sure the practitioner will find some calamitous malady in an obscure part of his unsuspecting body which won't leave. Either way, I would rather try to teach an Ox to fly than be assigned to get a Dog to go to the doctor, join a gym or take up some simple, healthy, organized sport. Deep down, Dogs feel that Mother Nature will take care of them.

Dogs usually thrive when allowed to follow their natural rhythms. Imposing any artificial schedules or sketchy, anarchic meal plans on these earth-bound creatures will upset their equilibrium and may establish negative patterns and undermine their sound metabolic structure.

The Dog is of a compact, hardy nature with tremendous powers of endurance which constitute a natural resistance to harmful environmental influences. Although he may appear rigid and even stiff, when put to the test, the Dog is very adaptable. A Dog can psych his spirit and body into 'going with the flow' of almost any circumstance. The Chinese say that the Dog's endurance increases with age. Because of his arthritis, he may not be a very comfortable old person but the determined Dog is unlikely to die young.

Most Dogs have skin problems. Their nervous tension is so often concealed that it emerges on the surface of the skin. Itching, psoriasis, hives and other types of annoying allergic reaction or urticaria will invade these people's epidermis at some point. The skin is usually dry and chafes or chaps easily and needs to be pampered. Even though most Dog people claim not to be able to live a single day without taking their ritual shower, vigorous washing and scrubbing with detergents, soaps and shampoos is definitely counter-productive. Gentle organic creams and lotions should be preferred and drastic allopathic remedies such as cortisone avoided, as the long-term side effects can be worse than the dermatitis discomfort itself.

Conditions such as hypotension and arteriosclerosis may cause trouble late in life. The Dog is never really active enough: he tends to prostration when depressed or melancholy, even when he is merely thinking something through. Dogs must be extremely vigilant about the state of blood and lymph circulation, have their immune system tested often and watch for the onset of the chronic diseases of old age.

Beware also of the possible early onset of gout. Watch out for stomach disorders, gall-bladder or pancreatic ailments. The Dog doesn't have a strong digestion. Although he claims to like everything and will gobble almost any food with gusto, the average Dog, although he loves it, cannot digest rich, greasy food. Like the rest of us, he would be better off without too much fatty meat in his diet. What Dogs need is calcium and lots of vitamins, grains, pulses and vegetables. Fish or chicken are fine, too. But for good assimilation, meat should be eaten only twice a week.

Dogs don't know how to handle illness. As they ordinarily push ahead, ignoring warnings and refusing to see doctors until symptoms have become emergencies, they are often surprised and angry when, one day, they can no longer lift their heads off the pillow. Being a stoic, the Dog is, however, a good patient. He doesn't complain unduly and readily learns to accept the discomfort of illness philosophically with good humor.

The way to lifetime good health for Dogs is remarkably straightforward. They must drink enormous quantities of liquid, avoid alcohol and drugs, eat natural foods, rise with the sun and sleep at dusk. Dogs only suffer serious illness and depression when they repeatedly break the simple laws laid down by their ruler, the earth.

Regular sexual activity is essential to the Dog's well-being, too. Nothing is more conducive to chronic joint pain and subsequent seizing up than preventing the flow of natural juices. Of all people, the potentially creaky Dog needs regular aerobic movement. He should walk or run, dance or ski, skip, swim or do something vigorous steadily for thirty minutes each day to raise the heartbeat and keep it there till the blood is oxygenated and the energy level has risen. Dogs do get rusty.

Hard work and movement are the Dog's friends. Sometimes he doesn't realize this and has to be prodded into action. Dog women must be extra careful not to allow osteoporosis to destroy their bones – luckily, they tend to be more physically energetic than Dog men but being self-abnegating, they need encouragement to take care of themselves.

If you love a Dog, don't hesitate to give him responsibilities which force him to move about. He is more apt to accept responsibility imposed by a loved one than to take it upon himself to exercise. Ask him to walk to the shops or take the kids to the playground on foot every day.

Activity also helps keep the Dog from sinking into the quicksand of his own anxiety. One of the most dangerous enemies of his good health is the permanently fluttering banner of panic that lives inside his head. He cannot forget certain painful childhood moments. He cannot put apprehension aside in favor of hope and anticipation. The Dog is constantly on the *qui vive*, worried, fearful of dire consequences. Inside his little head lives hundreds of flakes of virgin snow which require only the minutest stimulation to become great snowballs of misgiving. 'If this happens, that might happen, then what will happen?'

Dogs are not usually paralyzed by their fears and doubts; they are brave people, but, because of their uneasiness, they will often push on through a task or project in an unhealthy advanced state of private agitation: ulcerous types to a man. Need I add that Dogs are often hounded by insomnia, need utter quiet to sleep well and ought not to live in the city?

Dog futures

What the Dog should expect from the next twelve Chinese animal years

2008, the Earth Rat year – This Rat year will not be your most productive. You are completely unlike the Rat. Dog people are more idealistic than materialistic. It's just the opposite with Rats. Rats seek power (and cash) in any and all situations. Dogs like to have some power too. But for entirely different reasons. Dogs go after authority only if it gives them the necessary clout to effect social change. The Dog presidents or leaders of the pack in any organization want to see justice done. They rule to improve the world their way – not just to order people about. Rats rule to rule. So in this Rat year, you Dogs may bark as stridently as you wish, but no matter how fiercely you yap, you won't get much further than the bottom of your garden. The Rat simply doesn't give a damn what you want. Your personal life should be carefully monitored, as betrayal by a family member is afoot. This incipient treason could be about either money or property. It might also concern a young adult child who is threatening to leave school or home. Nip this in the bud by talking it through and offering just alternatives. Otherwise, although you won't feel that you are making much progress, you are maintaining a status quo. In Rat years, that's about as much as any Dog can ask for.

2009, the Earth Ox year – Although Dogs and Oxen are far from bosom buddies, you get on just fine as long as you stay out of each other's way. In other words, keep your revolutionary ideals to yourself and don't attempt to effect any political unrest this year. Your chances of success are not about to be foiled by the Ox's influence. He is not your enemy or your rival. He merely deems your enthusiasm for reform naive and childish. If an Ox person were to attempt to overthrow a government, he or she would simply take over by military force and set himself up as dictator. The Ox is He (and She) Who Must Be Obeyed. Nobody counters a determined Ox person and lives to tell the tale. So whatever plans you had for changing your world by peaceful, democratic means must be set aside till next year. Meanwhile, your family situation becomes clearer in the Ox year. Those members who were thinking treasonous thoughts have been discouraged from wreaking disaster on family harmony. And love re-enters the picture too. True, cozy, sweet lasting love will show up toward the end of this year in an interesting disguise. A blah workmate or an old school acquaintance turns up in some odd venue when you least expect it. Welcome this unexpected charmer into your life. You have earned it.

2010, the Metal Tiger year – You Dog people bask in Tiger years. Your money luck is good, the sun shines on your family and your heart throbs apace. Tigers and Dogs are sisters under the skin. You two agree on so many things that it's impossible to mention them all. But what is most salient about the character of your friendship is that you both seek to change the world. The Tiger, in his or her own way, blasts through barriers and carries banners high whilst you fret and worry that the cops will succeed in repelling the demonstration and perhaps even maim or kill someone in the process. You are the worrier. Tiger is the warrior. Tigers (God love 'em) are afraid of nothing. They espouse change, run after it and then roll around in it as though attempting to remove their stripes. But you can't do that. You are too afraid that something awful will happen. This year, put yourself in the capable, fearless paws of the Tiger. You will thrive and so will your loved ones. In return for his or her favors, you can be cautious for the Tiger. As the impetuous Tiger leads you into battle, remember to whisper that, confidentially, you, as his faithful lieutenant, do not think it wise to be exposing one's self without bulletproof vests. Tigers may listen and heed your counsel. And then again they may not. What do you have to watch out for? Your natural penchant for paranoia.

2011, the Metal Cat year – Initially, you may fear this year will be extremely uncomfortable. But the edginess will wear off when, after a couple of months, you realize that the Cat is not only friendly to

Dog people – but helpful and even comforting. In Chinese astrology, Cats and Dogs get along moderately well together. The Cat may not be your ally in guerrilla warfare; but he or she will not get in the way of progress and may even (if approached gently) be willing to finance one or two of your more charitable efforts. You will be pleasantly surprised as well by the way the general tone of the Cat year affects the sentimental side of your life. The person you love and have been wishing would accept your troth, might just concede. There is evidence of commitment now. It's time to start thinking of building a life together. If you fail to make the right moves at the right time, however, you could miss the love boat altogether in this Cat year. Keep your ears open for hints that your sweetheart is ready. He or she may not shout out a willingness to nest. You will need to read between the lines and listen for significant sighs for signs of acquiescence. Money starts to flow more freely into your coffers mid year. Keep some back for that honeymoon or better still, save it for the baby's nursery furniture.

2012, the Water Dragon year – You will find this year nerve-racking because of the excess noise and brouhaha which accompanies the reign of every Dragon. They just cannot keep still. Moreover, they require an obedient, willing and admiring audience. You Dog people tend not to gush. You give a 'woof' of approval and get on with the business at hand. For Dragons, your shrugging 'woofs' don't make the grade. So what does the Dragon do to pump up your volume? He shouts and prances and celebrates louder. You won't be able to tamp down his flamboyance. Just go with the flow and keep smiling. If you approach the Dragon with due respect and (fake it if necessary) a certain amount of awe, he will grant you excellent advice. Listen up. Dragons are the generals from whom you can learn some basic strategies with which to wage your perpetual war on injustice. Try not to display your irritation with the Dragon's style. Let there be noise. What do you care? You are there to absorb information. Family affairs may cause you to lose face this year. And you will no doubt be the unwitting source of the loss. As you are well aware, your biting comments can get you into deep hot water. Try not to tell your sister-in-law that her hair looks like dried cornstalks or disrupt the family reunion by opining that whoever made the potato salad this year should go back to cooking school. Tact, Doggie. Tact.

2013, the Water Snake year – Political unrest and even riots and wars are common in Snake years. Providing the turmoil might lead to justice for all, you won't be upset about what's going on. But where aggression is happening for its own sake, you will most decidedly not approve and may even decide to start your own battle against what's happening. The Snake will not be averse to your crusades and campaigns for the betterment of humankind, but neither will you receive masses of donations under the Snake's reign. Snakes prefer to spend their money on frivolities, luxuries and accessories. They never feel terrific about having to fund necessities. Paying the electricity bill annoys Snakes. So don't go barking for cash to hire mercenaries for your own causes this year. You won't find any willing philanthropists. You may, however, receive some very good advice. Snakes are philosophers. They understand what's going on under even the most baroque circumstances. So don't ask for charity, but do listen to all the Snake's speeches. They usually make infinite sense. Pay more attention to your private life. Your lover needs your support and comfort. When you get involved in your projects and plans, you tend to disappear both physically and mentally, cutting yourself off from relationships and sometimes even straying from the marriage bed. If your sweetheart finds out . . . you, my dear Poochie, will be relegated to the doghouse.

2014, the Wood Horse year – Oh lucky you! Horses can't get enough of Dog company. They are already mighty energetic people who never stop working and building and painting and writing and dancing. Horses are, in fact, a tad frenzied. Your presence is positively tranquilizing to the Horse. You are a person of reason, logic and good sense. Your way of thinking impresses the Horse and may even influence him or her to change certain major things about their lifestyle. Where you see wasted effort or extreme behavior, you do not hesitate to remark on it. You Dogs can be pejoratively critical. But you can also be constructively critical and help out a friend who is making a big mistake. The Horse (who just about never takes advice from anyone) will heed your counsel and even thank you for being more practical than he. Conversely, when the Horse is in power, the ambience is somewhat tense and laden with free-floating anxiety. This atmosphere is not your favorite. Why? Because you were born anxious so you simply don't need extra reasons to fret. Try working off some of that nervousness with meditation or yoga. Or . . . if

Eastern practices don't appeal to you, try scrubbing your floor, washing the car or running around the block 111 times.

2015, the Wood Goat year – In this year, insecurity tends to color everything. The Goat means no harm to you Dogs. In fact, Goat people get along swimmingly with their Dog cronies. Dogs, too, enjoy company of all types. But they particularly enjoy the company of open-minded Goat people who listen attentively to their complaints about everything from man's inhumanity to man to bias and discrimination against the poor and unwashed. So the Dog's causes and beliefs will not be threatened or undone in this Goat year. You may, indeed, get things accomplished that you did not expect to be able to carry through. However, you are more comfortable not having to bear the weight of more than yourself in life. You are not unreliable, but you do not wish to be depended on. The Goat lives to depend. So in this Goat year, you feel listened to – but you may also feel leaned on. Beware of offering your shoulder to cry on once too often and ending up with someone who wants to be able to count on you for support and rescue for the rest of their natural life. Your job this year is to fend off sycophants. Keep clear of freeloaders and wend your way speedily past any and all creatures who fancy living at *your* house and eating *your* food and watching *your* TV until they get back on their feet. If you let them in, they may still be there next year, in the Monkey year and the Rooster year and the next Dog and Pig years – on and on ad infinitum.

2016, the Fire Monkey year – Monkey years can be tricky. This one will be no exception. Monkeys know all the ropes and will use them to climb up and over the rest of the world as much as they can. As brilliant as you Dog people are, you are hardly ever guilty of hoodwinking merely for the sake of putting something over on someone. You want justice and mean to get things done right. But for once, in this complex year, you might just take a big risk and start a new business or do something daring. Why not try to strike it rich? Instead of remaining in the back seat, you can be in the forefront thinking up schemes to make money. It's about time you saw some financial gain and could take a break from wearing your bleeding heart on your sleeve. The family situation in the Monkey year will be happier than it has been in a while. You may be more the center of attention than you like to be. Take it in your stride. Invite your parents, your in-laws and your kids to share in the fun with picnics and barbecues, road trips and fun in the sun. You are always good to family. But the reverse has not always been true. Enjoy it while you can. Whilst everything is moving so smoothly, you might want to have a few check-ups. See your doctor for a general medical check. Go to an ophthalmologist or other specialist for any specific symptoms and don't forget to see the dentist every six months. There doesn't seem to be anything wrong with you. But better safe than sorry.

2017, the Fire Rooster year – This year has definite conservative overtones. Because of this, if you attempt to overthrow any governments or force the rich to give up their yachts to house the homeless, you will suffer great losses. Instead of trying to fight the system, I suggest you continue in last year's money-grubbing vector. It's about the only way for you to keep on winning. No amount of effort will make the Rooster smile on your campaigns to get more subsidies for the poor, better public education or health insurance for all. It just is not the time for that sort of do-gooding. So go with the flow and continue to strive for more personal income. If you apply yourself and make a lot of money in this Rooster year, you will have all the more to spend on crusading next year, which is (as you no doubt already know) the Dog year! Romance keeps avoiding your grasp in this Rooster year. Dogs are not happy campers without sexual gratification. The struggle for cash might not be much fun, but being a workaholic does have the advantage of keeping you off the streets. Don't overdo the gourmet business lunches. If you're not careful, your waistline could go to the dogs.

2018, the Earth Dog year – Phew! This twelve-year period has been a tough haul for you Doggies. Bravo for getting through it all with tails a-wagging. As promised, you now have a great deal more capital than you did in the past few years. In this Dog year, nothing stands in the way of success in your every endeavor. No use giving up the business you so wisely started a couple of years ago. But do slow down. No use sacrificing your health to the pursuit of wealth. You are not all that materialistic by nature. You could live comfortably in a one-room apartment with a single cup (no saucer) and a handful of takeaway phone numbers. You are not exactly a Spartan. But damn close. So if you are worn out from excelling at making money, take time off to drink some of your vintage wine out of your single mug and read a few good books. Please don't forget that, according to Chinese astrology, in your year you must sit down and plan the next twelve years of your existence. Where do you want to be in 2030? What will you be doing and with whom? Write down each year and put your priorities in order. If you want to have kids and don't have any, then start thinking about it now. Do you long to build a spanking new house, take a trip around the world, climb a challenging mountain or marry the beauty queen/king of your dreams? Make a point of filling in all the blanks so as to better manage your destiny.

2019, the Earth Pig year – Dogs always benefit from the Pig's benevolent influence. The Pig wants luxury. But not for the sake of buying more trinkets, owning flashy vehicles or being seen with 'the right people'. The Pig seeks authenticity first. If he makes a lot of money, he may invest it all in one work of art that he will treasure and cherish – even if it hangs alone on the wall of his log cabin in the woods. If a Pig person takes a spouse, you can be sure the person is someone of value whose heart is in the right place. Jewelry? Idem. Only the best. Even if she only has one earring – the Pig will choose an antique 18-carat pink gold bauble bought at Sotheby's or Christie's or in Florence or Venice or in Paris itself. So in this Pig year, tradition and value will be high on the list of priorities. Make it your business, Doggie, to use this propitious time to advance your causes and implement your crusades. The Pig loves you and admires what you stand for. You can count on him to boost both your morale and your reputation. Love (which has been patiently waiting in the wings) dances your way in Pig years. Feel free to fall madly in love and even get married this year. It's a no-holds-barred fun-filled year of pure satisfaction for Dogs.

猪

The Pristine Pig

Gallant Pig,

You are a model of sincerity, purity, tolerance and honor. You want to do everything right. You've got a fine feeling for aesthetics and a flair for authenticity. We seek your common sense advice and enjoy your convivial company. You delight in country living. Rustic sensuality and off-color jokes tickle you silly. Gourmet food is no stranger to your lips either. Face it, Piglet, you're a *bona fide bon vivant*. However, you are far too accommodating. People take advantage of your yielding nature. Then, when you've exhausted yourself by giving too much, you fly into fits, tantrums, blind rages. We all run for cover when you're angry, reappearing only when you are re-ensconced in your favorite velvet armchair, your attention riveted on an expensive art book, smacking your lips characteristically while downing a stunning box of imported chocolates. Phew!

You Pig people often become rich. You can't help it. You're mad about opulence. Silks, hand-crafted silvers and 18 carat gold candelabra befit your sumptuous tastes. In romantic matters, you get on very well with hot-blooded Dragons, creative Goats and classy, countrified Cats. Whatever you do, don't let an elegant Snake slither into your heart. Hands off practical Roosters, too. Peace of mind sets in once you have learned to say *no* loud and clear. Then, usually post middle-age, your surges of rage will abate and life will become a real wallow. Try, in the interest of healthy self-defense, to exercise your right to refuse to serve others. Just say *no*. And remember . . . practice makes perfect.

Scrupulously yours,

Suzanne White

In the twentieth and twenty-first century all Pigs were born between the following dates:

30	January	1911	and	17	February	1912
16	February	1923	and	4	February	1924
4	February	1935	and	23	January	1936
22	January	1947	and	9	February	1948
8	February	1959	and	27	January	1960
27	January	1971	and	14	February	1972
13	February	1983	and	1	February	1984
31	January	1995	and	18	February	1996
18	February	2007	and	6	February	2008
5	February	2019	and	24	January	2020

The Pig ID card

Lasting symbols have special powers. Enhance your self-image by surrounding yourself with tangible signs of your own identity. Make these symbols known to your friends and loved ones. Use them daily and they will bring you luck, security and a feeling of personal worth.

Your best	*Your favorite*
color is royal purple	food is delicacies
flower is cala lily	animal is cat
fragrance is ambergris	drink is bordeaux
tree is acacia	spice is cloves
flavor is sweet and sour	metal is purest silver
birthstone is moonstone	herb is oregano
lucky number is 5	musical instrument is harp

The Pig is yin *The Pig's motto is 'I preserve'*

When wallowing contentedly along, Pigs are sensible, sensual and sensitive, sweetly naïve, caring, self-sacrificing, erudite, talented, open-handed, candid, outgoing, amusing, charitable, obliging, graciously hospitable and virtuous.

But when their elastic generosity has been stretched beyond its limit, out pops Piggy's darker side. Then, he becomes hot-tempered, pessimistic, outrageously epicurean, earthy to a fault, sardonic, snobbish, snide, authoritarian, competitive, know-it-all, stingy, victimized and sometimes downright criminally mad at the world.

This little Piggy

In China, this sign is called Wild Boar. In America and Europe, one doesn't meet up much with wild boars so I prefer to use an animal we know and, as most other westernized Chinese astrologers, call this sign the Pig.

In rural communities the pig is the staff of life. Each small farmer or peasant in Europe kills at least one pig every year. Pig-killing is a messy process, the details of which I will spare you here, but for farmers, the pig is the main provider.

In human life, although most families don't go so far as to slaughter their Pig parents or spouses, the Pig of a family is the solid, settled pillar of strength upon whom everyone can count, in whom everybody confides and from whom one can always get a quick loan. Pigs are generous of spirit and kinder than the rest of us.

When you first meet them, Pigs seem too good to be true. They are careful and caring, worried about how they may strike you, courteously hesitant to call you by your first name and so opulently well-mannered as to make you wonder if they've been lobotomized.

Maybe this gentle, cultivated approach is one reason why Pigs are always so attractive. Marriage-minded men (swashbuckling slave-trader types) find docile, gracious, cultured Pig women irresistibly wifely. Pig girls are the easiest to marry off in Chinese culture. Then, too, marriage-craving women, reputedly an especially ruthless species, snap baby Piggy men right off Mama's apron strings and hog-tie them for life.

Pigs are the people everyone admires most. Make a list of the Pigs in your life: aren't they the nicest, most loving and scrupulously caring people around? Haven't they got the warmest, most graciously furnished living room, the most infallible good taste and a magical gift for making guests feel both satisfied and special? Whether for gourmet meals, a cup of coffee, fashionable cocktails or lavish wedding receptions, Pigs are born to receive.

Pigs are attuned to the *other*, geared towards exteriorizing their goodness. They almost seem born to give, to yield and to serve. They are constantly sacrificing their own happiness and comfort for the sake of somebody else: a child, a mate, a lover, a dog or cat, a neighbor who's sick or a colleague at work. If a Pig has a minute, he'll gladly bestow it on you with a smile and if he doesn't have a minute he'll probably tailor-make one just your size.

Complex machinations are definitely not a Pig speciality: Pigs are so innocently obliging that they are frequently misused in business by those less scrupulous than they. Pigs are so gullible that many are forever being dragged through inextricably messy love affairs, falling victim to long-winded stormy divorces and suffering enforced bankruptcies.

Not only are Pigs easy to fool, they like it that way. They cling to the idea that everybody is beautiful and good. No matter how old they get, they never cease to believe that man/woman is basically good. Sam is a New York attorney. Lately, he is walking around looking crushed and insomniac. Why, Sam wonders, did he not discover straight away that his first wife came from a family of criminals who would attempt to use his good name and professional reputation to reach their own ends? Why did he not suspect that family would order their daughter to drop him and take him for all the alimony she could get?

'Am I stupid or what?' asked Sam.

'No. You're brilliant. But you're stubbornly naïve,' I said.

Sam's serial divorces have exhausted his fortunes, depleted his strength and worn thin the patience of his most devoted cronies. But these marital mishaps have not broken his spirit or dampened his enthusiasm for repeatedly becoming embroiled in basket after basket of man-eating crabs.

When his affections are involved, Sam cannot see beyond the end of his carved oak desk. He pities people. He's non-judgemental and happily acts as everybody's Big Daddy. In business, he never charges people he likes for professional services. For a Pig, this is natural. He cares more than he ought to and furthermore . . . doesn't know how to say no.

'Well, what's going on in your private life now?' I asked Sam, hoping he'd learned his lesson.

'I'm having a thing with this really lovely woman. She's tall and shapely, strong as hell and verrrry intelligent. I like her a lot. But it's complicated. She's married – or, well – she's attached to somebody who doesn't want to let her go,' said Sam, making circles in the sand with a stick. 'He's her pimp. She's really stuck. Poor kid . . .'

Obviously, Sam's not really meant for this world. He loves purely for the sake of love itself – especially if he feels sorry for somebody.

Like so many Pigs, I suspect Sam of being in love with love. And, in his Piggish way, in love with traditions such as marriage and kids, houses in the country and sailing boats, Christmas, and cozy parties with friends round the fireplace. Soon he will probably get himself roughed up by his new lady love's pimp and I'll have to go and visit him in hospital – dear Sam all bandaged and meek, murmuring with some difficulty, 'How could I have known?'

I have a French girlfriend named Eve who fell in love with the biggest rake I have ever known, an American called Kevin. He is a self-proclaimed genius writer and philosopher. So far, aged fifty, Kevin has seduced and abandoned enough women to have become an entry in the *Guinness Book of Records*.

The beautiful Eve, like so many Pigs, is a rip-snorting success in her career. She founded and runs a large public relations firm in Paris as its managing director and president. Like all Pigs, Eve is not only shrewd and lucky in business, but she's bright, charming, warm-hearted and soap-opera romantic. A few years ago, Eve came with me to a jolly Parisian brunch given by Kevin in his digs in the Marais quarter. She didn't leave with me that day and, next thing I knew, was following Kevin to America to meet his family! Nobody had ever heard of Kevin's family meeting one of his conquests before. He must be serious about this woman, I thought.

They chased each other across the ocean before they announced that they were returning to Paris to live at Eve's apartment. Kevin would keep his flat in New York. Eve wanted a baby desperately – her biological clock was ticking away – and they decided that when she got pregnant, they would marry.

Before tying the knot, Eve had to get down to some serious work: she'd been flitting back and forth across the Atlantic, getting to know Kevin and his family, repainting his New York apartment at her expense, buying him new furniture and new clothes. While she went to the office each day, Kevin stayed at home writing his book.

One day, Eve's secretary felt ill and left the office early. Eve decided to follow suit and left for home at 4.30 p.m. At 4.45 p.m., she burst into her apartment unannounced to find Kevin and the ailing secretary rolling around on the carpet. The secretary started blurting excuses about how she'd only come to tell Eve she was feeling better and could come back to work. Eve calmed her down, gave the young woman her taxi fare and sent her home.

Eve was crushed and aghast at Kevin's blatant Don Juanishness.

'How could you?' she said, weeping. 'Not only are you unfaithful to me but you've humiliated me.'

Kevin said, 'Darling, that crazy girl tried to rape me. She came here to see you and then when I asked her in, she jumped me.'

Eve believed him and fired her secretary the next day. Then, she overheard Kevin in whispered conversation with a woman he had known in New York: 'Yes, sweetie. You know I love you but I have to do this. For me this woman represents a new security. I'll be able to write undistracted by material worries. I will spend hours with you when I come back for a week in January.' Then, lowering his voice, 'I miss your . . .'

Eve couldn't listen to the last few words. Was Kevin really still in love with that woman he'd met in New York three years ago?

Kevin came in and asked her, 'What's wrong with *ma petite chérie*?'

'I heard you on the phone,' she sniffled, 'talking to that woman . . .' She broke down.

'You silly goose. That was my mother! From Pittsburgh.'

'Then why did you say New York?'

'Because she's going to be in New York in January when I go there for a meeting with my publisher.'

Eve was ecstatic. Her innocent little pixie face lit up and she smiled through her tears. She took Kevin's greying head in her hands and said, 'I'm pregnant.'

They rejoiced and set a date for the wedding.

Meanwhile, Kevin had locked a shoebox full of Eve's letters into the linen cupboard in the lavatory. Whenever he went to the loo he read a few of her old love letters. One day, he forgot to lock the door. Eve burst into the bathroom and found him reading her mail. She shrieked at him. Kevin claimed that he had been sorting out her files, putting them in alphabetical order. She grabbed the box: the letters were out of order and lots were even missing. 'Liar!' she exploded. 'I hate liars!'

'So what did you do then?' I asked her a week later when she rang me up.

'I threw him out. You don't know how mad I was. I never want to see that disgusting, lying, cheating *personnage* again,' she said. Then she added, 'But I am going to have his child.'

'But why? A baby needs his father. If you're carrying Kevin's child, he is going to complicate your life. He has a right to see his child. He'll never leave you alone. The child may never forgive you either. You'd better do something while there's still time,' I said gravely.

'I shall marry someone else very soon and nobody will be able to prove anything,' protested Eve. 'I know what I'm doing, and I'll call you if I need you.'

She never rang back. And I never called her either. I sensed that a large portion of Eve's determination to give birth to Krazy Kevin's kid was inspired by a steamy Pig-like fury at Kevin's duplicitous antics.

A few weeks ago, three years after these events, I boarded an airplane to New York. I was making my way to my seat in the tourist section and whom did I pass but Eve – with a blond two- to three-year-old boy, playing with toy cars.

I nearly dropped my hand luggage. 'Eve . . . you had Kevin's baby.'

'Oh no,' said Eve. 'This is Colin's baby.'

'Who's Colin?'

'Oh, I met Colin a couple of years ago. We got married after Kevin Bartlett left Paris.' Eve gathered up her little boy. 'This is Kevin O'Connell.'

She named it after him. 'Bravo,' I said, unconvincingly. Indeed, this blond-haired blue-eyed sunny little boy looked nothing like the original brooding, swarthy, Kevin. 'He's not Kevin's son, then?'

'Oh, no,' she laughed her sweetest giggle. 'I lost Kevin's baby after six weeks. Kevin is named after Colin's dad. But Colin and I don't live together any more. He turned out to be an alcoholic.'

The situation was weird. Nevertheless, I was relieved. I knew that Eve was a Pig, hence too kindly and compassionate to bear someone's child out of spite. Dastardly, underhand, mean acts are out of character for such benevolent souls.

Obviously, as an executive Piglette, Eve must be canny and even shrewd in business. Yet, although she might threaten revenge in Piggish pique against someone who betrays her confidence, it seemed impossible that she would do anything damaging to another human being. Altruism comes first with Pigs. Hence, they are often disillusioned and frequently misused by bounders, cads and rotters.

Pigs are naïve, innocent, unwitting, artless, guileless, unsuspecting and childlike – and they prefer it that way. Would you have listened when Kevin said he had been raped by Eve's secretary?

One doesn't have to be a member of MENSA to see through such blatant ruse. But, Pigs, no matter their IQ, prefer to face each new day with a *tabula rasa*, non-judgemental frame of mind. Pigs never forget but they forgive easily. This is the positive side of the self-enforced innocence and hapless naïvete native to all Pigs. Pigs always give everyone breaks, indulge thieves, shield meddlers and try to understand the motives of fiends. It can be exasperating but it is admirable. Pigs are generous with the benefit of the doubt, incurably sympathetic to the underdog and rarely take issue with the behavior of someone for whom they have affection.

The Pig is a charmer. He knows how to appeal to people of all sorts, makes friends easily and is rapidly adopted as a crony by all. Pigs please without trying. The average Piggy uses honest praise wisely. He knows how to make everyone he likes feel more special than anyone else. As a result, everyone wants to be the Pig's best friend.

An invitation to Piggy's home is always flattering. If you're the guest of a Pig, you will be well received, and amply fed and spoiled by his hostly attentions. Drop an inadvertent hint about how much you adore *crème caramel* and next time you dine at Piggy's house, you will be served vast amounts of it. Let an invited Pig guest know that you won't have time to prepare the elegant dinner he might have enjoyed tonight and that Pig will show up with enough delicious food for thousands.

Food is one of Piggy's little sins. It is rare to see an adult Pig without a spare tire or protruding tummy. Pigs are all slightly epicurean and adore fresh wholesome food, and thriving on all the trimmings that go with the meal: cigars, port, cognac, liqueurs and after-dinner chocolates. Like his animal counterpart, the Pig often over-eats but unlike his gluttonly barnyard brother, the Chinese Pig is a cultivated, discriminating gourmet with a well-developed palate.

Pigs are often perceived as meek. They are confirmed pacifists and never exhibit visible signs of aggression. Always the gentleman, the Pig does more than his share of bowing and scraping. Many behave in an apologetic and meaninglessly self-sacrificing way. No matter their discomfort, it is the Pig who insists on riding in the back seat so you can sit next to the driver, especially if the driver happens to be their husband, wife or lover.

This self-effacing conduct may appear martyr-like or strike you as boy-scout overkill. Trust me, it is genuine: the Pig would do almost anything to avoid tension or guilt. He learns early on that one way to avert stress or self-recrimination is to surrender his position before he's even been challenged. Don't worry about abusing your friend's generosity. The peace-loving Piggy rolled acquiescently into that back seat before you noticed the color of the car.

Further, Pigs deplore quarrelling and despise open argument. When called upon to take a stand and be firm with a fellow human, Pigs usually avoid the issue or beat a quiet retreat. If attacked, however, Pigs are tough and will aim accurately at the jugular, but they refuse to clutter up their lives with malcontents. They flee from disgruntled folk who might incite them to a rare towering rage. Pigs are ultrasensitive and fragile: conflict upsets their placid natures. They are so non-violent that they would usually prefer to appear stupid or lose an argument rather than enter the fray. They are past masters at the art of changing the subject, skirting thorny issues and turning the music up to drown vituperation.

Of course, the Pig's passion for serenity and unwillingness to deal with life's sharper angles can handicap him. It can also be a pain in the hambone for his friends and family. He is so supremely emotional that his reactions are almost always subjective. When a jagged edge rises suddenly up before him, the Pig starts back in horror, bumbles, trips, apologizes profusely. Often, he wishes he didn't have such overwhelming emotional ups and downs. He dreams of being tougher and more heroic. Pigs are not lily-livered snivellers but their excessively active emotions curse them with a squirmy, uncomfortable, skinned-alive feeling of vulnerability. In reaction to tension, the Pig often becomes skittish or squeamish and may then behave irrationally. He will lead a more balanced lifestyle and view events more objectively once he succeeds in conquering his tendency to hyperemotivity and curbs his subjective reactions to emotional stimulus.

Pigs are born culture vultures. They may prefer to live in the country and lie about listening to music or baking rough country bread to consume with fresh butter and homemade jam but if they have access to a city, they never miss an exhibition, concert or ballet. They scour antique shops and haunt auctions for new treasures to buy for their sumptuous penthouse or opulent farmhouse retreat.

Pigs are traditionalists who believe fiercely in the lessons of the past as an example for the present and guide to the future. Avid readers of history, Pigs consult historical events, recall landmark battles when asked, can list hundreds of names of kings, generals, their mistresses and servants' middle names. To a Pig, the best way to do something is as it was done in the good old days.

In company, Pigs often wax pedagogical. They never tire of expounding on some moot point or reaching up into the bookshelf at the end of a big convivial meal, dragging down a heavy leather tome or two and relating wild and woolly tales of the intrigues of days gone by. In private, too, Pigs read books the way six-year-olds consume chocolate biscuits. Pigs also collect information to back up their basic theories. They love to uncover examples of how truth, purity and goodness invariably win out over wickedness and evil.

The Pig's secret inner life is chock-a-block with dreams of heroes rescuing damsels in distress, or princes and princesses whose blameless virtue saved the kingdom from destruction, of warring factions finding a peaceful means to a truce, for love to win out over hate and for hate, in its turn, to be given instant absolution. Deep down, the Pig sincerely longs for all to be well on earth which, in turn, is under the perpetual protection of a benevolent God and a spotlessly incorruptible band of merry saints who float around on gold-tinged clouds playing Mozart.

Some people claim that Pigs are snobbish. Manners, breeding and good taste are of enormous importance to them. I prefer to call them aesthetes: Pigs are born with an excellent nose for style in everything from dress to furnishings. Venture into any Pig's sitting room, no matter the social milieu or income level, and you will be astounded by the aura of *luxe*, the tasteful, comforting scale on which the living spaces are arranged, the precious antique plates on the mantelpiece, the walls embellished with fine drawings, prints and paintings. Authenticity is of optimal importance to Pigs. He would rather have one gold earring than thirty phoney ones, one real pearl to drawers full of beads.

To compound their reputation for the odd foray into snobbery, Pigs are inveterate name-droppers. They are always saying things like, 'You know I had lunch at 21. Whom do you think I saw? *Nina Truffaut*.'

Long pause while Piggy eyes you to note if you show signs of recognizing who the hell Nina Truffaut is, and God help you if you don't because then the quiz begins. 'Of course you know her. She's François Truffaut's sister-in-law. Don't you remember? She's in the decorating business in New York,' says Piggy.

Never heard of her? Well, shame on you. But never mind – Piggy will instruct you. 'You must know about her. Her father was the heir to the big Portuguese duck pâté fortune. It's sad really. Despite her good education, Nina's always in the tabloids . . .' If you're wise, you'll change the subject. Otherwise, Piggy will hammer bevies of big name acquaintances at you till you've forgotten what he was talking about in the first place.

Pigs are great people but they are far too easily impressed by hotshots. Ironically, they don't want anyone dropping their name. Another notable characteristic is their distinct lack of desire to change the world, to stand out from the crowd or be publicly honored for good deeds. Pigs swerve sharply away from competition and eschew scheming, wheeling and dealing. Yet, paradoxically, Pigs almost always manage to get their sticky little trotters on pots of money. In China, Pigs are identified with plenty and prosperity and are often endowed with great wealth. Good luck seems to pursue them in everything from playing the stockmarket to slot machines. Sometimes they inherit money but even if they do, although they may appear languid, Pigs perpetually and diligently engage in money-gathering. They are patently unafraid of hard work, purposeful, tenacious and intelligent. Success in almost any profession is assured.

Yet if Pigs believe everything they are told, flee from artful plots, reject shady deals, deplore conflict and are willing to give anyone the benefit of the doubt, *how* do they manage to accumulate so much money? Self-reliance and stoicism are two of the Pig's most salient features. A Pig rarely asks for help and cannot graciously accept it. A Pig who is ill won't tell you *how* ill he is and will probably refuse your aspirin and scoff hugely at your offer to run him to hospital.

An exquisite Pig friend called Paulette, whom I have known for over thirty years, is an arch example of stolid suffering. Whether Paulette is in acute physical pain, nervous tachycardia, depressed or besieged by flu or raging toothache, she sits elegantly in her little Chanel tweed, hands folded, holding court at her giant marble-topped dining table, listening to her guests recount their latest escapades, commenting, applauding or offering to help.

Not long ago, I was talking to Paulette's mother. 'I am so worried about Paulette,' she said. 'Last Wednesday, when you and the Rousseaus came to dinner, she had chronic tachycardia. I tried to get her to retire early and let us carry on without her but Paulette always thinks she knows best. I keep pleading with her to slow down. She won't listen to me – or anyone else. She keeps on rushing about all day and in the evenings, she sits up till 2 a.m., poring over her accounts and drafting petitions.'

'Can't the doctor order her to spend a few days in bed?' I asked.

'The doctor never stops ordering her to do just that,' replied her mother. 'But she won't listen. She just carries imperturbably on.'

Then I spoke to Paulette and asked her how she was. 'I'm fine,' she snapped. 'Why do you ask?'

'Well . . . your mother did hint that perhaps you were overdoing it a bit lately,' I tried, wanting to shelter her mother from daughterly reproaches for meddling.

'Listen, Suzanne *chérie*,' said Paulette hurriedly. 'I do appreciate your sweet call but I must rush off now. It's time for church and I am driving friends. What's worse, it's my week for flowers on the altar. By the way, I bought you masses of potted flowers for your garden while I was at the flower market. I'll bring them round next week. See you soon, *mon chou*,' and she rang off.

I would gladly have driven Paulette to church, picked up the flowers or the friends. But Paulette will not be helped. Rather, she is obsessed by her urge to give. She must indulge everyone around her but will take nothing in return. If she receives a gift, she giggles humbly, mumbles a quick *merci* and lays the gift discreetly aside so as not to draw attention to herself and away from you.

How wonderful it is to have a Pig for a friend! Lots of Pig friends is even more lovely. All my Pig friends and acquaintances are adorable in their personal *and* more general Piggy-sign ways.

But if you have a lifetime Pig friend, don't think that your worries are over. Pigs are steadfast, loyal, faithful and giving – *only* as long as they approve of you. A Pig's devotion is unfathomable as long as you are in his good graces. But God forbid you should step over his secret boundary line: if you do something of which your Pig friend profoundly disapproves, don't be surprised if you never hear from him again.

Take the advice of someone who has lost a couple of Pig cronies: never try to force your opinions or your unsolicited assistance on a Pig; never give undue attention to members of *his* entourage; never impinge on what he considers *his* moral or physical territory; never meddle in *his* private business.

Pigs are possessive, jealous and exclusive. They don't often make much noise about it but all Pigs are achingly conscious of trivia such as how much younger than her age Sarah looks, how much less James paid for his house than Piggy, how Peter can afford a new Mercedes when he said he was too poor to pay Piggy back the loan, how you said that you enjoyed so-and-so's party and didn't mention Piggy's last bash, and . . . how long you have been standing there staring lustfully at Piggy's lover!

Pigs keep impeccable books, pay their taxes on time and rigorously declare every last cent of what they earn. Yet they are wildly extravagant. The more anxious and fearful he is, the more the Pig tends to squander. He is always aiming to provide extra comfort and achieve grander grandeur. He covets, and buys, well-cut clothing of the best fabrics, sometimes has wardrobes full of softest leather shoes and is lavishly generous with those close to him. He is ever conscious of the need to create or provide some reliable form of endurable purity, a cocoon wherein he and his tribe can increase comfortably in opulence and generate a spirit of goodwill worthy of the Pig's noblest aspirations.

Ms Piggy

The Pig lady is whimsically unstable. Sudden changes of heart and mind cause her and her entourage some dreadfully insecure moments.

However, when Madame Pig is feeling hale and steady, no ill wind ruffles the smooth-sailing ambience in her peaceful, well-cared-for household. No one knows why but, at some point, the willies set in and slowly overcome her. When she starts to feel unsure of herself, put upon, unable to take the next step without fretting, making snide remarks or even griping openly about how others have mistreated her, the Pig lady has embarked on one of her downward spirals and may be subject to anything from a few days of grumpiness to a depression that requires medical care.

The very quality we all so love in this person's nature is also her worst enemy. We are attracted to Pig women because they are compliant, good listeners, suggestible, impressionable and loving. They serve their mates and families willingly, spend hours aiding friends and relatives with everything from their tax returns to doing their ironing, asking in return little more than peace of mind, love, comfort and security. Yet even when they have achieved that, some Pig women retain an unpleasant sensation that something is missing. This creepy awareness grinds away at their equilibrium and may cause these highly susceptible women to break down.

In a way, they are reacting to their own unwillingness to refuse to serve. They are furious because they did not say no often enough. Ms Piggy wishes she had had the guts to turn down those requests which she feels distract from what *she* really wants to do. Yet the pain is real. You can hear it in their plaintive songs as, during these periods of discomfiting awareness, Pig women often repeat the same type of refrain. With longing in their voices, they recite their wish list: 'I need more time to myself. I wish I could take a course in horticulture or painting. I want a studio where I can shut out everybody who keeps pulling at me.' The Pig woman's wish list is long and almost always consists of projects which would take her out of the house, reduce pressure, allow her to unwind and be alone. But she hardly ever gets round to insisting on having any of it fulfilled. Deep down, she doesn't dare to accept them. As a Pig she is naturally devoted, subservient, humble and modest. She is also gentle and self-sacrificing, loyal and committed to duty. To be brazenly selfish enough to put herself first is out of the question. Hence, her perpetually conflicted nature. She is happiest when she is fulfilling her obligations but because of her fine intelligence and multi-talented nature, the smart little voice in the back of her head constantly repeats that she should be doing something more edifying, that she should be a fully fledged portrait painter or a recognized actress or businesswoman.

Yet, she is reluctant to distinguish herself or in any way stand out from the crowd. Publicity makes her blush and public appearance causes her to sweat. Somewhere in her heart of hearts she believes that she wants attention from a public who loves her work, admires her style and applauds her good taste and manners.

It is rare to see a Pig woman give up home to pursue an independent career and live on her own. As my beloved departed sister, Sally-the-painterly-Pig used to say, 'Of course I want to be recognized as a painter. But it may snowball. Then what will I do?'

In my enthusiasm for her success, I would reply brightly, 'You'll be able to go on painting for ever.'

'Some future!' retorted Sally. 'If I become a well-known painter who sells a lot of paintings, I shall be *obliged* to go on painting for ever. What will happen to my family? What if my paintings don't continue to bring in good money? What if. . . .?'

'What if you fail?' I offered.

'I couldn't stand to fail,' answered the good Sally whose paintings now hang in museums.

As she was a genius, Sally never failed. But she always thought she would and feared the consequences.

Pig women are not usually startling beauties in the classical sense but they are almost always pretty and interesting to look at. They emanate the special sweetness and warmth, of the old-fashioned ideal wife and mother, and appeal to a variety of males. In the presence of men, Pig ladies know instinctively how to appear helpless. Men stand at the ready to lift them over puddles and help them on with their coats. Even well into middle age they retain an air of little girlishness which men find irresistibly charming.

Ms Piggy's complexion is exquisitely creamy and tinged with just the right pink (or sometimes freckles). Her figure is neither too thick nor too slim. She has an open, broad smile and an easy laugh. Her eyes are unusually big and often appear astonished, wide awake and even surprised by everything she sees. She is endowed with a fine head of densely planted robust hair which she wears in the simplest of styles. Her childlike enthusiasm is contagious. She seems unruffled and is rarely disturbed when dropped in on or asked for a favor. No matter her age, Ms Piggy is perpetually young at heart. She dresses in excellent taste and almost always embellishes her carefully color-coordinated ensembles with gold or silver jewellery. Ms Piggy is a traditionalist with a flair for the exotic.

The Pig woman always does things right. No half-way solutions for her. If she wants a house in the country, she finds the prettiest, remodels and decorates it with impeccable taste and gets it paid for by some miracle which only she knows how to cook up. She studies on her own, storing information and culture the way a rechargeable battery stores electricity. Her conversation is as intriguing as her cozy hospitality is attractive and endearing. She loves to gather people together and feed them delectable specialities that she has learned to cook on her sojourns abroad. She will hold *soirées musicales,* followed by a luxurious dinner and a midnight dip in her heated pool.

Take my good friend Elspeth Juda, who I first met in 1984 when she was seventy-three. I saw her first at a Saturday market, carrying two heavy baskets and walking uphill at a good clip. Full crop of crisp white hair, arms and legs seemingly made of steel (she swims twenty laps every day), Elspeth bustled up to our group of three wherein she knew one of us well, set down her baskets, kissed everyone and invited us all to dinner that evening.

That year alone I dined about thirty times at Elspeth's house. Each evening she would think up some tempting new meal and/or invite mystery guests to amuse us. She might bring in some chic and charming people from Texas who owned department stores or introduce us to famous textile designers from London or to a prima ballerina from some travelling Russian troupe. Elspeth cooked. We cleared up. Conversations went on long past our mutual bedtimes.

Elspeth is just as lively in her London life. Her answering machine is always on because she is always out and about: theaters, concerts, dinners, or just visiting. Her husband, the love of her life, died many years before I met her and she never even dreamed of replacing him. She is still driving hither and yon, ordering everyone about and showering us all with her special brand of loving curiosity and concern about our children, lovers, finances and work. Elspeth was a famous fashion photographer in her youth and now she is a very competent painter.

All the Pig women I know are not only tough-minded yet nurturing but also talented for care-taking and creating. My friend Roselyne paints fabric patterns, sews, decorates, lays tiles and designs theater costumes. Plus she drives her daughter Melodie to every school function, and picks up other kids and takes them all to a movie. She also runs a successful business with her husband and is always inviting everybody to dinner. When I was sick in 1978, Roselyne gave up her three-month holiday and flew to New York from France. She looked after my house, cooked and cared for my kids without a word of complaint or fatigue. Pigs have showed me a thing or two about devotion that I never even dreamed existed.

The Pig lady is tenacious, patient, long-suffering and, unfortunately for her, resigned to accept her lot. Never lie to her because, although she may pretend to believe you, her gut-level intuition is almost as spot-on as the Goat's. The Pig woman is both delicate and accurate in her judgement of others. She's patient, observant and seems to put up with a lot but when she's finally too disappointed in someone, she'll shut off her loving spotlight and leave you to shiver alone on the tundra of life.

Ms Piggy fears criticism. Guilt and sensitivity combine to prevent her from feeling secure in undertaking life changes, making a difference in her chosen field of endeavor or standing up for her rights. She bides her time – or at least she thinks she does. In fact, she is afraid of making waves, generating surprises or being responsible for upheaval. This fear, when blended with her tendency to self-pity, sometimes makes the female Pig difficult to deal with. You can suggest remedies for her complaints till you're blue in the face, but she will never accept them – at least not while you are suggesting them. There is, in Ms Piggy, a strain of 'Poor me, I'm victimized.'

This trait doesn't always show – and is certainly not always there – but her sensitivities are so finely honed that she sometimes grasps at straws and may deduce from her own panic and inability to cope that she is being wronged or mistreated by something outside her control. Then too, when unscrupulous or mean-spirited people *are* taking advantage of her good nature, she feels helpless to deal with it. She is easily wounded and weeps easily when hurt – a soft target for bullies.

Some Pig women refuse to grow up. They feel safe in the role of daughter where the flood of responsibility is not always up to their noses. Ms Piggy loves to be mothered and likes to know that someone bigger and stronger will fight the battles for her.

As astonishing as this seems in the light of the Pig woman's excellent marriage possibilities, many Pig women choose spinsterhood instead of marriage. Because of their eternal hesitancy, they frequently remain stuck in the Oedipal stage, so attached to their parents – especially fathers – that they never want to dilute that tie by diverging and loving outsiders as well. This same resistance to growing up may manifest itself in an inordinate attachment to things and events of the past. Pig ladies often save all high school mementoes, shreds of baby blankets, postcards, letters and even their first shoelaces. Rather than seeking to face her adult self openly and move ahead, Ms Piggy often harks back to, and even produces, specimens from her past to justify her current resistance to leaving home.

We are not examining the character of the most liberated of women. Ms Piggy is anything but a crusader for women's rights. She requires to be attached to a home base and must satisfy her domestic concerns before she will set out on any individual quest. Pigs are not women to leave their kids and hubbies to fend for themselves. If they have to travel, they plan ahead, fill the freezer and get someone in to replace them in the household.

Although Pig women are compliant, they can be infuriatingly obstinate. You will frequently hear ultimata in their discourse: 'I'll *never* call Jim again' or 'Don't *ever* ask me to come to your house when Mary is visiting.' Some Pigs like to call this *pride*. Certain more psychology-orientated folk might term it passive/aggressive acting out. I call it pig-headedness. When pride takes over, unenlightened Pigs can close up like Main Street on Sunday afternoon and stay that way for ever. Remedy? Some form of group therapy which will help them to take a good look at how obtuse they are at times and teach them not to go on using this negative trait as a wedge to get their own way.

Pig women are dreamers. They enjoy kaleidoscopic day- as well as night-dreaming. Their dreams can be as vivid as they are premonitory. As part of this dreamy quality, they have a marked tendency – a compulsion even – to rework and embellish reality, making any story much more charming than it actually is and often tinged with a smidgeon of self-aggrandizement. Ms Piggy's little white fibs, however, sometimes snowball into big black prevarications that Ms Piggy, because of her profound desire to see life through rose-colored glasses, believes are true.

She cannot help it. She has a built-in predilection for romanticizing, dreams of masked balls and carnivals. She devoutly wishes that all her existence were more gracious and glamorous. When workaday life isn't exciting enough Ms Piggy sometimes doctors it with a few homemade spicy details. Pig ladies will serve you a can of beans, call it 'Hearty New England Casserole' and keep a straight face.

I once knew a tranced-out Pig woman who gave a formal ball at a rough and ready farmhouse down a 3-mile rut-filled muddy track in the outermost reaches of Zimbabwe. Most of the guests had to come from four or five hours' away in Jeeps over roadless terrain, at the height of the rainy season in peanut-butter mud over desolate hill-country ruts and non-roads. But this didn't faze Jessica: she had lived in back-country Zimbabwe for twenty years. She had dreamed up her ball-gown scheme in London and just knew that everyone back in Zimbabwe would simply *love* a real old-fashioned ball with all the trimmings. Jessica wore a bouffant mauve moiré-silk floor-length gown from Laura Ashley. A few of her closest family members dutifully complied with Jessica's dress code. Hubby wore a dinner jacket, children and cousins wore European-bought elegant taffeta and silk tea gowns.

Most of the country people who were invited considered the ball scheme poppycock. They showed up but – eclectically garbed in everything from T-shirts and safari-type Bermuda shorts to clown costumes and ski togs. One man wore a Mexican sombrero, a serape and roller skates. Most drank gin instead of Jessica's imported champagne. Jessica was crushed. Her elegant ball was transformed into a bash – but it was, after all, being held in bash country. Another Piggy dream shot to bits because the reality was bigger than the dream.

As far as Ms Piggy is concerned, emotional and financial security are directly linked. She usually makes certain that there is plenty of loot in the coffers. Then, because she loves to spend, she goes shopping. She believes that money is made to be spent but, ordinarily, she is careful to spend it wisely on the best life has to offer. You'll notice a marked increase in her spending sprees whenever emotional problems crop up. As the stress increases, her purse empties. Then, when she's back on the straight and narrow, she yanks those strings tight, may become an outright miser, refusing to let any money out of her sight and making incomparable cheese-paring budget cuts.

No matter her petty faults, the Pig woman remains among the worthiest persons ever born. All my Pig women friends are kind and loving, devoted and true, compliant and self-effacing, forgiving and affectionate, compassionate and honest.

Just to highlight these upstanding moral qualities, let me tell you a bit about Colette Mercier, a farm-owning countrywoman who lives near me outside Paris. Colette was widowed in her early twenties. With three children to raise, she had to run the farm on her own. She was left with many farm animals plus cereals and other foodstuffs to grow, harvest, sell and keep the books on. The task was enormous but she did it and did it well. She never remarried. She never bought herself anything. She raised her kids and kept the farm going.

By the time I met her five years ago, two of her kids were already married and had good jobs. Her only son was a strapping boy of eighteen. Most of the animals had been sold or given to relatives. After her son graduated from agricultural school and came home full time, there was less work for Colette. As she wanted to make some money, she began helping weekend residents with their gardening or painting fences. I decided that I needed a helper too so I hired Colette.

In a few months, we had bonded. Colette had plenty of what I did not: knowledge of nature, animals, the forest, the seasons, herb remedies, village life, tradition and intuition about kids and grandparents. I possessed some of the things Colette had always longed for, like a pretty house which was easy to keep clean, no mud, no farm hands to feed, and I wasn't afraid to drive all over creation where Colette feared getting lost.

Over a period of two years of accomplishing things together, Colette became my best country friend, my right arm, my garden advisor and finally my gardener. Like all Pig women, Colette never commits to anything she cannot do. She rarely gets visibly angry and she worries when I'm pale or look stressed-out. She rings me when I'm in New York to tell me if the roses are blooming and what colors they are. She calculates her working hours fairly and always has a cup of tea when she drops off vegetables and fruit, jam, flowers and plants, newspaper clippings and exquisitely laundered clothes. When I'm at home, Colette and I chat incessantly on the phone, laugh about the same things, exchange war stories about our adult children or else play hookey and race off to see some fantasy castle on the Loire. I wish everyone had a friend like Colette-the-Pig Mercier. Her strengths are rich and numerous, her faults minor and few – and her sterling character provides the perfect model for our darling Ms Piggy.

Professionally, the Pig woman might employ her talent for nurturing and become a nurse or teacher or even a cook with her own restaurant. The Pig woman is usually artistic, musical and culturally sensitive, so any job involving the arts will suit her. She makes a terrific museum curator, might hold an important position at an elegant auction house or compose or conduct classical music. When confronted with difficult people or hard-to-tame animals, Ms Piggy is a genius at reaching through barriers and helping them express themselves. She has a penchant for psychiatry and will do well as a social worker or counsellor. She makes an excellent physician, vet or dentist. Farming or gardening suit her well.

As an artist, she is most gifted for graphic art, has an acute sense of color values and mixtures. She could become a famous painter or designer, sculptor or photographer. She may act or even sing. But if in the public eye, she will require a strong man to protect her from the treacherous types who people these industries. Her infallible eye for design makes her sought after as a decorator, architect, builder or antique dealer. She might also write perceptive psychological or romantic novels or even poetry.

Her hobbies range from collecting memorabilia to reading history, joining gourmet food clubs and always – yes – swimming. The Chinese attribute to the Pig an uncannily strong attraction to water. All Pigs will like aquatic sports and can be guaranteed to succeed at careers where shipping and/or liquids come into play.

There's no better person than Ms Piggy to engage in public relations or advertising. Although this woman hates crowds and being hustled or jostled, she has the common touch. Better still, her intuition allows her to read the public's mind and work out their reactions early.

In love affairs the Pig woman is rarely the aggressor. She wants to be courted, seduced and brought swooning to the marriage bed. As a young woman she dreams of a Prince Charming who will break her passivity's shell, sweep her off her feet and carry her to the land of love and lollipops. But she can never quite decide which of the gentlemen hanging about is best for her. Usually, she goes through heartwrenching pain and hand wringing before she decides. Then, she feels sorry for the rejects and gets herself into some hairy scrapes before she settles down.

Someone more romantic and intensely sentimental than Ms Piggy you are unlikely to find. She practically lives for the ideal of romantic love; she wants to submit, be taken and adored and, most of all, to give pleasure. Her sensuality and all-out investment in relationships makes getting over bad love affairs almost impossible. It takes years for the Pig lady's broken heart to mend.

Perhaps more than just a refusal to leave Oedipus behind causes the Pig woman to be attracted to older men: she doesn't usually marry someone her age the first time. Older men give her the security she needs. However, as an older woman, Ms Piggy is frequently involved with younger men whom she can mother and spoil.

During her marriage she is consumed with maternal instinct. The Pig woman is at her happiest when devoting herself to her kids and their welfare, which is sometimes detrimental to her husband who feels left out and even jealous of the time and attention stolen from him by his children. Never mind. The Pig woman is indulgent and understanding with her children. She is not usually a strict disciplinarian but nor does she spoil them rotten. Instead she encourages them to develop their best traits and handles each as though they were special only children. She defends their interests like a tiger; but otherwise she's gentle as a lamb. I know this well because my own darling mother was the Piggiest of Ms Piggies who always vigorously defended me and cheerfully advised me to follow my heart. I did it and I'm glad. Thanks, Mom.

Porky

For all my boasting about having masses of Pig friends, I admit that the majority of them are females. Out of twenty-two Pigs I know, only six are Porkies. None are male *chauvinist* Pigs. Have I ever had a serious Pig gentleman friend? No. Am I not drawn to the male of the Pig species? Well . . . a Pig man's hypersensitivity, so closely linked as it is to his hair-trigger temper, coupled with his imperious need to maintain a strong mother figure to whom he can tell little white lies does not pluck at the heart strings of the rashly independent Tiger such as I. Or perhaps it's the reverse. More than likely, my headlong, know-it-all Tigerish style puts off the discreet, understated Pig.

My lack of intimate knowledge of Pig men doesn't prevent them from being who they are – which is mostly verrrry appealing and opulently sexual. They are notoriously attracted to a wide variety of sensual experience – plastered, as though with thick cream, with rollicking ribaldry. If this description captivates your imagination, you should look into finding a Pig man to love. Go hunting for a boyishly handsome man with a fresh open face and an air of innocence. No matter his age, the male Pig's years rarely show on his face, which maintains its softness and immaturity well beyond fifty. If you look more closely, you'll also note traces of frailty and a gentle receptiveness in his eyes. He may look rather petulant too. And vulnerable.

One doesn't often meet a scrawny Pig man. He is roundish. His muscles are quite slack and surround a pillowy body. Even as a young man, he may be overweight – a bulging stomach, sloping, padded shoulders and a thick neck. His long chest, shortish limbs and very pale complexion are hardly considered athletic. Unless he takes appropriate measures to control his epicurean habits early on, this man's virility can diminish prematurely. Pig men sometimes remind one of a clown or jester but they are charming and attract lovers because of their keen intuition, merry countenance and intimate knowledge of the female animal.

The male Pig's round face is often host to an irresistible smile. Unless his face has already got too chubby for us to find them, his eyes are clear, usually wide open in wonder, bespeaking an endearing naïvete but with a dreamy look too. He has large sensual lips, his nose is short and slightly *pugged* – like a pig's. The picture is of sweetness and good nature.

The male Pig is the most lovable of characters. Even his ex-wives don't hate him. Like the female, the male Pig is kind, friendly, generous, tender, affectionate, honest, patient, modest, conscientious and loyal. Life without his conviviality to cheer us along and warm us when we're cold would be harsh, rigorous and bleak.

Pig men adore telling and hearing slightly vulgar, off-color stories and must sometimes be asked to pipe down in snooty, prudish company. However, they are extra sensitive to the feelings of others and will never insist or grow pushy if scolded. They please us effortlessly and are always concerned about how their presence is affecting a group. Can he get you a drink? Make you a fire so you won't have to get your hands dirty? Help you paint your house?

The Pig man's presence inspires confidence. Even the most mistrustful people tend to like him and open the gates of their most secret gardens to his probing curiosity. Look for the plumpish man, seated on the gilded settee, his ankles primly crossed under the seat, the one listening raptly to the prattle of a gorgeous damsel in distress. Soft sell all the way. Easy intimacy, using the gentleman's approach, offers the lusty Pig male many an opportunity to annex people – especially women who need someone masculine to talk to – to his entourage.

He is, however, a loyal husband. Once a Pig male is committed to a relationship or a project, he tries to be faithful. Remember, the Pig doesn't like to cheat or be seen to be dishonest. His basic belief in goodness as a weapon against evil usually keeps him straight.

Pig men sometimes appear meek. Rarely are they outwardly aggressive. Instead their behavior is apologetic and they never insist on being first or best. He hardly ever learns the meaning of firmness and is unable to avenge himself when harm has been done to him. He is baffled and confused by wickedness and naïvely insists on believing in the basic goodness of mankind.

The male Pig's imagination is fertile: it sometimes works overtime and causes him great anxiety. As a result, his emotional reactions are often over-reactions. If, by accident or mis-step, you offend the sensibilities of a Pig, he may respond irrationally. A friend of mine, Jim Jukas who comes from Chicago, was raised in a modest milieu and tough neighborhood where the father believed in 'putting up yer fists' whenever trouble loomed. Unlike his dad, who was a fighting Bull, by sign as well as girth, Jim is a gentle-natured Pig. All of his childhood, Father Jukas prepared his only son to be a scrapper, never to negotiate but to fight his way out of scrapes.

Grown-up Jim can't kill so much as a mosquito. His life has been a series of backings down and relinquishings of power to keep his sanity. But despite controlling his physical reactions in potentially violent situations, Jim constantly gets fighting mad. Once, his wife reminded him of a minor criticism he had made during the early days of their marriage which had hurt her feelings.

For days, Jim seethed and raved. 'How dare you say that to me? If you were so hurt, how come you didn't divorce me?'

Another time, his landlady asked for the rent a day early because she was leaving on holiday. Jim lost his rag. 'How could she? What kind of Nazi woman is that? How dare she ask me for a favor?'

These mini crises don't usually last long but typically flare up when least expected. It is almost impossible to predict what might trigger the Pig male's fragile temper. Sometimes Pig men react more vehemently when they feel they're being accused of wrongdoing. In this person, there is a large invisible chip on the invisible shoulder of the invisible little devil who stands on his shoulder. The devil is the one who prods Piggy with his pitchfork, tauntingly chanting, 'Hey, buddy. You don't have to take that crap. Stick up for your rights.'

It's easy to make a Pig feel guilty because his guilt quotient is so outrageously high. He's so afraid of his own possible misconduct that he borders on paranoia. Pig men live in a perpetual state of trepidation, concerned that someone might be trying to get the better of them, that they've unwittingly insulted someone or that they have made a *faux pas* which may cost them their job, their wealth or their life.

Pig men hate to be considered naïve but they are more naturally artless than almost any other sign. Having been betrayed so often by less scrupulous people, Pig men may develop a pernicious doubting streak. Also, not wishing to confront or deal with ugliness or anger, they often become manipulative and sneaky. They hesitate even more than usual, sizing up every aspect of new elements and wondering if *this* time the person or thing will turn on them.

Or, because of their grim determination to hang on to their innocence, gentler and more resilient Pig men repeatedly prepare to repeat their error, stubbornly believing in disreputable people whose moral rectitude you or I would have classified below subnormal.

The problem here is not the first mistake old Porky makes, but his eternal repeats. Over and over again, Pigs are duped, then complain about it. They extricate themselves by the hair of their *chinny chin chins* from Machiavellian scenarios in which they always get to play victim. Afterwards Porky is a-wallow in desolation. He cannot figure it out. Tremendous pain and suffering accompany these disappointments. You stand there helpless, wondering how you can step in and help. But before you can warn him not to take up with Peter Pirate, whom you know has a bad reputation and is surely conniving to steal Porky's jewels or wife or yacht, Porky is waving goodbye and taking off on a cruise with the scoundrel Pirate, plus wife, jewels and, of course, the yacht.

This pattern of repeating his mistakes constitutes a grave danger for the well-being of the Pig. While his female counterpart may suffer from mental instability and require medical care, Pig men are attracted to the anesthetizing effects of drugs and alcohol. The spectre of drug or alcohol dependency stalks the life of every male Pig. Porky needs to feel stronger and tougher than he really is to face up to the corrupt jungle in which he lives and works. The edge of comfort he derives from intoxicating substances gives him a false sense of his most favorite feeling of all . . . security. It may not be the drugs or alcohol on which he finds himself hooked but the safe sense they give him that he can and will triumph.

Opulence and plenty, high living and soft music, few angles and dark corners are what the male likes. When he feels good about himself, protected by his family and friends, confident in his career, the male Pig can perform wonders. He has remarkable tenacity and strength of purpose. He is patient and knows how, like the Ox, to take the long view. He is a redoubtable adversary for tax or debt collectors. Subtle, retiring and laid back in his business dealings, he probably invented the low profile. He's quiet and soft-spoken, reserved and knows how to stay out of the way.

In love, the male Pig rarely has to take no for an answer. As he is born with a natural understanding of the female side of himself, he can comprehend the baffling intuitions of women. He can instinctively foresee their need for constant communication, endow them with tenderness and never tire of supplying all those tiny delicious lies, the key to maintaining the health of the female ego.

Even though his success with women is legendary, he's hardly a Don Juan. Instead, his game is slow and calculated. The sexual observation period is long and may include a mystifying hands-off policy. Pig men are over-susceptible to pain and will not take up with 'just anybody' until they find out if that 'anybody' might break their heart. Like a rarely sick husband whose cold is always worse than his wife's, when a male Pig's heart is broken, it's more broken than anyone else's. He *dare* not take many emotional risks.

In love relationships, the male Pig is seeking to replace or improve on his mother. Love at first sight may smite him only if the lady resembles Mama. Also, the male Pig's frequent depressions make him so vulnerable to falling in love. Not surprisingly, he prefers clinging-vine women who stay close to home and see to his needs. He likes to play prince and princess games and will reward her participation handsomely, with lavish gifts and an opulent nest. The male Pig falls in love with romantic love and will be cozily satisfied as long as he feels he is king of the castle. Even if his wife is boldly unfaithful, cruel or even insane he is unlikely to instigate a break-up. Love, to him, is to be taken seriously. Marriage represents the fusion of two bodies and souls and to destroy it strikes the male Pig as sacrilege. He has no patience with such trivia as jealousy, suspicion and competition in love.

As for his ideal of friendship, the male Pig really deserves the prize. Not only is he loyal, but he's attentive to small needs, thoughtful and aware of his friends' personal tastes. The male Pig brings bottles of *your* favorite wine instead of his own, chooses to take you to *your* preferred night spot on *your* special occasion and never forgets your birthday.

If you have one of these sensitive sensualists for a friend, try to keep in mind that he has a difficulty accepting the same considerations that he generously hands out. Male Pigs rarely, if ever, request help or impose their will or presence on those they care about. Are they shy? Rather. They are almost sheepish towards strangers. Male Pigs don't sashay jauntily about meeting hordes of new people for the sake of being surrounded. Most Pigs have a few good old friends whose company they delight in. Here again, male Pigs definitely prefer quality to quantity.

Though convivial by nature and possibly the zodiac's best host, the male Pig is not a permanently cheerful soul. Given to melancholy, he is often pessimistic where a light-hearted attitude would be more appropriate. The Pig can be moody, his attachment to things and events of the past weighing heavily on his heart. He will always prefer stasis to change, the country to the city, nostalgia to speculation on the future. He devoutly wishes that his extended family, friends and neighborhood might remain always intact.

His respect for family and reverence for mothering make the male Pig the original family man, a wonderful father, whose memory bank is full of tearful childhood events, half-torn Valentines he received in the second year and homemade souvenirs from *his* kids' primary school. He is sentimental, an eternal child at heart and no matter how old he grows still yearns for the warm presence of a mother to whom he remains for ever attached. He sometimes perceives this as a negative emotion. He may even claim to hate his poor old ma but that he spends so much energy hating her is proof that he cannot and will not let her go. Whatever his age or social position, the male Pig seldom grows to full emotional maturity, remaining afraid of the unknown, strong emotion, new experience, and loath to confront danger (or what he perceives as danger) for fear of the imagined hideous consequences.

To fend off these mental bogeymen, the male Pig may use devious tactics. He may want people to think him more vulnerable and helpless than he is and to engage their sympathy, protection or approval, may even resort to emotional blackmail and vivid displays of paralysis.

A few years back, I was invited to dinner by an attractive male Pig we'll call Simon, who I didn't know very well. I had spoken with him once or twice at parties when he had been obsequiously attentive. I was charmed by his manners, jovial smile and obvious good breeding. I knew some members of his family slightly – they came highly recommended and seemed like 'nice' people.

The grapevine had it that Simon, a Washington lawyer, had recently divorced. Most single women shrink from just-divorced men as their fragile condition usually bodes an obligation to spend many long-winded dinners over too many bottles of wine, listening to diatribes against ex-spouses. But I was drawn to this tall, good-looking chap with his well-pressed jeans and casual Ralph Lauren checked shirts. I knew that he was a Pig. And I also knew that a *bona fide* hot-out-of-the-divorce-court male Pig is synonymous with an emotional basket case. Yet Simon seemed such a likeable Pig – a possible swain, even. So, at the risk of suffering an evening's worth of his personal home-grown soap opera, I accepted to meet him at his house at 7.30 p.m., have a drink and go out to dinner.

When I arrived, it was pouring with rain. I stood on the doorstep getting wet for a good five minutes, pounding on the door. Nobody came. There were lights on and a car in the drive. It looked like Simon was at home but not answering. I went through the routine mental horrors of having come on the wrong night. But no. It was the right night and time. I knocked harder, stamping and swearing about the sopping state of my hair and the by-now fetching swag of my well-moistened Sonia Rykiel velour pantaloons. Pound though I might, no sound came from inside.

In desperation, I tried the door. It was open. I walked in and called, 'Yoo hoo! It's me. Hellooooo!'

Nothing. Nobody in the living room. The kitchen was empty too. I knew this geezer lived alone but if I entered the bedroom I might find him in his pink Porky birthday suit, enlaced with Ms God-knows-who, having spontaneously dumped our cozy *dîner à deux* for a hotter engagement.

I decided to brave it, reminding the sceptical me that Simon had a kind face, a courteous manner, and was probably not an axe murderer.

I saw light coming from what looked like the bathroom. Seeing nobody lurking in the half-light of the bedchamber, I crossed it and ventured into the loo.

There he was. Unaccompanied. Fully clothed. Out cold, on his pink and white tiled floor, oozing blood from a small head wound. I screamed. He groaned. 'Simon!' I gasped. He rose in slow motion, weaving, dipping, grabbing at towel rails, to his feet. 'What happened to you?'

'I fell,' he mumbled. 'Schlipped right there by the john.' He giggled. 'Was looking at myself in the mirror and next thing I knew . . .'

Simon was drunk. Just plain old-fashioned three sheets to the wind and listing badly. Despite a pressing desire to leave him to bleed to death, I took Simon's arm and dragged/led him to the bedroom, where I dumped him on the bed saying sharply, 'OK, what really happened?'

'What time is it?' he asked.

'Seven forty-seven,' I said. 'How did you get like this?'

'You won't believe me,' said Simon then, hand to forehead, 'but this is the firsht time in my life I've ever been drunk.'

Sixty-five and never been kissed, I mused. I said nothing. I was in a dark blue rage but I felt sort of sorry for him.

'Did you eat something?' I asked.

'No,' said Simon. He rolled around and made motions to sit up. 'I better take you out to dinner,' he managed. 'I promished.'

'Stay there,' I said. 'I'll go out and get you something to eat.'

'Oh no. Never mind about me,' he said, grabbed my hand and didn't let go. 'I think I got drunk because I was so sad,' he said in a perfectly serious voice. 'You see, I saw my ex-wife last night and do you know what she said to me . . .?'

Here come the sob stories, I predicted. And they came indeed. First, Simon said he was sorry for this unbecoming breach of etiquette. Then he claimed that he got drunk because he was hurt when his ex-wife told him over last evening's dinner that he had made her suffer. He was convinced he had not. He paid her regularly every month, which was proof enough, was it not? Simon was further saddened by his ex-wife's disregard for his first ex-wife's feelings regarding son number one's marriage. Simon was in pain because he had tried a case on Thursday wherein a poor woman had been beaten by her awful Latin husband who was his client. He was suffering too because his ex-wife's daughter by her first marriage was selling her summer home and hadn't consulted him as she did when he was married to her mother.

I was now a nervous wreck and ready to bop this complicated, over-sensitive, snivelling Pig when suddenly I remembered, He's a Pig! And . . . he has not eaten.

I stood up, disengaged my sweating hand from his and announced, 'I'm going to run right out now and buy you a lovely hamburger and some french fries and that'll fix you right up.' I knew that no self-respecting Pig man could deny himself the pleasure of watching a woman take his welfare in her capable motherly hands. I grabbed my coat, raced for the hamburger joint, bought whatever they had, carried it, in all of its styrofoam splendor, lovingly to his bedside, pushed it at him and cried, 'Toodalooo!' on my way out. Then, I jumped in my car and drove like a bat out of hell.

Professionally, even if he isn't enjoying his work, the Pig man is conscientious and tenacious. He will go about tasks dutifully and without complaint. Though he may give the appearance of being slow, the male Pig is tremendously industrious, productive and unafraid of hard work. He is capable of deep commitment to protracted projects as he doesn't mind long hours of concentrated work. He is remarkably successful in business so long as he doesn't try to deal or negotiate with people of bad faith and duplicity. Here, he should engage advisors or partners whose acumen measures up to the tricky task of finagling with sharks.

Despite his profligate habits, wealth accrues to the male Pig. He is often proficient at turning his most romantic dreams into reality. As he enjoys staying out of the line of fire, he makes an excellent behind-the-scenes financier. He might be a first-rate stockbroker, foreign exchange dealer, banker or speculator. He makes a lucky gambler and often wins large sums at cards or other games of chance.

The male Pig also benefits from an extraordinary visual acuity and sensitivity to color and shape. He's keenly aware of symbolism and can uncover hidden meanings and works of great value where others might fail. Careers to do with image are therefore areas where Pigs often excel. Not a few Pigs have been hugely successful at photography, film-making, painting and sculpture. Poetry and literature are excellent fields for the countrified male Pig too.

Bad taste has no place in the life of any Pig. Hence he can make it as a decorator, fashion designer or landscape architect. His love of people and warm personality gives him a special talent for public relations and sales. In government he will do well only as an advisor. Entering politics, *per se*, would prove a real mistake: the Pig is incapable of ruse. The Chinese claim that one shady deal or dirty trick can undo the Pig's life for ever. He does not handle guilt or lack of peer approval well.

In guiding Pigs towards a career, we should remember that the Pig sign is yin. Although some may deny it, Pig males are essentially more female than male. Mothering suits them, as does education and other nurturing professions such as social work, nursing, gynecology and pediatrics.

Above all, male Pigs must not push their luck. They overspend funds they have not yet earned and are unduly magnetized by their dreams. They tend to head for mirages, leaving the prey at hand to escape. To ensure their survival, they must remain circumspect, not be afraid to ask for advice from those wiser than themselves and steer clear of deceit in all its tempting and seductive forms.

The five Chinese elements and how they influence the Pig

The Wood Pig

1755 Brillat-Savarin
1875 Maurice Ravel
1935 Johnny Mathis, Jerry Lee Lewis, Lee Remick, Nina Simone, Woody Allen, Bibi Andersson, Julie Andrews, Dudley Moore, Herb Alpert, Alain Delon, Sonny Bono, Judd Hirsch, Charles Grodin, Diahann Carroll, Jim Dole, Luciano Pavarotti, Jerry Orbach, Phil Donahue

Earnest and well-meaning, this Pig is the most kind-hearted and considerate of all. He is sweet-natured and accommodating, eager-to-please and giving of his time and effort for anything in which he believes. He rarely falls out with people as he is tolerant of their foibles and accepting of their faults.

Friendship with a Wood Pig affords one perpetual consolation. His most salient feature is compassion. Wood Pigs feel the pain of others more than they do their own. If you have a Wood Pig in your life you will surely recognize the outpouring of kindness: 'Have you got a cold?' 'How I wish I could be ill for you.' 'You look tired. Would you like me to bring you some soup?', etc . . . And he does things about your needs. Out of wood? He'll bring you a carful of his own logs to be sure that you don't get cold. Short of time? He'll volunteer to do your ironing so you can devote yourself to what you need to do. In a bad mood? He'll tell you jokes and cook you a huge *pot au feu* to cheer you up. The Wood Pig is a classic nice guy, loyal and devoted too.

Wood Pigs are creative and culturally involved. They crave art and music, enjoy reading books and keeping up with current events. Yet, these cultivated people have a rustic side and almost always choose to live away from the madding crowd (and if they don't they should). Wood Pigs are delicate of spirit, and don't fare well when surrounded by hordes of noisy humans, machines or traffic or if they are obliged to confront bustling daily street activity. Without a soothing rural atmosphere, the Wood Pig grows cranky and difficult to deal with, sniping and snapping at people, popping tranquillizers or hitting the bottle just to stay sane. Kids, animals and farms suit the testy Wood Pig down to the ground.

There is pessimism in the Wood Pig's nature too. He is subject to depression and often feels morose. But his depressions are not profound or long-lasting. When he is offended by the behavior of someone he likes, the Wood Pig may pull a long face for a few days. His message is: 'I thought you were superior to the rest of the world but now I have my doubts.' But it doesn't last long. He is not one to hold a grudge or seek revenge.

Essentially bashful, he is often crippled by his timidity. The Wood Pig has an excruciatingly hard time allowing others to know him and is often handicapped in his love life because he dares show no evidence of sexual interest or receptivity. This Pig may develop confidence but he will need encouragement and lots of practice. Don't be disappointed if he never metamorphoses into a social butterfly. He is born shy, retiring and reserved. He would never snub others nor is he rude to them but the Wood Pig will not walk up to a stranger and strike up a casual conversation. As he is secretly preoccupied with what others think of him, he tries to keep a low profile. He is famous for knowing how to mind his own business and stay out of others'. The Wood Pig may live next door to a criminal's hide-out but he will never turn him in. He can witness a bank robbery and pretend both to himself and the world that he didn't. This behavior might almost be thought to encourage crime but it is only that the Wood Pig feels compelled to be tolerant and indulgent. Besides, he thinks, those poor robbers probably needed the money.

The Wood Pig is first, last and always a householder and homemaker. If you're looking for your Wood Pig chum, you will almost always find him at home, puttering about, digging, weeding and planting in his garden, reading to his children or helping them with homework, refurbishing antiques or improving his home. For someone who likes to be out and about and wants a good mate waiting at his fireside, this character is the best bet. A word of warning to the Wood Pig – no matter how attractive you find him or her, don't marry a Snake. Snakes like to wrap themselves round the Wood Pig's soft center and then begin to crush him to a pulp.

The Fire Pig

1767 John Quincy Adams, Andrew Jackson
1887 Louis Jouvet, Boris Karloff, Raoul Walsh
1947 Dan Quayle, Bernadette Peters, Billy Crystal, Peggy Lipton, Jane Curtin, Steven Spielberg, Mikhail Baryshnikov, Marc Bolan, Carlos Santana, Karim Abdul Jabar, Pat Sajak, James Wood, Glenn Close, Meredith Baxter Birney, Arnold Schwarznegger, Anne Archer, Suzanne Somers, Kevin Kline, Richard Dreyfuss, Billy Crystal

This Pig is the energetic type. He's a combination of homebody and crusader and is always placing himself at the forefront of causes for the betterment of humanity. He'll do anything: carry placards, sign petitions, raise funds or even spend some of his own fortune for what he believes in. Justice for all is his goal. The Fire Pig fearlessly brandishes his ideas and ideals in an effort to make progress against inequities that he cannot tolerate.

In the same vein, the Fire Pig often plays patron to creative people, doling out money for an artist's livelihood, encouraging him to create unencumbered by the vicissitudes of earning a living. He doesn't attempt to gain anything himself but gives willingly for the sake of art. As he is a naïve and compliant Pig, he is frequently used by unscrupulous 'creative' types who take his money and run off to the South Seas to open a bar. When these unfortunate events occur, the Fire Pig's disappointment is grave and sorrowful. He cannot believe anyone could be so greedy and dishonest but such setbacks do not teach the Fire Pig much about prudence. No matter how many times he is cheated, he stubbornly remains on the look-out for somebody new to help.

The Fire Pig is always rigidly opinionated. If he thinks he knows that the woman presenting herself as candidate for chairman of the board once said she didn't like foreigners and he feels that this disqualifies her, nothing can sway him from his conviction. No proof to the contrary will be acceptable or sufficient. The Fire Pig knows what he knows. Perhaps this obstinacy comes from his inordinate need for security. He feels comfortable in his first belief and stays with it so as not to have to alter his viewpoint and lose his assuredness.

All Fire Pigs know that they are pig-headedly unswervable and most are unwilling to allow for much change in their ways and flatly refuse to become more flexible. All Fire Pigs need to remember that although holding rigid ideas as gospel truth feels good to them and gives them a solid sense of hanging on to something right, the image that this mental rigor mortis projects is absurd. Everybody knows that the truly secure thinker is he who can allow new thoughts to enter his mind, knows how to stir them around, mix and match them until he comes to some new conclusion. Learning how to blend the new with the old is true wisdom indeed.

To remedy their intransigence, Fire Pigs are advised to read more widely, pore over newspapers whose points of view differ from their own and travel to exotic lands where things are done differently from the way they have always known. They should seek to befriend people of different political views and sincerely try to understand them.

With all of his retrograde thinking, the Fire Pig is none the less a fervent idealist. He believes strongly in the future and sincerely wishes to work towards political and moral progress, to help establish brotherhood among men. He dreams optimistically of the toppling of tyrants, the elimination of borders, the end of racism. In some ways, he is Utopian.

As a result, the Fire Pig invests himself in noble (and often misguided) schemes and projects that he trusts will unseat the baddies and replace them with goodies. In real life there are no such absolutes and our Fire Pig is often a disappointed Pig. If he doesn't step back and take stock, get a grip on his exaggerated idealism and temper his dreams of a better world, he will grow cranky and even misanthropic in old age.

Fire Pigs don't usually want success for themselves but they love to be the power behind the throne, assisting their chosen favorite in his ascent to power and fortune. The Fire Pig is nature's helpmeet, cheerleader and caretaker. He will go to any lengths to see his partner win. He longs to bask in the reflected glory of his own personal winner. The Fire Pig gets a kick out of having ironed his wife's shirt the day she went in and got that big promotion. Fire Pigs are givers of love, born nurturers and make wonderful parents and supportive spouses.

But can they ever complain! Fire Pigs are frequently grumpy and testy because they feel victimized *because* they choose to dedicate themselves to the cause of someone they love. Whenever they realize just how much of their time and effort it takes to promote the other person, they gripe. It can be about everything from 'nobody picks up clothes around here any more' to 'When I think how brilliant I was as a textile designer, what I gave up when I came to live with you.' They grouse and harrumph, pout and cackle and threaten to leave for ever.

Occasionally, Fire Pigs leave. But they never leave for ever – because they are too good.

The Earth Pig

1839 Paul Cézanne
1899 Al Capone, Fred Astaire, Ernest Hemingway, James Cagney, Charles Laughton, Alfred Hitchcock, Noël Coward, George Cukor, Humphrey Bogart, Irving Thalberg, Jorge Luis Borges, Xavier Cugat
1959 Rosanna Arquette, Tracey Ullman

Strength, stamina and scope are the three words I like to use to describe Earth Pigs. This Pig is also bent on living the rural life and will try to stay out of cities. He is an out-and-out rustic who is often blunt. Occasionally, he exhibits rather coarse manners, tells off-color jokes and makes comments relative to the baser aspects of life in an effort to amuse his guests. I wouldn't go so far as to call the Earth Pig a hick as he is simultaneously attracted to the highest forms of sophistication but he's a bit of a bumpkin.

The Earth Pig is energetic, vastly creative and carries the burden of inventions on his own shoulders, taking full responsibility for their exploitation. He's unafraid of criticism and will go the full distance to realize a project. Often, he is involved in art. He may be a painter or writer, a curator or a collector of fine art. His goals are rarely more ambitious than to experience the fulfillment of creative expression and the joy of fashioning beautiful things from his imagination. Money comes naturally to him. The Earth Pig is forever receiving windfalls – marrying money, receiving an unexpected inheritance or landing the most lucrative contracts. He is lucky and doesn't have to do much fancy footwork to ensure his survival.

This character is reluctant to surrender his native innocence. If he had his way, the Earth Pig would live in a state of refined purity where right things never go wrong, where man is always humane to his fellows and where the scent of crime is unknown. As he thinks better in rarefied atmospheres, he has a tendency to hole up for work purposes in remote hideaways where the air is clear. Not only does the Earth Pig not want his life polluted by the poisons of a tainted or crowded life, but he knows how vulnerable he is to being hoodwinked by less scrupulous souls. Rather than taking undue risks, the wise Earth Pig avoids the jet set, the rich and the spoiled, sticking close to the soil and its restorative properties.

The Earth element contributes an even more intense need for tradition and closeness to history than with other Pigs. Earth Pigs are often involved in professions having to do with antiquity, anthropology, archaeology, history or even social history. Or they may prefer to open antique shops or galleries where ancient artifacts are viewed or sold. But whatever they decide to do, it is often closely related both to tradition and aesthetics.

Indecision is the Earth Pig's worst flaw. He is easily swayed and often confused about which direction he ought to take. He has trouble making up his mind. His exaggerated willingness to be tractable, negotiable and compliant constitutes a danger to his image among his peers. People always wonder what on earth the mixed-up Earth Pig is thinking and, very often, the last person to know is the Earth Pig himself. It is no good pushing him, trying to help him make up his mind as he is pig-headed about taking advice and resents interference from outsiders. If you push too hard, he'll fly into one of his epic rages and you'll be flattened.

The Metal Pig

1911 Ronald Reagan, Terry Thomas, Lucille Ball, Eugene Ionesco, Barbara Tuchman, Samuel Fuller, Paulette Goddard, Merle Oberon, Jean Harlow, Jules Dassin, Nicholas Ray, Ginger Rogers, Robert Taylor, Giancarlo Menotti, Lee J. Cobb, Vincent Price, José Ferrer

Metal endows this Pig with extra grit and endurance. Here is a person born with enormous personal integrity, who always tries to improve on his own previous performance. If, at first, he does not succeed, the Metal Pig will always try again. He is honest too. And forthright.

The worst crime you could commit against a Metal Pig would be to accuse him of a guileful act, suspect him of chicanery or mistrust his motives. Accusation, to the Metal Pig, is almost as damaging as being convicted. Conserving his trustworthy, solid-citizen image among his admirers keeps the Metal Pig sane.

He is reasonable too, the most unemotional of Pigs, malleable and easy to negotiate with. But, paradoxically, when pushed to the limits of his patience, the Metal Pig can grow very stubborn and refuse further compromise. However, he never allows himself too much latitude and rarely, if ever, follows any random urge to color outside the lines in the sketchbook of life.

Metal Pigs do not enjoy the fireworks of argument. They prefer discretion to belligerence. Decorous conversation suits their temperament, as does intellectual discussion or pure cultural exchange. If they find themselves confronted by a potential row, rather than being tempted to express a controversial opinion and perhaps riling their interlocutors, Metal Pigs usually choose to back off and change the subject. They are forever telling bawdy jokes or performing amusing spectacles for their friends. Whatever it takes, the Metal Pig makes the fewest enemies possible by deliberately keeping his public happy with his antics or simply chatting about the weather.

Metaphysics hardly interests the Metal Pig at all. He is not attracted to abstract thinking. Religion bores him and spirituality puts him off. He's even slightly suspicious of philosophy. Needless to say, Metal Pigs deplore the very existence of astrology and its sister sciences.

This character is not very ambitious – at least, not in the world-beater sense. He's even a little shy. He can be pushed and prodded into the limelight but if and when he arrives at fame or renown, it is usually the result of someone urging him until he grudgingly allows his private charms to enter the public domain.

The Water Pig

1923 Dexter Gordon, Henry Kissinger, Italo Calvino, Marcel Marceau, Roland Petit, Peter Lawford, Sylvia Montfort, George Roy Hill, Linda Christian, Prince Rainier, Marcello Mastroianni, Esther Williams, Estelle Getty, Richard Attenborough, Charlton Heston, Lindsay Anderson

Water confers soothing gentility and amiability on this Pig. He is a calm sort who doesn't get carried away by his own impulsive notions. In a crisis he keeps his head and never fails to return the affections of those who profess to love him and remain loyal to his beliefs. This Pig is a sweetie pie, a strong but silent soul who spends quality time in the wings but does not necessarily want to leave the green room to appear on the latest talk show. He's rather shy and retiring, a thinker with excellent manners and a giant store of self-discipline.

The Water Pig doesn't care for power or dominion over others. He would rather be thought of as a mediator than a dictator or managing director. Again, as with other Pigs, his talents lie in his emotional proximity to art and its cultural expressions. He loves to create and even to show off the results. But the Water Pig rarely aspires to anything more materialistic than perfection in his field. Using his talents for personal gain seems almost sacrilegious to the purity-conscious Water Pig.

The Water Pig must be surrounded by people. Although professionally he can function alone and turn out impressive amounts of hard work, at the end of the day this Pig wants company – someone to talk to, laugh with, share dinner and exchange ideas with. He's not particularly sociable in the grander sense, preferring to remain anonymous or, at least, out of the limelight. Yet he sorely needs conviviality, a family atmosphere, a happy cheerful environment in which to feel a sense of camaraderie.

The Water Pig is a born builder. He frequently undertakes construction projects wherein he designs and reshapes. He thrives on knocking down walls, creating large open spaces where his collections of *objets d'art* and old master paintings can best be appreciated.

He is not expansive in his gestures of affection or love. The Water Pig is profound, modest and poetic. He rarely gushes or rants. Emotions, he feels, are meant to be controlled, managed carefully and expressed decorously. His great loves are always physical passions. The Water Pig adores pleasurable experience and places sex high on the list of joys to be sought. Fine food comes next. Water Pigs are rather delicate and often suffer monumental indigestion from over-indulgence in gustatory delights. Something about the sight of a groaning board, laden with taste treats and drinks caves in the Water Pig's resolve to stay away from heavy repasts. He should beware of strokes.

Lastly, this Pig is economical. Unlike other Pigs who tend to squander and save by turns, this Pig keeps his money. He likes security and knows how to live well – even luxuriously – on a budget. The Chinese often say that because the Water Pig year comes round at the end of the sixty-year cycle, natives of that year have similar characteristics to the first symbol of the new cycle which is the Rat, who is a true master at hoarding and protecting his loot. Perhaps a little of his frugality rubs off on his zodiacal neighbor, the nice, kind, pure-hearted Water Pig.

Pig health

Excessive fragility often characterizes the Pig's health picture. Pigs often feel impelled to miss a day's work or feel the urge to slow down or slip out for a nap because of the onset or persistence of some chronic (and perhaps psychosomatic) ailment. Often the Pig is not as sick as he thinks or feels he is yet, physical discomfort – even the slightest headache – impresses his hypersensitive nature. Piggy is overwhelmed by the force of the unexpected intrusion. Even a broken fingernail can kick-start the Pig's overactive imagination, revving it into a whirlwind of self-examination, diagnosis and undue worry about the future. When can I get a manicure? What if the nail gets infected and falls off?

Does this sound hypochondriacal? Well, it is. Pigs are among some of the most panicky of panickers when it comes to conjuring themselves into a physically disabled state. Subconsciously, the Pig lives in incessant fear of both suffering and death. Sometimes, he frets so hard that he acquires the symptoms he fears and can, without trying, torment himself into an actual illness. If I had a Pig in my house, I would forbid him to read medical journals or books or to watch hospital dramas or documentaries on TV. One or two colorful dramatic and well-narrated heart bypass operations could have old Piggy jumping into his BMW for a quick trip to the cardiologist. With Pigs, nerves and emotions combine to create an almost constant state of apprehension and dread. Given that tenuous mental position, Piggy needs little convincing to begin to believe that every malady he so much as sniffs is his for ever.

If the Pig does fall ill he usually regresses: he wants to be spoiled and treated like a child. He needs enormous morale-boosting and moral support to resist the temptation to feel sorry for himself. An ailing Pig is demanding and insists on indulging in forbidden foods or drinking what he ought to leave alone. He will need at least third and fourth opinions on every minute aspect of his disorder and may phone his physician continually for clarification of every real or imagined new symptom. Be careful too, if you're the victim of a sick Pig's whims. He may manipulate your sentiments and play shamelessly on your sympathies to get you to take care of him.

Not surprisingly, Pigs often develop stomach trouble: the stomach is their weakest point and requires much coddling and careful attention. The average Pig is hardly unaware of his tummy's frequent dysfunctions. He really feels those stabbing pains and suffers with colic and cramps. But he has a hell of a time preventing himself from overeating or drinking. He regularly imposes an impossible workload on his fragile digestive system and is frequently laid up with every gastro-intestinal indisposition known to man – plus such gourmet's delights as gout and acnea rosacea, to mention only two. He gets ulcers and is besieged by attacks of embarrassing flatulence. Still . . . he eats and drinks and makes merry beyond all reason.

The Pig sometimes suffers from chronic insomnia. This inability to get to sleep stems from his persistent paranoia that death may strike him in the night. He hears non-existent prowlers who have come to beat him senseless in his sleep. He is jerked awake by the horrible hunch that he has forgotten to lock the downstairs door. He lies in bed from 4 a.m. till dawn, arms crossed corpse-like over his pounding chest, wondering how he will dare to face the unknown terrors stalking his new day.

A healthy Pig is a rural Pig. A Pig who lives amid big city life with all of its real dangers and frenzied vicissitudes is an afflicted Pig. He is born unarmed against the din, and his natural rhythms – the rhythms of nature – are thrown into confusion by the artificiality of the urban setting. When comfortably ensconced in peaceful, safe surroundings, the Pig will thrive. His tortured spirit will grow calmer. His fears will be quietened. His true self will emerge and allow him to get on with what really concerns him in life – family, sex, work, pets, friends, culture, reading and painting, gardening, viewing nature's glories and, of course, occasional royal banquet-giving.

Because they so often feel the need to calm a relentless inner raging, Pigs are bound to be drug and alcohol prone. If they have not developed the skill to relax in other, healthier ways, they will be tempted to abuse all sorts of drug. Sports, such as swimming, sailing and surfing, are good for Pigs. Strenuous sports, such as football, boxing or wrestling, requiring strong muscular structures don't suit him. He often excels at some gracious or noble sport such as tennis or golf.

Certain Pig ailments are specifically female. Ms Piggy tends to develop varicose veins and even high blood pressure at an early age. Her endocrine system is highly strung and can easily become unbalanced. Hyperthyroidism and its reverse, pancreatic disorders and diabetes are common among Pig women. Ms Piggy also has to keep a close eye out for breast problems such as recurrent cysts and occasional changes in the breast tissue. Mammograms are always a good idea after the age of thirty. Allergies, too, affect her more than her male counterpart and although they are rarely life-threatening, they can be life-altering and ought to be dealt with naturally, treated with proper diet, rigorously avoiding recourse to drugs.

To protect their health Pigs must learn to refrain from excess. The Pig's life is plagued by the desire to go to extremes in everything from food to sex to work, spending and over-exertion. Pigs are fragile. No Pig can commit himself to the fast lane for long or he will succumb to life's most dreadful ailments. He should eat in moderation and ingest only fresh organic foods. A good diet for the Pig includes dairy products (especially yoghurt), fish and shellfish (if he isn't allergic), fresh fruit and vegetables. All Pigs should refrain from eating sweets and avoid gaseous beverages. Alcohol? The rule for Pigs is the same for everyone else . . . only more so: Drink wine with food. Drink better and better quality wines and you will find you will drink less.

To ensure his emotional well-being, the Pig must also attempt to achieve a balance between his own exaggerated, anxiety-laden approach to life and reality. He must strive to be more casual and relaxed about his taboos, more open and free with things he resists and fears. However, if he can't do this by himself, he should seek the help of a therapist, psychiatrist or psychologist to gain both objectivity and perspective.

A stubborn, reactionary Pig who does not care for his chronic emotional difficulties and learn to cope with fear, frustration, anger and agitation can develop serious life-threatening health problems from the age of forty. Unresolved emotional problems cause him to become a sitting duck for psychosomatic illnesses such as tachycardia, asthma, anxiety attacks and depression. Curing these maladies is difficult, sometimes even impossible, unless the afflicted Pig agrees to become seriously involved in effecting a real lifestyle change. He must subject himself to many hours of soul-searching psychotherapy, develop relaxation skills through yoga, exercise and acupuncture and, in short, learn as an adult what his nature did not confer on him at birth – the art of being *cool*.

Pig futures

What the Pig should expect from the next twelve Chinese animal years

2008, the Earth Rat year – The Rat is a protector of those he loves. And he really fancies Pigs. You Pigs possess a brand of personal power that the power-hungry Rat respects. You are your own person. You depend on nobody and you know what you like and go after it in life. Rats are quite similar in that way. They are go-getters and are unafraid to take the reins and drive their own existence – their way. But Rats do not own the quiet peacefulness of Pigs. Rats are more urban dwellers than country folk. They live at a frenzied, city-like pace, are nervous and chatty and needful of admiration from others. Pigs don't much hurry. Nor do they care who admires them. They just carry on *tra la la* with their conviviality and their taste for the luxurious in life. Rats work at breakneck speed, and if things are not moving quickly enough, they can fly into fits of anger. Pigs handle leadership with great diplomacy and only fly into rages about once a year. So you Pigs can be comfortable this year in the knowledge that you are protected and admired and respected. You are, however, expected to perform. The Rat demands you make wise investments, put the brakes on excessive gourmandise and be sure to invite him to all your luscious country dinner parties.

2009, the Earth Ox year – Another twelve months of peace and quiet coming up for you Piggies! What could be better than that? The Ox is in charge and he wishes you no ill. In fact, Oxen and Pigs get on like two pings in a pong. Always content to meet up and banter back and forth about crops and flower varieties, exchange country recipes for jams and compare the qualities of their respective honeys. Good old-fashioned rural-living people. The only fly in your Ox year ointment has to do with work. You are anything but a lazy person. You enjoy producing and caring for what you produce. You take pleasure in buying expensive art and jewelry. And you covet golden sconces and antique furniture. All these lavish purchases cost money. In order to get that loot, you have to work hard. Fine. So far you see nothing amiss. However, the Ox is a demanding task-master. This year you will be working your squiggly little tail off. There be less time and therefore less likelihood you will stumble on someone irresistible at the beach or at a chic spa or even at your local outdoor market. So try to accept that this year will be most wisely used as a time to generate cash. Once you have done so, you will be able to kick back and take off for some museum-hopping in Amsterdam or Rome or Vienna. Nose to grindstone, Piggy. The Ox is watching.

2010, the Metal Tiger year – The Tiger has a tendency to irk Pigs. You two get on well enough. But there are not a plethora of intimate friendships between you. Why? Well, you have different energies and different goals in life. You Pigs thrive on culture, authenticity, purity and the joys of Mother Nature. Tigers prosper in the presence of movement, excitement, novelty and change. Whilst the Pig might sit all morning in a museum in New York City scrutinizing a single painting by Rembrandt, the Tiger would stride through the room where the Rembrandts hang, give each one a minute's stare and move on to the Picasso room. Tigers are impatient to get on with things. Pigs are content to relish the best things in life and revel in its pleasures. So although this Tiger year doesn't bode any ill for you Pigs, the frenetic pace and frantic haste with which everything is accomplished raises your bristles. My suggestion for Pig happiness in Tiger years is travel. This is the year for you to get moving. Go see all those museums you have been dreaming about. Visit those splendid temples in India and Vietnam and Cambodia and Thailand. And while you're at it, hie yourself and your new-found sweetheart to someplace green and lush and warm where one of you can pop the crucial question. As we head into the peaceful Cat year, it's time for Pigs to settle down.

2011, the Metal Cat year – You and people born in Cat years are both peace-loving sorts who honor nature and carry on their lives in relative tranquility. Cat usually make and keep their money under mattresses or buried in the cellar. They are not mad for the hurly-burly and prefer serenity to conflict. In fact, clashes, discord, dissension and argument cause the Cat to flee the premises and hole up under the nearest sofa. You are not one to say no easily. You have to force yourself to refuse any favor or demand made on you by almost anyone. 'Can you drive me to the airport at 3 a.m. on Tuesday? Will you take my four kids for a month while I go to Europe? Would it be too much to ask you to lend me your new Mercedes SUV for a race in the Sahara?' People request these outlandish favors of you because they know they might not get No for an answer. There is, however, a limit to every Pig's patience. And when that limit has been tested too many times, Pigs explode into blinding lightning-blue rages. However, in this Cat year, I strongly advise you to keep your temper under control so as not to offend the tender sensibilities of your host. You will have great good fortune in the money department, but must watch out for the incipient betrayal of your trust by a close family member. When asked to participate in something a tad shady by a cousin or nephew or aunt, just say no.

2012, the Water Dragon year – Looks like you are still in business or are somehow in the process of making money. Take it in your stride. You are someone who willy-nilly seems to attract wealth. And once you have it, you *always* know exactly what you want to do with it. The Dragon year is a celebratory time. Fireworks and parades, fairs and processions and all manner of rambunctious festivity accompany the Dragon throughout his year-long reign. You are a convivial type. You give dinner parties and invite guests for the weekend the way other people change their socks. Everybody loves to be entertained at your house. The difference, of course, is that you don't give huge bashes and throw gigantic shindigs complete with marching bands and majorettes the way the Dragon is wont to do. You are the low-key warm fuzzy hostess or host who cooks long hours to make scrumptious long-lasting meals for four to eight people. At your house everybody stays till 1 a.m. talking or singing, drinking your good wines and solving the problems of the world. So you will have money this year and your love life continues sunny and warmer. But the noise level and flamboyance of the general tone this year frankly gets on your nerves. Do yoga. Meditate. Take up the piano or study French. You are happiest when quiet and busy learning something culturally challenging.

2013, the Water Snake year – Here is a year to beware of. The Snake holds a mysterious – even mystical – attraction for you Pig people. When you meet a Snake person, you are almost instantly smitten. When the Snake meets you, he or she is instantly aware that they can pull great skeins of wool over your innocent eyes with impunity. You're a pushover for Snake charmers – and charming they are indeed! So this year constitutes a sort of emotional labyrinth where you Pigs may become disoriented several, if not many, times. Much of the confusion will go on in your personal life. You will be misled or gossiped about by someone you love and sorely disappointed to wake up to the fact that the said loved one is capable of such chicanery. You may also be cheated on by a lover or mistress. You might not find out about it until the whole neighborhood does – a humiliating situation. I don't see you losing any financial ground where your work is concerned. But you will have to tiptoe through this twelve-month period, and keep watching your back because the fates want to dupe you and cause you no little distress. Resist the temptation to be seduced by anyone or anything. Keep a cool head and analyze each new set of problems as they evolve. If you are extra careful this year, you will be able to hang onto your precious stability.

2014, the Wood Horse year – As you most likely will be in recovery mode after the year of the devious-minded Snake has wrenched the last of your gold coins from your hot little fist, I remind you to stop beating yourself up. Whatever happened to you last year was fate. Destiny for Pigs in Snake years means to be duped and hornswoggled and often to lose some of that native Pig innocence you so cherish and cling to. Snakes take Pigs for a big ride. This Horse year will be one of recuperation and re-centering. You will have to work excessively hard. You won't be able to holiday the way you like to. No bon-bons whilst reclining on your favorite moire *chaise longue*, leafing casually through the catalogues from auction houses in splendid venues. No caviar at those intimate gourmet suppers you are so famous for giving at your charming abode. Nope, Piggy, this year is shoulder to the grindstone and nose to the elbow grease. You won't be slaving for nothing. There is an objective. You need to rebuild your emotional and material self. Nothing like turning over the soil in two acres of garden or painting all the upstairs ceilings, to help restore one's confidence. Keep yourself occupied doing practical chores. The Horse smiles on a busy Pig.

2015, the Wood Goat year – You have certainly come to the right year! Pigs love and admire Goats. I have never seen this phenomenon explained, but whenever I meet a Goat person I am sure there is a Pig lurking around somewhere nearby: an adoring wife, a helpful husband or loyal kindly friend or lover will emerge from another room and I will ask their birthdate and almost invariably they divulge that they were born in a Pig year. Goats attract Pigs the way Pigs attract money (which may give us a hint as to why Goats are, in their turn, attracted to Pigs) and these two are often married or at least living together. We know that Goats need security and crave structure. And, as they don't usually know how to concoct their own security and structure, they seek it from outside themselves in another person or an institution or some sort of relationship to something strong that they can depend on. Although Pigs are not always the sort of people one can lean on, they are so taken by Goats that they allow themselves to open wide their doors and pocketbooks in order to give the Goat anything he or she may need. How does this compatibility affect the Pig in a Goat year? Well, of course, the Pig can do as he pleases in this year. And what most pleases a Pig? Love. Great gooey gobs of sweet, tender, sexy, bawdy, glorious *amour*. There will be more than enough of that precious commodity for you this year, Piggy. Everything from family love to puppy love and intimacy and passionate love will thrill you throughout this Goat year. You will be understood and adored. Wallow in it. But don't neglect your health.

2016, the Fire Monkey year – This year, your friend the Monkey is on your side. Monkeys are tricky and do manipulate others for their own ends. They are indeed far more guileful than Pigs, and have a lot to teach you naive characters. Watch for chicanery in the workplace this year. Someone who holds a higher rank than you will try to unseat you. Perhaps he or she wants to give your job to a niece or slot in a girl- or boyfriend. Keep a weather eye out for this double-crosser and nip him or her in the bud. No. Don't go trotting to the boss and rat on the person. This is a Monkey year. You must endeavor to be slyer than usual. Find a chink in the double-dealer's armour and subtly threaten to tell all if he or she persists in trying to get rid of you. Better to be tricky than sorry. Last year's love picture should go forward smoothly as well. The naughty Monkey encourages all manner of lecherous profligacy. I wouldn't advise you to engage in downright lascivious behaviour. But you Pigs enjoy the game of sex. Why not take advantage of the bawdy tone of this Monkey year and allow yourself some extra sexual latitude?

2017, the Fire Rooster year – Finally! A year to pursue all the cultural activities you so adore. The Rooster's years usually go forward in a climate of conservatism and economy. The Rooster is a hard-working person who approves of you Pigs and admires your good taste and refined sense of the authentic. Roosters are very real people. Artifice annoys them. They prefer the real to the synthetic in life. The Rooster's atmosphere doesn't jar you or demand much more than what you might normally do to get on with your life – your way. So whatever duplicities you had to endure last year will disappear and you will have your free time to yourself. You may, of course, be obliged to cut back on luxuries. The Rooster has us all tightening our belts. But as a Pig person who can't help but salivate at every mention of food or drink, a bit of belt-tightening might not be such a bad idea. Drag the *chaise longue* out of storage and set it up next to that pile of art books you've been promising yourself to read for a couple of years. Pig out on exhibitions and operas and concerts and theatrical events. Make use of this clement time to enrich your cultural life and slake that thirst for sophistication that you have been neglecting for too long.

2018, the Earth Dog year – You and the Dog are natural buddies. Although your goals are vastly disparate, you do enjoy a pleasant comradeship. You, for example, invite your Dog friends to your lovely, intimate dinner parties because you know that Dogs make fabulous conversation. They're always gabbling on about their various causes, shaking their paws at corruption and, in general, baying at the moon about some 'important' issue or other. As you are fond of lively meals where everyone sits late into the evening conversing about the problems of the world, hashing over current events and holding vivid arguments about everything from salmon-fishing quotas to illicit wars and scandals in high places in governments around the world, the Dog serves your purpose. Best thing about your fondness for each other is that your Doggie friends don't mind being invited along to add such animation. In fact, your hospitality rounds out their otherwise quasi-Spartan existence. So in this Dog year, you Pigs will hear more than your share of invective about the rampant shady deals going on in high places. And you will be asked to participate in all manner of crusades for the rights of the homeless, the mindless and the jobless. Give the Dog a hefty contribution. Then go home and cook a big meal for your friends to come and share in your conviviality. Love? Keeps on going like a Duracell battery this year. Be more open and generous with your affection.

2019, the Earth Pig year – A perfect time for you Pigs to initiate projects, get married, have a baby, build a house or start that brand new art gallery business you have been dreaming about. This is *your* year to influence others positively and refine your own goals. The objectives you set for yourself twelve years ago should by now have come to fruition and be giving you a sense of true pride and accomplishment. Because it is the Pig year, you must of course sit down with pen and paper (or computer) and write yourself a new list. Where do you want to be in 2031? How do you see yourself navigating to that place? Will you move house in 2023? Do you want to buy a boat in and sail around the world in 2025? Where will you be working in 2028 and what will your lifestyle look like then? If you want children and don't have enough, make some new ones now. The Chinese divide our lifetimes into twelve-year periods wherein we must endeavor to evolve from one stage to the next by applying ourselves to building our lives. This year, your job is to get to know yourself well enough to make a serious plan for your future. Take a hard look at the past twelve years. See where you went wrong, when and why. Then make resolutions to alter behaviors you wish to eradicate in order not to continue to get in your own way. This is your year to shine! Pure Piggy bliss.

Compatibilities

How you get along with people born under other Chinese signs

Rat with Rat

A marriage guaranteed to enrich the lives of both. Both partners fear loneliness; each clings to the unit with tiny tough teeth and claws. The Rat knows how to behave as a friend as well as a lover, taking a mate's part in business ventures as well as helping them over emotional rough patches. Rat showers Rat with presents and solicitude. Rat appreciates kindnesses, understands the Rat mate's gentle nature and gives complete support.

A few spiky moments may crop up. They both flirt – outrageously! He'll be eyeing some comely dinner guest while she plays footsie under the same dining table with the comely guest's hubby. Bitter accusations ensue: rifts, breaches of trust and days of mute tension. Early on, this couple should take a vow to discuss everything when it happens. Lay jealousies and suspicions on the carpet so they can be properly dissected and jettisoned before the week-long silences set in. They ought to restrain their social life. Too much *innocent* shoulder-rubbing with 'attractive' cocktail cronies may ultimately weaken their bond.

Normally, the sex is fantastic. Both parties require masses of cuddling and time together in bed. They also agree on adventurous sex. Rat bed games are enormously complicated – but harmless.

Rat with Ox

Union between these guarantees matrimonial stability. The Ox provides the rambunctious Rat with the grounding he lacks and the Rat peeks through the Ox's wall of convention and resistance to change, pepping up an otherwise dreary existence. This combination fits, each rounding out the other's sharper edges.

The Ox's steadfastness provides the Rat with much-needed security and the devoted Ox will be happy to take on the role of provider and family protector. The gregarious Rat will accept every invitation, always happy to spend the Ox's hard-earned money. All the better for the quiet Ox who, without the Rat's exuberant nature, would simply stay at home ruminating. Each is happy to fulfil their role. Alluring and meticulous, a Rat is a perfect helpmate for an Ox in business, doing backflips and handstands to encourage the Ox's career.

The Ox demands complete fidelity. Despite a desire to dash out on the town, the Rat will appear faithful but how he or she spends his spare time is nobody's business.

What about passion? Neither the Rat nor the Ox is preoccupied with the fanciful notion of tearing-up-the-bedsheets lovemaking. Their sex life will be routine. They are not bored by this, however: the Chinese claim that they prefer it.

Rat with Tiger

At first meeting these two charm the pants off each other. The Rat finds the Tiger alluring, and will love to show him off while the confident Tiger is amused by the Rat's vigor and lively sense of humor. But there is bound to be friction in the long run.

After the first spark of love, these two will find fault with each other. The rambunctious, adventurous Tiger will forever be seeking excitement – off on safari to Kenya, then on to San Francisco to watch the earthquake. The Rat, being more domestic, will come to hate the sight of suitcases.

The Tiger stalks instability, tempted by danger and the prospect of having a new job every year. Everything is challenging to this aggressive beast. The Rat will not always find the Tiger's inconsistencies appealing and will be plagued by worry. Rat's survival depends on material security and, with the Tiger job-hopping, the Rat will fret over money.

To endure, both must remember the initial reasons which drew them together. They have lots to talk about and agree on many things. If the Rat can recall how the Tiger roared attractively into his or her life, and the Tiger can appreciate the Rat's seductive charm, there is hope for an exciting, long-lived marriage.

Rat with Cat

This game of Cat and Mouse is one I would resist playing. Although both the Cat and the Rat have some similar traits, they are not compatible. Both have strong needs for a home. One might imagine them rummaging through the Bloomingdales' catalogue together and picking wallpaper for the kitchen but they disagree on just about everything.

Like Tom and Jerry, they will forever chase each other around, neither prepared to make concessions or take steps towards reconciliation. The Cat will forever be hissing and this relationship grows pickier and pettier by the day.

However dissonant a chord they strike, once joined, it will be hard for this team to separate. They both cling to security. Divorce would lead them into the unknown. They find the familiar reassuring and prefer to be mildly satisfied together than tossed out into the world of adventure.

Sexually, they tend to be excited by sado-masochistic games, tearing out each other's hair in the midst of a passionate embrace. In time such practices will lead to a sexually destructive relationship. Prolonged commitment is unadvisable.

Rat with Dragon

This is an absolutely delicious marriage: the Chinese claim it as one of their best-arranged unions. The restless Rat will be warmed by the heat of the dashing Dragon and the Dragon will bask in the Rat's generous applause. These two will complement each other beautifully. Guaranteed bliss.

With the strong-willed Dragon around, the Rat will be happy to give up total control: anxieties slowly subside, bringing peace and comfort. The Dragon is so emotionally effusive that the burden of worry will be taken off the poor little Rat's shoulders. Bigger and bolder, the Dragon will carry the weight of the loving Rat's turmoil. The Rat will not feel competitive about the Dragon's position of strength in this couple, happy to stand in the shadows of a fervent friend/mate.

The Dragon and Rat team will feel like king and queen. In the Rat's eyes, the Dragon does no wrong. All the better for the lucky Dragon who loves to preen. The dazzling Dragon is so bright and exciting that the Rat's usual hearty appetite for sex may be overwhelmed. Despite his wisdom, the proud Dragon may fail to see the problem and a bruised ego will make him or her believe the Rat to be either disinterested or incompetent. A relaxed, rational discussion will clear the air and in no time, the Dragon's conversational fireworks will reignite the Rat's temporarily diminished sensuality.

Rat with Snake

Although this alliance can often make for an interesting friendship I would not recommend it as a romantic relationship. Physically, they may attract each other and they are both gregarious. But this mutual social accord is only skin deep.

On an everyday level, Rat/Snake life will not be so charmed: upheaval, disagreement, and disappointment are in store. After the initial physical pull, the Snake will withdraw and keep compartments of his or her life safely tucked away. The serpentine innate weakness for flirtation will be even greater if the Snake is attached to a Rat.

The Rat will grow uneasy, and fearful of security. The Snake's investments will prove unfruitful and the restless Rat will have to take charge of the family accounts. Tempers will boil, especially the Rat's, who staggers under the weight of attempting desperately to hold up the crumbling fort. The Snake may storm out of the house to the nearest Dior, using overdrawn credit cards to supplement an overweight wardrobe.

The only moments of repose in this union will be spent between the sheets, passionately entwined for hours. The Rat will enjoy the sexual attention the slippery Snake contributes and, generous as ever, will be forgiving. Be wary, gentle Rat, of your enchanting Snake. If you are not careful, even you can fall victim. Snakes will reel you in with promises, love you to pieces, then eat you for breakfast.

Rat with Horse

In China, even the corner grocer shudders at the mention of this unlikely possibility. The Horse is far too self-centered for the Rat's kindly giving, dependent nature. Although initially attracted by their differences, they should flee each other instantly – before it's too late. Beyond a love of money and all it can afford them, no common ground exists between these two.

The Rat is likely to be mistreated by the haughty Horse. The Horse is moody, causing the Rat to feel unstable, and so individualistic that he will not even consider the Rat's feelings, which will unnerve the anxious rodent.

The Horse will not feel challenged by a Rat partner, criticizing and attacking at every opportunity, perhaps even growing to despise the Rat. The Horse's impatience may lead to a search for pleasure elsewhere and merciless infidelity. All the negative aspects of the Horse's personality will be drawn out by the Rat's frailties.

The usually strong Rat will be starved for security. A family and children could return Ratty to his or her whimsical self but when the child grows up, the Rat will grow sad. Yet no matter his unhappiness, the Rat, fearing disruption, will not be able to leave the punishing Horse and may grow bitter and vengeful. Bad vibes. A marital no-no.

Rat with Goat

This is a tricky one. The Goat enjoys the loving Rat but finds the Rat's nervousness unappealing. The Goat's peaceful nature appeals to the snuggly Rat but Goatly lack of interest in the menial tasks of everyday life will cause the Rat to fuss.

The Goat will not want to clear up messes or groom the home, and, being such a fusspot homebody, this laziness will grate on Rat's nerves. The Goat will spend money on unnecessary objects and it won't be long before the Rat feels overburdened by responsibilities and the lack of security brought on by the Goat's desultory attitude.

This household is in a constant state of cold war. The Rat worries quietly and the Goat lacks the necessary initiative to loosen up his troubled mate. All their battles will be fought with under-hand tactics, and vicious stares. The Rat will long for a partner with more oomph. The gracious Goat, not courageous enough to confront the

Rat, will resist lethargically. The Rat remains helpless in the face of rank ineptitude.

Their feelings of inadequacy will be put to rest when they have sex. The Goat is so sensual that he can exert power over the Rat. Filled with sexual excitement, the Rat will be happy to feel dominated. Confident, and clear of conflict, the Goat may see this as an opportunity to discuss some of their differences. If the physical union is strong, this couple may learn to iron out their basic differences on the pillow.

Rat with Monkey

If all else fails, these two can go on the road as a comedy duo. Humor, games, parties, and friends! What fun you'll have! How lucky you are to have been brought together! Shared, your lives will be a never-ending roller-coaster ride. The amusing Monkey, incessantly grimacing from the top of the jungle gym, has the Rat in perpetual stitches. Amid guffaws, the Rat suggests funnier, more clever antics, fuelling the witty Monkey with ever more hysterical moves. It's a picnic.

The sometimes repressed Rat will become a tiresome chatterbox alongside a mellow Monkey. But not to the Monkey, who never tires of the clever Rat, the walking radio show. Both so personable, they will always be dining out or entertaining at home. They have a multitude of friends and spend little time alone. As neither is afraid of hard work, money comes easily to them.

The Monkey sometimes uses characteristically diverse interests to justify a desire for sexual promiscuity. Should Monkey betray the ever-devoted Rat, the relationship will become strained. But dissension is rare. Mostly, this gleeful couple lives in an amusement park of joy.

Rat with Rooster

The Rat and the Rooster peck away at each other. They are equally jealous and possessive as well as anxious about their combined future. One would expect this alliance to devote long hours to mutual accounts, carefully monitoring each debit. Nervous and impatient, they've surely planned ahead, booking their flights to London months in advance. Not so! Each considers that the other should be the adult. Each wants freedom from financial responsibility. Rooster and Rat forever argue over money. Each deems the other too spendthrift.

A racy Rat with an active social calendar turns a jealous Rooster green. A Rat coupled with a Rooster feels stifled. The rebellious Rat accepts prestigious invitations and leaves the jilted Rooster at home. Confronted by the Rat's absence, the Rooster grows insecure and looks for new ways to imprison the racy Rat.

Using sex as a weapon, each deprives the other when they need to. Although capable of enjoying each other, their mundane conflicts surface in the bedroom. This allows for only intermittent pleasure on the occasional peaceful Tuesday.

The union is shaky, at best.

Rat with Dog

Providing the cards are played fairly, Rat and Dog can be satisfied in each other's company. But beware of kinks: be prepared for long tedious chats, sorting through political and social differences.

The materialistic Rat can find it difficult to reason with an idealistic Dog. Generous to a fault, the Dog gives money away, forgetting to save enough for the rent, and can't resist the opportunity to salvage the needy: the Dog's survival depends on being good, forgetting, in this fatal attraction to performing acts of charity, that it should begin at home. Rat, the hoarder, ravaged by anxiety, will worry about the savings, unable to understand his or her puppy-faced mate's desperate need to give it all away. This misunderstanding can cause the pessimistic Dog to mope. The cheerful Rat will gladly try to lift his or her spirits.

Loyal and kind, the Dog's love is unconditional, offering a gentle cradle in which to comfort the Rat's frenetic mind. The Dog is so sentimental that the Rat's raw sexual side may be neglected. If the Dog can learn to be more aggressive and the Rat less so, a decent night's frolicking is to be had. If not, I envy you the compensatory snuggling.

Rat with Pig

Indeed, these two make marvellous mates. In China, the Pig symbolizes affluence, which alone keeps a disquiet Rat from tooth-grinding. The practical Pig mellows the Rat, and is lucky with money, painting a big grin on the face of the contented Rat.

They share a common love for food, go on vacation to France and Italy to taste the glories of old-world cuisine. The restive Rat, now safe in the peaceable Pig's presence, finally lets go, surrendering worry beads and buying daring Parisian *toilettes*.

Despite this affluent couple's bent for squandering, they are both hoarders. Having robust savings to depend on will keep the jolly Rat jollier. Kind and sensitive, the lucky Pig is not always so clever with business transactions. Regarding money matters, the prospering Pig welcomes the circumspect Rat's counsel.

This gregarious and delightful couple is on every host's 'A' list. Genuine love marks this union. You can expect piglets to abound. Equally sexually satisfied, this pair delights in lovemaking. The sensual Pig delights the lusty Rat. Emotional and financial security allow the Rat to surrender fully in the act of sex. The solid Pig is wowed by the Rat's eccentric somersaults. A good time will be had by all.

Ox with Ox

The brute force of a double-Ox marriage could plough forty acres before breakfast. Dutiful and methodical, they mutually protect and provide. The household will be blessed with a rare harmony, so even-keeled that any outside influence might throw off the balance. Expect a certain *ennui*.

In their well-kept kitchen, this couple schemes to uphold their common idiosyncratic need for order. Despite basic concord, this willful pair sometimes has trouble sharing power. Oxen like to dominate. Each expects the other to obey.

Ox couples are mutually stubborn and will not be prepared to exhibit petty disagreements – not even to each other. Rather than convey dissatisfaction, Oxen will deny their differences, assume a façade of marital bliss, and suffer silently, plodding laboriously on, accepting the heavy cross they have to bear. Stasis becomes them.

Their wholesome loving brings steady sexual fulfilment to this marriage. There are some daring deeds to perform together in bed, but Oxen might have to express emotion to achieve fulfilment.

With both noses to this grindstone, an Ox-filled house will not lack financial security. Plenty of money will be earned but rarely foolishly spent. The Ox permits no frivolity.

Ox with Tiger

Disastrous. No matter how you slice it, this combo is in for a rocky ride. Both possess an iron will, backed by the power to exert it. Equally self-possessed and determined, the obstinate Ox and temperamental Tiger are better known as rivals than accomplices. Frankly, this quarrelsome duo is best off entangled at the center of a boxing ring.

Often, the Tiger jump-starts the Ox's tranquil day by stirring up trouble. The stoical Ox wants only to stay at home and plod: he must exercise much patience with the rambunctious Tiger. It's exhausting.

The rebellious Tiger roars off to a trade union demonstration, complaining bitterly about the humdrum, dreary Ox, while the Ox bullies the Tiger, accusing him or her by innuendo of everything from incurable restlessness to insanity.

If round three takes place under the covers, there is hope for reconciliation. The Tiger's raw sensuality thaws the Ox's glacial resistance. With the Tiger, the inhibited Ox feels free and performs at the most down and dirty. Twenty-four-hour truces may result. Even so, the union is best-suited for friendship or business partnership where dual iron wills can effect real progress. The Tiger/Ox emotional match is a tug of war. It is not romantically promising.

Ox with Cat

Cozy. Nestled against a solid-as-a-rock Ox, the Cat will have plenty to purr over. The Ox brings the anxious Kitty security, allowing the Cat to spend time on creative activities without having to fret over money. In return, the Cat, endowed with natural refinement, provides the coarser counterpart with much-needed class. Cat has season tickets to the opera.

The Ox's bossiness is handily managed by a Cat, who usually opts out of conflict. Quiet and submissive, the Cat is happy to take a back seat and let the Bull bully, safe in the presence of a strong, forceful mate. To show gratitude, the Cat lavishes love on the Ox but the self-sacrificing Ox finds excessive displays of affection difficult to endure – is sometimes so defensive about physical love that he or she almost believes those generous hugs are designed to poke fun.

This attitude could prove frustrating for the cuddly Cat who adores snuggling. But, in time, our feline friend will thaw the Oxen's iceberg of resistance and maybe even teach him or her a love trick or two.

Ox with Dragon

Be prepared for plenty of late-night squabbles in an Ox/Dragon combo. Both believe they are righter than right. The Dragon dictates his will over the opinionated Ox and the Bull bullies back.

The Ox has little patience with vanity. The Ox's indifference to the Dragon's fiery appearance is a perpetual disappointment to the Dragon's ego. The glamorous, extravagant Dragon loves to spend money but, with the Ox counting pennies, feels hampered and ill-at-ease.

The Dragon's wandering eye unsettles the faithful Ox.

With so much conflict, how can this duo reconcile? Their love of home and family could save them from total despair. Both enjoy sex, although the Ox's routine techniques may bore the Dragon, whose sentimental nature yearns for puff clouds of pink cotton candy to enhance lovemaking.

Also, the methodical Ox expects a regular living schedule. The Dragon, however, favors a more erratic time code, exorbitant stormy sex for a week followed by peace and quiet for three. An excellent business partnership, this union is not recommended for either marriage or romance unless the Dragon can be free to roam and hunt excitement elsewhere.

Ox with Snake

A slithery Snake wraps him- or herself around an Ox yoke. Content, the Ox welcomes this. But the valiant, seductive viper has enough *sang-froid* to strangle dead the cautious Ox.

A Snake feels cozy in the Ox's warm embrace. And why not? Well, the fickle Snake has an appetite for flesh – especially flesh as yet unexplored. Oxen are devoutly monogamous. Deep down, of course, the Snake is devoted to the Ox, whose stability is vitally important for the Snake's survival. If the Ox can learn to tame a love-wounded ego, and control a jealous temper, this beast can hold on better than anyone else to a Snake. After all, the Ox has all the money, power and patience.

Should the Ox start to fret over depleted reserves, the Snake must surreptitiously drag him or her off to bed. The Ox is happy to oblige with lusty quantity but, to keep the reptile's eye from wandering, must develop more imaginative foreplay. This union can be a good one, if the Ox can remain courageous and undaunted by a tricky Snake mate.

Ox with Horse

Exhausting! These two get along so poorly that the effort which goes into trying is hardly worth the result. What a struggle!

The conventional Ox wants to tame the wild, independent Horse, whose only urge is to gallop off far away from an over-authoritarian Ox. Horses like to make their own decisions, abhorring meddlesome suggestions, which the obstinate Ox fires constantly. If the Ox interferes too strongly with the Horse's single-mindedness, the haughty Horse will take revenge, jumping at every opportunity to mortify the unsuspecting Ox in public.

The Horse will simply *not* conform and drives the Ox mad with hyper-fanciful ideas of painting the house pink, getting married in black or taking home a STOP sign from in front of the police station. Ox steams and pouts. The Horse just laughs, convinced he or she is married to a dullard.

This willful combo will already be dissatisfied on their honeymoon. The Horse, like a wild bronco let loose in a corral, makes mincemeat out of the Ox's reserve. The slow-paced Ox is still in a state of undress when the Horse is riding the great white way. No harmony will cloud this union.

Ox with Goat

In the beginning, the delicate Goat seems like a great catch for a domineering Ox. But never judge a Goat by appearances! Although gentle, Goats are not easily bossed. I caution all Oxen against this union. First, you'll feel a surge of power next to this dainty mountain creature. But after several shared hikes, your puffed-up ego will flop like a tired soufflé. The Goat complains endlessly.

The patient Ox puts up with the Goat's lackadaisical attitude for a while, but soon comes to realize that the Goat is not only lazy, but directionless. A hard-working Ox simply can't understand the Goat's inertia. Happy to be dependent on others, the Goat just doesn't feel the need to work. Besides, the dedicated Bull brings home more than enough bacon.

After a while, as the Ox is so tame and responsible the Goat finds him or her dreary. The Goat likes to sleep on different sides of the bed every night just for the fun of it, which exasperates the rigid Ox who can't bear the thought of breaking routine. Even in bed, the stodgy Ox has trouble keeping up with all the different Goat positions. This is a clumsy couple. Each will be better off without the other.

Ox with Monkey

A happy Monkey can greatly improve the quality of an Ox's life, if the Ox can relinquish stubborn conformism and trust a beloved Monkey. In return for the Monkey's gift of freedom, the Ox will lend security to an able simian mate.

Much to everybody's surprise, the Ox, usually incensed by any disturbance of routine, is fascinated by the tricky Monkey – although won't altogether lose the characteristic resistance to change. This can annoy the free-thinking Monkey who doesn't deem any house-holding rituals important, but both are basically practical and project-oriented. Monkeys teach Oxen to step outside themselves, are kind to others, sacrificing their own comfort to help out – a valuable lesson for an inward-looking Ox.

Under the covers, expect the imaginative Monkey to spice up the Ox's humdrum technique. Under the Monkey's agile tutelage the Ox can expect to learn much more than a few dancing techniques and may even learn how to fly!

Ox with Rooster

Good idea! Should you be lucky enough to have found each other, stay put! People always notice an Ox/Rooster couple. 'Look how happy they are!' they comment. Astrologers in China recommend it as one of the best unions ever! Together, your lives will be filled with pink clouds of romance, mixed with a melodic tune of easy conviviality and hard-line security.

Independently, the Ox and the Rooster can be equally fussy and nervous about perfection. One would expect this match to come together and self-destruct out of such frenetic nit-picking. But, for some reason, they find peace.

This traditional couple lives by the book. The Ox does everything right and the Rooster follows. They buy their first house at the right time of life, have children when expected, and retire to their beautiful country home.

They are not much for social outings, preferring to stay at home. Children will be more than welcome here. This steady pair provides great security for a family.

Not known for passion or folly, their sex reflects their down-to-earth lifestyle. No frills, just basic normal lovemaking. Two naturally, harmonious people will make this happy marriage long-lived and successful.

Ox with Dog

Don't expect the loyal Dog to bay at the moon out of blind love for an adorable Ox: pleading a case for the homeless in Alaska is bound to take priority. And the Ox will be going to trial for a major corporation and grossing 50 per cent of the winnings. These two are so different in their philosophies that mini battles form craters in their living room.

Despite a gentle, loving nature, a puppy Dog, graced with lucidity, knows that this is a Dog-eat-Dog world, yet believes only in justice and equality. The Dog wants no part of the Ox's haughty domineering, answering only to the call of the wounded. The Ox believes that charity begins at home and will beg Doggy to leave the world's problems alone. Both are devout moralizers. But they don't see eye to eye: the Dog argues about starving children in India, trying to sway the Ox to contribute to the noble cause; the Ox fights for justice at home, complaining that the money used on creating a shelter for the homeless last month was really meant to pay for the children's private school.

Sex between them can be fun! This is the only place where an Ox's *roll over* command has clout. The Dog is tickled by and admiring of the Ox's relentlessness and brutally frank style in bed. This Ox/Dog match starts out rocky but as time goes by they learn to love each other with fierce devotion.

Ox with Pig

Indeed, these two get on famously. The good-natured Pig is so malleable that the Ox will be duped into thinking he or she really is boss.

At the summit of a beautiful hill in the mountains of some exquisite location, the Ox and the Pig own a home. This home is so well cared-for that it sparkles. Pig loves to cook. Before bedtime, the careful Ox turns off all the lights and this cuddly combo springs into bed.

Early morning, they wake to the sound of their neighborhood birds, who set a harmonious tone for the day. Of course, the birds are fed daily by the regimented Ox who keeps this ship running on the tightest of schedules.

Sex between these two country people is very satisfying. The Ox is a bit square and rude at first but the Pig's rich sensuality soon takes over and they have a lovely languorous time making a life's worth of love.

Tiger with Tiger

Two Tigers? Burn-out alert! Tigers believe fervently in love at first sight. A Tiger tandem is full of instant enthusiasms, quick takes, gigantic plans, and clever strategies.

Candlelight dinners. Vibrant witty foreplay. Banter and excitement. 'My place or yours?' decisions rapidly executed. Groans, throaty sighs, crackings of zippers, and tearings of clothes, twin Tigers are so turned on, they never make it to the bed. They *need* to consume each other. Afterwards, they'll sip champagne and pore over the world's fate. Their torrid embraces become passionate arguments. In combat, the Tiger twins are happy.

Come morning, two Tigers regain their respective lairs, freshen up, and dash off to work. No time lost, and no extra romantic palaver to cloud the clear purpose of a busy day.

Tigers are inveterate meddlers, always shoving their paws in where they ought to abstain. Two Tigers will contradict and wrongly advise each other all over the place, leaving no other alternative than to swim around in boiling water for the rest of their lives. Help! Perhaps they should forgo marriage. A love affair will be played out in fast-forward mode and promises to be ultra dynamic. But this marriage is unlikely to be either peaceful, long-lasting or productive. And . . . God help the Tiger cubs. The insecurity! The ever-changing domiciles and décors. Arrgh!

Tiger with Cat

A competitive style clash. This couple might very possibly enter into what your mum called 'a marriage of convenience', but underneath roils a mute tension that screams, '*Get me outta here!*' With a Tiger/Cat union, it's the Tiger who's doing the silent shrieking. What about the convenience, then? The Cat usually has the money, and the Tiger, who married the Cat for the loot, is busy with the nervous breakdown.

On the surface, this partnership could be cast in an ad for the Rock of Gibraltar Insurance Co. – everybody is so tolerant and well intentioned. From a rocker, the Cat muses and dreams while the Tiger inspects the estate grounds in Sunday-best attire. But lurking behind the scenes is much turbulence.

Trying to outwit each other, they stealthily compete for the household throne. The Tiger goes at it with typical self-serving vengeance and the Cat struts around the house seeking opportunities to entrap the Tiger. Imagine, two felines under the same roof: they tolerate yet avoid each other. An occasional playful interlude usually degenerates into a clawing, hissing brawl. Cats require security and build their nests with refinement and taste. The Tiger enjoys these surroundings but, unlike the Cat, craves change, favoring a more Bohemian lifestyle. The seductive Tiger could grab the Cat's dough and dash off to the Amazon, leaving only a deep skid mark outside the Swiss bank.

Even in bed, this pair is not apt to be compatible. The Tiger is so hearty and aggressive, possessing such a raw, frank, pushy sexuality that the Cat's delicate sensuality is overwhelmed. Cats require coaxing, seductive, slow-moving lovers and Tigers are ill-suited to satisfy this placid sexual type.

I see the Cat/Tiger match as either an intense summer romance, or perhaps a long-lived 'loving friendship' wherein they get together in bed once in a blue moon for old times' sake. Marriage? Only if the Cat has a private income and protects it from the Tiger's spendthrift clutches.

Tiger with Dragon

Sexeee! The Tiger/Dragon love relationship bears serious consideration. Combined, their strength is almost excessive. And energy! Enough to fuel several large power plants. There is EGO flashing in red neon all over this couple. Overbearing and self-propelled, they are both a bit *too much*. But as a pair, they can succeed.

Despite an excess of commando muscle, this combo lives peaceably together. Mutual respect and admiration offset the expected clashes. The dashing Dragon begs for constant flattery and applause. However, the strong-minded Tiger, finding the pontificating Dragon tiresome, teases the spotlight away. The Tiger is undaunted by fire-breathing antics. In fact, the intrepid Tiger loves a good shouting match and respects a worthy opponent. The generous Dragon is amused by and tolerates the Tiger's love of danger and precipitous behavior.

Tiger with Dragon is not only a sensual match. They carry themselves with bravado and flair. An air of madness colors everything they do. People flock to their home to bask in their aura and share in the high of their hazardous love. Not afraid to share power, they take turns sitting on the throne, complicity taking precedence over their individual roles.

This relationship is good for marriage. Battles will be waged but at the end of the day the force of their attraction ensures they will be lovers for life. Entwined in their own whirlwind of passion and steamy sex, this couple knows the road to heaven. The Dragon sets the tawny Tiger alight and the feline devors the dashing Dragon. Enjoy!

Tiger with Snake

The slithering Snake and tempestuous Tiger are irresistibly drawn to each other but, this union is not encouraged: it is one of the most disastrous alliances. As different as black and white, yin and yang, the Tiger/Snake combo just doesn't mesh. Should either of you be ill-fated enough to fall for the other, a preliminary restraining order could save you from disasters. If not, here's what to expect.

The slow-moving Snake will inflict tremendous frustration on the Tiger's psyche. Initially, the jungle pouncer misguidedly sees the enchanting serpent as quiet and submissive and attempts to dominate. But reptiles don't take kindly to bullying. They retaliate.

Snakes are aloof, independent-minded and strategic whizz kids. Haughty indifference and disdain are among their sharpest weapons and repeated bouts of infidelity shatter a Tiger's giant ego. The impressive tantrums of the Tiger make the Snake's life miserable.

Equally magnetic, Snakes and Tigers compete for attention. The Tiger does so aggressively and the Snake slyly bewitches. At their own cocktail party, Tiger/Snake hosts may appear quarrelsome. The Tiger tells stories about his days in the Sinai desert. Snakey treads on Tiger's territory, wooing the company with the Dance of the Seven Veils, learned (coincidentally) in the Sinai desert. One-upped, the Tiger trounces the Snake more loudly, recounting further desert treks. Subdued, the Snake joins the applause, but adds, in a cultivated, soft-spoken voice, that everything the Tiger knows about deserts was gleaned from the Snake.

Tigers are fast and alert, Snakes quiet and slow-thinking. Tigers think on their feet. Snakes rely almost solely on intuition. These creatures may cohabit for sensual pleasure but they don't see eye to eye.

Sex? The Snake's need for beautiful romantic foreplay is denied by an aggressive Tiger who just gets down to business. Best abstain!

Tiger with Horse

Auspicious, to say the least. Both parties have unruly natures. Individually, they are independent. They might clash, but the attraction between them is strong and so is the mutual respect. In love, they become wilting passion flowers of vulnerability. As a loving pair, their passion knows few bounds.

The Tiger and the Horse are equally inventive and creative. In family matters, the Horse's conservatism curbs the Tiger's hot-headedness. They work hard together to raise a fine family in a 'proper' way, yet, thanks to the Tiger's rebelliousness, the kids will get some relief from the seriousness of Horsey's approach.

Both are optimistic and strong. Usually, if a depression comes along, the Horse is up and the Tiger's down, or vice versa. And no boredom here: these two are active and lusty life-grabbers. Unless one learns to be practical with money, they may have financial crises. Both know how to earn and both love to spend.

The initial sexual attraction is volcanic and they are both imaginative and faithful enough to keep sex exciting over the long haul.

Tiger with Goat

This union is among the worst possible known to Chinese astrologers. Although the couple may make a fabulous start (in bed), from there on it's all downhill.

The practicalities just don't work out. Goat is charming, beautifully seductive and loving. Tiger is passion and mettle. But who will bring home the bacon? In this family, nobody wants the job. No concessions are made. The Goat remains laid back while the ambitious Tiger bombasts a hole in the kitchen ceiling. What was a great passion ends in lifelong misunderstanding and acrimony. Affairs? Yes. Marriage? Abstinence is advised.

Tiger with Monkey

These two make eager lovers. Initially, they will leap frequently on each other's bones, accomplishing astonishing feats of extreme passion but, in the long run, the ardor may die a natural death because Tigers hate to be clung to and innately neurotic Monkeys don't know how not to cling.

The strong intellectual tug between Tigers and Monkeys frequently keeps them together, anyway. The Tiger admires the Monkey's keen eye for strategy and the Monkey enjoys and applauds the Tiger's feisty wit and temerity. Monkey gives Tiger plenty of presents and kudos. Tiger gives Monkey spunk and encouragement. These two have an easy common viewpoint and, even if they cannot keep the love flame burning, will go far together as lifelong pals.

Tiger with Rooster

I don't recommend this as a marriage duo. Both parties are aggressive and opinionated; neither will back down easily and the atmosphere will be taut and arguments one-sided. Conflicts and collisions are guaranteed to hinder the harmonious progress of this couple. Tigers bounce back and forget every nasty word that was said. But Roosters carry grudges and cannot forget how badly they were treated by a Tiger last time they had a row. Impasses are common.

In bed, there may be some fairly exciting fireworks as the Rooster is imaginative and energetic enough to keep the demanding Tiger interested. They are both impetuous and uninhibited lovers capable of grand gestures and profound intensity. Unless the disagreements of the day carry over into the bedroom, this couple is well aspected for a long, healthy sex life.

Tiger with Dog

Harmony incarnate. Dogs and Tigers just plain get along. They have common causes and common philosophies. But they are very different. The Tiger is optimistic, the Dog pessimistic. But each helps the other to overcome basic character defects.

The Chinese call this pairing a happy alliance of muscle and heart. The Tiger has the strength to put the Dog's ideals across to the public. The disquiet Dog keeps watch and prevents the Tiger from leaping into the wrong frays. They are, simply, a great couple.

In bed, the Tiger usually takes the lead, which is felicitous for the tense, nervous Dog who needs to be thawed out before engaging in any heavy sexual activity. With time, this couple learns to blend eroticism with affection to achieve physical fulfilment. It is rare that such a marriage ends in divorce.

Tiger with Pig

The basic characters here are vastly different. Pigs are scrupulous and peace-loving. Tigers strategize every move and carry banners for their own noisy causes. Yet with the proper amount of gentle understanding from Piggy and the sort of generous reasonableness for which Tigers are famous, the pair can make a real go of marriage.

The Pig admires the Tiger's punchy gall and the Tiger the Pig's guilelessness and purity of spirit. Pigs are mostly even-tempered and good-natured while Tigers are pathologically changeable. Pigs find Tigers too mobile but they don't mind staying at home and holding the fort while Tiger rushes about being self-important. Instead of clashing, they complement one another.

Their physical relationship is full of tenderness and mutual understanding. The Pig is sensual, adores pleasure and is lavishly generous. Tigers need a lot of affection and cherish the sort of warmth and homeliness the Pig offers their restless nature. Steamy cuddling sessions abound in the Pig/Tiger household.

Cat with Cat

As long as they have loads of money, Cats can adore each other. Both need material comfort and love order. They are not deliriously reproductive: kids mess up the household and break the porcelain vases, are damned inconvenient and expensive, too.

Mr and Ms Cat are mutually cautious about cash. However, they usually live lavishly by budgeting and planning all expenditures. They collect cruise brochures and set up trips to the safest, most luxurious zones of the globe. Switzerland, New Zealand, Arizona or the Cotswolds will do nicely. *No* danger or funk, *thank you very much*.

The Cat couple's idea of fun at home is to snuggle in duvets, on a bed strewn with books about home decorating and gardening. They love to be pampered and may invite the chiropodist, hairdresser, masseur and yoga teacher to service them *in camera*.

Cats demand such perfection and find fault in so many areas that no one (least of all each other) ever measures up. Reciprocal nit-picking is usually at the center of any dissonance between them.

Cat with Dragon

The flamboyant Dragon's exaggerated pizazz factor does not suit the Cat's need for discretion. The fire-breathing monster goes about wowing crowds with his pyrotechnic displays while the Cat sits by disdainfully, calling the Dragon's antics vulgar. The classy Cat finds all grandiose public exhibits ridiculous; would rather stay at home and polish the silver coffee urn.

Although a Cat/Dragon marriage usually proves unfulfilling, there can be a positive aspect to this duo: a wise Dragon sometimes chooses a gentle, sensible Cat as savior. With much patience and forbearing on Kitty's part, their marriage might work.

Unfortunately, the gentle consideration the Cat lends to a tempestuous Dragon partner can never really be reciprocated. The Dragon needs to be in the limelight, to lead a gregarious life, careering around, currying ovation, and the domesticated Cat is often left at home, tending the household, where, overly sensitive to the Dragon's indifference, poor Kitty sits alone by the fire, doing a slow burn.

Cat with Snake

The intuitive Snake and the philosophical Cat find each other reciprocally interesting. Both have keen minds and are deep thinkers. Should they run into trouble, this couple can rely on their mutual innate wisdom to steer them out of difficulties.

The spendthrift Snake makes weekly shopping appointments with sales-people at Cartier and Dior. This upsets the careful, tradition-bound Cat who doesn't approve of the Snake's penchant for the extravagant. Conflicts are easily resolved if the Cat is allowed to be in charge of the dough. However, unless the Cat learns to understand the Snake's desperate need for the grandest accessories and surroundings, a powerful python may turn into a bored garden Snake. A Snake deprived is a hostile reptile. These two *bons vivants* can usually resolve their differences, whiling away an evening over a bottle of Pommard.

As a couple, this pair oozes charm. They make excellent guests and can expect invitations to all the best parties. In public, the Cat fears the Snake's incessant flirtations, finding the Snake's open, raw sexuality difficult to deal with. But Snakes have their irresistible ways with reticent Cat lovers. Both are potential psychics: if all else fails, they can always become travelling soothsayers.

Cat with Horse

The very name of this union is *catastrophe*. Cats are sedate, laid back and reserved. Horses are pushy, antagonistic and outspoken. Clashes in everything from decorating style to sexual frequency will stand in the way of this lop-sided couple's happiness.

Although both are devoted to pragmatism, each has a different way of dealing with material issues. Cats are cautious, even tight-fisted with money. Horses flaunt their wealth openly and try to impress with their generosity. No meeting of minds ever occurs on this touchy subject.

Cats are not much on public display. Horses love to show off. Cats like quiet, traditional surroundings. Horses adore bold fantasy settings. The Cat wants to stay at home listening to Brahms. The Horse wants to get up and boogie at the best disco in the funkiest section of town. Hard work is the Horse's religion. The Cat seeks ways to live and work in luxury without disturbing one immaculately coiffured hair. Does this sound like a harmonious pair? Hardly. Moreover, in sexual settings, the Cat needs soft music, satin sheets and filmy négligés while the Horse prefers a no-nonsense loft bed *sans* pajamas and plenty of loud marching music to reach ever greater heights of fancy sexual athletics.

Cat with Goat

Although initially they seem ill-suited, this pair will undoubtedly develop a solid love relationship. Cats and Goats are complementary. The Cat provides the dependent, creative Goat with just the right amount of down-home security and the hypersensitive capricious Goat amuses and keeps the Cat interested.

Cats are serious and steady. Goats hardly ever follow the rules. Although normally disconcerted by such nonchalance the Cat finds it disarming in a love partner. The Goat respects the Cat's sound judgement and takes solace in Kitty's ability to cope in a routine fashion.

The Goat's capacity for total surrender in love situations melts the sexually resistant Cat's frozen little heart. Their romantic life is dense with passion. Tenderness and marathon caressing sessions are the order of the day.

The fewer children this couple has, the better. The Goat requires so much personal attention and caring from a Cat spouse that a brood of children who distract the Cat might make him or her cranky and jealous.

Cat with Monkey

These two people are intellectually well matched. They both enjoy being in cultural situations, seeking out new exhibitions or museums and learning about subjects of particular interest to one or both of them. The meeting of two like minds can be the basis of a lifetime of wedded harmony.

Emotionally, however, there will be snags. The Cat hates change and does not enjoy surprises. Discretion, for the Cat, is nine-tenths of the law. Monkeys live for change, enjoy leaping about from place to place and adore being in the limelight, amusing cronies and carrying on high in public. Moreover, the Cat takes him- or herself very seriously. No jokes allowed. Monkeys make fun of everything (including their mates) and think of the world as a giant silliness.

The success and longevity of this relationship depends on the degree of passion the couple can extract from their intensely cerebral friendship. Neither lends much belief to the idea of syrupy romance, keeping their respective cynical distances from all 'sentimental' notions. A little shove from the pain of a complex love triangle or other potentially hot sexy intrigue may inspire them to give in to the natural human impulse to love and be loved – no matter what!

Cat with Rooster

This couple should think twice before taking the lifelong plunge into matrimony. The sex is mediocre at best. Although Cats are initially attracted by the haughty Rooster's natural nobility and aura of reserve, they may be misinterpreting the Rooster's real methods and motives. Basically, Roosters want to be free to roam and race about following the peripatetic bent of their roller-coaster existence. Cats like to stay at home, work long and hard at quiet jobs, get and stay rich.

Lifestyle would quickly become a problem for this pair. With their individual approaches being so gapingly different, who, I ask you, would take out the garbage?

Certainly not the refined Cat, who is too busy reading philosophical tomes and decorating magazines on a Louis XV *chaise longue*. As for the Rooster – hardly ever home long enough to create any garbage, or to make any babies. If the pair has the means (and nothing prevents them from earning money as they are both hard-working, serious types) to hire help for the baser human chores, they can establish a solid, functional family life.

Cat with Dog

In Chinese astrology, Cats and Dogs traditionally get on with each other. Although sexual intimacy is not the most salient point of contact here, companionship is. Everybody knows how important companionship is to animal Dogs. Cats like to be safe and well housed too. This couple's marriage is based on profound mutual affection and respect for each other's opinions and aesthetic choices.

Both Cats and Dogs have a marked tendency to mood swings. Both are critical and easily discouraged by the realities of everyday life and its various injustices. Although Dogs are more pessimistic, Cats can be testy and crotchety when the chips are down. Their complicity will be based largely on their mutual mistrust of human nature. Their shared cynicism is their consolation for putting up with an imperfect world.

Both parties are dutiful and unafraid of working hard. Money should not be an issue. Mutual participation in professional and para-professional projects will lend strength to their union. The Dog's spontaneous expressions of lapping affection might get on the Cat's taut nerves. But one thing for sure, the Cat can depend on the Dog's undying sexual loyalty.

Cat with Pig

Here's a pair tailor-made for successfully carving out a bucolic country life together. Both creatures love nature and thrive in rural bourgeois opulence. They both covet ownership of the finer things in life. With time, the Cat/Pig couple can expect to lead a civilized, charming life together in peace and tenderness without suffering want or lack of mutual respect.

The Cat, of course, has an artistic side, and will be the one to maintain decorum, keep neat flowerbeds and establish house rules. The Pig, an earthier character given to rustic manners and relaxed – even sloppy – habits will appreciate the Cat's attempt at forging a pristine existence for them. These people are both malleable enough to accept the other's shortcomings and honor their partner's needs.

Piggy is very sexual. Kitty is not. Piggy is rampantly erotic. Kitty is borderline prudish. At first, there may be some misunderstanding in this area but in the long run, the Pig's sensuality and open-mindedness about sex will break down the Cat's hesitancy and a good old sexual time will be had by both.

Dragon with Dragon

This relationship is almost too volatile for any long-term good to come of it. What we have here is a lifetime battle royal for supremacy. In competitive situations, neither Dragon can allow the other's gigantic ego to prevail so, whether it's a pitched combat over who gets to open the new potato chip bag or a tussle about who drives the car on the next trip to the supermarket, the air will aways be full of strife.

At first, all this emotional power play may seem to the Dragon couple like a love storm of glorious emotion. They are not ill-suited sexually and, even when they are furious with each other, may have some of the most exciting sex of their lives together. Yet, day-to-day living threatens to be so highly charged, so noisy and fraught with shouting and name-calling, that one wonders if a few moments of occasional earth-shaking sex is worth it.

Unless it's irreversible, I advise against this marriage. Two giant uncompromising fire-breathing beasts may well be doomed to set each other's hearts on fire – but they are patently unsuited to keeping the home fires burning.

Dragon with Snake

In Chinese astrological parlance, these two are considered kissin' cousins. The Dragon adores sporting a gorgeous, attractive, sexy Snake partner and the quiet, subtle Snake admires the Dragon's world-beating flamboyance and style. In turn, Dragon protects Snake. Snake coddles Dragon's ego and lets Dragon blab away without so much as a hint of criticism.

Of course, no relationship with any Dragon can ever be calm, but the Snake/Dragon duo comes close to being a level-headed, harmonious union. Wisely, the Snake never confronts the Dragon's overblown ego head-on. Snakes deal subtly with clashes, slithering and examining all sides before striking at just the right spot to get results.

Sexually – with the Snake's huge capacity for erotic activity and the Dragon's giant appetite and innate talent for same – you can just imagine ... the chemistry is sublime. They agree on living luxuriously, too. The Dragon buys endless scrumptious accessories for the Snake's pleasure and the Snake allows the Dragon – within reason – to indulge in filling the house with gadgetry. Their home life is peachy. They make a handsome couple. It's truly a match made in heaven.

Dragon with Horse

This couple will, no doubt, boast vociferously of having fallen in love 'at first sight'. Both of these effusive people are firm believers in *falling in love* as a way of life. The sex meter will be permanently set to hot and heavy mode. They won't be able to keep their hands off each other. Fact is, sex is about the only thing that distracts these two from a full-time war of wills which inevitably besets their relationship.

Horses are authoritarian and don't like to be told what to do. Dragons like to dominate and hate to be bossed around. Each one is proud, touchy, irritable, self-centered and headstrong. Neither is acquiescent. The Dragon, at least, is sentimental but the Horse is hard-nosed and tough-minded and knows how to make the Dragon cry. The Dragon is the less conventional of the two and will not hesitate to embarrass the socially correct Horse in public for revenge.

I also see money conflicts here. The Dragon and the Horse both like to spend. If allowed to have their way, they'll be broke and in debt all the time. This ill-suited couple is only happy during the initial sexy infatuation stage. From there on it's all downhill.

Dragon with Goat

In Chinese astrological circles, this is said to be a sound marriage. Goats are essentially weak-willed. They are easily swayed and don't mind being bamboozled and manipulated by their loved ones. Dragons need to command, direct operations and dominate. The Goat's good-natured passivity inspires the Dragon to protect and be chivalrous. He or she thrives in the security provided by the Dragon's big-time authority trip.

Their sexual life together will be as near to an erotic dream as you can get. Dragons like to take charge and Goats like to lie back and be loved. Being two very sentimental as well as sensual beings, these two will know instinctively how to blend sex with affection. Their intimacies will be satisfying and frequent.

Dragon with Monkey

Despite the obvious differences in their characters, these two have a lot going for them. The Dragon is bombastic and needs to be adored yet reveres the Monkey's keen intelligence and ability to see around corners. Monkeys love spectacle and invariably enjoy the show that Dragons put on. Dragons get themselves embroiled in world-class problems. Monkeys are born solvers of problems – big and little.

There is plenty of room for personal evolution in this couple too. Impressed by the efficiency of the Monkey's exceptional mind, the Dragon (atypically) will become dependent, let up on the accelerator from time to time and even take an occasional back seat to Monkey's brilliance. Monkeys enjoy being appreciated for their skillful talents, are not particularly interested in the number one position, and can let a Dragon bask in the footlights. As a result of this clever balance, the Dragon/Monkey match becomes a strong bond, built on compromise and mutual respect. Sex, however, may not be the strongest element that binds these two. The Monkey's normally healthy sexual appetite seems moderate by comparison to the Dragon's voracious and conspicuous need for consumption of his or her mate's most intimate favors.

Dragon with Rooster

Both passion and glamor are missing from this otherwise well-balanced relationship. It is workable. Dragon protects with gusto and Rooster obeys with serious intent to do the right thing. Neither is ecstatic in this arrangement but, then, neither is blatantly unhappy. It works.

Roosters recognize and respect the Dragon's need to shine, to assert superiority over others and go out and beat the world at its own game. Despite sometimes flamboyant outward appearances, the Rooster is a rank conservative who doesn't want to stand out from the crowd. Roosters want to be free to voice their truths and bandy their ideals. With a brave and daring Dragon, the Rooster can carry on merrily being just plain him- or herself.

I'm afraid the Dragon's exorbitant sexual needs may prove overwhelming to the less sensual Rooster. Rooster's rebuffs may destroy Dragon's ego. The solution will only be found in frank discussion with an objective third party. A therapist? A clergyman? A good family friend?

Dragon with Dog

Polarized outlooks might find happiness, providing the sex is sensational. But with the Dragon/Dog duo, this is plainly not the case. According to Chinese astrologers, few relationships are less likely to withstand the test of time. Dragon/Dog bickering and barking prevail.

Both Dragons and Dogs are full of enthusiasm, energy and vigor. But their styles are so different as to make them near enemies. Dogs hate making a fuss over nothing. Dragons intentionally create daily scenes complete with flames, smoke and noise. Dragons deem the moralizing, pessimistic, stern Dog a downright irritating bore. Dragons live primarily for themselves. Dogs live for others. The Dragon will wish the Dog a more obedient mate. But the free-thinking Dog will never buckle under to oppression. While the

Dragon boasts of successes, the Dog gloats over his or her mate's resounding failures.

The Dragon may try to take revenge in the bedroom. There is nothing that gentle Dogs hate more than violence. Moreover, the Dog is less interested in sex than in saving the world from superficial people like the Dragon. Unless there is a very compelling reason to keep it together, I advise giving this relationship a pass.

Dragon with Pig

Most Dragon/Pig marriages last for ever. The two have just enough in common and just enough differences to keep them both interested. The Pig is compliant and easygoing, always gives the benefit of the doubt to the other fellow and admires gutsiness and audacity in a mate. The Dragon needs an ally, a helpmate, a shoulder to cry on and someone nice to boss around – preferably someone who forgives easily. The Pig amply fills the bill.

Both characters adore opulence – the more gilt sconces they can stick on the walls of their *châteaux*, the happier they will be. The Pig applauds Dragon's successes and turns a blind eye to all chicanery. In turn, Dragon protects and admires the Pig's scrupulousness. In short, Pig helps Dragon maintain the shine on an overactive ego. Dragon adores being put on a permanent pedestal and makes it clear that Pig's homemaking talents are all he or she has ever dreamed of.

The sex is good. The Pig cleaves to sensuality and the Dragon just plain loves sex – lots of it. Piggy wants romance so Dragon must temper crudity and learn something about foreplay.

Snake with Snake

Drama. Sex. Luxury. Promiscuity. Passion. Ruin. Both Snakes will be potentially indolent. Both tend to dissimulate. Both want to be surrounded by beautiful things and unusual friends. The Snake couple's life will be fraught with intricate complexities and unexpected happenings.

A Snake couple is artistic. In tandem, they will enhance their cultural existence, regularly attending exhibitions, concerts and theater. As they also tend to be philosophical and are drawn to the metaphysical, they will often engage in exciting New Age activities and hold conversations which last far into the night.

This sexually compatible pair will entwine upon first meeting and subsequently have great difficulty disengaging for even the most important of practical matters. Tenderness, romance and passion are the very cornerstone of their intimacy.

Although the financial area of their joint life might be a real mess, an overwhelming physical attraction binds them together. Despite a philandering tendency on both sides, no jealousy will cloud their lovemaking. In fact, these two may hardly emerge from between their smooth satin sheets long enough to let the live-in full-time maid wash them.

Snake with Horse

These two are strongly attracted to each other. The Horse admires the Snake's natural ease with people and appreciates the Snake's considerate, generous nature. The Snake, on the other hand, likes and respects the Horse's spunk and native enthusiasm. Their social life will be rich and full.

Trouble sets in when the Horse realizes that the adored Snake mate is 'running around'. Promiscuity does not set well with the straight arrow, faithful, devoted Horse. So Horsey flips into recrimination mode. Which forces the Snake to conceal any extra-curricular activities more cleverly – but not give them up.

The Snake is hyper-generous and the Horse more conservative with money. This disparity will cause some world-class rows. Best to let Horsey take over running the finances and doling out money to Snake for fripperies. But don't expect the money-hungry Snake to sit still for that arrangement.

Almost everybody is happy with a sensual Snake person in their bed. Horses have little confidence in their sexuality, but Snakes have more than enough to go around. They make good considerate teachers. The match can work if Horsey can learn not to whine if Snake takes off on a sexy, romantic mission on their wedding night.

Snake with Goat

Charming and gracious, this pair of gentle, creative people can have the world eating out of their hands. The Goat's inherent beauty and seductive appeal, when combined with the Snake's elegance and sensuality, forms an enviably synergistic couple. Theirs will be a delicious complicity.

Unfortunately, neither of these gloriously attractive people is very handy with a calculator. They are both equally improvident, luxury-loving, even profligate about spending. Unpaid bills will pile up and each will call the other a spendthrift. Stalemate. Don't expect the Goat to find solutions. Snakes may overspend but they can also provide. Goats are determined to depend and be provided for.

Once again, the Snake's incurable infidelity slithers into the equation. Goats tend to be fickle too. But, even though the Snake understands the Goat's occasional need for a fling, the more stubborn Goat hates to share his goodies and will freak out at the idea of Snakey's infidelity. But never mind. Rows are the stuff of these people's lives: both are addicted to passionate drama. Romantically, this couple is sound. But when the harsh, overhead light of reality pierces the veneer of their relationship, the cracks and flaws may prove too numerous for its survival.

Snake with Monkey

Auspicious beginnings encourage these characters to join forces and operate as a team. The versatile Monkey finds wisdom and consideration in the Snake's personality. The Snake enjoys the Monkey's charm and peppy energy. They are truly a complementary pair.

After a time, however, they will see that all they have in common is a taste for helping others, a charitable bent which binds them ever-so-loosely together. Snake, of course, always takes off on extra-marital adventures. Monkey? Well, Monkey couldn't care less: if affairs turn up, so much the better. If not, too bad.

Snakes like elegance and want their lives carefully accessorized. Monkeys are bored by the very idea of accessorizing anything and dress down rather than dressing up. Monkeys are spontaneous. Snakes ponderous. Snake is romantic, Monkey logical. Snake is sophisticated, Monkey Bohemian and carefree. Dialogue becomes difficult because Snakes find it hard to divulge themselves. Breakdown in communications will be the death of this relationship.

Their sex life usually compensates for much of the strife they feel between them. Although sex is not always the Monkey's strongest suit, Snakes succeed in turning them on in a big way. The complicity of elaborate sex games may ensure a basis for this pair to consolidate their union – despite their essential differences.

Snake with Rooster

A love match if ever I saw one! The Rooster is rather bourgeois and conventional while Snakes like things to appear perfect. Although, at first glance, it may seem that the Snake is too sophisticated and elegant for the plain-living Rooster, the opposite is true. Roosters and Snakes form some of the best couples.

They are both secretive and like to keep to themselves. They are forever locked in intense discussion and consideration of every detail, from the quality of light inside their fridge to the leather on the soles of their expensive shoes. Roosters are forgiving, indulgent people whose loyalty knows no frontiers. Snakes may run around a bit, both socially and sexually, but they are careful never to get deeply involved with their conquests and hardly ever betray or leave their Rooster mates. Why? Because they truly love them.

In this marriage the Rooster should look after the finances. Snakes often waste money, while Roosters keep closer tabs on their pennies. The cultural side can be handled equally well by both. Sex should definitely be left up to the seductive Snake. Snakes know how to turn on hesitant Roosters, to make their bodies sing; Roosters are basically reserved about sensual things. The Rooster who lands a Snake mate will have much to crow about.

Snake with Dog

This partnership is lop-sided. We are dealing with two disparate types of people. Dogs are pessimistic, giving in to depression and worry. Snakes are naturally relaxed, less anxious and certainly less sarcastic. Sometimes the doubting Dog even mistrusts a pet Snake's indubitable charm and will whine and snap about it, criticizing the vulnerable Snake for frivolity and an easygoing nature.

However, basic personality differences do not have to destroy relationships. The Dog hates society, has few friends and stays at home a lot. Snakes are just the opposite yet need a home to go back to after their numerous forays into the big world. Returning to the cozy Dog home after imbibing a faceful of society's cupidity can be refreshing for the overly sociable Snake. Even though they snarl and threaten, Dogs always forgive, are loyal to a fault and never waver in their devotion to their loved ones.

Both parties are sensitive to causes, feel strongly about combating injustice and believe in right over might. This similarity of purpose can serve to harmonize their relationship and round out some potential hard edges.

Trouble is, their sexual selves are very different. Dogs are physically conventional and direct. Snakes are highly adventurous in bed and enjoy intricate sexual play. The two may not clash over this issue, but the Snake may eventually get bored, resume a natural bent for flirting and irrevocably damage the Dog's tender ego.

Snake with Pig

The Pig's nemesis. The Chinese sages always advise against this relationship. Pigs are earthy, warm-hearted pushovers for beauty and cultural *savoir-faire*. Inevitably, the first gorgeous sex-loving Snake to come along knocks the Pig for six.

Superficially the luxury-loving Pig has much to recommend him to a Snake lover. Pigs are scrupulous and mostly honest. They usually know how to make lots of money, which the Snake loves to lavish on their joint lifestyle. They both adore things traditional like antiques and vintage wines.

The problem here revolves around the weakness these two share. Neither the Snake nor the Pig is a world-record decision maker: Pig changes his or her mind as readily as Snake changes his or her outfit. Snake procrastinates. Pig wallows and wonders. They are sexually compatible to a fault, but little is accomplished in life by lying about sensually entwined in each other's arms.

Pigs don't much care about appearances, making rude noises and smacking their lips when they eat. Eventually, a fastidious Snake grows critical of a Pig's sloppy habits. Snake's jibes bring out the worst in Piggy, who whimpers, which only makes the Snake more impatient. The gracious Pig can never please the demanding

Snake enough, finally withering away under the Serpent's disapproval.

Horse with Horse

Not a perfectly harmonious couple. As the Horse is self-centred, two Horses will initially be attracted by their similarities. Merely sharing so many things in common will cement a solid friendship between two Horses. However, unless they can agree to slough off convention and each remain free to go their own way, excitement will be lacking and boredom will smother this hardworking couple in its own hair shirt.

These two are open-minded, so, with an extra dose of flexibility, they can function as a productive team. However, the hot-headed, headstrong, willfulness of two Horses can threaten their marriage with discord.

As both are gamblers, financial instability can also weaken the marriage. For money matters to tick along as they should, these two should hire an accountant and try to keep their social life active. The influence of softer, more gentle souls, will improve the double Horse *entente.*

Individualism is not always the best ingredient to ensure the success of a team. The Horse couple's tempestuous sex life will reflect excessive egocentricity on both sides which may cause the eventual demise of this otherwise effective and hardy couple.

Horse with Goat

This apparently odd combination sometimes works extremely well. Horses are strong-minded hard workers. Goats are languorous, creative and oh-so-independent. The Horse in this pair will always feel protective of the Goat mate. Horses like to feel superior and Goats know exactly how to inflate their egos. When decisions are to be made or actions taken, the Goat goes all flabby and swoons, 'Honey, you're so clever. I just know you're better at this than I am,' and the Horse rides off into the night to play hero.

The Goat's romantic side appeals to the stodgy Horse's sense of poetry. Even though their sensitivities are not too similar, Horses find ethereal Goats decidedly sexy. They complement each other. Goats are pessimistic, Horses are not. Goats are flaky. Horses are solid conservatives. Goats depend and Horses willingly provide. Horses like things their way and, as long as there's money in the bank, Goats are supremely flexible.

These two are so different that they will never be bored together. Of course, friction might occur because the Goat is jealous and possessive and the Horse needs to feel free. But usually, the Goat's sense of what is most practical for the future will win out and, aside from some mild disapproval, he or she will not tax their partner sufficiently to cause the Horse to bolt.

Horse with Monkey

A mutual desire to stay abreast of events, mingle in society and be part of what's happening in the outside world will constitute the initial attraction between these two. Monkeys are so versatile, imaginative and amusing that Horses have trouble in resisting their charms. Monkeys can feel that serious Horses need cheering up and are inspired to make them laugh. Monkeys also appreciate the hardy Horse's strict sense of duty and ability to endure hard work. They love to join forces and solve problems together.

Communication may not be their strongest suit. Monkeys are inveterate neurotics who cherish their unhealthy behavior patterns and don't open up easily. Horses are guarded and conservative about speaking up on their own behalf. Much tension may build. They should agree (before reaching the ulcer stage) to see a therapist regularly. Otherwise, unexpressed emotions will cause the death of their union.

A brilliant sex life is in store for the Monkey/Horse couple. They are mutually energetic and fanciful about romance. Horse may want more sex than does Monkey but Monkey's fertile imagination will more than compensate for lack of appetite. As long as these two don't sit around complacently patting each other on the back about how well their couple 'works', they can create a lasting bond.

Horse with Rooster

This relationship doesn't have much to recommend it. Unless stimulated by the right partner, both Roosters and Horses become stodgy and work-obsessed. Unless they have a professional or family connection they probably won't get together in the first place. There is not much charisma on either side at the outset.

Once together, the Horse will be flattered by the Rooster's possessive streak, but in time will resent it and dissension will set in. Horse wants to go out and play and Rooster wants them both to stay at home reading and playing records.

The Horse must learn to be less outgoing and the Rooster more tolerant of the Horse's need for social interaction. Roosters are so conservative that, although Horse's occasional outrageousness appeals to their rebellious side, they will worry nonstop about the negative outcome of their mate's follies. A Rooster's best bet is to give the Horse a longer and longer rein, and wait sanely by the fireside.

At first, their sex life may be limited by Rooster's excessive conservatism. The practical Horse will rise to the occasion and prod the Rooster to be more imaginative. In time, when they learn to satisfy each other's needs, their sexual rapport can become nigh unto perfect.

Horse with Dog

If this pair hires a nanny and a housekeeper, a laundress and a cook, they can probably establish a very sound love relationship. Neither of these two effective, active, project-oriented people is enchanted by a career as a horse drudge or nose-wiper, staying at home waiting for the other to appear.

Horses are characteristically profligate with money. They gamble it away and take chances others would not. This risky trait fills the nervous Dog with fear. The Horse hates to be reminded of profligacy but the sarcastic Dog cannot keep quiet for long. Fights – yes, I said *fights* – ensue.

As harmony reigns in their bedroom, these two usually end up better friends after vibrant lovemaking sessions wherein each bestows lavish pleasure on the other. The Dog is giving and the Horse is loving. It's a good sexual match.

The lovemaking may be salutary but what will ultimately hold this pair together is their deep respect for each other's integrity. They are mutually honorable people with a refined sense of social conscience and loyalty. Time will round off whatever sharp angles this pair encounters. A durable, solid relationship is assured.

Horse with Pig

Poor Piggy! Horses are notoriously headstrong and wilful. The Pig simply cannot say no to a Horse's winning ways. And even though a right-thinking Horsey knows better than to walk all over an acquiescent mate, he or she seemingly cannot help himself. Because they are often very striking, Horses attract Pigs in droves. In their turn, Pigs win the hearts of Horses because they are so willing, generous and tantalizingly compliant.

Sexually, they are well matched. The Horse finds the Pig's overt sensuality liberating. Pigs like the strong side of Horse's sexual nature and are turned on by their handsome appearance.

Pigs attract money. Horses work hard and know how to make money, but often gamble it away. The Pig is a natural home-builder and nurturer. The Horse is an outside person. They complement each other, a strength in such a relationship. Providing the Pig can endure the Horse's frequent absences and accept the outgoing side of his personality, this couple can create a sound basis for a prosperous family.

Goat with Goat

Immediate synergy! In bed, this couple performs well. They are so alike that everything flows naturally. Romance flourishes as they are both loving, sensitive and unusually in touch with and open about their emotions. At first glance, it would seem that these two might be able to live on *l'amour* alone.

Later on, however, when they have settled into a mild routine, a pair of Goats will cause each other much mutual pain. Being so alike in temperament, their sins and grievances will be similar. Each will learn quickly how to push the other's panic button.

The immaturity and pessimism of dual Goats could be their undoing. Neither wants responsibility for the finances, for the future of their emotional bonding or for the workaday continuity of the household. Neither is able to depend on the other. When things go wrong, each will dream of having a stronger partner.

The best way for this union to work well would be if one party (or better still both) had a private income. Then, they could hire a 'take charge' domestic staff and have all the time in the world for creative joint projects.

Infidelity is another Goat trait. Imagine two randy Goats running loose in the same marriage. Awful rows, pouting and shrieking occur. Moreover, Goats are possessive and jealous. Each, in his turn, will be devastated by the other's betrayal. 'Iffy' at best.

Goat with Monkey

A mutual lightheartedness will draw these two creatures into a joyous relationship. The Monkey's energy alone can carry the couple financially and, as the Monkey is very generous, he or she will not mind being the sole provider. If Monkey is doing well, their whole existence can consist of fun and games.

The sex will be less than wonderful, though, because Monkey is not the same sort of sensitive lover as the Goat. Goats need constant caresses, are romantic and sentimental, while Monkeys are practical, literal lovers whose lovemaking resembles a healthful gymnastic more than a swooning match.

The Goat's moral dependence may become irritating to the carefree Monkey who longs to move about freely without undue constraint. Having to stay at home, coaxing a grumpy Goat out of pessimism and inertia may be more than the independent Monkey can bear.

If this couple has a family, it may help to hold them together. Goat can stay securely at home while Monkey wanders free. It's a sound combination, providing the Monkey can eventually support the Goat in an appropriately high and leisured style.

Goat with Rooster

This is a dicey combination. Roosters are conservative and individualistic. They deplore laziness and cannot tolerate lackadaisical attitudes in others. Goats like to take it easy. They don't believe in work for its own sake, would rather sit still than move about and are ever ready to get someone else to take care of their basic needs.

As the Rooster often has great difficulty scratching out a living, he or she will be impatient with the idea of anybody living off the fat of the land and will wish the Goat would find a real job like a normal person. Goat's feelings are readily hurt. Tensions can mount in this household and very little will be talked through because the Rooster hates discussing his emotions.

The fickle Goat will wander sexually, causing the staid and faithful Rooster untold pain. Trouble is, the Goat needs more sex than the Rooster, which creates feelings of inadequacy and a lack of self-confidence in the Rooster.

If Goat could be persuaded to stick around all the time and teach the willing Rooster how to be more sensual, their relationship might have a good chance at success. At least it would give purpose to the otherwise idle Goat's home life.

Goat with Dog

Not much love is lost between these two. The Dog is all moral standard and high-mindedness. Very often, the Goat's ideals begin and end with where the next meal is coming from. Goats are often on the side of the person carrying the wallet. Dogs deplore pandering. Goats know no other way of life. As a couple, unless the Dog decides uncharacteristically to shoulder the burden of changing a poor misunderstood Goat whom he or she believes to be a hidden genius, they will be two very different people going in opposite directions.

The Dog likes things to be clear, just and fair. The Goat doesn't even know what those terms mean. Goats are dreamers whose ephemeral plans often go up in smoke. Dogs dream too, but their dreams are founded in concrete and seek real solutions to real social problems.

Goats, of course, love sex and favor open relationships wherein they have full freedom. Dogs wouldn't think of being unfaithful –

even if their partner handed them the world to roam in search of new sexual horizons. To a Dog, devotion and loyalty come first. To a Goat, blind devotion and loyalty are for fools who don't know which side their bread is buttered.

It would be too optimistic to expect harmony from this essentially unbalanced romantic equation.

Goat with Pig

In this pairing we find one of the happiest possible combinations. The atmosphere between Goat and Pig is mellow and smooth. They may have minor differences of opinion over small things, like taste in furniture or which sort of friends to frequent most, but the Goat likes the security he finds with Piggy and Piggy, in turn, enjoys the whimsical, creative nuttiness of the charming Goat.

Pig is lucky in money matters so he can support the gentle Goat and allow him free rein to dream, aimlessly inventing and reinventing his daily life. Pigs have endless patience and seem to be composed of goodwill and indulgence for the capricious Goat mate. Goat could not be better matched where emotional stability is concerned either. The Pig usually stays in the country, away from madding city life where the Goat can safely cavort unhindered in fertile fields.

The sexual side of this affair is enviably harmonious. The parties have similar sensitivities. Noble Piggy will undoubtedly be wounded by the Goat's incessant dalliances and disapprove of Goat's unfortunate tendency to try to take up with almost every attractive person who comes to call – the flirtatious Goat lacks tact. But, never mind. Once Piggy's pain has passed, the darling Goat will be forgiven and both will return to the familiar devil-may-care bucolic existence.

Monkey with Monkey

These two make great companions. They love in a hands-off fashion. Neither interferes with the other's progress merely to seek ego-strokes. Two Monkeys usually create a project-oriented family atmosphere wherein each member of the group has individual responsibilities and householding belongs to everyone. Cooking and washing up, shopping and even ironing may be shared equally. The male Monkey is never too proud to do laundry. And Ms Monkey doesn't mind changing the oil in the family car. Sexually slanted competition doesn't exist here.

Problems (and there aren't many that two Monkeys cannot solve better than one) will arise in the financial arena. Neither Monkey likes doing accounts, writing checks or letters protesting gas and electricity bills. As a couple, they may fall behind and ruin their reputation. As both are work- and people-oriented, these Monkeys will need to hire a part-time bookkeeper to hold their finances together.

Sex is not often the foremost consideration between two Monkeys. They both enjoy it and even prefer having sex with each other. But they are not overly preoccupied by the intensity or endurance of their sexual lives. If and when it happens, they are excited and happy. Without it, neither curls up and dies. Promiscuity might be a dot on the horizon, but dalliances are of no consequence as Monkeys make committed couples who believe in personal freedom.

Monkey with Rooster

Not much is going on sexually between these two characters. Roosters are possessive and anxious about their position in relationships. Their instinct is to anchor their prey. Monkeys are freedom freaks who need miles of rope to feel good about themselves. They have to roam amid people, jabber with others and find solutions to ever more important problems.

Roosters are conservative thinkers. Monkeys are all for liberation, gentler laws and personal liberty. This couple may be constantly at odds over policy. Decisions become difficult to make. Tensions rise and Rooster suffers – because Rooster makes the untenable scenes which send the Monkey packing. Rooster must accept Monkey's devil-may-care side to enjoy the benefit of his or her humor. It's up to the Rooster to be more flexible. And that is a tall order.

These two are not exactly Romeo and Juliet. Monkey is interested in sex, but he's also fascinated by life's other aspects, above all its practicalities. Rooster is also practical and appreciates Monkey's delight in solving concrete issues. But Rooster needs softening, romancing, loving and cuddling to appreciate the joys of sex. Now it's Monkey's turn to adapt, to become more languorous and spend time petting and nuzzling. Or Rooster (God forbid!) might begin scratching around in another barnyard for sexual understanding.

Monkey with Dog

The Dog is a blazing idealist. The Monkey lives for the opportune moment. They may well meet up and fall in love when engaged in a great social struggle together. Each possesses qualities lacking in the other. Although this might make them seem perfectly matched, it takes more than dovetailing qualities to make two such impervious individualists communicate. Each is so accustomed to living on his own wavelength that they have real trouble shifting gears to make themselves understood to someone on another plane. The remedy is talk. These two nervous souls must sit and yammer for hours, days and months before they reach comprehension. The Dog will have to give up blurting nasty remarks and the Monkey must accept being tethered for at least part of the time.

Faithful Dogs don't take kindly to philandering, but Monkeys must constantly prove themselves in sexual freedom. Monkey seems carefree and Dog laughably frustrated. Being of basic good intention, if they wish to stay together, this pair can work out a harmonious sex life together. This relationship's harmony is possible but will not be won without effort. Unless the union is inevitable, I advise against imagining it can work for ever.

Monkey with Pig

Poor Piggy! The Pig must treat this relationship with less blind indulgence for the opposite party. Monkeys can be ruthless when necessary. The Pig's naïvete is no help when it comes to dealing with a beloved, yet sometimes unscrupulous, Monkey.

Unlike the Snake, whose intentions in the Pig's regard are plainly lethal, the Monkey means no harm. Pigs' and Monkeys' tender hearts are mightily compatible – but their thinking processes are worlds apart. The Pig must adapt to the Monkey's ways or the couple is doomed.

As Pigs are very malleable, adaptation is not an unreasonable demand. But Piggy must be careful not to lose his or her purest ideals in Monkey's constantly expanding bag of tricks. Pigs live by their intuition. Monkeys cleave to logic. If they can teach their mutual talents to co-operate, it will assist their union's progress. If not, there will be major rows. An angry Monkey is a hopping mad mini volcano who forgets about it two minutes after the eruption. A mad Pig is fearsome, relentless, dangerous and vengeful.

Monkey should accept and enjoy Pig's smothering and homely charms. And Pig should try to see how innocently the Monkey needs room to wander and squander. If these concessions are made they can have a lovely long-lasting life together.

Rooster with Pig

This partnership can succeed brilliantly. Roosters who find themselves in bed with willing, sensual Pigs are truly in luck. My advice to this lucky Rooster is to hang on tight: you will not find such amiability, charm and easygoing service anywhere else in the zodiac. Pigs are willing to adapt and change, modify their personalities and lifestyles to suit the one they love. With all of your ups and downs, resounding successes and failures, you will definitely benefit from the presence of a kindly, nurturing, understanding Pig.

As for the Pig in this relationship, you will gain much from the pure rigor and frank style of a Rooster partner. Roosters like things as they are. They are not revolutionaries. Pigs, too, enjoy tradition and respect the basic tenets of a good society. Your common interests will flourish and after the first few years will take you both very far towards achieving dreams and goals you only dreamed of before meeting.

Sex, too, is favored in this couple. The Rooster can take charge in lovemaking. Pigs appreciate being moved to exotic heights in bed, adore almost anything sensual and make excellent cuddlers for the roughshod Rooster to learn to snuggle with. If I were a Rooster, I'd seek a Pig mate. Your lifetime happiness and financial security (Pigs attract money) would be assured.

Rooster with Rooster

Difficult at best, this couple's inevitable clashes over everything from money to styles of clothing and which schools to send the children to are practically never worth sorting out.

What we face here are two opinionated egotistical people. They are, first of all, victims of themselves and require jollier, more acquiescent partners than either can be for the other. Roosters need to be cushioned and coaxed. I hardly see any Rooster accepting to do the coaxing for another – unless in a war where the other Rooster was a fallen buddy.

The war metaphor is perfect: each Rooster engaged in a Rooster/Rooster couple wants to be the boss. Each needs to feel superior to the other. Each is conservative and shy, unsure of their image and feisty beyond feistiness. Battles royal rage daily, viciously pulling harmony apart.

Roosters often befriend each other. They think alike and have similar views. They can even work together – providing one takes a back seat. But first love between Roosters rarely produces equilibrium. The sex is lukewarm: neither is able to express passion without help from a more vigorously self-assured partner.

A second marriage later in life could be blissful between Roosters as many basic Rooster problems would already have been worked out.

Rooster with Dog

Incompatibility reigns supreme in this couple. Dogs and Roosters are equally flinty and raw-nerved. Dogs are forever blurting criticisms and bruising the egos of those around them. Roosters are cocky but deeply unsure of themselves. One yelp from the Dog's storehouse of biting blatancies can put the Rooster under for days, depress him and undo his hard-earned stance.

Do these people fight? They never stop backbiting, carping, bickering over details. They don't agree on anything. Dogs are classically left wing, kindly and trustworthy. Roosters are born conservatives who believe in the system, adhere to society's basic tenets and cleave to traditional ways. This couple's home life is a constant push-me pull-you of political unrest.

Dog wants revolution. Rooster devoutly wishes for status quo. Dog thinks mismatched china and a pallet on the floor will do nicely. Rooster wants Spode or Limoges set with crystal glasses on an heirloom table. Dog wants to spend money on causes. Rooster wants to keep his money in the bank.

Rooster demands more and varied sex than Dog has to give. Rooster needs to puff up his ego and preen his feathers. Dog couldn't care less what he looks like in bed. He feels sex rather than performing it. Besides, Dogs are slightly puritanical. They don't believe one should over-indulge in pleasure. Leave this relationship alone.

Dog with Dog

Seriousness and anxiety could cloud the union darkly between two Dogs who want to live together as a team. There exist, of course, areas of mutual understanding regarding causes and social ills, justice and humanitarian issues. But their abrasive Dog personalities and incessant caustic remarks will make pain the order of the day.

There is much reciprocity here. One Dog will always want to help the other with everything from grocery shopping to projects. There are few, if any, artificial barriers about who is male and who female and which tasks befit either. Respect for the other's time and understanding of their partner's desire to be effective in the world are given here.

Trouble crops up in this relationship because of an age-old enemy: boredom. Both Dogs will be hyper-puritanical, chronically anxious, guarded, sceptical, cynical, critical and lacking in joy and light-heartedness. Life around the Dog house could be Gloomy Gus City. Stodgy moralities will be the rule rather than the exception. Self-righteousness will be knee-deep in the very kitchen.

Sex will be limited. There is not much natural chemistry between Dogs so the act of love will be healthful but unimaginative. Intimacy frightens Dogs; they mistrust closeness. A second Dog sniffing along behind them for a quick pop in the grass is about as much fun as this couple will ever have in bed.

Dog with Pig

Intimacy between Dog and Pig subjects promises great enduring love, respect and sex. The Dog and Pig are complementary in thought and feeling. They both believe in the basic good of humankind. They both love the countryside and adhere to sanity as a fine way to live.

Mind you, there are some basic differences to contend with: Pigs like opulence and Dogs couldn't care less about luxury. Pigs are conservative, Dogs are liberal. Pigs are sensualists – there's nothing they love better than a good dirty story – Dogs are puritanical and sober-faced.

But all these differences are worked out between the Pig and Dog because they are each willing to respect and even admire the other for their individual tastes and preferences. Dog loves the cosy house Pig provides and Pig sees Dog's politically active friends as the perfect guests – feeds them to death.

Pig may at first be flummoxed by the Dog's seeming sexual indifference. But Pigs have clever (sometimes devious) ways of getting people's attention and will always find a way to their Doggy's heart. Also, Pigs are infinitely patient. They know how to bide their time and cajole until they get what they want and need out of their kindly sweet-tempered Dog partner.

Providing they husband and promote their mutual talent for goodwill, this pair will be blissfully content for a very long time.

Pig with Pig

An excellent match. Here we have two interesting, nature-loving, sensitive and sensual people whose mutual quest for culture, and respect for creative imagination are guaranteed to fend off boredom for a lifetime.

Money will never be a problem: Pigs attract piles of it. They are not only lucky, but they are hardworking and fair-dealing in all transactions. Two Pigs are better than one in the financial arena as they will be able to advise each other as to spending: which art treasures to buy and which to sell, what stocks and bonds to invest in, and which houses or other property would protect their future.

There is a streak of masochism in the Pig character, so one or the other might, following an unfortunate incident or business betrayal, slide into a depression and be beset by pessimistic notions. If luck is with them, the other will know how to respond and help their mate out of the doldrums.

When things are going well, both Pigs have real talent for pleasure. They enjoy a dirty joke and have few inhibitions about things sensual. The sexual conjugality of this couple is sublime. They are likely to be very vocal in bed, just as they make lots of noise when they eat. Neither will ever correct the other's manners, so the ambience at table around the Pig house might resemble something akin to 'Dining with Wolves'.

The Chinese Calendar Pre-1900

1516–1599

Year	*Sign*	*Element*	*Year begins*	*Year ends*
1516	Rat	Fire	3 Feb 1516	21 Jan 1517
1517	Ox	Fire	22 Jan 1517	9 Feb 1518
1518	Tiger	Earth	10 Feb 1518	30 Jan 1519
1519	Cat	Earth	31 Jan 1519	19 Jan 1520
1520	Dragon	Metal	20 Jan 1520	6 Feb 1521
1521	Snake	Metal	7 Feb 1521	27 Jan 1522
1522	Horse	Water	28 Jan 1522	16 Jan 1523
1523	Goat	Water	17 Jan 1523	3 Feb 1524
1524	Monkey	Wood	4 Feb 1524	22 Jan 1525
1525	Rooster	Wood	23 Jan 1525	10 Feb 1526
1526	Dog	Fire	11 Feb 1526	31 Jan 1527
1527	Pig	Fire	1 Feb 1527	21 Jan 1528
1528	Rat	Earth	22 Jan 1528	8 Feb 1529
1529	Ox	Earth	9 Feb 1529	28 Jan 1530
1530	Tiger	Metal	29 Jan 1530	17 Jan 1531
1531	Cat	Metal	18 Jan 1531	5 Feb 1532
1532	Dragon	Water	6 Feb 1532	24 Jan 1533
1533	Snake	Water	25 Jan 1533	13 Jan 1534
1534	Horse	Wood	14 Jan 1534	1 Feb 1535
1535	Goat	Wood	2 Feb 1535	22 Jan 1536
1536	Monkey	Fire	23 Jan 1536	9 Feb 1537
1537	Rooster	Fire	10 Feb 1537	30 Jan 1538
1538	Dog	Earth	31 Jan 1538	19 Jan 1539
1539	Pig	Earth	20 Jan 1539	7 Feb 1540
1540	Rat	Metal	8 Feb 1540	26 Jan 1541
1541	Ox	Metal	27 Jan 1541	15 Jan 1542
1542	Tiger	Water	16 Jan 1542	2 Feb 1543

1543	Cat	Water	3 Feb 1543	23 Jan 1544
1544	Dragon	Wood	24 Jan 1544	12 Jan 1545
1545	Snake	Wood	13 Jan 1545	23 Jan 1546
1546	Horse	Fire	24 Jan 1546	21 Jan 1547
1547	Goat	Fire	22 Jan 1547	9 Feb 1548
1548	Monkey	Earth	10 Feb 1548	28 Jan 1549
1549	Rooster	Earth	29 Jan 1549	17 Jan 1550
1550	Dog	Metal	18 Jan 1550	4 Feb 1551
1551	Pig	Metal	5 Feb 1551	25 Jan 1552
1552	Rat	Water	26 Jan 1552	13 Jan 1553
1553	Ox	Water	14 Jan 1553	1 Feb 1554
1554	Tiger	Wood	2 Feb 1554	22 Jan 1555
1555	Cat	Wood	23 Jan 1555	10 Feb 1556
1556	Dragon	Fire	11 Feb 1556	29 Jan 1557
1557	Snake	Fire	30 Jan 1557	19 Jan 1558
1558	Horse	Earth	20 Jan 1558	6 Feb 1559
1559	Goat	Earth	7 Feb 1559	26 Jan 1560
1560	Monkey	Metal	27 Jan 1560	15 Jan 1561
1561	Rooster	Metal	16 Jan 1561	3 Feb 1562
1562	Dog	Water	4 Feb 1562	23 Jan 1563
1563	Pig	Water	24 Jan 1563	13 Jan 1564
1564	Rat	Wood	14 Jan 1564	31 Jan 1565
1565	Ox	Wood	1 Feb 1565	20 Jan 1566
1566	Tiger	Fire	21 Jan 1566	8 Feb 1567
1567	Cat	Fire	9 Feb 1567	28 Jan 1568
1568	Dragon	Earth	29 Jan 1568	16 Jan 1569
1569	Snake	Earth	17 Jan 1569	4 Feb 1570
1570	Horse	Metal	5 Feb 1570	25 Jan 1571
1571	Goat	Metal	26 Jan 1571	14 Jan 1572
1572	Monkey	Water	15 Jan 1572	1 Feb 1573
1573	Rooster	Water	2 Feb 1573	22 Jan 1574
1574	Dog	Wood	23 Jan 1574	10 Feb 1575
1575	Pig	Wood	11 Feb 1575	30 Jan 1576
1576	Rat	Fire	31 Jan 1576	18 Jan 1577
1577	Ox	Fire	19 Jan 1577	6 Feb 1578
1578	Tiger	Earth	7 Feb 1578	26 Jan 1579
1579	Cat	Earth	27 Jan 1579	15 Jan 1580
1580	Dragon	Metal	16 Jan 1580	3 Feb 1581
1581	Snake	Metal	4 Feb 1581	23 Jan 1582
1582	Horse	Water	24 Jan 1582	23 Jan 1583
1583	Goat	Water	24 Jan 1583	11 Feb 1584

1584	Monkey	Wood	12 Feb 1584	30 Jan 1585
1585	Rooster	Wood	31 Jan 1585	17 Feb 1586
1586	Dog	Fire	18 Feb 1586	6 Feb 1587
1587	Pig	Fire	7 Feb 1587	27 Jan 1588
1588	Rat	Earth	28 Jan 1588	14 Feb 1589
1589	Ox	Earth	15 Feb 1589	4 Feb 1590
1590	Tiger	Metal	5 Feb 1590	24 Jan 1591
1591	Cat	Metal	25 Jan 1591	12 Feb 1592
1592	Dragon	Water	13 Feb 1592	31 Jan 1593
1593	Snake	Water	1 Feb 1593	19 Feb 1594
1594	Horse	Wood	20 Feb 1594	8 Feb 1595
1595	Goat	Wood	9 Feb 1595	28 Jan 1596
1596	Monkey	Fire	29 Jan 1596	15 Feb 1597
1597	Rooster	Fire	16 Feb 1597	5 Feb 1598
1598	Dog	Earth	6 Feb 1598	26 Jan 1599
1599	Pig	Earth	27 Jan 1599	13 Feb 1600

1600–1699

Year	*Sign*	*Element*	*Year begins*	*Year ends*
1600	Rat	Metal	14 Feb 1600	2 Feb 1601
1601	Ox	Metal	3 Feb 1601	22 Jan 1602
1602	Tiger	Water	23 Jan 1602	10 Feb 1603
1603	Cat	Water	11 Feb 1603	30 Jan 1604
1604	Dragon	Wood	31 Jan 1604	17 Feb 1605
1605	Snake	Wood	18 Feb 1605	6 Feb 1606
1606	Horse	Fire	7 Feb 1606	27 Jan 1607
1607	Goat	Fire	28 Jan 1607	15 Feb 1608
1608	Monkey	Earth	16 Feb 1608	3 Feb 1609
1609	Rooster	Earth	4 Feb 1609	24 Jan 1610
1610	Dog	Metal	25 Jan 1610	12 Feb 1611
1611	Pig	Metal	13 Feb 1611	1 Feb 1612
1612	Rat	Water	2 Feb 1612	18 Feb 1613
1613	Ox	Water	19 Feb 1613	8 Feb 1614
1614	Tiger	Wood	9 Feb 1614	28 Jan 1615
1615	Cat	Wood	29 Jan 1615	16 Feb 1616
1616	Dragon	Fire	17 Feb 1616	5 Feb 1617
1617	Snake	Fire	6 Feb 1617	25 Jan 1618

1618	Horse	Earth	26 Jan 1618	13 Feb 1619
1619	Goat	Earth	14 Feb 1619	3 Feb 1620
1620	Monkey	Metal	4 Feb 1620	21 Jan 1621
1621	Rooster	Metal	22 Jan 1621	9 Feb 1622
1622	Dog	Water	10 Feb 1622	30 Jan 1623
1623	Pig	Water	31 Jan 1623	18 Feb 1624
1624	Rat	Wood	19 Feb 1624	6 Feb 1625
1625	Ox	Wood	7 Feb 1625	27 Jan 1626
1626	Tiger	Fire	28 Jan 1626	15 Feb 1627
1627	Cat	Fire	16 Feb 1627	4 Feb 1628
1628	Dragon	Earth	5 Feb 1628	23 Jan 1629
1629	Snake	Earth	24 Jan 1629	11 Feb 1630
1630	Horse	Metal	12 Feb 1630	31 Jan 1631
1631	Goat	Metal	1 Feb 1631	19 Feb 1632
1632	Monkey	Water	20 Feb 1632	7 Feb 1633
1633	Rooster	Water	8 Feb 1633	28 Jan 1634
1634	Dog	Wood	29 Jan 1634	16 Feb 1635
1635	Pig	Wood	17 Feb 1635	6 Feb 1636
1636	Rat	Fire	7 Feb 1636	25 Jan 1637
1637	Ox	Fire	26 Jan 1637	13 Feb 1638
1638	Tiger	Earth	14 Feb 1638	2 Feb 1639
1639	Cat	Earth	3 Feb 1639	22 Jan 1640
1640	Dragon	Metal	23 Jan 1640	9 Feb 1641
1641	Snake	Metal	10 Feb 1641	29 Jan 1642
1642	Horse	Water	30 Jan 1642	18 Feb 1643
1643	Goat	Water	19 Feb 1643	7 Feb 1644
1644	Monkey	Wood	8 Feb 1644	27 Jan 1645
1645	Rooster	Wood	28 Jan 1645	15 Feb 1646
1646	Dog	Fire	16 Feb 1646	4 Feb 1647
1647	Pig	Fire	5 Feb 1647	24 Jan 1648
1648	Rat	Earth	25 Jan 1648	10 Feb 1649
1649	Ox	Earth	11 Feb 1649	31 Jan 1650
1650	Tiger	Metal	1 Feb 1650	20 Jan 1651
1651	Cat	Metal	21 Jan 1651	8 Feb 1652
1652	Dragon	Water	9 Feb 1652	28 Jan 1653
1653	Snake	Water	29 Jan 1653	16 Feb 1654
1654	Horse	Wood	17 Feb 1654	5 Feb 1655
1655	Goat	Wood	6 Feb 1655	25 Jan 1656
1656	Monkey	Fire	26 Jan 1656	12 Feb 1657
1657	Rooster	Fire	13 Feb 1657	1 Feb 1658
1658	Dog	Earth	2 Feb 1658	22 Jan 1659

1659	Pig	Earth	23 Jan 1659	10 Feb 1660
1660	Rat	Metal	11 Feb 1660	29 Jan 1661
1661	Ox	Metal	30 Jan 1661	17 Feb 1662
1662	Tiger	Water	18 Feb 1662	7 Feb 1663
1663	Cat	Water	8 Feb 1663	27 Jan 1664
1664	Dragon	Wood	28 Jan 1664	14 Feb 1665
1665	Snake	Wood	15 Feb 1665	3 Feb 1666
1666	Horse	Fire	4 Feb 1666	23 Jan 1667
1667	Goat	Fire	24 Jan 1667	11 Feb 1668
1668	Monkey	Earth	12 Feb 1668	31 Jan 1669
1669	Rooster	Earth	1 Feb 1669	20 Jan 1670
1670	Dog	Metal	21 Jan 1670	8 Feb 1671
1671	Pig	Metal	9 Feb 1671	29 Jan 1672
1672	Rat	Water	30 Jan 1672	16 Feb 1673
1673	Ox	Water	17 Feb 1673	5 Feb 1674
1674	Tiger	Wood	6 Feb 1674	25 Jan 1675
1675	Cat	Wood	26 Jan 1675	13 Feb 1676
1676	Dragon	Fire	14 Feb 1676	1 Feb 1677
1677	Snake	Fire	2 Feb 1677	22 Jan 1678
1678	Horse	Earth	23 Jan 1678	10 Feb 1679
1679	Goat	Earth	11 Feb 1679	30 Jan 1680
1680	Monkey	Metal	31 Jan 1680	17 Feb 1681
1681	Rooster	Metal	18 Feb 1681	6 Feb 1682
1682	Dog	Water	7 Fcb 1682	26 Jan 1683
1683	Pig	Water	27 Jan 1683	14 Feb 1684
1684	Rat	Wood	15 Feb 1684	2 Feb 1685
1685	Ox	Wood	3 Feb 1685	23 Jan 1686
1686	Tiger	Fire	24 Jan 1686	11 Feb 1687
1687	Cat	Fire	12 Jan 1687	1 Feb 1688
1688	Dragon	Earth	2 Feb 1688	20 Jan 1689
1689	Snake	Earth	21 Jan 1689	8 Feb 1690
1690	Horse	Metal	9 Jan 1690	28 Jan 1691
1691	Goat	Metal	29 Jan 1691	16 Feb 1692
1692	Monkey	Water	17 Feb 1692	4 Feb 1693
1693	Rooster	Water	5 Feb 1693	24 Jan 1694
1694	Dog	Wood	25 Jan 1694	12 Feb 1695
1695	Pig	Wood	13 Feb 1695	2 Feb 1696
1696	Rat	Fire	3 Feb 1696	22 Jan 1697
1697	Ox	Fire	23 Jan 1697	10 Feb 1698
1698	Tiger	Earth	11 Feb 1698	30 Jan 1699
1699	Cat	Earth	31 Jan 1699	18 Feb 1700

1700–1799

Year	*Sign*	*Element*	*Year begins*	*Year ends*
1700	Dragon	Metal	19 Feb 1700	7 Feb 1701
1701	Snake	Metal	8 Feb 1701	27 Jan 1702
1702	Horse	Water	28 Jan 1702	15 Feb 1703
1703	Goat	Water	16 Feb 1703	4 Feb 1704
1704	Monkey	Wood	5 Feb 1704	24 Jan 1705
1705	Rooster	Wood	25 Jan 1705	12 Feb 1706
1706	Dog	Fire	13 Feb 1706	2 Feb 1707
1707	Pig	Fire	3 Feb 1707	22 Jan 1708
1708	Rat	Earth	23 Jan 1708	9 Feb 1709
1709	Ox	Earth	10 Feb 1709	29 Jan 1710
1710	Tiger	Metal	30 Jan 1710	16 Feb 1711
1711	Cat	Metal	17 Feb 1711	6 Feb 1712
1712	Dragon	Water	7 Feb 1712	25 Jan 1713
1713	Snake	Water	26 Jan 1713	13 Feb 1714
1714	Horse	Wood	14 Feb 1714	3 Feb 1715
1715	Goat	Wood	4 Feb 1715	23 Jan 1716
1716	Monkey	Fire	24 Jan 1716	10 Feb 1717
1717	Rooster	Fire	11 Feb 1717	30 Jan 1718
1718	Dog	Earth	31 Jan 1718	18 Feb 1719
1719	Pig	Earth	19 Feb 1719	7 Feb 1720
1720	Rat	Metal	8 Feb 1720	27 Jan 1721
1721	Ox	Metal	28 Jan 1721	15 Feb 1722
1722	Tiger	Water	16 Feb 1722	4 Feb 1723
1723	Cat	Water	5 Feb 1723	25 Jan 1724
1724	Dragon	Wood	26 Jan 1724	12 Feb 1725
1725	Snake	Wood	13 Feb 1725	1 Feb 1726
1726	Horse	Fire	2 Feb 1726	21 Jan 1727
1727	Goat	Fire	22 Jan 1727	9 Feb 1728
1728	Monkey	Earth	10 Feb 1728	28 Jan 1729
1729	Rooster	Earth	29 Jan 1729	16 Feb 1730
1730	Dog	Metal	17 Feb 1730	6 Feb 1731
1731	Pig	Metal	7 Feb 1731	26 Jan 1732
1732	Rat	Water	27 Jan 1732	13 Feb 1733
1733	Ox	Water	14 Feb 1733	3 Feb 1734

1734	Tiger	Wood	4 Feb 1734	23 Jan 1735
1735	Cat	Wood	24 Jan 1735	11 Feb 1736
1736	Dragon	Fire	12 Feb 1736	30 Jan 1737
1737	Snake	Fire	31 Jan 1737	18 Feb 1738
1738	Horse	Earth	19 Feb 1738	7 Feb 1739
1739	Goat	Earth	8 Feb 1739	29 Jan 1740
1740	Monkey	Metal	30 Jan 1740	15 Feb 1741
1741	Rooster	Metal	16 Feb 1741	4 Feb 1742
1742	Dog	Water	5 Feb 1742	25 Jan 1743
1743	Pig	Water	26 Jan 1743	12 Feb 1744
1744	Rat	Wood	13 Feb 1744	31 Jan 1745
1745	Ox	Wood	1 Feb 1745	21 Jan 1746
1746	Tiger	Fire	22 Jan 1746	8 Feb 1747
1747	Cat	Fire	9 Feb 1747	29 Jan 1748
1748	Dragon	Earth	30 Jan 1748	16 Feb 1749
1749	Snake	Earth	17 Feb 1749	6 Feb 1750
1750	Horse	Metal	7 Feb 1750	26 Jan 1751
1751	Goat	Metal	27 Jan 1751	14 Feb 1752
1752	Monkey	Water	15 Feb 1752	2 Feb 1753
1753	Rooster	Water	3 Feb 1753	22 Jan 1754
1754	Dog	Wood	23 Jan 1754	10 Feb 1755
1755	Pig	Wood	11 Feb 1755	30 Jan 1756
1756	Rat	Fire	31 Jan 1756	17 Feb 1757
1757	Ox	Fire	18 Feb 1757	7 Feb 1758
1758	Tiger	Earth	8 Feb 1758	28 Jan 1759
1759	Cat	Earth	29 Jan 1759	16 Feb 1760
1760	Dragon	Metal	17 Feb 1760	4 Feb 1761
1761	Snake	Metal	5 Feb 1761	24 Jan 1762
1762	Horse	Water	25 Jan 1762	12 Feb 1763
1763	Goat	Water	13 Feb 1763	1 Feb 1764
1764	Monkey	Wood	2 Feb 1764	20 Jan 1765
1765	Rooster	Wood	21 Jan 1765	8 Feb 1766
1766	Dog	Fire	9 Feb 1766	29 Jan 1767
1767	Pig	Fire	30 Jan 1767	17 Feb 1768
1768	Rat	Earth	18 Feb 1768	6 Feb 1769
1769	Ox	Earth	7 Feb 1769	26 Jan 1770
1770	Tiger	Metal	27 Jan 1770	14 Feb 1771
1771	Cat	Metal	15 Feb 1771	3 Feb 1772
1772	Dragon	Water	4 Feb 1772	22 Jan 1773
1773	Snake	Water	23 Jan 1773	10 Feb 1774
1774	Horse	Wood	11 Feb 1774	30 Jan 1775

1775	Goat	Wood	31 Jan 1775	18 Feb 1776
1776	Monkey	Fire	19 Feb 1776	7 Feb 1777
1777	Rooster	Fire	8 Feb 1777	27 Jan 1778
1778	Dog	Earth	28 Jan 1778	15 Feb 1779
1779	Pig	Earth	16 Feb 1779	4 Feb 1780
1780	Rat	Metal	5 Feb 1780	23 Jan 1781
1781	Ox	Metal	24 Jan 1781	11 Feb 1782
1782	Tiger	Water	12 Feb 1782	1 Feb 1783
1783	Cat	Water	2 Feb 1783	21 Jan 1784
1784	Dragon	Wood	22 Jan 1784	8 Feb 1785
1785	Snake	Wood	9 Feb 1785	29 Jan 1786
1786	Horse	Fire	30 Jan 1786	17 Feb 1787
1787	Goat	Fire	18 Feb 1787	6 Feb 1788
1788	Monkey	Earth	7 Feb 1788	25 Jan 1789
1789	Rooster	Earth	26 Jan 1789	13 Feb 1790
1790	Dog	Metal	14 Feb 1790	2 Feb 1791
1791	Pig	Metal	3 Feb 1791	23 Jan 1792
1792	Rat	Water	24 Jan 1792	10 Feb 1793
1793	Ox	Water	11 Feb 1793	30 Jan 1794
1794	Tiger	Wood	31 Jan 1794	20 Jan 1795
1795	Cat	Wood	21 Jan 1795	8 Feb 1796
1796	Dragon	Fire	9 Feb 1796	27 Jan 1797
1797	Snake	Fire	28 Jan 1797	15 Feb 1798
1798	Horse	Earth	16 Feb 1798	4 Feb 1799
1799	Goat	Earth	5 Feb 1799	24 Jan 1800

1800–1899

Year	*Sign*	*Element*	*Year begins*	*Year ends*
1800	Monkey	Metal	25 Jan 1800	12 Feb 1801
1801	Rooster	Metal	13 Feb 1801	2 Feb 1802
1802	Dog	Water	3 Feb 1802	22 Jan 1803
1803	Pig	Water	23 Jan 1803	10 Feb 1804
1804	Rat	Wood	11 Feb 1804	30 Jan 1805
1805	Ox	Wood	31 Jan 1805	17 Feb 1806
1806	Tiger	Fire	18 Feb 1806	6 Feb 1807
1807	Cat	Fire	7 Feb 1807	27 Jan 1808

1808	Dragon	Earth	28 Jan 1808	13 Feb 1809
1809	Snake	Earth	14 Feb 1809	3 Feb 1810
1810	Horse	Metal	4 Feb 1810	24 Jan 1811
1811	Goat	Metal	25 Jan 1811	12 Feb 1812
1812	Monkey	Water	13 Feb 1812	31 Jan 1813
1813	Rooster	Water	1 Feb 1813	20 Jan 1814
1814	Dog	Wood	21 Jan 1814	8 Feb 1815
1815	Pig	Wood	9 Feb 1815	28 Jan 1816
1816	Rat	Fire	29 Jan 1816	15 Feb 1817
1817	Ox	Fire	16 Feb 1817	4 Feb 1818
1818	Tiger	Earth	5 Feb 1818	25 Jan 1819
1819	Cat	Earth	26 Jan 1819	13 Feb 1820
1820	Dragon	Metal	14 Feb 1820	2 Feb 1821
1821	Snake	Metal	3 Feb 1821	22 Jan 1822
1822	Horse	Water	23 Jan 1822	10 Feb 1823
1823	Goat	Water	11 Feb 1823	30 Jan 1824
1824	Monkey	Wood	31 Jan 1824	17 Feb 1825
1825	Rooster	Wood	18 Feb 1825	6 Feb 1826
1826	Dog	Fire	7 Feb 1826	26 Jan 1827
1827	Pig	Fire	27 Jan 1827	14 Feb 1828
1828	Rat	Earth	15 Feb 1828	3 Feb 1829
1829	Ox	Earth	4 Feb 1829	24 Jan 1830
1830	Tiger	Metal	25 Jan 1830	12 Feb 1831
1831	Cat	Metal	13 Feb 1831	1 Feb 1832
1832	Dragon	Water	2 Feb 1832	19 Feb 1833
1833	Snake	Water	20 Feb 1833	8 Feb 1834
1834	Horse	Wood	9 Feb 1834	28 Jan 1835
1835	Goat	Wood	29 Jan 1835	16 Feb 1836
1836	Monkey	Fire	17 Feb 1836	4 Feb 1837
1837	Rooster	Fire	5 Feb 1837	25 Jan 1838
1838	Dog	Earth	26 Jan 1838	13 Feb 1839
1839	Pig	Earth	14 Feb 1839	2 Feb 1840
1840	Rat	Metal	3 Feb 1840	22 Jan 1841
1841	Ox	Metal	23 Jan 1841	9 Feb 1842
1842	Tiger	Water	10 Feb 1842	29 Jan 1843
1843	Cat	Water	30 Jan 1843	17 Feb 1844
1844	Dragon	Wood	18 Feb 1844	6 Feb 1845
1845	Snake	Wood	7 Feb 1845	26 Jan 1846
1846	Horse	Fire	27 Jan 1846	14 Feb 1847
1847	Goat	Fire	15 Feb 1847	4 Feb 1848
1848	Monkey	Earth	5 Feb 1848	23 Jan 1849

1849	Rooster	Earth	24 Jan 1849	11 Feb 1850
1850	Dog	Metal	12 Feb 1850	31 Jan 1851
1851	Pig	Metal	1 Feb 1851	19 Feb 1852
1852	Rat	Water	20 Feb 1852	7 Feb 1853
1853	Ox	Water	8 Feb 1853	28 Jan 1854
1854	Tiger	Wood	29 Jan 1854	16 Jan 1855
1855	Cat	Wood	17 Jan 1855	5 Feb 1856
1856	Dragon	Fire	6 Feb 1856	25 Jan 1857
1857	Snake	Fire	26 Jan 1857	13 Feb 1858
1858	Horse	Earth	14 Feb 1858	2 Feb 1859
1859	Goat	Earth	3 Feb 1859	22 Jan 1860
1860	Monkey	Metal	23 Jan 1860	9 Feb 1861
1861	Rooster	Metal	10 Feb 1861	29 Jan 1862
1862	Dog	Water	30 Jan 1862	17 Feb 1863
1863	Pig	Water	18 Feb 1863	7 Feb 1864
1864	Rat	Wood	8 Feb 1864	26 Jan 1865
1865	Ox	Wood	27 Jan 1865	14 Feb 1866
1866	Tiger	Fire	15 Feb 1866	4 Feb 1867
1867	Cat	Fire	5 Feb 1867	24 Jan 1868
1868	Dragon	Earth	25 Jan 1868	10 Feb 1869
1869	Snake	Earth	11 Feb 1869	30 Jan 1870
1870	Horse	Metal	31 Jan 1870	18 Feb 1871
1871	Goat	Metal	19 Feb 1871	8 Feb 1872
1872	Monkey	Water	9 Feb 1872	28 Jan 1873
1873	Rooster	Water	29 Jan 1873	16 Feb 1874
1874	Dog	Wood	17 Feb 1874	5 Feb 1875
1875	Pig	Wood	6 Feb 1875	25 Jan 1876
1876	Rat	Fire	26 Jan 1876	12 Feb 1877
1877	Ox	Fire	13 Feb 1877	1 Feb 1878
1878	Tiger	Earth	2 Feb 1878	21 Jan 1879
1879	Cat	Earth	22 Jan 1879	9 Feb 1880
1880	Dragon	Metal	10 Feb 1880	29 Jan 1881
1881	Snake	Metal	30 Jan 1881	17 Feb 1882
1882	Horse	Water	18 Feb 1882	7 Feb 1883
1883	Goat	Water	8 Feb 1883	27 Jan 1884
1884	Monkey	Wood	28 Jan 1884	14 Feb 1885
1885	Rooster	Wood	15 Feb 1885	3 Feb 1886
1886	Dog	Fire	4 Feb 1886	23 Jan 1887
1887	Pig	Fire	24 Jan 1887	11 Feb 1888
1888	Rat	Earth	12 Feb 1888	30 Jan 1889
1889	Ox	Earth	31 Jan 1889	20 Jan 1890

1890	Tiger	Metal	21 Jan 1890	8 Feb 1891
1891	Cat	Metal	9 Feb 1891	29 Jan 1892
1892	Dragon	Water	30 Jan 1892	16 Feb 1893
1893	Snake	Water	17 Feb 1893	5 Feb 1894
1894	Horse	Wood	6 Feb 1894	25 Jan 1895
1895	Goat	Wood	26 Jan 1895	12 Feb 1896
1896	Monkey	Fire	13 Feb 1896	1 Feb 1897
1897	Rooster	Fire	2 Feb 1897	21 Jan 1898
1898	Dog	Earth	22 Jan 1898	9 Feb 1899
1899	Pig	Earth	10 Feb 1899	30 Jan 1900